Children's
Literature
Review

Guide to Gale Literary Criticism Series

For criticism on	Consult these Gale series
Authors now living or who died after December 31, 1959	*CONTEMPORARY LITERARY CRITICISM (CLC)*
Authors who died between 1900 and 1959	*TWENTIETH-CENTURY LITERARY CRITICISM (TCLC)*
Authors who died between 1800 and 1899	*NINETEENTH-CENTURY LITERATURE CRITICISM (NCLC)*
Authors who died between 1400 and 1799	*LITERATURE CRITICISM FROM 1400 TO 1800 (LC)* *SHAKESPEAREAN CRITICISM (SC)*
Authors who died before 1400	*CLASSICAL AND MEDIEVAL LITERATURE CRITICISM (CMLC)*
Black writers of the past two hundred years	*BLACK LITERATURE CRITICISM (BLC)*
Authors of books for children and young adults	*CHILDREN'S LITERATURE REVIEW (CLR)*
Dramatists	*DRAMA CRITICISM (DC)*
Hispanic writers of the late nineteenth and twentieth centuries	*HISPANIC LITERATURE CRITICISM (HLC)*
Native North American writers and orators of the eighteenth, nineteenth, and twentieth centuries	*NATIVE NORTH AMERICAN LITERATURE (NNAL)*
Poets	*POETRY CRITICISM (PC)*
Short story writers	*SHORT STORY CRITICISM (SSC)*
Major authors from the Renaissance to the present	*WORLD LITERATURE CRITICISM, 1500 TO THE PRESENT (WLC)*

ISSN 0362-4145

volume 43

Children's Literature Review

Excerpts from Reviews,
Criticism, and Commentary
on Books for Children
and Young People

Diane Telgen
Linda R. Andres
Editors

GALE

DETROIT · NEW YORK · TORONTO · LONDON

STAFF

Diane Telgen and Linda R. Andres, *Editors*

Joanna Brod, Sheryl Ciccarelli, Charity Ann Dorgan, Alan Hedblad, Motoko Huthwaite, Paul Loeber,
Sean McCready, Thomas F. McMahon, Zoran Minderovic, Gerard J. Senick, Kathleen L. Witman, *Contributing Editors*

Marilyn Allen, *Assistant Editor*

Joyce Nakamura, *Managing Editor*

Susan M. Trosky, *Permissions Manager*
Maria L. Franklin, *Permissions Specialist*
Edna M. Hedblad, Michele M. Lonoconus, Maureen A. Puhl, *Permissions Associates*

Victoria B. Cariappa, *Research Manager*
Cheryl L. Warnock, *Project Coordinator*
Gary J. Oudersluys, *Research Specialist*
Laura C. Bissey, Tracie Richardson, Norma Sawaya, *Research Associates*
Alfred A. Gardner, Sean Smith, *Research Assistants*

Mary Beth Trimper, *Production Director*
Deborah Milliken, *Production Assistant*

Sherrell Hobbs, *Macintosh Artist*
Randy Bassett, *Image Database Supervisor*
Robert Duncan, Mikal Ansari, *Imaging Specialists*
Pamela A. Reed, *Photography Coordinator*

∞™ This book is printed on acid-free paper that meets the minimum requirements of American National Standard for Information Sciences—Permanence Paper for Printed Library Materials, ANSI Z39.48-1984.

Library of Congress Catalog Card Number 76-643301
ISBN 0-8103-9986-5
ISSN 0362-4145
Printed in the United States of America

10 9 8 7 6 5 4 3 2 1

Contents

Preface

Literature for children and young adults has evolved into both a respected branch of creative writing and a successful industry. Currently, books for young readers are considered among the most popular segments of publishing. Criticism of juvenile literature is instrumental in recording the literary or artistic development of the creators of children's books as well as the trends and controversies that result from changing values or attitudes about young people and their literature. Designed to provide a permanent, accessible record of this ongoing scholarship, *Children's Literature Review (CLR)* presents parents, teachers, and librarians—those responsible for bringing children and books together—with the opportunity to make informed choices when selecting reading materials for the young. In addition, *CLR* provides researchers of children's literature with easy access to a wide variety of critical information from English-language sources in the field. Users will find balanced overviews of the careers of the authors and illustrators of the books that children and young adults are reading; these entries, which contain excerpts from published criticism in books and periodicals, assist users by sparking ideas for papers and assignments and suggesting supplementary and classroom reading. Ann L. Kalkhoff, president and editor of *Children's Book Review Service Inc.*, writes that "*CLR* has filled a gap in the field of children's books, and it is one series that will never lose its validity or importance."

Scope of the Series

Each volume of *CLR* profiles the careers of a selection of authors and illustrators of books for children and young adults from preschool through high school. Author lists in each volume reflect:

- an international scope.

- representation of authors of all eras.

- the variety of genres covered by children's and/or YA literature: picture books, fiction, nonfiction, poetry, folklore, and drama.

Although the focus of the series is on authors new to *CLR*, entries will be updated as the need arises.

Organization of This Book

An entry consists of the following elements: author heading, author portrait, author introduction, excerpts of criticism (each preceded by a bibliographical citation), and illustrations, when available.

- The **Author Heading** consists of the author's name followed by birth and death dates. The portion of the name outside the parentheses denotes the form under which the author is most frequently published. If the majority of the author's works for children were written under a pseudonym, the pseudonym will be listed in the author heading and the real name given on the first line of the author introduction. Also located at the beginning of the introduction are any other pseudonyms used by the author in writing for children and any name variations, including transliterated forms for authors whose languages use nonroman alphabets. Uncertainty as to a birth or death date is indicated by question marks.

- An **Author Portrait** is included when available.

- The **Author Introduction** contains information designed to introduce an author to *CLR* users by presenting an overview of the author's themes and styles, biographical facts that relate to the author's literary career or critical responses to the author's works, and information about major awards and prizes the author has received. The introduction begins by identifying the nationality of the author and by listing the genres in which s/he has written for children and young adults. Introductions also list a group of representative titles for which the author or illustrator being profiled is best known; this section, which begins with the words "major works include," follows the genre line of the introduction. For seminal figures, a listing of major works about the author follows when appropriate, highlighting important biographies about the author or illustrator that are not excerpted in the entry. The centered heading "Introduction" announces the body of the text.

- **Criticism** is located in three sections: **Author's Commentary** (when available), **General Commentary** (when available), and **Title Commentary** (commentary on specific titles).

    - The **Author's Commentary** presents background material written by the author or by an interviewer. This commentary may cover a specific work or several works. Author's commentary on more than one work appears after the author introduction, while commentary on an individual book follows the title entry heading.

    - The **General Commentary** consists of critical excerpts that consider more than one work by the author or illustrator being profiled. General commentary is preceded by the critic's name in boldface type or, in the case of unsigned criticism, by the title of the journal. *CLR* also features entries that emphasize general criticism on the oeuvre of an author or illustrator. When appropriate, a selection of reviews is included to supplement the general commentary.

    - The **Title Commentary** begins with the title entry headings, which precede the criticism on a title and cite publication information on the work being reviewed. Title headings list the title of the work as it appeared in its first English-language edition. The first English-language publication date of each work (unless otherwise noted) is listed in parentheses following the title. Differing U.S. and British titles follow the publication date within the parentheses. When a work is written by an individual other than the one being profiled, as is the case when illustrators are featured, the parenthetical material following the title cites the author of the work before listing its publication date.

      Entries in each title commentary section consist of critical excerpts on the author's individual works, arranged chronologically by publication date. The entries generally contain two to seven reviews per title, depending on the stature of the book and the amount of criticism it has generated. The editors select titles that reflect the entire scope of the author's literary contribution, covering each genre and subject. An effort is made to reprint criticism that represents the full range of each title's reception, from the year of its initial publication to current assessments. Thus, the reader is provided with a record of the author's critical history. Publication information (such as publisher names and book prices) and parenthetical numerical references (such as footnotes or page and line references to specific editions of works) have been deleted at the discretion of the editors to provide smoother reading of the text.

- Centered headings introduce each section, in which criticism is arranged chronologically; beginning with Volume 35, each excerpt is preceded by a boldface source heading for easier access by readers. Within the text, titles by authors being profiled are also highlighted in boldface type.

- Selected excerpts are preceded by **Explanatory Annotations,** which provide information on the critic or work of criticism to enhance the reader's understanding of the excerpt.

- A complete **Bibliographical Citation** designed to facilitate the location of the original book or article precedes each piece of criticism.

- Numerous **Illustrations** are featured in *CLR*. For entries on illustrators, an effort has been made to include illustrations that reflect the characteristics discussed in the criticism. Entries on authors who do not illustrate their own works may also include photographs and other illustrative material pertinent to their careers.

Special Features: Entries on Illustrators

Entries on authors who are also illustrators will occasionally feature commentary on selected works illustrated but not written by the author being profiled. These works are strongly associated with the illustrator and have received critical acclaim for their art. By including critical comment on works of this type, the editors wish to provide a more complete representation of the artist's career. Criticism on these works has been chosen to stress artistic, rather than literary, contributions. Title entry headings for works illustrated by the author being profiled are arranged chronologically within the entry by date of publication and include notes identifying the author of the illustrated work. In order to provide easier access for users, all titles illustrated by the subject of the entry are boldfaced.

CLR also includes entries on prominent illustrators who have contributed to the field of children's literature. These entries are designed to represent the development of the illustrator as an artist rather than as a literary stylist. The illustrator's section is organized like that of an author, with two exceptions: the introduction presents an overview of the illustrator's styles and techniques rather than outlining his or her literary background, and the commentary written by the illustrator on his or her works is called "illustrator's commentary" rather than "author's commentary." All titles of books containing illustrations by the artist being profiled are highlighted in boldface type.

Other Features: Acknowledgments, Indexes

- The **Acknowledgments** section, which immediately follows the preface, lists the sources from which material has been reprinted in the volume. It does not, however, list every book or periodical consulted for the volume.

- The **Cumulative Index to Authors** lists all of the authors who have appeared in *CLR* with cross-references to the biographical, autobiographical, and literary criticism series published by Gale Research. A full listing of the series titles appears before the first page of the indexes of this volume.

- The **Cumulative Index to Nationalities** lists authors alphabetically under their respective nationalities. Author names are followed by the volume number(s) in which they appear.

- The **Cumulative Index to Titles** lists titles covered in *CLR* followed by the volume and page number where criticism begins.

A Note to the Reader

CLR is one of several critical references sources in the Literature Criticism Series published by Gale Research. When writing papers, students who quote directly from any volume in the Literature Criticism

Series may use the following general forms to footnote reprinted criticism. The first example pertains to material drawn from periodicals, the second to material reprinted from books.

[1]T. S. Eliot, "John Donne," *The Nation and the Athenaeum,* 33 (9 June 1923), 321-32; excerpted and reprinted in *Literature Criticism from 1400 to 1800,* Vol. 10, ed. James E. Person, Jr. (Detroit: Gale Research, 1989), pp. 28-9.

[1]Henry Brooke, *Leslie Brooke and Johnny Crow* (Frederick Warne, 1982); excerpted and reprinted in *Children's Literature Review,* Vol. 20, ed. Gerard J. Senick (Detroit: Gale Research, 1990), p. 47.

Suggestions Are Welcome

In response to various suggestions, several features have been added to *CLR* since the beginning of the series, including author entries on retellers of traditional literature as well as those who have been the first to record oral tales and other folklore; entries on prominent illustrators featuring commentary on their styles and techniques; entries on authors whose works are considered controversial; occasional entries devoted to criticism on a single work or a series of works; sections in author introductions that list major works by and about the author or illustrator being profiled; explanatory notes that provide information on the critic or work of criticism to enhance the usefulness of the excerpt; more extensive illustrative material, such as holographs of manuscript pages and photographs of people and places pertinent to the careers of the authors and artists; a cumulative nationality index for easy access to authors by nationality; and occasional guest essays written specifically for *CLR* by prominent critics on subjects of their choice.

Readers who wish to suggest authors to appear in future volumes, or who have other suggestions, are cordially invited to contact the editor. By mail: Editor, *Children's Literature Review,* Gale Research, 835 Penobscot Bldg., 645 Griswold St., Detroit, MI 48226-4094; by telephone: (800) 347-GALE; by fax: (313) 961-6599; by E-mail: CYA@Gale.com@GALESMTP.

Acknowledgments

The editors wish to thank the copyright holders of the excerpted criticism included in this volume and the permissions managers of many book and magazine publishing companies for assisting us in securing reproduction rights. We are also grateful to the staffs of the Detroit Public Library, the Library of Congress, the University of Detroit Mercy Library, Wayne State University Purdy/Kresge Library Complex, and the University of Michigan Libraries for making their resources available to us. Following is a list of the copyright holders who have granted us permission to reproduce material in this volume of **CLR.** Every effort has been made to trace copyright, but if omissions have been made, please let us know.

COPYRIGHTED EXCERPTS IN *CLR,* VOLUME 43, WERE REPRINTED FROM THE FOLLOWING PERIODICALS:

America, v. 139, December 9, 1978. © 1978. All rights reserved. Reproduced with permission of America Press, Inc., 106 West 56th Street, New York, NY 10019.—*American Artist,* v. 46, January, 1982. Copyright © 1982 by Billboard Publications, Inc. Reproduced by permission.—*American Reference Book Annual 1984,* v. 15, 1984. Copyright © 1984 Libraries Unlimited, Inc. All rights reserved. Reproduced by permission.—*Appraisal: Children's Science Books,* v. 13, Winter, 1980. Copyright © 1980 by the Children's Science Book Review Committee. Reproduced by permission.—*Appraisal: Science Books for Young People,* v. 15, Fall, 1982; v. 17, Fall, 1984; v. 20, Fall, 1987; v. 21, Winter, 1988; v. 22, Winter-Spring, 1989. Copyright © 1982, 1984, 1987, 1988, 1989 by the Children's Science Book Review Committee. All reproduced by permission.—*The Atlantic Monthly,* v. 197, June, 1956 for a review of "Knight's Castle" by Charlotte Jackson. Copyright 1956 by The Atlantic Monthly Company, Boston, MA.—*Best Sellers,* v. 31, September 15, 1971. Copyright 1971, by the University of Scranton./ v. 40, May, 1980. Copyright 1980 Helen Dwight Reid Educational Foundation. Both reproduced by permission. —*Book Window,* v. 7, Winter, 1979; v. 7, Summer, 1980; v. 8, Winter, 1980. ©1979, 1980 S. C. B. A. and contributors. All reproduced by permission.—*Bookbird,* v. 32, Fall, 1994. Reproduced by permission.—*Booklist,* v. 73, November 1, 1976; v. 73, July 15, 1977; v. 74, June 1, 1978; v. 74, June 15, 1978; v. 74, July 15, 1978; v. 75, January 1, 1979; v. 75, January 15, 1979; v. 76, November 1, 1979; v. 76, April 1, 1980; v. 77, October 15, 1980; v. 77, May 15, 1981; v. 77, July 1, 1981; v. 78, November 15, 1981; v. 78, December 15, 1981; v. 78, July, 1982; v. 79, March 15, 1983; v. 79, August, 1983; v. 80, October 15, 1983; v. 80, August, 1984; v. 81, November 1, 1984; v. 82, March 15, 1986; v. 82, July, 1986; v. 83, January 15, 1987; v. 83, May 15, 1987; v. 84, September 1, 1987; v. 84, October 1, 1987; v. 84, November 1, 1987; v. 84, December 1, 1987; v. 84, June 1, 1988; v. 84, July, 1988; v. 85, January 1, 1989; v. 85, March 1, 1989; v. 85, May 15, 1989; v. 86, October 1, 1989; v. 86, March 15, 1990; v. 86, May 15, 1990; v. 86, August, 1990; v. 87, October 1, 1990; v. 87, December 15, 1990; v. 87, February 1, 1991; v. 87, May 1, 1991; v. 87, August, 1991; v. 88, September 1, 1991; v. 88, November 15, 1991; v. 88, February 1, 1992; v. 88, February 15, 1992; v. 88, June 15, 1992; v. 88, July, 1992; v. 88, August, 1992; v. 89, October 15, 1992; v. 89, November 1, 1992; v. 89, December 15, 1992; v. 89, April 15, 1993; v. 89, July, 1993; v. 90, October 1, 1993; v. 90, November 15, 1993; v. 90, February 1, 1994; v. 90, May 1, 1994; v. 90, June 1 & 15, 1994; v. 91, October 1, 1994; v. 91, October 15, 1994; v. 91, February 15, 1995; v. 91, April 15, 1995; v. 91, July, 1995. Copyright © 1976, 1977, 1978, 1979, 1980, 1981, 1982, 1983, 1984, 1986, 1987, 1988, 1989, 1990, 1991, 1992, 1993, 1994, 1995 by the American Library Association. All reproduced by permission.—*The Booklist,* v. 70, May 15, 1974; v. 72, October 15, 1975. Copyright © 1974, 1975 by the American Library Association. Both reproduced by permission.—*The Booklist and Subscription Books Bulletin,* v. 63, October 1, 1966. Copyright © 1966 by the American Library Association. Reproduced by permission.—*Books and Bookmen,* v. 23, December, 1977 for "Weirdies and Horrible" by Alan Hull Walton.—*Books for Keeps,* n. 30, January, 1985; n. 62, May, 1990; n. 74, May, 1992. ©School Bookshop Association 1985, 1990, 1992. All reproduced by permission.—*Books for Young People,* v. 1, December, 1987 for a review of "Pay Cheques and Picket Lines: All About Unions in Canada" by Eva Martin. All rights reserved. Reproduced by permission of the author.—*Books for Your Children,* v. 15, Autumn-Winter, 1980. ©*Books for Your Children* 1980. Reproduced by permission.—*Books in Canada,* v. 13, August-September, 1984 for a review of "The Minerva Program" by Mary Ainslie Smith; v. 17, April, 1988 for "Doers and Seekers" by Welwyn Wilton Katz. Both reproduced by permission of the respective authors.—*British Book News*

Children's
Literature
Review

Mabel Esther Allan

1915-

(Also writes as Jean Estoril, Priscilla Hagon, and Anne Pilgrim) English author of fiction, poetry, and nonfiction.

Major works include *The Sign of the Unicorn* (1963), *We Danced in Bloomsbury Square* (as Jean Estoril, 1967), *The Wood Street Secret* (1968), *Climbing to Danger* (1969; U.S. edition as *Mystery in Wales,* 1971), *An Island in a Green Sea* (1972), *The View Beyond My Father* (1977), *Mills Down Below* (1980).

Major works about the author include *To Be an Author: A Short Autobiography* (1982), *More about Being an Author* (autobiography, 1985), *My Background Came First: My Books and Places* (1988).

INTRODUCTION

A prolific and widely respected author, Allan has written scores of books for young readers over a literary career spanning seven decades. Although the majority of her works are directed to middle schoolers and older adolescents, she has also created many stories for primary graders that have been well received. Allan's earliest published efforts were works for this younger audience; thereafter, her career may be delineated according to a very rough grouping of her titles: "career books for girls" and other stories for older readers, usually with romantic endings, during the 1950s and early 1960s, and more introspective, autobiographically based tales thereafter. These later efforts, including the critically acclaimed *An Island in a Green Sea* and *The View Beyond My Father,* are less formulaic and demonstrate more freedom from convention than Allan's earlier writings, and are regarded among her finest stories for their strong central characters and emotional depth. Her entire body of fiction, however, is distinguished by a number of elements common to virtually all of her works: adventure, mystery, romance, family relationships, and—especially—carefully detailed and accurate settings in which the author took great pride. Zena Sutherland, reviewing Allan's *May Day Mystery* (1971), commented: "Although all of Mabel Allan's books follow a set pattern (English girl away from home becomes involved in mystery and also acquires a man), they are capably written and provide a background that usually has some interest." An avid traveler, Allan has successfully recreated a variety of international locations in her books, and has been frequently commended for her skill in evoking these settings. Reviewing *Home to the Island* (1962), a *Junior Bookshelf* critic noted that Allan "always writes against a real and vividly presented background," adding that "she also sympathizes with young people on the threshold of a career or in the throes of difficult family relationships or unhappy love affairs." Allan has also written a number of school stories, often with boarding school settings, that she considers ahead of their time, because they call for students' self-discipline rather than educator-administered discipline, student involvement in curriculum issues and other forms of decision making, and the elimination of letter grading in favor of learning for its own sake. Many of her later works also address other concerns that Allan has come to embrace, including women's rights and the plight of urban working-class youth.

Biographical Information

Allan was born in Wallasey, England, a Cheshire town on the Mersey River near Liverpool. As a child she suffered from very poor eyesight, the result of a vision disorder that plagued her until the age of twenty-nine, when she experienced a sudden reversal of her condition. Allan attended private schools in Wallasey until she was seventeen, and was greatly troubled by teachers who seemed unaware of the gravity of her eye problems and did not sense her frustration. She sought solace in books and reading, although her father discouraged this pursuit because of his concern for her vision. Spending hours at the local library, Allan devoured the boarding school books popular in her day. She began writing at an early age and composed her first book-length story when her father gave her a typewriter at the age of twelve. After finishing school, Allan continued to write while busying herself as a teacher of dance at girls' clubs and children's homes in Seacombe, Liverpool and Birkenhead. She sent stories to various sources of publication without success until one story for small children was purchased by a magazine called *Fairyland Tales*. Thus encouraged, Allan continued to write and sell short fiction, eventually offering stories for adolescents and older readers that were also accepted for publication. With the onset of World War II, she joined the British Women's Land Army and later worked as a teacher and warden in nursery schools. When the war in Europe ended in May of 1945, Allan had two reasons to celebrate: she had just sold her first book to publisher Frederick Warne. Although paper shortages and other post-war crises prevented the publication of this first or any subsequent work before 1948, Allan continued to write prolifically, completing dozens of books for young people as writing became her full-time career. During the 1950s she experienced grave setbacks with her eyesight, suffering a detached retina that greatly restricted her activity though sparing her vision. At the same time, however, her fiction was finding an audience outside of Britain: three of her books were published by three different New York publishers in 1957, and a translated version of one of her stories won an award in France in 1960. Over the course of more than three decades since, Allan has continued to write almost continuously, publishing a wealth of stories that have been well received by U.S. and U.K. audiences as well as readers in Poland, France, Holland, Italy, Portugal, Japan, and elsewhere.

Major Works

The Vine-Clad Hill (1956) (*Swiss Holiday,* 1957) was one of the first of Allan's works to be published in America. In this story, heroine Philippa Wynyard travels to Switzerland, where her aunt will pay her to look after her three young cousins during the holidays. Although aunt and cousins prove to be a handful for Philippa, a newfound romance makes the whole adventure worthwhile. While acknowledging that the storyline is something less than innovative, Zena Sutherland noted that the "modest plot is convincingly compounded of natural incidents which are well-related to the attitudes of the characters." A reviewer for *Virginia Kirkus' Service* enthused: "Few authors writing for adolescents show the respect for their readers' intelligence that Mabel Esther Allan does. A British writer, she achieves a synthesis of scene, romance, characterization which is poetic, ironic and observant." Many others of Allan's earlier works feature similar subjects and themes, in harmony with her penchant for depicting a heroine who leaves home and matures notably in the process. Sutherland described *Black Forest Summer* (1957) as "[a]nother good book about adolescent girls whose lives reach a turning point during a vacation

away from home," adding: "As in Miss Allan's previous novels, the new setting gives perspective, so that the protagonists face—and solve—their problems." In *Home to the Island,* eighteen-year-old Helen must leave Edinburgh, her schooling, and her sophisticated English boyfriend and travel home to the remote, barren Scottish island of Lindra to care for her motherless siblings. Another of Allan's early heroines, Julia Conway, is kidnapped after becoming entangled in mystery while visiting Paris in *The Sign of the Unicorn,* which a *Junior Bookshelf* reviewer called a "rattling good story."

Allan's later books are more introspective in nature, and more often feature settings closer to her childhood home. *We Danced in Bloomsbury Square,* one of a number of ballet stories Allan wrote under the pseudonym Jean Estoril, introduces Deborah and Doria Darke, twins who depart Liverpool for London and the rigorous life of a boarding house and ballet school. Allan was praised by many reviewers for her characterization of the twins in this story. Susan Stanton wrote that "the author avoids making the ambitious, outgoing girl a villain, and the deep-feeling, introverted one a genius, and instead shows very fairly the dark and light sides of both kinds of temperament." *The Wood Street Secret* also was acclaimed by many commentators for its realism, especially in the depiction of urban poverty and working-class children. In this story, young protagonists Ben and Cherry, new to Liverpool's old warehouse district, are invited by five new friends to the group's condemned, closed-off Wood Street hideaway. Margery Fisher commended *The Wood Street Secret* as having "[p]lenty of sense, good characterisation, [and] a strong flavour of Liverpool." Allan recounts protagonist Mairi Gilbride's 1920s childhood on an isolated island of the Scottish Outer Hebrides in *An Island in a Green Sea.* Despite poverty and hardship, Mairi is content with her circumstances—until her grandmother dies, her brothers emigrate to Canada, and her sister leaves to seek work in Glasgow. Mairi is comforted by the arrival of an English girl who has come to learn the language and customs of the island and offers Mairi a view of the world beyond. Of this highly regarded work, E. Colwell stated: "The book has a purpose—to give the succeeding generations of emigrants now living in Canada and the United States an impression of the 'islands in a green sea' which they may never see. This it does admirably and often movingly." *The View Beyond My Father,* which has especially strong ties to the author's own childhood experiences, has been praised for its depth of emotion and strong central characters. In this work, Mary Anne Angus, blind for two years of her adolescence before regaining her vision in an operation, experiences the frustration of an overprotective father who stifles her independence. Zena Sutherland wrote that *The View Beyond My Father* was written with "far more depth than Allan's usual travel-and-adventure stories," adding that the story "is especially fine in the characterization of a domineering Victorian father." Denise M. Wilms also praised the book, asserting that "Allan writes with insight; the story has an autobiographical cast that commands both interest and empathy."

Awards

Mystery in Wales was named runner-up for the Edgar Allan Poe Award by the Mystery Writers of America in 1972. *An Island in a Green Sea* was selected as a *Boston Globe-Horn Book* honor book the following year.

TITLE COMMENTARY

📖 *HERE WE GO ROUND: A CAREER STORY FOR GIRLS* (1954)

The Junior Bookshelf

SOURCE: A review of *Here We Go Round*, in *The Junior Bookshelf*, Vol. 18, No. 4, October, 1954, pp. 203-4.

Many career stories are really pill-coated sugar-lumps, and conjure up visions of young readers rushing into uncongenial occupations in the expectation of the notoriety and romance found in fiction. But only a girl who really liked young children and the idea of working with them would choose nursery work after reading this scrupulously honest little book.

In the first person the heroine, Mary McBride, looks back at the recent period when she worked as helper in a dock-side nursery school. Not yet 17, fastidious, and not very anxious to teach or to plunge into adult life, she encounters drudgery, discomfort, and dirt for the first time, and very uncongenial she finds them. The conditions and the school personnel all ring true, and there is a particularly just portrayal of Mary's fellow helper, a younger girl, always jolly and good with children, but lacking the professional qualities which Mary comes to recognize in herself. There are a few excitements—Mary's stories are accepted by the B.B.C., and she saves a child from fire—but they seem unconvincing in contrast to the very convincing central theme of Mary's growing interest and pleasure in her vocation. It would have been easy to make the repulsive old char-woman a comic figure, the young man turned from enemy to friend more romantic, and the impersonal but able superior suddenly sympathetic, but the author courageously resists. Her account is sober and fair-minded, but readable. It should appeal to many older girls, and those considering work with little children would be well advised to read it. Others, too, might profit from the picture of slum-area schools and teaching conditions presented in this unpretentious, but unusually sound career story.

The Junior Bookshelf

SOURCE: A review of *Here We Go Round*, in *The Junior Bookshelf*, Vol. 18, No. 5, November, 1954, p. 255.

Here we go round is more competently written [than E.

Forbes's *Brenda buys a beauty salon*], being by a professional author, and more satisfactory, probably because it covers a shorter period and takes unusual pains to be fair; possibly because teaching demands more human qualities than most work. Mary McBride, the heroine, is not sure she wants to teach at all and chooses nursery work as a lesser evil. To test her choice she spends her pre-college year as helper in a slum-area nursery, and gives in her first-person report, an unromanticized picture of the drudgery, the dirt, the dock-side children and exciting staff, and of her growing interest and pleasure in her work. A few excitements are allowed her, but far more are avoided—like the young man turned from slight enemy to mere friend, and the neighbourhood nuisance who remains unreformed—and there is a particularly good portrayal of her fellow-helper, a jolly, buoyant girl whose acknowledged way with children will never be a professional way. Few girls unfitted to teach would choose nursery work after reading this book, and few born to teach would be deterred by the grimness, while many might benefit from the picture of slum and teaching conditions.

M. J. P. Laurence

SOURCE: A review of *Here We Go Round*, in *The Junior Bookshelf*, Vol. 20, No. 3, July, 1956, pp. 108-9.

Here We Go Round is by the same author and purports to be a career story for girls who might like to know what it is to be a Nursery School teacher. Instead of centring the tale on a Nursery School, it tells of a pre-training year that the girl is taking as Nursery Assistant in a Nursery class attached to an Infants' School. This is a dubious device, as it is not the best approach to training; the girl would be better advised to remain in full-time education until 18. But granted that the framework be accepted, cannot a more up to date Nursery class be chosen? The Headmistress says blandly, " . . . Here we have so many difficulties," said Miss Wyckham. "Ideally the children should be much more free. They should have a safe playground out-of-doors, preferably with grass, trees and flowers. You'll learn when you go to college that the best way to organise the nursery day is to let the children join in activities only if they wish. Start a story with just a few and let the other children either join the group or carry on with their own amusements. . . ."

But that is no reason for all the techniques which make the trained Nursery School teacher shudder:—"Marshalling the children into quite an orderly line," "The Morning Ring," "calling the register," "marching out and making a train," "playing organised games," free play interpreted as "a bit of a melee, even when reasonably orderly, for the big boys always seem to like to do something vigorous," giving out percussion band instruments, "organised expeditions," a "period" for water play. There is even an item at the concert for the Nursery class. Beds are prepared for the children and not with the help of the children. Gardening, which should be such a natural, happy background for the Nursery school, with constant opportunities for a few children to take part, is a crowded, community activity with the teacher and the bigger children on the plot and everyone else standing round looking.

It is a great pity that the author did not take specialist advice before she wrote the book; for example, from the Nursery School Association. Even the title, *Here We Go Round,* is alien to the spirit and content of a good Nursery school.

JUDITH TEACHES (1955)

The Junior Bookshelf

SOURCE: A review of *Judith Teaches,* in *The Junior Bookshelf,* Vol. 19, No. 4, October, 1955, pp. 242-3.

In this addition to the Career Books for Girls the facts and realities of a teacher's first years are most skilfully interwoven with the fictional narrative. We have not only been given a story interesting in itself; Miss Allan has managed to establish throughout the book the attitude of mind which must be developed by any teacher who is to maintain her competence without infringing on her sanity. No doubt in some quarters Judith Prestwood's outlook on children and teaching might be condemned as sentimental but I am of the opinion that schools would be happier and more effective if her attitude were more widespread than it seems to be. Naturally, within the limit of its length the book telescopes much and emphasises the heights and depths of elation and despair while the longer, duller interludes of school life tend to appear to have been eliminated but there are definite indications that such do exist. The reasonable teacher knows this and knows also that the occasional triumphs of temporary perfection are worth aiming for, for the sake of the teacher and the taught. Both benefit from a feeling of accomplishment and this idea is certainly demonstrated here. On the Career side, the bias is for girls who are likely to take up work in a secondary modern school, and in larger towns. There is no attempt to glamorise the profession or its prospects, but the compensations and reliefs to be derived from keeping a sense of proportion about the job are clearly set out. In this book, to put it briefly, the reader is shown what teaching is really like.

M. J. P. Laurence

SOURCE: "Soldier, Sailor, Tinker, Tailor . . . ," in *The Junior Bookshelf,* Vol. 20, No. 3, July, 1956, pp. 107-8.

Judith Teaches is rather better than *Here We Go Round.* Specially interesting is the emphasis on individual children, the sense conveyed of the strain of a teacher's life and its interest and fascination for the teacher. . . .

The story itself is somewhat tuppence-coloured. The school is rather too successful in its competitions, the child's novel is a little too incredible, a little too good to be true. The references to Training College and the Inspectorate

seem rather old-fashioned. The Training College curriculum as described is certainly out of date and the Training College staff would have been horrified to find Judith teaching the first year Secondary Modern class "Noah and the Flood," or contemplating setting compositions on "My Favourite Pet" or "A Day at the Seaside." Judith's references to a teacher of folk dancing . . . "The woman who teaches them does not know the first thing about it, she only did it in a College," seems a curious remark in a book which is, presumably, to persuade some girls to teach and also to train for teaching. The attitude to the Inspectorate is similarly out of date. The Headmaster who takes every "opportunity to put the school on the map," says, "But we can almost certainly expect a General Inspection by the summer term at the latest. By then we must have something to show."

The book, however, is a pleasant reconstruction of the first year in a teaching post in a Secondary Modern school.

STRANGERS IN SKYE (1956)

Virginia Kirkus' Service

SOURCE: A review of *Strangers in Skye,* in *Virginia Kirkus' Service,* Vol. XXVI, No. 2, June 15, 1958, p. 36.

Elizabeth Falcon summered with her painter brother, John, on the isle of Skye. The youth hostel which John directed aroused bitter hostility in Colonel Kinloch, a neighbor, and for a time it seemed John's romance with Fiona, his granddaughter, would founder. Two local brothers Charles, glamorous but superficial and Grant, the steady native son loyal to the land, spar for Elizabeth's affection. The youth hostel gains a better name as the group helps in the search for a missing child and John undertakes a rescue mission on the mountains. The characters in their pastoral setting are deeply realized: the conflicts and crises of the plot are not compelling enough to bring this up to the earlier *Swiss Holiday* but it does project a sensitive heroine in her late teens with more conviction than most.

The Junior Bookshelf

SOURCE: A review of *Strangers in Skye,* in *The Junior Bookshelf,* Vol. 20, No. 2, March, 1956, pp. 73-4.

Mabel Esther Allan has written another unpretentious, cheerful book for girls who have grown out of holiday adventure stories. Her heroine is on holiday, but it is an enforced one (she has had trouble with her eyes), and soon she will be going to a university. Her interests are not ponies and sailing and lost treasure, but the people she meets in Skye, and the job she does with her painter brother who is in charge of a Youth Hostel there. New friends, quarrels, walks up mountains, a disaster, a feud with a local Colonel—these are the matter of her days. Elizabeth Falcon is no very strong or endearing character but she is a pleasant girl with whom many readers will identify themselves. Her eventual enjoyment of Skye, and satisfactory budding romance with a young man whose home is there, are happy things in which to share vicariously. A slight, simple story for many girls to enjoy, and then forget.

THE VINE CLAD HILL (1956; U.S. edition as Swiss Holiday)

The Junior Bookshelf

SOURCE: A review of *The Vine Clad Hill*, in *The Junior Bookshelf*, Vol. 20, No. 4, October, 1956, pp. 200-1.

This is another junior novel for the older girl, that resembles so many of its type. Philippa Wynyard is invited to Switzerland by an aunt, to look after her three young cousins during the holidays, before she, Philippa, goes to the University. The job is to be a paid one, and because she needs such a temporary job and cannot resist the temptation of Switzerland, Philippa accepts the offer, although her aunt and cousins are anything but likable. The author seeks to gather together a group of widely differing characters, all impingeing upon one another and needing a sorting and a straightening out. Her attempts at such a junior psychological novel are not very successful. Her writing is too naive and too immature, while her characters are not much more than caricatures. The story makes only happy light-hearted entertainment but there are a few pointers to true values and the good things of life, making the book a mild stimulant in a romantic and soothing way. The production is pleasing and attractive.

Virginia Kirkus' Service

SOURCE: A review of *Swiss Holiday*, in *Virginia Kirkus' Service*, Vol. XXV, No. 19, October 1, 1957, p. 745.

Few authors writing for adolescents show the respect for their readers' intelligence that Mabel Esther Allan does. A British writer, she achieves a synthesis of scene, romance, characterization which is poetic, ironic and observant. Furthermore in the story of Phillipa Wynward, a girl from a middle class London family who needs money for her studies at Cambridge, we meet a credible heroine, who finds romance. The author closes the story with the implication that *later* the romance may develop into serious committal. She achieves a wholesome balance by neither overemphasizing the importance of the attraction Phillipa feels for Timothy Randal nor underestimating her heroine's determination to continue her education. Phillipa takes advantage of a chance at a Swiss holiday when Aunt Millicent Hamlin, a patronizing upper-class matron asks her to look after the Hamlin children, Clemency, beautiful, almost 18, her mother's darling, Gay and Gordon, rebellious, troublesome nuisances and Tilda, the awkward poetic girl who enters adolescence overshadowed completely by Clemency's grace and beauty. Phillipa's adjustment to a more privileged milieu is interwoven with incidents of conflict and danger in the pastoral peace and crystal altitudes of Switzerland and its resorts.

Carefully wrought, and in style a little reminiscent of Daphne du Maurier.

Zena Sutherland

SOURCE: A review of *Swiss Holiday*, in *Bulletin of the Children's Book Center*, Vol. XI, No. 9, May, 1958, p. 89.

A teenage novel successfully presented in the first person. Phillipa, who is planning to get a job in the summer before college, is invited by her aunt to spend the summer in Switzerland helping to care for her younger cousins. Phillipa is stable and intelligent; her relationships with some of the members of her family are described with sharp perception. Especially moving is the portrayal of her younger cousin Tilda, who has been eclipsed all her life by a beautiful older sister. The modest plot is convincingly compounded of natural incidents which are well-related to the attitudes of the characters. Without moralizing, the author illustrates the possibility of effecting a change in others by one's own behavior.

Grace P. Slocum

SOURCE: A review of *Swiss Holiday*, in *The Saturday Review*, New York, Vol. 42, No. 19, May 19, 1958, p. 38.

The summer in Switzerland with wealthy, snobbish Aunt Millicent and her family had all the drawbacks Phillipa had anticipated but more real pleasures than she had dared to hope for. The youngest cousins were difficult to handle, fourteen-year-old Tilda's shy reserve almost impossible to break through, and the poised, well-dressed Clemency (just Phillipa's own age) made her feel as gawky and ill at ease as she always had. But Phillipa loved the Alps and the people she met there and was determined to enjoy the months before returning to London in time for her first term at Cambridge.

In this well-written, romantic novel for teen-age girls the author presents real people in an authentic setting who come to understand each other without losing their own identities.

ANN'S ALPINE ADVENTURE (1957)

The Junior Bookshelf

SOURCE: A review of *Ann's Alpine Adventure*, in *The Junior Bookshelf*, Vol. 21, No. 3, July, 1957, pp. 125-6.

One or two characters familiar to readers appear again in this story for girls. Ann, an English girl, goes to stay in Andermatt, Switzerland, where she helps her Swiss companion to overcome her shyness, makes friends with a group of young people and travels round one or two interesting places. The feeling for the country is well portrayed through Ann, though at times it becomes sentimental. There is no definite plot since the book mainly concerns Ann and her doings, the chief of which is her friendship with Leli. For the author to do this successfully requires thorough characterisation and in this case it is not thorough enough. The blossoming of Leli is unconvincing right to the end of the book. Ann herself seems a paragon of all that a young girl should be, but this, in a heroine, can, I suppose, be encouraged. Pussy Alleyne is the most lively and interesting character and therefore the most convincing. The Italian children complete the happy group. There are one or two adventures, together with one or two tremendous pieces of "good luck." The book will appeal to most girls over eleven to be read and enjoyed until the next M. E. Allan book comes along.

M. E. Ellis

SOURCE: A review of *Ann's Alpine Adventure,* in *The School Librarian and School Library Review,* Vol. 8, No. 5, July, 1957, p. 365.

Miss Allan has added another pleasant story to her list of "adventures abroad". Ann, at fourteen, has her first visit to Switzerland when she goes to spend some weeks with an old school friend of her mother's. She is a friendly girl, whose pleasure in her new experiences is slightly dimmed by having to cope with the shy, awkward daughter of the household; at first Ann is too eager to help, but when she knows Leli better and lets her become acquainted in her own way, a friendship of benefit to both girls begins to develop. Other children holidaying in the district come into the story, there are the usual kind of excursions and adventures, Leli proves herself something of a heroine, and all ends happily.

Miss Allan knows her Andermatt district well, and writes with sincerity and enthusiasm.

📖 *SUMMER OF DECISION* (1957)

Virginia Kirkus' Service

SOURCE: A review of *Summer of Decision,* in *Virginia Kirkus' Service,* Vol. XXV, No. 16, August 15, 1957, p. 586.

A summer at Glenvara in Ireland with her cousins gave Sheila O'Mara, a young British girl faced with a choice of vocations, the opportunity to persuade her father, a school principal in England, that writing offered good possibilities for a career. And Sheila's visit gave her cousin, Mairin, 17, the audience and encouragement she craved to further an acting career. The family and their British cousin initiated performances of short plays by Irish writers, with consequences affecting all their lives. Credible characterization, a lively plot and authentic background on Ireland as a country and a culture add up to a superior teen-aged story. Also, the exposition of parental attitudes toward the arts as a livelihood is valid. Wholesome entertainment with positive value.

Zena Sutherland

SOURCE: A review of *Summer of Decision,* in *Bulletin of the Children's Book Center,* Vol. XI, No. 8, April, 1958, p. 77.

Sheila O'Mara and her younger sister Mops leave Lancashire for a summer with relatives in Ireland. Sheila, 17, wants to be a writer; her cousin, Mairin, the same age, wants to become an actress. The parents of both girls are opposed to their plans and want them to do something more sensible. The three girls and Mairin's brothers Terry and Lanty do such a spectacular job of putting on a play for their own entertainment that they are pressed into forming a theater company. Sheila takes a part-time job and has a story printed in the local paper. By the end of the summer, both girls have convinced their parents to let them try to achieve their goals. Especially well-expressed by the author is the conflict which both the young people and their parents feel about a choice of career; the solution for Sheila is a realistic compromise in which she is to try writing while she works. Romance is introduced with less exaggeration than in many teen-age novels: Lanty falls in love with Sheila, but it is clearly compounded of proximity, novelty and moonlight.

📖 *BLACK FOREST SUMMER* (1957)

Zena Sutherland

SOURCE: A review of *Black Forest Summer,* in *Bulletin of the Center for Children's Books,* Vol. XIII, No. 6, February, 1960, p. 93.

Another good book about adolescent girls whose lives reach a turning point during a vacation away from home. As in Miss Allan's previous novels, the new setting gives perspective, so that the protagonists face—and solve—their problems. Here three sisters, newly orphaned, adjust to the loss of their mother and to their new status while they visit an uncle in Germany. The girls also learn to adjust to a family life more formal and old-fashioned than their own. Writing style is smooth, and the characters are interesting and highly individual. The ending of the book is slightly weakened by the appearance of an aunt who is a famous and wealthy artist, and who decided to return to England so that they may all live together. Not quite a pat reprieve, since the girls had already had an offer of help from Uncle Gustav, but an unnecessary last ornamentation of the plot.

Elizabeth Stafford

SOURCE: A review of *Black Forest Summer,* in *Junior Libraries,* Vol. 6, No. 8, April, 1960, p. 72.

Like this author's previous book, **Swiss Holiday,** this story is well worked out and satisfying and presents successfully life in present-day Germany. Three girls, Londoners, after the death of their mother, go, pretty much against their will, to spend the summer with an unknown uncle and his family. Their opposition is eventually overcome as they are given opportunities to indulge their various, very definite interests in painting, the ballet, and foreign language study. Dramatic presentation of the beauties of the Black Forest, good family relationships, and good, plausible plot. Recommended.

BLUE DRAGON DAYS (1958; U.S. edition as *Romance in Italy*)

M. E. Ellis

SOURCE: A review of *Blue Dragon Days,* in *The School Librarian and School Library Review,* Vol. 9, No. 3, December, 1958, pp. 233-4.

Jane Graydon, eighteen years old, pretty and vivacious, dislikes her work in an insurance office, and is delighted when a chance of taking a junior post with the Blue Dragon travel agency in Genoa is offered to her. Here she makes friends with her Italian cousins, so far estranged from her parents by a family quarrel, and the story ends with the possibility of her marriage to the eldest cousin Andrea. Miss Allan is fond of Italy and describes the sea-coast villages with affection; she also understands the feelings of a young girl set to work among strangers, with an eager interest in everything that is new around her and yet having strong loyalties to her parents. There is colour and life in her writing, but it is sometimes marred by her way of letting the older women in her stories patronize the younger ones; it is an irritating trait which she would do well to lose.

Zena Sutherland

SOURCE: A review of *Romance in Italy,* in *Bulletin of the Center for Children's Books,* Vol. XVI, No. 4, December, 1962, p. 53.

Jane has always longed to travel, and she is overjoyed at the offer of a travel agency job in Genoa, particularly since her mother was born there. Cast off by her father because she had married an Englishman, Jane's mother extracts a promise that her daughter will never divulge the relationship. In Genoa, Jane becomes involved with her relations and falls in love with Andrea, an adopted son of the family; when her grandfather dies, matters come to a head: her mother comes to Genoa in response to a letter of confession, and Jane and Andrea decide they will marry in another year. Much in the pattern of other books by this author, with foreign background, career interest, and quite good characterization and values. The story is weakened somewhat by dependence on coincidence: on the train to Genoa, Jane returns a lost pin to the girl who turns out to be her cousin—when Jane goes sightseeing, she helps another cousin who has hurt her ankle and so is invited to the family home—when Jane goes on holiday with two other girls they again run into the cousins when they are stranded on an expedition.

CATRIN IN WALES (1959)

The Junior Bookshelf

SOURCE: A review of *Catrin in Wales,* in *The Junior Bookshelf,* Vol. 23, No. 3, July, 1959, p. 163.

Catrin is a young girl who has just left school, and who goes to visit her mother's sister in Wales. She finds her aunt acting as guide to an historical building; almost immediately on her arrival the old lady falls and breaks her leg, and Catrin is left in charge. The author includes the romantic element necessary for the teen-age girl by permitting a neighbouring farmer to fall in love with Catrin—a farmer who also turns out to be a successful playwright.

This then is the admittedly unlikely situation from which the author creates a thoroughly pleasant story. Catrin proves to be a very likeable girl who is not too proud to admit how petrified she is to remain living alone in the eerie ruined abbey. The local folk think she will not have the courage to stay, but stay she does and is amply rewarded, not only by the meeting with her future husband, but also by the friendliness of some of the neighbours, the gradual awareness of her love of all things Welsh, and the mounting excitement as the annual Eisteddfod visits Llangollen.

Virginia Kirkus' Service

SOURCE: A review of *Catrin in Wales,* in *Virginia Kirkus' Service,* Vol. XXVIII, No. 16, August 15, 1960, p. 686.

Eighteen-year-old Catrin leaves her London home for a walking trip in Wales. An accident in which her elderly aunt is injured launches Catrin into the unexpected career of Priory custodian. At first the city girl detests the eerie ruins of the convent and the quiet Welsh countryside, but friendship, romance, and a deep spiritual involvement with the people and their customs convince her, finally, that Wales is the country in which she must permanently make her home. Rich in detail of the Welsh countryside, this quiet story has moments of singular poignance and sensitivity.

Virginia Haviland

SOURCE: A review of *Catrin of Wales,* in *The Horn Book Magazine,* Vol. XXXVII, No. 1, February, 1961, p. 54.

Miss Allan manages to make acceptable a most unlikely situation, that of an eighteen-year-old London girl alone taking over residence and guide service in priory ruins in a lonely Welsh valley. Catrin tells her own story, with considerable introspection. It is the unusual setting coupled with a girl's appreciation of regional antiquity and the Eisteddfodd that recommends the book. Not the best from this author, but no less rewarding a background than usual.

📖 *A PLAY TO THE FESTIVAL* (1959; U.S. edition as *"On Stage, Flory!"*)

The Junior Bookshelf

SOURCE: A review of *A Play for a Festival,* in *The Junior Bookshelf,* Vol. 23, No. 3, July, 1959, p. 164.

Flory Ronald comes of a theatrical family on her mother's side and is very anxious to go on the stage. With the help of her great aunt, a famous actress, she goes to the Edinburgh Festival as an "extra" in a long verse play, the success of which is problematical. Her friend Joanna is acting in another play on the "fringe" of the Festival and the two girls share lodgings. Of course there is the fortuitous accident to one of the principals which gives Flory her chance of a speaking part in which she is successful. The story ends with the probability that the play will continue in London and elsewhere but the love interest makes it seem likely that Flory will not long pursue a stage career.

The love interest is pleasantly introduced without sentimentality and the author also gives the reader some idea of the City of Edinburgh and the Festival arrangements. Nor is the glamour of the stage overdone and though the story itself shows no great originality in its plot it is of average quality and not so obviously a "career book" as some.

Zena Sutherland

SOURCE: A review of *On Stage, Flory!,* in *Bulletin of the Center for Children's Books,* Vol. XIV, No. 8, April, 1961, p. 121.

Flory Ronald, having convinced her parents to let her try a career on the stage, gets a job with a company that is putting on an experimental play at the Edinburgh Festival. She is successful in a small part and she falls in love with the young producer of an amateur group that is also performing. The theatrical background is interesting, and it is handled in realistic—not melodramatic—fashion. The characterizations are not quite as well done as they are in other books by this author, and the story is so heavily saturated with Edinburgh atmosphere that it competes with the theatrical details in a rather obtrusive manner.

Peggy Sullivan

SOURCE: A review of *On Stage, Flory!* in *Junior Libraries,* Vol. 7, No. 8, April, 1961, p. 57.

The Edinburgh Festival provides the colorful, romantic setting for this story of a London girl. Flory's exuberance and interest in the play, the people around her, and the picturesque and historic city make her a delightful heroine. If the happy accident which gives Flory a speaking part seems too fortuitous, the book has value enough to offset this flaw. Readers in the early teens will relish the romance with an older man (of 20).

📖 *DRINA DANCES IN ITALY* (as Jean Estoril, 1959; U.S. edition as *Drina Dances on Stage*)

The Junior Bookshelf

SOURCE: A review of *Drina Dances in Italy,* in *The Junior Bookshelf,* Vol. 24, No. 2, March, 1960, p. 86.

This is the fourth in a series of books about Drina Adams, daughter of a famous ballerina, and an Italian father. An orphan, Drina lives with her English grandparents and attends the Dominick ballet school in London. Later she visits her Italian grandmother and finds the Dominick are to dance in Milan.

The whole story is interesting and can be read without knowledge of its predecessors. There is sufficient information about the ballet itself but the girls live a natural life and make their own friendships. In Italy the background scene is well painted and though Drina "stands in" for a girl who is ill, this is nothing very spectacular or incredible. Altogether a very good type of "career" book mainly because the "career" is kept in its place and not presented as the whole of life. Nor is it over glamourised or used as an excuse for silly nonsense—it is just a chosen career entailing hard work and skill like any other.

Zena Sutherland

SOURCE: A review of *Drina Dances in Italy,* in *Bulletin of the Center for Children's Books,* Vol. XV, No. 7, March, 1962, p. 109.

A sequel to ***Ballet for Drina;*** Drina, now fourteen, is back at her old ballet school in London. Invited to Italy by the grandmother she has never seen, Drina is apprehensive until she learns that her school's company will be performing there. While in Geona, Drina substitutes for a dancer who is ill, and receives commendation in a review of the ballet. The book is unhappily burdened by too many characters, too many small sub-plots, too many detailed descriptions of excursions or performances. The writing style is turgid and the characterizations are shallow.

📖 *A SUMMER IN BRITTANY* (1960; U.S. edition as *Hilary's Summer on Her Own*)

The Junior Bookshelf

SOURCE: A review of *A Summer in Brittany,* in *The Junior Bookshelf,* Vol. 24, No. 2, March, 1960, p. 95.

Eighteen year-old Hilary Ashford answers an advertisement for a companion to the children of a Breton family for the summer holidays. The idyllic setting, the clash of temperaments within the family, the arrival on the scene of a boy-friend in the shape of a school-teacher temporarily turned author, are some of the ingredients which help to make this novel for the older girl pleasant light reading. The author reveals the charm engendered by the romantic old town of La-Trinité-sur-Cronne, and she also reveals a brisk, commonsense attitude towards the various domestic situations which arise as the plot unfolds. The author is to be congratulated upon providing a series of books, for the adolescent girl, with an interesting geographical background, and a sensible outlook on everyday life.

The Times Literary Supplement

SOURCE: "Further Instalments," in *The Times Literary Supplement,* No. 3038, May 20, 1960, p. xiv.

A Summer in Brittany by Mabel Esther Allan has a newcomer as the heroine, but plot and locality are disturbingly similar to other books by this author. Eighteen-year-old Hilary answers an advertisement asking for an English girl to live with a French family during the summer. She accepts the position with some trepidation and soon becomes involved with the tempestuous Sylvestres. The characterization is clear and precise, especially the French family, and the story has many ingredients for popularity. But although a lot of thought has gone into this book, there is an overall feeling of flatness.

Zena Sutherland

SOURCE: A review of *Hilary's Summer on Her Own,* in *Bulletin of the Center for Children's Books,* Vol. XIV, No. 7, March, 1961, p. 104.

Hilary was eighteen and about to enter Oxford; for three years she had been living with an aunt who was her only relative. Shy, but determined to have a change, Hilary answered an ad for a summer job: companion and English teacher to three French girls. Her two months in Brittany were more troublesome than she had expected, because all three girls had problems; her summer had a happier aspect than she had ever expected, however, because she fell in love. Good writing style, good characterization, and interesting background. The author is perceptive about family relationships, but the book is slightly weakened by the fact that almost everybody has a problem and by the ending, in which all of the problems are solved.

The Christian Science Monitor

SOURCE: A review of *Hilary's Summer on Her Own,* in *The Christian Science Monitor,* May 11, 1961, p. 46.

Normally a story which shows a young person living in a country other than her own has much to commend it, for the more we know about how other nations live, the better under standing we gain. [In *Hilary's Summer on Her Own*] Hilary, an 18-year-old English girl who has been orphaned and lives with an aunt, takes a job in Brittany, where she cares for children in a French family which also includes a German girl. The author is apparently English, for the story includes many phrases and words which will fall unfamiliarly on American ears. The real disadvantage, however, is a point of view, which seems to condone deceit on Hilary's part, as well as a justifying of wine drinking. Also, this tale seems to include more inharmony than constructive family relationships, and altogether makes a less than satisfying whole.

THE FIRST TIME I SAW PARIS (as Anne Pilgrim, 1961)

Virginia Kirkus' Service

SOURCE: A review of *The First Time I Saw Paris,* in *Virginia Kirkus' Service,* Vol. XXIX, No. 18, September 15, 1961, p. 847.

A young English girl abandons her plan to attend a teachers' college in London following her father's death and decides in favor of a position in a Parisian boarding school run by her aunt. Roberta leaves her boy friend Edward, who disapproves of the whole idea, and becomes immersed in the problems of her wards, especially in helping two step-sisters learn to get along. Romance comes her way in the form of Philippe, a French student, but in the end Roberta must differentiate between spun sugar romance and real love. The plot—in some ways routine—is actually incidental to the enchanting travel log that unfolds as the reader sees Paris for the time through the appreciative and wondering eyes of the sensitive young girl. There are impressive trips to the Louvre, to the Bois de Boulogne, and Versailles. Enjoying dinner on the Left Bank, riding to the top of the Eiffel Tower, living in the picturesque Montmartre of Utrillo's canvases allow Roberta to realize her dreams. The book is imbued with a scenic life that fairly emits the odors of springtime in this fabulous city.

Zena Sutherland

SOURCE: A review of *The First Time I Saw Paris,* in *Bulletin of the Center for Children's Books,* Vol. XV, No. 2, October, 1961, p. 32.

Newly orphaned and eighteen, Roberta leaves London to work on the staff of her aunt's Parisian school for British and American children. She falls in love with a French youth whose arranged engagement he has been keeping secret; at the close of the book Roberta has decided to marry the steady and gentle old friend from home. The second theme of the story is the unhappy relationship between two small girls who have just become stepsisters and sent together to the school; a theme that is handled with realism. Adequate characterization, but the story is weakened by the somewhat obtrusive details of local color, and by a rather pretentious style of writing.

The Junior Bookshelf

SOURCE: A review of *The First Time I Saw Paris,* in *The Junior Bookshelf,* Vol. 29, No. 5, October, 1965, p. 307.

Anne Pilgrim is the pen-name of a writer of popular novels for the 'teen-age girl. Recently she has given us some junior thrillers, but in this book she has returned to her formula of heroine of 17, lonely in London, taking a temporary post abroad and after an unsatisfactory first romance, returning to "the boy next door." It is pleasantly done, and with no illustrations and an adult-approach in the cover design, it may well appeal to the girl who has outgrown school stories but is not ready to read adult novels entirely. The author knows the kind of things a sensitive, well-brought up girl will be interested in in a foreign city, and followers of Roberta's adventures will find themselves in sympathy with her as she explores Montmartre, ascends the Eiffel Tower, and makes friends with French families, sorting out her own problems as she learns to cope with her small charges at the school where she works. Not one of the year's outstanding books, but pleasing and helpful to readers who need to gain confidence in themselves.

HOME TO THE ISLAND (1962)

The Junior Bookshelf

SOURCE: A review of *Home to the Island,* in *The Junior Bookshelf,* Vol. 26, No. 4, October, 1962, p. 187.

A few years ago Miss Allan made a name for herself as a popular writer of school and family adventure tales; now she is our chief exponent of the "junior romance." The best part about her stories is that she always writes against a real, and vividly-presented background. This time it is one of the thinly-populated isles of the Outer Hebrides. She also sympathises with young people on the threshold of a career or in the throes of difficult family relationships or unhappy love affairs; several of her heroines, like eighteen year-old Helen in this story, have to face giving up what they had planned for the future, and only after considerable readjustment do they find happiness in a new environment. Unfortunately, one is now only too ready to guess what will happen from the first page; here Helen abandons Edinburgh and the sophisticated George for the island of Lindra and (eventually) John Angus the village schoolmaster. The background may vary, the incidental characters and events may be different, but "plus ça change, plus c'est la même chose." This is not to deride Miss Allan's books; they are good straightforward tales which one can safely recommend to girls of eleven to thirteen or so. They are always enjoyable, and serve to widen a young reader's background.

Ruth Rausen

SOURCE: A review of *Home to the Island,* in *Library Journal,* Vol. 91, No. 13, July, 1966, p. 3541.

Eighteen-year-old Helen must go home to one of the Scottish Outer Isles to help care for her motherless family. She is reluctant to leave the busy city of Edinburgh for the remote, barren island where nothing ever happens, where Gaelic is spoken, and everything is so old-fashioned. She comes to find beauty in the land, the people, the songs; she meets an agreeable, intelligent, young schoolmaster, organizes a festival, and sheds her regrets. Well-written with the local color smoothly worked into the plot.

Sister M. Lucille

SOURCE: A review of *Home to the Island,* in *Catholic Library World,* Vol. 38, No. 4, December, 1966, p. 271.

When eighteen-year-old Helen Galbraith is asked by her father to leave Edinburgh for the small remote island of Lindra off the coast of Scotland to take up her responsibilities in the home, she resents the request because it means giving up her education and leaving her sophisticated English boyfriend, George. But Lindra promises more to Helen than she had anticipated. Helen learns a new set of values and meets John Angus MacKelloch, who adds a new note in her life. An unusually well-written light romance with flesh and blood characters. Recommended.

A SUMMER IN PROVENCE (as Anne Pilgrim, 1963)

Virginia Kirkus' Service

SOURCE: A review of *A Summer in Provence,* in *Virginia Kirkus' Service,* Vol. XXXI, No. 17, September 1, 1963, p. 871.

The author's latest (earlier titles include *The First Time I Saw Paris*) does not contain much insight into a foreign country or many descriptions of its sights and scenes, as do her earlier books. After conveniently killing off the parents and eliminating confusing intervention of close relatives, the author launches into a far-fetched story of Emily and her proud brother Simon, both in their late teens or thereabouts. Their summer in Provence consists of association with a mysterious child, Maryvette (the child's pearl-like quality is never explained), a few romances, and three expected marriages. It is all disjointed and poorly plotted; the false dream world aura which hangs over all is abruptly withdrawn toward the end, without explanation.

Margery Fisher

SOURCE: A review of *A Summer in Provence,* in *Growing Point,* Vol. 2, No. 9. April, 1964, pp. 291-2.

Anne Pilgrim, dispensing with drama, concentrates on the personal dilemma of a brother and sister (Simon and Emily

Mountwood, aged twenty and seventeen) who need to earn money while Simon finishes his teachers' training. Their work at Mrs. Payne's guest-house is hard enough even before it is complicated by her daughter Marigold, whose caprices cut across Emily's gentle romance with the son of a local celebrity. Again, characterisation is slight and conventional—except for one person; brother and sister seem cardboard figures beside Mrs. Payne, a person drawn in the round, a woman selfish and greedy through circumstance, uncertain of herself, aggressive, an adult's character in a book which has otherwise been watered down for young people.

THE SIGN OF THE UNICORN: A THRILLER FOR YOUNG PEOPLE (1963)

Virginia Kirkus' Service

SOURCE: A review of *The Sign of the Unicorn*, in *Virginia Kirkus' Service*, Vol. XXXI, No. 19, October 1, 1963, p. 965.

Alone in Paris at the age of eighteen, Julia manages fairly well for herself, but chances to become involved with two strange individuals. Curiosity leads Julia into the center of blackmail and murder; she knows her French friends are connected with the intrigue, and sets out to uncover details. By withholding information from both the reader and J., the author creates a realistic amount of suspense and maintains tension nearly to the end. Mainly mystery with a minimal romance, it is smoothly written—for girls.

The Junior Bookshelf

SOURCE: A review of *The Sign of the Unicorn*, in *The Junior Bookshelf*, Vol. 27, No. 6, December, 1963, p. 354.

When this author's *A Summer in Brittany* was published we congratulated her on this series of short stories for adolescent girls "with an interesting geographical background and a sensible outlook on everyday life." The same can be said about her new book with the addition that it is a rattling good story too. It is referred to as a "thriller for young people" and space-gazing young males will enjoy it too, including the quite credible love interest in it. The Parisian scene is well described and we feel the atmosphere of that city. If one or two events seem unlikely by our police notions then we must put this down to the difference between coppers and gendarmes.

Zena Sutherland

SOURCE: A review of *The Sign of the Unicorn*, in *Bulletin of the Center for Children's Books*, Vol. XVII, No. 5, January, 1964, p. 73.

As in other Allan books, a story in which an English girl has adventures in another country; here Julia Conway becomes involved in more mystery and melodrama than the author has hitherto permitted her heroine. Julia, unexpectedly alone in Paris, becomes acquainted with a French girl, Annette; it is clear that Annette and her brother are in serious and frightening trouble. Julia herself is followed by a suspicious character; the mystery is solved after a highly dramatic conclusion in which Julia is kidnapped, is rescued by her British suitor, and escapes being run down by the car in which two criminals crash and are killed. The pace is good, the plot construction tight-knit if not credible, and the mood of suspense is well-maintained. The melodramatic plot and some of the coincident episodes within the action weaken the story.

NEW YORK FOR NICOLA (1963)

Virginia Kirkus' Service

SOURCE: A review of *New York for Nicola*, in *Virginia Kirkus' Service*, Vol. XXXI, No. 20, October 15, 1963, pp. 1010-11.

Stricken with poliomyelitis just when she is beginning to succeed as a concert pianist, nineteen-year-old Nicola stays far from the keyboard and clings to her home in London for security. An invitation—which her parents accept for her—from an aunt to spend a few months in New York City forces Nicola to face herself. Although she incurred no physical defects from the disease, at first she seems only half alive. She is partially cured by the boat trip and completely rehabilitated by New York—a city she finds more friendly and exciting than her native London. A brisk, preoccupied aunt, two bewildered children, a friendly uncle, and—of course a handsome young man (who proposes at the end of the N.Y.C. visit) fill out the cast. The author has provided a refreshing perspective of New York realistically, but she weakens the book considerably by tacking a few unnecessary paragraphs on to the end in which all the problems of all the characters are settled with a few words as Nicola trips off to the pier to meet her American beau, who ever true, has left the stars and stripes behind. By the author of *Romance in Italy*, this is a low level story—for girls.

Zena Sutherland

SOURCE: A review of *New York for Nicola*, in *Bulletin of the Center for Children's Books*, Vol. XVII, No. 6, February, 1964, p. 89.

Deviating slightly from the pattern of previous heroines-away-from-home, a book in which an English girl comes to New York City reluctantly, and immediately falls in love with the town as well as with Gray, a young man who lives there. Nicola is a young pianist whose recent illness has made her feel dubious about pursuit of her career and about the fact that a concert pianist must travel. She gets over her doubts and her depression by helping a young actress who has had some of the same emotional problems; she achieves additional security when she finds her love for Gray is reciprocated. The author writes well, the characters are interesting, the plot is adequate; the weakness of the book is in the emphasis on New York sights and scenes, an emphasis that, in some chapters, has almost the quality of a travel brochure.

STRANGERS IN NEW YORK (as Anne Pilgrim, 1964)

Virginia Kirkus' Service

SOURCE: A review of *Strangers in New York*, in *Virginia Kirkus' Service*, Vol. XXXII, No. 18, September 15, 1964, p. 965.

Anne Pilgrim, whose earlier books have romanced through Paris, Holland, and Provence, now brings the three motherless Saxon children from London to New York. Only Anthea, 18, is pleased. She may see Clyde again. But she's less pleased when she sees him with another girl. The Saxons get to know New York, the streets, shops, museums, Lever and Seagram buildings; they walk in the parks and take a trip to Staten Island; they find an apartment and Anthea gets a job; and they look up the old friends of their mother who had been an American. At last all adjust. . . . A rather storyless story, but there are lots of moods, dreamy, restless, poignant, lonely and finally radiant.

Zena Sutherland

SOURCE: A review of *Strangers in New York*, in *Bulletin of the Center for Children's Books*, Vol. XVIII, No. 6, February, 1965, p. 91.

Three young people who have never been in the United States come from London to live in New York, the city where their dead mother had grown up. Anthea, eighteen, is especially excited because she is in love with a New Yorker she had met at home; all three are bent on tracing friends of their mother's, a pursuit they hide from their father. Anthea, disappointed in love, finds a new beau and a job; father, startled by the fact that the children have met friends of his wife (whose loss is still so hard to bear that he cannot talk about it) realizes that his children need to remember their mother. The city scene is described in a style a bit too much like a tour-brochure to be interesting; writing style and characterization are adequate, but not polished; the story line is believable but labored.

THE BALLET FAMILY AGAIN (1964; U.S. edition as The Dancing Garlands)

The Junior Bookshelf

SOURCE: A review of *The Ballet Family Again*, in *The Junior Bookshelf*, Vol. 28, No. 5, November, 1964, p. 301.

This is a sequel to *The Ballet Family* and, though there are plenty of explanatory references to the first book, not to have read it is a slight disadvantage. It tells of the doings of the Garland family and the Thorburg ballet school during the cold winter of 1962. There are several vague themes, but on the whole it is a sprawling family chronicle, a harmless story with a little light romance for added flavour. There is a great deal of repetition, for example Pelagia, the eldest daughter and a budding ballerina, an ethereal dancer, is constantly to be found "munching chocolates" and eating enormous meals. The youngest child is an "enfant terrible" whose reactions are tiresomely predictable. There are some good passages, telling the stories of various ballets and of the technicalities of composing a ballet, which will certainly interest young fans.

In short this is a "run-of-the-mill" novel lacking depth of perception and nothing is added by the illustrations, which are very unimaginative. It is probably suited to the 10–14 age group. All the ingredients for a good, strong story are present, but a less hidebound treatment would have given it a much wider appeal.

Nancy Berkowitz

SOURCE: A review of *The Dancing Garlands: The Ballet Family Again*, in *School Library Journal*, Vol. 15, No. 8, April, 1969, p. 120.

The English Garlands are back on stage, beset with new problems. Pelagia can't make up her mind whether or not to marry devoted Timothy—she claims to be completely dedicated to her career as a dancer. Edward has his first brush with romance and finds to his disgust that the girl is really interested in his famous parents. Anne must adjust to the loss of her best friend, who leaves the ballet school for another career, and young Delphine has an accident that may prevent her from ever dancing again. Cousin Joan faces the unpleasant fact that she has outgrown her old home in the provinces, and struggles to create another ballet to prove that her first successful attempt was not just a fluke. At last, everyone gathers in Paris during April, and happy solutions are meted out by the author to all. Contrived—yes, but smoothly written, and the kind of story young teen-age girls, especially those interested in ballet, will enjoy.

FIONA ON THE FOURTEENTH FLOOR (1964; U.S. edition as Mystery on the Fourteenth Floor)

The Junior Bookshelf

SOURCE: A review of *Fiona on the Fourteenth Floor*, in *The Junior Bookshelf*, Vol. 28, No. 6, December, 1964, p. 388.

Fiona is on her way to America to meet her father when she realises that something rather strange is going on around her. Her handbag is stolen, and the only reason for this seems to be the letter in which her father tells her that he has discovered that something criminal is happening in his block of flats in New York. Father fails to meet her when the ship docks and Fiona is alone in the vast city and it soon becomes obvious that she is in danger. It takes time to find her father who is in hospital, but she then finds that she has unearthed too many facts about a spy ring. However she is saved in the nick of time and her shipboard romance culminates in an engagement ring.

Plenty of action here and the bustling, teeming life of New York makes an excellent setting. The author also shows that there is a more peaceful gracious side to the American life and countryside.

Virginia Kirkus' Service

SOURCE: A review of *Mystery on the Fourteenth Floor,* in *Virginia Kirkus' Service,* Vol. XXXIII, No. 3, February 1, 1965, p. 115.

This mystery, which begins on the 14th floor of a New York house apartment where Fiona, from London, goes to join her long absentee writer-father, ends on the 15th floor where a spy ring has been operative. In between Fiona has had the unnerving experience of finding herself alone—her father has disappeared—being followed by strange men, and finally being held by, but escaping, the spies whom her father had tried to expose. The story, a little underweight to begin with, is force-fed with activity by the close—her father is found, amnestic, in a hospital; and there's her own new romance. But there's lots of detail about seeing and sightseeing in New York (and Washington) and the American setting should extend the readership. Congenial.

Zena Sutherland

SOURCE: A review of *Mystery on the Fourteenth Floor,* in *Bulletin of the Center for Children's Books,* Vol. XVIII, No. 11, July-August, 1965, p. 157.

Fiona, eighteen, sails from England to New York; nervous about living with the father she hasn't seen for some years, she is shattered when he doesn't meet her at the pier. He is not in his apartment, and none of his acquaintances know where he is. Fiona makes a few friends and begins to feel more at ease although she is very worried about her father. She becomes more and more convinced the two men on the floor above are criminals and that they are responsible for her father's absence; she finds that the men are indeed spies and that she is in danger. Father's absence is, however, only a coincidence, since he turns up in a hospital as an accident victim. Although the plot has heavy elements of coincidence and of contrivance, the writing style is good and the reaction of a young English girl to New York is mildly interesting.

IT HAPPENED IN ARLES (1964; U.S. edition as *Mystery in Arles*)

The Christian Science Monitor

SOURCE: A review of *Mystery in Arles,* in *The Christian Science Monitor,* February 25, 1965, p. 7.

Mabel Esther Allan is fast becoming the Mary Stewart of the 12's up. This tale is a glittering mixture of mystery, suspense, and romance. As its title implies, it is set in the South of France where an 18-year-old English girl is spending her summer holiday. Like all good heroines of her type, she is attractive and cannot help falling into love or into danger. Visits to the Roman amphitheater in Arles and to the bridge at Avignon provide an opportunity for some good descriptive writing.

Zena Sutherland

SOURCE: A review of *Mystery in Arles,* in *Bulletin of the Center for Children's Books,* Vol. XVIII, No. 7, March, 1965, p. 97.

Damaris Cleveland goes to France with her cousin Celia, and there she becomes involved in a mystery that culminates in a murder in the Roman Amphitheater at Arles. The man Damaris is in love with is suspected and arrested; she helps clear his name with the help of a fellow Briton, Thomas, in a dramatic and dangerous confrontation with the criminals. The plot is a bit contrived, characterization is adequate, writing style is good, and the details of locale are vivid.

A SUMMER AT SEA (1966)

The Junior Bookshelf

SOURCE: A review of *A Summer at Sea,* in *The Junior Bookshelf,* Vol. 30, No. 1, February, 1966, p. 56.

Gillian thinks she has a broken heart when her boy friend lets her down and she resolves never to reveal her feelings again. A bad dose of influenza leaves her weak and depressed and in an effort to restore her to health an aunt offers to get her a job helping with a shop on board ship. At first Gillian is not too impressed with life at sea as she has to share a very cramped cabin with her aunt, but it is not long before she is fascinated by the foreign towns they visit and involved in the lives of the passengers. Of course a new young man is soon taking an interest in Gillian and all ends in the best possible way.

Not inspired writing but good material for girls of thirteen and over who think they are too old for children's books but who have not developed enough to enjoy really "grown up" novels. Mabel Esther Allan is adept at giving them some romance while still keeping their feet on the ground.

Kathleen Kennedy

SOURCE: A review of *A Summer at Sea,* in *School Library Journal,* Vol. 14, No. 3, November, 1967, p. 72.

An 18-year-old English girl, Gillian Manson, after an unhappy romance, takes a job aboard a cruise ship for the summer. Glimpses of the ports of call—Amsterdam, Copenhagen and Bergen—are colorful but do not make this more than a poorly plotted, weakly characterized girl-loses-boy, girl-meets-new-boy story. Gillian's fellow crew members and passengers fare just as well with their problems, and happy endings are the order of the day as the ship returns to London. The text and illustrations are not well coordinated, though both are equally mediocre.

Zena Sutherland

SOURCE: A review of *A Summer at Sea,* in *Bulletin of the Center for Children's Books,* Vol. 21, No. 10, June, 1968, p. 153.

As do other books by this author, this offers a combination of romance, travel, and some personal problems; this is a slight variation from the pattern in that the protagonist is on tour, rather than residing in a foreign place. Gillian, who has had an unhappy love affair, takes a job on a small cruise liner sailing from England to Holland, Denmark, and Norway. She gets over her chagrin and finds a new love, copes with the ship's enfante terrible, makes friends. The rather patterned plot is alleviated by a competent writing style, with good but not deep characterization; a certain amount of travel information is incorporated, not always smoothly.

THE WAY OVER WINDLE (1966)

The Times Literary Supplement

SOURCE: "Stepping-Stones," in *The Times Literary Supplement,* No. 3351, May 19, 1966, p. 446.

Mabel Esther Allan, in *The Way over Windle,* has been . . . successful in interweaving ancient history and modern plot, probably because for her character and story are of paramount importance and the old road over the moors, which Simon and Betsy rediscover, is a useful and solid thread on which to hang a good tale. Not only Simon, who has recently moved to the moors from the Chilterns, but the reader too soon become immersed in moorland talk, customs and people—and lost in its "capricious mist". Raymond Briggs, who illustrates, is superb with scenery and spaniels but should only be asked to draw fantasy human beings.

Margery Fisher

SOURCE: A review of *The Way Over Windle,* in *Growing Point,* Vol. 5, No. 4, October, 1966, pp. 772-3.

Mabel Esther Allan uses a form unusual for her, in *The Way over Windle,* and this book is so good that I wish she would give 'teenage romance a rest and write more stories in the disciplined length of the Pied Piper series. For it is a discipline to direct a story so short and simple and make it seem full and strong. This is the description of a journey—straightforward in plan, difficult in execution. The Harlows have come from suburban Bucks. to live on the moors near Manchester and are not sure they like the change. But Simon makes friends with Betsy Thorpe next door and they decide to go and look for the lost road over Brown Windle to Ogleshaw. They have to wait for their expedition till Cousin William comes to stay, for he is fourteen and may be trusted to look after them. But William is a know-all and the journey shows him up as he loses his way and prolongs the outing alarmingly. The merits of the story lie in its simplicity and smoothness of style and in the direct, pleasing way the author manages the moorland setting, not exaggerating detail but using it as an element of the plot.

The Junior Bookshelf

SOURCE: A review of *The Way Over Windle,* in *The Junior Bookshelf,* Vol. 30, No. 5, October, 1966, p. 306.

The North Country beyond Manchester struck ten year-old Simon as bleak and ugly after his native Chilterns. However, the people seemed friendly enough, especially Betsy, the girl next door, who showed him the moors. Once on the moors, Simon was caught by their beauty and the feeling of freedom their vastness gave him. When he discovered the remains of an old road over Brown Windle, he determined to follow it and get it replaced on the O.S. map of the area.

Well written and with good family relationships, this simple book for 7–10 year-olds has plot, character and suspense.

SKIING TO DANGER (1966; U.S. edition as Mystery of the Ski Slopes)

Margery Fisher

SOURCE: A review of *The First Time I Saw Paris* and *Skiing to Danger,* in *Growing Point,* Vol. 4, No. 9, April, 1966, pp. 681-2.

It would be a good exercise for a correspondence course in writing if students had to write a story about a pretty eighteen-year-old in Paris and her attendant swains, one a sober Britisher working in a bank, the other a smooth Frenchman—the story to be designed successively for ages 14, 17 and for adults. It would not be hard to make a far better story on this theme, treating it with moderate realism, than Anne Pilgrim has done by treating it sentimentally. The point is, rather, should girls be encouraged to read terrifyingly readable stories like *The First Time I saw Paris* or should they be firmly directed to more stringent reading. Those who are advising girls in their 'teens may like to know that, apart from the glossy ups and downs of Roberta Branding's romance in this book, there is a sub-plot of greater point. Roberta is helping in her aunt's school for English and American children, and the problem of Karen and Gwyddy, whose widowed parents have married and who hate each other on sight, is treated with intelligence and humour—by heroine and author alike. *Skiing to Danger,* is, again, easy to read and as easy to forget. The plot starts with a rather dangerous assumption. Binnie Webb has disappeared on a skiing holiday in Switzerland and it is suspected that she has been kidnapped by employees of a Master Power trying to get her scientist father to defect from the West. The Foreign Office is helpless. Their only course (as the author sees it), is to send Binnie's cousin Perdita to pose as an innocent holiday-maker while doing some detecting. The action on ski-slopes and in a conveniently isolated mountain village follows the course of such stories. The heroine achieves her aim, in romance and against crime, sundry red herrings are removed, the rascally inn-keeper is arrested, and a high degree of story-telling skill has been, I feel, completely wasted.

School Library Journal

SOURCE: A review of *The Mystery of the Ski Slopes,* in *School Library Journal,* Vol. 13, No. 3, November, 1966, p. 112.

The Mystery of the Ski Slopes by Mabel Esther Allan is a slightly different version of a book published in England under the title *Skiing to Danger.* It is a spy story for teen-age girls set in the Swiss Alps, where 14-year-old Binnie, daughter of a British scientist, has disappeared. The fact that she has been kidnapped by the Russians in an effort to subvert her father is being kept secret, and Perdita Webb, Binnie's 18-year-old cousin, is sent by the British government to hunt for her. Disguised with a dark wig and a false passport, Perdita poses as an ordinary skier while she makes frantic efforts to find Binnie. She has been warned to work alone and does not even confide in David, the young man who arrived on the same train she did and who openly displays his interest in her. Somebody suspects Perdita, however, and attempts to push her over a cliff. The fact that the British Foreign Office would hardly trust this delicate espionage operation to one 18-year-old amateur will probably not bother other teen-age girls, who will enjoy the exciting and romantic story. For additional purchase in libraries that can afford trivia.

Zena Sutherland

SOURCE: A review of *Mystery of the Ski Slopes,* in *Bulletin of the Center for Children's Books,* Vol. 20, No. 9, May, 1967, p. 134.

Another rather patterned mystery-and-romance in the usual Allan formula, in which a British girl goes abroad and finds adventure, romance, and often danger. Here Perdita

comes in disguise to a Swiss pension, searching for her lost young cousin, Binnie. The story is saved from mediocrity by the competence of the writing style and by the deviations from formula characterizations.

CRUISING TO DANGER (as Priscilla Hagon, 1966)

Zena Sutherland

SOURCE: A review of *Cruising to Danger,* in *Bulletin of the Center for Children's Books,* Vol. 20 No. 1, September, 1966, p. 11.

A good mystery and adventure story, told in first person by Joanna, who has just finished attending a London high school. When she answers an ad that asks for an "ordinary" girl to help care for two children on a cruise, Joanna hears a conversation that makes her realize that she must hide the fact that she has a scholarship to Oxford and pretend to be stupid. She becomes increasingly suspicious of the children's father: suspicious that he is an enemy agent, that he is the cause of his wife's illness, and that he is using his little daughter's dolls as a front for an operation concerning stolen information. The story has pace, suspense, love interest, and the colorful setting of a Mediterranean cruise ship. The author deviates from the patterned mystery for the young reader in having the criminal be the father of two children; it adheres, happily, to a logical development and conclusion based on the premise that Joanna's intelligent apprehensions are correct: no hidden facts, no sudden contrivances.

The Booklist and Subscription Books Bulletin

SOURCE: A review of *Cruising to Danger,* in *The Booklist and Subscription Books Bulletin,* Vol. 63, No. 3, October 1, 1966, p. 182.

A job caring for two children on a Mediterranean cruise involves Joanna Forest in intrigue and danger. Despite too much dependence on coincidence and the improbable situation in which the villain confesses everything to Joanna before he attempts to kill her, this is an adequate mystery in which the teen-aged heroine is instrumental in saving atomic secrets and breaking up a spy ring. Faults in the plot and in the depiction of characters are counterbalanced by sustained suspense and the unfamiliar background.

The Junior Bookshelf

SOURCE: A review of *Cruising to Danger,* in *The Junior Bookshelf,* Vol. 32, No. 3, June, 1968, pp. 180-1.

It all began when Joanna answered an advertisement for a "sensible ordinary girl as companion for two children during a Mediterranean cruise". Joanna was sensible, but she had to keep up a long pretence that she was ordinary.

The plot in which she became involved and the events described are not ordinary either. This is a well-written and exciting story, suitable, as the jacket tells us, for 10+, but will be much enjoyed by those who have several more years than that. The characters and scenery, including the ship, are well drawn.

WE DANCED IN BLOOMSBURY SQUARE (as Jean Estoril, 1967)

The Junior Bookshelf

SOURCE: A review of *We Danced in Bloomsbury Square*, in *The Junior Bookshelf*, Vol. 32, No. 2, April, 1967, pp. 119-20.

It is strange how the headmistress of any fictional ballet school is full of insight, sympathetic kindness, and a wide knowledge of the thoughts and feelings of her pupils— quite the reverse of the fictional headmistresses in most school books. Madame Lingeraux of the Lingeraux Ballet School is no exception to the usual pattern. In Doria Darke, the twin who is always left behind, she sees qualities which no-one has ever recognised before. In fact Doria is so surrounded by sympathetic, understanding people that it is hard to understand why she should, for most of the book, feel so out of sorts with the world around her. Nevertheless Jean Estoril has written a story which is full of life. The sights of London are described and will seem real to the reader. Above all each character is an individual in her own right, vivid and recognisable. The ballet part of the book plays a minor role to the development of the characters, and yet the whole is well blended to make a very readable story.

Margery Fisher

SOURCE: A review of *We Danced in Bloomsbury Square*, in *Growing Point*, Vol. 6, No. 1, May, 1967, p. 926.

Deborah and Doria Darke are twins, Deborah as diffident as Doria is self-assured. Both are ballet-mad and both— after nerve-racking weeks—leave Liverpool for London with scholarships to the Lingereaux Ballet School. Life in Aunt Eileen's boarding house, rigorous training at the school, are described with a sure domestic touch, and the conflict between the sisters lifts the story from the woodenness that so often afflicts this type of story.

Susan Stanton

SOURCE: A review of *We Danced in Bloomsbury Square*, in *School Library Journal*, Vol. 17, No. 2, October, 1970, p. 138.

A realistic ballet story for older girls. Twelve-year-old twins Debbie and Doria Darke dream of someday being ballerinas. When a scholarship is offered at a famous London ballet school, the twins have to compete for one place. The bitterness that results when Debbie is chosen and Doria is not takes a long time to heal, even though both girls do get to attend the school. The conflict in character between cheerful, extroverted Debbie, whose feelings are somewhat superficial, and "dark," sensitive, quiet Doria, the story's narrator, is especially well portrayed. The author avoids making the ambitious, outgoing girl a villain, and the deep-feeling, introverted one a genius, and instead shows very fairly the dark and light sides of both kinds of temperament. The spectacular success which usually comes so unrealistically to heroines of this type of story is also refreshingly lacking. Both girls gain small but well-earned parts in the school show, and Doria comes to realize that although Debbie's perfect body won her the scholarship (another extremely realistic touch), Doria has qualities of her own which are also important, so that she need not always be in her sister's shadow. The author's prose is rather pedestrian, but it is equal to that of most ballet stories, and the quality of plot and characterization more than make up for it.

IT STARTED IN MADEIRA (1967; U. S. edition as The Mystery Began in Madeira)

Kirkus Service

SOURCE: A review of *The Mystery Began in Madeira*, in *Kirkus Service*, Vol. XXXV, No. 9, May 1, 1967, p. 564.

Mabel Esther Allan writes form-fitting mysteries with globe-trotting locales and this one is more strongly plotted than many of its predecessors. Betony, leaving Madeira for England, has taken a picture which earns her the unwanted attention of ?????? Aboard ship (and yes, a romance with attractive Miles) her stateroom is vandalized, there is an attempt to drown her, and in Lisbon she is almost kidnapped. Then there's Fergus Winter, who handles children's books, the Silly and Solly series, and our Dick and Jane, oops—we mean Betony and Miles—realize that the Silly and Solly books are solanders (you'll need the *new* Random House dictionary for that one, or read the book) for caching drugs. . . . Undemanding girls will give it their undivided attention.

Margery Fisher

SOURCE: A review of *It Started in Madeira*, in *Growing Point*, Vol. 6, No. 4, October, 1967, p. 984.

Be warned, it does only start in Madeira; from the sun-baked first scene we move quickly to a liner en route to England via South Africa and thence to Liverpool (the most interesting and best drawn setting of the three). In this highly competent 'teenage thriller you can learn what a 'solander' is, meet a group of likeable young people and an increasingly unpleasant villain. Suspense and circumstantial detail are cleverly manipulated; characters are drawn in outline and the reader is not intended to probe too far.

The Junior Bookshelf

SOURCE: A review of *It Started in Madeira*, in *The Junior Bookshelf*, Vol. 31, No. 5, October, 1967, p. 326.

Three teenagers voyaging on a liner from Madeira to Liverpool stumble on mystery and crime that has almost disastrous consequences. Here are all the ingredients of the adult light thriller adapted to the teenage reader. There is a murder, a sinister stranger, mysterious threats and an attempted kidnapping. The plot unfolds to a hectic climax in the fog of Liverpool, and needless to say "we" win.

Mabel Esther Allan is an experienced writer for the teenage market, and this, one of her better books, is a lively well constructed story for "light entertainment".

📖   *SELINA'S NEW FAMILY* **(as Anne Pilgrim, 1967)**

Kirkus Service

SOURCE: A review of *Selina's New Family,* in *Kirkus Service,* Vol. XXXV, No. 22, November 15, 1967, p. 1370.

When her widowed mother remarries, Selina Gilruth, fourteen but young for her age, must adjust to the move from Liverpool to Ireland and accept a stepfather and stepbrother. Her brooding presence shortens the family honeymoon; she never admits being pleased with her newly decorated room; she even avoids responding to her stepbrother's dog. But there's no chance the gloom will continue for long because the new family is just too nice to resist (but not too nice to believe), and apologies are stammered and accepted with relief. Selina's ambivalence ("I hate having to be grateful") is justifiable but overjustified, resulting in overt expression ("a voice said in her mind") where subtle treatment would render her frustration more evocatively. A glossary and map may help readers as unfamiliar with the new country as Selina. Nothing to write home about but something to think about if so much had not already been written.

Marilyn Goldstein

SOURCE: A review of *Selina's New Family,* in *School Library Journal*, Vol. 14, No. 5, January, 1968, p. 90.

This is a maudlin treatment of a serious family problem. When her widowed mother marries an Irishman with a young son, 13-year-old Selina Gilruth, born and reared in Liverpool, must adjust to a new way of life in Ireland. Selina is attracted to the beauty of Ireland but remains extremely resentful towards her stepfather whom she considers an intruder into her formerly happy family life. She wallows in self-pity and bitterness until she finally realizes her mistake. Selina's change of heart, however, is too sudden to be convincing and is typical of the book's melodramatic tone and superficial characterizations.

The Junior Bookshelf

SOURCE: A review of *Selina's New Family,* in *The Junior Bookshelf,* Vol. 32, No. 3, June, 1968, p. 187.

Anne Pilgrim's latest story shows her understanding of the problems of adolescence when, however strong the realisation that one is wrong, one seems powerless to make oneself behave better. Selina's situation is not within every teenager's experience—her mother, widowed when Selina was five, suddenly marries again, after some eight years when they had no-one but each other. Selina's refusal to accept her new circumstances, however, the move to Ireland, her new father and brother, is entirely realistic, and so are her friends' efforts to reconcile her to her very pleasant lot. A somewhat dramatic series of accidents brings her to her senses but the basic situation is again true to life. In addition, Miss Pilgrim has captured vividly the colours and freshness of the Western Irish countryside, the character of the small seaport of Galway, and the thrill of exploring Aran and Connemara—even if occasionally, her characters sound rather like guide books.

📖   *MISSING IN MANHATTAN* **(1967)**

The Junior Bookshelf

SOURCE: A review of *Missing in Manhattan,* in *The Junior Bookshelf,* Vol. 32, No. 1, February, 1968, p. 56.

Miss Allan gives teenagers the ingredients they enjoy, romance, mystery and authentic teenage interests, and at the same time, from a literary viewpoint, her characters are thoroughly natural and as always there is an unusual and vividly conveyed background. It is New York again, the Manhattan district and the countryside round, and it is refreshing to see it through English eyes which recognise the subtle differences from English customs and behaviour. The sultry summer heat broods over charming old American architecture and parks, modern apartments, streets and dockland: a whole new world. The heroine helps a girl newcomer to New York, rescues her sister from a gang of jewel thieves after exciting narrow escapes and not too savage violence. The beautiful selfish sister achieves maturity while for the heroine herself wedding bells are obviously near.

Madalynne Schoenfeld

SOURCE: A review of *Missing in Manhattan,* in *School Library Journal,* Vol. 15, No. 1, September, 1968, p. 196.

Three years in Manhattan have made 18-year-old Gay Selby love the excitement of the city, but she sometimes misses the British accents of home. She becomes friendly with two sisters just arrived from London, and is immediately involved in robbery, kidnapping, and murder. The unravelling of the mystery takes readers from Central Park to Greenwich Village to Brooklyn Heights. Though the characterizations are stereotyped, the background material is well integrated and the suspense is effectively sustained.

Zena Sutherland

SOURCE: A review of *Missing in Manhattan,* in *Bulletin of the Center for Children's Books,* Vol. 22, No. 8, April, 1969, p. 121.

Gay Selby, walking in Central Park, was caught by the sound of two accents more British than her own; she had been living in New York for some time, and she learned that Cressida and Annabel Newton were new arrivals. She and Annabel became friends, and Gay found that the younger sister was worried about Cressida's boy friend. And with good reason. Cressida was kidnapped, and the other two girls began a hunt (with the help of Gay's boy friend) for four criminals who were jewel thieves. The plot leans heavily on coincidence and chance, the love interest seems superimposed, and the characterization is believable but shallow; the saving graces of the book are the author's relish for the city, as expressed through Gay's enthusiasm, and a practiced, easy style of writing.

THE WOOD STREET SECRET (1968)

The Junior Bookshelf

SOURCE: A review of *The Wood Street Secret,* in *The Junior Bookshelf,* Vol. 32, No. 5, October, 1968, p. 302.

An author better known for her teen-age stories here successfully turns her attention to a novel for younger readers. Half-a-dozen children living in a largely non-residential area of Liverpool make themselves a secret playhouse in one of a terrace of condemned cottages tucked away behind a derelict warehouse. Excitement, suspense and danger form the climax of the story, but no serious harm befalls any of the children, who are led to safety by the calmness and resourcefulness of the eleven-year-old hero. There is a moral, though it is not too blatant, and the children are real people, shown in life-like surroundings, with normal, though unobtrusive, family relationships. An enjoyable book, with pleasing illustrations [by Shirley Hughes].

Kirkus Reviews

SOURCE: A review of *The Wood Street Secret,* in *Kirkus Reviews,* Vol. XXXVIII, No. 2, January 15, 1970, p. 55.

Where do the five children disappear to, that's what Ben and Cherry want to know. New to Liverpool's old warehouse district, they've spied the three O'Donnells, red-haired Mary Ellen, and West Indian Julius on a ferry, admired their camaraderie, and followed them until . . . pouf. One rescue of Mary Ellen's Siamese Shang (for Shanghai) admits them to the gang on a part-time, play-time basis, another ("They deserve it. We'll show 'em in

the morning") lets them in on the secret of condemned, closed-off Wood Street Terrace where the O'Donnells used to live and the five now hide away. But the houses in the court *are* unsafe, as they discover during a thunderstorm when falling bricks block the passage and they are imprisoned. For a very young mystery, it has uncommon texture and integrity—thanks to readily distinguishable kids, an integral leadership crisis (upstart Ben vs. accustomed Mayo O'Donnell), a setting and circumstances as tangible as the worn cobbles. All kept moving by Miss Allan's practiced hand.

Frances B. Kelly

SOURCE: A review of *The Wood Street Secret,* in *School Library Journal,* Vol. 16, No. 9, May, 1970, p. 65.

A mild, contrived adventure story about Ben and his sister Cherry who, when displaced from their home, go to live with their aunt in Liverpool, England. There, they make friends with the Wood Street Gang and learn of the secret entrance to an abandoned old home. The children enjoy the pleasures of this hideaway until a storm traps them inside, and they are forced to seek another exit. Finally, firemen respond to a fire that the children start in desperation to get attention, and a rescue is effected. Characterizations are weak, and American children would need explanations of some of the typically British terms used and customs mentioned.

Zena Sutherland

SOURCE: A review of *The Wood Street Secret,* in *Bulletin of the Center for Children's Books,* Vol. 23, No. 11, July-August, 1970, p. 171.

Ben and Cherry Stanton, eleven and ten, have just moved from West Derby to Liverpool and are feeling a bit strange in the city. They follow a group of five children who vanish suddenly into what seems a solid wall of houses. Friendship flourishes. Ben and Cherry are admitted to the inner circle of the Wood Street Gang, and they are enthralled by the hideout, an abandoned house adjoining industrial property. The dramatic focus of the book is the gang's imprisonment when a storm damages the building and blocks the children's egress. The children are diverse and believable, although not deeply characterized; the story line is slow to start but subsequently moves along at a good pace.

THE WOOD STREET GROUP (1969)

The Times Literary Supplement

SOURCE: A review of *The Wood Street Group,* in *The Times Literary Supplement,* No. 3572, August 14, 1970, p. 909.

A West Indian boy is a leading member of the Wood

Allan in the Women's Land Army, Brook Farm, Plumbley, Cheshire, 1940.

Street Group in Mabel Esther Allan's story of Liverpool kids making music. Children will undoubtedly seize on this title for its contemporary theme and it's a pity that the writing is so undistinguished, the language so thin.

Margery Fisher

SOURCE: A review of *The Wood Street Secret* and *The Wood Street Group,* in *Growing Point,* Vol. 9, No. 3, September, 1970, p. 1590.

In the earlier of these lively tales a group of children in a back street find a centre for their activities in an empty house until a heavy storm brings danger and reveals their secret. In the second book they forward their musical ambition (their instruments ranging from guitar and pipe to castanets) and after some disappointments are lent an unused committee room for their shows. Plenty of sense, good characterisation, a strong flavour of Liverpool.

The Junior Bookshelf

SOURCE: A review of *The Wood Street Group,* in *The Junior Bookshelf,* Vol. 34, No. 5, October, 1970, p. 286.

All too often story books for the younger children have a good plot, an interesting background and plenty of action

but they have characters which are lifeless and uninteresting. In *The Wood Street Group* all the attributes of a good younger-reader story are combined with life-like characters. The author has not chosen extraordinary or unusual characters, just types one can find in a gang in any street; they fall out, get cold, get into trouble, and try to overcome boredom. The outcome is a book which will appeal to all children and actively encourage those reading their first "real" book.

CLIMBING TO DANGER (1969; U.S. edition as *Mystery in Wales*)

The Junior Bookshelf

SOURCE: A review of *Climbing to Danger,* in *The Junior Bookshelf,* Vol. 33, No. 2, April, 1969, p. 130.

In the realm of stories for the early teenage group, Mabel Allan's novels are especially welcome. The mixture of suspense, adventure and romance is carefully blended. In order not to get too far from what her readers can associate, if not with their everyday knowledge then with what they hear about, she incorporates circumstances similar to some which have actually happened—a train robbery, and holding captives at gun point. Four young people set off for Snowdonia to stay at a farm where two of them, Bronwen and Robert, have stayed previously. There they get themselves involved in a very serious situation. The story is related with no little breathlessness, and the characterisation truly makes individuals of the main participants. The climbing scenes too, whether undertaken for pleasure or of necessity, have considerable realism.

School Library Journal

SOURCE: A review of *Mystery in Wales,* in *School Library Journal,* Vol. 18, No. 4, December, 1971, p. 73.

[*Mystery in Wales*] is a stereotyped mystery-romance not worth anybody's consideration. The story concerns Bronwen Parry, who returns to her native Wales for a mountain-climbing vacation with her brother, Robert, and their friends, Adam and Tina. They spend the night in an abandoned manor house where they disturb a mysterious tramp; then, upon arriving at the Owens' farm, they find their old friends very formal and inhospitable. When it's almost too late to escape, they discover that the Owens' son, wanted for murder, is reputed to be hiding out in the vicinity. Largely because of Adam's resourcefulness and courage, the young people eventually escape by climbing a dangerous mountain, and the villain obligingly falls to his death while pursuing them.

THE KRAYMER MYSTERY (1969)

Zena Sutherland

SOURCE: A review of *The Kraymer Mystery,* in *Bulletin*

of the Center for Children's Books, Vol. 23, No. 9, May, 1970, p. 139.

For years Karen Kraymer has been titillated by the mystery, half a century old, of a murder and a lost necklace in the old Kraymer brownstone. Now, coming to New York with her actress mother, she falls in love with the city (her dead father's city) and with her cousin Drew. Together they track down the answer to the puzzle, always trailed by two criminals who have heard about the necklace by sheer chance. Chance accounts for too many aspects of the story, in fact; there are also notes of contrivance throughout, and an unconvincing relationship between Karen and her mother. The story does have suspense and plenty of action, mild love interest, and a background drawn with affection; despite the weaknesses of plot and characterization, the writing style is competent enough to incorporate both into an adequate mystery story.

J. Murphy

SOURCE: A review of *The Kraymer Mystery,* in *The Junior Bookshelf,* Vol. 38, No. 2, April, 1974, p. 103.

Karen Kraymer comes to New York with her mother who is a famous actress opening in a new play there. Karen is attracted to the city because it was her dead father's birthplace, and he had told her of the mystery concerning the death of the great grandmother and a valuable necklace which had disappeared. She tells the story to a shipboard acquaintance, and unfortunately is overheard by an unsavoury character called Ben Kelly. On arrival in New York Karen meets her distant cousin Drew who is interested in the mystery as well, in fact he has rented a room in the old Kraymer home, and the plot concerns their attempts to solve the mystery before Kelly and his uncle who are simply after the cash. It is an exciting, fast-moving story with just enough give-away clues to keep the reader a step ahead of Karen, Drew and sister Delia. There is also the romance which develops between Karen and Drew plus a very accurate creation of the atmosphere of New York. All this adds up to a very good book for the 12 to 15-year-old girl who is not quite ready for adult fiction.

THE MYSTERY OF THE SECRET SQUARE (as Priscilla Hagon, 1970)

Kirkus Reviews

SOURCE: A review of *The Mystery of the Secret Square,* in *Kirkus Reviews,* Vol. XXXVIII, No. 7, April 1, 1970, p. 381.

Priscilla Hagon's mysteries for older girls have taken place on cruises or at finishing schools; this comes home and talks small. It's about Heather and Sam, and their new friends the twins Melantha and West, who live in uptown Manhattan off "the secret square." Believing that a film documentarist who grows plants on his terrace is their

enemy, they watch and witness an accident, a fire and a final scuffle which enables them to help apprehend the member of a spy ring. Writing down for this audience, the author obviously underestimates it—this is no more than instant nothing.

Publishers Weekly

SOURCE: A review of *The Mystery of the Secret Square,* in *Publishers Weekly,* Vol. 197, No. 20, May 18, 1970, p. 39.

This mystery is really not a mystery at all, just a series of incidents that are tied together loosely. Its possible salability stems from the fact that it takes place in a city—Manhattan to be exact—should give it a certain attraction for city children wanting a mystery with a familiar setting.

DANGEROUS INHERITANCE (1970)

The Times Literary Supplement

SOURCE: "Post-School Zone," in *The Times Literary Supplement,* No. 3583, October 30, 1970, p. 1266.

As for **Dangerous Inheritance,** one can but admire the author's insouciance in plucking so well-tried a plot from the yarn-cupboard, and in serving it up with so mere a dash of new paint. Not a hint of current pedestrian strains and anxieties. Sabrina Redmond (orphan; 18 but looks younger; gold hair; blue eyes; living in S.W.3; working as secretary) learns that she has been left the main part of her grandfather's vast dollar fortune, as well as his great Gothic (nineteenth century) mansion on the Hudson River. Uncles Jasper and John—she has never met either—receive but a modest share. Straightway she sails for New York to stay with Uncle Jasper and wife (*Jasper* indeed!) and an eerie pair they seem. The lawyer, Mr. Schultz, is not much more reassuring. And the young man Penrod Hadden, is *he* to be trusted, with his "crisp hair", straight nose and "fine dark eyes"? At least he takes our heiress to hear Weber in the park.

> Mystery there was afterwards, and danger and almost death. But that was perfect, quite perfect, and it set the seal on my love of my mother's city. Riots, strikes, poverty, problems. . . . Yes, of course. But also a mysterious incredible beauty that almost stopped my heart. And so, on that first day, I was committed. To being part of it.

Readers who can take the strain of the heroine's inordinate guilelessness as she places her foot in trap after trap will find it the only strain in a speedy read. After a decent interval they might try a Wilkie Collins.

Margery Fisher

SOURCE: A review of *Dangerous Inheritance,* in *Growing Point,* Vol. 9, No. 5, November, 1970, p. 1617.

Dangerous inheritance is set in New York, a milieu in which this author has already involved one or two of her trouble-prone heroines. Sabrina Redmond has inherited a large sum of money from her mother and has been invited to stay with an uncle she has never seen. This uncle she finds unexplicably fussy and increasingly unpleasant and it is no surprise (to the reader, at least) to learn that this is the "wicked" uncle masquerading as the good one. Attentive and admiring friends, male and female, help to rescue Sabrina from an entanglement that belongs so obviously to melodrama that it seems entirely suitable that the final scene should be played out in a Gothic mansion on the Hudson. The mystery and excitement are skilfully contrived.

The Junior Bookshelf

SOURCE: A review of *Dangerous Inheritance,* in *The Junior Bookshelf,* Vol. 34, No. 6, December, 1970, pp. 360-1.

Mabel Esther Allan has a formula for success but she has the good sense to vary her setting and her plots. Her heroines are usually the threatened persons; there is usually a dusting of romance thrown in for good measure, but Miss Allan's strength lies in the fact that her characters live and breathe and her environmental descriptions are excellent. Anyone who has suffered New York in August will vouch for this.

Sabrina, aged eighteen, inherits a vast fortune from her mother's father in New York and goes there alone to claim it. She is met by an uncle whom she distrusts on sight and taken to a seedy apartment. Luckily she has two friends in the city, the nephew of a neighbour in London and a girl she met on the ship out. The plot concerns her uncle's plan to murder her and thus get her fortune and her eventual escape, thanks to her own ingenuity and the help of her friends.

This is not great writing, but it is a stepping stone for those addicts of "the mystery of . . ." type of book towards adult thrillers and detective stories.

THE WOOD STREET RIVALS (1970)

Margery Fisher

SOURCE: A review of *The Wood Street Rivals,* in *Growing Point,* Vol. 10, No. 6, December, 1971, pp. 1847-8.

There is little enough room in books for the middle years to indicate emotional development in swiftly drawn characters but, all the same, emotional change must be put forward to the reader in something more than bald statement. *The Wood Street Rivals* describes how children in Liverpool belonging to rival gangs reconcile their differences after an awkward clash over identical plans for May Day processions. Setting and street atmosphere are admirable, characterisation rather less than adequate. Possibly

the author is relying on her two earlier stories about Bronwen, Julius and the rest to distinguish them one from the other but some of the space she fills with the padding of casual chat could have been better spent in providing particular touches of personality.

Authors of short books like this have a choice to make. Should they look for peer relationships as being more easily appreciated by the young or should they satisfy their own more mature preoccupations by bringing children and grown-ups face to face? If they choose the latter course, they have to keep the delicate balance between what the young see in adults and what adults see in themselves and in the young; this is the rock on which so many junior stories founder.

The Junior Bookshelf

SOURCE: A review of *The Wood Street Rivals,* in *The Junior Bookshelf,* Vol. 35, No. 6, December, 1971, p. 370.

A treasured guitar is broken during a scuffle between groups of children in one of the poorer districts of Liverpool, and ways and means of making money to pay for its repair occupy most of the book; not a very original theme and not particularly well told, the dialogue at times being altogether unreal. However, the children from several racial backgrounds get on well together which alone is something these days, especially as the author does not make an issue of this but treats it as entirely normal, which indeed it usually is. The final fund-raising effort is to be a May Day parade inspired by the Padstow May song, which for those who know it is understandable but for others, the majority, a mere description of its compelling quality is unconvincing. It is a pity that so many books for this seven to eight age group are concerned with the making of money and that the pleasure of the May Day parade had to culminate in the winning of a money prize for a photograph of it in the local paper. [Shirley Hughes's] pictures, as usual, are pleasant, as is the story, indeed, with the above reservations.

THE MAY DAY MYSTERY (1971)

Mrs. John Gray

SOURCE: A review of *The May Day Mystery,* in *Best Sellers,* Vol. 31, No. 12, September 15, 1971, p. 277.

A mystery-romance with a folklore background. The setting is a village in Cornwall, England, and the action revolves around the First of May custom—a man parades through the town dressed in an ancient horse costume. During the charade, the "horse dies" (symbolizing winter) and then is teased back to "life" (spring) by the townspeople. Naturally a perfect setup for real danger! Too many plots and sub-plots (stolen treasure, hippies, attempted murder, romance, mistaken identity—you name it, it's here!) are developed, and the story needs to be tied together a little more neatly.

Zena Sutherland

SOURCE: A review of *The May Day Mystery,* in *Bulletin of the Center for Children's Books,* Vol. 25, No. 6, February, 1972, p. 85.

Although all of Mabel Allan's books follow a set pattern (English girl away from home becomes involved in mystery and also acquires a man) they are capably written and provide a background that usually has some interest. Here the protagonist, Laura, has been invited by a Cornish friend to visit at the time of the May Day rites that preserve many ancient procedures. Laura falls in love with her friend's brother, who by the end of the book responds in full; she also is instrumental in resolving an old mystery with new developments, and through all of the days of her stay in Cornwall, Laura learns about the celebration of the May. The plot is undistinguished, but there is plenty of action, romance, and good atmosphere.

📖 *AN ISLAND IN A GREEN SEA* (1972)

Kirkus Reviews

SOURCE: A review of *An Island in a Green Sea,* in *Kirkus Reviews,* Vol. XL, No. 15, August 1, 1972, p. 858.

Through the softening filter of memory, Mairi Gilbride recalls her adolescent admiration for Isobel, the young Englishwoman who comes to share the life of the crofthouse, learn Gaelic and work on a book of Hebridean legends and songs. Isobel introduces Mairi to the world of books and photography—and to the mainland itself in a brief summer visit—and fills the void created by the death of old greatgrandmother and sister Jean's departure to work in Glasgow. Mairi's dreams of a marriage between Isobel and the young Gaelic scholar Ros McBride are thwarted when Ros chooses Jean instead, and her mother's decision to emigrate to Canada brings an abrupt, hopefully temporary, separation from her beloved Glen Gaoth. It's hard to really share Mairi's affection for Isobel's idealized perfection, but the dominant theme in any case is nostalgia for the Outer Isles as they were in the 1920's—a mood which mixes charm and inertia in equal measure.

Carol L. Stanke

SOURCE: A review of *An Island in a Green Sea,* in *School Library Journal,* Vol. 19, No. 3, November, 1972, p. 72.

An engrossing tale about a girl living on a bleak, isolated island of the Scottish Outer Hebrides in the 1920's. Saddened by her two brothers' emigration to Canada and her older sister's departure for a job in Glasgow, Mairi Gilbride finds friendship with an English girl who has come to learn the language and customs of the islands. Mairi eventually realizes that she must leave the island in order to develop her capabilities, but she retains her dream of returning to help improve island life. The story's quiet

pace and theme of realizing one's potential will appeal primarily to mature readers.

The Times Literary Supplement

SOURCE: "The Call of the Wild," in *The Times Literary Supplement,* No. 3742, November 23, 1973, p. 1429.

Mabel Esther Allan's new book, *An Island in a Green Sea,* is the story, written in the first person, of the childhood of Mairi Gilbride on a remote island in the Hebrides in the 1920s, and how its tough crudities are alleviated by the arrival of a rich English girl who comes to share and study. The story, though far more familiar in theme, yet has something in common with *Julie of the Wolves*—the clash between the old ways and the new. It is to North America that the Scottish families turn, looking for a new life, when it is obvious that their beautiful island offers them nothing but poverty and hard work. This is a straightforward, old-fashioned book, with the ends neatly tied. It has no pretensions and no flashing insights but a solid core of good sense and an interesting background.

E. Colwell

SOURCE: A review of *An Island in a Green Sea,* in *The Junior Bookshelf,* Vol. 38, No. 1, February, 1974, pp. 32-3.

A re-creation of life on a remote Scottish island in the 1920's. There is poverty and hardship but it is set against a wild background which has many moments of beauty and grandeur. Mairi is at first content with her simple life on the island, for she knows no other and she has the security of her loving family. As she grows up her brothers are compelled to emigrate, her sister has to go to Glasgow to earn a living and her grandmother dies. The company of a young woman writer shows her how much wider life can be. Like so many islanders she and her mother emigrate to Canada.

The book has a purpose—to give the succeeding generations of emigrants now living in Canada and the United States an impression of the "islands in a green sea" which they may never see. This it does admirably and often movingly. The story interest is a little weak but the relationships within the crofter family are warm and convincing. An interesting and human record of a way of life which has almost disappeared.

Lucinda Fox

SOURCE: A review of *An Island in a Green Sea,* in *The School Librarian,* Vol. 22, No. 1, March, 1974, p. 75.

The story of a Hebridean childhood in the late 1920s, this story tells of when the outer isles were really remote and life was harsh and unrewarding. Mairi Gilbride was happy and secure in her home despite this life and then after her eleventh birthday everything familiar is threatened by changes. Her brothers are forced to emigrate, her sister goes to Glasgow to work in a household. Mairi herself begins to accept the changes and see the world beyond the island through the eyes of Isobel, a young English visitor.

Told in the first person, this is a convincing and warmly related tale with an interesting background. An unpretentious book but one which will have a lot of appeal to girls of eleven onwards.

TIME TO GO BACK (1972)

Sylvia Mogg

SOURCE: A review of *Time to Go Back*, in *Children's Book Review*, Vol. II, No. 4, September, 1972, pp. 111-12.

The 'generation gap' and lack of understanding between parents and children is an eternal problem and although better publicised today, it is no nearer a solution. Consequently the subject continues to be the source of much literary exploration which, while entertaining, does sometimes also contribute a degree of understanding. In *Time to go Back* sixteen-year-old Sarah becomes ill after a protest march which turned out to be far from the peaceful affair she had anticipated. During the boredom of convalescence she finds some poems written by her mother's dead sister during the Second World War. Through the poems she begins to take an interest in the dark war days of her mother's childhood. Sarah and her mother go to stay in Wallasey, where her mother grew up and Larke wrote her poems, and while seeking out the house where they had lived, Sarah finds herself back in 1941 at the time of the dreadful series of air-raids on Liverpool. She makes her way to her grandmother's air-raid shelter and there, during this and other nights, when she slips back in time, she gets to know the young girl who became her mother and her aunt, Larke, who died in the flames of Liverpool. She is surprised to find the way in which people continued to live their lives in spite of the dreadful things going on around them and what she learns so vividly, because of her experiences, helps Sarah to view her mother and older people generally, in an entirely new light. The events of 1941 are well-described and obviously part of the author's life, but the attempts to understand the young protestor of today are feeble in the extreme, the whole matter being dismissed as some kind of delinquency; an attitude which might so easily alienate those who could obtain most from the story. The 1941 part of the book, however, and the consequent growth of understanding is worthwhile and could do much to help bridge the eternal gap.

Kirkus Reviews

SOURCE: A review of *Time to Go Back*, in *Kirkus Reviews*, Vol. XL, No. 18, September 15, 1972, p. 1105.

Sarah at 16 is something of a problem: she dismisses her parents' memories of wartime England as "those old days," gets arrested in a protest march, and has "unkempt and very messy" friends with long "untidy" hair who are "loud, aggressive, and rather rude to Mother." But all this changes when Sarah discovers the poems of Mother's sister Larke who was killed in an air raid shortly before her fiance's death in battle. The poems literally bring Sarah back to 1941, when she lives through bombing attacks with her mother as a young girl and watches Larke go off to her fatal appointment confiding that "if David dies I would sooner be dead too." Sarah also meets Hilary who kisses her and seems to pop up later when she returns to the present, but it turns out that this second Hilary is the first one's son. You can be sure that Sarah "came out of the experience a different girl," rejecting her "shallow and silly" old friends for nice Mary Garrick (who has "nothing to do with drugs" and invites Sarah to join the dramatic society) and finally marrying Hilary II who tells her that "Protest is the great thing nowadays, but . . . I loathe violence for its own sake." The fact that Larke's poems are really the author's own, written during World War II as the bombs fell, makes this dreadful novel all the more embarrassing.

E. Colwell

SOURCE: A review of *Time to Go Back*, in *The Junior Bookshelf*, Vol. 36, No. 5, October, 1972, p. 322.

A story which helps to bridge the generation-gap and to bring home to modern young people the fact that war is not just history but the suffering of people like oneself.

Sarah is unhappy, a protester against modern society, and has even been arrested for her part in a march. By chance she finds the poems written by her Aunt Larke who lost her life in the Second World War. She goes to Liverpool, her Aunt's home, and there her intense interest in the poems brings about her journeys into the past. On several occasions she shares the terror of air raids with her Aunt and her own mother, then a child. Through this experience she realises the emotion that inspired Larke's poems and that made her death less tragic than it seemed at the time. Meeting her mother as a girl, she understands how much they are alike.

This is an over-simplification of a complicated story which, because it is partly autobiographical and the poems which inspire Sarah are the author's own, rings true. Although the story is a little slow in getting under way and the end rather drawn out, the total impact for young people is probably considerable, especially as a love story develops for Sarah through her experiences.

A FORMIDABLE ENEMY (1973)

C. Martin

SOURCE: A review of *A Formidable Enemy*, in *The Junior Bookshelf*, Vol. 37, No. 3, June, 1973, p. 194.

The reader knows what to expect from this author: rapturous young love which ends happily after a series of fearsome entanglements with red spies, drug smugglers or what have you, the former in this case. It does not do to be too critical, and Isobel's adventures in Edinburgh may well serve to while away an idle hour for a twelve-year-old. Indeed, with a willing suspension of disbelief, some of it is really quite spine-chilling.

Sarah Law Kennerly

SOURCE: A review of *The Formidable Enemy,* in *School Library Journal,* Vol. 21, No. 9, May, 1975, p. 71.

The Formidable Enemy is a spy story which mixes large dollops of Scottish scenery with some exciting and dangerous adventures. An 18-year-old Londoner, Isobel Leigh, who is visiting her grandmother in Edinburgh meets Fern Forster, an American tourist, staying with her aunt. Fern suspects that her aunt is a spy and that an accident which resulted in amnesia was really attempted murder. Her suspicion is confirmed when the enemy spies, whom Aunt Mary was chasing, capture both girls as hostages. The exciting chase and rescue scenes seem authentic, and the plot is more believable than most spy stories for the age group.

Ralph Lavender

SOURCE: A review of *A Formidable Enemy,* in *Children's Book Review Service,* Vol. 3, No. 12, June, 1975, p. 93.

In a final shoot-out, the good spies kill the bad spies, but since both groups are flat, dull people, we don't care. Unbelievably bad spying coupled with coincidence and inadequate foreshadowing flaws the plot. Drab, cliché-ridden language tells rather than shows. Hastily cranked out, the mystery fails on grounds of plot, character, theme and style.

A CHILL IN THE LANE (1974)

Barbara K. Rodes

SOURCE: A review of *A Chill in the Lane,* in *Children's Book Review Service,* Vol. 2, No. 7, March, 1974, p. 63.

The author of 17 other books has once again combined an interest in mood and physical setting (Cornwall, England) with sensitive character (Lyd, a 16-year-old girl) and mysterious plot (Lyd has troubling visions of former witchcraft in Trelonyan). Teenage girls will enjoy this Gothic tale as the adopted Lyd, on her way to being a liberated woman, is exploring her identity and roots and has a wholesome—much restraint—romance with Saul, an attractive, caring young man.

Kathleen Roedder

SOURCE: A review of *A Chill in the Lane,* in *Childhood Education,* Vol. 51, No. 6, April, 1975, p. 325.

Prone to fears and premonitions, Lyd has come unwillingly to the Cornish fishing village on the Lizard. The terrifying chill at one spot on the lane to the coast more than justifies her reluctance. Through the following days Lyd faces and explores the dimensions of the growing apparitions revealing the unhappy history of the village. Well done and exciting, with a bit of love and a bit of witchery.

THE NIGHT WIND (1974)

Kirkus Reviews

SOURCE: A review of *The Night Wind,* in *Kirkus Reviews,* Vol. XLII, No. 8, April 15, 1974, p. 422.

Clare Court, as we are continually reminded, is *not* the dreary sort of orphanage found in Dickens and *Jane Eyre,* and since this begins as a memoir written by a Robin all-grown-up and happily married, we know that she will survive the emotional pangs of institutionalization. After the death of her middle class parents Robin goes through some hard times, living with a dull aunt and an uncle who drinks, but her reservations about Clare Court are decorously expressed ("no one knew how much I shrank from the inevitable crudities of communal living"). And though the compensations—the arrival of spritely, ballet dancing Tafline who becomes a best friend, and their three-day runaway idyll to an abandoned farm—would match the best fantasies of any lonely outsider, they also reinforce the conviction of superiority to her fellow orphans which is rather simplistically accepted here as personal growth. Given that the theme of a sensitive girl fallen on hard times by the deaths of her parents is hardly new in British juveniles, Allan might have been expected to add some psychological depth to substitute for the traumatic deprivation that has no place at Clare Court.

Booklist

SOURCE: A review of *The Night Wind,* in *Booklist,* Vol. 70, No. 18, May 15, 1974, p. 1054.

A sensitive first-person narrative by an English woman recalling her twelfth year when, orphaned by the death of her mother, she was sent first to her hard-drinking uncle's house and then to a children's home in Illingborough. There she was caught between loneliness for a kindred soul and irritating dormitory contact with others until the appearance of an imaginative girl Tafline, the first person with whom she made deep and loving contact—and got in trouble. The characters and events are developed slowly but three-dimensionally into the very real world of a withdrawn girl who begins by being someone nobody wants and ends by creating a place for herself in several hearts and in society. For readers who can become absorbed in the subtle development of a special personality and friendship.

SHIP OF DANGER (1974)

Margery Fisher

SOURCE: A review of *Ship of Danger,* in *Growing Point,* Vol. 13, No. 4, October, 1974, p. 2477.

Readers around twelve and thirteen, if they are fortunate in enjoying working-holidays in school ships, may look at the travel-romance askance from one point of view while, from another, they might wish that ships like *Uganda,* with their lectures and guides, could have been more like the *Golden Star,* in which Nella Pallant travels on a courtesy ticket because her father is the Purser. The frothy whip of danger and glamour in *Ship of danger,* given a certain substance by the topical theme of hi-jacking, also hides a shrewd if rapid survey of another theme still more topical, the generation gap. During the capture and recapture of the ship—events as slickly described as they are improbable—Nella comes to realise the reason for her father's charming manner to the passengers, which she finds so dishonest, and may even be said to have acquired a little wisdom in the course of an adventure which the author handles with her usual expertise.

Kathleen Roedder

SOURCE: A review of *Ship of Danger,* in *Childhood Education,* Vol. 51, No. 4, February, 1975, p. 215.

Nella Pallant vaguely despises her father's job as purser on a great ocean liner so her trip to the Canaries on the *Golden Star* is reluctant. However, when "pirates" hold the ship and passengers for ransom, her father's personality and experience avert panic. Details of shipboard life, the role of Nella's deaf friend at the center of the action, an exciting climax and a dollop of romance make for pleasant light reading about a vanishing holiday lifestyle.

MYSTERY IN ROME (1974; England edition as The Bells of Rome)

Barbara Elleman

SOURCE: A review of *Mystery in Rome,* in *Booklist,* Vol. 73, No. 5, November 1, 1976, p. 405.

Flavia's excitement about working in Rome as a secretary to author-traveler Emily Agnew turns to apprehension and later terror during their stay at the villa of Mrs. Agnew's friends, Ethel and Luigi Giannino. Overheard snatches of conversation and several suspicious events lead Flavia to suspect Ethel and Luigi of plotting to kill Luigi's mother, the 80-year-old Signora, and thus secure a hold on the Giannino fortune. Flavia's involvement results in a terri-

fying night alone in the villa and a deadly chase through the Coliseum. A subplot develops as Flavia's interest in vacationing Ashley Bainbridge grows to a more serious level. Although at times the story breaks down under travelogue-type descriptions of Rome, this should appeal to readers looking for a light romantic mystery.

Zena Sutherland

SOURCE: A review of *Mystery in Rome,* in *Bulletin of the Center for Children's Books,* Vol. 30, No. 5, January, 1977, pp. 69-70.

This follows the usual Allan formula: a girl has an adventure while abroad and also finds romance. Here Flavia Scott, an American who has learned Italian from her mother, travels as secretary to a writer of travel books, Mrs. Agnew. They stay with the Giannino family, whose original invitation had been rescinded (the letter had not reached Mrs. Agnew) and whose reception of their unwanted guests is icy. In fact, Flavia suspects that the Gianninos want them out of the house because they are planning to do away with the octogenarian mother who controls the family business. Several attempts are made on Mrs. Agnew's life, and there are suspicious characters who lurk about; Flavia herself is clearly in danger. After a not-quite-credible chase scene, Mr. Giannino is killed. "I guess fate meant me to be there," says Ashley, the young American Flavia had met en route, and with whom she had done some sightseeing in Rome. Here and there throughout the story are descriptions of Roman sights, guidebook style: "Mrs. Agnew pointed out the Circo Massimo (or Circus Maximus) opposite, just south of the Palatino Hill . . ." By such techniques, the author detracts from the setting; the characters are without any depth; the plot is labored. There is action, there is suspense, but the book seems contrived.

CROWS' NEST (1975)

Margery Fisher

SOURCE: A review of *Crows' Nest,* in *Growing Point,* Vol. 14, No. 2, July, 1975, pp. 2667-8.

Mabel Esther Allan is not one to turn from the way of the world in her books, even when they are designed for the under-tens. The old houses in Almond Street are justifiably condemned and the inhabitants accept rehousing in a high rise block readily enough—all but Mr. Crump, a retired sailor who is afraid of lifts, and who, because there is no first floor flat available, barricades himself in his house and stands siege till the children, who have a real affection for him, persuade him to come out to Samantha's birthday party. He is lured by lift to the top floor, where a flat is available, and finds he can see the sea and ships from its windows; thus easily is the problem solved. Rose-coloured but shrewd, highly professional in style and structure, the story has a Liverpool atmosphere that gives it solidity for all its brevity and simple manner.

📖 *BRIDGE OF FRIENDSHIP* (1975)

David Rees

SOURCE: "Cosy Contact," in *The Times Literary Supplement,* No. 3826, July 11, 1975, p. 763.

Mabel Esther Allen's *Bridge of Friendship* is concerned with a family of Irish immigrants and their first few weeks of growing used to the problems of life in New York City. The bewilderment and sense of disorientation is very convincing. The change has been from rural County Mayo to Manhattan's decaying West Side; the children inevitably adjust to the new life more quickly than the adults, and the stresses this produces within the family are conveyed in the writing with considerable insight and compassion. In a sense it is the story of any immigrants uprooted and coming to terms with their new environment, but the Irish have their own particular problems, and their own capacities for coming to terms with them: it all has a ring of authenticity. Less successful perhaps is the parallel story—rich-girl Katya, a New Yorker of Russian-Jewish descent coping with the problems of her parents' divorce. Katya and the Irish children meet on the boat coming over to America and their friendship continues after they arrive, in spite of the cultural and social differences.

There is perhaps too much of a feeling of something documentary hiding in this novel, and the ending is a bit too easy. Also, one wonders about the ease with which children walk around modern New York; its crimes, murders, drug problems are mentioned, but Katya and her friends do not come into contact with them. However, the author knows her Manhattan, and she may well be right in telling us that life there is a lot easier than press reports suggest.

Denise M. Wilms

SOURCE: A review of *Bridge of Friendship,* in *Booklist,* Vol. 73, No. 22, July 15, 1977, p. 1725.

The O'Connells, newly arrived from Ireland, are fearful and apprehensive about making a new life in New York City. Their unease is heightened by the discovery of Uncle Padraig's poverty; his tiny apartment in a shabby tenement is a distressingly uncomfortable base from which to confront the city. Twelve-year-old Nuala and her older brother Liam provide the focus for examining the family's plight: they chafe at their mother's sudden overprotectiveness each time they want to explore; Nuala is upset by her father's inclination to forget his troubles in drink and worries over the sudden fragility of the family bonds. The crucial bright spot in their lives is Katya Pushkoff, a wealthy uptowner whom Nuala and Liam met on the ship. She proves genuinely friendly, tactfully overcoming Mr. O'Connell's prejudice toward her wealth, and eventually becomes a blessed catalyst in securing the O'Connells a proper apartment as well as a job suited to Mr. O'Connell's abilities. Characters and situations are thoughtfully developed, and some significant stereotypes are breached: the setting is present-day New York, Katya's money is not an excuse to cast her as a snob, and the run-down neighborhood where the O'Connells first meet the city is brightened by friendly neighbors of differing races and nationalities. Moreover, the differences between rural Ireland and bustling New York are subtly made clear so the reader's appreciation of the O'Connells' situation is deepened. The story's happy ending is not unbelievable; told as it is here, it just could have happened that way.

Zena Sutherland

SOURCE: A review of *Bridge of Friendship,* in *Bulletin of the Center for Children's Books,* Vol. 31, No. 1, September, 1977, p. 2.

Lured by the boasting letters of his brother, Cormac O'Connell brings his family to Manhattan from rural Ireland, only to find that Padraig lives in a shabby tenement and has a menial job. Mrs. O'Connell is heartsick and homesick, dreading the heat and the dangers of the city, even fearful when her children, Liam and Nuala, go to visit their shipboard friend, Katya Pushkoff, who is adjusting to her parents' divorce and her father's imminent second marriage. Katya and her mother help the O'Connells find a better home and a job for Cormac, and the children all begin to adjust to the changes in their lives. The characterization is flat, and although the message of brotherhood is worthy, its delivery is labored, with a writing style weakened by irrelevant bits of description (Katya's stateroom is "decorated in fawn and a lovely shade of lime green") and by some instance of convenient coincidence.

Patricia S. Butcher

SOURCE: A review of *Bridge of Friendship,* in *School Library Journal,* Vol. 24, No. 1, September, 1977, p. 119.

Twelve-year-old Nuala O'Connell leaves her rural Irish home and sails to present-day Manhattan with her older brother and parents. Settled into a decaying apartment building, the family slowly and painfully learns to adjust to urban life and different kinds of people. Katya, a wealthy Jewish girl who was a shipboard friend, helps to ease their numerous problems. The story is marred by stereotypes—a braggart uncle who frequents bars, a "hippie" with "long, greasy hair" who lives in a "smelly room"— and while the cultural assimilation of contemporary immigrants has potential as a theme, this British import does not probe deeply enough into the characters or their actions.

📖 *ROMANSGROVE* (1975)

Elizabeth Haynes

SOURCE: A review of *Romansgrove,* in *School Library Journal,* Vol. 22, No. 2, October, 1975, p. 93.

An old pendant takes Clare and Richard back 70 years to the old manor house on Romansgrove estate. Invisible to all but Emily, the daughter of the house, they try to sensitize her to the plight of workers on the estate who are treated little better than slaves. Clare and Richard eventually learn that a fire destroyed the old house and make one more trip back to save Emily and her family. This ends their excursions into the past, but from Victoria, the modern-day daughter of the estate, they learn that Emily, whom they thought dead, is still alive and anxious to see them. Although the ending is left hanging, the swift pace and good characterizations keep readers enthralled.

Denise M. Wilms

SOURCE: A review of *Romansgrove,* in *The Booklist,* Vol. 72, No. 4, October 15, 1975, p. 295.

As Clare and Richard Manley explore ruins of the first manse at progressive Romansgrove, where their father has taken an accounting job, they stumble into the harsh manor world of 1902. A pendant unearthed by Clare seems to precipitate the time transition, and in this bygone era they establish a friendship with Emily Roman, the spoiled but intelligent daughter of the estate owner. The children regard each other with mutual interest; Emily is intrigued by Clare's and Richard's free appearance as well as by their liberal beliefs on the status of women and the rights of servants. They, in turn, seek to acquaint Emily with life in the 1970s and to foster in her a sense of social awareness. As Clare and Richard ponder the significance of their strange experiences Clare discovers that the anniversary date of the mansion's burning is upon them. She and Richard rush to warn Emily of the danger, arriving just in time. The notion of past and present coexisting is basic to this gently crafted story; though the children are never able to explain the dynamics of the odd experience, there is satisfaction enough in knowing that they were somehow instruments for positive change.

Virginia Haviland

SOURCE: A review of *Romansgrove,* in *The Horn Book Magazine,* Vol. LII, No. 1, February, 1976, p. 54.

One more time fantasy, moving from today back to 1902, the year that Romansgrove, a Cotswold manor house, burned down. Clare and Richard, just arrived on the estate where their father is to be the new accountant, find an old pendant during the first of their daily explorations in the surrounding woods. Through its magic, they see the place in its former grandeur and meet young Emily Roman, a wealthy and difficult child. All three children, as well as present-day Victoria Roman, are susceptible young teenagers gaining awareness of social differences—period contrasts in women's liberation, workers' rights, and class distinctions—presented with didactic intent by the author. Details of Cotswold background and society give credence to the book; however, the characterizations are superficial, though smoothly contrived to suit the story.

THE FLASH CHILDREN (1975)

Margery Fisher

SOURCE: A review of *The Flash Children,* in *Growing Point,* Vol. 14, No. 7, January, 1976, p. 2798.

The Flash Children, like so many of Mabel Esther Allan's stories, demonstrates that children do have a sense of class and shows in a simple, optimistic way how readily they overcome differences. The three Briggs children are unhappy at the move from the hilly freedom of Shropshire to a flat salt-plain in Cheshire, and resent the fact that though their father is cowman on the nearby farm, they are not allowed to play or help there. They get rid of their spleen by scorning and avoiding Dan and Edith Brown, rough, motherless children who have made themselves a nuisance locally. Harmony, not implausibly, is restored by hard work. Exploring the district, the Briggs children find a schoolfellow helping his parents in the task of restoring a derelict family manor to some kind of order. Money troubles and sabotage by louts from Manchester are dealt with by the good luck prevalent in junior fiction; even so, we can believe that Arthur and Dilys are left a little more open-minded at the end of their adventure.

Karin K. Bricker

SOURCE: A review of *The Flash Children,* in *School Library Journal,* Vol. 22, No. 5, January, 1976, p. 42.

A flash is a lake formed in salt country by land subsidence. The surrounding soil is not easily cultivated and the landscape bleak. Arthur, Dilys, and Megan Briggs find their new home depressing and dull, but things pick up when they become involved in the restoration of the vandalized Pelverden Manor house. Dilys befriends partially-sighted Brian Pelverden and helps him to accept this handicap. The angelic Briggs are contrasted with budding delinquent school mates and bands of teenage vandals. The plot lines are too rapidly and neatly joined; the characters, with two exceptions, entirely good or bad. Annabel Farjeon's *The Seige of Trap's Mill* succeeded in creating a much more complicated and realistic contrast of the good and the bad in the behavior of children.

AWAY FROM WOOD STREET (1976)

Margaret Meek

SOURCE: A review of *Away from Wood Street,* in *The School Librarian,* Vol. 24, No. 2, June, 1976, pp. 126-7.

A strong story line, some really good characters and an authentic-seeming Liverpool setting make this story a good addition to an already successful series. I like Bridget and Esmeralda. Dad, home from sea and fretful, threatens the gang security of his children. Mum is the usual shadowy character who has to worry. But there's something here for young readers, not least a splendid black print and pictures [by Shirley Hughes] that fill out the author's outlines.

J. Russell

SOURCE: A review of *Away from Wood Street,* in *The Junior Bookshelf,* Vol. 40, No. 4, August, 1976, p. 194.

There have been four earlier books about the Wood Street gang, a group of tough Liverpudlian children who live near the Cathedral and have to find their own amusements in the drab city centre. In this latest book the three O'Donnell children are forced to move away from their flat near Wood Street to a tiny terrace house which has been rented to their parents very cheaply following their father's accident at sea. Mr. O'Donnell is a sailor and rather a remote figure to his children, their romantic view of him alters slightly after he returns from hospital, his leg in plaster, a hero no doubt after rescuing his mate, but a very short tempered one at times who is always wanting to know just where they have been, what they have been doing. Inevitably with such restriction one of them was bound to get into trouble, and it is only because of his sister's common sense that Mayo is not caught by the police. The happy ending is handled very skilfully and so too is the friendship between Bridget and the handicapped girl next door. The author has a sure ear for the tempo of life for the 8–12 years olds, their style, speech and attitudes, and she uses them with panache here.

THE RISING TIDE (1976)

Ann Evans

SOURCE: A review of *A Home of Your Own,* in *The Times Literary Supplement,* No. 3900, December 10, 1976, p. 1544.

With Mabel Esther Allan, writing for a slightly older age group, one is again immediately aware of the practised craftsman. She may be sensational, sentimental and facile but she does know what she is about. The theme of *The Rising Tide* is, rather unexpectedly, Welsh nationalism. Eighteen-year-old Fennel Chalfoat inherits a group of remote islands off the coast of Wales and decides to try living on one of them with her friend Sue. With the help of a boyfriend apiece, the two girls discover that the caves beneath the island contain a sizable bomb factory in full production, run by unscrupulous Welsh Nationalists. At great danger to themselves they expose to the police a desperate plot to blow up half the public buildings of Liverpool. . . . Far-fetched, but undeniably a splendid read. Those who belong to the "Nothing but the best . . ." school will find little to applaud in such a book. It is not of any great literary worth. It is not meaningful, symbolic or psychologically important. As comfortable padding, however, I can think of nothing better.

Drew Stevenson

SOURCE: A review of *The Rising Tide,* in *School Library Journal,* Vol. 24, No. 9, May, 1978, pp. 85-6.

The Rising Tide is another of Mabel Esther Allan's Gothics set in a remote area of England and revealing the author's eye for detail in the descriptions of the wild beauty of three coastal islands inherited by the 18-year-old heroine, Fennel Chalfont. Fennel and her friend Sue find the islands deserted except for a sullen caretaker and his granddaughter, a disturbed child named Ceiridwen. While fixing up the main house which is in disrepair, Fennel and Sue encounter strange lights in the night, a possible ghost, and several suspicious near-accidents. With the help of Michael who lives in a nearby town, the girls try to link the odd happenings to the activities of the Servants of the Red Dragon (the Welsh equivalent of the I.R.A.) and soon find themselves trapped on the island. Readers will like the girls' determination to get to the bottom of things, and, if the love between Fennel and Michael seems too Victorian, even that works out for the best.

Alethea K. Helbig

SOURCE: A review of *The Rising Tide,* in *Children's Book Review Service,* Vol. 6, No. 11, June, 1978, p. 106.

This is a somewhat better-than-average mystery set on islands just off the English coast in sight of the Welsh hills. If eighteen-year-old Fenny Chalfont had not inherited the three Seal Islands, she and her school friend, Sue, would not have met thirteen-year-old Ceiridwen and her grandfather, the Welsh tenants there. They would not have become involved in preventing Welsh revolutionaries from bombing public buildings in Liverpool to keep the British from constructing a dam in Wales. Although any mystery fan can predict what is going to happen, events are plausible, the story moves fast and holds interest well, and the sense of place is strong. Since Fenny and Sue are self-reliant and do not need friends Alex and Michael to bail them out of their difficulties, the happy-ever-after ending with marriage and domestic bliss strikes a wrong note, particularly for today. Still, it is a good introduction for the young to the Gothic novel.

Barbara Elleman

SOURCE: A review of *The Rising Tide,* in *Booklist,* Vol. 74, No. 20, June 15, 1978, p. 1614.

When 18-year-old Fenny Chalfont inherits three small islands off the west coast of England near Wales, she and her friend Sue decide to take up winter residence to pursue writing. Their arrival is met with hostility from caretaker Mr. Parry-Jones and his granddaughter Ceiridwen, who use scare tactics and threats in an attempt to get rid of them. Entranced by her islands and intrigued by the lonely, strangely behaved Ceiridwen, Fenny is determined to stay. A developing interest in Michael, Ceiridwen's teacher, also proves to be a motivating factor. Explosives hidden in a cave and a marked map of the city of Liverpool point to Parry-Jones' involvement with a radical Welsh cause, and the girls suddenly realize their own lives are in danger. Quick action prevents catastrophe, and the story ends on a romantic note with Fenny and Michael planning to marry and adopt Ceiridwen. Compensating for the overdramatic plot and idealized conclusion are the swift pace and culminating suspense. An involving read for mystery fans.

THE VIEW BEYOND MY FATHER (1977)

Cyrisse Jaffe

SOURCE: A review of *The View Beyond My Father,* in *School Library Journal,* Vol. 25, No. 2, October, 1978, p. 152.

Brought up in a conventional household, ruled by her domineering father, Mary Anne Angus, 14, has had failing eyesight all her life. When she goes blind at 12 her family becomes oppressively protective, squashing any sense of independence or individuality. Out on a walk one day she meets Dennis Weston who, along with his liberal family, gives her the confidence to defy her father. With a new awareness of the unjust class system which determines British foreign and domestic policies in 1930, Mary gets to know Gwyn, a 14-year-old Welsh servant from a poor mining family. ("Gwyn . . . Dennis . . . *He* was more important, but I seem to have made two new friends . . ." she says.) When an operation restores her sight in one eye, Mary's life begins to take on new meaning and vitality. Unfortunately, the story suffers from melodramatic writing and poorly developed characters—apart from Mary. And even in her case, her supposed burgeoning consciousness is belied by her dependence on Dennis and Dr. Perry (the eye surgeon) and by her condescending attitude toward Gwyn.

Denise M. Wilms

SOURCE: A review of *The View Beyond My Father,* in *Booklist,* Vol. 75, No. 9, January 1, 1979, pp. 747-8.

Mary Anne Angus finds her parents' stifling overprotectiveness almost as much of a problem as her blindness. Growing up in Britain in the 1930s, she's impatient to get on with living as best she can since becoming totally blind but finds that her parents' refusal to send her out to school, out with friends, or anywhere on her own compounds her handicap. An emotional refuge develops in her friendship with Dennis Weston, who accepts her openly and whose ideas, borrowed from his freethinking, intellectual parents, stimulate Mary Anne's own thinking to more positive lines. Her growing sense of self is further encouraged by a forthright surgeon who operates successfully to restore some of her sight. That pushes Mary Anne further toward independence, most concretely demonstrated in her move to accompany her family's servant girl home to the town where the girl's father has been killed

in a mining accident. The favorable outcome of a showdown between Mary Anne and her father signals her substantial progress toward a self-determined future. Allan writes with insight; the story has an autobiographical cast that commands both interest and empathy.

Zena Sutherland

SOURCE: A review of *The View Beyond My Father,* in *Bulletin of the Center for Children's Books,* Vol. 32, No. 7, March, 1979, p. 109.

Written with far more depth than her usual travel-and-adventure stories. Allan's first-person novel about a young adolescent who has been blind for two years and recovers her sight after an operation has pace and insight, and is especially fine in the characterization of a domineering Victorian father. Set in an English town in the 1930's, the story describes—from Mary's viewpoint—the struggle to be independent, and the joy she found when a boy who became her friend introduced her to his sympathetic, intelligent parents. The plot denouement may be, for most readers, Mary's joy when she realizes she can see again, but the more profound victory is in her finally convincing her father that she is capable and self-reliant. Mary's parents have shielded her too much because of her blindness, but most adolescent readers will recognize to some degree the conflict between parental protection and adolescent rebellion as a phenomenon of most teenage lives.

Ann A. Flowers

SOURCE: A review of *The View Beyond My Father,* in *The Horn Book Magazine,* Vol. LV, No. 2, April, 1979, p. 197.

Mary Anne Angus's life is bounded by the fact that she is blind and kept a virtual prisoner by her overprotective family. Her blindness, hereditary in nature, struck when she was twelve, and now several years later she has almost given up hope. An operation by a brilliant and sympathetic surgeon restores her sight; her mind is set free by exposure to new and interesting ideas, especially those of the family of Dennis Weston, a boy who befriends her. But her long struggle against the narrow ideas and regulations of her domineering Victorian kind of father is only successful when she openly defies him and performs a necessary and charitable action. Set in England in the 1930s, the book surprisingly never mentions the Great Depression, and the writing style is rather flat; but the portrayal of Mary Anne, a strong, responsive character, in contrast to her father, who is loving but insensitive, gives the book an almost autobiographical feeling.

TOMORROW IS A LOVELY DAY (1979; U.S. edition as A Lovely Tomorrow)

A. Thatcher

SOURCE: A review of *Tomorrow Is a Lovely Day,* in *The*

Junior Bookshelf, Vol. 43, No. 6, December, 1979, p. 331.

This sensitive portrayal of a young girl's dedication to her chosen career as an actress is compulsive reading. Fifteen-year-old Frue Allandale, a pupil at a stage school, tragically loses both her adored artistic parents when a V2 rocket falls on their home on New Year's Eve, 1944.

Her Great Aunt Mildred, a tough seemingly insensitive woman, comes to collect the badly shocked girl, and takes her to the house she shares with her unmarried thirty-nine-year-old daughter Muriel in the Chiltern village of Little Hartshorn. Their neighbour is Robert the Earl who had once lived at Great Hartshorn House, now an expensive boarding school for girls.

Rebellious and miserable, Frue misses London and the stage school, the family friends, the Tremartins, and especially their son Paul whom Frue was just beginning to realise was someone special in her life. Then she is enrolled as a pupil at Great Hartshorn House School.

After a very unhappy few months, during which she attempts to run away, and helps lonely little Annie—a Duke's daughter—Frue at last settles down. A special new friend, Nicola, turns out to be the daughter of Great Aunt Mildred's estranged daughter, Molly. Frue begins to love the beautiful Buckinghamshire countryside.

By the end of August, after a wonderful working holiday in Cornwall with the Tremartins, life once again holds promise of joy and happiness. She and Paul are closer than ever. She is to return to the stage school. Muriel and Robert are married. Tomorrow may well be a lovely day after all.

Master craftswoman Mabel Allan carries the reader back to Britain in 1944. But this delightful novel is far more than just nostalgia. The story lives. The characters are real people in real situations against an authentic and very lovely background.

Cyrisse Jaffee

SOURCE: A review of *A Lovely Tomorrow,* in *School Library Journal,* Vol. 26, No. 8, April, 1980, p. 119.

Aspiring drama student Frue Allendale lives an unconventional life with her parents in London until a fatal New Year's Eve, 1944, when a bomb leaves her a 15-year-old orphan. She must go and live with her only surviving relatives, very proper Aunt Mildred and her passive, obedient daughter Muriel, in the country. All the ends are tied up (too) neatly: Frue gains respect for Aunt Mildred; Muriel gets up the courage to marry the local lord, Robert; Frue befriends Nicola, who just happens to be the daughter of Aunt Mildred's runaway daughter Molly; Frue inherits a lot of money from a film her father made years earlier; and in an especially phony manner, Paul (the romantic interest who pops up unconvincingly

throughout) and Frue meet and she decides, "Paul was the one I wanted. I had known that months ago, in another life." Although the descriptions of life in wartime Britain are accurate, the writing style is detached and dry with occasional melodramatic passages. Frue, like other Allan heroines, is a shallow character whose feelings, thoughts, and development are constantly spelled out, not shown.

Denise M. Wilms

SOURCE: A review of *A Lovely Tomorrow,* in *Booklist,* Vol. 76, No. 15, April 1, 1980, p. 1120.

When her parents are killed during a 1944 New Year's Eve rocket hit in their London flat, Frue Allendale's life alters abruptly and irrevocably. Her story is one of painful adjustment—to the loss of her parents, to the countryside where her crotchety, iron-willed great-aunt Mildred brings her to live, and later to the nearby boarding school that Aunt Mildred dictates she will attend. Allan allows local affairs to soothe Frue's raw, unsettled psyche naturally. She gradually comes to appreciate the area's beauty; her unmarried Aunt Muriel arouses her curiosity and sympathy. When Frue reluctantly attends Hartsthorn House Girls' Academy, her determined aloofness cracks at the routine of school activities and her classmates' friendship. A strong subplot concerns Aunt Mildred's relationship with her grown daughters (one of them estranged) and the prospect of Muriel's being in love with the local earl. Frue's character is plausibly imperfect; she's not above snobbery or patronizing her aunt, yet is open-minded to her surroundings and in touch with herself enough to realize her shortcomings and work around them. The story's ending seems pat, however. Aunt Mildred's reconciliation with her daughter and her agreement to Frue's returning to London seem too easily accomplished. That wrapup is not without appeal, however, and seasoned readers won't really mind.

Linda Coslick

SOURCE: A review of *A Lovely Tomorrow,* in *Best Sellers,* Vol. 40, No. 2, May, 1980, p. 78.

A Lovely Tomorrow is an appealing book about a girl whose life is blown apart by a stray V-2 rocket falling in London, WW II. Frue Allendale loses both her parents and a budding career as a stage actress when the rocket falls on her home on New Year's Eve, 1944. Filled with an overwhelming sense of loss and despair, Frue is rushed to the hamlet of Little Hartsthorn to live with her Great Aunt Mildred. Frue hates the quiet countryside, the beechwood trees. She's a city girl. Mostly she hates Aunt Mildred and her country ways. She will never be able to understand, or be understood by, Aunt Mildred.

This well-written book will easily hold the interest of a young female reader: sympathy for Frue's plight, interest in her cousin's clandestine (though innocent) love affair, curiosity about the posh girls' school Frue is sent to, excitement over Frue's own love interest.

By the end Frue has learned a lot about herself and a lot about her Aunt Mildred. She realizes with a shock that she has learned to love both Little Hartsthorn and Aunt Mildred. The only aspect of this book that teenagers might not like is that Aunt Mildred turns out to be all-knowing. Every one of her do's and don't's turns out to be right on the money. And teenagers don't like to be reminded that mother—or in this case Aunt—knows best.

If the book has a moral, it's that time heals. By the end of the year, Frue is at peace, happy with Hartsthorn and happy with Aunt Mildred.

Zena Sutherland

SOURCE: A review of *A Lovely Tomorrow,* in *Bulletin of the Center for Children's Books,* Vol. 33, No. 11, July-August, 1980, p. 205.

A story set in England during World War II is based in part on the author's experiences; her heroine, Frue, is precipitated into a wholly different kind of life when a bomb kills her parents. Frue has to give up a part in a London play and her plans to go to drama school, since her stern, brisk Aunt Mildred comes to London and takes Frue back to the country with her. Lonely, bored, and frustrated, Frue longs to get away, and she's increasingly resentful when Aunt Mildred places her in a nearby girl's school. There she finds a friend who later proves to be her cousin (there has been a rift in the family) and she is delighted when her no-longer-young cousin Muriel (long under the thumb of her tyrannical mother Mildred) marries the local Earl, and life looks even brighter when her London friend, Paul, shows that he returns her affection. To add to a promise of a lovely tomorrow, Aunt Mildred decides it will be acceptable for Frue to go back to London and the drama school if she lives with her new-found cousin (sister of Muriel, mother of the school friend). So all ends very neatly, with tomorrow promising all that Frue desires. Allan creates a fairly vivid picture of the vicissitudes of the blitz period, and the writing style is adequate, but the plot is thinly stretched, the ending of the story weak, and the characterization variable: one or two minor characters (the headmistress of the school, for example) seem stereotypical, most have little depth; a few (cousin Muriel) come alive; Frue herself is not a memorable character.

THE MILLS DOWN BELOW (1980)

Anne Strachan

SOURCE: A review of *The Mills Down Below,* in *Book Window,* Vol. 7, No. 3, Summer, 1980, p. 29.

Elinor Rillsden's life centred on the school-room of the Jacobean mansion of her family. She led a dull, boring existence, suffocated by her parents' desire to make her a lady. Her brother Teddy went to Eton, but she was not to be allowed to go to school. But the year was 1914. An entire way of life was being questioned and was about to be wiped out of existence by a war. In this year Elinor discovered the Suffragette movement and began to think. She gradually awoke to the realities of her position as a pre-war female and was amazed to find her conservative mother doing the same. Despite a more serious appearance, there is an element of childish humour in this story, as it is seen through the eyes of a friendly fourteen-year-old with a sense of humour growing up in difficult times. Altogether a very enjoyable book.

D. A. Young

SOURCE: A review of *The Mills Down Below,* in *The Junior Bookshelf,* Vol. 44, No. 4, August, 1980, p. 184.

It is 1914. Fourteen-year-old Elinor is the daughter of the mill-owner and the grand house in which she lives is more of a prison than a home. Also she is growing up into a world of change which she cannot, even if she so wished, escape. She makes friends with children in the town: her cousin comes to stay and fills her mind with women's rights and suffragettes: war breaks out and the death of her father strangely releases her finally to face the prospect of freedom undreamed of some months before.

It may not be a very original story but it works uncommonly well. It manages without violence and the emotional climate is calm. Nevertheless Elinor comes alive as an interesting person and her awakening to the social changes of her time is shown with commendable credibility.

Wendy Dellett

SOURCE: A review of *The Mills Down Below,* in *School Library Journal,* Vol. 27, No. 8, April, 1981, pp. 135-6.

In the summer of 1914, a young girl learns about Life, Death, and Women's Rights. The unpleasant heroine is haughty, sneaky Elinor Rillsden, who lives in a large mansion on a hill, rarely sees her parents, listens at keyholes (because it's the "only way to learn anything . . .") and hates her governess, her lessons, her father, her brother, her life and herself. The characters are all vaguely delineated—most are never physically described—and yet Elinor (who is telling the story) is sensitive to their repulsive features: she is especially disgusted by her brother's acne, which she refers to often, as if it were a nasty habit he should correct. Elinor's father is a despicable man who browbeats his wife, his servants and his employees in the "mills down below"; and Elinor (justifiably) feels that things have become "better because my father had died and Mother had somehow come alive." But the sudden mellowing of the unreasonable father, the brief camaraderie with the ill-mannered older brother, the abrupt blossoming of the repressed mother when her domineering husband dies so conveniently—all these changes are obviously contrived and the outcome boringly predictable. In just three months Elinor "becomes a woman," overcomes her class snobbery and gets everything she always wanted from her transformed mother. Allan's often trite phrasing, ill-constructed paragraphs and unconnected thoughts make her book tedious and unrewarding.

Denise M. Wilms

SOURCE: A review of *The Mills Down Below*, in *Booklist*, Vol. 77, No. 18, May 15, 1981, p. 1250.

Feminism is at the heart of this story of wealthy, sheltered Elinor Rillsden, who realizes that her Victorian father's ironfisted rule of his family and his weaving mills (which employ women and children) is insensitive and destructive. Characters are sure to generate tension: Elinor's father is a narrow-minded snob who thinks women are inferior; her cousin Amy, who comes to stay when her parents are killed, is a feminist; Elinor's mother, seemingly meek and mild, turns out to have both sense and spirit in the wake of her husband's death. Plotting is somewhat predictable, with hints that Mr. Rillsden won't last and that mother might not be so demurring; but that doesn't matter, thanks to Allan's sure hand at sketching the story's victims.

Zena Sutherland

SOURCE: A review of *The Mills Down Below*, in *Bulletin of the Center for Children's Books*, Vol. 34, No. 11, July-August, 1981, p. 205.

The overprotected daughter of a stern Victorian father, Elinor was well aware that she must keep her friendship with two of the children from the mill town a secret. Owner of the mills, Father wanted Elinor to be a proper young lady; Father wanted Elinor to stay quietly with her governess, whose teaching was inept and dull. It was the summer of 1914, and with the announcement of war Father became so furious that he had a fatal stroke; unexpectedly, Elinor's quiet mother became a firm and outspoken manager of the family's affairs, and Elinor's dearest wish came true: not only would she be allowed to go to school, but to the school in the town below. The difference in location is paralleled by the difference in social status, and the book—a competent but not stimulating period piece—is indicative of the changing status of women (feminine suffrage is one of the issues it explores, education for women another) and of the breakdown of the rigid class system. The writing style and characterization are adequate if not impressive; the story line is cohesive but sedate.

📖 ***STRANGERS IN WOOD STREET* (1981)**

Janet Fisher

SOURCE: A review of *Strangers in Wood Street*, in *Brit-*

ish Book News, Children's Supplement, Spring, 1981, p. 21.

Strangers in Wood Street is the seventh book in the series about the Wood Street gang set in a rather run-down area of Liverpool. In this story the gang track down two boys who have run away from home and rescue them. Although this tale stands alone, it would help to have read the others in the series in order to be familiar with the eight members of the gang and their families. However, the tensions within the gang and the different family relationships are well drawn and make this a readable adventure story for sevens to elevens.

Geoff Fox

SOURCE: "Home and Away," in *The Times Educational Supplement*, No. 3394, July 10, 1981, p. 26.

[When] one of Mabel Esther Allan's Liverpudlian Wood Street Gang says, "Well, I vote we seek out those boys", or "Oh rot!", it doesn't *sound* like a Scouser. Young readers may not be worried about this at all, however, for although the plot involves runaway children and the possible loss of jobs and homes, we are not much concerned with social realism here. This is one of a series, and children read series for predictable plots with cheerful endings and equally predictable characters. Whilst the book is rather more than a kind of *Eight have Fun in the Liverpool Slums*, its intentions are modest and well-defined, and Mabel Esther Allan meets her readers' needs for a satisfying, secure read.

📖 ***A STRANGE ENCHANTMENT* (1981)**

Janet Fisher

SOURCE: A review of *A Strange Enchantment*, in *British Book News, Children's Supplement*, Autumn, 1981, pp. 22-3.

It is difficult for today's youth to understand the fervour with which people volunteered to undertake war work in 1939. This book does little to alter this state of affairs but paints a somewhat rosy picture of life as a land girl. Although the physical discomfort, long hours and unpleasant nature of some of the work is described, it somehow does not come alive. Prim herself, and Jane and the little girl Eileen are well drawn but the romance with Peter is predictable and the war seems far away. It is a pleasant, undemanding read for girls of twelve and upwards.

Denise M. Wilms

SOURCE: A review of *A Strange Enchantment*, in *Booklist*, Vol. 78, No. 21, July, 1982, p. 1439.

Farming appeals to Prim and, like everyone around her, she wants to do her part for Britain's war effort. So she joins the Land Army to be trained in farming skills and assigned a place in some shorthanded rural household. Prim's experiences shape an informative story that exposes a little-known aspect of World War II. As Prim's rude awakening to real-life farm duties gives way to a genuine liking for the job, readers learn about farming conditions, the precarious livelihoods of farmhands, and the unfair working conditions under which many labored. Although story development is somewhat predictable, it is quite satisfying, thanks to well-realized characters and a romantic thread that leads to marriage for Prim. A sharp, absorbing look at the not-too-distant past.

Ellen Fader

SOURCE: A review of *A Strange Enchantment,* in *School Library Journal,* Vol. 29, No. 1, September, 1982, p. 114.

It is 1939. Primrose is 16 and too young to join Britain's armed services. She adds a year to her age, volunteers for the Women's Land Army and is sent to an agricultural college for training before going to work on a farm. Prim's romantic ideas about farm life are quickly changed to reflect the realities of hard work, extreme temperatures and long hours. She is eventually assigned to a farm in Shropshire and is upset to discover living nearby an instructor from the college who had made her life miserable. Prim is not happy with the family with whom she is living, but does find solace at a neighboring farm and, in time, in Peter Blane, her former instructor. Prim is an intriguing character who is determined to enjoy the "strange enchantment" of country life; she also begins to establish a reputation for her satirical political cartoons. The romance, as described, is quite innocent; the war seems very distant and appears to make little difference in the daily lives of most of the characters. This is very mild historical fiction. Although the plot will carry readers through, there is a certain remoteness in this story that makes engagement with the characters difficult.

Zena Sutherland

SOURCE: A review of *A Strange Enchantment,* in *Bulletin of the Center for Children's Books,* Vol. 36, No. 3, November, 1982, p. 42.

The experiences Primrose has as a member of the Women's Land Army in the English countryside during World War II are based on the author's service in that group, and give the book enough validity and variety to compensate for the hackneyed plot. Prim, sixteen, pretends to be older so that she can enlist; during her arduous training, she becomes angry at one young man who is a teacher, but as the book progresses it becomes increasingly clear that an intensive rapport will be established. Not impressive structurally or stylistically, the story should appeal to readers because of the verisimilitude of the details of farm work and the local color.

📖 *THE HORNS OF DANGER* (1981)

Drew Stevenson

SOURCE: A review of *The Horns of Danger,* in *School Library Journal,* Vol. 28, No. 4, December, 1981, p. 83.

Summoned to Darkling Farm by a frantic phone call from her friend Sabrina Wallace, Marissa Fen finds Sabrina alone, her aunt and uncle recently killed in an automobile crash. Sabrina claims to have seen ***The Horns of Danger*** near the farm and believes the horns (part of an ancient ritual in which village men don antlered headdresses and parade through the countryside) had something to do with her relatives' accident. But the vicar of the church where the horns are kept swears that they haven't been taken from storage since last year. Dubious at first, Marissa becomes a believer when she, too, sees the horns in the wood one night. The young women are convinced that the villagers are conspiring to scare Sabrina into selling the farm. But why? This is the kind of reading that will be savored by suspense lovers. Author Mabel Esther Allan knows her village and its characters and knows how to draw readers into the nightmare of Darkling Farm.

Zena Sutherland

SOURCE: A review of *The Horns of Danger,* in *Bulletin of the Center for Children's Books,* Vol. 35, No. 8, April, 1982, p. 141.

Marissa is delighted when her friend telephones and asks that she leave Liverpool and come out to the country—but why, Marissa wonders, is Sabrina frightened? The horn dancers, observers of an ancient and symbolic rite, have been used as the theme of several adolescent novels; here the plot is based on the mystery of how the horns can be seen when it is known that they are safely locked in church? The two girls and their boyfriends have already deduced a great deal about an old murder and a lost treasure when, in a final melodramatic episode, a fire leads to the discovery of the treasure itself. The story line is obscured by a plethora of minor characters and unessential details; the writing style is weakened by a plethora of gasped details and exclamation points.

📖 *A DREAM OF HUNGER MOSS* (1983)

Denise M. Wilms

SOURCE: A review of *A Dream of Hunger Moss,* in *Booklist,* Vol. 80, No. 4, October 15, 1983, p. 354.

The stretch of English countryside called Hunger Moss is a place Allie has heard about often enough from her mother; now that her mother is about to have an operation, Allie and her brother Adam are to stay near there with the same farming couple their mother summered with years ago. Both are apprehensive about the visit, for country living is alien to their working-class, Liverpool lives.

But Allie discovers that although she misses some of the amenities of town, she has the same affinity for the area her mother had. Even Adam, who is headed for delinquency at home, seems grudgingly to accept his new surroundings. That's all just as well, for World War II is declared, and the children learn they can't go back to Liverpool. In the meantime, Allie befriends Reuben, another visitor on a nearby farm, and watches with fascination as their relationship seems to parallel one that her mother had years ago with a boy of the same name. The story's British setting is clear but not overbearing; characterizations of Allie and her brother are quiet and true, with the war and a light touch of mystery adding enough complexity to make the story interesting and absorbing.

Margaret C. Howell

SOURCE: A review of *A Dream of Hunger Moss,* in *School Library Journal,* Vol. 30, No. 5, January, 1984, p. 83.

For years Alice's mother has told her about her girlhood summers at Guelder Rose Farm, the friend, Reuben, whom she met on Hunger Moss, a marsh crossed by an old Roman road and of Reuben's sudden disappearance. Now Alice and her brother Adam are going to Guelder Rose while their mother has an operation. In the quiet style of her other English country books, like *A Strange Enchantment,* Allan weaves a story about what happens to Alice during the next few weeks as she goes on the Moss, meets a modern Reuben and his great-grandmother and finds the answer to the mystery of what happened to the original Reuben 20 years before. Woven into Alice's story are lovely descriptions of the countryside and a subplot about the first children evacuees from cities during World War II. Alice discovers something of her mother's feel-ings by reliving some of her experiences. Alice is a realistic character, as are Mrs. Farmer of Guelder Rose and Mrs. Carey, Reuben's great-grandmother. The other characters are not as well developed and it is not clear why Adam, who is afraid of cows, agrees to work on the farm. The ending is a little too pat, as a fire in a cowshed helps Adam overcome his fear and a bombing of the Bakers' store brings the whole family to Guelder Rose. Considering these flaws the story does have the warmth and atmosphere of the English country in the '40s and would be of interest to those looking for a gentle story rather than a problem novel.

Zena Sutherland

SOURCE: A review of *A Dream of Hunger Moss,* in *Bulletin of the Center for Children's Books,* Vol. 37, No. 6, February, 1984, p. 101.

Because of her mother's hospitalization, Alice (the narrator) and her brother Adam are sent to stay on the farm near Oxford where Mother had spent her childhood holidays. Alice loved the place; Adam, afraid of some animals, was less pleased until he started working and found he enjoyed it. Both were fascinated by Hunger Moss, a dangerously boggy piece of land that held a ruined tower. It was there they met Reuben, and Alice found it mysterious and intriguing that Mother had once had a friend by the same name, whom she'd met secretly in the same place, and who had disappeared. Because England goes to war, local families take in city children, and it is partly through that fact that Alice gets to know Reuben's imperious great-grandmother and solves the mystery of her mother's lost friend. The story is nicely knit, capably written, and structured with good pace and some suspense.

Additional coverage of Allan's life and career is contained in the following sources published by Gale Research: *Contemporary Authors New Revision Series,* **Vol. 47;** *Major Authors and Illustrators for Children and Young Adults; Something about the Author,* **Vols. 5, 32, 75;** and *Something about the Author Autobiography Series,* **Vol. 11.**

Daniel Cohen

1936-

American author of nonfiction.

Major works include *The Last Hundred Years: Medicine* (1981), *ESP: The New Technology* (1986), *When Someone You Know Is Gay* (1989), *Ancient Egypt* (1989), *Ghostly Tales of Love and Revenge* (1992).

INTRODUCTION

Prolific author of a wide range of nonfiction for children and young adults, Cohen is known primarily for his books about ghosts, monsters, and psychic phenomena. He also writes on other subjects of appeal to young readers, such as rock video superstars, UFOs, movies, and dinosaurs. Together with his wife, Susan, a social worker, he has written successfully for the reluctant teenage reader on social issues like drugs, drinking, and homosexuality. Critics praise him for his easy, colloquial, noncondescending style in dealing with sensitive topics and his contagious enthusiasm for ancient history as well as animal behavior and the supernatural. Above all, his open-minded attitude towards the bizarre and unexplainable stands him in good stead with believers and nonbelievers as he edifies and entertains his readers.

Biographical Information

Born in Chicago during the Great Depression, Cohen graduated with a degree in journalism from the University of Illinois and married sociology student Susan Handler. After a brief stint with Time, Inc., he joined the staff of *Science Digest,* moving with his wife to New York City when the office relocated. There, he began contributing his own articles to the periodical, including his controversial review of John Fuller's UFO book *Incident at Exeter,* which led to guest appearances on television and radio programs. Cohen next explored the subject of extrasensory perception (ESP) in a *Science Digest* article, making record-breaking sales for the magazine, and culminated his success with his first book, a collection of pieces on such topics as the Loch Ness Monster and flying saucers entitled *Myths of the Space Age* (1967). Once launched as an author, Cohen left the publishing business and moved to a farmhouse north of the city to continue writing not only popular science type articles but also supernatural subjects—aliens, ghosts, witches, etc. He encountered some hostility from religious fundamentalists, who accused him of Satan worship and spiritualism, and subsequent pressure resulted in the banning of his books from some school libraries, notably his popular *Curses, Hexes, and Spells* (1974). Animal lover and history buff, Cohen wrote rapidly on subjects as diverse as

Talking with the Animals (1971) and *The Body Snatchers* (1975), the latter about ancient tomb robbers of Egypt, but found himself getting behind on his numerous commitments. In desperation, he enlisted his wife's help. The ensuing collaboration not only met deadlines but enabled the two to achieve a new goal: writing about social issues for the reading-resistant teenager, including *When Someone You Know Is Gay.* Inspired by their daughter, Theodora, they also did a well-received rock video book, which led to other books on movies, music, and television. Tragedy, however, struck the family in 1988 when Theodora was killed in the bombing of Pan Am 103 over Scotland. Cohen continues to write on a great variety of subjects and regularly lectures at schools and colleges.

Major Works

One of Cohen's informative tomes for young adults, *The Last Hundred Years: Medicine* covers a century of medical advances, controversies, major contributors, and health care, enlivened with anecdotes and placed in historical perspective. Critics acclaimed it for its clear and comprehensive account of the breakthroughs in medicine and such related fields as nutrition, the drug industry, and the training of physicians. Cohen and coauthor wife Susan submitted *When Someone You Know Is Gay* to over fifteen children's publishers before it was accepted. Directed to the average nongay reader, it contributes well-researched, responsible, sympathetic information on homosexuals—their history, experiences, and relationships to families and churches—promiscuity, and AIDS, including frank interviews and quotes from teenaged gays. Although there is no index or bibliography, there is a directory of gay organizations and an annotated list of movies, videos, and books. On a topic most often associated with the author, Cohen provides an impartial introduction to parapsychology in his *ESP: The New Technology* by exploring both the strengths and weaknesses of differing approaches, from early times to modern laboratories, and supplying useful definitions and a helpful bibliography. Forerunner of his books for younger children on early civilizations like Greece and Rome, *Ancient Egypt* is a collection of short essays on the geography, history, religion, art, and way of life of the people known for their pyramids, pharaohs, hieroglyphics, and mummies. Following his popular *The Ghosts of War,* which dealt with male ghosts, *Ghostly Tales of Love and Revenge* deals with female ghosts from around the world—women who died and had reason to return to haunt the living. Some are based on real people, others are legends from various times and places as far away as Scotland or Japan, back in the seventeenth century to contemporary times. The brief stories make for excellent read-alouds.

GENERAL COMMENTARY

Alan Hull Walton

SOURCE: "Weirdies and Horrible," in *Books and Bookmen,* Vol. 23, No. 3, December, 1977, pp. 61-2, 64.

Magicians, Wizards, and Sorcerers, by Daniel Cohen, commences with a chapter on 'The Secret of the Pyramids', which includes a description of the initiation of postulants into the great brotherhood of the Magi; wherein, if they passed the terrifying ordeal, they learned the powers of theurgy and the secrets of universal life—after seven further years of study. 'The Magician's World' reveals that modern scientists have been able to discern the beginnings of magical rituals among some animals, such as the chimpanzee. Contagious magic and voodoo are dealt with in this section (not forgetting Sir J G Frazer), together with what modern medicine describes as the 'placebo effect', and the magical and medicinal use of herbs.

'The Ancient Magicians' adequately covers the Pythagoreans (Pythagoras was a most important magical figure), Apollonius of Tyana, Simon Magus and the Gnostics. 'Mediaeval Magic' covers Faust, Cornelius Agrippa, John Dee and others; and is followed by a beautifully concentrated and informative chapter on the Alchemists and the Rosicrucians, exposing details of the ancient Hermetic tradition, and the lives of Nicolas Flamel and Paracelsus.

The remainder of the volume is devoted to the Comte de Saint-Germain, Cagliostro (*ie,* Joseph Balsamo, whom Goethe describes so tantalisingly in his *Italian Letters*), and Mesmer. These eighteenth century figures are followed by Eliphas Levi, MacGregor Mathers (and 'The Golden Dawn' group, which included such celebrities and geniuses as W. B. Yeats, Arthur Machen, Algernon Blackwood and others of lesser eminence), Aleister Crowley, and that most exotic (and learned) of all creatures, Madame Blavatsky—who is honoured with a goodly number of pages. A final short chapter deals with the practising magicians of our own time—and gives a warning about the dangers of becoming involved in such ceremonies.

Curses, Hexes and Spells, by the same author, is just what its title indicates. The first chapter ('The Old Family Curse') relates a strange belief which is completely new to me. This is the so-called twenty-year curse attached to the Presidency of the United States. It is, it seems, undeniable that every president elected at intervals of twenty years, commencing with the election of 1840, has either been assassinated, or has died in office. A complete list, with dates and details, is reproduced, up to the time of John F. Kennedy. Mathematically, the odds against this happening by chance are a hundred to one. 'But improbable things sometimes happen'. The remaining chapter headings concern themselves with 'Accursed Places', 'Accursed Creatures', 'Curses of Wanderers and Ghosts', 'Everyday Curses', 'Black Magic' and 'Amulets and Talismans'.

The next volume is *The Body Snatchers,* also by Daniel Cohen, who appears to have devoted a great deal of careful research to the subject. The dissection of human bodies for purposes of medical study has, of course, gone on for many hundreds of years. Nevertheless, especially in Europe, the first three decades of the nineteenth century appear to have been its golden era. One of the principal sources for this grisly supply of human flesh was the gallows, the bodies of the executed being speedily despatched to some hospital or surgery. The criminals themselves were terrified of what were described as 'miracle revivals'—that is, that they would be cut down before they were truly dead, and come back to life on the dissecting table. Such events must have been infinitely more frequent than imagined in those days of unscientific hanging. Apparent death (even when medically certified) is not necessarily true death, as Lyall Watson went to great pains to stress in his important book, *The Romeo Error*; and even today—as witness a number of separate reports on the BBC—dead people have suddenly come to life in the mortuary, or even on the autopsy table, hours after 'dying'. In one case the heart and lungs of a man had ceased to function for eleven hours—yet back to life he came.

Mr Cohen covers the entire subject in a thorough manner. As one might expect, Burke and Hare are given their fair share of attention; the profit of the game is investigated; much attention is given to Egyptian mummies and tomb-robbing; and a political section considers the honoured and dishonoured dead, with some mention of Stalin. The penultimate and final chapters are 'Restless Corpses' and 'Screaming Skulls', the first of which relates much concerning Zombies and Vampires—with suitable illustrations!

TITLE COMMENTARY

📖 *CURSES, HEXES, AND SPELLS* (1974)

Harriet Miller

SOURCE: A review of *Curses, Hexes, & Spells*, in *School Library Journal*, Vol. 21, No. 3, November, 1974, p. 61.

Cohen discredits all supernatural explanations for family curses, the disappearance of ships and planes in the Bermuda Triangle, the curse on the ship *Mary Celeste*, and the legend of the Wandering Jew. Yet he drums up mystery, sometimes to the point of confusion, to maintain the "chill and thrill" ambience of the Weird and Horrible Library series. This tendency is apparent in his misleading comment that the Knights Templar worshipped devils and were adept at putting curses on people. While more detailed than the author's *Superstition,* this is not as openminded as Gary Jennings' *Black Magic, White Magic.*

Publishers Weekly

SOURCE: A review of *Curses, Hexes, and Spells,* in *Publishers Weekly*, Vol. 206, No. 22, November 25, 1974, p. 46.

Most of the author's examples of creepy phenomena are old hat (the Bermuda Triangle, the Kennedy tragedies, the Hapsburg curse, etc.) which seem to be leftovers from his other books on similar subjects. What is interesting in this book is that Cohen gives a picture of the society and culture that apparently *needs* curses and superstitions. His explanations of how the modern fascination with the occult originated is delivered logically and with no moralizing. (Incidentally, he says it's traditionally o.k. to curse someone who has wronged you; it's not o.k. to curse someone who hasn't, no matter how you dislike him or her.) Mr. Cohen also seems to get a lot of pleasure out of elaborating on the scariness of curses, hexes and spells, an attitude which may distress some and bring a grin to others.

📖 *THE WORLD OF UFOS* (1978)

Booklist

SOURCE: A review of *The World of UFOs*, in *Booklist*, Vol. 74, No. 19, June 1, 1978, pp. 1543-4.

In a brisk, informal overview of the modern UFO scene from its beginning in 1947, when the term "flying saucer" was coined, to the present, Cohen objectively traces the course and controversy of contemporary "ufology," citing a number of classic sightings and highlighting U.S. Air Force projects, the Condon Committee, and its report. His skepticism is evident when he delves into some of the more outré fringe elements—contactees, monsters, von Däniken's ancient astronauts, hollow-earth theory, and UFO religions, among others. While most of Cohen's account will be familiar to readers who have kept up with the world of UFOs, it provides a good introduction for those who want to satisfy a casual curiosity, generated perhaps by the motion picture *Close Encounters of the Third Kind.* The bibliography can be used as a list of books (pro and con) for further reading.

Kirkus Reviews

SOURCE: A review of *The World of UFOs,* in *Kirkus Reviews*, Vol. XLVI, No. 11, June 1, 1978, p. 600.

Case by case Cohen points out how most reported UFO sightings have been frauds or misinterpretations; the unexplained remainder are classed simply as "still debated" and not played up for ambiguous sensation. Further, Cohen repeatedly points to UFO enthusiasts' ignoring of negative evidence; he debunks favorite "proofs" and dismisses prominent crackpots (Van Daniken); and neither his reportage of disputes within and without official investigating circles nor his citation of theories linking UFOs to everything from the Kennedy assassinations and Watergate to the Loch Ness monster and Irish fairies would tend to encourage credulity. As with Cohen's own *Ancient Visitors* (1976), the only question concerns the need to rake over the same old coals yet again; however, where the demand for further close encounters is compelling, this will serve.

Anne C. Raymer

SOURCE: A review of *The World of UFOs,* in *School Library Journal*, Vol. 25, No. 1, September, 1978, p. 155.

An informal, opinionated narrative that debunks celebrated UFO encounters, mainly of the last 30 years, and treats UFOlogy as genuine American folklore. Cohen supports official explanations for reported sightings (temperature inversions, ball lightning, etc.). He elaborates on the investigative work of individuals and groups (both federal and civilian), favorably highlighting the conclusions of the Condon Committee and the Air Force's Project Bluebook researchers. A questioning of witness reliability exposes hoaxes and half truths, and the reasons people want to believe in outer space visitors (space people may save us from nuclear holocaust or nullify Darwin's theories of evolution!). A less biased coverage would be more convincing in content, but Cohen's points are well reasoned and highly readable and this is more articulate, amusing, and coherent than Strickland's *Aliens on Earth.*

THE WORLD'S MOST FAMOUS GHOSTS (1978)

Judith Goldberger

SOURCE: A review of *The World's Most Famous Ghosts,* in *Booklist,* Vol. 74, No. 22, July 15, 1978, p. 1738.

This survey of some of the more dramatic and better-known ghosts is a collection that falls between fiction and "well substantiated" sighting—in the author's words, "ghostly legends." Unfortunately, Cohen tends to present his material in an implicitly factual manner, which may be misleading to the unversed reader. Aside from this ambiguity and the somewhat simplistic style of description, there are aspects of the book that will appeal to an unsophisticated reluctant reader: basic occult terms are explained throughout, and a large number of different legends are contained within 10 short chapters.

Anne C. Raymer

SOURCE: A review of *The World's Most Famous Ghosts,* in *School Library Journal,* Vol. 25, No. 1, September, 1978, p. 132.

In ten engaging chapters, Cohen presents accounts of ghostly apparitions of Abraham Lincoln, Anne Boleyn, Aaron Burr, and other well-known figures from history. The potpourri also includes tales of the nameless but equally legendary Man in Gray, the Flying Dutchman, and the Horror of No. 50 Berkeley Square in London. What with screaming skulls, eerie houses, and spectral trains, this selection should be a hit with children, and it has special appeal to reluctant readers since the vocabulary is simple and the tempo swift.

YOUNG GHOSTS (1978; revised edition, 1994)

Kris Preslan

SOURCE: A review of *Young Ghosts,* in *School Library Journal,* Vol. 25, No. 2, October, 1978, p. 143.

Imagine a juvenile ghost who pulls covers from the bed, talks in codes, and swoops around shrieking about her lost tooth. This collection of ghost lore concentrates mainly on English child-ghosts, but there is a chapter on American ghosts, too. Included is a novel section on Christmas ghosts with a discussion of Charles Dickens' *A Christmas Carol.* The book includes photographs, prints, and a bibliography of delicious titles for further reading. A refreshing approach to the subject of psychic phenomena.

Barbara Elleman

SOURCE: A review of *Young Ghosts,* in *Booklist,* Vol. 75, No. 10, January 15, 1979, p. 808.

"At one time or another all of these stories have been represented as being true," states Cohen in the introduction to this account of children-as-ghosts and children-seeing-ghosts. He discusses the situations surrounding each incident, retells the supposed appearances, and goes on to cite the results of investigations telling why many have been discredited by nonbelievers. Strange legends of the Radiant Boys who appear in a glowing light and foretell death, a poltergeist that troubled a Tennessee family, and a young ghost named Rosalie who appeared in the flesh during a seance, as well as some stories authenticated by the British Society for Psychical Research, are included. The photographs and drawings are sometimes confusing as they don't always correspond to the narrative. Those interested in probing the validity of ghostly appearances will enjoy sharing Cohen's lively, if somewhat meandering, explanations.

Elaine E. Knight

SOURCE: A review of *Young Ghosts,* in *School Library Journal,* Vol. 40, No. 10, October, 1994, p. 132.

Cohen has a knack for selecting ghost stories with unusual angles. In this revision of his 1978 book, the focus is on child specters. Few new accounts have been added, but the audience appeal has definitely been enhanced. The writing style is crisper and more conversational. A larger typeface and a truly haunting jacket will attract readers. Many of the stories date from the 18th and 19th centuries, and some, such as the Wesley family poltergeist and the Tennessee Bell Witch, have appeared in many other sources. There is a fascinating chapter on modern young haunts, drawn from a 1992 magazine survey. The book strikes just the right balance between belief and skepticism, allowing young readers to evaluate the accounts for themselves.

DEALING WITH THE DEVIL (1979)

Booklist

SOURCE: A review of *Dealing with the Devil,* in *Booklist,* Vol. 76, No. 5, November 1, 1979, p. 438.

Using a historical approach, Cohen sifts through trial testimony, legends, literature, folktales, the Bible, apocryphal writings, and the like to relate the ways in which people have identified and tried to deal with the devil (making pacts and/or trying to outwit him). He also describes some of the demons who are devil's helpers, ideas about hell, and the practice of satanism. Some repetition mars an otherwise interesting, nonsensational treatment for the curious teenager or the student.

Janice F. Giles

SOURCE: A review of *Dealing with the Devil,* in *School Library Journal,* Vol. 26, No. 8, April, 1980, p. 121.

This is a factual and objective account of the origins and

history of human contact with the Devil and Devil worship from Old Testament to modern times. Historical facts and figures are documented in the text which emphasizes literature and legends of the devil; Cohen stresses the difference between what actually appears in scripture about the Devil and Hell and what has grown up around those subjects through legend, early church ideological differences, pagan influences, etc. Carefully researched and written, Cohen expresses throughout his viewpoint that there were more people afraid of Devil worshippers than there were actual Devil worshippers. The title promises sensationalism and some readers will be disappointed that Cohen doesn't deliver; but this approach is more satisfactory.

James McPeak

SOURCE: A review of *Dealing with the Devil*, in *Voice of Youth Advocates*, Vol. 3, No. 1, April, 1980, p. 39.

The devil and all his works. Cohen examines Biblical and mythological bases for demons and devils, and then probes the many legends and stories that maintain that man can conjure up the devil for his own devices. Of course the price for this privilege is the man's soul. Cohen explains some of the conjuring spells that were used during the Middle Ages, and also identifies the minor spirits whose names form part of the conjuring litany. He also explains the difference between witchcraft and Satanism—they definitely are not the same.

WHAT'S HAPPENING TO OUR WEATHER? (1979)

David G. Hoag

SOURCE: A review of *What's Happening to Our Weather?*, in *Appraisal: Children's Science Books*, Vol. 13, No. 1, Winter, 1980, pp. 14-15.

In spite of the title, this book is more concerned about patterns of weather as manifest in different climates than it is in the details of short term weather variations themselves. The various theories which attempt to explain possible causes for major climate changes to dry, wet, hot or cold are described well. There is good balance in the presentation of competing theories. Another book on exactly the same subject and almost the same title, *What's Happening to our Climate* by Malcolm Weiss, is of essentially the same quality as a children's science book but is simpler, easier reading, and intended for a younger audience than is this present volume. Both are technically and editorially well done.

Ralph J. Folcarelli

SOURCE: A review of *What's Happening to Our Weather?*, in *School Library Journal*, Vol. 26, No. 6, February, 1980, p. 64.

Perhaps, promoted by the severity of recent "good old-

fashion" winters, 1976-77 and 1977-78, there is a need for a straightforward, popularly written account which attempts to answer the oft-asked question: is our weather really changing? Theories on the effects on our weather of natural phenomena (such as volcanic dust and sunspots) and man-induced problems (such as air pollution and nuclear radiation) are discussed in both historical and current context in the non-technical explanation of what has caused the changes and what we can expect in the future. The illustrations are sparse but well placed and generally add interest. There is really very little new information added to an already crowded field of weather lore and history; however, this highly readable account should appeal to the non-scientific minded.

THE GREAT AIRSHIP MYSTERY: A UFO OF THE 1890s (1981)

Kirkus Reviews

SOURCE: A review of *The Great Airship Mystery: A UFO of the 1890s*, in *Kirkus Reviews*, Vol. XLIX, No. 15, August, 1, 1981, pp. 978-79.

Though UFOs are widely considered to be a post-WW II phenomenon, in November 1896 (well before the Wright brothers and the zeppelin era) the citizens of Sacramento reported seeing a "mysterious airship" flying overhead—characterized by a "bright light" (sometimes two or more lights) and a dark, indistinct, cigar-shaped body. Other observers reported wings, wheels, propellers, or (often hilariously) occupants, both human and non-human. The airship uproar spread rapidly up and down the West Coast, then eastwards to Nebraska, Kansas, Texas—and eventually as far as Chicago and Indiana, where reports died out in 1897. Cohen, prolific writer of juveniles on otherworldly subjects, traces the airship's progress from surviving records and also attempts an analysis. Astonishing as it may seem today, journalistic hoaxing was a widespread and acceptable circulation-booster in 19th-century newspapers; and Cohen ascribes the bulk of the reports to this very-earthly phenomenon. Other factors were wishful thinking, mass hysteria, misidentification of commonplace objects (such as the planet Venus), a conspiracy among railroad employees (whose telegraph was the main means of long-distance communication), and the newspaper serialization of Verne's *Robur the Conqueror*, which features just such an airship. Most of the sightings, are, indeed, explicable in these terms; but Cohen unjustifiably extends "most" to "all," while ignoring or glossing over a small number of queer and potentially important points. Could there have been, in particular, a mysterious backwoods inventor? Cohen, after investigating a number of likely candidates, thinks not. Solid exposition, then, but debatable analysis—so the conclusions will not satisfy either UFO believers or skeptics.

George M. Eberhart

SOURCE: A review of *The Great Airship Mystery: A UFO*

of the 1890s, in *Library Journal,* Vol. 106, No. 18, October 15, 1981, p. 2043.

The modern phase of UFO studies began in 1947, when the media first ran reports of strange "flying disks." But anomalous aerial objects have been seen throughout history. One of the most interesting series of early American observations was in 1896-1897, when thousands of communities in the West and Midwest reported a lighted "airship" sailing through the sky. Cohen's is the first major book to treat the airship wave exclusively. He examines the journalistic style of the period, current science fiction, contemporary aviation technology, and 19th-century popular culture, as well as the airship reports themselves. The result is a very insightful glimpse into American life in the 1890s. However, Cohen seems to have done very little original research; he is apparently unaware of extensive airship sightings in Ohio, Michigan, West Virginia, and other states east of Indiana, where he claims the sightings stopped.

Sally Estes

SOURCE: A review of *The Great Airship Mystery: A UFO of the 1890s,* in *Booklist,* Vol. 78, No. 8, December 15, 1981, p. 524.

A self-dubbed "long-time UFO skeptic," who, nonetheless, relishes the challenge of UFO investigation, Cohen digs into the past to chart the course of a colorful but generally forgotten, mysterious-airship flap that took place in the U.S. some seven years before the Wright brothers' famous first flight. Quoting and examining the florid newspaper reports of the day—both the serious and the facetious—and other evidence, Cohen shows how widespread the sightings were and considers a variety of possible explanations, including factors that may have inspired some of the tales and the confirmed hoaxes. A lively entertainment for fellow skeptics, Cohen's book will prove small comfort for believers.

Leslie Burk Chamberlin

SOURCE: A review of *The Great Airship Mystery: A UFO of the 1890s,* in *School Library Journal,* Vol. 28, No. 2, February, 1982, pp. 86-7.

If you have UFO enthusiasts, or if you have Daniel Cohen fans, and if they know how to use the card catalog, this book is heartily recommended. The title and, especially, the cover art are grossly misleading, generating the impression of a tacky science-fiction mystery novel. The cityscape beneath the starry night sky has too many skyscrapers to match the 1890 of the title. The contents explore numerous sightings of the first UFO—an "airship" that was often seen in 1896 and 1897. Cohen admits to skepticism in his wrap-up after presenting many reports of newspaper accounts and theories suggesting hoax possibilities. A thoroughly researched historical analysis.

THE LAST HUNDRED YEARS: MEDICINE (1981)

Stephanie Zvirin

SOURCE: A review of *The Last 100 Years: Medicine,* in *Booklist,* Vol. 78, No. 6, November 15, 1981, pp. 432-3.

Using just the right combination of information, anecdote, and description, Cohen highlights a century of advancement in medical science and puts the stereotype of the kindly old doctor who makes house calls into proper perspective. Significant discoveries (X rays, etc.) of the late nineteenth and early twentieth centuries serve as a platform for his discussion of cause, control, and/or cure of such dread diseases as polio through improved diagnostic and surgical techniques and the use of drug therapy. Controversial aspects of modern medicine related to drugs, genetic engineering, and the connection between the environment and human well-being along with insights into the changes in medical education and hospital care are also touched on. A wide-ranging, well-balanced treatment that considers the difficulties as well as the benefits of medical progress.

George Barr

SOURCE: A review of *The Last Hundred Years: Medicine,* in *Children's Book Review Service,* Vol. 10, No. 9, August, 1982, p. 87.

Anyone interested in medicine, doctors, hospitals, and nurses will be intrigued by this fascinating account of the state of the art a mere hundred years ago. Gigantic advances have wiped out many dread diseases and changed the way we think and live. This book describes how great discoveries came about and also tells of mistake scientists made along the way. A chapter on the future of medicine rounds out this excellent report.

Esther Nussbaum

SOURCE: A review of *Last Hundred Years: Medicine,* in *Voice of Youth Advocates,* Vol. 5, No. 2, June, 1982, p. 42.

About midway through this history of recent "advances" in medical care are chapters dealing with the diet factor in health, both the deficiency caused disease and the additives or simply the food habits which contribute to specific conditions. I began to think of the author as an enzyme which had broken down mounds of information, predigested it and made it palatable by mixing in anecdotes and archival photos and illustrations.

Concise and accurate, the book also traces the major changes in health care and delivery in the last century (mainly in the industrialized countries). The dramatic strides are inextricably linked with major personalities whose laboratory discoveries and clinical observation have virtually eradicated or brought under control once dreaded, usually fatal diseases. The story of Yellow Fever is the story of William Gorgas and Walter Reed; Smallpox of Edward Jenner; Polio of Jonas Salk and Albert Sabin; Tuberculosis of Robert Koch; and Diabetes, the work of Banting and Best on insulin.

Other major figures parade across the pages; the great surgeons who understood the role of antisepsis in control of infection; the pioneers in brain and heart surgery and organ transplantation; and many others whose dominating personalities and zealousness left permanent imprints on contemporary health care delivery.

The author manages to touch on all aspects: preventive medicine, quackery, the drug industry, addiction, physician training and health care costs—all neatly and lucidly presented. If "chance favors the prepared mind" as the author fondly quotes Louis Pasteur, perhaps some YAs will be inspired to turn their efforts to medicine or the allied health professions.

Lynn Pollino

SOURCE: A review of *The Last Hundred Years: Medicine,* in *Appraisal: Science Books for Young People,* Vol. 15, No. 3, Fall, 1982, p. 19.

The Last Hundred Years includes some good anecdotes, but it attempts to take on too large a scope. Medicine has changed so much in the last 10-20 years that to try to review all areas of health even in the last few years would be a major undertaking. For example, Cohen has left out new techniques in ultrasound, brain and body scans, microsurgery, etc. The book fails to capture the excitement of the health field by encompassing too many areas in too long a time span.

Susanne S. Sullivan

SOURCE: A review of *The Last Hundred Years: Medicine,* in *Appraisal: Science Books for Young People,* Vol. 15, No. 3, Fall, 1982, pp. 18-19.

Clear, lucid and easy to follow text describes breakthroughs in medical science over the last hundred years. A number of useful topics are included, from the discovery of aspirin and penicillin, to the first operation for appendicitis, and the elimination of dread diseases like yellow fever, typhoid, and cholera.

Current concerns about the hazards of air and chemical pollution and the dangers of drug and cigarette use are put into historical perspective as current theories and research techniques are compared to those used in the past to determine the causes of disease.

Cohen's book makes interesting browsing: it is certainly graphic in parts in its description of awful diseases of the past. Report writers will find access to specific topics through the index, but will find generalized chapter headings of meager guide value.

David T. Mininberg

SOURCE: A review of *The Last Hundred Years: Medicine,* in *Science Books & Films,* Vol. 18, No. 1, September-October, 1982, p. 21.

This informative book is written in a clear and enjoyable style that should be a delight to any junior high school student. Cohen introduces each of his topics with an illustration to establish an historical perspective. He then proceeds to develop the subject in detail and provides useful information while maintaining a light, essay style. The subjects he selects are suitable for these readers, covering many of the significant advances in medical science. The surgical advances, diagnostic breakthroughs, and therapeutic successes are well discussed, with proper focus on the historical perspective. The inclusion of public health problems and nutrition broadens the scope of the book in an appropriate way. Cohen also deals with the evaluation in the roles of physicians and nurses in a realistic and thoughtful manner.

📖 *THE ENCYCLOPEDIA OF MONSTERS* (1983)

Michael Schuyler

SOURCE: A review of *The Encyclopedia of Monsters,* in *Library Journal,* Vol. 107, No. 20, November 15, 1982, p. 2162.

All sorts of monsters and weird creatures, such as fur-bearing trout and aliens kept in the freezer, inhabit this book, each described in a few anecdotal pages. Many of the monsters are variations on a theme. Thirteen variations of Sasquatch-like creatures, for example, are described. Others, like unicorns, griffins, and dragons, are taken directly from mythology. This volume does not present new material, nor does it offer much analysis. Where interest is unusually high, the book very well may be a reasonable addition. Most collections, however, will not be hurt by its absence.

Maureen Ritter

SOURCE: A review of *Encyclopedia of Monsters,* in *Voice of Youth Advocates,* Vol. 6, No. 3, August, 1983, pp. 151-2.

Scare yourself silly or satisfy all your curiosities. This volume could be the monster lovers' bible. Arranged in categories, such as: Humanoids, Sea Monsters, Visitors from Strange Places, and Weird Creatures in Folklore, it includes lengthy discussions about more famous monsters, the likes of Big Foot, Loch Ness Monster, Giant Octopus, and Dragons. Less attention is given to minor creatures such as Chessie (the Chesapeake Bay monster), Little

Green Men, the Jersey Devil, and the Beast of Truro (a town on Cape Cod where I go for vacation!). These are just a sampling of the more than 100 monsters presented. Includes illustrations and photographs, when available. Short annotated bibliography is included. Cohen has again written an informative book on a favorite topic of his. An excellent volume which will provide hours of entertainment. Buy it for your fright freaks. You will not be sorry.

Charles R. Andrew

SOURCE: A review of *The Encyclopedia of Monsters,* in *American Reference Book Annual 1984,* Vol. 15, 1984, p. 501.

In what is essentially a collection of popular essays, "monster" specialist/enthusiast Cohen has lucidly and charmingly presented about 100 accounts of creatures that "lie somewhere in a misty realm between zoology and folklore." Although Cohen admits that for his purposes the dictionary definition of "monster" is not wholly satisfactory, he applies, with some expanding and bending, "an animal of strange and terrifying shape." He excludes those humans with extreme physical deformities, who have been cruelly called monsters, as well as those who have stained the pages of history with their inhumanity. Neither does he include purely literary or cinematic monsters.

This modestly priced volume is divided into eight sections—humanoids, land monsters, monster birds and bats, phantoms, river and lake monsters, sea monsters, "Visitors from Strange Places," and weird creatures in folklore—each of which lists its subjects alphabetically. Many are familiar, such as the abominable snowman, bigfoot, thunderbird, Loch Ness monster, leviathan, griffin, hydra, and mermaid; others are less so—Jenny Hanivers, Minnesota iceman, Ogopogo, Oannes, and the *Daedalus* sea serpent.

Perhaps more for browsing than for reference, the encyclopedia is without an index, which would have enhanced its reference value. The work concludes with a three-page annotated bibliography.

Reference departments would not go wrong in adding this highly readable, inexpensive, and well-illustrated volume. Even the casual reader will find it monstrously hard to put down.

THE LAST HUNDRED YEARS: HOUSEHOLD TECHNOLOGY (1983)

Kirkus Reviews

SOURCE: A review of *The Last Hundred Years: Household Technology,* in *Kirkus Reviews,* Vol. L, No. 23, December 1, 1982, pp. 1295-6.

Though he acknowledges that some advances such as the TV-dinner are of dubious value, and that many others depend on energy consumption that can't long be sustained, the drift of Cohen's hundred-year survey is that nostalgia for the days of graceful homes and servants is misplaced: "You" would more likely have been a servant than have had them; Granny's cheerful bustling in the kitchen involved such drudgery as starting up the wood stove and hauling and heating water from the pump; Dad's chilly chores included visits to the basement coal furnace on rising and retiring; and most people of all classes bathed infrequently and smelled accordingly. The bulk of the book, though, is not an argument. In separate chapters Cohen traces a century's changes in the kitchen (the main advances being efficient layout, gas and electric stoves, and the electric refrigerator), the bathroom ("Now don't snicker"; city streets were open sewers without them), and in heating, lighting, shopping (the rise and fall of mail order), and home entertainment—the last of which has evolved from "stereopticon slides and singing 'Daisy Bell' around the piano" to TV news, video games, and the home computer that promises to transform life in the '80s. Realistically, except for this likely development, Cohen doesn't predict any glittering technological advances; major changes may be dictated by water and energy shortages and the declining opportunity for home ownership. His analysis of the interaction between custom and technology is sometimes simplistic or second-hand, but it makes for a readable summary which never bogs down into lists and mechanics.

Margaret M. Hagel

SOURCE: A review of *The Last Hundred Years: Household Technology,* in *School Library Journal,* Vol. 29, No. 7, March, 1983, p. 189.

Cohen traces the evolution of the home over the last 100 years, emphasizing the manner in which a particular invention changes the life style of most Americans, pointing out drudgery where it existed. Kitchens, bathrooms and the areas of heating-cooling, lighting-power, cleaning and home entertaining are covered. Included also is how the founding of the great mail order houses changed the lives of both country and city dwellers. The style is casual and chatty. Cohen begins with a day in the life of "Mr. and Mrs. Imaginary." Reproductions of turn-of-the-century appliances and home scenes, and photographs of newer merchandise and life styles are superb and provide added dimension to the book. Interesting personal sketches of various inventors throughout add interest and supplement other biographical materials in the library. This book can be used on many levels in the school and public library. It is fascinating general reading about a changing America and it is also useful for supplementary reading in American history, general science and ecology.

Ilene Cooper

SOURCE: A review of *The Last Hundred Years: Household Technology,* in *Booklist,* Vol. 79, No. 14, March 15, 1983, p. 964.

Cohen takes a look at how our homes have changed in the last 100 years. His style is chatty (he even tells readers not to snicker when he talks about bathrooms), but he packs a lot of information into the discussion. He paints a picture of what life was like for an imaginary family from the time they woke up in the morning to rattle the furnace grate and shake out the ashes till evening, when the family had to provide its own entertainment. Cohen takes readers through the kitchen, the bathroom, the heating and cooling systems, the cleaning advances, and the astounding changes in home entertainment that are still evolving. Highly readable and full of fascinating detail, this is buttressed by illustrations and comparative black-and-white photographs.

Choice

SOURCE: A review of *The Last Hundred Years: Household Technology,* in *Choice,* Vol. 20, No. 10, June, 1983, p. 1495.

An excellent introduction to the study of technology in the home. Synthesizing materials from the standard sources on the history of technology and studies of modern culture, Cohen traces the evolution of household technology in the 20th century. Not only does he consider these changes in the various rooms of the house, but he also discusses the developments in public utilities, garbage disposal, and home heating. Particularly valuable are the final chapters showing the diffusion of household technology from the private residences of the middle classes to public housing projects designed since WW II and speculating on the future impact of technology on the American home. Although Cohen does not go into the implications of his research for the history of the American family and the history of American women, the facts he presents provide a point of departure for those interested in studying the interrelationships between technological changes and social developments in the 20th century. The short but well-selected bibliographical suggestions are useful for scholars planning to do additional work in the field, and the illustrations offer visual evidence of just how much American life-styles have changed since the turn of the century.

SOUTHERN FRIED RAT AND OTHER GRUESOME TALES (1983)

Denise M. Wilms

SOURCE: A review of *Southern Fried Rat & Other Gruesome Tales,* in *Booklist,* Vol. 79, No. 22, August, 1983, p. 1463.

This is a collection of urban legends, defined by Cohen as "a branch of folklore that centers on stories told by people who live in cities or suburbs today." They are the apocryphal tales kids (and adults) love to tell as truth, and perhaps believe: how a girl bites into a piece of fried chicken that she discovers is fried rat; or how a bully gets his fatal comeuppance after one too many harassment episodes; or how a spaced-out baby-sitter puts the baby in the microwave because she thinks he's a turkey. Some of the tales are very funny; others are quite gruesome. A few, such as one about a man who on his fortieth birthday is lured to his secretary's apartment for a surprise party and winds up greeting his family with his drawers dropped, are adult in appeal. Mostly though, the tales are squarely on target for a junior high audience, who will love the unorthodox mix of humor and horror.

Rebecca Sturm

SOURCE: A review of *Southern Fried Rat & Other Gruesome Tales,* in *School Library Journal,* Vol. 29, No. 10, August, 1983, p. 63.

This is another collection of what the author calls "urban legends" or "urban belief tales"—stories that people (especially children) pass on to each other as factual. They are the stories we all told (or heard) at camp as true, and sickened or scared, retold to someone else as fast as the opportunity arose. While not of great literary or artistic merit (people generally look alike and bear the same expression), *Southern Fried Rat* is sure to be popular where readers devour (excuse me!) Cohen's *The Headless Roommate* and Alvin Schwartz's *Scary Stories to Tell in the Dark.* Bait with which to hook nonreaders.

Neil K. Citrin

SOURCE: A review of *Southern Fried Rat and Other Gruesome Tales,* in *West Coast Review of Books,* Vol. 9, No. 5, September-October, 1983, p. 40.

Ever wondered where today's horror writers get their ideas? Cohen provides a partial answer to this problem with a distinctly American collection of urban folktales. Though funny. informative and, to the true horror fan, tasty, this book lacks depth.

The stories here vary from the simply funny to the grisly. Some of the more well-known tales include variations on the phantom hitchhiker theme, in which a person meets someone who turns out to be the dead relative of a long-lost friend. In another tale a melancholy young woman. on the day of her marriage to a lively and fun-loving man, locks herself in a trunk in her attic. Other morsels include the "rodent in the fast food" tale and the story of the none-too-bright girl who tried to dry her hair in a microwave oven.

Like the proverbial Chinese dinner, this collection provides a lot to eat that never quite fills you up. In addition to the tales themselves, we get the author's frequent and condescending assurances that they probably never happened. He never bothers to explain this, or to explore how these tales reflect American culture. The meanings remain locked in the attic trunk, and this otherwise well-written and entertaining book remains a simple list of stories.

Ruth Kline

SOURCE: A review of *Southern Fried Rat and Other Gruesome Tales,* in *Voice of Youth Advocates,* Vol. 6, No. 4, October, 1983, p. 222.

Illustrated by Peggy Brier and very fast reading with short episodes and to-the-point narrative, this book will be popular with storytellers of all ages. Based on urban legends and folktales, many of these stories have been oral tradition and have now found their way into newspapers and folklore collections. Some of the stories are disgusting, gruesome, and gross, but they will be popular for reading and retelling. Teachers could use the book to stimulate students to collect folklore of their own, and to compare versions of their stories with these. This book is a springboard for language arts activities rather than an end in itself. Oral language and written stories are a natural outgrowth. Some of the stories included are the southern fried rat which was consumed before the girl realized it wasn't chicken; the solid cement cadillac; the microwave oven stories; and test-taking tricks for students. Although many of the stories are unpleasant, young readers will relish and retell them.

MONSTER DINOSAUR (1983)

Kirkus Reviews

SOURCE: A review of *Monster Dinosaur,* in *Kirkus Reviews,* Vol. LI, No. 21, November 1, 1983, p. 195.

What Cohen actually has to say about dinosaurs—a look at the 19th-century reconstructions of B. W. Hawkins, the "bone wars" between collectors Edward Cope and O. C. Marsh, a brief rundown of modern ideas on what dinosaurs were really like (evidently based on a superficial reading of Adrian Desmond's *The Hot-Blooded Dinosaurs*) and why they disappeared—isn't very reliable or informative. And the remainder of this frankly personal, very eccentric, and ill-informed grab-bag wanders off into such non-dinosaur topics as pterosaurs, plesiosaurs, fabulous beasts like the African *mokele-mbembe* and the Loch Ness monster, sea serpents, dinosaurs in literature (e.g., Conan Doyle's *The Lost World*), and dragons. Altogether dispensable.

George Barr

SOURCE: A review of *Monster Dinosaur,* in *Children's Book Review Service,* Vol. 12, No. 7, February, 1984, p. 72.

Since childhood the author has been fascinated by dinosaurs and has studied every aspect of the subject. This informal ramble through the science, history, lore, and art of these interesting creatures will be enjoyed by all dinosaur lovers, although it is often too heavy with detail for the average elementary student.

Katharine C. Payne

SOURCE: A review of *Monster Dinosaur,* in *Science Books & Films,* Vol. 19, No. 5, May-June, 1984, p. 296.

This book is a find for any classroom, library, or home with young people who want to learn everything they can about dinosaurs and other earthy monsters. In elementary language, here is the literary and cinematic history of the dinosaur in a self-described "fun" book. Cohen covers the history of the dinosaur's discovery and popularity and describes the early scientific rivalry of paleontologists Cope and Marsh. He then questions the accepted theories that all dinosaurs were reptiles, coldblooded, and prehistoric. Cohen lastly explores historic monster sighting and ends the book by mentioning famous dinosaurs in ancient myths and modern literature.

Ronald J. Kley

SOURCE: A review of *Monster Dinosaur,* in *Appraisal: Science Books for Young People,* Vol. 17, No. 3, Fall, 1984, pp. 22-3.

The author is a talented writer, but perhaps more adept as a propagandist than a scientist. In seeking to convey new ideas about dinosaurs, Cohen has sometimes failed to draw appropriate distinctions between the documentable, the probable, the possible, and the barely conceivable. He has tended to ignore or dismiss evidence contrary to his frankly revisionist suggestions, and to pyramid unsubstantiated hypotheses and speculations into structures of fascinating shape, but with minimal underlying substance. Fully one quarter of the book is openly labeled as being drawn from and related to the realm of science fiction, and it might well be argued that an even greater proportion could be placed under the same heading.

This is not a first-rate science book; yet it is a first-rate book that relates closely and constructively to science. It should not be seen as a substitute for more rigorous and more systematic treatments of the same subject matter, but it may be a stimulating, entertaining and thought-provoking supplement.

THE RESTLESS DEAD: GHOSTLY TALES FROM AROUND THE WORLD (1984)

Zena Sutherland

SOURCE: A review of *The Restless Dead: Tales from Around the World,* in *Bulletin of the Center for Children's Books,* Vol. 37, No. 10, June, 1984, p. 183.

Demons ride, poltergeists throw things, zombies sit down to dinner, and half-rotted corpses seek revenge in this high-interest low-vocabulary collection of eleven ghost stories from around the world. In the folktale tradition, the gruesome erupts in the everyday world, and the occult subject matter will fascinate readers. The type is well-spaced and the cover luridly appealing, but the prints and photographs which illustrate the stories are poorly reproduced. The style is flat: "the thing waved its arms, and fell to its knees"—and it could be Haiti, ancient China, or Australia.

Denise M. Wilms

SOURCE: A review of *The Restless Dead: Ghostly Tales from Around the World*, in *Booklist*, Vol. 80, No. 22, August, 1984, p. 1624.

Cohen serves up 11 ghost stories from around the world. None of the starring specters are what you would call friendly; some are downright vicious. The most interesting tale is perhaps that of a peculiar chair, alleged to bring death or mayhem to those who sit in it. According to a historical drawing, one of its victims would seem to be Napoleon, who is shown sitting in it to plan strategy on the eve of Waterloo. Cohen occasionally interjects a comment or note on the story or its background; for example, he shows the motif of **"A Ride for a Corpse"** to be the same one operating in today's common "phantom hitchhiker" tales. Simply written, varied, and gritty, these will easily please fans of the genre.

HIRAM BINGHAM AND THE DREAM OF GOLD (1984)

Nancy C. Hammond

SOURCE: A review of *Hiram Bingham and the Dream of Gold*, in *The Horn Book Magazine*, Vol. LX, No. 5, September-October, 1984, pp. 605-6.

Reputed to be the model for the popular film character Indiana Jones, the handsome, rugged adventurer Hiram Bingham thrived on physical hardship and danger. Despite several careers—university professor, author, World War I aviator, and United States senator—his greatest feat came during nine years of exploring: the discovery in 1911 of the spectacular Peruvian Inca city Machu Picchu. Yet his life has been singularly unexamined. Two-thirds of the volume is focused effectively on this period; it relies heavily on Bingham's own dramatic account: *Lost City of the Incas: The Story of Machu Picchu*. Creating a dramatic biography rather than a definitive one, the author—like Bingham himself—pursues action; the volume is a pastiche of periods and places. Yet, despite some overdramatic writing, the book tantalizes as it flits from Inca history and Spanish conquistadors to the Hawaiian Islands (where Bingham's grandfather was a powerful, contentious missionary); from the Gilbert Islands, where his parents were failed missionaries, to American politics in which landslide victories brought Bingham two years as lieutenant governor, two days as governor, and seven years as a senator who was eventually censured. "The very picture of the adventurer on the run from the restrictions of ordinary life," Bingham was a man whose attributes became assets in one career and liabilities in another.

Will Manley

SOURCE: A review of *Hiram Bingham and the Dream of Gold*, in *School Library Journal*, Vol. 31, No. 3, November, 1984, p. 130.

According to Cohen, Hiram Bingham "is clearly the inspiration for Indiana Jones, the popular film hero professor-explorer right down to the battered hat." And although there is no way that Cohen could capture on paper the excitement of *Raiders of the Lost Ark* or . . . *Temple of Doom*, he has done a solid job of writing a fast moving, balanced account of the man who made some of the greatest archaeological discoveries of the 20th century. Bingham's most adventurous work was done between 1905 and 1915, when he fearlessly explored the mountains and jungles of Peru for the lost cities and buried treasures of the Incas. He found little gold but his discovery of Machu Picchu, the secret hiding place of the last Inca emperors, was a spectacular archaeological find. This is a true adventure story that many young people will read for its sheer excitement, but from which they will learn a great deal about some very interesting South American history.

Ilene Cooper

SOURCE: A review of *Hiram Bingham and the Dream of Gold*, in *Booklist*, Vol. 81, No. 5, November 1, 1984, pp. 364, 366.

Hiram Bingham, university professor and explorer, was the primary model for Indiana Jones, hero of two popular movies. A dashing adventurer, handsome, brave, and rich (thanks to his long-suffering wife's money), Bingham's happiest days were spent in the remote Peruvian mountains where he eventually discovered several of the Incas' lost cities. The son and grandson of missionaries, Bingham later became a pioneer aviator during World War I, and when that career was finished, he was elected to the U.S. Senate. With such a subject, Cohen obviously has plenty to work with, and he plays his material to the hilt, providing a biography that is as full of highs and lows as any movie. Despite all Bingham's glory, Cohen does not overlook his less desirable qualities. A philanderer who neglected his seven sons, Bingham was censured by his colleagues in the Senate and near the end of his life became a happy participant in Joe McCarthy's witch-hunts. A full-bodied, rip-roaring real-life adventure, illustrated with a small center section of black-and-white photographs. Bibliography appended.

THE ENCYCLOPEDIA OF GHOSTS (1984)

Ben Nelms, Elizabeth Nelms, and Regina Cowin

SOURCE: A review of *The Encyclopedia of Ghosts*, in

English Journal, Vol. 74, No. 6, October, 1985, pp. 80-1.

"The essence of telling a good ghost story," Cohen writes in his introduction, "is to tell it with a straight face and with absolute conviction. No campfire ghost story is ever supposed to be less than absolutely true." There is "truth" aplenty in this collection, *and* some interesting speculation on the origin and nature of some of that "truth." The 106 entries are grouped under such headings as ghosts of the famous, poltergeists, apparitions, animals ghosts, and ghostly legends. Some are familiar, some are new and strange, but most readers will find at least one story they grew up with. We were delighted to find an old friend, the Bell Witch, whom we have been hearing about since we were eighth graders in Robertson County, Tennessee. Most of your students will be able to add their own oft-repeated and half-believed stories, especially to the section on high school and college ghosts. There is raw material here for many storytelling sessions and oral reports all recorded with wit and clarity and from just enough of a "scientific" distance to provide a balanced perspective.

📖 *ESP: THE NEW TECHNOLOGY* (1986)

Ilene Cooper

SOURCE: A review of *ESP: The New Technology,* in *Booklist,* Vol. 82, No. 21, July, 1986, p. 1611.

In chatty fashion, Cohen presents the history of parapsychology and describes the various ways *psi* (a common term for psychic events) is being tested. The views of psi debunkers—like former magician Randi—are aired, but, in general, Cohen supports the work of the psychic researchers and describes the new tests being used to actually measure this elusive phenomenon. The author's frequent interjection into the narrative is disconcerting, and the bland black-and-white photographs add little. For those interested in the subject, this is a useful, nonsensational, and evenhanded introduction to an always fascinating subject.

Leslie Chamberlin

SOURCE: A review of *ESP: The New Technology,* in *School Library Journal,* Vol. 33, No. 2, October, 1986, pp. 170-1.

A balanced, noncondescending, factual, and credible book. Cohen explores old and new means of scientific analysis of the paranormal and debunks pseudo-scientific approaches as well as a number of hoaxes. The vocabulary and language are far more complex than Cohen's usual style. This is an advanced book for older readers with a real interest in this area. The chapter on ESP in pets is particularly good, even as it explains away the mystique. Other areas of special interest include reincarnation, poltergeists, ghosts, and ESP laboratory tests. Enough real names and

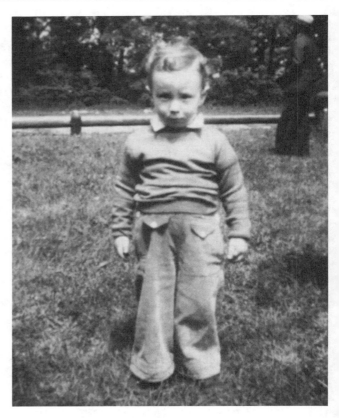

Cohen, age two.

dates and bibliographical citations are given to make this a useful research tool. One quote from the text pretty well sums up the whole book: "as in the investigation of so many other poltergeist cases, no one's mind was really changed about the reality of the phenomena. The skeptics were still skeptical, the believers still believed, and everybody else was puzzled."

F. Elizabeth Gillis

SOURCE: A review of *ESP: The New Technology,* in *Appraisal: Science Books for Young People,* Vol. 20, No. 4, Fall, 1987, pp. 16-17.

ESP is a fascinating subject. The author describes its ancient history, a modern ESP lab with computers and isolation rooms, accounts of telepathy, clairvoyance, and remote viewing. There is some emphasis on the frauds, magicians who claim to be psychic. Those such as Uri Geller who say they are capable of psychokinesis are shown to be deceiving their audiences. Cohen debunks ghosts and poltergeists and animals that supposedly can add or substract. Black-and-white photographs are adequate (although one caption has a typo in Dr. Rhine's name). The coverage is competent and entertaining. However, I found the lack of an index and glossary a serious deficiency. It was frustrating to read about PK and either have to remember that several pages before it referred to psychokinesis or leaf back through to find the original use of these letters. At times I wanted to go back to a previous topic but, unless it was listed in the Contents, I had to waste time trying to locate it.

James Minstrell

SOURCE: A review of *ESP: The New Technology,* in *Appraisal: Science Books for Young People,* Vol. 20, No. 4, Fall, 1987, p. 17.

ESP: The New Technology is a book, carefully written by an award winning author with a long standing interest in parascience as well as normal science. All through the book Cohen clearly describes evidence for and against various psychic events, including ESP, psychokinesis, ghosts, contact with the dead, and poltergeist. Without dictating what to believe and not believe, the book allows the reader to explore each of the ideas from both the rational and emotional sides. It compromises neither the views of science nor of parascience. The author describes his personal visits to modern, computerized ESP laboratories, and it reminds us of the well publicized, historical and contemporary, sensational "happenings." For the upper intermediate or older person interested in these ideas, the book is a good first source and suggests other resources in order to further explore the world of ESP.

Marilyn Braschler

SOURCE: A review of *ESP: The New Technology,* in *Science Books & Films,* Vol. 23, No. 1, September-October, 1987, p. 22.

Cohen gives an overview of the field of parapsychology, presenting the material in a balanced way by providing both the pros and cons of various research approaches. A chronology of developments in parapsychology, from early Greece to modern computer labs, provides a very readable framework. All technical terms are well defined, and the bibliography lists some excellent sources for greater detail on various aspects of ESP. This book is a good starting point for young readers newly interested in this area. Its broad scope and balanced presentation avoid the sensationalism typical of the many popular media reports on ESP.

A SIX-PACK AND A FAKE I.D.: TEENS LOOK AT THE DRINKING QUESTION (with Susan Cohen, 1986)

Sari Feldman

SOURCE: A review of *A Six-Pack and a Fake I.D.,* in *Voice of Youth Advocates,* Vol. 9, Nos. 3-4, August-October, 1986, p. 173.

Susan and Daniel Cohen have written a lucid and interest-ing book about alcohol use and teenagers. Shifting between hard fact and stories of teen experiences, the authors deal with topics such as false identification, parental pressure, hangovers, and many of alcohol's greatest myths. While they also focus some attention on the disease of alcoholism, the book is mainly an account of emotionally painful or physically dangerous situations that can arise out of a particular "drunk."

A good concluding summary reviews the factual information and there is descriptive information on organizations concerned with drinking. This is a good addition for public or school libraries and programs serving youth. The book will be well used because of the currency of information, the attractive title and the interest in the issue.

Paul Leung

SOURCE: A review of *A Six-Pack and a Fake I.D.,* in *Science Books & Films,* Vol. 22, No. 2, November-December, 1986, p. 95.

The Cohens' book was difficult to review. I did not see any glaring errors in content accuracy; however, there were occasional generalizations not supported by fact, such as, "Teens are chronic overreactors." The book's basic purpose and audience are not clear. The subtitle is "teens look at the drinking question," but little is reported about what teens actually say. The perspective is clearly one of adults speaking to teens, but the authors indicate that the book is not about the problem of teen-age drinking. A clearcut purpose—such as, "it's o.k. to say no," or even that one should be moderate in using alcohol—would have helped provide a focus. The book's major fault is its assumption that teen-agers are a homogeneous lot. Cultural, ethnic, rural, and urban differences are not dealt with, and the vignettes presented give a limited view. As a book for teen-agers, *A Six-Pack* is not particularly appealing. Illustrations and even some tables would have added a great deal. While the basic information about alcohol use is there and the information is basically sound, the book's weaknesses will probably limit its usefulness. Teachers may wish to use it to supplement health education classes at junior and senior high school levels.

CARL SAGAN: SUPERSTAR SCIENTIST (1987)

Patricia Manning

SOURCE: A review of *Carl Sagan: Superstar Scientist,* in *School Library Journal,* Vol. 33, No. 11, August, 1987, p. 81.

A comfortable approach to a popular scientist. While this book deals primarily with Sagan's achievements as an outstanding scientist and his amazing (and enviable) ability to promote his enthusiasm and erudition to the general public as well as to his peers, the glimpses given of a young Sagan will reassure readers that he is, after all, quite human. Cohen supplies little information on Sagan's personal life, although he assures readers that Sagan is a very private individual, despite his international recognition. Indeed, Cohen has done an admirable job of presenting this multi-faceted persona—his career as an academician, a NASA planner, an investigative researcher, a popularizer of seemingly unpopularizable subjects, and a concerned citizen of a threatened world. Photographs of Sagan appear in a central insert. It is a pleasure to read about a live scientist, rather than one whose discoveries lie in the distant past, a pleasure from which young adults on the verge of choosing career paths might benefit.

Stephen L. Gallant

SOURCE: A review of *Carl Sagan: Superstar Scientist,* in *Voice of Youth Advocates,* Vol. 10, No. 4, October, 1987, p. 185.

Cohen's book is a portrayal of Carl Sagan and his work that will interest the many young adults who have seen the famous astronomer on television or who may have read his books. While it will provide a useful introduction or supplement to his writing, the book has some limitations as a biography. Just as in a previous biography, *Henry Stanley and the Quest for the Source of the Nile,* Cohen sacrificed objectivity by overly relying on Stanley's own writing, so it may be for this one in which information as well as its interpretation are supervised to some extent by Sagan himself. The resulting book is concerned not so much with depicting his character and personality, and less with his personal life, as it is with summarizing his books and explaining what makes Sagan such an important public figure.

In the first chapter Cohen describes some early influences on Sagan and traces the history of his interest in science and his educational attainments. While he states that the writings of Paine and Russell may have been more influential than those of science fiction writers, he does not explain this, possibly to avoid having to mention Sagan's controversial views on religion. The author stresses the fact Sagan has done serious research and has published scientific papers, but never fully tells the reader what his accomplishments have been in this area. After a good discussion of the work of scientists, Cohen describes Sagan's contributions to the space program. Subsequent chapters summarize the themes and content of Sagan's popular works. The chapter on *Cosmos* covers its production more than its content, while the chapter on nuclear winter presents the theory's origins well. Throughout the book Sagan's responses to his critics are given. This is an interesting book and Cohen will have done well if he leads the reader to Sagan's own writing.

Sarah Lamstein

SOURCE: A review of *Carl Sagan: Superstar Scientist,* in *Appraisal: Science Books for Young People,* Vol. 21, No. 1, Winter, 1988, p. 26.

In this lively biography of contemporary scientist Carl Sagan, Cohen succeeds in conveying the utter expansiveness of the man in regard to both his achievements and his intellectual and emotional outlook. As a successful astronomer, teacher, consultant to the space program, television host and producer of *Cosmos,* activist and writer, Sagan's focus is the universe and his passionate interest in the possibility of life in outer space. His arms are open both to the uninstructed whom he wishes to engage in his passion and to the international scientific community whom he would like to see working and sharing together. Sagan attends to life on earth as well. He was part of the group that studied the effects of nuclear war and came up with the theory of nuclear winter. He now speaks out in favor of disarmament.

Cohen gives us a good sense of Sagan's boyhood and shows how as an adult he has remained true to his earliest interests. As a result, the book has a rounded feeling, like a life coming full circle. Cohen includes the views of Sagan's detractors, who are few, which Sagan would heartily approve. He admonishes us to question closely those beliefs we most dearly hold, the hallmark statement of a man whose mind and heart are open wide and who aims to tear down all barriers.

At the end of the book, one is left feeling in awe of the talents and achievements of Carl Sagan, but also grateful that he is among us. This book will be fascinating reading for everyone.

Indira Nair

SOURCE: A review of *Carl Sagan: Superstar Scientist,* in *Appraisal: Science Books for Young People,* Vol. 21, No. 1, Winter, 1988, pp. 26-7.

"Science is a joy. It's not just something for an isolated, remote elite. It's our birthright."; Carl Sagan is quoted as saying. No one person has ever done as much to convey the marvels of the universe to the public, to evoke wonder and promote knowledge as Carl Sagan has in this generation.

Here is a well-written biography of this optimistic scientist-author-educator. The book starts with young Sagan's absorbing fascination for stars and his learning about stars from books in the library. His interest in extraterrestrial intelligence was first captured at the age of ten by Edgar Rice Burrough's science fiction stories about Mars. The budding scientist in young Sagan questioned the many inaccuracies in Burrough's stories, but was fascinated by the possibility of life on other planets.

Cohen presents a well-written chronicle, that both maintains a reader's interest and gives a clear, human and interesting picture of Sagan to the young reader. Sagan's contributions to astronomy, and his recent work about the possibilities of a nuclear winter which would result from the burning of forests and cities during a nuclear war are clearly explained by tracing the origins of the ideas. Similarly traced are the origins of his popular books *Dragons of Eden* and *Broca's Brain.*

Cohen's presentation gives a clear understanding of the man and the scientist. It conveys the enormous energy and dedication Sagan has devoted to the popularization of science, as well as to his rigorous scientific work. It closes with Sagan's hope for better human understanding of the Universe and each other. It is an inspiring book that could provoke several discussions on several themes in a science class, including that of a scientist as a public, rather than an isolated person.

DINOSAURS (1987)

Cathryn A. Camper

SOURCE: A review of *Dinosaurs,* in *School Library Journal,* Vol. 33, No. 11, August, 1987, pp. 65-6.

Dinosaurs is just what most kids want when they ask for a book about dinosaurs. It's big (but not thick), and has plenty of colorful illustrations [by Jean Zallinger] and just enough text to cover the dinosaur basics. Clear charts of dinosaurs' lifespans and locations of dinosaur fossil finds decorate the endpapers, and an index makes the text (if not the charts) more accessible. Best of all, Cohen has included some of the latest theories about dinosaurs, including the possibilities that they were warm-blooded, that they were related to birds, and that some species gave birth to live young. Comparable to, but more current than, McGowen's *Album of Dinosaurs,* this book will update collections and provide lots of big pictures of dinosaurs.

Phillis Wilson

SOURCE: A review of *Dinosaurs,* in *Booklist,* Vol. 84, No. 1, September 1, 1987, p. 61.

The voracious appetite of *Brachiosaurus* is only equaled by that of the young child in search of a new dinosaur book. Given the predilection of small children for large dinosaurs, this new offering by Cohen and [illustrator Jean] Zallinger will fill the bill. If the earth's history could be reduced to a single 24-hour period, dinosaurs would appear less than an hour before the day's end, and the whole history of human civilization would take only about the last half-second. In a lively text readers learn that "the dinosaurs ran . . . jumped, stomped, waddled, and crawled across the earth's surface for over 140 million years," and "the lowly, slow-moving opossum was as much at home in the dinosaur's world as it is in our suburbs." Bold headings on each page effectively break up the text into concise units. Though

the actual colors of dinosaurs are not known, Zallinger exercises poetic license in vividly rendered illustrations. Pages in full color coupled with an oversize format make the book well suited for hold-up presentations with groups. The report-oriented child will benefit from the double-page spreads giving a time-line chronology of the Triassic, Jurassic, Mesozoic, and Cretaceous eras, and a world map showing where fossils have been found.

Robert M. Schoch

SOURCE: A review of *Dinosaurs,* in *Science Books & Films,* Vol. 23, No. 2, November-December, 1987, p. 104.

Dinosaurs is not a typical children's dinosaur book. It does not solely illustrate various types of dinosaurs; it also reconstructs the dinosaurs' milieu. Each page addresses a different relevant subject often posed as a question—"How do we know about them [dinosaurs]?" or "What are fossils?" Topics as diverse as continental drift, geologic time, dinosaur classification, dinosaur social life, dinosaur metabolism, the relationship between dinosaurs and birds, reptiles contemporary with the dinosaurs, and the meteorite/asteroid extinction hypothesis are covered. Throughout, the book explains how scientists are able to reconstruct the world of the dinosaurs. For controversial issues, such as the terminal Cretaceous extinction hypotheses, the author presents various theories in a balanced manner. This is a large book (10 x 12 inches) with exceptional color drawings [by Zallinger] on every page. The illustrations will intrigue even very young children. *Dinosaurs* is sure to attract any child's curiosity.

PREHISTORIC ANIMALS (1988)

Publishers Weekly

SOURCE: A review of *Prehistoric Animals,* in *Publishers Weekly,* Vol. 233, No. 19, May 13, 1988, p. 275.

Following the age of dinosaurs, mammals became the next dominant species, from which latter-day mammals (including humans) are descended. Cohen focuses on these and smaller creatures of the Cenozoic era—e.g., birds—and attempts to give simple but complete descriptions of them, from the ancient opossum to the giant ground sloth, which is said to have been the size of an elephant. The book is almost a series of small articles on each of the animals, so that readers may learn only about those that interest them rather than proceed chronologically. But, after speculating that, with his new discovery of fire, primitive man made some species of animals extinct, the author preaches conservation for the present. That message seems out of place, given the scope of the rest of the material, but does not detract from an otherwise intriguing look at the past.

Denise M. Wilms

SOURCE: A review of *Prehistoric Animals,* in *Booklist,* Vol. 84, No. 21, July, 1988, p. 1833.

Cohen offers a bright, oversize album of prehistoric mammals and birds. Visuals are important; each spread features a box of text surrounded by a page-filling illustration [by Pamela Ford Johnson]. The text is smooth and economical, first describing the ascendancy of birds and mammals after dinosaurs died out and then looking at an array of other beasts that walk the earth no more. The lineup includes familiar types such as the woolly mammoth and saber-toothed cat, but by and large most of these animals will be unknown to all but those who haunt natural-history museums. Unfortunately, the book's design is garish. The cover, for example, filled with bright oranges and dusky purple, depicts two woolly mammoths fleeing a fire. This loudness continues inside as text appears on chartreuse, intense pink, lavender, or bright green. The pictures are quieter, though they are not particularly well drafted; nor is there mention of the source for these figures. Is it *really* known what some of these creatures looked like or are these the illustrator's speculations? Obviously aimed at browsers and casual readers, Cohen's information is nevertheless substantial enough to suit students needing report material; the endpapers feature miniature portraits of each animal.

Cathryn A. Camper

SOURCE: A review of *Prehistoric Animal,* in *School Library Journal,* Vol. 35, No. 1, September, 1988, p. 176.

Prehistoric mammals are as varied and as intriguing as dinosaurs, and Cohen, as in his book ***Dinosaurs***, introduces some of these strange creatures to a young audience. Kids will like the book's large size and realistic, bright pictures [by Johnson]; they'll also find it a helpful book for reports, because of its index and its well organized text. However, several minor points detract from the book's overall excellence. One problem is that not all of the animals mentioned are illustrated, a frustrating predicament when the text teases with descriptions of deer with "horns on their noses" or other equally intriguing accoutrements. Too, the illustrations have a tendency to homogenize these creatures' anatomical oddities into a watercolor fuzziness. The illustrations in Stidworthy's *Mighty Mammals of the Past* and *Prehistoric World* by Berger are more accentuated and more detailed. Sadly, a twist of fate has already dated the text; the dusky sparrow, which Cohen mentions as an example of an endangered species, just recently became extinct. In spite of these shortcomings, none of them add up to a big enough reason to reject this otherwise appealing book.

Michael Jury

SOURCE: A review of *Prehistoric Animals,* in *Science Books & Films,* Vol. 24, No. 2, November-December, 1988, pp. 95, 97.

Prehistoric Animals is a compendium of some of the more famous ancient mammals that have become extinct. The descriptions typically consist of [Johnson's] nicely done color illustrations of an animal accompanied by a few paragraphs of text and pronunciation guides for the names. The animal's habitat, diet, approximate size, and eating pattern are discussed. A wide variety of mammals, ranging from ancient horses to giant sloths, is covered. There is also a description of some prehistoric birds. The organization of this book is good because Cohen sets these prehistoric mammals in their proper place in earth's history. The rise of the mammals to importance after the end of the age of the dinosaur is presented, as are possible explanations for the extinction of these beasts. Also mentioned are the relationships of early man to these prehistoric animals. This is more than just a children's book. Enough information is given in a sufficiently sophisticated manner to entice just about anyone's interest.

Dana Richard Freeman

SOURCE: A review of *Prehistoric Animals,* in *Appraisal: Science Books for Young People,* Vol. 22, Nos. 1-2. Winter-Spring, 1989, pp. 27-8.

Oh no! Not another book on Dinosaurs. No, actually a somewhat needed book on prehistoric animals. Many prehistoric animals. Daniel Cohen's book will probably fill in some gaps between the plethora of dinosaur books and encyclopedias. He presents us with a parade of animals not often written about. They existed and we ought to know what scientists know about these animals. The illustrations by Pamela Ford Johnson are very well done and faithful to what scientists believe these animals looked like.

Many of the animals presented in the book were larger forms of something that resembles them today. All are extinct. Daniel presents some of the more popular views as to why they became extinct and, in a short segment, discusses the future in light of the fact that they became extinct. The message is "We have to think about the future."

As is probably the case with any book of this nature, it falls short in ways that it probably can't help. You see, when we write about the distant past—were you there? I know I wasn't—in definitive ways without pointing out that this is not "fact" fact but, the best-information-we-have-fact, we run the risk of compromising science. I know we all have concrete views on what's been happening lately in the realm of origins. *But,* at least the Creationists have caused some of us to stop and think about what we are pronouncing as the truth in equally dogmatic ways. Having said that, it is important to point out that this book can't—and shouldn't—address all of those arguments we are more than familiar with by now.

I wrestled with the rating on this as being one that (Good) would fill in some gaps and (Very Good) is fully up to relevant standards. To me, it falls in between. However, because it is a desirable purchase that fills in some gaps, it is very nicely done, and it will stimulate further study and curiosity, I went with the VG. Be careful, though, how you use it. It has some gaps and is a little too definite as to what *did* happen back then. It's all in the interpretation.

WHEN SOMEONE YOU KNOW IS GAY (with Susan Cohen, 1989)

Stephanie Zvirin

SOURCE: A review of *When Someone You Know is Gay,* in *Booklist,* Vol. 85, No. 18, May 15, 1989, p. 1630.

Considering lesbians as well as gays, the authors contribute a perceptive, well-organized perspective, written largely to supply information to non-gays rather than to provide self-help and support to teenage homosexuals. Experiences and comments by gay teens are used throughout, but the bulk of the book reflects the Cohens' own informal voice. This is particularly apparent as they consider mainstream religion and homosexuality, discussing biblical references and church-related gay support groups. Candid, nonsensationalized interviews with a drag queen, a transvestite, and a transsexual successfully clear up typical confusions about behaviors. With equal sensitivity and forthrightness, the authors present information about gay parents, coming out, and gay sex and promiscuity, and they answer common questions realistically: "If I'm the friend of somebody gay, won't everybody think I'm gay too?" "Not everybody, but . . . some will . . . if you can't face being the friend of a gay person now, at least don't become an enemy." A look at how AIDS has affected the gay community follows highlights of gay history in Western civilization. Strong in its debunking of myths and misconceptions, this is a responsive introduction that gays can read without feeling put down and straights can read for a better understanding of a different way of life.

Robert Strang

SOURCE: A review of *When Someone You Know is Gay,* in *Bulletin of the Center for Children's Books,* Vol. 42, No. 10, January, 1989, pp. 245-6.

While it's billed as a "book written for straight teenagers on the subject of homosexuality," gay teens will find much here to inform and reassure themselves as well. Writing in a casual, sympathetic voice, the Cohens discuss the nature of homosexuality and its existence throughout history; theories as to its causes; the relationships of gay people with their families, friends, and churches; and the special concerns of gay youth. Controversial topics such as gay parenting, promiscuity, and AIDS are addressed fairly and responsibly, and throughout there are welcome

touches of pithy humor: in responding to the question as to whether homosexuality can be cured, the Cohens write "You can make someone miserable but you can't make them straight." Occasionally, the tone gets a little too laid back (calling Lord Alfred Douglas an "upper-class twerp," for example). A reliance on those handy "experts" who "say" is no substitute for attribution and footnoting; in one case where the experts are named, one would still like to know how Drs. Ellis and Ames arrived at their definitive conclusion that "sexual orientation is determined between the second and fifth months of pregnancy." Far more enlightening (and engaging) are the anecdotal quotes from gay teens as well as kids whose friends or parents are gay. There is neither an index nor a bibliography, although a directory of gay organizations and a list of books and movies of gay interest are appended. Despite its technical flaws, this commonsensical treatment of a controversial topic is the best YA book on homosexuality currently available.

Carolyn Polese

SOURCE: A review of *When Someone You Know Is Gay,* in *School Library Journal,* Vol. 35, No. 13, September, 1989, p. 261.

An estimated one in ten teenagers is homosexual. This book addresses the other nine. The Cohens discuss emotions, attitudes, and facts that shape our perceptions of gay and lesbian people in America today. One informative chapter answers questions "you would be too embarrassed to ask," such as "Is it catching?" and "What should I do if a gay person comes on to me?" Another chapter gives a short history of social attitudes toward homosexuality. There is a frank discussion of the spread of AIDS and, at the back of the book, an annotated list of films, books, and videos. Interviews with teenagers who are struggling to come to terms with their sexual orientation help straight readers understand the realities that their gay and lesbian counterparts face. In trying to address the subject on a teenager's level, the Cohens have used some highly charged language (Oscar Wilde's lover, Lord Alfred Douglas, is referred to as an "upper-class twerp"). Statements such as, "Being gay is a social disaster. Who wants to be known as 'the faggot's friend?'", while intended to show that the authors understand teens' feelings, also sell readers short. Elaine Landau's *Different Drummer* offers a more even-toned presentation of similar material. Unique to the Cohens' book is an excellent and thorough discussion of religion and homosexuality.

ANCIENT EGYPT (1990)

Publishers Weekly

SOURCE: A review of *Ancient Egypt,* in *Publishers Weekly,* Vol. 237, No. 3, January 19, 1990, p. 111.

This attractive volume consists of short essays on the art,

religion, history, geography, agriculture and way of life of the ancient Egyptians. The book is written in a friendly though slightly pedagogical tone, with an emphasis on familiarly dramatic aspects of ancient Egyptian culture. Entries such as "Picture Writing," which defines the basics of hieroglyphics as well as offering a truncated history of the Rosetta Stone, or "The Mummies," describing the embalming and preservation of the dead, make for brisk reading. [Gary Lippincott's] atmospheric watercolor illustrations, too, aim only for the dramatic jugular with bold colors, broad composition and strong lines. As a basic introduction to the land and society, this is perhaps more entertaining than last season's *Exploring the Past: Ancient Egypt* by George Hartand, illustrated by Stephen Biesty, but offers less in the way of both detail and a cohesive, panoramic view of its subject.

Deborah Abbott

SOURCE: A review of *Ancient Egypt,* in *Booklist,* Vol. 86, No. 14, March 15, 1990, p. 1444.

The mysteries of ancient Egypt will attract younger readers to this oversize volume. In smooth prose that begins with Howard Carter and Lord Carnarvon's discovery of King Tutankhamen's tomb, Cohen continues with short articles (in conversational prose) about the land, history, pyramids, mummies, religious beliefs, and rulers. The boxed text is set against panoramic watercolor paintings [by Lippincott] executed in muted tones. The drama of these effective double-page spreads is lessened by the wooden quality of some of the figures. While students researching life in ancient Egypt will find that Oliphant's *Egyptian World* and Hart's *Ancient Egypt* contain more in-depth coverage in a structured format, those reading to contemplate the wonders of ancient civilization will find this book an enticing introduction. The endpapers contain neatly bordered, artistically designed time lines.

David N. Pauli

SOURCE: A review of *Ancient Egypt,* in *School Library Journal,* Vol. 36, No. 4, April, 1990, p. 130.

In his brief overview covering more than 3,000 years, Cohen has managed to bring a coherent unity to his topic. The introductory page captures the amazement of Howard Carter when he first breached the wall of Tutankhamen's tomb. This is followed by informative double-page watercolor spreads [by Lippincott] on such topics as pyramids, mummies, hieroglyphics, religion, warfare, and tombs. Readers will find a clear, direct text combined with oversized illustrations that brings a lively immediacy to the subjects. A bonus is the provision of a brief but thorough debunking of the so-called "curse of King Tut" that supposedly plagued those associated with opening the pharaoh's tomb. By no means a comprehensive reference, but a concise and attractive introduction.

THE GHOSTS OF WAR (1990)

Kirkus Reviews

SOURCE: A review of *The Ghosts of War,* in *Kirkus Reviews,* Vol. LVIII, No. 12, June 15, 1990, pp. 871-2.

Since ghosts are often spawned by traumatic circumstances, it's hardly surprising that many battlefields, soldiers, and soldiers' relatives are haunted. Cohen has assembled dozens of modern stories of such hauntings, "told as true," mostly from British sources. He does include one from Japan and several from the US, but reports a paucity of ghosts from the wars in Korea and Vietnam. He points out that credibility varies: the ghostly re-creation of the battle of Edgehill (1642) has been seen by responsible observers; but the **"Angels of Mons,"** supposedly witnessed by many at the beginning of WW I, are traced to a short story by Arthur Machen. Both incidents provide insight into the origins of ghostly lore. Ghosts never seem to photograph well, but disembodied voices and other hard-to-explain sounds have been captured on audio-tape.

Cohen's careful reasoning and simple, conversational style serve his subject well. The stories here have a chilling cumulative effect, expertly capped off with an RAF officer's particularly macabre vision. Readers will be informed as well as entertained.

Susan H. Patron

SOURCE: A review of *The Ghosts of War,* in *School Library Journal,* Vol. 36, No. 8, August, 1990, p. 152.

A collection of "true" ghost stories, each framed within the context of war, from the 12th-century Japanese Gempei War to World Wars I and II. (An introductory note speculates that the Korean and Vietnam Wars are probably too recent to have inspired ghostly lore.) Cohen's understated, conversational tone is convincing and effective, although fragmented sentences frequently mar his style. As with the genre of the urban folktale (to which these predominately contemporary tales are related), readers have the impression of hearing the story from a close or reliable witness. These stories have been collected and retold, but Cohen does not cite his sources for them. Like his other collections, the book is well suited for reading aloud and invites retelling among children.

Betsy Hearne

SOURCE: A review of *The Ghosts of War,* in *Bulletin of the Center for Children's Books,* Vol. 44, No. 1, September, 1990, p. 4.

Starting with his usual apologia, "The Reader is Warned (Again)," Cohen launches his first chapter with several random examples of haunted British battlefields before settling into a pattern of one story per chapter. These include ghosts of 12th-century Samurai, World War I, the American Revolution, early 19th-century U.S.-British naval conflicts, the War of 1812, the Civil War, and World War II, from which most of the tales are drawn. The best of the tales are tightly shaped and haunting; in one, an RAF mechanic shares a beer, during a North African desert sandstorm, with a German tank driver whom the British soldier later discovers to have been dead for a month. Occasionally, however, the narrative is anticlimactic, as in the case of some taped voices that provide " . . . just another interesting bit of evidence about ghosts that has been collected. It's the sort of thing that keeps you wondering." More or less chronologically arranged, this suffers from a few organizational lapses, with a World War I story sandwiched between Samurai and 1776, but the title alone will make sure the book circulates among even the most reluctant readers, who can savor the blend of legend and history.

GREAT GHOSTS (1990)

Julie Corsaro

SOURCE: A review of *Great Ghosts,* in *Booklist,* Vol. 87, No. 3, October 1, 1990, p. 329.

Nine ghost stories of the British haunted-house variety are based on reported sightings but lack documentation. The haunters here include an apparition whose performance at a London theater guarantees a successful show and another whose bookstore appearances promise unhappy endings. Although the collection is flawed by uninspired writing and careless errors in the text, the title and cover portrait of a dapper skeleton will entice genre buffs.

Molly Kinney

SOURCE: A review of *Great Ghosts,* in *School Library Journal,* Vol. 36, No. 11, November, 1990, p. 121.

Nine retellings of encounters with ghosts—six English, one Dutch, one Greek, and one Middle Eastern that are lively and easily read. Each succinct, concisely told story is from three to four pages long, and sports an illustration. Other versions of the stories can be found in Cohen's *Real Ghosts,* Seymour Simon's *Ghosts,* and David Knight's *Best True Ghost Stories of the 20th Century.* The cover art is dynamite—a skeleton appears in dark, somber tones, wearing a suit and fixing his tie. Cohen has done it again—he has created a real crowd pleaser.

PHANTOM ANIMALS (1991)

Kirkus Reviews

SOURCE: A review of *Phantom Animals,* in *Kirkus Reviews,* Vol. LIX, No. 12, June 15, 1991, p. 786.

From the demon cat said to stalk the U.S. Capitol building's "confusing tangle of . . . winding passageways" to the swarming "rats of the Rhine," who take terrible vengeance on a man who ordered a peasant massacre, Cohen presents an array of animals who die but refuse to rest, or appear from nowhere only to vanish mysteriously. As always, his reports are drawn from folklore ("King of the Cats"), accounts of psychic investigators, newspaper articles (the Nottingham lion, the recent Chicago kangaroo), or regional ghost story compilations; he relates them calmly, and in an evenhanded manner. Cohen doesn't include source notes; nor does he claim that everything here can be substantiated—but if readers "happen to believe the story while . . . reading it, so much the better."

Linda Waddle

SOURCE: A review of *Phantom Animals,* in *Booklist,* Vol. 87, No. 22, August, 1991, p. 2140.

With tales of ghostly dogs, scary kangaroos, and menacing birds sandwiched between stories of phantom cats, Cohen presents another collection for the "creepy entertainment" of his readers. The short, easy-to-read selections have been chosen from legend and folklore the world over. Each chapter contains not only the tale but also the author's speculations about its origin and truth. As with Cohen's other collections, reluctant readers and browsers will be attracted to the stories, which are also well suited for reading aloud—especially on Halloween.

Kathleen F. Redmond

SOURCE: A review of *Phantom Animals,* in *Voice of Youth Advocates,* Vol. 14, No. 3, August, 1991, pp. 187-8.

For those who enjoy stories of ghostly appearances, poltergeists, and hauntings Cohen's **Phantom Animals** will be appreciated. It is a collection of ghost stories with a twist. All of the ghosts are animals; some are even pets! In the introduction, Cohen explains that while he does not guarantee that all the tales are factual, the sources for the stories certainly believed!

In this collection of 17 tales, we meet the expected quota of werewolves, demon dogs, and phantom lions. However, there are other, less obvious spiritual creatures whose presence casts fear into even the most stalwart hearts. These animal ghosts include a menacing pet rabbit, a terrifying kangaroo, and an ominous white bird. Also present are the ghost of an enormous chicken as well as the ferocious spirit of a roaring bull!

Phantom Animals is an enjoyable book. While it is not a required purchase, it will certainly find an enthusiastic audience in middle and junior high school students.

📖 *RAILWAY GHOSTS AND HIGHWAY HOR-
RORS* (1991)

Molly Kinney

SOURCE: A review of *Railway Ghosts and Highway
Horrors,* in *School Library Journal,* Vol. 37, No. 10,
October, 1991, p. 134.

Another of Cohen's efforts to cover new material in the
ghost/phantom arena. He uses popular folklore and researched accounts of train and highway accidents; apparitions appearing along tracks and roads; and strange
encounters in abandoned buildings and other sites. The
information is accurate, and locations are authentic.
Unfortunately, the book lacks the excitement of some of
the author's earlier work in this genre. Several of the
selections appeared in **Phantom Animals**. While the stories themselves are adequate, the presentation is lacklus-
ter.

Stephanie Zvirin

SOURCE: A review of *Railway Ghosts and Highway
Horrors,* in *Booklist,* Vol. 88, No. 6, November 15, 1991,
p. 619.

Cohen draws his latest anthology of ghostly yarns from
the vast stores of American and British travelers' lore.
Readers will find tales about phantom hitchhikers, accident victims, ghosts on trains, and a variety of spooky
creatures who haunt the highways and byways. Adding
appropriate background (and a sprinkling of exclamation
marks), he relates each story in easy-to-read third person,
arranging his tales in loosely linked topical chapters.
Though amateurish, the full-page black-and-white illustrations [by Stephen Marchesi] break up the text. A competently done book that kids familiar with Cohen's other
spooky-stuff roundups will want to read.

📖 *PROPHETS OF DOOM* (1992)

Chris Sherman

SOURCE: A review of *Prophets of Doom,* in *Booklist,*
Vol. 88, No. 12, February 15, 1992, p. 1097.

Without belittling or condemning, Cohen provides readers with an intriguing and entertaining analysis of some
of the soothsaying men and women who have predicted
the end of the world—among them, the oracles of Delphi,
the Roman Sibyls, Jeanne Dixon, and Elizabeth Clare
Prophet. Merlin, Edgar Cayce, and Nostradamus are also
included, along with a number of lesser-known doomsay-
ers and seers. Cohen describes a variety of methods used
over the years to foretell the future—omens and portents,
comets, UFOs, and pyramidology. By providing information about the soothsayers and their times and traditions,
Cohen attempts to show how Western culture has accepted doomsday scenarios as "reasonable and even attrac-

tive." An intriguing choice for browsers and students in
search of material for reports.

Kirkus Reviews

SOURCE: A review of *Prophets of Doom,* in *Kirkus
Reviews,* Vol. LX, No. 4, February 15, 1992, p. 251.

The Second Millennium is at hand. Aren't you just a wee
bit anxious? Cohen claims that, deep down, you probably
are but (probably) shouldn't be, since one of the oldest
features of Western culture is the recurrent and (so far)
always mistaken conviction (or sneaking suspicion) that
the end of the world is nigh. The author deftly analyzes
the attractions of this belief, amidst a wide-ranging discussion of omens, oracles, millennial movements, natural
disasters, plagues (including AIDS), pyramidology, UFOs,
mass extinction theories, and a skeptical history of prophecy and prognostication from the ancient sibyls to Jeanne
Dixon and Elizabeth Clare Prophet. He barely mentions
the Old Testament prophets or Asian practices; devotes
an entire chapter to the life and writings of Nostradamus;
and closes with a reassuring message to readers, plus a
relatively hefty bibliography.

Ann G. Brouse

SOURCE: A review of *Prophets of Doom,* in *School
Library Journal,* Vol. 38, No. 5, May, 1992, pp. 138,
140.

This examination of prophets and their prophecies throughout history takes a skeptical view of the ability of anyone
to predict future events precisely. Included are discussions of the Millerites, Jehovah's Witnesses, the Greek
oracles, omens and portents in nature, the Cumaean Sybil,
Mother Shipton, the use of astronomical events such as
eclipses and comets, Jeanne Dixon, Nostradamus, etc.
People such as 16th-century Anabaptist leader John of
Leiden have been both hailed and persecuted as shown by
the first chapter's description of his rise and gruesome
end. As each person's methods and notable predictions
are related, Cohen points out their general failure to be
specific or, when exact, to come to fruition. This body of
evidence backs his assurance, among others, that the world
will not end in 1999 or 2000. Prophecies, beliefs, and
occult practices of Asian, African, South American, and
indigenous peoples are not included. The information
selected seems logical, reasonable, and comforting, although unlikely to dissuade believers in the "sixth"
sense.

John R. Lord

SOURCE: A review of *Prophets of Doom,* in *Voice of
Youth Advocates,* Vol. 15, No. 3, August, 1992, p.
183.

This book falls into the category of those books which

serve as basic resources on intriguing, somewhat sensational topics. In this case, rather than finding the real Camelot or discovering who really shot President Kennedy, the YA reader has the opportunity to delve into the realms of the past, the present, and the future. *Prophets of Doom* provides us with the chance to read quickly and succinctly about the end of the world—in 1844, the position that prophets and seers held in ancient civilizations, interesting predictions made during the Middle Ages about the late 20th century, and the men and women who made those predictions.

The book is well written, focusing on one topic after another in a very orderly fashion. The narrative is characterized by nearly a *National Geographic* style that flows easily and conveys a great deal of factual information in a very pleasant manner. The author succeeds in meeting his objective to inform his readers.

In chapters four and five (*Omens and Portents,* and *The Puzzle of Prophecy*), we get a chance to read about the early Sibyls, the roles played by augurs and haruspices (the latter are the people who divined the future from reading the entrails of sacrificed animals), and the prophets who peopled the Renaissance. Here we have the opportunity to discover that the portents in *Julius Caesar* were really part of the ancient Romans' lives, and that predictions supposedly made during the reign of Henry VIII of England were actually first recorded during the mid-19th century. So factual and not so factual as they may be, all serve to make good reading.

Two other chapters deal with religious predictions and prognosticators who foretold the end of the world—all of which have so far passed uneventfully. The author also includes topics such as the end of the dinosaurs, the prophecies of Nostradamus, and others.

Ultimately, the strength of this book is its entertainment value coupled with its effective presentation of information. Without seeming to be sensational and weird, Cohen gives his readers, young and old, an enjoyable respite from more tedious reading. At the same time, for the younger end of the YA group, the book can actually serve as a resource for research into one of the topics covered in the book.

GHOSTLY TALES OF LOVE AND REVENGE (1992)

Kirkus Reviews

SOURCE: A review of *Ghostly Tales of Love and Revenge,* in *Kirkus Reviews,* Vol. LX, No. 12, June 15, 1992, p. 776.

Cohen's **Ghosts of War** (1990) were men; here, women's ghosts comprise most of the cast—women who died betrayed or abandoned, by murder or accident; who returned for love, vengeance, or (in one case) jewelry. Most haunt the British Isles, Japan, or the US and date back no more

than a century or two; the "Headless Lover" of Brooke End and New York's "Empire State Building Ghost" are of particularly recent vintage. Cohen's lucid style is well-suited to creating chills, and he seasons his narrative with an occasional grisly touch—"His face had become a mask of skin tightly stretched over a grinning skull." "Put aside your doubts," he advises, "and read on." Perhaps not at night.

Susan R. Farber

SOURCE: A review of *Ghostly Tales of Love and Revenge,* in *School Library Journal,* Vol. 38, No. 7, July, 1992, p. 72.

A collection of 13 ghostly tales with the themes of love and revenge. Most are sad, and many feature women who have been scorned and return for vengeance or those who have died waiting for their lovers. The locations vary, from Japan to Scotland to Manhattan, and most of these well-written, suitably creepy, and very short tales retain their timelessness. As books on ghosts and love are perennial favorites (especially in this format, which has a high appeal for reluctant readers), so too will this one be. The cover is a wonderful added incentive, and will attract lots of readers.

Kay Weisman

SOURCE: A review of *Ghostly Tales of Love & Revenge,* in *Booklist,* Vol. 88, No. 22, August, 1992, p. 2003.

Cohen relates 13 eerie tales revolving around the themes of ill-fated love and revenge. He introduces each story by providing setting and historical information that leads smoothly into the legend itself. The subjects range from "Pearlin Jean," a jilted seventeenth-century specter who haunts her lover's house even after he marries another, to the apparition of a young woman said to visit the rooftop of the Empire State Building. Some narratives are based on the lives of actual people, such as Marian Hooper Adams (wife of John Quincy Adams' grandson), whose spirit is reported to frequent a statue placed near her grave in a Washington, D.C., cemetery. Cohen offers no source notes, but young readers swept up in these ethereal yarns are not likely to care. A good choice for read-alouds and storytellers.

Doris Losey

SOURCE: A review of *Ghostly Tales of Love and Revenge,* in *Voice of Youth Advocates,* Vol. 15, No. 4, October, 1992, p. 250.

These 13 short ghost stories from around the world with the theme of love and revenge are perfect for middle and junior high school readers not yet familiar with King and Koontz. Cohen's style and language is more appealing than Schwartz's *Scary Tales* and evoke images of fog, phantoms, and ghouls. **"Demon Lover,"** from northern Germany, is about Lenore whose lover Bruno suddenly appears after months of being lost. When Bruno takes her for a ride, he suddenly points to an empty grave and says, "This is our wedding bed." Cemetery workers later wonder at the fresh grave.

English Journal

SOURCE: A review of *Ghostly Tales of Love and Revenge,* in *English Journal,* Vol. 82, No. 1, January, 1993, p. 78.

This is a delightful, spine-tingling collection of documented ghost stories from a variety of cultures and times. Most focus on the ghosts of betrayed and abandoned lovers returning to haunt their betrayers; others relay tales of romance in which the ghosts serve as reminders of their never-ending love. Two tales are set in Japan: one in which a betrothed woman dies, yet promises to be reborn and return to her lover; another in which a woman's ghost returns to destroy a long-kept secret love letter from her past. Another tale is set in Spain and relays the heartbreak of a woman who, learning of her lover's deceitfulness, kills herself and then returns to haunt him and his family. Other tales focus on historical figures. In **"Grief,"** the ghost of Marian Hooper Adams, wife of the grandson of President John Quincy Adams, continues to haunt the statue erected in her memory in Rock Creek Cemetery in Washington, DC. The collection ends with a story set in 1985 in which New York City native Lucy Brenner finally visits the top of the Empire State Building, only to encounter the ghost of a woman who jumped to her death in the 1940s after she learned of her lover's death in World War II.

These fifteen ghost stories provide wonderful read-alouds for both middle-school and high-school students.

📖 GHOSTS OF THE DEEP (1993)

Kirkus Reviews

SOURCE: A review of *Ghosts of the Deep,* in *Kirkus Reviews,* Vol. LXI, No. 12, June 15, 1993, p. 783.

Cohen adds to his corpus of corpses (***Ghostly Tales of Love and Revenge,*** 1992, etc.) with an assortment of European and American nautical apparitions—some widely known (the Flying Dutchman; hammering aboard the *Great Eastern,* frequently presaging misfortune), others of local interest, including several tales of Cornish ghosts from 19th-century collector William Bottrell. Most of the incidents follow typical patterns: an admiral who goes down with his ship in the Mediterranean appears that evening at a London reception; a drowned woman haunts a Bahamian beach calling for her child; the faces of two sailors buried at sea "follow" their ship. The ghosts are mostly friendly or passive, but readers will still find cause for an occasional shudder (in one tale, a hotel guest wakes to

find himself sharing a bed with a dead sailor), while Cohen's unsensational reportage adds, as usual, an air of credibility. The author closes with a chapter on the *Constellation* and the *Queen Mary,* both haunted ships that can be visited.

Ellen Mandel

SOURCE: A review of *Ghosts of the Deep,* in *Booklist,* Vol. 90, No. 6, November 15, 1993, pp. 615-16.

Using an objective journalistic style, Cohen delves into the mysteries enshrouding a variety of ghosts of the sea. Relating names of people involved and often citing precise dates of sea battles, pirate attacks, or ghostly sightings, the straightforwardly delivered narratives include the account of a wealthy nineteenth-century merchant, forced to stay overnight in an undesirable inn, who awoke to find a sailor sleeping alongside of him. It wasn't until morning that he learned his roommate was the ghost of a sailor who had been murdered at the inn and secretly buried in its backyard. Also included is an account of a ship, bound from England to Canada, influenced to change its course by a ghostly intruder in the captain's cabin. In changing course, the ship happened on a vessel that was grounded on an iceberg. Among the wrecked ship's survivors was the very stranger who had visited the captain's cabin. Concluding with notes about haunted ships that can be visited in the U.S., this nonsensationalized collection of salty sightings will intrigue readers.

Myrna Feldman

SOURCE: A review of *Ghosts of the Deep,* in *Voice of Youth Advocates,* Vol. 16, No. 5, December, 1993, p. 318.

Sailors have had a strong tradition of ghostly lore and Cohen has put together a collection of intriguing and scary tales. They include the story of the admiral seen greeting his guests in his London home when at that moment his body lay at the bottom of the Mediterranean, the story of the sailor who shared his room with a stranger purported to have been murdered days earlier, and the story of the three men whose faces appeared in the sea after they had been buried. The chapters are brief and readable and will appeal to the YAs with a taste for the mysterious.

Journal of Reading

SOURCE: A review of *Ghosts of the Deep,* in *Journal of Reading,* Vol. 37, No. 5, February, 1994, p. 440.

This is a chilling new collection of ghost stories, 16 tales that deal with incidents related to the sea. The stories have a historical perspective, ostensibly with some basis in truth. The eerie tales include the grisly **"Sleeping Sailor,"** a saga of a weary traveler who awakens to find a sailor bathed in blood sharing his bed. **"Faces in the**

Water" is an account of an oft reported sighting of the faces of two crew members who were buried at sea. Cohen ends this collection with a chapter on the haunted ships readers may visit in the United States.

Elaine E. Knight

SOURCE: A review of *Ghosts of the Deep*, in *School Library Journal*, Vol. 40, No. 3, March, 1994, pp. 226-7.

A haunting collection from the dean of the "true" ghost hunters. These accounts of ocean-going specters—from sailing ship days to World War II—are dramatically written, and many include corroborating historical detail, heightening the impression of authenticity. Most of the stories are not well known, although a few, such as **"Ocean-born Mary,"** have been previously anthologized. The book reflects Cohen's open-minded attitude toward the uncanny—neither credulous nor scornful. Sure to be welcomed by fans of the supernatural.

ANIMAL RIGHTS: A HANDBOOK FOR YOUNG ADULTS (1993)

Chris Sherman

SOURCE: A review of *Animal Rights: A Handbook for Young Adults*, in *Booklist*, Vol. 89, No. 21, July, 1993, p. 1954.

While much of the information and many of the examples Cohen provides on animal exploitation can be found in other books (Pringle's 1989 *The Animal Rights Controversy*, for example), the author does offer arguments and insights that will make this a valuable addition to most library collections. He discusses the use of animals for medical experimentation; conditions in zoos, marine theme parks, and rodeos; factory farming and hunting (including traditional regional events such as pigeon shoots and rattlesnake hunts); puppy mills and dog breeders; and classroom dissection. He also questions the motives of some animal rights groups, notably PETA (People for the Ethical Treatment of Animals), discusses vegetarianism, and offers practical suggestions for young adults who are interested in animal rights issues. Cohen attempts to present a balanced point of view, but his bias toward animal rights is quite evident. Students debating animal rights or preparing persuasive speeches will find the book very helpful. A list of organizations, a bibliography, and source notes are appended.

Kirkus Reviews

SOURCE: A review of *Animal Rights: A Handbook for Young Adults*, in *Kirkus Reviews*, Vol. LXI, No. 13, July 1, 1993, p. 857.

Cohen's subtitle expresses his activist theme; though it's evenhanded, this what-to-do volume, dedicated to the animals in the author's life who have "given me so much more than I was ever able to give them," communicates a strong sympathy. Acknowledging the occasional ferocity of the animal rights movement, Cohen views its history as comprising issues beyond respect for nonhumans, pointing out that SPCA groups led to SPCChildren and that their early members were also actively anti-slavery and pro-feminist. The author's research revealed many horrors: chickens debeaked and female chicks kept in egg-producing plants while males are gassed; fast-food burger meat imported from former tropical rain forest lands; pet-shop pups, raised in "puppy mills," maturing into vicious or nervous dogs. As far as it goes, the material is striking; but medical research is inadequately covered here. Still, Cohen offers a range of levels of commitment to the cause, describing possible actions such as refusing to buy animals or supplies in pet shops or to dissect animals in class but leaving readers to make their own choices.

Eva Elisabeth Von Ancken

SOURCE: A review of *Animal Rights: A Handbook for Young Adults*, in *School Library Journal*, Vol. 39, No. 8, August, 1993, p. 193.

The right of animals to a safe, pain-free life is one of the philosophical debates of our time. Advocacy roles range from those who believe that humans should practice simple kindness to lesser beings to those who believe that all creatures have intrinsic rights similar to those of humans. Cohen does an admirable job of presenting all sides of this issue fairly and without prejudice. He is opposed, unquestionably, to cruelty toward all animals, but is evenhanded in his discussion of the various ideologies. There is a thorough discussion of the history of animal-rights movements as well as the history of man's attitudes toward animals. The author discusses the question of terrorism on behalf of animals, vegetarianism, laboratory testing, and cruelty-free products as well as giving a reasonable list of things to do to help save animals. A complete bibliography and lists of related organizations and magazines are also included. A valuable, informative volume.

GHOST IN THE HOUSE (1993)

Janice Del Negro

SOURCE: A review of *Ghost in the House*, in *Booklist*, Vol. 89, No. 21, July, 1993, pp. 1959-60.

Cohen's nine brief accounts of haunted houses and places include the discussion of a Washington, D.C., mansion said to be haunted by Dolly Madison, a house owned by a confessed warlock, and the famous case of Anne Moberly and Eleanor Jourdain and their experience at Versailles. Cohen does not depart from his usual, popular approach. The stories are very simply told in very simple language and will serve to whet the appetite for additional information.

Kirkus Reviews

SOURCE: A review of *Ghost in the House*, in *Kirkus Reviews*, Vol. LXI, No. 15, August 1, 1993, p. 999.

Nine brief tales of odd or supernatural doings in and around buildings—from the well-documented hauntings of Captain Despard's house in England and Vermont's Eddy farmhouse (the "Spirit Capital of the World") to the strange history of California's Winchester House and the many apparitions (including one of Dolley Madison) reported at Washington's Octagon. Cohen has delivered previous accounts of some of these incidents, but this simply phrased offering will draw less practiced readers. No source notes.

Elaine E. Knight

SOURCE: A review of *Ghost in the House*, in *School Library Journal*, Vol. 40, No. 3, March, 1994, p. 226.

Cohen has assembled nine "true" accounts of haunted places in the United States and Europe, ranging from churches to the White House. While some of these ghost haunts, such as the Sarah Winchester house, appear in many collections, others are less well known. Some of the tales are rather gruesome, featuring spectral revenge and demonic activity. Written in short simple sentences with large type and copious white space, this attractively designed book will appeal to reluctant readers. . . .

⬜ *CULTS* (1994)

Jack Forman

SOURCE: A review of *Cults*, in *School Library Journal*, Vol. 41, No. 2, February, 1995, p. 116.

Defining cults as being insular, leader-driven, apocalyptic, paranoiac, doctrinaire, and often dangerous, Cohen proceeds to argue that although such groups have existed and do exist today, they are not as harmful to society as some may think. He feels that the increasing number of single-minded, scattershot attacks on cults that have spawned wide-spread public fear about witchcraft and satanism have lead to the persecution of innocent people. Because he believes that it is very difficult to identify a cult as such, he implies that society should concentrate its efforts on teaching people how to think for themselves instead of engaging in forced deprogramming of cult members and scaring the public about the powers of cults. His examination of cults recognizes some bona fide dangers—such as James Jones's People's Temple, David Koresh's Branch Davidians, and COG (Children of God). To show that such groups are difficult to pinpoint, the author discusses the ambiguities of the TM movement, the Mormons, and the Lubavitcher Hasids, but unfortunately he also includes some misleading information about them. And, he fails to discuss clearly dangerous secret organizations such as Synanon, the Identity Church, and the KKK. He writes forcefully and clearly and succeeds in raising valid questions about overreactions to such groups—especially in regard to satanism and child abuse—but his libertarian stance toward cults generally ignores the dangers they pose to young people.

Drue Wagner-Mees

SOURCE: A review of *Cults*, in *Voice of Youth Advocates*, Vol. 17, No. 6, February, 1995, pp. 354-5.

The author proposes that the history of America was shaped by the actions of groups that could be defined as cults. Over two hundred years later we are still allowing people to believe and live as they wish, as long as they do no harm to others, no matter what the rest of us think of them. It is difficult to estimate the hundreds and perhaps thousands of small, essentially harmless groups considered to be cults functioning in the United States and in the world today.

Most of the members of cults have been treated badly by society and life in general. They are described as "society's walking wounded." The cult gives them a sense of community, they don't have to think for themselves, and are never lonely, or for that matter, alone. Despised and set apart from the rest of the world, they possess a knowledge that makes them better than the rest of the world. There are a number of characteristics which seem to define a cult: a group of people devoted to a particular set of ideas and individual; this set of ideas and this individual are more important than the other people in the usually small, though not in every case, group; members tend to be isolated from the rest of society and their families; cults tend to be apocalyptic and on the verge of great change; they believe themselves to be persecuted by the outside evil world; every world event is explained in terms of the beliefs of the cults; they tend to be short-lived, or, if not, their philosophy is moderated over time; they are perceived to be potentially dangerous, possessing secret doctrines and extra-ordinary powers of mind-control over the members.

Brief chapters explore the Branch Davidians and David Koresh; Jim Jones and the Peoples Temple; Mormons; Rabbi Schneerson and the Lubavitchers; Dr. William Reich and his medical theory of orgone energy; mind control, brainwashing and deprogramming as they relate to the Assassins of the Shia Muslim group, the SLA which kidnapped Patty Hearst, the Korean War POWs; Lyndon LaRouch; Satanism, witchcraft and Anton LaVey; Father Divine; the Sullivanians; Transcendental Meditation and the Maharishi Mahesh Yogi; the Moonies and Sun Myung Moon and the Children of God. By presenting short overviews of many groups, this introduction to the subject will not really whet the appetite of those interested in researching the individual groups. For some young adults delving into the subject for the first time, it may give them a taste for heavier and more complete information to be found elsewhere. The index includes a wide variety of sources but not the main source for most Christians, Walter Martin's *Kingdom of the Cults*. The sources cited are also, for the most part, old—many from the 1960s and 1970s—and dated in their usefulness in libraries. There are very few titles on cults in juvenile literature and this one may fill a niche for some teens who don't wish to pick up a 500 page tome on the subject. For current information, I would still refer the students to magazine indexes, newspapers, and current reference items on the topic. The author is a noted young adult writer and some of his personal life experiences show through his discussion of the subject.

Additional coverage of Cohen's life and career is contained in the following sources published by Gale Research: *Authors and Artists for Young Adults*, Vol. 7; *Contemporary Authors New Revision Series*, Vol. 44; *Major Authors and Illustrators for Children and Young Adults*; *Something about the Author*, Vols. 8, 70; and *Something about the Author Autobiography Series*, Vol. 4.

Tessa Duder

1940-

New Zealander editor and author of fiction, nonfiction, short stories, and plays.

Major works include *Night Train to Kawau* (1982), *Jellybean* (1985), *Alex* (1987; published in the United States as *In Lane Three, Alex Archer*), *Alessandra: Alex in Rome* (1991; published in the United States as *Alex in Rome*).

INTRODUCTION

Considered a talented and insightful writer of books for young adults and middle graders, Duder is regarded as an author whose rich, varied works have helped to define contemporary juvenile literature in her native New Zealand. The creator of fiction that features strong, independent young women as protagonists and nonfiction that focuses on subjects about which the author has intimate knowledge, Duder is praised for her rounded characterizations, keen evocation of place and atmosphere, and graceful, craftsmanlike writing style. She is best known for writing the "Alex Quartet," a series of young adult novels about Alexandra Archer, a teenager in the New Zealand of the late 1950s and early 1960s who becomes an Olympic swimming champion. Duder takes Alex, a spirited fifteen-year-old whose experiences often mirror those of her creator, from the race qualifying her for the 1960 Olympic Games in Rome to her triumph as a bronze medalist and her decision to move beyond swimming when she returns home. Throughout the series, which is acknowledged as both an effective example of sports fiction and a revealing depiction of the challenges facing women of the era, Duder outlines the personal growth of her protagonist, a feature shared by the author's other works of fiction. Commended for her understanding of young people, Duder is also acknowledged for the strength of her narratives and for the range and accuracy of the background details that she includes in her books.

Biographical Information

Duder's father was a physician and her mother was a cellist. Born in Auckland, New Zealand, Duder later wrote of her family, which also included a younger brother, that they were "very much like the one I gave Alex Archer." At six, Duder was sent to a small Catholic boarding school on the south coast of England; she notes that her experience as a non-Catholic in this environment led her to discover "what it was to be an outsider, bullied and humiliated by adults." She also lived briefly in London and Edinburgh before returning to Auckland. A voracious reader, Duder decided at the age of twelve to become a writer. The year before, however, she began competitive swimming; like Alex Archer, she also participated in piano, ballet, hockey, and school dramatics. After integrating the butterfly stroke and dolphin kick into her approach, Duder became New Zealand's national champion in butterfly and medley and later held the medley record for her country; at eighteen, she won the silver medal in the Commonwealth Games and was one of the few medal winners in the British Empire Games in Wales in that year. Shortly after being named New Zealand's first Swimmer of the Year, Duder retired from swimming after losing and regaining her title. She notes that she set the "Alex" books in this period of her life "partly to try and analyse just what were the pressures that so shaped my adult life." Duder claims that the character of Alex is a composite of two of her daughters, the Australian swimmer Dawn Fraser (who appears peripherally in one of the volumes of the series), and a second swimmer of the period. Although there are strong parallels between Duder and her most famous creation, the author notes that Alex "is actually far more forthright, confrontational, and interesting than I believe I was as a teenager. No, I was never an Alex."

After she ended her swimming career, Duder became a cadet journalist for the Auckland *Star.* She then became the paper's swimming correspondent as well as a columnist and editor of the women's page. After marrying in 1964, she became the mother of four daughters. Duder and her family lived in England and Pakistan before returning to New Zealand, where she worked as a freelance journalist and as a musician; she also supervised a parent-run play group and became influenced by the feminist movement. In 1978, she began writing her first book, *Night Train to Kawau,* an adventure for middle graders set on New Zealand's Kawau Island where Duder had a holiday cottage. After its publication, Duder moved to Malaysia for a year and then back to New Zealand. In 1981, she writes, Alex Archer "sprang fully formed into my consciousness and stayed there, rumbling away. . . . In 1986, I was ready for her." In the late 1980s and early 1990s, the "Alex" books became a publishing phenomenon in New Zealand; Alex Archer is now considered the best known character to have emerged from the country's current literature. The first book of the series, *In Lane*

Three, Alex Archer, was made into a film entitled *Alex* in 1993; Duder served as script consultant for this project.

In recent years, Duder has continued to write fiction, nonfiction, short stories, and plays for young people and to edit short story collections for this audience. In 1988, she lost her daughter Clare to illness, an event that affected her deeply. However, she continued to work, forming a theater company and writing, producing, and acting in a play about Joan of Arc; in 1991, she became writer-in-residence at the University of Waikato, New Zealand and has been a speaker at international children's literature conferences, a book reviewer, and an officer of the New Zealand Children's Book Foundation. She has also been experimenting with writing fiction about a Maori boy, Freddie Bone, while exploring new ways of representing the New Zealand experience to young readers. "I believed," she wrote of her work, "New Zealand children had a right to books set in their own culture, as American and English children took for granted; indeed that they had *yearned* for them. As a child I had been denied that." She adds, "My motivations are to explore my own emotional and literary boundaries, while at the same time helping young New Zealanders to develop a strong sense of identity through fiction."

Major Works

In Duder's first novel, *Night Race to Kawau,* twelve-year-old Sam Starr finds herself in charge of the family sailboat when her parents become incapacitated during the annual race across the Hauracki Gulf north of Auckland. Although she faces fear and anger as well as bad weather, Sam guides the boat safely through the night. Margery Fisher notes in a review of *Night Race to Kawau* in *Growing Point* that "In its kind, this book is a small triumph." Duder's next book, *Jellybean,* describes how ten-year-old Geraldine, nicknamed Jellybean, struggles to establish her identity while dealing with the focus of her single mother on her career as a cellist. As Geraldine's frustration mounts, Gerald, an old friend of her mother's for whom Geraldine has been named, appears in their lives. Gerald, who is himself a cellist, helps Geraldine to become less resentful of her mother and to achieve one of her own dreams when she conducts a school orchestra. Betsy Hearne writes in *Bulletin of the Center for Children's Books* that "the novel has immediate appeal by virtue of its depth and development."

With the "Alex Quartet," Duder made her first contribution to literature for young adults. The series, which includes *Alex* (U.S. edition as *In Lane Three, Alex Archer*), *Alex in Winter* (1988), *Alessandra: Alex in Rome* (U.S. edition as *Alex in Rome*), and *Songs for Alex* (1992), is often recognized as a stellar account of the growth of a young woman who is strong, talented, and likable. In her quest to define herself as an individual, Alex—who becomes the youngest swimmer on the Olympic team and the only one from New Zealand—surmounts such challenges as the death of her boyfriend, the attentions of a new suitor, the rivalry of her teammates, grueling practices and swimming meets, and the sensation of becoming a celebrity; at the end of the series, Alex has matured enough to be ready to make swimming a secondary interest. In her review of the first book in *Booklist,* Stephanie Zvirin says, "This is as impressive for its sports drama and backdrops as it is for its depiction of the emotional turmoil of coming-of-age," while Jennifer Mc-Dougall calls the story "un-put-down-able" in *Reading Time.* In her review of *Alessandra: Alex in Rome* in *Magpies,* Robyn Sheahan observes, "This novel has all the careful structuring and subtle development of character which one looks for in a work for the teenage reader." Duder has continued to direct several of her later works to young adults, such as three short story anthologies that also contain her own fiction. In addition, she has written educational readers for small children, plays with Martin Baynton, and nonfiction on New Zealand and the ancient Olympics.

Awards

Duder received Esther Glen Awards from the New Zealand Library Association for three of her "Alex" books: *Alex* in 1988, *Alex in Winter* in 1990, and *Alessandra: Alex in Rome* in 1991. She also received the AIM Children's Book Award for story book of the year for *Alex* in 1988 and *Alex in Winter* in 1990; she was a finalist for story book of the year for *Alessandra: Alex in Rome* in 1992. Duder was the recipient of the Choysa Bursary for Children's Writers in 1985 and received the Queen Elizabeth II Arts Council Special Writing Bursary in 1990. She was made a member of the Order of the British Empire in 1994.

GENERAL COMMENTARY

Judith James

SOURCE: A review of *Alessandra: Alex in Rome,* in *Reading Time,* Vol. 36, No. 4, 1992, p. 30.

The Alex Quartet which began with **Alex** and **Alex in winter** is now complete. The first two titles in the quartet were well received on both sides of the Tasman, with awards from the New Zealand Library Association. Therefore, it is with a degree of expectation, that the reader approaches the final two books. Alex is in Rome, having overcome difficulties which still leave her scarred. The details which are provided to refresh the reader's memory at times became intrusive. Alex is the only swimmer in the New Zealand team, and also a female, an obsessive point with Alex. The amount of detail of Alex's trip to Rome is excessive: her diet, menstrual cycle and wardrobe give her all the hallmarks of a Mills and Boon heroine. There are unusual sentence structures which irritate and puzzle. Both books swap narrator—Alex, then Tom; Book four uses letters from Tom as an alternative to Alex's narrative.

There is more to Alex than that, however. A closer look at the quartet reveals a considerable depth to Alex's character. Tucked in under the dust jacket of the final book, printed on the end papers, are two current (1992) *Who's Who* entries, detailing the lives of Alex and Tom, her expatriate opera singer friend from Rome. It is not easy for the reader to become involved in the last two books. Two experienced teenage readers found them unrewarding and gave up. Yet the detail of New Zealand in the 1960's is accurate. The emotion is real, and there is quite a lot to explore in the treatment and expectations we have of sporting hero/ines. The peripheral information Tessa Duder gives to the reader ranges over Rugby, politics, Opera, music and drama—on an international and New Zealand level. The effect of the detail is to distract, as the reader is told everything, with no gaps left. Choose carefully with your readers in mind for these two unusual books.

TITLE COMMENTARY

NIGHT RACE TO KAWAU (1982)

Margery Fisher

SOURCE: A review of *Night Race to Kawau,* in *Growing Point,* Vol. 24, No. 3, September, 1985, pp. 4490-91.

The roles which children of school age are given to play in most junior adventure stories are not in themselves notably convincing. Usually the reader is won over either by the strong topicality in the plot or by circumstantial details, which may be geographical or technical. Only rarely does an author achieve that unanimity of place, person and event which lends what we call authenticity to a piece of fiction. This unanimity seems to me to have been reached in an unpretentious tale from New Zealand, **Night Race to Kawau.** The author obviously writes from first-hand knowledge of sailing but she has arranged her setting and described her characters with craftsmanlike neatness so that there is none of the give-away, untidy spill over of details which betrays autobiography disguised as fiction. The structure of the adventure is firm and simple. The Starr family has entered for the celebrated annual race across the Hauraki Gulf north of Auckland. Sam, who is twelve, and the younger Jill and Jeremy, are to be included in the crew, but Dad and a student friend will oversee everything. In theory, that is. In practice Terry never turns up, Dad is knocked out by a mast early in the evening, Mother is grievously seasick and Sam finds herself called on for heroic efforts—improvising, steering, controlling her fears. There is no sensationalism here. Sam is afraid but she is also, at times, angry with the discomfort of cold and fatigue and even bored by a danger that won't go away and by parents whose authority has been so drastically curtailed. Her feelings are part of a mixture of sailing points, weather hazards and, most important, the behaviour of her companions on this unexpectedly difficult night sail. We watch her making rapid adjustments, both emotional and physical, until the adventure ends in a wholly plausible landfall and rescue. In its kind, this book is a small triumph.

JELLYBEAN (1985)

Margery Fisher

SOURCE: A review of *Jellybean,* in *Growing Point,* Vol. 25, No. 1, May, 1985, p. 4625.

Mother-daughter relations are described in **Jellybean,** not in a portentous style but with speed and grace in the writing, with conversations that go far to suggest personal feelings and readjustments; in this short book the action moves quickly, particularly when for greater immediacy the author changes from the storyteller's 'and then' to the historic present. The theme is serious enough, the need of a child to find her own way to independence. Geraldine, almost eleven, has for years been used to sitting in rehearsal rooms or concert halls while her mother, a single parent, plays the 'cello in groups or orchestras to earn a living for them. Their mutual affection is as clear as their respect for one another but Geraldine is beginning to suffer from a frustrated ambition to earn a reputation, preferably in what she sees as the powerful position of a conductor, in spite of the deficiencies of her own musical talent. A meeting with a 'cellist waiting for an audition for a place in an orchestra, a man who seems to know something about her, leads to the moment when she does have a chance to conduct at her school, but this extraordinary widening of her life is in the end less important to her than the way she learns to accept her new friend's old links with her mother and its possible future. Humour and good humour combine in a tale told with sympathy for the young; the scenes in a New Zealand city are well devised to establish the characters domestically and to ensure that young readers will understand the changes which a few weeks bring to them.

Sue May

SOURCE: A review of *Jellybean,* in *The School Librarian,* Vol. 34, No. 3, September, 1986, p. 265.

Neglected by her hippy mother and laughed at by her peers, Geraldine feels she might as well not exist for all the notice people take of her. Are they not aware that she has feelings, opinions and needs? Apparently not, and a range of people—from her mother's musical friends to the snooty sweetshop lady—treat her with little respect. Despite this well-worn theme of eccentric parent and isolated child, the 'progressive' mother is less patronising and insensitive than is often the case, in fact to some extent mother and daughter are quite good friends; but it is ironic that the obsessively musical mother fails to recognise the causes of frustration in her own 'Jellybean'. It

takes a bearded stranger to understand Geraldine's ambition. What is the connection between the stranger and the mother? This is a believable account of feelings, reactions and situations, but the ending is a little contrived and somewhat predictable.

Betsy Hearne

SOURCE: A review of *Jellybean,* in *Bulletin of the Center for Children's Books,* Vol. 40, No. 3, November, 1986, p. 47.

Geraldine, nicknamed Jellybean, lives with her mother and her mother's cello, very often in conflict with the latter. Concerts, rehearsals, and trio work crowd out their time together and often leave Geraldine in the company of various babysitters. The story begins one night when the sitter fails to show up and Geraldine must accompany their mother to a restaurant where she is scheduled to perform. There appears a stranger who sits at Geraldine's table, seems to know her already, and shows up again at an orchestra rehearsal. Geraldine first suspects he is her father, but it turns out he is an old friend of her mother's, come to renew their courtship and his own musical career. In the meantime, he wrests from Geraldine her secret ambition to be a conductor and proves to be the friend she needs so desperately to relieve her loneliness. The writing here is beautifully crafted ("the harpist is already in her seat, dropping icicles of sound into the silence"), the characters closely portrayed, the scenes intensely played. Particularly vivid are the passages of Geraldine experiencing certain pieces of music, as in the section where she listens to the Nutcracker Suite from her hiding place in a corner of the orchestra pit. Although the setting is Auckland, New Zealand, the novel has immediate appeal by virtue of its depth and development.

Donna Rodda

SOURCE: A review of *Jellybean,* in *School Library Journal,* Vol. 33, No. 5, January, 1987, p. 73.

As the only child of a single musician, Geraldine (nicknamed Jellybean) has always played second fiddle to her mother's career. Resentful and lonely, she has to arrange her life around her mother's rehearsal and performance schedule as a concert cellist. A man from her mother's past helps Geraldine discover her own passion for music and helps her to better understand her mother and herself. This book is a commentary on the dedication and single-mindedness that a musician must have in order to succeed. The characters are real people who deal with real problems and who grow and change during the course of the story. This well-written novel, set in New Zealand, is slow paced but solid. It should appeal not only to those interested in music, but also to children who may sometimes feel that they are not getting enough attention from or spending enough time with their parents.

📖 *ALEX* (1987; U.S. edition as *In Lane Three, Alex Archer*)

Margery Fisher

SOURCE: A review of *Alex,* in *Growing Point,* Vol. 27, No. 4, November, 1988, p. 5064.

The central theme of *Alex* is competition—in this case the rivalry during several years of two New Zealand girls who in 1959 were in contention for a place at the Rome Olympics. However, the fact that the actual swimming heats and finals are described in italicised sections separated from the main text suggests that this is not just a sequence of sporting events. Alexandra Archer, who tells the story herself, has many interests for a girl of fifteen. She takes leading part in school plays, she attends ballet classes and plays games strenuously and she is studying hard for School Certificate. Besides this, she has to recognise changes in her friendship with Andy, her lifelong ally in times of stress; his untimely death is cruelly hard to bear in her state of emotional change. A first-person story sometimes means an unpleasantly self-absorbed central character but Alex, besides being very self-critical, is an outgoing person, well able to understand her rival Maggie and to sympathise with her frustration as her wealthy mother tries to ensure victory for her in the swimming contests. We never learn which of the girls finally goes to Rome, for it is through preliminaries, of swimming and also of personal development, that the book makes its effect. It is a substantial tale, based on a firm background of Auckland society, school and home life and taking every chance to deepen the reader's understanding of a likeable heroine with a high standard and a high personal goal to aim at.

M. Hobbs

SOURCE: A review of *Alex,* in *The Junior Bookshelf,* Vol. 53, No. 1, February, 1989, p. 27.

This is a really enthralling account of a girl swimming for a place in the Rome Olympics in 1959 (though as the setting, like the author, is from New Zealand, the historical aspect of the story is not at first apparent). Short italicised sections take the reader from the beginning to the end of the race; they alternate with long flash-backs telling continuously the background story to Alex Archer's struggle this night to beat her close rival Maggie Benton for the place in the Olympics. Tessa Duder was herself once a champion swimmer, but the authentic detail unfolds absolutely naturally, without distracting. The book is so much more than the race, just because Alex herself (in contrast to Maggie, whose mother devotes her whole life and considerable wealth to Maggie's swimming career) tries to lead an all-round life. This is a drawback when, for instance, she breaks a leg at hockey and misses months of training, and when the boy to whom she becomes very close (their romance is for these days conducted on pleasantly old-fashioned lines) is killed. On the other hand, he gives her something to work for; she wants

the Olympic place for his sake—he too was a swimmer. The whole gamut of adolescent hopes, fears and passions is grist to this mill: difficulties at home and at school, reactions, physical and mental, to growing up—Alex is fortunate in that the adults of her family are lovingly supportive throughout. The book in addition gives a splendid insight into a specialist world few will encounter.

Publishers Weekly

SOURCE: A review of *In Lane Three, Alex Archer,* in *Publishers Weekly,* Vol. 236, No. 14, October 13, 1989, p. 54.

Although sports enthusiasts in particular will be attracted to this story about a competitive swimmer, Duder writes for a larger audience. In addition to examining the makings of a champion, she profiles a teenaged feminist who breaks the boundaries of her conservative society in 1959. Fifteen-year-old Alex Archer is a multidimensional character whose dedication to sports does not preclude a wide variety of other interests, concerns and ambitions. Qualifying for the New Zealand Olympic team is only one of the pressures Alex endures. She must also contend with slanderous gossip, the failing health of her beloved grandmother and then the death of her boyfriend. Even in the darkest moments, Alex's spirit remains undaunted. Her griefs and triumphs are beautifully expressed through clear narrative interspersed with stream-of-consciousness excerpts. Readers will not fail to be uplifted by this talented writer's thoughtful novel.

Jennifer McDougall

SOURCE: A review of *Alex,* in *Reading Time,* Vol. 34, No. 1, 1990, p. 23.

The year is 1959 and Alex Archer is swimming the race of her life. The prize? A place on the Olympic team that is headed for Rome and Alex is not at all sure that she can best her long-time rival Maggie. Maggie's ambitious mum keeps her focussed on swimming but Alex comes from a family that encourages her to set her own goals and be a self-starter. The result is that Alex is an over-achiever who divides her time and her energy fairly evenly amongst all the things she loves and excels at—theatricals, hockey, ballet, piano and, of course, school work. She has also fallen in love and suffered a tragic loss.

Alex tells her own story in flashback but in between chapters there is the clever use of a device that allows the reader into Alex's thoughts as she swims that all-important race. Fragments of thought, innuendo, reference to people and events not yet entered into the main body of the narrative all serve to make this story un-put-down-able and to push the reader on.

It will appeal most to adolescent girls but if boys could be brought to a story featuring a female in the main role, they also would find it relevant. A most enjoyable book and a desirable addition to both the public and private library shelf. Tessa Duder won the New Zealand Story Book of the Year Award of 1988 and also the Esther Glen Award for children's writing for her book about Alex. It is not difficult to understand why.

JoEllen Broome

SOURCE: A review of *In Lane Three, Alex Archer,* in *Voice of Youth Advocates,* Vol. 12, No. 6, February, 1990, pp. 342-3.

The young girl as Olympic champion has intrigued Western viewers since the onset of medal-winning Eastern bloc gymnasts in the early 70s. We have been made aware of the fact that hard work and sacrifice are standard entrance requirements into that circle of elite hopefuls who grace our television screens every four years. Beyond the superficial media interviews, we know little about the long, hard drive leading up to the Olympic limelight. Entrants often appear to be driven youngsters backed by driven parents unless they are products of the state systems in the Soviet bloc countries where financial duress is not felt by the families of the athletes.

What is the climb really like for these dynamos? One powerful insight into the making of a female champion is offered by Duder as she follows a swimmer, 15 year old Alex Archer of New Zealand, through the steps that lead to the Rome Olympics of 1960. This is a highly dramatic account, jam-packed with daily workouts, love, jealousy, death, performance anxiety on stage as well as at the poolside, burnout, family love and sacrifice, self-centeredness, and treachery. Overachievement in almost every form is examined. Still, Alex manages to appear human and her plights touch us as well as her successes and fears and incredibly involved lifestyle. This is a gritty, determined champion who is on the verge of womanhood. She is not conventionally pretty or petite and this is a source of anxiety for this heroine because her fiercest competition fits that description.

This is a tightly crafted novel where all of the hormonal and psychological stresses that fall on a young champion are looked upon with honesty and occasional humor— and the reader easily hangs in there to find out what happens next. The death of her handsome boyfriend and the impact upon her and the stricken families is very, very moving, even though it did not seem necessary to burden the heroine with such pain and tragedy amid all of the other situations that she endured on the route to Rome.

Linda Newbery

SOURCE: A review of *Alex,* in *Books for Keeps,* No. 62, May, 1990, p. 19.

Tessa Duder's book has already won two awards in her native New Zealand, and it's not difficult to see why. The year is 1959, and Alex, a talented swimmer, hopes to qualify for the Rome Olympics. For all her numerous achievements, Alex has self-doubts and anxieties enough to make her a thoroughly sympathetic and likeable character. Whereas a lesser writer would have gone on to show Alex winning an Olympic Gold, Tessa Duder leaves her at the qualifying races with a sense of having overcome her personal tribulations—a satisfying end to a moving and engrossing book.

ALEX IN WINTER (1989)

E. Colwell

SOURCE: A review of *Alex in Winter,* in *The Junior Bookshelf,* Vol. 54, No. 3, June, 1990, p. 147.

Alex, aged 15, is a competitive swimmer who is hoping to win a place in the New Zealand team for the Olympics. The author is well qualified to write on this theme as she has been a champion swimmer herself.

Any athlete, especially one who aspires to qualify for the Olympic Games, must of necessity lead a disciplined and monotonous life with restricted social relaxation, while he or she is in training. An author, therefore, who chooses such a subject for a novel must find other material to give her story sufficient interest for the reading public. Tessa Duder has used the natural theme of rivalry and its emotions and the actions of all-important selectors who will make the final decision. Alex feels that these men are prejudiced against her and have plans to pass her over, although she has won the trials.

Alex's fortunes are much influenced by her temperament, She is naturally independent, outspoken—sometimes unwisely—and resents being treated 'as a child' because of her age. Added to this, her 'boy-friend' has been tragically killed in an accident, an emotional shock which still disturbs her. As a result, she is 'difficult' at home. Her rival, Maggie, is good-tempered and kind so that Alex feels guilty when she triumphs over her.

Suspense is well maintained. Will Alex be selected to go to Rome with the team? The reader doesn't know until the last page of the book. Will Maggie's unscrupulous mother succeed in winning her daughter a place also and— most important—will Alex win the battle with her own temperament and become a wiser and better person.

A story for adolescents which, while a little tedious at times, is well-informed and interesting.

Julia Wright

SOURCE: A review of *Alex in Winter,* in *The School Librarian,* Vol. 38, No. 3, August, 1990, p. 120.

Throughout the book Alex feels alone and out of touch with her usually helpful and caring family. The training schedules are punishing. She faces hostility from one of the selectors, the temporary loss of her coach, and the plotting of her rival's mother. The subtle intrigues and attempts to wear down her resolve are fascinating, but her determintion is inspiring. Alex is still grieving over the recent death of her boyfriend and is suffering from a depression which is so well conveyed that the reader is often sucked into a similar mood! There is no event which can lift her spirits but time brings a small blossoming of hope. An impressive book which is intellectually demanding but well worth the effort.

Jacquie Frew

SOURCE: A review of *Alex in Winter,* in *Magpies,* Vol. 6, No. 2, May, 1991, p. 33.

In this book, Alex is recovering from the death of her boyfriend. She's also coming up against some of the barriers faced by sportswomen thirty years ago, particularly the perception that what she is doing is unfeminine and unnatural. Alex is a strong character who tells her story well but the point of view also changes from time to time to give other perspectives. The real strength of *Alex in Winter* is Duder's handling of Alex's emotional turmoil and tension. There are a couple of clear goodies and baddies but otherwise reality is what Alex makes of it and changing views reflect a world of realistic, engaging complexity.

Val Randall

SOURCE: A review of *Alex in Winter,* in *Books for Keeps,* No. 74, May, 1992, p. 21.

Alex is 15—a champion swimmer hoping to be selected to swim for Australia in the 1960 Olympic Games.

She is, however, in the winter of grief and self-doubt. Her boyfriend was killed in a hit-and-run accident and she can no longer communicate with friends and family, choosing instead to lock herself into training and confrontation with the petty bureaucracy which seeks to deny this unconventional girl a place in the Olympic squad.

The story is immediate and powerful. The vocabulary and ideas challenge and stimulate the reader. The '60s setting throws the exploration of women's role in society into sharp relief and examines the sexual and political stereotyping from an historical perspective which illuminates contemporary concerns. Well worth buying for library or book box.

📖 *ALESSANDRA: ALEX IN ROME* (1991; U.S. edition as *Alex in Rome*)

Kirkus Reviews

SOURCE: A review of *Alex in Rome,* in *Kirkus Reviews,* Vol. LX, No. 15, August 1, 1992, p. 988.

In Lane Three, Alex Archer introduced a thoughtful, independent-minded champion swimmer. Now Alex, still not quite 16, is representing New Zealand in the 1960 Olympics, where—against her own expectations—she wins a bronze. Despite a conscientious chaperon she calls Bulldog, she also makes friends with another "Kiwi," a 23-year-old singer who studies in Milan but is temporarily in Rome. Tom, a clever impersonator as well as fine baritone, has the rest of the team convinced that he's an accommodating Italian; but, in the briefer alternating chapters he narrates, it's clear that his growing affection for Alex is genuine. Here, Duder re-creates the 1960s, the Roman ambience, and the Olympic experience in vivid, authentic detail, while Alex's narrative beautifully captures her heightened perceptions and sense of unreality as—disoriented in mind and body by the tension—she trains and swims to win. Meanwhile, she's wary of Tom but charmed by him; in turn, he's enchanted with her, for the right reasons. Divided, in the end, by geography and career plans as well as age, they have exchanged just one chaste kiss and are not devastated by their parting; yet they are so nice, well suited, and ultimately sensible that it's hard to imagine they won't find each other eventually. Alex frequently refers to events and characters in the first book; reading it would enrich this one, but it also stands well on its own. Well crafted and satisfying romantic. A scrupulous note separates fact from fiction—the protagonists only *seem* real.

Susan Knorr

SOURCE: A review of *Alex in Rome,* in *School Library Journal,* Vol. 38, No. 10, October, 1992, p. 140.

Readers who enjoyed the first novel will be disappointed by this one, which lacks the insights and descriptions of aspects of competition so crucial to the earlier story; those unfamiliar with the first title will be confused or kept in the dark by several references. With rival Maggie ill in New Zealand, the swimming takes on a mechanical, secondary role. Alex practices and wins the bronze, but her long-awaited dream takes a back seat to another, never fully developed thread—her relationship with Tom. The alternating first-person chapters do not convey to readers just what these two see in each other. Tom doesn't seem to know what he wants other than to pursue a singing career; a revelation about his true identity, which readers anticipate, is hardly climatic, and his reasons for leaving his native New Zealand are vague and minor. The unsatisfying plot, along with abbreviated or run-on sentences, awkward phrasing, overblown phrases and descriptions, and Kiwi jargon, will lose all but the most determined readers.

Stephanie Zvirin

SOURCE: A review of *Alex in Rome,* in *Booklist,* Vol. 89, No. 4, October 15, 1992, p. 417.

A sequel to *In Lane Three, Alex Archer,* this probably

won't grab as many readers as its predecessor. More complex, it has the sophisticated feel of an adult novel, with little of the first book's extraordinary sports drama and none of its tragedy or feminist underpinnings. The setting is one of literature's most romantic—Rome—which Duder vividly captures from its sidewalk cafés to its stunning historical landmarks. Told through the alternating perspectives of 23-year-old Tom, a disaffected New Zealander in Italy to study music, and Alex, in Rome to represent New Zealand in women's swimming in the 1960 Olympics, the story focuses mainly on the pair's gradually evolving affection. There's no physical, fall-into-bed romance in the story. Rather, Duder concentrates on her characters' growing understanding of each other, and in a challenging role reversal. It's 15-year-old Alex, not Tom, who turns out to be the more mature of the two. Filled with internal monologues, the plot is both convoluted and slow; the European setting and even some of the author's allusions will be too obscure for American teens. Yet the story is about the kind of teenage character that appears too infrequently in YA novels these days, and Duder's artful probing yields a vision of a confident, determined young woman who validates her already strong sense of herself.

Ellen Fader

SOURCE: A review of *Alex in Rome*, in *The Horn Book Magazine*, Vol. LXVIII, No. 6, November-December, 1992, p. 727.

In ***In Lane Three, Alex Archer,*** readers first encountered the feisty and independent New Zealander; now almost sixteen, Alex is in Rome to represent her country in the 1960 Olympics. In spite of her rigorous training schedule and her overprotective chaperone, whom she nicknames Bulldog, Alex manages to spend a considerable amount of time with twenty-three-year-old Tom, another Kiwi who is temporarily living in Rome. Readers discern early on that his attraction to Alex is sincere, even as he constructs an elaborate hoax by passing himself off as a helpful Italian to the rest of the Olympic team. While in the end the disparity in their ages and their differing career goals cause them to part after having exchanged only one innocent kiss, a continuing attraction between the two hints of future encounters. Told in the alternating first-person voices of Tom and Alex, numerous details about Rome, competitive swimming, and the Olympic experience add a sense of vivid immediacy and help to draw readers into the dramatic plot. An author's note preceding the story explains that many of the medal winners mentioned—Dawn Fraser, for example—are real people, but that no swimmer from New Zealand competed at the Rome Olympics; it is a testament to the author's skill that Alex's success in winning a bronze medal seems so authentic. Alex makes a number of references to events that happened in the previous book; while knowing it would embellish the reading experience, ***Alex in Rome*** stands strongly on its own.

Robyn Sheahan

SOURCE: A review of *Alesssandra: Alex in Rome,* in *Magpies,* Vol. 8, No. 1, March, 1993, p. 33.

Poised on the edge of the Olympic pool for the swim of her lifetime, Alessandra is aware of the 20,000 people watching her, and of the fact that, win or lose, her life will never be quite the same again. As the third in the tetralogy, this carefully researched volume continues Alex's story with her arrival in Rome for the seventeenth Olympics in 1960. . . .

A sense of complete veracity is achieved by the author's clever meshing of the entirely fictitious presence of an NZ swimming team of one (Alex!) competing in the historically accurate competition against Dawn Fraser et al.

The dual narrative technique employed is a common device in recent young adult fiction, and contributes added dimensions and interest to Alex's very personal narrative. Her breathless reactions to the grandeur of her first international swimming meet in Rome is interspersed with the story of Tom, an ex-patriate New Zealander who has been studying opera singing. Alex's voice is fresh, engaging and intriguing. The sense of time past conveyed by the author manages to give a nostalgic impression whilst attaching a present feeling to this tale of fierce exhilarating competition and first love. Tom is equally engaging though his tone is a little "arch" in spasmodic bursts. His boater and devilish sartorial elegance also occasionally make one grimace, but then, when in Rome! This novel has all the careful structuring and subtle development of character which one looks for in a work for the teenage reader, and manages to avoid the often self-conscious tone of the first person narrative. Even the romantic undertones remain just that, with a nice sense of the excitement of first love, mixed with the uncertainties of it.

Tessa Duder is deservedly an award-winning author of books for young people, whose final book in this Alessandra Quartet will be looked forward to with mixed feelings of anticipation, and disquiet at losing an acquaintance of some stature and significance.

SONGS FOR ALEX (1992)

A. R. Williams

SOURCE: A review of *Songs for Alex,* in *The Junior Bookshelf,* Vol. 57, No. 3, June, 1993, p. 108.

The progress of Alexandra Archer on her return to New Zealand after her Olympic successes continues with the overriding theme of conflict which is Alex's destiny as a firmly individual personality. Her attitude within her community strikes friends and foes alike as at best wilful and at worst obstreperous. She firmly refuses the status of celebrity and eschews the threat of role model. She will neither exploit herself nor be exploited. Swimming rapidly becomes a secondary interest except for one last, pointed assertion of superiority. There is so much else with which to be concerned: family responsibilities, personal adjustment, exams to be passed and a permanent career to be prepared for. All her decisions create dismay or resentment. As Tomas Alexander so often warned her in Rome, she is about to be discarded as an achiever, but fame is not her forte. To round off her story Tessa Duder reintroduces 'Tomaso' as Dunois to Alex's Joan in Shaw's play in a relationship not altogether dissimilar to their own to date. When Alex, as Joan, rebels against her inquisitors with: 'What other judgment can I judge by but my own?' she just, incidentally, encapsulates her individuality and the source of her conflict with friends, officials and educators, even with Tomas.

The treatment of the play and its implications is a masterpiece grafted on a triumph. Miss Duder continues to write at a furious pace with details smoothly entwined in the flowing narrative. It cascades past the reader like a mountain stream, turbulent and fast-flowing yet crystal clear. If, as seems to be indicated, Alex Archer's story is for the time being to cease, it is a good point at which to pause. Alex is about to enter a largely adult world with serious intentions, leaving childhood behind.

Monica Dart

SOURCE: A review of *Songs for Alex,* in *The School Librarian,* Vol. 41, No. 3, August, 1993, p. 122.

A life absorbed in swimming and acting might be seen as enviable. Not so. Conflicting demands coupled with the hard grind of school work give Alex endless problems. The reader is drawn convincingly into the world of a New Zealand swimming champion, of international status, who is persuaded to take a major role on the stage with its disciplines and required rehearsals. Authenticity is the keynote of this gripping tale. The play is Shaw's *Saint Joan,* no less. We understand the anxiety of the swimming coach whose patience is tried; also the disappointment of the headmistress whose plan to fill the vacancy for head girl with her star pupil, Alex, is thwarted. Another thread throughout the story is the turmoil of our heroine's friendship with Tomas Alexander, a promising opera singer; and excellent supporting characters include the family. This is a worthy successor to the previous three books in the series.

📖 CROSSING: AUSTRALIAN AND NEW ZEALAND SHORT STORIES (edited with Agnes Nieuwenhuizen, 1995)

Lyn Linning

SOURCE: "Crossing: Australian and New Zealand Short Stories," in *Magpies,* Vol. 10, No. 4, September, 1995, p. 10.

The stories in **Crossing** are always interesting, sometimes intriguing, and occasionally illuminating. Because many and varied facets of the transition from childhood to adulthood are explored, most young readers will find at least one story memorably resonant with their real or imaginative experiences.

Tessa Duder's introduction, unmistakably aimed at the young adult reader, clearly explains possible interpretations of the term 'crossing', the genesis of the collection, and the principles on which contributors were selected: eight Australian and eight New Zealand authors; some who write for both adults and teenagers; a gender balance; and a place for emerging talents along with established writers. Caroline Macdonald (numbered amongst the Australians) sets her story, "Miranda Says", in New Zealand, exploring further the life of the protagonists in *Talking to Miranda* from the point of view of her half-sister. This highlights the fruitful interaction of the two writing cultures.

Stories firmly set in the era when the authors were young adults thirty to fifty years ago are no less relevant than tales of the nineties. "Annie's Brother's Suit" (Gillian Rubinstein) recaptures the characters and atmosphere of a girls' boarding school in the 1950's but the protagonist's timely realisation that she does not have to sacrifice her femininity to fulfil her intellectual potential comes to some, but sadly not all, girls today. Owen Marshall's "The Tank Boat" reveals, without comment, the timeless truths that reality sometimes falls short of expectations and that shared guilt can permanently separate friends. William Taylor's "At the Big Red Rooster," arguably the most sparkling story in the collection, satirises small town and suburban life forty years ago, but Brett's resistance to the supermarket culture and Lisa's eventual appreciation of his act of defiance epitomise that ability, consistently attributed to even ordinary young people ever since *The Catcher in the Rye,* to see through the false values of their elders.

Crossings are achieved in some stories through the interaction of past and present. The protagonist in Fiona Farrell's "Market Pointers," a compassionate social worker, reflects on an incident from her primary school days when she was one of the peer group who excluded a girl desperate for acceptance. The mother and daughter in "No Blood for Oil" by Peter McFarlane work through their intergenerational differences to unite in demonstrating for peace during the Gulf War when the mother regains the ideals of her own activism in the 1970's. Patricia Grace's multi-layered "Manners Street Blues" touches on police brutality to indigenous people, colonisation, and the enduring nature of some societal problems as a young Maori woman comes to realise, through the synthesis of her recent experience and the war-time memories of an elder, *'plus ça change, plus c'est la même chose'*.

Characterisation leans towards caricature in some of the stories set solely in recent years, which enhances their dramatic impact at the cost of convincing motivation and thematic insight. Gary Crew's suspenseful "One Step Behind," an engrossing read, and Witi Ihimaera's "Who are you Taking to the School Dance, Darling?," an amusing satirical view of the 90's 'liberated' middle-class family, are cases in point, as is Tina Shaw's pseudo-mysterious "Holly."

However, three contemporary stories have memorable, realistic characters and wide appeal. Christopher Thompson's convincing story of a young man's developing sense of competence as a valued member of a group of road-workers after years of ridicule at school brings to mind Bill Naughton's classic *The Goal-Keeper's Revenge* (a personal favourite). Garry Disher's "Another Word for It" demonstrates the potential of the short story form to recount a dramatic incident vividly while revealing a range of characters and the complexities of their relationships in just a few pages. The African setting extends the collection's geographical range. The oppressed brother and sister in Judith Clarke's "Flying Horses" are roundly drawn as they grow into an understanding and appreciation of each other.

Tessa Duder effectively draws on the ancient myth of Narcissus to develop her theme—the dangers of succumbing to the modern myth of the 'beautiful people'—in "**White Daffodils**." Both her story and Gaelyn Gordon's "Don't Do Anything I Wouldn't Do" lean towards 'magic realism'. In a racy letter to her Australian pen-friend, Gordon's protagonist innocently reveals her shallow scattiness, the power (natural and supernatural) and integrity of the neighbour she purports to scorn, and her steps on the path to mindless promiscuity: a clever, thought-provoking story for those who can read between the lines.

Glyn Parry's "Shadowstrangers" is the only futuristic story and seems out of place here. It sits better as previously published in Parry's own collection *Radical Take-Offs*.

On the whole, the collection has the potential to fulfil the hope Tessa Duder expressed in her introduction: that it will explain some of the readers' crossings whether they are 'currently on this youthful journey' or looking back on it. *Crossing* provides excellent opportunities for readers on both sides of the Tasman to extend the range of accessible authors they know and like and to explore cross-cultural similarities and differences. It is therefore a valuable addition to the growing body of thematic collections of short stories for young adults.

FALLING IN LOVE: ROMANTIC STORIES FOR YOUNG ADULTS (edited by Tessa Duder, 1996)

Jo Goodman

SOURCE: A review of *Falling in Love*, in *Magpies*, Vol. 11, No. 3, July, 1996, p. 33.

The sub-title reads Romantic Stories for Young Adults, and the ten New Zealand authors represented in this collection have of course as many different responses to the theme, although the prevailing tone is one of bitter-sweet poignancy—not all these romances lead to a happy ending. The confronting "Angel Hotel" by Bill Payne is set in a drug rehabilitation centre, and in this story and a couple of the others racial tension underlies the romances. Kate de Goldi's "Kissing Cousins" sets the scene of tentative first love at a family death and funeral; and in Martin Baynton's "Samara Jane" a school performance of *Romeo and Juliet* threatens to turn into tragedy, and all because of Juliet's (Samara Jane's) perfect breasts.

This is a varied and enjoyable collection which provides an interesting sample of contemporary New Zealand writers for young adults.

Additional coverage of Duder's life and career is contained in the following sources published by Gale Research: *Contemporary Authors*, Vol. 147; *Something about the Author*, Vol. 80; and *Something about the Author Autobiography Series*, Vol. 23.

Edward Eager

1911-1964

American author of fantasy fiction and picture books.

Major works include *Half Magic* (1954), *Knight's Castle* (1956), *Magic by the Lake* (1957), *Magic or Not?* (1959), *Seven-Day Magic* (1962).

INTRODUCTION

Through a series of seven novels, Edward Eager ably continued the tradition of "everyday fantasy" pioneered by British author E. Nesbit. His fantasies for middle graders have been praised for their humor, realistic characters and family relationships, and believable magical devices that follow logical rules. The author's protagonists are regular children who encounter extraordinary things; his magic is brought to life not by focusing on how it works but on how the characters relate it to their own modern world. Like the young heroes of many of Nesbit's works, the children in Eager's stories are enthralled with books, and his novels celebrate the imaginative spirit aroused by reading. Nevertheless, these readers discover they cannot blindly accept all of what they read as true—usually after some humorous episode that points out the necessity of thinking for oneself. Along with realism and an often subversive wit, Charlotte S. Huck observed, "[l]ogic and humor are characteristic of the many books of fantasy that were Eager's legacy of modern magic for today's children."

Biographical Information

Eager was born and raised in Toledo, Ohio, where he developed a fondness for children's books that was to last his entire life. He began his writing career not as an author of fiction, however, but as a playwright. While an undergraduate at Harvard University, Eager wrote a play, *Pudding Full of Plums,* that proved so successful that he lived off the royalties for some time. He left Harvard for New York City, where he attained modest success as a lyricist and adaptor, collaborating with Neil Simon and others on the musical *Adventures of Marco Polo* (1956) and adapting operas by Mozart and Offenbach for production on NBC-TV. After his son Fritz was born, he rediscovered his love of children's literature and began writing his own stories; his first, *Red Head* (1951), was directly inspired by his son's own fiery coloring. Two more picture books followed, the result of the author's belief that many of the old favorites he was reading to his son, particularly the animal stories, had unsatisfying texts.

It was while in pursuit of more tales to read to his son

that Eager made his most important "discovery," that of the books of British author E. Nesbit. Her stories of ordinary children and unusual magic inspired the writer to create his own novels of "daily magic," works that added his own brand of wit and invention to the Nesbit model. His fantasies are frank tributes to—some say imitations of—Nesbit's works, such as *Wet Magic* and *The Magic City,* and he always took care to make reference to her novels within his stories "so that any child who likes my books and doesn't know hers may be led back to the master of us all." Eager's successful new career as a children's author lasted just over a decade, however, for he died of lung cancer at the age of fifty-three. The seven novels he left behind remain popular with today's children, who can identify with his ordinary protagonists and can believe, as Eager intended, that the magic he described "could all happen to *you,* any day now, round any corner."

Major Works

Told in an energetic, bouncing rhyme, *Red Head* relates how Fritz, fed up with being nicknamed after his flaming hair, runs away only to discover that leaving home doesn't solve his problem. Eager wrote two more picture books after *Red Head,* both featuring animals and inspired by Beatrix Potter: *Mouse Manor* (1952), a subtly humorous tale of a country mouse in London, and *Playing Possum* (1955), a realistic story of a child's comic encounter with nature. It was with *Half Magic,* however, that Eager found his natural subject; this tale of how the dull summer vacation of four fatherless children is transformed by a talisman that grants only half of the bearer's wish was hailed for its humor, charm, and realism. "For his character drawing," a *Times Literary Supplement* reviewer asserted, "no praise can be too high." *Knight's Castle* features the children of the four siblings from *Half Magic* in a scenario inspired by Nesbit's *The Magic City.* Using a toy fortress supplemented with everyday household items, the cousins create a model of the castle from Sir Walter Scott's *Ivanhoe;* they are then magically transported to the world of Torquilstone. In a satirical twist, the children fail to stick to Scott's story and improvise their own ending; critics praised this imaginative variation on the original as well as the children's inventive, entertaining mixture of modern and literary idioms.

The four children from *Half Magic* return to rent a cottage for the summer in *Magic by the Lake.* While some critics found *Magic by the Lake,* a sequel to *Half Magic,* less spontaneous than its predecessor, others believed that this tale of a lake and its magical inhabitants had humor enough to appeal to adults as well as children. The cousins from *Knight's Castle* return in *The Time Garden* (1958), where a summertime visit turns up a garden toad called the Natterjack who, like Nesbit's Psammead, guides them through history—including the fictional history in *Little Women.* Although the story contains the same lively dialogue as the earlier books, several observers found this entry in the series somewhat formulaic. Eager varied his method in *Magic or Not?,* a story of a wishing well that only works if the wish is for someone else, by making it ambiguous whether actual magic or coincidence is at work. Despite the debatable nature of the magic, the novel contains the same realistic dialogue and entertaining episodes that make it "unmistakably an Eager book," according to Margaret Warren Brown. In a sequel, *The Well-Wishers* (1960), the truth behind the magic remains in question, even though more wishes just happen to come true; the work is distinguished by being the only one of Eager's works to use first-person narration. In his final work, *Seven-Day Magic,* the author most obviously depicted his belief that reading creates its own kind of magic by making his talisman a library book. Five friends start out on a series of humorous adventures after they open their library book and find themselves starring in it. They travel through Frank Baum's Oz, and tidbits from other literary classics appear throughout the work. While Eager "borrows elements from many stories," Joel D. Chaston noted, he "reinvents them, making them into something unique." The inspiration for his novels may have come from the stories of Nesbit and others, the critic added, but the author's genius lay in his ability to take these ideas and rewrite them, "transforming them into something original, going far beyond mere imitation."

Awards

Half Magic and *Magic or Not?* received Honor Book citations at the *New York Herald Tribune* Children's Spring Book Festival.

AUTHOR'S COMMENTARY

Edward Eager

SOURCE: "Daily Magic," in *The Horn Book Magazine,* Vol. XXXIV, No. 5, October, 1958, pp. 349-58.

[In the following excerpt, Eager explains the appeal of E. Nesbit's work, the acknowledged inspiration for his novels.]

It is customary, in writing of E. Nesbit, to begin by telling how one first read her stories in *The Strand Magazine,* either devouring the installments one by one as they appeared, or perhaps even better, coming upon them unexpectedly in old bound volumes in some grandmotherly attic.

This did not happen to me. My childhood occurred too late for the original Nesbit era, and too soon for the revival sponsored in this country by William Rose Benét, Christopher Morley, May Lamberton Becker, Earle Walbridge and others (not to mention the firm of Coward-McCann, which earned everlasting honor by beginning to reissue her books in 1929, and has continued to do so ever since).

I was dimly aware of the renewal of interest in Nesbit in the early thirties, but since I was then entering my own early twenties, with no thought of ever again having anything to do with the world of children's books, it all seemed very remote.

It was not till 1947 that I became a second-generation Nesbitian when I discovered a second-hand copy of *Wet Magic,* while casting about for books to read to my son. I have not got over the effects of that discovery yet, nor, I hope, will I ever.

Probably the sincerest compliment I could pay her is already paid in the fact that my own books for children could not even have existed if it were not for her influence. And I am always careful to acknowledge this indebtedness in each of my stories; so that any child who likes my books and doesn't know hers may be led back to the master of us all.

For just as Beatrix Potter is the genius of the picture book, so I believe E. Nesbit to be the one truly "great" writer for the ten-, eleven- and twelve-year-old. (I don't count Lewis Carroll, as in my experience the age when one stops being terrified by, and begins loving, *Alice* is about thirteen and a half. And Kenneth Grahame, whose *The Golden Age* had an undoubted influence on the Nesbit style, is an author to wait for, too, I think. As for Mrs. Ewing, so sadly forgotten of late, she is best come upon a bit earlier, except for *Mary's Meadow,* which might almost have been written by E. Nesbit herself.)

How to describe the Nesbit charm for those who don't yet know it? Better for them to stop reading this article and read the books themselves. I have read all I could find of those that matter (she wrote countless potboilers that are not worth searching for). . . .

[Her] books for children were never the mere potboilers she claimed they were. Every page shines with the delight the writer took in fashioning it, and this is a thing that cannot be faked. I know. In truth it is her "adult" writing that bears a synthetic stamp. Her poems and novels are mere self-conscious attitudinizing, the little girl playing "lady" in borrowed clothes, and all of them have long been forgotten. It was when the child in her spoke out directly to other children that she achieved greatness.

I do not mean to equate genius with arrested mental or emotional development. But there are lucky people who never lose the gift of seeing the world as a child sees it, a magic place where anything can happen next minute, and delightful and unexpected things constantly do. Of such, among those of us who try to write for children, is the kingdom of Heaven. And in that kingdom E. Nesbit stands with the archangels.

Of course there are other people who plainly have never known what it is like to be a child at all, who would suppress fairy tales and tell children "nothing that is not true." (I once knew a lady who denied her children Santa Claus, till they rebelled and forced her to relent. And when one year she so far relaxed as to say that he had been there and brought *one* of the presents, her little girl cried, "And did he wear a red coat and a white beard?" "No," said the lady, stubbornly progressive to the end. "He wore a business suit!")

Tragically, toward the end of E. Nesbit's life, the fantasy-haters were in vogue (again)! One of the saddest chapters in Doris Langley Moore's book is the one that tells of her sending stories to publishers, only to have them returned with the comment that there was no longer any demand for "her sort of books."

The thought of these lost, unpublished Nesbits is enough to make the reader weep. "Bitter unavailing tears" indeed! It is true that the books of her later years are not so strong as her first work, but who knows? She might have found a second wind and finished in a burst of triumph, like Verdi. And if not, even second-rate E. Nesbit is better than no E. Nesbit at all. Which is my justification for having dared to write second-rate E. Nesbit myself.

Still, even without these forgotten manuscripts (what one would give to know even the titles!) there remain in print today, on one side or the other of the Atlantic, fifteen

books. And fifteen books of such golden quality are a priceless treasure for any child.

First in any listing of E. Nesbit's works always must come the three books dealing with the Bastable children, delectably titled *The Treasure Seekers, The Wouldbegoods* and *The New Treasure Seekers.* (There is a fourth book, *Oswald Bastable and Others,* obtainable in England, which contains four additional Bastable adventures, as well as eleven other short pieces.)

Who could forget the Bastables, particularly the noble Oswald? One sees them as perpetual pilgrims, marching forever down the road with peas in their shoes and a brave plan in mind to save the family fortunes, stopping by the way to dam the stream (and later cause a nearly disastrous flood), forgetting in their zeal the cricket ball left lodged in a roof-gutter (which still later is to cause a flood of another kind).

And yet, so short are the memories of critics that one frequently sees the Bastable books listed as fantasies, or among "magic stories." They are of course nothing of the kind, but belong firmly in the realistic tradition of heroic naughtiness, or naughty heroics. And surely of all the naughty children in literature, none were ever so heroic as they, nor any heroes so (unintentionally, of course) very naughty!

Nevertheless, in spite of all the fun, in spite of the unforgettable, endearing Oswald, I question whether the Bastable stories are the best introduction to E. Nesbit today, at least for American children. Because they are realistic books, the details seem more dated, the "Britishness" more marked, than in the Nesbit magic stories. The things these children do are too different from the things children do today for them to qualify as "easy reading." Thus the very elements which make these books unique may be the elements which stand in the way of their acceptance.

If there is resistance to E. Nesbit on the part of some American children in these days, I think it may well be because they encounter the Bastable stories first. Certainly every child should know the Bastables, but if on first exposure he doesn't see their charm, let him meet E. Nesbit instead in the world of fantasy, where background counts for less and once the story gets going, all is gas and gaiters. Then, if he is a right-minded child, he will be won to her forever, and Oswald and his brothers and sisters can follow later. . . .

With *The Wonderful Garden* one comes close to the very best of E. Nesbit, yet it is a book hard to define. Is it "real"? Is it fantasy? It is either or both. Here is a book in which every event *could* have a prosy, dull, boring, logical explanation. Or there could be magic at work, and of course the children in the book, Caroline and Charlotte and Charles, know that there is. This "magic or not" formula is one oddly challenging and tempting to the writer, and devilish hard to bring off. I know, because I've just finished trying it, myself. E. Nesbit handles it with consummate skill, to make an almost perfect book.

The Wonderful Garden, with its incidental and fascinating flower-magic lore, is a book peculiarly attractive to the adult reader, and for this reason I would hesitate before pressing it over-enthusiastically on any non-Nesbit-inoculated child. Again, let him meet her first in the purely "magic" books. Then he will demand all the rest.

Of these magic books there are eight, and of these eight two, The Magic City and Wet Magic, are late works and, authorities agree, inferior to her best writing. Perhaps. But who could forget Philip waking in the night and walking over the bridge and into the city he has built himself, of blocks and books and bric-a-brac? Who could forget those engaging dachshunds, the cowardly Brenda and the heroic Max? Who could forget the languishing mermaid in Wet Magic ("We die in captivity!") and, later, the battle of the books, with its picture (by H. R. Millar, of course) of Boadicea vanquishing Mrs. Markham and the Queen of the Amazons dealing with Miss Murdstone? (Here again, however, adult appreciation may be different from a child's.)

We are left with a golden half-dozen. There are the "five children" books (Five Children and It, The Phoenix and the Carpet and The Story of the Amulet). There are the Arden stories (The House of Arden and Harding's Luck). And, shining proudly by itself, there is The Enchanted Castle.

Who can choose among them? Who can describe perfection? Given only one choice, I would take The Enchanted Castle for my desert island, but Doris Langley Moore would not agree, though Roger Lancelyn Green (in Tellers of Tales, Edmund Ward, England) feels as I do.

But why make comparisons? Read them all. Step up, step up and meet the Psammead and the Mouldiwarp (and the Mouldierwarp and the Mouldiestwarp). Learn how to make Ugly-Wuglies (and then see what happens)! Find out how it feels to own a magic carpet and a phoenix at the same time. And what takes place when the magic carpet begins to wear out and develops a hole in the middle? Explore the lost kingdom of Atlantis. Go seeking for the real head of the house of Arden and follow the adventures that begin when a crippled boy in a London slum plants strange seeds in his back garden.

And always remember that magic has a mind of its own and will thwart you if it can. So that if you wish, for example, to be invisible and the magic ring you happen to have on you is geared to twenty-four hour cycles (or twenty-one, or fourteen, or seven; you never can tell with magic), invisible you will remain till the time is up. Or four yards high, as was poor Mabel's fate on one historic occasion. And think of the complications, as you go about your daily round.

For if there is one thing that makes E. Nesbit's magic books more enchanting than any others, it is not that they are funny, or exciting, or beautifully written, or full of wonderfully alive and endearing children, all of which they are. It is the *dailiness* of the magic.

Here is no land of dragons and ogres or Mock Turtles and Tin Woodmen. The world of E. Nesbit (except for some elaborate and debatable business with magic clouds toward the end of The House of Arden) is the ordinary or garden world we all know, with just the right pinch of magic added. So that after you finish reading one of her stories you feel it could all happen to *you*, any day now, round any corner.

The next time you pick up what you think is a nickel in the street, make sure it *is* a nickel and not a magic talisman. And don't go scrabbling about in sandpits unless you want your fingers to encounter a furry form and your startled ears to hear the voice of a Psammead begging to be allowed to sleep undisturbed for another thousand years.

But of course you *do* want your fingers and your ears to encounter just that; all right-minded people do.

The next best thing to having it actually happen to you is to read about it in the books of E. Nesbit.

GENERAL COMMENTARY

Eleanor Cameron

SOURCE: "Fantasy: Edward Eager," in The Green and Burning Tree: On the Writing and Enjoyment of Children's Books, Atlantic-Little, Brown, 1969, pp. 92-6.

Edward Eager, who is always having the children in his stories read E. Nesbit's books, has written six deft and amusing fantasies, much beloved of American childhood. Of them, three are time tales, **Half Magic, Knight's Castle,** and **The Time Garden,** and the best of the three by far is **Knight's Castle.** The least good, **The Time Garden** is, it seems to me, an example of the danger of admiring too greatly the work of another writer. For behind **The Time Garden** one distinctly senses "Blueprint for a Time Tale" hanging up somewhere out of sight, a blueprint worked out from Nesbit's The Story of the Amulet, and **The Time Garden** whipped up almost matter-of-factly as if, "Once you get the idea, there's nothing to it. You settle on some sort of magical creature who has the power of sending the children around in Time, and then you just move them backward and forward." (Of course in Nesbit's fantasy it was the spirit of the Amulet and not the Psammead who had this particular power.) Indeed, it is all so matter-of-fact and one-two-three that one of the children even complains that so far their forays into Time have "all been kind of non-fiction! Like those books where you get Highlights of History, with kind of a story wrapped around. Or those television shows where You are There. We've had the Revolution and the Civil War. Any day now we'll get around to the election of Calvin Coolidge. There's no variety." They therefore persuade the Natterjack to mix in a little literature—and get Louisa May Alcott.

Which makes it all as magical and subtle as the Automat, where you put in your dime and get a cup of coffee or, if you'd rather, a glass of tomato juice. Only instead of a dime, substitute the Natterjack who, on several occasions, is used by the children almost as unfeelingly as one uses a dime. He is an English toad, and though toads are abundant only in the south of Surrey, W. H. Hudson, the naturalist, tells us, this Natterjack happens to be a cockney, thus reminding us almost too clearly of the Mouldi-warp. And perhaps the measure of difference between Nesbit's Psammead, with his passionate likes and dislikes, his unforgettable appearance, his eternal unpredictability, his piques and flare-ups and sudden givings-in, and the, by contrast, far less unique and various personality of the Natterjack, is one measure of the difference between *The Time Garden* and the story that inspired it.

It is a pity, because Eager gave himself opportunity for an original and meaty creation, his basic premise being that the Natterjack inhabits the thyme garden of a very strict old lady upon whom several children descend for a prolonged visit. The possibilities of the thyme garden are innumerable: there are wild thyme and wild time, old English thyme and old English time, common thyme and common time, all the time in the world, time out of mind, the last time and time that is ripe, and the Natterjack sleeps under woolly thyme. It is a potent premise and Eager, to a certain extent, takes advantage of it, amusingly, deftly but not richly. A piquing basic idea, it would seem, is only a beginning and a very small beginning at that, and it is as though Eager played over his melody most cleverly, but left depth and abundance to his inspirer, her extraordinary unexpectedness, her variety and vividness of detail, her "fancy as free and inventive as that!"

Again, in his best time tale, *Knight's Castle,* Eager borrows from E. Nesbit, but now from *The Magic City,* and he is as frank about this as he is open in his admiration for her work. On page 53 of the book he writes:

> *The Magic City* proved to be all about a boy named Philip, who built a town of blocks and books and ornaments and peopled it with all his toys, and then one night the town came to life, and Philip found himself in the middle of it, and the magic adventures began.
>
> "This," said Ann, after chapter one, "is a good book."
>
> "This," she said after chapter two, "is one of the crowned masterpieces of literature which have advanced civilization."

Doris Langley Moore, in her *E. Nesbit,* says that no one has ever been able to imitate Nesbit's books, though several have tried. And I think that this accounts for the difference between *The Time Garden* and *Knight's Castle.* In *The Time Garden* Eager was echoing, in a way, rather palely imitating his predecessor. But in *Knight's Castle* he has taken the central idea of the magic city, built out of small objects found around the house (which Nesbit, in her turn, took from someone else) and reimagined it, reshaped it to his own completely fresh use. A

literate wit and an ability to develop any potently magical situation to the highest degree of risibility transforms *Knight's Castle* into something *The Time Garden* was not: the kind of book that can be thoroughly enjoyed by most adults who remember their own childhood imaginings, and especially by those who have read *Ivanhoe.* It also betters *Half Magic,* for though *Half Magic* is far and away more original than *The Time Garden,* even here the often repeated word *magic* does not always keep the working of it from at times deteriorating into formula.

In *Knight's Castle,* as in Nesbit's *Harding's Luck,* the children go into the past through dream. The children's dream feeling, it is true, is different from Dickie Harding's, for he lived so completely and knowingly and self-consciously in dream that eventually the past experienced there becomes as real as the waking present, whereas Eager's children know quite well which is day experience and which night. Yet there can be no sense of disappointment in the reader, for at the end one is not in the least inclined to exclaim, as at the end of *Alice,* "So it didn't really happen after all!" (Doris Langley Moore in this connection contrasts two kinds of dream fantasies: the kind in which waking dreams of children are realized, and the kind in which sleeping dreams are crystallized as in *Alice.*) It *did* happen to Eager's children—magically— and the children know it happened and discuss their adventures during the day and make further plans. They *did* shrink to the size of the small knights and ladies in the toy castle, which becomes the mighty Torquilstone with Ivanhoe and Brian Bois-Guilbert and de Bracy on their doughty chargers pricking across the carpet (become a great plain covered with some sort of strange stubble), and Rowena and Rebecca peering out anxiously across the vast distances of the bedroom from the battlements of the castle. It is around Torquilstone that the children innocently build their city of odds and ends.

E. Nesbit's *The Magic City,* begun as a serial in the *Strand Magazine,* grew out of Hoffman's story (so Mrs. Moore conjectures) of the small boy Reinhold, who built a city of toys which grew larger and larger until its buildings were as tall as those in actuality and its inhabitants as big as himself. Once the book was begun, both Nesbit and her friend Lord Dunsany became fascinated with the idea of building little cities out of candlesticks, chessmen, books, silver and glass boxes, dominoes, brass bowls, ashtrays and ivory figures. A room, Lord Dunsany told Mrs. Moore, is full of miniature domes and cupolas if you turn things the wrong way up, and it was at his Irish castle that E. Nesbit's story continued to take shape while they built one city after another and compared the respective virtues of clay bricks in the garden with wooden blocks indoors, which of course were only the base of their fantastic concoctions. So clever did Nesbit become, in fact, that one of her finest cities was put on public display at Olympia, and there is a photograph of it in Mrs. Moore's book.

But of course Eager's own little city, or rather the children's, was not so elegant as those constructed at the Irish castle, seat of the Dunsanys, but was put together with milk cartons, tea and baby-powder cans, bars of soap, bottles of nail polish, match boxes, and that all-important, enormously crucial, can of pea soup. And it never grew in size as Reinhold's did, but stayed clustered about the skirts of the castle and the children grew down to fit it when they entered another time, only to find that within its cardboard and tin and plastic and glass and polyethylene confines, the knights and ladies had turned vulgarly modern under the sheer power of looming influence. The knights had slacked off from the old high days of pageantry, jousting and knight-errantry and were playing baseball and indulging in Rhubarbs, riding in Wedgewood flying saucers, working up traffic snarls in their toy motor scooters, and sprawling around watching wrestling matches on television, their reverberant knightly language debased into modern slang. It all so sickened the children that they were not too regretful when one of their mothers in present time destroyed the city entirely by putting all the objects back where they belonged.

Anyone can borrow, and most of those working in the field of the arts constantly borrow—ideas, sometimes the whole feeling of other works of art, wittingly or unwittingly. Nabokov can be a clever skater, one reviewer said of him, in the way he stylishly traces another's figures: the Conradian *Laughter in the Dark,* or the Kafkaesque *Invitation to a Beheading.* But "an idea, like a ghost, according to the common notion of ghosts, must be spoken to a little before it will explain itself." In other words, each borrowed idea must be made indelibly and uniquely one's own, imbued with one's own light, transformed by an original cast of mind and a private manner of seeing. No one who is going to borrow from a master, or indeed from anyone, should attempt it if he has not spoken to the ghost a little—no, more than a little: he should have held communion for a year or two at the very least.

Charlotte S. Huck

SOURCE: "Modern Fantasy: *Half Magic,*" in *Children's Literature in the Elementary School,* third edition, updated, Holt, Rinehart and Winston, 1979, pp. 274-5.

The children in the many books of fantasy by Edward Eager frequently possess a magic object, know a magic saying, or have magical powers themselves. In *Half Magic,* Jane finds what she believes to be a nickel, but it is a magic charm, or at least half of a magic charm, for it provides half of all the children's wishes. For example, Katherine wished that their cat would talk, but no one could understand its garbled language. Thereafter, the children learned to double their wishes, so that half of them would come true. Each child in the family has an exciting adventure, including a trip to the Sahara Desert and one through time to the days of King Arthur! Another of Eager's stories, *Seven-day Magic,* tells of a magic book that the children borrow from the library. When they open the book, they find it is about themselves; everything they had done that morning was in the book and the rest of the book was shut tight waiting for them to create it. The children all agree that the best kind of book is a magic one, where:

. . . the people in the book would be walking home from somewhere and the magic would start suddenly before they knew it. . . . and then they'd have to tame the magic and learn its rules and thwart it.

When their wonderful book is due to be returned to the library at the end of seven days, they take it back. Logic and humor are characteristic of the many books of fantasy that were Eager's legacy of modern magic for today's children.

Joel D. Chaston

SOURCE: "Polistopolis and Torquilstone: Nesbit, Eager, and the Question of Imitation," in *The Lion and the Unicorn,* Vol. 17, No. 1, June, 1993, pp. 73-82.

In a 1958 essay in the *Horn Book,* "Daily Magic," Edward Eager acknowledges his debt to E. Nesbit, explaining that his own books for children "could not have existed if it were not for her influence." In fact, he feels obligated to mention her in them so he can lead his readers back to "the master of us all" and justified in imitating her work because "second-rate E. Nesbit is better than no E. Nesbit at all." Anyone who has read Eager's books will know that he is not exaggerating—they are filled with allusions to Nesbit's fiction. For example, Eager's characters often praise Nesbit's books, as when Abbie of *Seven Day Magic* (1962) complains that she has read everything Nesbit wrote and "nobody seems to do books like that any more." In *Knight's Castle* (1956), Ann and Roger's father is always wanting to read Nesbit's books to them. Later, Ann pronounces *The Magic City* (1910), "one of the crowned masterpieces of literature which have advanced civilization." In Eager's *Half Magic* (1954), the children believe Nesbit's works are "the most wonderful books in the world" and their magical adventures begin only after they have finished reading Nesbit's *The Enchanted Castle* (1907).

So effusive is Eager's praise of Nesbit and so frequent are his references to her books that critics such as Zena Sutherland, Ann Flowers, and Eleanor Cameron have dismissed his fiction as formulaic, agreeing that it is indeed "second-rate E. Nesbit." In particular, Cameron complains that Eager's *The Time Garden* (1958) is a mechanical imitation of Nesbit's *The Story of the Amulet* (1906). She explains that it is "as magical and subtle as the Automat, where you put in your dime and get a cup of coffee or, if you'd rather, a glass of tomato juice. Only instead of a dime, substitute the Natterjack who, on several occasions, is used by the children almost as unfeelingly as one uses a dime."

A quick glance at Eager's books seems to support the notion that he is mechanically copying Nesbit, that his imitations are a "dumbing down" of her work. But *Half Magic* and its sequel, *Magic by the Lake* (1957), borrow liberally from Nesbit's "Five Children" series. Like *Five Children and It* (1902), Eager's books involve the problems that result from the magical granting of children's capricious wishes. While this is a common plot device in children's fantasy, Eager is clearly imitating Nesbit. For example, in *Five Children and It*, a wish transforms the infant Lamb into a snobbish grown-up who has no time for his siblings. A similar wish has the same effect on Katherine and Jane in *Magic by the Lake*. Both Eager and Nesbit's fictional children wish themselves into medieval settings and onto desert islands and travel through time, often finding themselves in danger as a result. They also ask for rules to help them control the magic, so that grown-ups won't notice the magic's effects. At the same time, the cantankerous magical turtle of *Magic by the Lake* is clearly the Psammead of *Five Children and It* in disguise. Both creatures have lived for centuries, are reluctant to help the children, and are far from polite.

Eager's debt to Nesbit is also evident in both of his other series. In Eager's *Magic or Not?* (1959) and its sequel *The Well-Wishers* (1960), the protagonists compare their adventures to those described in Nesbit's *The Wonderful Garden* (1911) with good reason. In each of these works, the characters pretend they have discovered a source of magic, such as a wishing well or a garden. In the end, however, they are themselves the source of the "magic" they find. Perhaps Eager's most conscious imitation of Nesbit is *Knight's Castle,* in which characters travel to a toy city composed of books and household objects, much like the one in *The Magic City*. As already noted, Eleanor Cameron has criticized the sequel to this book, *The Time Garden,* because its Natterjack is yet another imitation of Nesbit's Psammead and Mouldiwarp.

One of the greatest similarities between the fantasies of Nesbit and Eager is their interest in childhood reading, Julia Briggs argues [in *A Woman of Passion: The Life of E. Nesbit*] that "all Edith's children's stories are preoccupied with the effect of reading upon the child, even though only a small number of them actually allow books as objects, with their contents, to be reified and figure significantly in the narrative." Nesbit's first children's book, the nonmagical *The Story of the Treasurer Seekers* (1899) and her last, the water fantasy, *Wet Magic* (1913), are excellent examples. Early in *Treasure Seekers*, Nesbit provides the reader with a list of the books the Bastables have read, which includes works by Sir Arthur Conan Doyle and Rudyard Kipling. During the course of the novel, the children are inspired by their reading to become detectives, search for a princess, and seek out a rich gentleman benefactor. Reading is so important to them, that they dub their simpering neighbor, Albert, "foolish and ignorant" because he has not read as many books as they have. In *Wet Magic,* one of the protagonists is greatly affected by Charles Kingsley's *The Water Babies* (1863). His love of fantasy, along with a few lines of Milton's poetry, send him and his siblings off on a journey that resembles the one in Kingsley's novel.

Eager's own concern with reading is, of course, evident in his references to Nesbit's books, although his fictional children are also influenced by other writers. In *Seven Day Magic,* the children read widely, including works such as *Little Women* (1869-70), *The Wizard of Oz* (1900),

Little House on the Prairie (1935), and Eager's own *Half Magic*. They also often discourse on the value of reading, sounding a little too much like Eager's 1948 essay in *The Horn Book,* "A Father's Minority Report."

Both Nesbit and Eager, however, go beyond mere allusions to other books, dramatizing their interest in childhood reading by allowing their protagonists to meet characters from the works they have read. For example, Nesbit's *The Enchanted Castle* features gods and goddesses from Greek mythology in the form of statues who come to life and *Wet Magic* includes a battle between villainous book people, such as Uriah Heep and the Giant Blunderbore, and heroic characters like Ivanhoe and the Queen of the Amazons. Eager's children have similar experiences, as in *Half Magic,* where young Katherine meets and defeats Sir Launcelot in a jousting match and wishes Morgan le Fay into a pond and, in *Seven Day Magic,* where characters meet Dickens's Tiny Tim and Little Nell as they frantically search for their friend, Barnaby.

Both Nesbit's *The Magic City* and Eager's *Knight's Castle* include similar encounters with literary creations as part of their authors' most developed explorations of the power of childhood reading. A close study of the way these two books treat this topic reveals that Eager is not merely a second-rate imitator, but that he rewrites Nesbit's books and those of others, transforming them into something original, going far beyond mere imitation. Moreover, in many ways *Knight's Castle* is more subversive than *The Magic City*. In Nesbit's book, while she occasionally pokes fun at other literary texts, she argues for the value of imaginative literature. The city itself, which becomes a metaphor for the power of reading, transforms its protagonists into heroic characters like those of their favorite stories. In *Knight's Castle,* however, Eager outwardly appears to celebrate reading, but actually criticizes the very works he seems to praise, arguing for his own brand of "daily magic," as well as the importance of imitation and reinterpretation of earlier works. Eager's miniature city, too, represents the world of reading, but it is its literary characters who are changed by the children who come from the real world.

Like many of Nesbit's characters, Philip, the protagonist of *The Magic City,* bases his conception of the world on his reading, which, in the tradition of *Don Quixote,* sometimes misleads him. At the beginning of the book, Philip senses that a misfortune has occurred and he guesses that his older sister, Helen, has lost all of their money or been accused of forgery. The reader is told that all "the books Philip had ever read worked together in his mind to produce these melancholy suggestions." Clearly, Nesbit is highlighting the lack of reality of some of the melodramatic books Philip has read. Although they are unfounded, these fears heighten his concern over his sister's impending marriage.

Nesbit continues to mine other literary works for humor after Philip and Lucy, the daughter of Helen's new husband, are magically transported to the magic city. On their trip through the desert, the children are accompanied by a parrot who frequently recites *The Aeneid,* which is described as "poetry of a rather dull kind that went on and on." This same parrot attacks the nursery rhyme, "Polly put the kettle on" because it is "quite false." She maintains that Polly "never did put a kettle on, and . . . never will." Later, after various historical figures have escaped from the books that line the city, Nesbit suggests that the schoolmasters will lose their jobs if these fictional creations don't go back where they came from.

Nevertheless, most of the time, *The Magic City* celebrates the value of reading, making a strong case for the relationship between reading and the development of the imagination. To begin with, the magic city itself has been created from books and becomes a symbol of the power of reading. Even its weather has come from a book of poetry. As the parrot explains:

> We got a lot out of that page, rain and sun and sky and clouds, mountains, gardens, roses, lilies, flowers in general, "Blossoms of delight" they were called in the book and trees and the sea, and the desert and silver and iron—as much of all of them as anybody could possibly want. There are no limits to poets' imaginations, you know.

A whole island of people has also come to life from a few lines of poetry which speak of "gentle islanders."

When the children seek out the Great Sloth, other elements escape from books and affect their adventure. As their ship, the *Lightning Loose,* rushes on through the darkness, Philip remarks, "All this is out of a book. Some one must have let it out. I know what book it's out of, too. And if the whole story got out of the book, we're all right." He is referring to *The Last Cruise of the Teal,* which he calls, "a ripping book." Lucy's nurse, the "Pretenderette," has opened it up in an attempt to prevent the children from achieving their quest. She quickly shifts to other books. As a result, the children encounter an underground lake from a book about Mexico and an empty bucket from the *Arabian Nights,* which takes Lucy up into the sky.

Even the people and animals who populate the magic city have come from works of literature, for instance, the Hippogriff, the parrot, and the Great Sloth. Although they began as toy figures, Noah and his wife have become modern versions of their Biblical counterparts. In fact, Noah builds an ark to save the Happy Islanders who, along with Lucy, are rescued from a miniature version of the deluge. Later, the children must defeat "the barbarians of Gaul," whom the Pretenderette has released from a book. As the captain of the guard tells the children, when she opened up the giant books in the Hall of Justice, "soldiers came marching out. The Sequani and the Aedui they call themselves." The children respond by calling forth, from the same book, a very literary and heroic Julius Caesar, who also resembles Lucy's father.

In the end, it is the power of reading that helps the children successfully complete their quest and vanquish the

barbarians and the Nurse. For Philip, reading provides comfort and vicarious experience, which keep him from being afraid. His comments about *The Aeneid* notwithstanding, Philip tells one of the citizens of Polistopolis that he loves poetry. This is borne out later, when he recites a long poem while waiting for his bath. The poem, "Dreams of a Giant Life," has been written by Philip's sister and describes how a young boy's imagination transports him to a fantasy world while bathing, only to be reluctantly called back to reality. The poem, which validates his own fantasizing, provides him with some comfort, which he has not received from a single person he has met since Helen's marriage.

In Polistopolis, it becomes clear that Philip's reading has helped prepare him to become the "Deliverer," a title he hopes to earn. In part, this is because his literary experience makes every new adventure familiar. As he enters the city, everything about it reminds him of something he has read. The ground makes him think of the prairie in one of his books and a ladder recalls Jack's beanstalk. Later, when he returns home, the empty rooms make him think of *Sleeping Beauty.* His prior reading also instills in him certain notions of chivalry, providing him with courage because he has read that knights are not afraid; and he remembers the story of St. George, which taught him that heroes always defeat their enemies.

Eventually, the children themselves are transformed into figures of romance, acting out stories they have read as they complete the seven deeds of power that will save Polistopolis and return them home. Philip, like his hero, St. George, slays a dragon. Like many folk heroines, Lucy completes an impossible domestic task, in this case, the unraveling of a gigantic rug. Later, they both save the Happy Islanders from drowning, Polistarchia from the oppressive Sloth, and Polistopolis from the Pretenderette. As part of their heroic roles, both children also dress the part. Philip adopts the armor of a crusader and Lucy the finery of a princess. At the end of the novel, Philip and Lucy become less ordinary and more heroic. Philip finally appreciates Lucy and is willing to accept his sister's marriage. Lucy makes friends with Philip and proves to him her own abilities. When they return home, their adventures only make them want to read more. As Philip tells Caesar before he leaves, "I'll swot up my Latin like anything next term, so as to read all about you."

Many of these same ideas are present in Eager's **Knight's Castle,** and a superficial reading of this book may suggest that it is, in fact, little more than a mechanical imitation of *The Magic City.* Indeed, as the children embark on their adventure, they have Nesbit's book in mind, particularly Ann and Eliza who have just read it. In chapter 3, which is actually called "The Magic City," Nesbit's book inspires the two girls to add on to Jack's toy castle. When completed, their city is a modern version of Philip's, in *The Magic City:*

> A sidewalk of stone blocks led away from the castle, flanked by a double row of glittering columns that ended suddenly where the supply of old ginger ale

bottles had given out. There was an imposing building made of books, labeled "Public Library," and another beautiful one made of different-colored cakes of soap, labeled "Public Baths." And since you can always find more drinking glasses and glass ashtrays and perfume bottles than you can anything else when you're building a magic city, the whole area sparkled with transparent domes and pinnacles.

As in *The Magic City,* the children of **Knight's Castle** soon magically travel to the city they have created. In this case, instead of meeting Noah and Caesar, they interact with the characters of Sir Walter Scott's *Ivanhoe.* Like Philip and Lucy, they, too, embark on a quest to help save the castle, this time from Prince John and his army.

Like *The Magic City,* **Knight's Castle** is preoccupied with its characters' reading. Its four children—Roger, Ann, Eliza, and Jack—are all great readers, which gives rise to some sermonizing about the value of literature. The book begins by describing Roger's and Ann's reading habits. They both love fantasy, particularly Nesbit's, which their Eager-like father insists on reading to them, although they like other books as well. Roger devours science fiction and "yeomanly" books like *The White Company* and *The Scottish Chiefs,* while Ann leans toward *Little Women* and the Betsy-Tacy books. Their cousins also have been exposed to fantasy, although Eliza feels she has grown into more adult books and that magic is babyish, while Jack likes factual and scientific works. All four of the children love *Ivanhoe,* although Jack and Eliza know it primarily through the film version.

Despite their love of books, however, the four children often discover that what they have read is false. For example, because of a few lines in an encyclopedia, Ann mistakenly deduces that everything in Baltimore is orange. Later, Roger is surprised to learn that his social studies book is wrong and that the castle was not always the hub of activity in medieval times. Because he relies so heavily on books to interpret the world, the other children claim it has given him a feeble brain.

While at the castle, Torquilstone, the four children eventually come to realize that they can not rigidly adhere to what they have read. Their fantasy world, like Nesbit's magic city, has been created from parts of books. Yet, it has taken on a life of its own and its fictional inhabitants refuse to follow Scott's *Ivanhoe.* In Roger's first visit to the castle, he inadvertently alerts Bois-Guilbert that the castle will catch on fire. When Bois-Guilbert moves to prevent this from taking place, Roger exclaims, "You can't do that: it's not in the book!" As the book continues, the inhabitants of Torquilstone refuse to follow Scott's narrative. Ivanhoe does not act heroically, and spends most of his time on a couch reading science fiction, and Rowena shows her true colors by helping the Normans. Later, when the children have to rebuild the dismantled castle, Roger tells them that they "ought to go by the book," keeping the adventure as close to *Ivanhoe* as possible. Eliza counters that the characters aren't following the story, which makes what happens more interesting.

Ultimately, **Knight's Castle** is actually quite subversive, a quality which Alison Lurie finds in most "great works of juvenile literature." Lurie claims [in *Don't Tell the Grown-ups: Subversive Children's Literature*] that such books "express ideas and emotions not generally approved of or even recognized at the time; they make fun of honored figures and piously held beliefs; and they view social pretenses with clear-eyed directness, remarking—as in Andersen's famous tale—that the emperor has no clothes." Throughout the book, the same Eager who seems to indiscriminately praise childhood reading criticizes many other works of fiction as he defends his own brand of fantasy. Early in the novel, the four children discover an inherent, underlying falsity in *Ivanhoe*—that the character, Rowena, is, in reality, stiff, whiney, and selfish and that Ivanhoe ought to have married the superior Rebecca. When Eliza makes this point, Roger explains, "That wasn't what the author wrote . . ." "Oh, that old Sir Walter Scott," Eliza retorts, "A lot he knew about anything!" As the novel progresses, the children manage to rewrite Ivanhoe to their liking. In particular, Ivanhoe now marries Rebecca and becomes friends with his enemy, De Bracy.

Eager is not content to merely criticize Scott and knightly romances. In the miniature world, the children also act out other fictional genres, including science fiction, domestic fiction, and sports stories, each of which Eager also satirizes. Like Roger, Ivanhoe becomes obsessed with reading science fiction, which Roger's father has previously defined as "having bad dreams on purpose." This prompts the children to embark on an unpleasant journey to another planet in a flying Wedgewood saucer, which feels "like a thousand Empire State Building elevator rides mixed up with a thousand merry-go-rounds." Later, they have a horrifying encounter with giant dolls who act out a very unimaginative, dull, realistic family story. Shortly after this, the knights of Torquilstone are transformed into baseball players. The siege becomes a sports story which, as the children discover, does not settle their differences.

Like Eager's own books, the city the children create is based on imitation of and borrowing from other works of literature. Like Nesbit's magic city, it becomes a metaphor for reading, but it also suggests Eager's own feelings about imitating the works of others. The city and the children's adventures there have been created from *Ivanhoe,* mixed with elements from other literary sources. Eager and his fictional children, however, are not content with merely following the stories of others rigidly. They must create their own story, making something new and original from the pieces they have borrowed.

At the same time, the romance of Ivanhoe and his castle is increasingly transformed into the sort of fantasy Eager praises—that in which magic is held to a minimum and made real through its connection to the modern world. This is the kind of book that he believes Nesbit wrote. In it, there are "no dragons and ogres or Mock Turtles and Tin Woodmen." It is "the ordinary or garden world we all know, with just the right pinch of magic added. So that after you finish reading [it] you feel it could all happen to *you,* any day now, round any corner." Thus, Eager's magic city becomes modernized with knights riding motorcycles and buildings with "glass and chromium, and glaring electric lamps and neon signs . . ." At times, the children find it a little too modern, especially when Ivanhoe gives up any desire to perform great deeds, and Sir John becomes a neo-Nazi, requiring that Roger's World War II toy soldiers defeat him.

In the end, however, it is the castle's balance of realism and fantasy that attracts the children. What has engaged them is that the magic is happening to them; it is everyday magic and the fictional characters they meet are rather ordinary. At the end of the novel, after Roger has re-enacted an episode from Arthurian legend by pulling a can-opener out of a gigantic can of peas, Ivanhoe and his friends return to their original chivalric states and the children, who are realistic and ordinary, are thrust back into their own world by the words of power. Their adventures have not changed them; instead, they have changed the story of *Ivanhoe,* altering it to one of their own liking.

Ultimately, Eager has transformed *The Magic City* into something original, a work which, like the castle he describes, borrows elements from many stories, but reinvents them, making them into something unique. He does not rigidly adhere to either *The Magic City* or Scott's *Ivanhoe.* Instead, he creates his own kind of fantasy, one which deserves critical attention beyond its association with Nesbit's earlier book. It is readily apparent that Eager is not merely an imitator. Perhaps it is for this reason that his books are still popular today. Clearly, both *The Magic City* and **Knight's Castle** validate the importance of reading and literary imitation, particularly for the writer who, like the young architects of Polistopolis and Torquilstone, creates literary worlds for young readers to explore.

TITLE COMMENTARY

📖 *RED HEAD* (1951)

Virginia Kirkus' Bookshop Service

SOURCE: A review of *Red Head,* in *Virginia Kirkus' Bookshop Service,* Vol. XIX, No. 18, September 15, 1951, p. 528.

Rhymed nonsense of comfort to all red heads who cringe or have tantrums when the nickname "Red" blisters the air. "Fritz" was a perfectly nice name, but because of his flaming top-knot people said "Hi, Red!" Running away didn't help either because bees, bulls, and even ships at sea were much too curious, or angry or entirely mistaken about the luminous noggin. But Fritz is very glad he has such an unusual head of hair when his crowning glory lights him home to safety. Bumpity rhyme with appropriately ridiculous pictures in sunset colors by Louis Slobodkin.

New York Herald Tribune Book Review

SOURCE: A review of *Red Head,* in *New York Herald Tribune Book Review,* November 11, 1951, p. 12.

If there is a boy under six within your ken who has red hair and hates it, offer him an odd little book **Red Head** by Edward Eager, with many pictures by Louis Slobodkin. Rollicking verses carry poor Fritz off on adventures that change from unhappy to heroic, and he comes home at last glad that his hair is so red. For non-red-heads, it seems very forced and not important.

Phyllis Fenner

SOURCE: A review of *Red Head,* in *Library Journal,* Vol. 76, No. 20, November 15, 1951, p. 1942.

This book is lots of fun with its clever rhymes about a little redheaded boy who dislikes his hair so much that he runs away.

> "Fritz didn't like it; his name was Fritz.
> And he blamed his hair, 'cause the fault was its."

He was chased by a bull who "saw red," by bees who thought he was a red flower, and numerous other individuals. He was glad to get home again. Pictures are typical Slobodkin, colorful and vague.

Jennie D. Lindquist and Siri M. Andrews

SOURCE: A review of *Red Head,* in *The Horn Book Magazine,* Vol. XXVII, No. 6, December, 1951, p. 403.

I thought I was tired of stories written in rhyme, there has been such a flood of them; but of course it's never safe to generalize and I wouldn't have missed **Red Head!** The amusing turn of phrase and clever use of rhyming words as well as the plot give it real humor. The young hero was called "Red" for obvious reasons. "Fritz didn't like it; his name was Fritz! And he blamed his hair, 'cause the fault was its, . . ." Louis Slobodkin is just the artist to picture Fritz's adventures.

📖 *MOUSE MANOR* (1952)

Virginia Kirkus' Bookshop Service

SOURCE: A review of *Mouse Manor,* in *Virginia Kirkus' Bookshop Service,* Vol. XX, No. 15, August 15, 1952, p. 451.

In the British tradition of the humanized animal story, this is a charmingly illustrated vignette of a lonely Victorian country mouse's adventures in the city. Miss Myrtilla Mouse, fed up with a dreary existence as sole tenant of draughty, dusty Mouse Manor, goes to London. In town, acquaintance with some palace mice, the Cheesebiskers and cavortings in the throne room where Myrtilla frightens an officiating Queen Victoria result in marriage with dapper Bertie Cheesebiskers and joint efforts that turn Mouse Manor into a prosperous country inn. Beryl Bailey-Jones' softly-hued drawings of exquisitely clad mice are fetching glimpses of tickling escapades.

Louise S. Bechtel

SOURCE: A review of *Mouse Manor,* in *New York Herald Tribune Book Review,* October 5, 1952, p. 8.

Quite a few stories, long and short, have had their climax in boy or cat looking at Queen Victoria. Here a procession of all the cats of London is allowed to "look" on Christmas Day among them the sworn enemy of Miss Myrtilla Mouse, who is also looking on. How she left her lonely big mansion to come to London, how there she found Mr. Albert Cheesebrisker, married him, and turned the mansion into a hotel, is the gist of this picture-story for ages six to nine. Both text and pictures slightly satirize the Victorian era, the pictures, of which nine are in full color, giving amusing details of costumes and interiors.

One hesitates to be too critical of a talking animal fantasy dreamed up by a father who was inspired by reading aloud from Beatrix Potter. As he himself says, it is neither "coy nor slapstick." To like it, you will have to find fun in rabbits who exchange hand-painted calendars, a mouse nibbling on the manuscript of *A Christmas Carol* and finding it "most succulent," and a finale in which "We are not amused" has become a byword. We cannot rate it high, but we expect the pictures [by Beryl Bailey-Jones] will sell it widely.

Ellen Lewis Buell

SOURCE: "Off to London," in *The New York Times Book Review,* November 9, 1952, p. 52.

Victorian in setting, whimsical in approach, **Mouse Manor,** says its author, was inspired (like a great many other books) by Beatrix Potter. Such a statement, even by its creator, invites an unfair comparison. Certainly this bears little resemblance to any of Miss Potter's stories, being longer, more complicated in plot and lacking her pristine simplicity. Nevertheless, this story of a timid country mouse who journeys to London to see the Queen has a charm of its own. I doubt if young children will appreciate fully Miss Myrtilla's brief encounter with Mr. Dickens and her introduction to *A Christmas Carol* or the slightly satirical portrait of Bertie Cheesebisker, the dashing Cockney mouse. They will, however, enjoy the cozy details of Miss Myrtilla's housekeeping, her adventures on the train and the comic uproar she creates when she arrives in court. Beryl Bailey-Jones' sharply defined black and white illustrations are more successful in catching the humor of the story than are her rather gaudy colored pictures.

Virginia Haviland

SOURCE: A review of *Mouse Manor,* in *The Horn Book Magazine,* Vol. XXVIII, No. 6, December, 1952, p. 399.

Intended by this American writer to carry the tradition of Beatrix Potter to children older than the *Peter Rabbit* audience, this story has captured something of English style and humor. [Bailey-Jones's] charming illustrations, many full-page, with lovely colors and quaint Victorian details, help much to tell the tale of shy, genteel Miss Myrtilla Mouse Manor and her surprising Christmas trip to London. Her meeting with Bertie Cheesebisker, a gallant cockney mouse who becomes her suitor; her ride in Charles Dickens' pocket, where a nibble of *A Christmas Carol* proves not quite to her taste; and her unexpected visit to Queen Victoria's court provide plenty of adventure for young children who may miss some of the subtleties and allusions.

HALF MAGIC (1954)

Elizabeth Nesbitt

SOURCE: A review of *Half Magic,* in *The Saturday Review,* New York, Vol. 37, No. 20, May 15, 1954, pp. 62-3.

This story belongs to the E. Nesbit school of fantasy, in which magic pursues its inevitable course. The author ingeniously and ingratiatingly acknowledges his debt in the first chapter. At the beginning of the summer vacation, four children bring home from the library a copy of *The Enchanted Castle.* Quite naturally they wish that they were like the children in the book, to whom exciting things happen. The fact that Jane finds something which she at first takes to be a nickel does not relieve their boredom. However, since their states of mind are those in which children say "I wish" every minute, they soon begin to notice, with awe, the instantaneous effect of Jane's wishes, which come true, but only half true. Before long, they make the association between Jane's possession of the presumed coin and the half effectiveness of her wishes. A few startling experiences with the half magic of the charm enable them to master the arithmetic which will enable them to phrase their desires so that their wishes will be granted entire. The children accept without question the idiosyncrasies of the magic which has fallen into their hands, but disconcerted adults attribute the results to mental aberration.

The chief effect of such a book is humor, arising from the ridiculous yet logical situations due to the unyielding laws of magic in conflict with the modern world. To be acceptable, such humor must be unforced and inherent in incident and situation. With one possible exception, **Half Magic** meets this requirement. Some may prefer that the children had not wished themselves back to the days of King Arthur. Here the story loses its sureness of touch, and the humor seems strained. But this is a minor fault in a book whose total contribution is one of fun and relaxation.

New York Herald Tribune Book Review

SOURCE: A review of *Half Magic*, in *New York Herald Tribune Book Review*, May 16, 1954, p. 10.

The four children whose magic coin changed one summer completely and brought them a stepfather were great readers. Their adventures began after one of them had read one of Mrs. Nesbit's books aloud, and they mourned that such things couldn't happen to them. Their mother was "the pride of the Toledo Blade," (actually, its Women's Club editor; with one of their final rubs of the coin the children tried to give her her dreams too) and they were left to a stern housekeeper most of the time. Their wishes took them first to the world of Sir Lancelot and the Knights (exciting but possibly not successful unless children recognize satire on this period); then, by a mistake about the "half," to the Arabian desert instead of to a desert island. Each child's wish works out with surprising revelations for that special one; in a satisfying final chapter, they agree about the strange good worked on them by this weird week, and also about disposing of the coin.

The value and charm of this unusual modern fantasy have been debated by critics and will be by children, too. They will either appreciate heartily or dislike the honest child talk of these three girls and one brother, put down with a wit and realism seldom achieved since Richard Hughes or perhaps in both books about *Homer Price*. Like many of the most honestly portrayed book children, these four are not always too lovable, and the thirty-year ago setting, so wonderfully well caught by the able illustrator [N. M. Bodecker], will seem funnier to adults. The bit of satire on the child psychologist is off key; Jane deserved a better adventure.

We enjoyed it. There is a masterly quality in Eager's lively style. originality in his interweaving of adventures in time and space on the level of nine to twelve, and satisfaction in the character changes he works out. Many American children who are not in the least lured by Mrs. Nesbit, or even *Alice,* will find this the sort of fantasy they do like. And the mother's love story really is hilarious, done truly from the point of view of children of this age. The sections less liked will be few and different for each reader; our favorite is the part where the four see their own mother, still wearing her hat of the twenties, riding bareback under the Big Top.

Jennie D. Lindquist

SOURCE: A review of *Half Magic*, in *The Horn Book Magazine*, Vol. XXX, No. 3, June, 1954, p. 174.

Mr. Eager and his young son have long been devoted admirers of E. Nesbit, and this is frankly in the E. Nesbit tradition—about a family of American children who love

her books so much that they are on the lookout for some way of making magic themselves. Wonder of wonders, it comes to them in the shape of a mysterious coin that grants them half of any wish they make and lands them in all sorts of amusing situations. It is an unusually good book: the humor never falls flat; the author never rides any situation to death; the story holds up to the very end. It is shorter than the E. Nesbit books and may well lead many children to hers. Nothing, we feel sure, could please Mr. Eager more.

The Times Literary Supplement

SOURCE: "The World of Magic," in *The Times Literary Supplement*, No. 2755, November 19, 1954, p. vii.

Never begin with the fairies. If it were possible to formulate a set of rules for the writers of children's fantasies derived from the classic models, this would certainly be the first. Alice playing with the kitten, the Five Children digging in the grave-pit, Griselda of *The Cuckoo Clock,* disconsolate in the dull house with elderly aunts—these are the necessary preludes to the pervasive magic which suspends disbelief. It is the smooth passage from the real to the fantastic, the strange turning which it seems so simple for anyone to take that delights the readers of Carroll, Nesbit and Molesworth.

There are no writers to-day who achieve quite this effortless fusion of two worlds, but there are several who come near it. This year, Mr. Edward Eager with **Half Magic** is far and away the best. Frankly inspired, as he is, by the tales of Mrs. Nesbit, Mr. Eager contributes a most original and pleasing touch of his own to this story of four children in an Ohio town who do not go away for the holidays because their father is dead and their mother "worked very hard on the other newspaper, the one almost nobody in the street took." With his first paragraphs, Mr. Eager brings the children instantly to life. "Katharine was the middle girl, of docile disposition and a comfort to her mother. She knew she was a comfort, and docile, because she'd heard her mother say so. And the others knew she was, too, by now, because ever since that day Katharine *would* keep boasting about what a comfort she was, and how docile, until Jane declared she would utter a piercing shriek and fall over dead if she heard another word about it." The children complain that the sort of things which happened in *The Enchanted Castle* simply do not happen in Toledo, Ohio. Only, with the discovery of the funny little coin which looks like a bus token, they do. The idea of a charm which gives you only *half* your wish is a very good one though it naturally leads to a lot of complications, particularly for those who have not learnt fractions. How for instance, to make the cat stop half-talking in a spitting kind of way, was a problem in itself. The holidays, at any rate, are very far from dull, either for the children or for Mr. Eager's readers. For his character drawing no praise can be too high. If a criticism is to be made, it is that Mr. Eager allows himself in one chapter to guy the Court of King Arthur in a way of which few children will approve.

The Junior Bookshelf

SOURCE: A review of *Half Magic,* in *The Junior Bookshelf,* Vol. 18, No. 6, December, 1954, p. 292.

At the beginning this fantastic story promised well, with the adventures of some children when they picked up a lucky coin. Their adventures follow too fast and become muddled. Quick, smart and funny, the story will carry the child reader along but it has nothing of permanent value and as a story of magic falls far below a number of English stories with a similar interest.

May Hill Arbuthnot

SOURCE: "Magic and Make-Believe for the Middle Years: Half Magic," in *Children's Reading in the Home,* Scott Foresman and Company, 1969, pp. 157-8.

Mr. Eager may call his book **Half Magic,** but there is no question that his own magic as a writer of fantasy for children is full strength. He commands absorbed reading interest from the first page to the last. In **Half Magic,** Jane, Mark, Katharine, and Martha are facing a dull summer in the city with their widowed mother hard at work. Then Jane finds what she thinks is an ordinary nickel, but it isn't. Jane discovers that it grants wishes, not entirely, only half way. However, the children soon learn to manage that by wishing twice as far or once again. So Mark got them all to the Sahara desert, Katherine took them back to the time of Sir Lancelot, and their mother, having borrowed what she thought was Jane's nickel, found a stranger who brought her safely home and eventually played an important and happy part in their lives. The magic in this story is so rooted in everyday life that it seems plausible enough to happen to any of us.

Noél Perrin

SOURCE: "Magic That Endures: Two Classic Children's Spellbinders Turn 40," in *The New York Times Book Review,* November 14, 1993, p. 54.

[In] 1954, in the United States, another late-blooming children's writer published a book—not his first, but his first really good one. Edward Eager was 43 when *Half Magic* appeared. He too had already lived a lot. He had dropped out of Harvard to write plays, having already written one while still an undergraduate, a play so successful that he lived for some time on the royalties. When he turned out not to be a major playwright, he drifted into the then-new world of television and discovered he had a talent for adapting grand operas, so as to make them sufficiently ungrand for small screens. He married, became a father and grew passionately fond of reading aloud to his son. While doing so, he first encountered the classic children's writer E. Nesbit. That encounter led to his book.

[Lucy Boston's] *The Children of Green Knowe* and *Half Magic* have more in common than the fact that they are very good books by authors who started late. The important thing they have in common is magic itself. One has solemn magic and the other a more playful kind, but both are able, in an almost literal sense, to hold children spellbound. . . .

[*Half Magic*] takes place in Toledo, Ohio, in the early 1920's. There is a really nice family consisting of four children and their mother. The mother works for a Toledo newspaper, making just enough money to scrape by. It is summer, but there is no way she can afford a lakefront cottage or anything like that. So how are Jane, Mark, Katharine and Martha spending their days? Reading, mostly. One good thing about the Toledo library is that in the summer you can check out 10 books at a time, instead of winter's measly 3.

By chance they bring home one of E. Nesbit's stories about four English children who have magical adventures. Like Edward Eager, they instantly fall in love with the book. Soon they have read all of Nesbit. A few days later, their own magic begins.

Jane spots a shiny round bit of metal in a crack in the sidewalk. She takes it to be a nickel and puts it in her pocket. Later the same day, feeling a little bored, she wishes there would be a fire. Within minutes firetrucks go screaming by. The children naturally follow. Eight blocks away, they find a rather elaborate child's playhouse crackling in flames. Apparently Jane got her wish, but on a small scale.

After two more events like this, the children have worked everything out; what Jane found is truly a magic charm, but one that grants only half of what you ask. For example, Martha, the youngest child, only 6, gets hold of the charm and wishes that Carrie, the family cat, could talk. "Purrxx," says Carrie "Wah oo merghtz, Fitzahhh!" Carrie is half-talking.

Carrie hates being compelled to talk, even in this garbled way, and demands to be returned to mewing. Jane has an idea. "I wish that Carrie the cat may in future say nothing but the word 'music,'" she says. She is thinking, of course, of the first syllable.

"'Sick,' said Carrie the cat. 'Sick sick sick sick sick. . .'

"She *looked* sick."

This is the sort of thing that makes the book such a pleasure. The children always have to guess how the half magic will work. They get almost as clever as lawyers at wording things carefully, but they get tricked from time to time, right to the end.

Meanwhile, they have spent a good while in King Arthur's England, a shorter time in a strange house in Toledo where Jane has by mistake turned herself half into someone else, and so on. *Half Magic* is a funny, charming, timeless book, as much pleasure to read to a child now as it was

40 years ago. Those who had it read to them then may even have an obligation to pass on the pleasure.

Lucy Boston wrote six books about Green Knowe during her long life, and Edward Eager . . . wrote eight that employ magic. Nearly all are worth reading. But in each case the first is the best. *The Children of Green Knowe* has a special claim in that it ranks with Dickens's *Christmas Carol* and possibly Rumer Godden's *Story of Holly and Ivy* as a perfect thing to read just before Christmas. But *Half Magic* is so joyous. Both books are all magic.

📖 *PLAYING POSSUM* (1955)

Virginia Kirkus' Service

SOURCE: A review of *Playing Possum*, in *Virginia Kirkus' Service*, Vol. XXIII, No. 7, April 1, 1955, p. 248.

Here's a marvellous bit of realism that puts little embroidery on an incident common to everyday life but seldom found in picture books. A possum is trapped in a barrel, and a family—mother, father and young son—are at odds as to the animal's identity and what to do about it. Parental distaste and misinformation bring on the exterminator, *and* firm instructions to young Billy to let the poor creature "die in peace." But Billy, who knows it is only a possum playing p . . . . . ., sneaks out to tip over the barrel and let the possum escape. Paul Galdone's drawings, many of them from a possum's point of view, are sharp commentaries, not without satire, on human and animal nature.

Heloise P. Mailloux

SOURCE: A review of *Playing Possum*, in *The Horn Book Magazine*, Vol. XXXI, No. 4, August, 1955, p. 258.

The possum only meant to investigate the new people's rubbish barrel; he climbed in, but he couldn't climb out. Unfortunately, the new man and his wife thought the possum was a "big old rat," and though their little boy knew better, nobody would listen to him—at least, not at first. A combination of obtuse adults and bright child is, perhaps, a lazy device for moving a plot, but the laziness of the possum seems to atone for it in this story. Children think it very funny that, realizing himself trapped, he merely observes, "Oh well, eight hours' sleep never hurt anybody." His subsequent reactions to dangers like the exterminator seem progressively funnier. The illustrations [by Paul Galdone] show a properly rakish possum and add a good bit of humor.

📖 *KNIGHT'S CASTLE* (1956)

Ethna Sheehan

SOURCE: "Magic-Prone," in *The New York Times Book Review*, February 26, 1956, p. 30.

From the moment the old lead soldier warmed to life in Roger's hand, magic was in the air. Things really began to move when Roger, Ann and their cousins marshaled the knights and ladies of the toy castle into position for a reenactment of the siege of Torquilstone in *Ivanhoe*. During several nights the children enjoyed extraordinary adventures in the castle, Ann's doll house and a magic city modeled from a story by E. Nesbit. The events were as wildly out of kilter as the props were incongruous: Prince John organized a collective farm; Saxons and Normans contended on the baseball diamond; Ivanhoe rode to Rebecca's rescue in a Flying Saucer. In blithe defiance of Scott, Rebecca became the bride of Ivanhoe and the insipid Rowena married De Bracy.

The children were magic-prone for their mothers in their youth and had a part in *Half Magic*, an earlier book by Mr. Eager. *Knight's Castle* is slower than its predecessor in getting under way. The plotting is somewhat complex and the writing is underlaid with poetic tags and references to characters of romance and fairy lore. This will confuse some readers; others may well be led to sampling the good things that influenced Roger and Ann.

Louise S. Bechtel

SOURCE: A review of *Knight's Castle*, in *New York Herald Tribune Book Review*, March 4, 1956, p. 8.

That bold author who had the idea of reviving the fantasy method of Mrs. Nesbit in *Half Magic*, now gives us more fun in a still better book. A brother and sister aged eleven and eight (the age range of probable readers or listeners, according to brightness of wit and reading background) for a sad reason must visit their wealthy cousins in Baltimore. Roger takes along his wonderful collection of model soldiers; some had belonged to his father and his grandfather, and one special one went way, way back in their family. To cheer them, the children are given a marvelous toy castle. They take properties from an unwanted new doll house to supplement the soldiers, and start to act out the story of Ivanhoe.

Now we have no "half magic" but whole, as first Roger, then Ann and the cousins, through the "Old One's" doings, are swept back into the world of Ivanhoe and Robin Hood, of King Richard and wicked Prince John. There are battles and wild escapes, there is the mystery of the "words of power" that must be spoken and acted out truly. Each time the children are swept into their dream world, it is more exciting. The magic involves not only the real castle of Torquilstone but the statue of St. George Peabody in Baltimore. It also works toward Roger's "earning" his father's recovery.

The children are modern, lively indeed, and real. The talk of the characters from Scott is a priceless mixture of old and new, possibly much as children would imagine it. This sort of partly satiric fun may even lure readers who thought they were beyond the fairy-tale age.

Aileen O'Brien Murphy

SOURCE: A review of *Knight's Castle,* in *The Saturday Review,* New York, Vol. XXXIX, No. 10, March 10, 1956, p. 30.

An ancient toy Crusader is the talisman which thrusts four children out of their play with toy soldiers, a castle, a doll's house, and dolls into a world peopled chiefly by characters from *Ivanhoe.* Scott's creations have been refined and modernized by the imagination of the children, and their conversation is a marvelous mixture of language borrowed from Scott and Howard Pyle and liberally enlivened by modern idiom. This is a delicious spoof which can be enjoyed on more than one level. It has validity as a fairy tale for those who have never read *Ivanhoe* and as a nonsense story for those who have. The parents of the children were the heroes of *Half Magic,* the author's first book.

Charlotte Jackson

SOURCE: A review of *Knight's Castle,* in *The Atlantic Monthly,* Vol. 197, No. 6, June, 1956, p. 83.

Knight's Castle by Edward Eager is another highly entertaining book where the author has skillfully combined believable magic and the feeling of warm family relationship. The children, with their lively imaginations, do exactly the sort of thing that children everywhere will recognize and appreciate. This would be a good time for rereading *Ivanhoe* and *Robin Hood* and several others of the old classics that helped Roger and Ann to enjoy their magical journeys thoroughly.

The Junior Bookshelf

SOURCE: A review of *Knight's Castle,* in *The Junior Bookshelf,* Vol. 20, No. 6, December, 1956, p. 336.

This is another story by the author of *Half Magic.* Not quite so original as that first book, it is still highly successful. The setting is Baltimore, Maryland. A family are unwillingly there, staying with relations, instead of holidaying in some more romantic place, because the father has to go into a particular hospital. As compensation, the three children are given certain magical powers. These are unpredictable, and like all magic, not entirely satisfactory, very much akin to the magic that works through rings and amulets in the books of E. Nesbit. Indeed the main enchantment of this book is based on Mrs. Nesbit's *Magic City* idea. The children, who are very civilised young Americans, interested at the moment in knights and tin soldiers and experts on *Ivanhoe,* extend their toy fort by building round it a city of books and bottles. Into this they are drawn to have their adventures.

These goings on happen at night, but they seem too solid to be dreams. There is no airy fairy fancy about Mr. Eager's work. He writes with the careful pedantic touch of a grown up playing a child's game. His children, in their real lives, are very well drawn; the conversation between them, and their observations, are never dull.

Betty Brazier

SOURCE: A review of *Knight's Castle,* in *The School Librarian,* Vol. 8, No. 4, March, 1957, p. 317.

Knight's Castle is a disappointing successor to *Half magic,* this author's earlier attempt to follow directly in the Nesbit tradition. In this book, the magic is no longer "real"— it is restricted and consequently unbelievable. There is a feeling that the children are not really enjoying themselves in the world of magic, an essential quality of a successful fantasy. The theme is one where children play with a toy castle, setting it up as a city in different periods, and peopling it with characters from *Ivanhoe.* The city becomes reality and the children enter into its life, taking part in the romantic and chivalrous adventures which follow. A fantasy turned into the fantastic.

MAGIC BY THE LAKE (1957)

New York Herald Tribune Book Review

SOURCE: A review of *Magic by the Lake,* in *New York Herald Tribune Book Review,* May 12, 1957, p. 18.

"Wottest thou not that all magic goeth by three," wise Eliza, one of the lively children in *Knight's Castle,* said as they ended their adventure with Ivanhoe and Robin Hood. We were therefore prepared for a third slice of Edward Eager's peculiar and delicious enchantment. Opening the attractive blue cloth book, N. M. Bodecker's drawings again gave us a vivid sense of the fun to come. Here to our delight are the quartette from *Half Magic* and, for a short time, Eliza and her group too. *Magic by the Lake* finds Jane, Mark, Katherine and Martha almost overwhelmed by magic, "a whole lakeful of it." Badgered, scolded and sometimes aided by a wise old turtle they learn something of its rules. It gradually becomes manageable although Martha, the problem child, by wishing at one point that all rules would be broken, almost ruined the whole thing utterly and completely, to say nothing of nearly dumping them all into a cannibal stew. They succeed in having adventures with mermaids and pirates, and even a share in the Ali Baba and Sinbad stories, but it did "take a lot out of the lake." The enchantments that are interwoven with favorite stories are more convincing than the "canoe" and "the storm," but all have Edward Eager's satisfying combination of realism and logical absurdities. The magic adheres to its odd rules. Young readers eagerly sharing the amazing experiences will sigh for more. Which brings us back to the magic number three. Jane, Katherine and Martha have been in only two books and they do so want to meet the *Knight's Castle* children again. Well, "Time will tell," as the turtle said. We, like Martha, add, "In a book that's always a good sign. At least it's better than No."

Heloise P. Mailloux

SOURCE: A review of *Magic by the Lake*, in *The Horn Book Magazine*, Vol. XXXIII, No. 3, June, 1957, p. 221.

In which the vacationing children of **Half Magic** discover not "magic by the pound . . . or by the day . . . or by threes, the good old-fashioned way . . ." but a whole lake, brimful of it. To me the adventures—which include a trip to a pirate island, Katherine's and Jane's suddenly turning sixteen, a visit to the North Pole, a particularly hard time at the hands of cannibals, and a hunt for buried treasure—seem less spontaneous than those of the first book and more consciously clever. (The influence of E. Nesbit, and particularly of *Five Children and It,* is very apparent.) But if the story falls short of the standard set by the first book, it is still better than average fantasy, and its humor will make it popular even with children who usually prefer realism.

Ethna Sheehan

SOURCE: "Voice of the Turtle," in *The New York Times Book Review,* June 23, 1957, p. 22.

"Don't you wish it were true?" asked Martha, as she and Mark, Katharine and Jane read the name on their vacation cottage—Magic by the Lake. "Now you've done it," muttered the ancient turtle Mark had captured and sure enough, the children were to find that a whole lakeful of magic entailed problems as well as pleasures. For instance, teasing Chauncey Cutlass and his pirates proved a fearsome joy, but it was uncomfortable to spend the remainder of that eventful day encased in turtle shells as protection. And it was exhilarating to visit the South Pole until the explorers realized they might have to spend the long polar night in the Antarctic.

There is here the same mélange of realism and fantasy, witty talk and believable characterization that has come to be the hallmark of Mr. Eager's stories. Many readers will hope for still another E. Nesbit-like expedition, in spite of Jane's reluctant conclusion, "No more magic for us."

The Junior Bookshelf

SOURCE: A review of *Magic by the Lake*, in *The Junior Bookshelf,* Vol. 21, No. 5, November, 1957, p. 259.

Perhaps it is a help to a tale of magic to be set slightly in period as the presence of a Model T Ford in this tale suggests. It is also more credible when the magic occasionally goes wrong, with sometimes uncomfortable consequences, as it does here. Mark and Katherine and Martha and Jane have a very active and bewildering time with the magic of the lake they visit for a vacation with their mother and stepfather. For English readers there is added interest in the American setting of fairly lonely territory and the

turtle which is the intermediary between the children and the lake is quite a character in its own right. Naturally there is treasure, though that goes very wrong right up to the end. The general atmosphere is very much that of spontaneous dreams of the kind that all happy children enjoy (or suffer) from time to time as the result of stories read or told to them, and within that framework of probability all is feasible and there is any amount of fun to be found.

P. E. Mansley

SOURCE: A review of *Magic by the Lake,* in *The School Librarian,* Vol. 9, No. 1, March, 1958, p. 80.

This American story has a strong Edith Nesbit flavour and the illustrations [by Bodecker] indicate a 1920 setting. The four children, one boy and three girls, encounter a magic turtle in a lake and subsequently experience unusual, amusing adventures. This writer's style flows smoothly and the book has a quality which will appeal to adults too, a sure test of a successful children's book.

THE TIME GARDEN (1958)

New York Herald Tribune Book Review

SOURCE: A review of *The Time Garden*, in *New York Herald Tribune Book Review,* May 11, 1958, p. 12.

While their parents are in England working on the production of a play, the four lively and literate children, whose magical adventures were so absorbing in **Knight's Castle** and who appeared briefly in **Magic by the Lake,** discover (in a bed of thyme in the garden of an old house, where they are spending the summer) a Natterjack. A Natterjack? It is "a British species of toad having a light yellow streak down its back." With a Cockney accent this old toad promptly makes a suggestion. "Pluck a spring o' this 'ere an' rub it once and sniff the breathin' essence of it. I wouldn't say what'd 'appen but it wouldn't be uninteresting. An' I wouldn't say when the tim'd be, but it wouldn't be now."

Mr. Eager's children are never dull—Eliza in fact is one of the pertest little pieces one would be likely to meet—so it didn't take them long to work that magic. Sniffing away at the thyme, they have a bit of fun on the "eighteenth of April in seventy-five" and with fugitive slaves somewhat later. Then, when Eliza finds it all too much like "Highlights of History" or those television shows where You Are There, they try for something livelier and get it. They talk to "Little Women," Queen Victoria and Queen Elizabeth I, and are even present at the first performance of their parents' play in London.

The dialogue is lively but the scenes in the past are somewhat stilted. They do not compare with the handling of this theme in *The Ship That Flew, Curtain of Mist* or *Bedknob and Broomstick*. Although we know Mr. Eager's ten- and eleven-year-old fans will keenly enjoy the book, we wonder if an author so gifted in making magic convincing might not vary the formula a bit more. For much as we delight in Eliza we feel perhaps it is time for a change.

Margaret Warren Brown

SOURCE: A review of *The Time Garden*, in *The Horn Book Magazine,* Vol. XXXIV, No. 4, August, 1958, pp. 265-6.

"Anything can happen when you have all the time in the world," said the sundial in old Mrs. Whiton's garden somewhere on the shore south of Boston. Ann, Roger, Eliza and Jack, of **Knight's Castle,** have all the "thyme" in the world—a magic herb which carries them back into the past. Perhaps the most entertaining adventure is a visit to the March family in Concord. The children make a traditional Alcott visit to succor a family—poor, but in this case dishonest—and manage to reform them in an un-Alcott-like fashion. Though these four children seem to get more smart alecky with each book and their adventures more contrived, the stories are still full of humor and ingenious fantasy. They make good reading aloud.

Phyllis Fenner

SOURCE: "Rub-It-Once," in *The New York Times Book Review,* August 17, 1958, p. 24.

"O you was to pluck a prig o' this 'ere," said the remarkable toad in the thyme garden, "an' rub it once an' sniff the breathin' essence of it, I wouldn't say what'd 'appen, but it wouldn't be uninterestin'. An' I wouldn't say *when* the time'd be, but it wouldn't be *now!*" That was all those extremely interesting children, Roger and Ann and their cousins, Jack and Eliza, needed (having previously experienced magic in **Knight's Castle** and other tales) to start them off in search of unusual happenings.

The children were spending the summer with an eccentric old lady while their parents were in England. The words on the sundial—"Anything Can Happen When You've All the Time in the World"—were translated by the toad to "when you've all the thyme in the world." Having time and thyme, and an unswerving belief in magic, they plunged into adventures, some funny and some dangerous, in olden and even future time.

The children are as amusing as ever and the play on words is lots of fun, perhaps especially so to adults. The adventures, however, seem a little contrived. As Eliza so smartly says, "Oh, it's been all right in its way, so far. Only it's all been kind of non-fiction! . . . Highlights of History, with kind of a story wrapped around." That, I think, is its trouble.

The Junior Bookshelf

SOURCE: A review of *The Time Garden,* in *The Junior Bookshelf,* Vol. 23, No. 2, March, 1959, pp. 71-2.

The author has had a good idea here, an imaginative conception which could, one feels, have produced a story of great depth and richness. Unfortunately, however, the initial inspiration quickly fades. The American children who have been involved in magic in previous books come to stay with an old lady in a big old house while their parents are abroad. In the garden is a bank of thyme where lives the Natterjack, a toad-like creature who is able with the help of the thyme to spirit them back into other times. The imagination plays upon the words "time" and "thyme," their respective uses and meanings. The idea is suggestive of much thought and the author has entered to some degree into the detached world of fantasy. But then he loses himself and though the children are taken back into various ages many of the instances are trite and stereotyped while some of the episodes read like a not very original dream. The Natterjack speaks in a strong cockney accent and while this in itself is not undesirable it does add to the rather coarse and uncouth impression he makes which is scarcely in keeping with the definitely "old time" garden.

MAGIC OR NOT? (1959)

Phyllis Fenner

SOURCE: "Connecticut Spree," in *The New York Times Book Review,* March 8, 1959, p. 40.

Take four children (three beautifully normal with charming parents and one friend-shy with "a witch" for a grandmother). Add one obnoxious rich woman with a toothily obnoxious son; a rich, understanding young man with an actress wife; a wishing well that works—if the wishes are for the good of someone else. Put them against a suburban Connecticut background where there is a normal amount of trouble (mortgage foreclosures and fights for new schools). Have everything end happily even to a forced change of heart in one obnoxious character, and you have an everyday story that will please almost all of the girls and some of the boys.

The children are lots of fun, as are all of Edward Eager's people, and there are the usual references to books in their conversation (even to the author's own books). Mr. Eager has a beautiful time, tongue in his cheek, and readers will have too. Those who believe in magic will say it was magic. Those who have to be convinced will say it wasn't. I say it was!

New York Herald Tribune Book Review

SOURCE: A review of *Magic Or Not?,* in *New York Herald Tribune Book Review,* May 10, 1959, p. 4.

Few writers for children now have as great a respect for magic as Edward Eager. He knows its rules, those inexorable logical rules that make magic believable. Wild conjecture there may be, but the details must be consistent and believable, and before any magic starts the children in the story must be clearly established as natural, un-magical human beings, just-like-you. Mr. Eager, in the Nesbit tradition, always has in his stories a small horde of children who are pleasantly literate, in a limited way, rather overemphasizing *Alice.* His admirers, and they are many, will therefore expect Laura, her brother James and the young neighbors in Connecticut, in the present book, to become involved in something elaborate in the way of magic such as delighted them in *Half Magic* and the rest. Indeed, Laura herself expects it. There is a well on the place. Surely it is a wishing well. *Well,* something elaborate does happen, several somethings, engineered by the wishing children, but is it magic, or not? On the whole we should say *not,* and we were as disappointed as Laura, but at the very end we were not so sure. The realists will be quite contented and the others can re-read *Half Magic.*

Margaret Warren Brown

SOURCE: A review of *Magic or Not?,* in *The Horn Book Magazine,* Vol. XXXV, No. 3, June, 1959, pp. 213-14.

Is it as good as the others? All Eager enthusiasts will ask immediately about the fifth "magic" book. The answer is "Yes, even better," at least to this reviewer. A new set of engaging children is involved this time. When Laura and Jane move to the country, they find an old well in their garden, which could easily be a wishing well. Jane decides to test it by wishing for a kitten—"a dull wish, but her own." Her wish is granted, but by magic? If magic, the well is certainly temperamental in its response, or lack of response, to a number of wishes. Everything that happens just could be coincidence—the reader, along with the children, will have to decide for himself. In any event, a real mystery develops. Characters and events are fresh and lively, for although unmistakably an Eager book, it is not written to formula.

The Junior Bookshelf

SOURCE: A review of *Magic or Not?,* in *The Junior Bookshelf,* Vol. 23, No. 5, November, 1959, pp. 285-6.

Imitation may be the sincerest form of flattery, but Mr. Eager's attempts to flatter E. Nesbit by assiduously copying some of her mannerisms can hardly have won any readers for Nesbit and may have lost him a few who liked his own first series begun by *Half Magic.* When E. Nesbit says something was "the work of a moment" she is a boy trying to sound literary; when Mr. Eager uses the phrase, which he does rather too often, he is simply himself, trying to be E. Nesbit.

If only he would *be* simply himself, he might have a great deal more to offer, for in this book he has created a character from a caricature, the spoiled son of an overbearing woman, and given him a curtain line which ends the story on such a satisfactory note that it seems cruel to criticise the rest. But too much that has gone before is less successful, and the central theme, a wishing-well which might really work, is weakened because the events described would have had more shape and cohesion if magic *had* been at work while if it had *not* been at work, the most climactic event could not have been engineered at all. The book reads smoothly on the whole and there is little doubt the author has considerable possibility if he will give rein to his natural ability without thought of famous predecessors.

John Coleman

SOURCE: A review of *Magic or Not?,* in *The Spectator,* Vol. 204, No. 6857, November 27, 1959, p. 782.

Frances Browne bewailed the disappearance of magic: 'Kings make no seven-day feasts for all comers now. . . . Chairs tell no tales. Wells work no wonders; and there are no such doings on hills and forests, for the fairies dance no more.' In his very elegant little upper-middle-class American *Magic or Not?* Mr. Eager sets about rehabilitating the wishing well for today's children. James and Laura have gone to live with their family in the Connecticut countryside, where they quickly make friends with surly Lydia and bouncing Kip ('My Pop works in New York. He's in advertising'). They're all very well read in children's fiction—Mr. Eager slips in a plug for a couple of his own—and hopefully trick one another into believing the garden well can grant wishes. Their further adventures—*no* violence—bring the community closer together; and that, as they agree, is a kind of magic after all. This is a wholesome, pertly written book, with some sharp portraits of locals and firmly delicate illustrations by N. M. Bodecker.

The Times Literary Supplement

SOURCE: "The Wisher and the Wish," in *The Times Literary Supplement,* No. 3014, December 4, 1959, pp. xiv-xv.

A variation worth noticing in the fantasy stories is in Edward Eager's summer holiday story *Magic or Not.* This easy and effervescent author, an open disciple of E. Nesbit, has been playing with the theme of magic for some time, trying to vary its range with ingenious conditions. Here, by suggesting that human desire and effort can produce very similar results, he has produced what is possibly the best of his books. There *is* a wishing well in the garden, but is it the cause of the wishes coming about? Even the reader is not quite sure. We know how the kitten is found and why the mortgage is not foreclosed, but are these the work of magic or of human resourcefulness? Even the children realize, at last, that the two can also be one.

THE WELL-WISHERS (1960)

Ruth Hill Viguers

SOURCE: A review of *The Well-Wishers,* in *The Horn Book Magazine,* Vol. XXXVI, No. 2, April, 1960, p. 129.

The readers of **Magic or Not?** will be pleased to know that the children did not use up all the wishes in the well and that in this new book a whole new set of wishes—all doing good to humanity—gives the children a very busy fall. This time the adventures are related by the children themselves, each taking a turn, but readers who are prejudiced against "I" stories will be disarmed in the first paragraph. Mr. Eager has an audience as loyal as was that of E. Nesbit (whose books inspired him to write his "magic" stories) and this book will be very welcome.

Bulletin of the Center for Children's Books

SOURCE: A review of *The Well-Wishers,* in *Bulletin of the Center for Children's Books,* Vol. XIII, No. 9, May, 1960, p. 145.

The continued adventures of the group of children of **Magic or Not?,** this time told by the children themselves. Each of the six youngsters takes a turn at recording events, and the device is not successful: in part this is due to the fact that the author has a writing style that is not simple and seldom reads like the writing of a child, and in part the lack of success is due to the fact that there is not enough differentiation between the writings of the various children. The plot involves the efforts of the children to propitiate and use a magic wishing well; action is episodic to the point of being choppy. One episode has to do with some blitzkrieg therapy practiced by one child; another—most laudable in intent—concerns the concerted effort of the children to welcome some new neighbors against whom some of the townspeople have indicated hostility; there is a great deal written about the adverse sentiments; the shame of prejudice, etc. There is never any direct mention of the fact that the new family is Negro, although this eventually becomes clear; it seems unnecessarily evasive—for no apparent reason, since the author's whole purpose is to derogate prejudice.

Ethna Sheehan

SOURCE: "Magic Again," in *The New York Times Book Review,* August 7, 1960, p. 26.

"You never can tell with magic," says James who begins this sequel to **Magic or Not?** And so it is that the Connecticut wishing well, which had seemed to do all it was going to do for the children of Silvermine Road is induced to grant again those unselfish wishes which lead to noble deeds. These deeds are not old-fashioned quests but strictly mid-twentieth-century operations. Each of the six youngsters reports on his own adventure in his own way, and all the reports demonstrate the appalling ease with which the children could penetrate the motives of their elders, analyze their thought process and reproduce their jargon.

The plotting of the episodes is grand (although I am not sure how an anxious parent might react to Lydia's vigil in an isolated clubhouse) and the telling is superb.

SEVEN-DAY MAGIC (1962)

Alice Low

SOURCE: A review of *Seven-Day Magic,* in *The New York Times Book Review,* November 11, 1962, p. 49.

Luckily for Edward Eager's fans, the children in his latest book—headed by a dynamic boy named Barnaby—are just as lively and literary as those in **Half Magic.** In the library they find a book which, mysteriously, is about *them!* Only the first part is written—which means, says Susan, "there's a whole book still going to happen to us." And happen it does, in variety for "to each person it was the . . . book that person had . . . longed to find." There is a magic adventure that takes them to Oz before that book was written, a humorous sequence that brings a storybook character from **Half Magic** into their world, and Barnaby's trip into his own unfinished book—which seems contrived, yet just what a well-read boy's first book might be. There is also a delightful spoof on T.V. wherein the magic turns against them and creates bedlam. **Seven-Day Magic,** Mr. Eager's seventh book in this realistic-fantasy vein, proves that his pen works magic with just about any number.

The Christian Science Monitor

SOURCE: A review of *Seven-Day Magic,* in *The Christian Science Monitor,* November 15, 1962, p. 126.

Now ring all the bells of Oz, Narnia, Pooh's forest, Never Never Land, and all such true places, for Edward Eager has written another of his "magic" books—and the best one yet. This book is about a book—a seven-day book—and it is no wonder that Miss Dowitcher, the children's librarian, had a strange look when Susan decided to borrow it. Its magical properties made the most wonderful (and sometimes frightening) things happen to John, Susan, Barnaby, Abbie and Fredericka. We could mention the clever and unusual plot with its surprise climax, the delightful humor, the human understanding, the nuggets from world literature tucked (some slyly) here and there, the sustained interest and the quality of the writing, but there isn't space. What—we've already done it? So we have. But now there really isn't any more space, except to say that the specified age group is 8-12, but we don't know why. Everybody should read it.

Margaret Warren Brown

SOURCE: A review of *Seven-Day Magic,* in *The Horn Book Magazine,* Vol. XXXVIII, No. 6, December, 1962, p. 602.

Mr. Eager makes the reading of books an exciting part of life and the sharing of magic a believable adventure for the reader. His children, though they are steeped in books, are real; they are persons; their characters and responses are varied and specific. Although he, like E. Nesbit, always writes the same kind of magic book, the magic itself is always different and never foreseeable. This time the book describes itself in an early conversation among the children. When they open the small, shabby book they have just taken from the public library, they find the story beginning with the very words of their conversation and carrying on right up to the point where they open the book. The rest of the pages seem to be stuck—and stay so until the children live the rest of the story. The present characters have not appeared before. Three of them are the children of a struggling singer currently forced to take part in TV commercials to support his young family. The reader will be delighted to find out what happened to the little girl who found the coin at the end of *Half Magic*.

The Junior Bookshelf

SOURCE: A review of *Seven-Day Magic,* in *The Junior Bookshelf,* Vol. 27, No. 3, July, 1963, p. 146.

This is the seventh magical story by Edward Eager, and illustrated by N. M. Bodecker, and is in many ways the best of the seven. The book which the five children in this story borrow from their public library is only a plain book with very worn covers, but the librarian gives them a quizzical look before she stamps it for them, and it is not long before they find that the book has two kinds of magic—it is able to record their own adventures, and to grant their wishes in the same way as their wishes have been granted in the other books, but with some differences! Particularly to be commended in this seventh story of Barnaby, Abbie, Fredericka, John and Susan is the subtle way in which the author weaves into the text references to other children's books—a way which means that children reading *Seven-day Magic* will want to read these other books mentioned—*The Wizard of Oz, On the Banks of Plum Creek, At the Back of the North Wind* and *Robinson Crusoe.* The author also hints successfully at some standards in this book—for instance the confession of the father of some of the children that he sings rubbishy pop-songs for money, rather than better material which he is capable of singing, but which the public do not want. A thoroughly enjoyable book, which will give young readers things to think about afterwards.

Additional coverage of Eager's life and career is contained in the following sources published by Gale Research: *Contemporary Authors,* **Vol. 73-76;** *Dictionary of Literary Biography,* **Vol. 22;** *Major Authors and Illustrators for Children and Young Adults;* **and** *Something about the Author,* **Vol. 17.**

Claire Mackay

1930-

Canadian author of fiction and nonfiction.

Major works include *Mini-Bike Hero* (1974), *Exit Barney McGee* (1979), *One Proud Summer* (with Marsha Hewitt, 1981), *The Minerva Program* (1984), *Pay Cheques and Picket Lines: All about Unions in Canada* (1987).

INTRODUCTION

Claire Mackay is a popular Canadian writer of fiction and nonfiction for middle school children and young adults. Her stories have been praised by readers and critics alike for their believable characterizations, clever story lines, and situations to which young people can easily relate. Her nonfiction is celebrated for its fresh, lighthearted, and well-researched approach. While many of Mackay's works of fiction are inspired by her sons' interests and experiences, the characters and themes are often drawn from her own childhood. As a young person, Mackay viewed herself as an outsider and liked to imagine herself as a rebel; similarly, her characters tend to be outlaws and misfits who often take a step toward adulthood in the course of their adventures. In addition, the author's early exposure to her parents' radical politics has led her to explore the struggle for justice in works such as *The Minerva Program* and *Pay Cheques and Picket Lines: All about Unions in Canada,* and Mackay's difficult relationship with her father is revealed in many of her books, most notably *Exit Barney McGee.* Jon C. Stott commented that "Mackay's books, in their clear and sympathetic portrayal of young teenage boys and girls facing the difficult choices involved in growing up, have justly earned a place as important Canadian novels about contemporary life."

Biographical Information

Mackay was born in Toronto, the daughter of staunch Communists. With the Great Depression came the loss of her father's job as an accountant and the onset of his alcoholic tendencies. The family moved frequently throughout the author's childhood, making it difficult for the young Mackay to form lasting friendships. She compensated for the lack of companions and luxuries by reading library books, particularly adult classics. Her first job, at the age of ten, involved shelving and dusting books in the library's children's division. Although she was associate editor of her high school magazine, Mackay decided to study political science and economics at the University of Toronto. She received her B.A. in 1952, and was married to Jack Mackay, an engineer, the same year. The author then worked as an assistant research librarian for

three years, until she became pregnant with the first of her three sons. In 1967, when her youngest child was eight, Mackay returned to the University of British Columbia, and her first essay prompted her teacher to suggest that Mackay try her hand at creative writing. Mackay was encouraged by this and for the first time began to believe she could become an author. In 1969 her husband was transferred to Saskatchewan. There the author began writing poetry and found a job as a social worker at a hospital rehabilitation center. The patients she worked with had powerful real-life stories to share, and the author composed long, detailed case histories which helped prepare her for a writing career. In 1971 Mackay's husband was transferred once again, this time to Toronto, and from 1972 to 1978 the author worked as a research librarian for the Steelworkers' Union and wrote a women's column for their newsletter. She began her first book, *Mini-Bike Hero,* when her youngest son was unable to find any books on the subject of mini-bikes in the library. It was published in 1974 and led to two sequels. Mackay became a full-time writer and researcher in 1978.

Major Works

Mackay's first book, *Mini-Bike Hero,* is about Steve, a young boy striving to establish his own identity. He secretly saves money and purchases a mini-bike against the wishes of his father, but then must reveal his knowledge and skill when a man is injured and an Indian village needs to be warned of an encroaching flood. Steve almost loses his best friend to jealousy, witnesses a robbery, and is taken hostage in the sequel *Mini-Bike Racer.* In the last of the "Mini-Bike" series, *Mini-Bike Rescue,* Julie defies her mother by becoming Steve's riding partner and a hero in her own right. *Exit Barney McGee* is another story of a strong-willed teenager. Barney has difficulty adjusting to his new step-family and runs away to find his long-lost father. When his father, who abandoned him ten years ago, turns out to be an alcoholic, Barney learns that the adult world is more complicated than he had imagined and that heroes come in all shapes and sizes. Thirteen-year-old Lucie La Plante is the heroine in *One Proud Summer,* a work of historical fiction based on a 1946 textile workers' strike in Valleyfield, Quebec. Lucie is a worker who has been forced to work long hours and whose pay has been unfairly docked. She joins family and friends in a 100-day strike for better working conditions. The success of the strike has an empowering effect on her. Mackay writes of yet another female character in her mystery story *The Minerva Program.* Minerva, an awkward seventh grader, discovers her talent for computers and thus gains some much-needed confidence, only to be accused of tampering with the school's program and altering the grade she receives in gym class. Her friends and younger brother rally around her, and together they discover who is trying to defraud the school board.

In the late 1980s the author began focusing on nonfiction works, including *Pay Cheques and Picket Lines: All about Unions in Canada,* which uses humor and stories about real people to explain the subject of unions and the labor movement to children; *The Toronto Story,* which includes facts about past and present life in the city; and *Touching All the Bases: Baseball for Kids of All Ages,* which provides facts of interest to baseball fans and beginners alike. In each case, Mackay uses her research skills to dig up unusual true stories about individuals, which she complements with equally surprising trivia tidbits. She presents the information in appealing, inventive formats that have been well received by both children and adults.

Awards

One Proud Summer received the Ruth Schwartz Foundation Award for best children's book in 1982. Mackay received an honorable mention for the Canada Council Children's Literature Prize in 1982. In 1993 she earned the Vicky Metcalf Award from the Canadian Authors Association for her body of work for children. Mackay received two Parenting Publications of North America Awards of Excellence, in 1990 and 1991, and was a finalist for the City of Toronto Book Awards in 1991. In addition she received a City of Toronto award of merit in 1992.

AUTHOR'S COMMENTARY

Dave Jenkinson

SOURCE: "'Claire Mackay' Mini-Bikes, Strikes and Mini-Computers," in *Emergency Librarian,* Vol. 15, No. 2, November-December, 1987, pp. 59-64.

When next you read one of Claire Mackay's books, pay particular attention to her characters' names. "I've been interested in words all my life. I've always read dictionaries as if they were the most exciting novel that ever was, and I can get tempted away from the work at hand by picking up a dictionary. And names! I always research the names of my characters."

"Every name in *The Minerva Program* means something. I usually try to have an extra connotation and have it fit in with the time period or the ethnic derivation of the person. 'Minerva Wright—'wright'—a maker or doer, and I saw her as a making kind of person. 'Minerva' is the goddess of wisdom, and Minerva had to learn some wisdom about computers. In a sense, what I was trying to get across with the book's title was that we all need to use as much wisdom as we can muster to cope with this rapid advance in technology. Minerva's father's name is Gregory, and that means 'one who watches'. He's a watchman at the hospital, and I saw him as a watchful father. The villian's name was Richard Campbell. I tell kids that if you're really smart about names, you'll know who the villain is right away because 'Richard' means 'hard ruler'. I saw the book's Richard as the despot of the computer and without a conscience. 'Campbell' means 'crooked mouth' in Gaelic and so, of course, he was a liar too. Every name was researched and fitted in. I 'wasted' a lot of time."

Claire's many readers may also think that she "wasted" a lot of time before she became a writer. Born in Toronto on December 21, 1930, Claire did not publish her first book until she was 43, though numerous occurrences in her life suggested that writing would become her career. With her brother, Claire at age 8, wrote, co-published and delivered the "Parkside News" which had a circulation figure of nine. The printing press consisted of "those tiny printing sets where you pick up the print with tweezers one letter at a time. You'd stamp it on the stamp pad and then on the piece of paper. Laborious! We sold it for a cent or two which was a lot of money then. It was bought partly because adults are often generous to children, but I think we reported on neighborhood items, and I suspect some of the neighbors were interested in what the people down the street were doing."

At Jarvis Collegiate, Claire was the associate editor of the school's magazine, *The magnet,* and at the University of Toronto where Claire, in 1952, received an Honors BA in Political Science and Economics, she was a reporter for the university newspaper, *The varsity.* Claire was also the writer, editor and publisher of *The blue water aquarist* whose circulation figures were almost four times that of the "Parkside news". "When we lived in Sarnia, Ontario—which is called the Blue Water Area—my husband got very interested in tropical fish, and we had fish all over the house, tank upon tank upon tank. He naturally met other people with similar enthusiasms, and we decided we would start this little newsletter. I leaped into it. I even wrote poetry about fish! I think all of these things were inference arrows, weren't they, of my wanting to be a writer and using any excuse almost. And in a way I was fighting against being a writer. I just never thought that I could join that "noble breed".

In 1968, Claire returned to the University of British Columbia. There, one of her professors, Frances McCubbin, had a very profound effect on Claire's perception of herself. "I'll be forever grateful to that woman. Here's this frightened-to-death mature student convinced that all these young people around her are brilliant. After my first essay, she came to me and said, 'Have you ever thought of creative writing?'" That was just the encouragement that Claire needed. "My first poem was to her and was called 'Thursdays at Nine' which was when her class was. She said, 'Claire. That's a little too much, you know!' I tend to get florid sometimes. We got to be very good friends and she encouraged me. 'You should be writing every day, and I'll have a look at it if you want.' Really though, it was then that I started thinking, 'Maybe I can do it'. It was a turning point."

Moving from short pieces to longer writing efforts was a large hurdle for Claire. "I did feel, 'I've got to try something of some length.' Most of the things I had done earlier, published or unpublished, had been pretty short. I'd been doing a lot of poetry. I'm really a failed poet you know. What I do are Spenserian sonnets, and they haven't been in style for some time. I hope they'll come back. I'm really good at them and at occasional verse. But I had reached a point where in my own feeling about writing, it was a kind of do or die. I never felt I could write well enough. I didn't publish much. Just little bits. 'Why bother with something bigger?' 'Why burden the world with another book?' But finally I thought, 'I have as much right as anyone else. I may have my own voice. I think I certainly have my own experience. Even if it's not very good, I'm going to do it anyway!'

. . . Reflecting on her childhood reading habits, Claire says, "To tell you the truth, I hardly read any children's books. I guess I must have, but none of them leap to mind. I got into heavy stuff relatively soon." Amongst those "heavy" tomes were such titles as [Sigmund] Freud's *Psychoanalytic theory,* [Giovanni] Boccaccio's *Decameron,* [Geoffrey] Chaucer's *Canterbury tales,* and the complete works of Alexandre Dumas, all of which had been read by the time Claire was in grade eight. In grade nine, she added Karl Marx's *Das kapital* to the list. "It was completely indiscriminate reading, and I had no particular guidance. I could just help myself to what was around, and we had some strange material because my parents were political radicals, very left of left. We were all pretty heavily involved in the Communist Party which is hard for people to understand now. Communism has developed a whole cluster of negative associations, but certainly, in the Thirties, if you weren't a Communist something was wrong with you, we felt. All the people we knew who were out of work and who were thinking drifted to the Party one way or another. I had a political consciousness very early or a sense of injustice. Any early aspirations to be a writer got covered under the political stuff, but I think in a way I see them as part of the same impulse: you want to leave something or make something that hasn't been in the world before. I see both of these desires as springing from the same general store of emotional idealism, and all adolescents, it seems to me, go through this period when they like to be revolutionary. Those were colorful years growing up in that kind of family atmosphere. Our record player played Paul Robeson and 'The Internationale', and our dinner table was the scene of discussion, argument and debate."

Claire Mackay

SOURCE: "Real Plums in Imaginary Cakes," in *Canadian Children's Literature,* No. 54, 1989, pp. 26-30.

In a metaphor both homely and elegant, one I cheerfully purloin today, Mary McCarthy has observed that the link between life and literature is one of "putting real plums into an imaginary cake." What I propose to do is to extract, from the half-dozen imaginary cakes I have baked, a handful of plums for our mutual inspection, plums plucked from my own life or the lives of people close to me, which have found their way, directly or circuitously, into my books.

To push the metaphor further—a bad habit of mine—plums come in several varieties: some are sour, others sweet; a few are fibrous, tough-skinned and gaudy; the flesh of others is soft, the skin fragile, the colour delicate. And in the process of baking, the plums change: some stay solid and almost whole; some shrink and blur around the edges; some swell far beyond their original dimensions; some nearly disappear in what surrounds them, leaving only a sort of vestigial spoor; and a few disintegrate altogether, and what remains is the memory of a plum, a phantom plum, known only to the cook. At least until now. It is this last sort of plum, the phantom plum, that I'd like to talk about most, because I believe it flavours—or haunts, you may pick your own image—everything I've written.

When I stand a little distance from my books and look at them askance, before they can notice what I'm doing, so to speak, I glimpse a common theme or pattern running through them. And this pattern, this theme—the phantom plum—springs from the favourite book of my childhood.

Its title, which nobody has ever heard of, is *Og, son of fire*. To my shame, I can't remember the author. But I do remember it was the 12th book on the second shelf of the bookcase in the northeast corner of the children's department of Yorkville Public Library in Toronto, and it had a maroon cover with embossed black printing on it. I know because I read it 17 times. I suspect that I also dusted it 17 times, since, when I was ten years old, I worked at the Yorkville Public Library, at a wage slightly below that of a Victorian ratcatcher. (By the way, I should dearly love to own a copy of *Og*, and stand ready to offer my next royalty cheque—which is not as generous a gesture as you might think—to a willing vendor.)

I wish I could claim that *The secret garden*, or *Anne of Green Gables*, or perhaps Oswald Spengler's *The decline of the west* was my favourite childhood book. But no. It was *Og, son of fire*. *The decline of the west* was my second favourite. Og is—I use the present tense because for me Og lives—a paleolithic prepubescent boy who is the despair of his father, for when it comes to spears and clubs and stone axes, Og is all opposable thumbs. Nor is poor Og held in high esteem by his peer group: he is always the last to be picked when the kids play Kick-the-Skull or Run, Mammoth, Run. Og never gets elected class president. Og is not an opinion leader in his neighbourhood. (Nor as it happens, am I. I have never been asked for my opinion on anything, except where I got my rugs cleaned, and I couldn't have given a satisfactory answer, because no one has phoned me since.) Og is a misfit, an outsider, a quiet revolutionary, a wanderer and a wonderer, with a talent for solitude, a knack for the romantic, a love for the larger than life, and a capacity for epiphany. He dreams of noble deeds, of valour, of glory and sacrifice, and of a place in the sun of his father's eyes. Because Og is what he is, to him is granted, courtesy of a serendipitous local lightning bolt, the gift, the transmuting power, and the terrible magic of fire. He brings that gift, with appropriate accompanying heroics, to his people, to his father. His dream comes true.

Why did I love Og? Why did I read his story with such intensity and devotion? You will have guessed the obvious: yes, I was Og, no matter that he and I were separated by sex, 500 millennia of alleged civilization, and several other infinities of difference. I was Og—but not, I fear, nearly so brave. There is a family story, which I haven't yet managed to suppress, that as a child I was frightened of grass. I've come a long way: it doesn't scare me anymore. Except at night, sometimes. I was an undercover Og, a closet Og. I dreamed Og dreams, of quest and discovery, of impossible bravery, even of martyrdom when I was feeling especially dramatic or melancholy and later, when I had 3 children in 3 years, I got a chance at it. I wanted a place for myself; and I longed, often, to make a gift to my father, to bring a light to his eyes. I also thought it would be terrific not to wear shoes.

Og, or a part of him, is in all the books I have written. The children in my books, like Og, like the secret me, like most of us perhaps, tend to be passionate, if reluctant, outlaws. Because they are so, they win through to a fuller sense of themselves as human beings who are valid and powerful. And sometimes they bring gifts, too.

So Steve, in my first book, **Mini-bike hero** (written for and drawn from my remarkably Og-like third son) upsets his father, his teacher (modelled on a real, if unbelievable, teacher who was heavily into bondage and discipline), and six or seven commandments in pursuit of his dream, finally risking, if not life, then certainly limb, in a redeeming act of heroism that heals all wounds with the exception of the limb, as the sun sinks slowly in the west.

So Julie, in a later book in the series, rebels at cultural stereotypes and parental expectations, even as Og did, even as I did, although I happened to be 35 at the time and it was my children's expectations I rebelled against, then rescues her friend Colin—another outlaw—from despair, not to mention a magnificently described forest fire, and brings about for both of them a deeper understanding of, and reconciliation with, their parents, as the sun rises slowly in the east.

So Barney in **Exit Barney McGee** (the surname meaning, by the way, "son of fire," as does MacKay, which might be why I married the fellow), his place usurped by a too-strict stepfather, runs away in search of his real father, only to find that some dreams are false, that gifts come in odd packages, and that heroes may wear humble disguise.

So Lucie Laplante, the young French-Canadian millworker in **One proud summer,** whose father's death has split her life in two, musters the courage to fight injustice, breaking several laws, a dozen factory windows, and a few heads along the way, and discovers not only her own power, not only the power of herself joined to like-minded others, but also the thrill of subversion, as I did when at age 11 I delivered illegal midnight pamphlets calling for the violent overthrow of the government.

And so Minerva, in **The Minerva program,** built like a large wading bird, inclined to lose control of her limbs and her temper, feeling left out at home and at school, desperate to be good at something, to know her own excellence, and finding it in the two-edged magic of computers, is tempted by *hubris* into disaster, and must mend a shattered friendship, burglarize the school, and engage in some dazzling derring-do before she wins her place.

You will not have failed to note that fathers figure largely in my books. And you will further not have failed to infer that my father figured largely in my life, even, or perhaps especially, when he wasn't around. Our relationship was intense, often troubled—I am very like him—but I have neither the time nor is this the appropriate place for me to enlarge on the matter. I will say only that like Steve, I fought with him. Like Barney, I searched for him. Like Lucie, I mourned him when he died too soon. Like Minerva, I remember him. But she can speak for herself:

> Minerva glanced at the . . . photograph, . . the one of her father . . . and herself when she was four. She still remembered that day. They'd been at the beach, with

the sun hot and white in the middle of the sky, and her father had called to her. She had run to where he stood, tall as a tree it seemed then, and he had swept her up to the place he kept for her on one warm shoulder. And she had looked out from that great height and seen farther than she'd ever seen.

That passage . . . is plagiarized from a sonnet I wrote for my father when he was dying. Like Og, I wanted to bring him a gift. It's entitled "Snapshot, 1934":

> . . . And this was taken at the beach one day
> When I was only three, or maybe four.
> I remember I was busily at play
> Building moats and minarets along the shore
> When he called. I ran to where he stood.
> He was stronger, taller than a tree,
> And I climbed the tower of his limbs till I could
> Nestle in the place he kept for me
> On one warm shoulder . . . Ah, in that hour
> I was a queen! My lifted finger hurled
> Suns, made mountains dance, and deserts flower!
> For as long as he held me, I held the world.
> . . . Scared? No, I was never scared at all.
> I knew my father would not let me fall.

I have never managed to get that piece published; now I grab at the chance.

This particular sequence is, I suppose, rather like the "begats" in the Bible. The real event, the story plain, is my father and I on the beach in 1934, which begat the photograph. (Unfortunately my brother is in it too, which rather spoils it.) The photograph begat the sonnet. The sonnet begat the passage in *The Minerva program*. And now, together, we have just engaged in a further begetting: as I tell you of these things, you bring your own perceptions and experience to the understanding of them. The story is no longer plain, but suffused with colour. Each step in the genealogy, from the ancestral plum to the finished cake, is, in a way, a step further from reality, since it is shaped by, if not art, then certainly artifice. We might legitimately ask what is left of the original event, the first plum. I believe that however far we—and I'm sure I speak for most writers in this respect—may stray from the *fact* of the matter, we never abandon, indeed we may enhance, the *truth* of the matter. And the truth of the matter—in this case the faith of a child in her father's desire to keep her safe—is doubtless why we later pick the plum.

"What a writer has not experienced in his heart," said the biographer Edgar Johnson of [Charles] Dickens, "he can do no more than coldly image from without. Only what he has proved within emerges from those depths with irresistible power, . . . no matter how thoroughly the mere surface details may have been changed and disguised."

Two hundred and fifty years ago John Newbery, that hustling, merry pioneer of children's books, opened his shop in St. Paul's Churchyard in London. Above it he hung a sign, with a slogan inviting all children to enter and find books they might love, books that might show them their place in the world, books that gave them, in Nina Bawden's words, "a little hope, and courage for the journey." The slogan read: "Trade and Plumb-Cake forever, huzza!" I am trying with my own few plums, with my own small cakes, to live up to that grand ideal, so that one day, if I am lucky, a child will say of one of my books, as I said of Og, "This is my story, my own story."

Claire Mackay with Barbara Michasiw

SOURCE: An interview in *Canadian Children's Literature*, No. 64, 1991, pp. 6-25.

[The following interview between Barbara Michasiw and Claire Mackay occurred in two parts. The original conversation took place in 1989. A postscript was added in 1991, when the author and interviewer reviewed the text for publication.]

Michasiw: Is it accurate to say that writing is your third career?

Mackay: I've had any number of careers; I fell into things. It had to do with geography and availability of jobs. I started out in a library, when I was ten years old, dusting the books. I've tried to avoid dusting ever since. And then, in a delightfully circular way, my last paying job was at a library. In between, when I was a student, I had about nineteen jobs, then I was a librarian again right after marriage. Later, as a social worker having to write social histories, I found my way into what I really should have been doing all my life.

Michasiw: That was one of the things I wanted to ask you. Was professional writing your ultimate goal all along?

Mackay: Yes, but not consciously for a long time. Only as a dream somewhere at the back of my mind perhaps. I abandoned it for most of my young adulthood thinking that my ability was small and my talent mediocre. I was perfectly aware that a ton of mediocre garbage was out there floating around. That didn't encourage me to add to it. It just persuaded me that we didn't need any more, that I should maybe turn my talents, whatever they were, elsewhere.

Michasiw: When the time came, why did you venture into children's literature?

Mackay: It was largely accident but I had reached the point in my life (just turned forty) when major decisions are made or unmade, when I felt if I was going to do any writing at all I had better get at it. I had developed a little more confidence because of returning to school as a mature student, and receiving encouragement from a magnificent woman, a professor of human behaviour at the University of British Columbia, who felt that I did have some talent in writing. At the same time my son was going through an identity crisis, trying to establish a place for himself in the family. His older brothers, who were strong personalities, had areas of competence that gave them a sense of self, I suppose, and poor Grant didn't. He chose as his interest—which kids often do—something he knew was regarded by his parents as disreputable and proceeded to become an armchair expert first. It was of course, mini-bikes. Considerable family trauma was connected with his selecting an interest that didn't meet with his parents' approval, and then pursuing it to the point of obsession. It was uncomfortable in the household for a while with father and son at war. When Grant asked for a story about a mini-bike it coincided with my long-suppressed, but now very vigorous, desire to write something longer than a sonnet. So that's how it came about and I suppose I've called it an accident on more than one occasion, but is there any real accident in life? Then I had the temerity to send the manuscript to a publisher in the expectation it would be immediately returned. So, that's how I got into children's writing and it's largely been a matter of being weak-willed thereafter. The first one was such a success, I was persuaded to try another and then it's just been one thing after another. No, no. It was strictly unplanned.

Michasiw: . . . but I am struck when I read them by the action, the suspense that you build, the straightforward but not over-simplified vocabulary. How did you know how to do this? How did you know how to write to keep readers—even adult readers—turning the pages?

Mackay: First I'd have to say that I knew how to do it because I had absorbed it unconsciously from all the reading I'd done. I started reading as soon as I knew what books and letters were. I learned (almost osmotically) by reading all those years, how a story went together. And the kinds of stories I liked as a child continue to be the kinds children like. I still like stories, narratives, people having problems and working their way out. I like plot and it's my feeling that most kids do too. Most children will not sit down and read an experimental novel. Even in adult fiction I like a story. So I think that's part of the explanation. I suppose another part of the answer is that the age group I write for was a particularly satisfying one for me as a mother. My three sons were willing to communicate—in fact they sometimes communicated more than I really wanted to know—at that age, and I was willing to listen. We had a close and talkative relationship throughout all those years, say ten to fifteen. I know that teenage boys are supposed to clam up at the age of twelve but mine didn't, particularly the boy who started me writing. The house was full of boys and girls at that time. Because I felt close to them, I felt I could communicate well—I could even hear the things they weren't saying—and perhaps that's given me an edge.

Michasiw: I find a pattern of development through the mini-bike books. The first book is primarily action. Yes, there's the conflict between Steve and his father, but primarily it's action. In book two there is more of a conflict built up between Steve and Kim, the friend from whom he becomes alienated, and there is more of an attempt to examine character, moving away from straight action. When you come to the third one where you are talking about Julie Brennan and her problems, I find a greater

consciousness of setting, a greater depth of characterization. Now is this because the book came after *Exit Barney McGee,* because you had done the very different treatment of another kind of subject, or is this just natural development? Perhaps I'm asking the same question in two different ways.

Mackay: Yes, you may be. But there's another angle to this. For the first two books, obviously I utilized my sons, their friends, their experiences, their conversation, and their behaviour. I felt unsure about mining my own childhood, even though I think I was doing it in a minor way, because I could probably not have written the early books without doing so. But in the third mini-bike book much of Julie is me. The first scene is right out of my own life because my mother happened to throw away a favourite sweater of mine. It was a lucky sweater. I wore it for exams. I obviously couldn't pass anything without wearing that sweater. When the book came out, I sent my mother a copy. She phoned immediately and with a great wail said, "I'm sorry, I'm sorry!" I started to be sure enough of myself (and you have to remember that part of *One proud summer* was written before *Mini-bike rescue*) to feel that it was okay to use one's own childhood—why I didn't think so before or why I didn't *consciously* think of using it, I don't know—and it opened up a huge resource for me. I also felt the publishers would let me get away with a lot more, to tell you the truth. For Scholastic I had already written two, three successful books and when *Rescue* finally got written—which they'd been waiting for with bated breath for some time—I pretty well had my way. Now I think they might have been a little tougher with me. I've reread portions of that book and have discovered that it's overwritten here and there.

Michasiw: Only a little.

Mackay: You should have seen it before, Barbara. I know my editor sent me back a page at one point and she said, "Claire, do you realize that you have twelve similes on this page? Would you mind reducing them to half a dozen maybe?" I feel this is the last residue of Claire trying to be a poet, thinking in images and trying to express it.

Michasiw: Still I like the images . . . particularly when Julie is out looking at birds and the dead swamp.

Mackay: Yes, but I think they probably slow things down. I've had letters, from boys in particular, saying, "I really liked the first two, but there's too much scenery in *Mini-bike rescue.*"

Michasiw: I'm not sure whether you agreed with me that there's development.

Mackay: I think there's development because I was beginning to know that I could use more inner resources. I was allowing myself to do more. This is important because the expectation set up after the first book was "Here's a writer of page-turners, the fast-action stories for young people, especially boys who don't like to read a lot." I was labelled immediately. That happens to children's writers more than any other group. And I even also resented for some time, and occasionally still do, being called a children's writer. We don't call Margaret Atwood an adults' writer. I got crammed into a double pigeonhole. You're a children's writer and apart from that you write action-filled, fast-moving page-turners.

Michasiw: Well, since you left the Mini-bike series, you have been much harder to pigeonhole. Each book is quite different from the books that have gone before. Maybe this is something you have done consciously.

Mackay: It was partly because I was asked to do a certain kind of book too. *Mini-bike racer* had been written mostly in response to the publisher desperately wanting another book that would sell a quarter of a million copies and in response to fan mail. There were hundreds of children who wrote letters, in addition to that first and now moderately famous fan letter from a boy who had never read a book in his life, wanting another adventure with Steve. And in response to those letters, I sat down in some bewilderment because my life had simply been turned upside down—people were calling me a writer, of all things—and put together that second book. I have occasionally regretted that I didn't take longer with it. I've often felt I should rewrite it, but of course you can't. So those two books came out relatively close together and then I sat back and took a deep breath and with great trepidation began to write *Exit Barney McGee.*

Michasiw: But *Barney* was not commissioned, was it?

Mackay: No, *Barney* was a voyage of discovery. I felt I could try a few different techniques. There are at least four different points of view and one critic took me to task for that, I remember. I tried to make it a novel more of character than action.

Michasiw: It's obviously a quest novel, but it's also a novel of initiation.

Mackay: What do you mean by a novel of initiation? You're not going to use jargon on me, are you?

Michasiw: Just this once. In it we take Barney from a protected, limited knowledge of the world. Although he thinks he's been taking care of himself and his mother since he was a little guy, in fact when he sets off on his trip to Toronto, he's pretty naive. He learns not only about his father, he also learns a lot about himself. He learns that he cannot turn his back on someone and let him drown, no matter how hard it's going to be to save him, no matter what that person has done to him before. He is initiated into some of the street smarts of Toronto. He is initiated into the failure of adults. He thinks his stepfather has failed him, but this is a different ball game from the failure of Mike McGee. So it seems to me two things are at work in the novel: quest and initiation. Which do you feel is more important—the quest for his father, the search for his identity—or his initiation into the adult world?

Mackay: I have to say that they're both important and I

don't think you can separate them. You don't sit down and say "Well, I think I'll write a quest novel today." The critical grid is put on afterwards. I was delighted to discover I had written a quest novel. I adore quest novels. Joseph Campbell has this pattern: separation, adventure, return. I read it and realized I did that! Smart me! But, of course, it's in our culture, this prototypical kind of story. It's hard not to write a quest novel in a way, isn't it? Every novel is a kind of quest.

Michasiw: Especially if you are writing for young people, because growing up is a kind of quest and ultimately what most children's stories are about is growing up.

Mackay: The fact that it's a physical quest, a geographical search, is incidental. It's nice to have that underpinning, that support for the novel, but he might have been able to do it in his own home town. Now, I think there's another important aspect to the novel and that's the search for the father. That's in a lot of books too as you well know. I didn't do it because it's a powerful thing, but when I say *Barney* came out of my own desires and, in some respects, my own childhood, that's exactly so. My father resembled Barney's and in some ways I felt, certainly as a child and even as a young woman, cheated of a father. It wasn't until I was grown that I came to understand that my father was ill. And before I wrote *Barney* I was conscious of the fact that many children had nothing but contempt for some of the pathetic creatures whom they saw downtown. At any rate that element of the search for the father, the longing, I suppose, of every child for a hero father entered into the writing of it too. So there's a whole lot of stuff in *Barney* and I just felt I had to write it, but when I finished I thought, "I haven't done a good job." Of course no book is what it is when it's a dream in your head. I can write a book in my head in ten seconds and it's perfect. It's perfect! Then I try to put it down and it becomes imperfect. I suppose that's why some people keep writing, keep trying for the vision that they see.

Michasiw: The next one will always be the perfect one. But back to *Barney*. Do you feel that the problem of alcoholism concerns children?

Mackay: It certainly does. The fan mail on *Barney* is heart-breaking and an indication of how widespread this problem is. I've had continuing correspondence with a number of young people, with some of them for eight years, and, at the risk of being immodest, I think that my letters have helped them get through difficult patches. Things they couldn't perhaps say to their own parent or parents, they have felt comfortable saying to me. This is quite rewarding though it has nothing to do with being a writer. But I think it's not uncommon in the children's writing field. I've talked to other writers sufficiently to know that in the letters they get the children open up their hearts and their homes. They say things they probably shouldn't, these kids, and it's a huge compliment that children feel that comfortable with you just from reading something you wrote.

Michasiw: I hesitate to break off this part of the discussion about children's letters, but I would like to move on to another aspect of your work. One of the remarkable things about your books is that once you accept the commission you make the book uniquely your own. *One proud summer* was a book that you were not only approached to write but you were also asked to collaborate on it with another person, so in this instance you had two constraints on you.

Mackay: Well, the major constraint, of course, was the historical event itself. One of the people who had to approve the manuscript (for the very practical reason that she wouldn't release the pictures that appear at the end of it unless she did approve) was Madeleine Parent, who is a real character in the story of the strike in Quebec in 1946. Madeleine remembers almost photographically everything that happened. She took exception to several portions of the completed manuscript. We wanted her marvellous shot of the nine-year-old being arrested by the Quebec strike squad, so we did change some of the events to correspond more closely to her recollections. One thing that I refused to change was the scene where Lucie at the dinner table begins to twist her linen napkin. Madeleine pointed out that this was a poor family and they would not have linen napkins, but I said, "If she twisted a paper napkin, it would come apart in her hands," and I didn't want that to happen in that particular scene. I saw the napkin as one valuable thing that had been passed down, a tangible piece of family memory. I pleaded and Madeleine conceded the point. So the first constraint was history. This novel is almost documentary fiction. It's so close to what truly happened. As for collaborating, that worked marvellously well because Marsha Hewitt, who had been working away on this book for a year before I came on the scene, has skills that are different from mine and strengths different from mine. Her skills in primary research helped in interviews, and then being thirty-five miles from the scene in Montreal meant she could get me information in a hurry or elaborate on descriptions. Her major discovery was the grandmother who is indeed based on a real person. She was a marvellous woman who actually had participated in this strike. In the final writing I think a touch of my own grandmother crept in. She was an independent-minded, radical woman who had to make her own way in the world and did a number of things to disturb the bourgeoisie. After an initial period of awkwardness between us, both emotional and creative, Marsha and I got along extremely well and our talents seemed to mesh so it was a very happy collaboration. We are at present negotiating the film rights for *One proud summer*. There's a scoop for you. It will be in French, naturally. One could hardly expect Lucie to be chattering to her grandmother in English, so it will appear in French first. There were the constraints of history, the constraints of having to be faithful to Madeleine Parent's recollections, the constraints of working with somebody else. There were others because the publisher, Women's Press, has a certain way of looking at reality and a certain desire to publish a kind of book that perhaps other publishers don't wish to. The manuscript was read by eight women at the press. We either did an end run around their comments or

accommodated them in ways that were satisfactory to us. Eventually out the book came. I am delighted that you think it and the other books don't seem like commissioned works, though why "commissioned works" should be a pejorative phrase I'm not exactly sure.

Michasiw: I think it's a hangover from the Romantic Movement, the idea that one had to be inspired by the Muse. But it's well to remember that Dickens wrote *Pickwick Papers* as a commissioned work. Did you have difficulty meshing the fiction and the fact in *One proud summer*? It reads without a seam, but I'm wondering if this was a particulary difficult challenge for you.

Mackay: It's hard to remember the nature of the difficulties—this is, after all, almost ten years ago. All books are very difficult for me. I do not write books easily nor do I write them quickly except for the one that should be rewritten, *Mini-bike racer*. There are times in the writing of every book when you are convinced that you cannot do it, you will never finish it, you have failed. The one thing that sometimes keeps you going is that you have signed a contract. You've got to do it no matter what if you are a person of honour, which I think I am. The other thing that gives one courage at these points is the sure knowledge that every other writer goes through this including the great and the mighty. We all get to that stage and knowing we have been there before and somehow miraculously finished the book gives enough, not courage maybe, but determination to persist for three hours of the day and see what happens. . . . Back to the difficulties of *One proud summer*. Because the fiction is almost confined to the character of Lucie, I was not conscious of that particular difficulty or constraint. I felt that I could successfully live inside this girl's body for the hundred days of that summer, partly because I was just about the same age in 1946 and probably of the same cast of mind even though I was not a young French Canadian mill worker who had to quit school. But you will note once again the relationship with the father. The father is gone when the novel begins, but the father is much loved.

Michasiw: The father's loss is part of the grievance against the company.

Mackay: That's right, but I certainly drew on my own childhood there once again and the funeral scene is my father's funeral. So all of those parts which I hope give some depth and colour and verisimilitude to the characters in the book are not dependent on the things that befall those characters. Let me make myself clear. If Lucie's character came through as legitimate, as real, as true, as genuine, then it didn't really matter what piece of history she was moving through. Naturally she was reacting to this history. I hope she reacted in a credible way. I suppose this is what every writer hopes. Really you paid me a high compliment by saying the book seemed to be mine. Do you want money?

Michasiw: No, I want some further discussion. I'd like to move on to *The Minerva program* which is a real departure, it seems to me, from what happens in *One proud* *summer*. Once again I know you were asked to write it, this time by Lorimer. And one of the things I find fascinating is that as Minerva was learning to use a computer, you were also learning to use a computer, so I would like to start this section of our discussion by asking you whether you found a computer affected the way in which you write?

Mackay: That may be a sensitive subject at this point. *Minerva* came out in 1984 which is five years ago now. You will not have failed to observe, as I have, that I have not written a full-length fiction work since that time and . . .

Michasiw: I didn't think it was that long.

Mackay: It doesn't seem that long because *Minerva* is still doing very well. But it struck me recently that I've done a non-fiction work and I've written quite a number of short pieces—but I have not written a full-length fiction work. Now I'm not going to say it's all the computer's fault. I had written most of the first draft of *Minerva* before I switched to the computer even though, as you pointed out, I was trying to be like my young heroine and learning how to use a computer. There are some drawbacks; there are also some wonderful advantages but I don't think the wonderful advantages have anything to do with creativity. The computer can do a whole lot of mechanical things very rapidly, but it can't write the book. The person who owns the computer has to write the book. The drawbacks that I'm beginning to see are these: in all my other fiction works the page I was working on was always in the typewriter, visible as I walked by. Its imperfections were also visible and every time I sat down I looked at it, I knew very well it was not my final draft. All its blemishes were there in front of me as evidence. With the computer, because you can correct on the screen, you make your mistakes disappear almost right away. You can print a perfect page every time. Half the time it's very imperfect and full of things that shouldn't be there.

Michasiw: I would worry that I might eliminate something that afterwards I wanted back.

Mackay: Exactly. That can happen too. Now I even save the little notes I take on the computer. I save everything in the hope that if I'm going to reuse something it won't have vanished into the ether. The other thing that happens, at least with my word processing program, is that you have to go through a whole lot of things to call up what you're working on. You turn the machine on. There are clicks and buzzes. A menu comes up and you select from the menu what you want; then you sub-select and finally up comes page one of your manuscript. What you want is page forty-nine, the last page written, but before you can get to page forty-nine, you eyes fall on page one. Because you see each page on the way to forty-nine, you feel compelled to change and polish. On page one you remove a comma, on page twelve an adverb which seems to throw the rhythm of that entire paragraph out, so you work on that. Often by the time you get to page forty-

nine, where you would have been had you been using a typewriter or a pen and a piece of paper, it's time to get lunch. And what you have done is rewrite a whole lot of little bits. You've lost the momentum of the story. This is what has happened to the novel that I'm working on. I have written the first hundred and ten pages at least eight times and I'm in the middle of the story and I'm not at all sure that I can get to the end. The other thing is that because there's an element of play in using a computer, because the keyboard is so responsive, the screen so delightfully obliging, you run off at the keys. There's more physical work involved in writing and correcting on the typewriter, consequently you tend to be a little more careful with your words. And you may even get it right the first time or the second time or the fifth time. With the computer, you put down any old thing because you don't want to lose the thought and then sometimes you think that any old thing is good enough; but it's not. *Because you can print a perfect page, you think you have written a perfect page.* So those are the real drawbacks and I'm even considering for this novel going back to the typewriter. Maybe it's just one of those writer's superstitions. Hemingway wrote standing up and another fellow always used purple ink. I went so far as to buy a $79.00 secondhand typewriter and put it in my little den at home just in case. Some writers have gone right back to pen and paper. Audrey Thomas, for example. She says there's actually a neuromuscular connection and perhaps even an emotional connection between her brain and her hand and it gets lost in electronics. She may have a point. Certainly I cannot write poetry on the computer. I write poetry with a pencil and paper.

Michasiw: So this really underlines the emotional connection. There are two other questions I would like to ask you about *Minerva*. One of them is about the names and I know, because you've spoken to my classes about this, that you gave careful thought to all the names in *The Minerva program*. Is this just a writer's game or has it the significance of naming that we find in fairytale and myth?

Mackay: It's probably a bit of both because words and the names of things have always fascinated me. I don't think that any writer lightly chooses a name. When Katherine Paterson named Gilly Hopkins she wasn't exactly sure where it came from. She was thinking of writing a story about a foster child and as a family the Patersons were reading *The Lord of the Rings* aloud. When Galadriel entered the story, she knew she was going to use that name. It seemed to fit and immediately she knew more about the mother of Gilly. She wasn't at all sure where Hopkins came from until she remembered Gerard Manley Hopkins, her favourite poet. So even when she doesn't choose names consciously, she *is* choosing them.

Michasiw: They choose her.

Mackay: Yes. They pop up. And I know Jean [Little] does the same thing. It's no accident that Emily appears in the book *Kate* and again later in the poems. There are Emily Brontë and Emily Dickinson, who is Jean's favourite poet, and Emily Carr, all big influences, the writing Emilys. Back to my own exercise in naming. I thinks it's evident early c.. in my work. There's a section in *Mini-bike rescue* where Julie talks about how she likes to name things. By naming things you own them.

Michasiw: This is what I was thinking of when I suggested the fairytale and myth connection, that to name something is to have power over it.

Mackay: Well, I believe that myself deeply. I look back on my own childhood and I *had* to name things; I had to know the names of things, just like Julie. Then I could make order. Otherwise the world was chaotic and menacing. I know I've read other writers, perhaps wiser writers, who say they don't want to know the names of things. It robs them of their emotional appeal and power, their mystery. To me it adds to the power, it adds to the significance of that object or event or person to know its name. It adds a whole other dimension and this is what I try to do when I'm naming—add an extra dimension. Whether young or older readers pick up on the significance of the names—the code in the names—doesn't matter to me. They may, even if they don't realize it, because we all carry a huge store of unrealized knowledge in our minds and hearts, the almost Jungian racial memory. I think many of the names will ring a faint bell, or a very loud one, with some people even though they don't realize it. They will add the little bit of extra resonance that I want and will give the character depth and credibility. In the article I've written on names in *Writers on writing* I mention Sue Alderson's "Bonnie McSmithers" is a stroke of genius, a wonderful name and very musical. And I note in this article too what Janet Lunn does in *Shadow in Hawthorn Bay* when her spelling counts. The second word in the book, I believe, is Mairi, M-a-i-r-i. With that one stroke, Janet made her whole story reverberate because there's the magic of second sight in that name, there's the music of the Highlands, there's a sense of differentness, of other-worldliness, all implied in that name. Whether or not Janet knew she was doing it or not, it's there and the reader will pick it up too.

Michasiw: I even want to say it differently with my inward voice.

Mackay: Sure, you drag out the central vowels. So important, very important, the names. I took immense care—apart from having a few private jokes of my own—throughout the book.

Michasiw: Your sense of humour really doesn't come into its own until *The Minerva program*. Was there something about this particular story or your approach to it or maybe even about the computer that released your sense of humour to its full potential?

Mackay: I would hope, Barbara, it's not my full potential, not yet. Once you reach your full potential, that's when you retire.

Michasiw: Sorry! To its greater potential. Can I say that?

Mackay: You're not the first person who has observed this. It was a question of giving myself permission to write this way. I've had to learn the courage to be more and more myself in my books. All writing, I suppose, is self-revealing, but some more than others. And this was an aspect I was both unsure I should reveal and unsure whether I could reveal. Now, that's part of the answer, but you raised another point. Was it because of the story? Yes, in large part it was because of the story. It's a contemporary story of kids who are in a way street-wise and sophisticated and it's also a genre book. I can glibly call it a computer mystery and it's almost true. Not quite true, but almost true. Very consciously in my mind, during the writing of this, was a recent development that I see in modern fiction, a development that has been designated by a woman writer as "exploding the genre." That is you use the genre say of a mystery story, a detective story, a science fiction story, so that the reader says, "Oh yes, that is what this is." And then you proceed to push against the boundaries of that genre, take some risks within it. The reader isn't at sea, but all kinds of rather interesting things are occurring within this set of expectations. That intrigued me. It seemed delightfully subversive, to tell you the truth, and I thought that if I could, using a mystery form—and you can see, it's pretty classical where you have all the suspects gathered together in the final scene.

Michasiw: Everyone except the butler.

Mackay: Yes. No butlers in Minerva's life. So it's a very classical form, it's a genre form, but some odd little things are happening throughout. There's the subplot, of course, which, in a sense, deals with what I was originally charged to do and that's write about the social implications of high tech. Certainly that was in my mind. If I could explode the genre, that might be kind of satisfying.

Michasiw: Well, basically humour is subversive.

Mackay: Of course, and once again I felt freer to use some of my own high school experiences. My five-year battle with my gym teacher . . . at last I got revenge. So a lot of it is straightforward development, as you said, and the beginnings of some degree of certainty about where to put my feet which I didn't have before. Naturally I think it is the best written of my novels, and thank heaven because it's the latest written too. It would be awful if you just kept getting worse. Now, before we move from this, I have to pay tribute to my editor.

Michasiw: To what degree have you relied on editors? Are editors an aid or a hindrance?

Mackay: They have been both. They have been a real pain in the neck a couple of times because they weren't being editors. They wanted to rewrite the book, please. They were frustrated writers. I have forgotten their names.

Michasiw: Good, we'll avoid a libel suit.

Mackay: They were freelancers hired by one of my publishers; but when I came to write *One proud summer*, I

.was assigned by Women's Press this particular editor, Charis Wahl, and in every book since then I have acknowledged her help in a foreword or an author's note. She has managed to convince me that I can write, which I think is a marvellous thing for an editor to do for a writer. Even though she's superbly critical of early drafts, and unerring when I do put a foot wrong, she ends all her written comments with "I really loved this book" or "This is a good story and only you could tell it." Fortunately, she has a sense of humour. But without her organizational intelligence, without her way of being cruel only to be kind, the three books I've written with her help would not be as good as they are. It's too bad we can't do a whole interview on editing sometime. Indeed, it might be worth devoting a whole issue of *CCL* to editing.

Michasiw: Yes. Think of some of the great editors! I was rereading the interview with Christie Harris that appeared in *CCL* last year and included her tribute to Jean Karl. I was fortunate enough at the Pacific Rim Conference to meet Jean Karl, I have never forgotten that.

Mackay: With the first couple of books, because I didn't know anything about the whole game, I just let them do whatever they wanted to do and it backfired. Backfired with the first book right into the pages of *Canadian Children's Literature*, where I was taken to task for being racist. That charge would not have been levelled had several paragraphs in my original manuscript of *Minibike hero* been allowed to stand. But they were edited out and that was a real gaffe. I should never have let it happen, but what did I know? Scholastic should not have allowed their editor to do it, but they just felt that it wouldn't play in Australia with all this history stuff in it, so it was out. In a later edition of that book, we essentially rewrote it so that all mention of native peoples was removed because both of us, as publisher and as writer, were very upset over this charge.

Michasiw: Understandably.

Mackay: Understandably, not just because we wanted to appear to be without prejudice, but also because of my own background and work settings to be accused of racism against Métis children with whom I had spent two years of my life was a really tough charge.

Michasiw: I hate to leave *The Minerva program* without further comment because I find it such a pleasing book, but perhaps we should move on to *Pay cheques & picket lines*. I know that labour and the union movement are causes you have had sympathy with for a long time, but when you were faced with the task of making them accessible to children was it a challenge that you welcomed or did you find it initially rather daunting?

Mackay: Initially I was very excited and unless I'm excited by the idea there's no way that I'll undertake it, just no way at all. This I was excited about. I was also, I suppose, feeling a little bit like a missionary. I was well aware there was nothing on the shelves (or not very much) on this topic for children and also I felt that, generally speaking, the establishment media give unions a bad rap and always have. In talking to kids before I even started the book, I had discovered a kind of contempt for workers who were on strike, an impatience with the desires of folks who weren't lawyers and stockbrokers and doctors. So I felt emotionally committed to it right from the beginning. But then the work began. It wasn't so much the difficulty in explaining complex and sophisticated concepts, I could find the words for that, it was the compression of what amounted to something like two hundred years of history (three hundred maybe) into what the publisher at first said was going to be sixty-four pages. It was quickly determined that I could not do this in sixty-four pages and do any sort of justice to the topic, so I begged for a few more pages: "Can I have eighty?" "Well, maybe." The final number of pages is a hundred and eight. And still I wonder if I did the whole topic justice. Compression was the big difficulty. How to get this mass of information into something not just comprehensible, but also something almost fun to read, and if not fun to read at least easy to read. This was the big problem.

Michasiw: The organization must have been an enormous task. It is partly the tone and the way in which the material is presented, but also partly the organization that makes it so accessible to young readers.

Mackay: Yes, and once again a tip of the hat to my editor and also to the in-house editor, Val Wyatt. The lot of us decided early on that we had to compartmentalize the material and we also knew that it was going to have *x* number of sections which made it easier for me to write. Much of it fell into place once we had that safety net of the form. Probably most non-fiction can be characterized that way: once you know the form, once you have it sliced into appropriate chunks, then at least you know this little piece of information is going in there. It's like sorting buttons. The other difficulty, and it's a corollary of the necessity for compression, is that when you compress facts into general statements or overviews, you might not do justice to the real truth of that particular event. So I had to be conscious all the time that yes, I must compress; yes, I'm forced to generalize; yes, I'm forced to deal with thirty years of history in two paragraphs; but at the same time I must not bend the truth. Yet because I write (I hope) in an illustrative way, even when I was generalizing, I wanted to pick out colourful bits which would illustrate the compressed general truth I had just stated. So I was always on the lookout for the detail that would lend drama, the detail that would jump off the page, and make a child see the truth of that general statement. All of these processes were going on at once. That's where the difficulty was. Also the research . . . one entire room in my house is now the union book.

Michasiw: I can believe that. I think the time chart that you include at the very end is a particularly useful device for a child.

Mackay: Oh, that's good because it almost didn't get in there. We almost didn't have room for it.

Michasiw: Given the chart, the parts of the book fell into place. You've mentioned already the fan letters you get. What sort of response have you got from children towards *Pay cheques?*

Mackay: Not a lot. I think I've only had two, maybe three, letters so far. The book still has to filter its way down through the system. It goes to older kids and usually I speak to junior grades. Just this past week I was in Mississauga talking to four grade eight bunches, I guess three hundred kids altogether in four sessions, and they had been primed a little bit ahead of time. One boy showed up with a Canadian Auto Workers' sweat shirt on. I asked how many of their parents belonged to a union. Half the kids put their hands up. Half again of those had parents who had been on strike, so there was a lot of prior knowledge and a lot of interest particularly, of course, in strikes. We had an extensive discussion about how strikes were really a rotten way to settle anything, but that in North America we seem to be stuck with it, at least for now, and that in the last analysis it's the only thing a worker can do, the ultimate weapon. I've also talked to some kids in Saskatchewan about this book. They had studied it ahead of time and when I arrived there was a complete picket line around the school! They had written a play based on that first little anecdote about Mary and the biscuit factory and it was just splendid. Oh, and they had formed a union in the school and the teachers were quite fearful of what it might bring in its wake. So if the book is presented in the proper manner, I think kids will turn on to it. Again, one of the reasons I wrote the book and why it may appeal is that labour union history is full of colour and drama and violence and humour and, up to now, in any exposition of this matter for kids none of that colour and drama has appeared. I hope it does in this book, enough so kids will see this is worthwhile and it's part of our history.

Michasiw: I like the way you use the microcosm of the Piggin' Out Restaurant to bring a union within the sphere of understanding of the young reader who has his or her first job.

Mackay: I hope you also noticed that I use the second person pronoun throughout that particular section which was really a ruse, a little technique to get the young reader right into the spot. It seemed to work.

Michasiw: Because you've brought up the subject of working with students in the schools, I'd like to move from *Pay cheques* to ask you about your experiences as a Creative-Artist-in-Schools and then a Writer-in-Libraries. What is entailed and what kinds of contacts did you have with the students?

Mackay: This is a special program under the Ontario Arts Council where writers, storytellers, visual artists, illustrators, any number of people can go in for *x* number of hours per week and deal with an assorted group of children. I had two classes of twelve children, from grades four to six, each for one morning a week for six successive weeks. Given the size of the groups and the extended period of time that I had with them, we were able really to take a project through to completion. At the end of that time, most of the children had completed either a poem or a story. One even did a non-fiction. Because the kids were preselected for interest in writing, the level of creative activity was pretty high. I think possibly the person who learned the most was me. I don't think I had ever analyzed, in an intellectual way, what was involved in writing, so I was forced to examine some of my own habits.

Michasiw: This was another stage in your development.

Mackay: Yes, I think so because I had to think critically about what I was going to say to them about the craft of writing, because I had to review their work and say, "Well, you've lost it here," or "Do you need ten words when one will do?" or "Really, we don't need to know that he breathed in and then he breathed out." That just boomeranged right back into my own work where I could see, to my discomfiture, some of the same things cropping up. So I hope they learned something. They claimed they did, the school was very pleased, and the kids were just delightful. Some of them are still writing which is very gratifying. I'll say one other thing: just because you write doesn't mean you can teach. I began that gig with great trepidation. I really did it because the school librarian is a friend of mine and she has had me to the school several times and she begged me. Once again I was responding to someone who was asking me to do something. I found it quite stressful. Then, about two months later, the librarian called me up and invited me to the school for a special ceremony. They had put together all the kids' writings in a specially bound volume with their pictures and a little note from each of them. One child—a little wee kid in Grade 3 who had hardly said a word and wouldn't read her work, she was so shy—had written a story about the kidnapping of a chipmunk. She wrote it from the chipmunk's point of view and it was quite wonderful. She had become the chipmunk. First person. This little nine-year-old. As far as the children were concerned, I guess it was a worthwhile experience. Now, Writers-in-Libraries. Once again I was responding to someone asking me to do something. This was another wonderful program from the Ontario government that all of us writers want to continue. It was a scheme to place a fairly well established writer in a local library and serve the community of aspiring writers that everyone assumed was out there. The children's librarians in Toronto asked me to take it on for all their six boroughs and I was the first appointee, a real pioneer. It was a bit of a burden placed on me immediately that I had better try to make the program work or the government, in its capriciousness, would simply stop writing cheques. It involved eighteen hours of work a week officially . . .

Michasiw: That's a fairly heavy schedule.

Mackay: . . . and the established writer who was in residence was supposed to be writing his or her own work during the rest of the time. Unfortunately it didn't work out quite that neatly. I got an enormous response: not just from the six library systems. Because the publicity was run in national newspapers and on national radio, I actually dealt with manuscripts from as far away as London, England, Vancouver, and every spot in Ontario and a couple of spots south of the border.

Michasiw: Eighteen hours a week!

Mackay: It was not eighteen hours a week. My particular charge in this was to interview and help writers who wished to write for children, to do workshops for them and also for children who had shown some promise in writing. I did thirty-five workshops in five months, lasting one to two hours each. I read in the neighbourhood of three hundred and fifty manuscripts, and wrote to or saw I don't know how many children. I must have talked to about eleven hundred people. A young girl, age fourteen, came from Haliburton one day and landed in a Scarborough library. She's going to be a writer. People wouldn't arrive with just one manuscript. They would bring their last six—since we had neglected to set up guidelines. I'm not ascribing blame to anyone; we just didn't know what was going to happen. It was as if we had offered water to a bunch of thirsty people. They just came in droves, especially as it percolated through the community: "Hey, there's a writer in the library!" Considering travelling time, it was almost like a full-time job. So very little of my own writing got done and since this was one of the prime concerns of the government, I was a little disturbed about that. I am now a kind of informal advisor to writers who take these positions and I immediately send them a bunch of caveats: be careful you don't do this . . .

Michasiw: Lay down some rules.

Mackay: Yes, have some guidelines about the number of submissions at a time. The response is still coming in. This was two years ago and I had a letter just last week from a woman who had neglected to thank me. She said "The local newspaper just published my story." A lot of people really only needed someone to take them seriously. From the point of view of the ministry and the point of view of the community it was a raving success. From the point of view of the writer—I needed a rest. I entered a sort of catatonia around the fourth month.

Michasiw: I was wondering how close you came to a nervous breakdown.

Mackay: It was a tough job, but I wouldn't have missed it for the world. Besides I found three wonderful writers, two magnificent illustrators, and ten kids who are going to be writers. One young woman actually had a story published in *Canadian Children's Annual* after she came to try my workshops.

Michasiw: That's your triumph, Claire. Now, before we finish, there are two additional questions I would like to ask. You have already mentioned that you are working on another book, tentatively titled "Waiting for the sunrise" . . .

Mackay: I'm waiting and waiting and waiting . . .

Michasiw: . . . and you've said a little bit about the difficulties of writing it and the slowdown, thanks to the computer. We've been talking also about your development as a writer. You may regard it as a kind of jinx to say anything in advance about this book; but if you feel comfortable talking about it, would you comment on the further development you're finding in this new work which is obviously coming out of your own life and experience?

Mackay: First I want to go right back to your third sentence about the computer slowing me down. I don't want to use the computer as a cop-out here. I suspect that much of the slowdown does not lie in the computer. It lies in the writer. Part of the difficulty with this book, I believe, is a desire not to upset certain members of my family who took part in some of the events which will appear in it. My view of those events then and now is quite different from their perceptions. I'm always reminded of that Japanese movie, *Rashomon,* which is told from four different points of view, a completely different view of the same event each time.

Michasiw: Or Browning's *Ring and the book.*

Mackay: Much more literary. Part of it has to do with the fact that—yes, you are right—I am another rung up in my development because the book doesn't know what form it wants to be in and I've become very sensitive to the power of form. I know you can't separate form and content. At the same time I have tried this in several different ways, one way being what I've termed a clothesline approach (it may not be original with me, that term). I mean there are a series of connected stories.

Michasiw: Do you mean like *A bird in the house?*

Mackay: *A bird in the house,* even Alice Munro's work to some extent where there is the same protagonist in many of the stories. And for a while I was almost settling nicely into that; then I felt that especially for a young reader, and I still had in my mind that this would be for young readers, it might not be as satisfying as a longer narrative. Also I was feeling some loss of dynamic in it myself. Even though the separate stories might be connected through character and chronology, the form didn't allow for much growth in the character. Given the set of events that I am immersing myself in, which is the Depression and essentially the politicization of a family, how they dealt with the Depression, considerable growth has to be demonstrated. So I went back then and tried to make it a continuing narrative but changed the voice from third to first person. Then I decided I didn't think I could sustain first person throughout a fairly lengthy novel, especially if the first person is a fifteen-year-old girl.

Michasiw: Well, she is going to have limited perceptions of what's going on.

Mackay: Exactly and she has to be on the scene or you have to use those really corny devices of someone telling her about an event or she gets a letter or she overhears a conversation. They're really too tired to even consider unless you do it so skillfully. . . . But mostly it was what I've noticed in some of young people's fiction I've read that is first person: there's such tunnel vision. The narrator is intrinsically a boring personality and you get so sick of that voice after eight chapters or so that you just say, "I've had it."

Michasiw: Especially in a trying situation, that voice tends to develop self-pity which really grates on the reader.

Mackay: So then I went back and did what is almost first person, that is, third person subjective which is used in *Minerva*. I was fairly happy with that for a while; then I discovered the events were forcing the characters to behave in ways I didn't wish them to behave and at that point I just stopped. That's where it is right now. I've decided to go back to first person and I've rewritten the first sixty pages with a voice I think I can live with. The voice is faintly ironic, the way Minerva's is in a sense, but definitely not Minerva. I suppose in many ways it's my own young self and you're quite right that in this book, more than in any other book I have tried, I'm utilizing huge areas not only of my background, but also of my family's background, my grandmother's background. So it may be rather longer than what I have written so far, it may be for older people, for older kids. It may be for adults. This is another thing I find a little alarming. It may be crossing over . . . if it's ever done.

Michasiw: It will be.

Mackay: I'm nervous about it. I'm scared to show it to anybody even. It's in a tender state. My editor has seen some and made some comments, useful as usual; she has backed off a little because she knows that I am going through some difficulties with it and there's no point in pushing it. I did read some bits to Jean Little and I was so nervous I could hardly believe it. She thinks it's terrific (I don't believe her) and well worth going on with. She also sees it as a leap forward from previous work. So I'm bearing out your thesis here. Maybe that's why I'm having difficulty finishing it. Maybe I haven't really gathered together sufficient courage to go on with it yet. Every bit of growth comes out of a certain amount of pain and cowardice . . .

Michasiw: And overcoming that.

Mackay: So I'll have to persist because the bottom line is I want to tell this story; I hope I can do it justice. To me it's the story of ordinary people triumphing. I hope I can tell it so that it's a tribute to my parents and grandparents. And maybe that's part of what's holding me back.

Michasiw: That seems like the right place to stop and yet there may be something else you would like to say.

Mackay: Well, I guess this has been said before, but I think I was very lucky to be in the right place at the right time. Fifteen years ago I might not have been able

to make a career, let alone a decent living from writing. Fifteen years from now we might all be back numbers. I have a sense that children's literature in Canada is fashionable right now and while there is a promise of another few years of popularity, it may end. It seems to me that my own desire to see if I could be a writer coincided with a number of other things happening in the country and in society that prepared the way for me. Once again I ask, is there such a thing as coincidence? The other thing I would like to say is this: I am profoundly grateful my books have found readers and grateful too that this affirmation has lent me the courage and confidence to proceed. It has made me believe, almost, that I am a writer.

[Post-script, 1991]

Michasiw: Since we last talked, Claire, you have won two awards from Parenting Publications of America, an Honourable Mention in 1989 and a First Place Award in 1990.

Mackay: These were for a monthly column I write for a Toronto tabloid newspaper called *Kids Toronto*. I'm allowed to write almost anything I please as long as it's remotely connected to children and nobody edits me. One I wrote recently arose from a walk down a street where I used to live. The walk evoked memories of the late thirties and early forties in Toronto, all grist to the particular mill I use for the column.

Michasiw: And some grist too for your most recent book, *The Toronto story*.

Mackay: All the writing I'm doing—nonfiction, journalism, novel—is part of the same motherlode especially for *The Toronto story*. I used my mother's diaries, my mother's stories, my mother's recollections, my own recollections, in reconstructing the nineteen thirties and forties. That was just *part* of a massive job of research.

Michasiw: I was struck on every page of *The Toronto story* with the enormous amount of research you had to do.

Mackay: It took two and a third years of many ten-hour days.

Michasiw How did you find all those human tidbits about people and history?

Mackay: Much of it was in letters or diary entries and I owe a great deal—as does my illustrator—to Edith Firth, who collected all the early papers of the town of York. She included things many people may find boring. But where else could I have discovered the great variety of merchandise that Toronto's first department store sold, or the long list of items that purchased Toronto from the Mississauga tribe? I looked always for the colourful detail. Any touch of character or idiosyncrasy, comedy or tragedy, I filed away, especially where it concerned children.

Michasiw: But you don't pull any punches either. For instance, the description of the American attack on York in 1813.

Mackay: I suppose that springs partly from my own *Weltanschauung.* It was a ghastly scene—all carnage is— and when I discovered that the apprentice-surgeon, William Beaumont, had kept such graphic notes, I knew I had to use them. Violence has been glorified for, or at least distanced from children through television and videos so that they don't make a connection between what they are watching and being hurt and bleeding and dying. I myself was shocked when I read these entries and I tried to be *there* with these characters. Above my computer was a quotation from Penelope Lively and it operated as a watchword. It reads " . . . places have a past, . . . they are now but also were then, and . . . if peopled now, they were peopled then." I wanted young readers especially to experience firsthand the many-layered history that they move through every day and the reality of the people who have gone before then. I'm concerned that children, that all of us, have a sense of continuity. The other characteristic of both my nonfiction works is that I put myself in the books. I didn't hesitate to insert my personality, to express my own convictions in my prose, a departure from earlier nonfiction written for children. It's more fun for the writer this way and I believe it's more fun for the reader too.

Michasiw: But *The Toronto story* is different from any other books you have written because of the illustrations.

Mackay: It was serendipitous that Johnny Wales had dropped off his portfolio to Annick about three months before we conceived this book. Johnny is a Torontonian from way back. His style complements mine and we share a similar sense of humour. Anyone who looks carefully at the illustrations will notice all kinds of delightful detail and hidden jokes. In the 1930 double-spread, for example, one can see that a stockbroker has heaved himself out a window and is lying on the street with an ambulance beside him. Every illustration, small or large, has an element of fun in it. But also—and I'm sure Johnny would want me to make a point of this—every illustration is historically and architecturally accurate. It was an enormous amount of work and I think it shows.

Michasiw: It's a beautiful book that bears repeated reading not only of the text, but also of the illustrations. You were both mining a wealth of Toronto reference.

Mackay: But, Barbara, my investment in *The Toronto story* may have robbed the novel. I suspect some of the novel's narrative energy got redirected into *The Toronto story,* even into my columns because of the similarity of the material. I'm fearful about reentering the novel. Some of the stories I was going to tell in the novel, I have already told. Whether I will want to tell them again is a question I'm not sure I can answer right now. Although worthwhile in many respects, *The Toronto story* was a detour from the novel emotionally and creatively. Soon I must find out whether the novel is still alive.

TITLE COMMENTARY

📖 *MINI-BIKE HERO* (1974); *MINI-BIKE RAC-ER* (1976)

N. B. Johnson

SOURCE: A review of *Mini-Bike Racer,* in *The World of Children's Literature,* Vol. II, No. 2, Fall, 1977, pp. 26-7.

Open the contemporary adventure novel and a chase scene almost always appears—or a fast car—or a daring motorcycle. Sometimes there is a reasonable plot that justifies the vehicle, sometimes there is even a hint of character development. And, occasionally, the motorcycle, etc. simply serves as the device that sets up the adventure.

. . . Mackay's book, a paperback reprint, is intended for the 10-14 year old. A sequel to the author's *Mini-Bike Hero,* it continues the adventures of Steve MacPherson, Kim Chambers, and Julie Brennan. The plot is undistinguished. Steve, recovering from the injuries incurred during his previous heroism, loses the friendship of his best friend, Kim. Julie Brennan, an accomplished mini-bike rider too (and an outspoken advocate of women's rights) becomes Steve's riding buddy. Involved as a hostage in the hold-up of the cycle repair shop, Steve shrugs that off to concentrate on the big mini-bike races coming up. While riding around in an effort to fix his bike on race day, Steve discovers the robbers' hideout and is captured. The rescue attempt draws in all the characters (and the Mounties, of course) and neatly resolves all the problems. Standard plot, standard characters, and standard ending make this a standard book. There is one thing in its favor however; Mackay does have some knowledge of motorcycle and mini-bike riding and uses that to good advantage.

Gertrude Barrett

SOURCE: A review of *Mini-Bike Racer,* in *In Review: Canadian Books for Children,* Vol. 11, No. 1, Winter 1977, p. 36.

In this sequel to *Mini-bike Hero* reviewed in *In Review* Autumn 1975 there are many of the components of a good adventure story. Unfortunately they are not combined in the proper proportions or with enough literary skill to make it successful.

Twelve year old Steve, his broken arm just mended from his last adventure, encounters a sudden coolness which soon turns to outright hostility from his best friend and rival racer, Kim Chambers, as they prepare for the biggest race of the season. In a rather obvious attempt to be non-sexist, the author introduces Julie Brennan as a new friend and racing partner, almost as competent as the boys. Together they rescue a young German shepherd which is the most true to form character in the book and becomes the real hero.

One evening when he is working on his bike in Pete Sikorsky's shop, Steve witnesses a robbery and Julie narrowly escapes getting struck by the getaway car. On the day of the big race Steve goes off alone to work some bugs out of his bike—and you guessed it—is taken hostage by the robber, an escaped convict. Of course the dog leads Julie and a repentant Kim to Steve and the police, alerted by the exploding bike, arrive just in the nick of time for a successful rescue. The kids get the $500 reward which the other two agree to give to Steve to replace his bike which was destroyed by the robber. Finally in a most improbable ending, the dog which had been left for dead by Steve bounds up to greet him.

This book is very simple but not well written; the characters are not realistically developed and I cannot recommend it for general purchase.

Vicki Wright

SOURCE: A review of *Mini-Bike Hero and Mini-Bike Racer,* in *Canadian Children's Literature,* No. 7, 1977, pp. 36-8.

It is easy to see why **Mini-Bike Hero** and **Mini-Bike Racer** are immediate hits with junior readers; the novels are escapist literature. Such stories are pleasure-giving because the imagination is minimally challenged, there is no preaching, the uncomplicated characterization is readily acceptable, the action is abundant, thrilling, suspenseful, and each plot and sub-plot has an upbeat ending. Although we bookish types would have it otherwise, the fact is that light reading is preferred by most children, as it is by most adults. Moreover, it is especially suitable for nine-to-twelve year olds who are stepping out of childhood but not quite into adolescence when one must face up to the confusing task of "growing up". Thus, *Mini-Bike Hero* and *Mini-Bike Racer* are highly satisfying, TV-like entertainment packages for this in-between age-group.

Contrary to expectations occasioned by the titles, the stories are not about mini-bikes and racing. Rather, the plots feature the activities and adventures of Steve, age eleven, who functions as an adult, and who is indeed superior to the adults with whom he interacts. He also outclasses his age-mates.

Mr. Svenson of the Strathemeyer Syndicate (Hardy Boys and others) says, [in *The Girl Sleuth,* by Bobbi Ann Mason] "Our big success has been to let the young heroes do the doing, and to keep adult interference to a minimum". Claire Mackay also uses this technique. She has the protagonist lead a double life in each of the books. In *Mini-Bike Hero,* Steve's Dad has forbidden him to even utter the word "mini-bike", so Steve is forced to lead a normal conformist life coupled with a secret life of earning money for, and learning about mini-bikes. This tantalizing duplicity ends suddenly with Steve in a state of grace: circumstances confront him with a chain of tasks wherein he takes a wild ride down a treacherous slope to assist a

friend pinned under a motorcycle, hurries on through a punishing storm to warn an Indian village about an imminent flood, daringly rescues an Indian baby for its screaming mother, then continues on a nightmare, miles-long ride in rain and darkness with a broken arm into town to contact the police and lead them back to the injured man. All of this happens on his first trip to the hills with his mini-bike. Steve never looks back.

In **Mini-Bike Racer,** his surface life provides him with opportunities to maintain and polish his hero role, while his inner life is one of hurt, and of toughening up to be a loner, a man. His best friend gives in to jealousy and becomes Steve's challenger. A resolution occurs when Steve becomes the hostage of a dangerous thief.

Steve is a protagonist with whom young readers can readily identify. As noted, this age group is about to begin the process of breaking away from their psychological, emotional, and financial dependence on parents. Steve's determination to have a mini-bike typifies their own capacity to be absorbed in hobbies or sports or some other interest. His display of expertness on the mini-bike and his derring-do makes their own dreams seem attainable. The demands of Steve's various job commitments, the strain of the terrible secret, the opportunities to perform heroically, allow for the vicarious trying on of adult-like responsibilities, roles and satisfactions. Julie's presence in the second story is the provision for exploring a relationship and friendship with the opposite sex. They even "play house" for an afternoon, babysitting Kate. Kids need such fictional experiences to expand their sense of developing individuality and values. Unconsciously, readers take at least a few steps in Steve's shoes.

The underlying story thread consists of Steve's developing manhood. Children are well aware that Canadian society places high premiums on masculinity and on financial independence. The stories reinforce their growing understanding that financial independence is symbolic of adulthood, and that to be masculine is to be adult. Steve, always the man-child, is a fine model. He doggedly earns every penny for his mini-bike. He displays incredible physical prowess. From these stories boys are reassured of what they have to do, to be, while girls are reminded that it is okay to attempt new competencies but they should keep their expectations low. This indeed is in keeping with the shaping children receive in the real world.

Although Steve is a highly likeable superhero, his story would have been better in the telling had he been merely a hero. In the unfolding of Steve as a paragon, Mackay overdoes situations and events. The story thus becomes cluttered and sometimes ludicrous, as shown earlier in Steve's return to grace.

Another example is seen in Steve's acquisition of a dog. Steve and Julie are babysitting wee Kate, who wanders off from her country home. Steve locates her just as she is about to pet a snarling dog made cranky by a steel trap that is biting into its leg. Steve's father and teacher are attributed the same unlikely transformation. When the facts are in, they instantly undergo a change from insensitive misusers of adult power, to warm, supportive devotees.

A final example of clutter, and the worst of its kind, is seen in the inclusion of an "Indian" episode. The negative depiction is entirely thoughtless and unnecessary. Consider the images that the following words and phrases portray as the episode evolves: "settlement"; "shack"; "a wrecked car with its engineless hood half in the river" (the wreck is right in front of a house). After Steve's alert about the flood (to a people who have a heritage of closeness to nature), " . . . the whole village . . . crowded together in a knot . . . gazing in fear at the crumbling dam." "His shout startled them into flight and they ran to the safety of higher ground . . ." A woman " . . . gave a piercing scream. 'My baby!' she wailed." Only Steve moves to rescue the child from the wrecked car as the wall of water rushes upon it.

The passage portrays the native people as slobs, dimwits, and cowards. When was it ever necessary for young white heroes to get a step up by standing on the necks of the native people? How can the scales fall from our children's eyes if they haven't fallen from the eyes of our authors and editors? Hopefully, in another printing of the story, this section will be removed.

According to her editor, Mackay did not intend to write a series, nor does she perceive the two books, her first, from that point of view. However, the framework has that kind of potential. The introduction of a female mini-bike racer in the second book promised interesting possibilities. As it turns out, Julie is no slouch, but neither is she any threat to the status quo, because Mackay cops out. Gender aside, Julie has the potential to be an equal peer in the story, and a positive role model for both girl and boy readers. Instead, she is repeatedly rendered ineffectual, as when she wins the Big Race only because the two top contenders, Steve and Kim, were not in it. She participates in Steve's rescue by staying back, albeit under protest, to keep the dog quiet! In keeping with the majority of storybook females, Julie is a background character, a prop for the male hero. Nevertheless, the structure is there so that Julie need not remain in that fringe position, should another story be forthcoming.

Mackay is an author whom children will recognize as being on their side. She raises mini-biking from the realm of disreputableness to one of respectability. She chastens a too-critical father, caricatures a dragon-teacher, then chastens her, too. For just a spot of fun, a cops-and-robbers chase becomes a cops-and-mini-bike chase, in which the law is foiled. So when plausibility is strained by the introduction of incredible situations contrived to enhance the hero, the kids cheerfully suspend judgement and accept them as delightful extras.

Merle Smith's illustrations capture the glamour of owning a set of wheels, and the excitement of action and spills. Word and picture come together neatly and the books have sold extremely well. It is this reviewer's hope that Julie will dry her tears, stop the phony protesting, the settling for third best, and get down to the solid action of which she seems capable. Her creator must know that there are countless readers who hope that both Julie and Steve will ride again.

EXIT BARNEY MCGEE (1979)

Jean Blair Simms

SOURCE: "Journeying to Maturity," in *Canadian Children's Literature*, No. 20, 1980, pp. 67-9.

Claire MacKay's *Exit Barney McGee* . . . deals with a teenager's attempt to find a place where he is wanted, needed and loved. As the novel opens, Barney is faced with two new and unfortunate circumstances. First, his new step-father uproots him by taking him to the suburbs with all their inconveniences, and secondly, his newly arrived half-sister, Sarah, usurps his place. As far as Barney can see, his step-father calls all the shots, and Barney's mother loves her husband more than her son. Barney makes a decision as a result: "He couldn't stay here. They didn't need him. They didn't want him. They didn't understand him. And he knew, he just knew, his real father would."

Thus the stage is set for new experiences and emotional adventure as the boy makes his way to Toronto in search of a father who deserted him and his mother ten years earlier. He envisions his father as an "adventurer" who is "free of all ordinary things, the dull routine stuff, the ruts of time and money. He had fled the road that Conrad [his stepfather] had chosen, the narrow road to nowhere". He imagines his natural father to be lively, reckless and bold—all the things that his step-father is not.

Finally, Barney reaches his intended destination where he encounters Maggie, whose smile vanishes when the boy tells her that he has come to see his father—Michael McGee. "Her face was unreadable. Emotions flickered across it like the twitching illuminations of a strobe light, there and gone too fast to decode." She turned away from him as she asked if his father knew he was coming. Barney finds harsh truths to face. He sums it up himself later: "running away just doesn't work. All you get is a whole new set of problems, some of them tougher than the ones you had before. *Maybe being free was something else altogether . . .*"

In this novel, you laugh at the antics of Barney's pet mouse, Saki; you suffer the agonies of a parent who loses a son; and you are deeply touched along with Barney, at the startling condition of alcoholics: "Barney had a sudden painful sense that Mike was the child and he the father". Barney learns that along with life's privileges go responsibilities. He learns that freedom, responsibility, and maturity are all intertwined.

Sandra Burke-Pidhurskyj

SOURCE: A review of *Exit Barney McGee*, in *In Review: Canadian Books for Young People*, Vol. 16, No. 1, February, 1982, pp. 45-6.

Last year Mr. Conrad was Barney's grade six teacher but now he is Barney's stepfather. On top of this, Barney also resents his new baby brother. One day Barney is trying to make some tea for his mother when his stepfather interferes and a special teapot breaks. This teapot had cost Barney three months' paper route money; it had been a present for his mother's birthday. Breaking it only adds insult to injury.

Barney is so mixed-up he thinks it would be best to find his father, Mike. He locates him and finds that Mike is a down and out street alcoholic. The emotions ride high in this book, especially when Mike rescues Barney's pet mouse Saki from a fire and ends up in the hospital in serious condition. Barney's father is now a hero. When Barney's stepfather finally finds Barney it is Mike who tells his son to go back to his family and his real home.

Exit Barney McGee is a realistic novel that tackles difficult problems facing a teenager. The book moves at a fast pace and the description of Barney's search to find his father is quite dramatic and believable. Its audience would be the 12 to 15 year olds who love "problem" books.

Lynn Wytenbroek

SOURCE: "Raw vs Clever," in *Canadian Literature*, Nos. 138-139, Fall-Winter, 1993, pp. 172-3.

In Mackay's *Exit Barney McGee,* a book about a pre-adolescent boy facing some real problems, the problems are neither endless nor completely unsolvable. . . . In fact, *Exit Barney McGee* is a surprising little book. It presents a fairly light-weight story about a boy who runs away from home after increasing problems with his new stepfather to join his real father who left when he was a baby. He has a series of predictable adventures along the way, meets a series of predictable people, and predictably finds his father is not all he had hoped he would be. The plot, especially once Barney gets to the city, becomes increasingly complicated and contrived, and the coincidences grow to a roaring crescendo when his stepfather, suitably humbled, arrives at the moment of Barney's greatest crisis, and wins the boy back through his sympathetic and uncharacteristic sensitivity.

Despite the irritating predictability and coincidences, this novel is actually both engaging and moving. Mackay has achieved these effects through the very humanness of the central character and through the unusual yet delightful relationship between the boy and his pet mouse, Saki, which he carries everywhere with him. Barney's own internal struggles with what is happening to him and the people he loves are well-drawn and convincing. Despite

some negative features, this novel is one of the best to come out of Scholastic for some time.

ONE PROUD SUMMER (with Marsha Hewitt, 1981)

Eva Martin

SOURCE: A review of *One Proud Summer*, in *In Review: Canadian Books for Young People*, Vol. 16, No. 1, February, 1982, p. 39.

This novel focuses on a small but vital event in Canadian history of which children today might be unaware. In the summer of 1946 the textile workers, men, women and children of the town of Valleyfield, Quebec, went on strike for 100 days for better working conditions and fair treatment by management. A previous strike in 1909 had been unsuccessful and the bitter memories of that strike spur the townsfolk on to greater effort making them determined to win. The strikers resist Maurice Duplessis' goons who were sent in to quell the uprising, and only resort to violence, rock-throwing and automobile rolling under the threat of tear gas and rifle fire from management. Finally, they are successful and jubilantly win their demands.

Lucie La Plante at age 13 is a worker who is prey to the whims of the plant manager, is forced to work long hours and overtime, and is continually docked in pay for imaginary offences. Lucie, her family and friends, and all of the strikers remain high-spirited and staunch in their convictions throughout the strike. Winning the strike restores Lucie's human dignity and her faith in people working together for a common cause.

This is an excellent portrayal of an important summer in a young girl's life. The characters are developed well, growing and learning as the situation progresses. The action is fast, full of passion and humour, and the background is historically accurate. This is a good all-around Canadian tale for young people which should be purchased for all libraries.

MINI-BIKE RESCUE (1982)

Linda Granfield

SOURCE: A review of *Mini-Bike Rescue*, in *Quill and Quire*, Vol. 49, No. 5, May, 1983, p. 12.

While young mini-bike enthusiast Julie Brennan believes her summer vacation will be spent on Suzukis, her mother has made other arrangements. Julie is to fly from her Saskatchewan home to Ontario to work at her Aunt Maureen's motel. Leaving behind mother-daughter confrontations about messy bedrooms and unladylike behaviour, Julie anticipates a boring summer. However, she soon finds herself astride a borrowed bike and enmeshed in a myriad of adventures, including robberies, forest fires, and cliff-top rescues.

Mini-Bike Rescue is the third of Claire Mackay's bike books, following *Mini-Bike Racer* and *Mini-Bike Hero,* aimed at the 10 to 12-year-old reader. Many aspects of her books appeal to the pre-adolescent: references to current films such as *Star Wars;* plenty of adult-adolescent confrontations; intense action and quick-tongued retaliations; the use of adolescent jargon; and the search for one's self, a theme common to most young-adult fiction. In *Mini-Bike Rescue,* Julie overcomes her fears in order to rescue her new friend Colin, and comes to respect the individuality of others, particularly her mother's.

Mackay's often overblown prose ("The night sighed with the death of many small things") and frequent references to Thoreau's "different drummer", may not be appreciated by a grade 4 reader. The story is satisfying enough, but if the book is looked to as an example of effective prose, the satisfaction is indeed short-lived.

📖 THE MINERVA PROGRAM (1984)

Mary Ainslie Smith

SOURCE: A review of *The Minerva Program,* in *Books in Canada,* Vol. 13, No. 7, August-September, 1984, p. 32.

Minerva, the heroine of Claire Mackay's *The Minerva Program,* is not a success at school. Self-conscious and awkward, she is the sort of girl to whom accidents are attracted. Gym classes are particular nightmares for her, but mathematics fascinates and delights her, and when she is picked to be part of a special course in computers she realizes she has found her niche. Then disaster strikes. At report card time, Minerva's gym mark has been altered, and she is accused of tampering with the school's computer programming. Unjustly banned from using the school's computers, she sets out to clear her name.

Minerva's feelings for the computer are sympathetically presented, and many young programmers will identify with her. It is also reassuring to be told that computers will not replace—and can even enhance—the values of friendship and loyalty.

Jean Little

SOURCE: "Talent In, Talent Out," in *Canadian Children's Literature,* No. 43, 1986, pp. 47-8.

The Minerva program has, to my certain knowledge, kept an eighty-three-year-old, a fifty-three-year-old and an eleven-year-old up long past their bedtime, because none of them could bear to stop before reaching the end. It has all the necessary ingredients of an irresistible story: suspense, surprise, humour, an engaging heroine with a difference, a mysterious villain, dialogue so real that its author has to be an inveterate eavesdropper on today's kids, an ingenious plot satisfyingly resolved and, to add a special,

new flavour, a computer. All of these, joined by flawless writing, would seem to be more than enough. Yet this book has other elements which make it worthy of special attention.

Minerva is a seventh grader with a low opinion of herself. Until a year before the story begins, her family has lived in a small apartment on St. Clair Ave. After they move out to "the eastern edge of Toronto" Minerva is lonely until she discovers Sophie, her best friend and faithful ally. Even Sophie cannot help Minerva to be less than a klutz at gym or to bear patiently with her lively small brother James.

The fact that Minerva is black while Sophie is white is just that, a fact. It is refreshing to read a book where a diversity of ethnic backgrounds are represented without this resulting in the Problem which provides the focus for the story. This lighthearted approach to something deeply serious, when added to the attractiveness of this heroine and her little brother, will do more for the cause of anti-racism than a plethora of admonitory lectures. Not only are black children respected and enjoyed in this book but so are many other "minority groups": the elderly, the kids at the video arcades, the cashiers at the supermarket, the teenagers who follow "punk" styles, even the teachers at the school Minerva attends. Each character in turn becomes a personality rather than a token figure.

The inventiveness of James, his energy, his maddening effect on his sorely tried older sister, his irrepressible high spirits plus his ingenuous charm and his unusual climbing ability cannot help but win laughter and affection from the most sophisticated reader. James is one of the book's greatest assets.

Other books have contained endearing kids and have handled minority groups with sympathy. This story adds an insight into the subtler dilemmas and delights which have arrived with computers. Minerva is instantly in thrall to her computer when she realizes magical success through it. Her preoccupation with it jeopardizes her friendship with Sophie; she must weight her relationship with a machine against her relationship with a person. The machine is easier to control, more predictable, more fun at times. Yet Sophie matters more.

The fear people have of computers is dealt with sensitively. Minerva's mother hates the machines that "spy" on her and the other cashiers, reporting what they do to the manager. Children reading the book will understand better the apprehension felt by those whose jobs are threatened through the use of technology. Yet they will also see, as Minerva does, where the responsibility lies—not with the computers but with the people who program them and use the results inhumanly.

The way Minerva solves her mother's problem and later foils the villain who attempts to defraud the school board keeps her the pivotal figure in the novel. Yet the unlikely but endearing gang who rally to help her will warm the hearts of kids. The plot is far-fetched, at this point, and its resolution is outrageous. If the reader wants fun though, this is the book of her or his dreams.

One final "minority group" which is included in this novel should not be left unmentioned. Dedicated readers! Sophie is reading her way through [Charles] Dickens. When she gives Minerva a synopsis of the plot of *Oliver Twist,* Minerva, shocked, inquires, "Soph, does your dad know you read stuff like that?" Well said, Minerva Wright. Well read, Sophie Michaloff. Well written, Claire Mackay!

Margaret Campbell

SOURCE: A review of *The Minerva Program,* in *The School Librarian,* Vol. 35, No. 3, August, 1987, p. 255.

From Canada comes *The Minerva program.* . . . Brisk, funny chat between the young crackles and sparkles from the opening page, as Minerva searches her fifth-floor flat to find her younger brother James. Elevators are boring, so he has climbed out of the window and is practising sliding down the building. Their school day has its ups and downs. The form master is so absent-minded that the pupils run a weekly pool on how many things he will forget. Minerva is excited to be chosen for a computer course but later, when she is accused of cheating and banished from the computer room, her friends rally round and, with the help of James acting as Spiderman and climbing up the building, they manage to get into the room at night and discover the truth.

PAY CHEQUES AND PICKET LINES: ALL ABOUT UNIONS IN CANADA (1987)

Eva Martin

SOURCE: A review of *Pay Cheques and Picket Lines: All About Unions in Canada,* in *Books for Young People,* Vol. 1, No. 6, December, 1987, p. 7.

The presentation and format of non-fiction for children have undergone major changes in the past few years. No longer is information presented in vast blocks of print illustrated with a few black-and-white photographs, charts, and graphs. Publishers and editors have realized that, because of the explosion in the video industry, children look at things differently and learn differently. They have become used to fast-paced action and sometimes a slightly irreverent view of the subject under discussion.

Book design for contemporary non-fiction has changed to reflect that phenomenon. Often, each page is broken up in such a way that the serious student will find the information required, and interested browsers will find tidbits and asides that may lead them towards a fuller consideration of the subject. The subject can be illustrated in varying formats, using cartoons, special typography, and photographs both in colour and black and white. The results can be either trashy and ill-conceived—flashing information like television commercials—or beautifully designed

packages that make basic information palatable to the modern child.

. . . . Claire Mackay's *Pay Cheques & Picket Lines* may well be the outstanding work of non-fiction for children published this year. Mackay, author of *The Minerva Program* and co-author of *One Proud Summer,* has succeeded in making the subject of unions and the labour movement accessible and interesting to children.

Pay Cheques & Picket Lines is well organized and stimulating from cover to cover. The historical background is illuminated by photographs and stories of personal tragedy arising from the exploitation of workers before the union movement was established. Mackay describes the growth of the union movement in various sectors, from steel workers to restaurant workers to public-service employees. The circumstances that usually precede the formation of a union, the steps taken to form a union, and the benefits a union can bring to a working person are clearly explained. Mackay also humanizes the chronicle by including biographical material about individuals who have been instrumental in the union movement. A discussion of some of the terminology that has come to be associated with unions is also useful. Canadian content prevails, although it is placed in context with events in Great Britain and the United States. Mackay's particular brand of humour, in which we learn of carpenters with chips on their shoulders, a grave situation when Montreal cemetery workers refused to "bury the hatchet", and "car wars I" and "car wars II", is a bonus, yet the book remains a well-balanced mix of humour, serious information, and human drama.

Pamela Young and others

SOURCE: A review of *Pay Cheques and Picket Lines,* in *Maclean's Magazine,* Vol. 100, No. 49, December 7, 1987, p. 56.

Explanations of how 19th-century Irishman Capt. Charles Boycott gave his name to a labor dispute tactic—and of the medieval origins of the term "shop steward"—are among the many anecdotes that *Pay Cheques* delivers with snappy quiz-show punch. Aimed at middle-grade readers, the pun-ridden text by Claire Mackay is a lively guide to the history, purpose, operation and future of frequently unpopular or misunderstood institutions. While clearly written from a labor perspective, it is a thoughtful, fair-minded work.

Welwyn Wilton Katz

SOURCE: "Doers and Seekers," in *Books in Canada,* Vol. 17, No. 3, April, 1988, p. 36.

Claire Mackay's *Pay Cheques & Picket Lines,* illustrated by Eric Parker, is an amusing, passionate account of how and why unions came about, what they do, and what is likely to happen to them in the future. In Mackay's hands, union history is not a long list of facts and figures, but real stories about real people. No one could read the story of John Gale (whose arm was chewed up like a sausage in a mill accident when he was 12 and who "had a good boss and so was paid for the whole day") without feeling an almost personal sense of outrage. Mackay has the fiction writer's understanding that, even in nonfiction, child readers need child characters they can identify with, particularly characters who do things the reader might wish to have done himself. Her book fills a notable gap, too; before *Pay Cheques & Picket Lines* there had been virtually nothing written for children on unions in general or Canadian union history in particular.

Mackay's humor lightens even the most grim statistics and photographs. The photo caption of a bank littered with paper during the Visa strike of 1985 is "Is that trash or Visa?" and the comical illustrations are appropriate and lively. The design of the book is rich, with illustrations, photographs, or inserts about word derivations on almost every page. This usually enhances the writing, though in a few places the main narrative feels interrupted by the inserts. I learned a great deal from this book, and I laughed a lot as I read it.

John D. Crawford

SOURCE: A review of *Pay Cheques and Picket Lines: All about Unions in Canada,* in *CM: Canadian Materials for Schools and Libraries,* Vol. XVI, No. 4, July, 1988, pp. 150-51.

This book is a sympathetic account of the historical development of trade unions in Canada. *Pay Cheques and Picket Lines* is designed to introduce children at the Intermediate level to a topic previously only treated in a cursory manner in school textbooks. Like other potentially difficult topics, trade unions tend to be considered in a very bland manner in school materials. This particular book presents the facts of the past in a manner that underlines the cruelty and reactionary attitudes to trade unions while at the same time managing to avoid cynicism.

The book has a number of strengths. Among these are the illustrations, which should have some effect on young readers, who will see their counterparts from the past looking out at them. The text also contains numerous examples to which young readers will be able to relate. The organization of the content is simple and effective. A section entitled "What Happened When" provides a very good time line; an index rounds out the volume. Perhaps a glossary would have been useful.

The most compelling feature of the book seems to me to be the sad reminder it provides of the casualties of the union struggle: the thousands of victims of industrial cruelty and carelessness. This book should inform children about an often neglected but important part of their heritage and perhaps enable some of them to avoid repeating the errors of the past.

THE TORONTO STORY (1991)

William Kilbourn

SOURCE: "Toronto's Tale Well-Told," in *Quill and Quire,* Vol. 56, No. 11, November, 1990, p. 13.

At last there's a history of Toronto one can recommend to anyone and everyone who enjoys lively writing and superb illustration—to city visitors, newcomers and native-born alike; to book collectors, school teachers and very young children. There are few history students familiar with the myriad stories, images and facts about life in Toronto from the French and Indian days to the present that author Claire Mackay and illustrator Johnny Wales have managed to include in *The Toronto Story*.

In a bookful of delights and surprises, the most stunning tour de force consists of eight huge, minutely detailed ink and watercolour cartoons depicting the Front, Church and Wellington Streets area (presently the Flatiron Building and Berczy Park) at eight different points in time, from Indian village to modern metropolis. Illustrator Wales, a student of Far Eastern art, returned to his native Toronto last year an accomplished artist. Besides the Japanese influence, I detect touches of Breughel, Giles and Maurice Sendak, all made brilliantly his own.

Also born in Toronto, author-historian Mackay is particularly good at linking her evocations of place to more than one point in time (e.g., happenings on the site of the Family Compact house where the gold-sheathed Royal Bank towers now stand). She connects the sights and sounds of Yorkville in the sixties with the shops and restaurants of today, with the dance studios there that taught Toronto to foxtrot and Charleston in the twenties and with the entertainments in the Red Lion coaching inn at the old Bloor-Yonge tollgate.

Women appear often, from pioneers Simcoe and Stong and Dr. Stowe to the jailing of June Callwood, another of the book's heroines. Children are actors in this history, not just victims or statistics—from the deGrassi girls' bold adventure in the 1837 rebellion to the mass extermination of house flies for which the children were paid by the city at a penny a hundred.

Two defects: the breezy style sometime lapses into arch, cute, or flip (Col. Simcoe was "no big fan of democracy" but gets a "gold star" for stopping the slave trade); disasters, and such oddities as Casa Loma, are given excessive space that might have been shared with more about the realities of religion, class, race and politics (the author's Orange Parade is colourful but what realities did it express?).

There are excellent suggestions for site visiting and further reading (e.g., James Reaney, Dennis Lee and Joy Kogawa) at appropriate points in the text, and wonderful evocations both of the city's far distant future and of Toronto's flora and fauna as the last mile-high ice sheet receded north beyond the escarpment 14,000 years ago.

Terence Scully

SOURCE: "Toronto Is Still Its Past," in *Canadian Children's Literature,* No. 64, 1991, pp. 80-1.

As the two hundredth anniversary of the settlement of Toronto as a permanent community approaches (1993), booksellers will undoubtedly be coping with a flurry of histories of the city. One of the most colourful of these will surely be *The Toronto story.* While its large format seems to indicate that it is intended for a young teenage reader, it would be a shame if very much older readers as well did not have a chance to open it. They would be captivated. Everything about the book is delightful. From the wit of Mackay's prose and the cheery vigour of [Johnny] Wales's line-and-wash sketches to the attractive elements of the work's apparatus and design, the book will quickly win a warm place in any reader's heart.

This is a survey of Toronto's past—from the ice-ages to the Sky Dome—with facts and figures and quotations from diaries; above all, though, it is not dry history. The author and illustrator, kindred spirits sharing a lively style, have indeed managed to narrate the story of their book's title, and one that is full of vitality.

The author does it by choosing to relate the experiences of real individuals, children and adults, who helped make the city. As an historian, however, she nicely balances this concern for the human with an obligation to recreate the complex tableau of a period. A series of vignettes turn the historian's erudition into understandable phases of the city's story: Sophia and Francis, children of John Graves Simcoe, explore the Don Valley in 1793; Lieutenant Ely Playter watches the American raiding fleet enter Toronto Bay in 1813; housewife Elizabeth Strong labours at her year-round chores in the 1820's. The author's voice is always present to comment or to criticize, always suggesting that whatever happened in the past involved real human beings and can be understood by us today in real human terms. Mackay writes with literate clarity and constant humour: William Lyon Mackenzie is described "with eyes of blue lightning, a jaw like a tombstone, a nose like an axe—and a tongue like a flamethrower;" Edwin Boyd (the bank robber) is described as a bill collector—"the bills were tens, twenties and fifties," and his gang "shared his enthusiasm for instant banking."

The illustrator's device for making history "real" is to show us, with often whimsical but always accurate detail, eight views of the changing "city-scape" at Wellington and Church Streets—from the time when settlers there were still pulling stumps until today when the venerable Flatiron Building seems overwhelmed by the skyscrapers of continuing history. The wide margins are also used for a wealth of charming miniatures, truly "illuminations" of life in Toronto's past, painstakingly researched in part from historic photographs.

Among the book's end matter, two big pages of Timelines offer such invaluable information as: "1800—Hogs are no longer allowed to run free in York;" "1835—Toronto's first garbage collector, called a 'scavenger,' starts collecting;" "1904—Second Great Fire makes charcoal of downtown T.O. Wood is banned for city buildings;" and "1950—Shoppers greet the credit card. Sunday sports are legal." A helpfully detailed Index occupies four pages. And, entirely typical of the earnestness of the author's purpose, a bibliography of 28 items is offered the young (and not-so-young) Torontophile and is entitled "More stories to read."

It is clear that this has been a work of love. The enthusiasm of the author and the illustrator for their city, its people and its story, is matched by their historical competence and a marvellous skill in transmitting both the enthusiasm and the history. They have given the reader a truly delightful book.

TOUCHING ALL THE BASES: BASEBALL FOR KIDS OF ALL AGES (1994)

Pat Steenbergen

SOURCE: A review of *Touching All the Bases: Baseball for Kids of All Ages,* in *CM: Canadian Materials for Schools and Libraries,* Vol. XXII, No. 6, November-December, 1994, pp. 224-5.

Claire Mackay has written a book that will be enjoyed by both fans and casual observers of the game of baseball. Her previous publications include *Mini-bike Hero, The Minerva Program,* and *The Toronto Story.* She is the recipient of the Ruth Schwartz Children's Book Award and the Vicky Metcalf Award. . . .

In a lively style, Mackay introduces all the aspects of the game and its history. "What's a ground rule double?" someone new to the game may want to know. Mackay explains it better than any sportscaster. On the other hand, there is lots for the fan as well: for example, did you know that one day in April 1986 there were nine shortstops from the Dominican Republic playing in major league games—four from the same town.

The chapters are arranged as innings starting with the development of baseball from "rounders" to the game we know today. This is followed by descriptions of the equipment and how it has changed; the ball parks; and the players. Naturally, since this is a baseball book, there is a chapter of statistics; however, this also includes a lesson in reading the box score and on how to keep score.

Throughout, there are sidebars giving tidbits illustrating the topic discussed. These references are often to the Negro League, the early history of baseball, or Canadian players. Although the Blue Jays were a dominant team when the book was being written, they do not dominate player or statistical references.

The illustrations include colourful drawings and photographs in both black and white and colour. The layout of the pages with main text, boxes and illustrations is attractive and not distracting, as sometimes happens when there is a lot of information on a page.

There is a glossary and index.

Highly recommended for both school and public libraries.

Adèle Ashby

SOURCE: A review of *Touching All the Bases: Baseball for Kids of All Ages,* in *Emergency Librarian,* Vol. 22, No. 3, January-February, 1995, p. 56.

I am not a baseball fan. Living as I do in the home of the Toronto Blue Jays, two-time World Champions, I may well be a minority of one. But despite my lack of enthusiasm for the game itself, three of my favorite movies and several of my favorite books deal with the sport. In this, the year in which the season did not finish, every young fan will be looking for something to tide his/her enthusiasm over until the players and the owners come to their senses. Fortunately, there is a host of lively new books that look at every aspect of the sport. . . .

Toronto writer and baseball fan Claire Mackay gives us *Touching all the bases: Baseball for kids of all ages.* Organized in nine innings, it covers the history of the game (No, it is not an American invention. John Newbery's *A little pretty pocket book* [London, 1744] has a verse entitled "Baseball"), the equipment, the ballparks, the players, the managers, umpires, fans and the media, followed by ballpark figures (scores and how to read them), baseball around the world and its distinctive language. It concludes with a glossary and an index. An appendix offers a more literary slant on the subject with the famous Abbott and Costello baseball sketch and "Casey at the bat." An earlier chapter includes the complete lyrics to "Take me out to the ball game," not just the familiar chorus. The lively text is accompanied by an array of illustrations of all kinds, and almost every page has a sidebar that offers fascinating highlights. For example, when Toronto hosted the 1991 All-Star game, the grounds crew "sped onto the field in a stretch limo and performed their tasks in tuxes." For every fan.

Jörg Müller
1942-

Swiss author and illustrator of picture books.

Major works include *The Changing Countryside* (1973), *The Changing City* (1977), *The Bear Who Wanted to Be a Bear* (written by Jörg Steiner, 1976; British edition as *The Bear Who Wanted to Stay a Bear*), *Rabbit Island* (written by Jörg Steiner, 1977), *Peter and the Wolf: A Musical Fairy Tale* (written by Sergei Prokofiev, retold by Loriot, 1986).

INTRODUCTION

Müller is the creator of sophisticated picture books that are characterized by their strong social messages, evocative illustrations, and appeal to both children and adults. Praised for his imagination and insight as well as for his superior artistic technique and the thought-provoking

quality of his books, Müller uses traditional narratives—the texts in his books are often by Jörg Steiner—as well as wordless formats to comment on the state of contemporary society. Müller is best known for creating *The Changing Countryside* and *The Changing City*, books that are considered powerful expressions of the disturbing effects of industrialization on two Swiss landscapes, one rural and one urban. These textless works, which Amy Scholar called "unique and unparalleled" in her *School Library Journal* review and Denise Von Stockar called "complementary masterpieces" in *Horn Book,* are recognized internationally for their relevance, universality, and the beauty and detail of their illustrations. In his subsequent books, some of which have been published in English, Müller has continued to address themes that have social resonance, such as the effects of pride, greed, and conformity on individuals as well as on whole cultures. He underscores his works, which critics often call parables or fables, with a sense of respect for both humanity and the environment. Although Müller includes images in his books that are considered grim, surreal, and disturbing, he is acknowledged for allowing his messages to speak for themselves and for including humor to offset their seriousness. As an artist, Müller characteristically works in oil, pencil, and airbrush and favors a style influenced by photographic realism; his paintings are often lauded for their clarity, precision, and stunning composition. In his essay in *Bookbird,* Jeffrey Garrett lauds both "the power of [Müller's] imagination" and "the conscience reflected in the message he seeks to impart as a thinking artist—a quality of all great illustrators. . . ."

Biographical Information

Born in Lausanne, Switzerland, Müller studied graphic arts at the Arts and Crafts School in Biel. After completing his education, he moved to Paris where he worked as a graphic artist for several advertising firms; he has also been associated with agencies in Zurich and Berne. In 1967, he returned to Switzerland, where he focused on creating picture books. The first of these was a collaboration with writer Bendicht Fivian, a portfolio depicting the urbanization of an idyllic country landscape that became *The Changing Countryside.* Müller was inspired to create his illustrations for this project when he realized that there had been "gradual but irreversible changes that have led to the eradication of the flying of kites, the football game in the street, the swim in the little country stream." Müller based his paintings on photographs he took as he traveled around Switzerland. After the success of *The Changing Countryside,* which was published in English without the original text, the pair published *The Changing City.* "Together," writes Jeffrey Garrett in *Bookbird,* "these two books revolutionized a generation," because they portrayed progress as destroying, rather than improving, the quality of life. Müller has collaborated with Jörg Steiner on the majority of his books since; Müller does the illustrations and Steiner supplies the text. Recently, Müller presented four large paintings at an exhibition in Zurich on urban life in the Middle Ages, a period that has a special interest for him; he is planning to use the paintings as illustrations for an upcoming book for young people on the Middle Ages.

Major Works

In *The Changing Countryside,* Müller presents a portfolio of seven paintings that portray the Swiss farming community of Gullen at three-year intervals during the period 1953–1972. The pictures depict the landscape's transformation from bucolic countryside to a busy suburb complete with shopping centers, highways, and a factory. *The Changing City,* which covers the period 1953–1976, records the transformation of a quaint city neighborhood into a cold urban area where, in nearly every picture, some kind of upheaval or accident is taking place. Documenting the effects of these changes on both the people and the physical environments, Müller is praised for making a powerful statement about progress in pictures re-

markable for their accuracy and detail. Writing in the *New York Times Book Review,* Karla Kuskin says that the two books "have so much to say that they make far wordier volumes seem inarticulate." In their first collaboration, *The Bear Who Wanted to Be a Bear,* Müller and Jörg Steiner address a theme similar to that expressed by Müller in his city and countryside books: the dehumanizing effect of progress on the individual. In this story based on a film that Müller had created for German television, an old brown bear awakes from hibernation to find that there is a factory built above him. When he wanders into the factory, the workers are so numbed by their dull routine that they do not notice that he is not one of them; against his will, the bewildered bear is put on the assembly line until he is fired for sleeping on the job as the next winter approaches. A review in *Publishers Weekly* calls *The Bear Who Wanted to Be a Bear* "another one of the marvels among children's books with a strong appeal for children and adults."

In their next collaboration, *Rabbit Island,* Müller and Steiner contrast two rabbits, Big Grey and Little Brown, who are trapped in a rabbit factory. When they escape, Big Gray, who is uncomfortable in the wild, chooses to return to the factory and impending doom. Sarah Hayes in *Times Literary Supplement* calls the book "clever but quite horrible" while Olga Richard and Donnarae MacCann note in *Wilson Library Bulletin* that Müller "compensates for [the deficiency of the text] with his powerfully desolate, surrealistic illustrations." With *The Sea People* (1981), Müller provides the illustrations and shares credit for the text with Steiner. In this oversized picture book, the team tells the apocalyptic story of two islands with very different cultures. Greater Island has a king, organized farming, and a social class system, while on Lesser Island the people spend most of their time singing and dancing. A mysterious shower of gold disturbs the peace between the islands by causing the people of the Greater Island to become greedy, steal land, and force the Lesser Islanders to become their slaves; when the Greater Islands begin to crack, the islanders flee to the Lesser Islands, where they are recolonized according to humane and artistic values. *Times Literary Supplement* critic Elaine Moss describes *The Sea People* as a "magnificent picture book which asks more questions than it answers. . . ." Müller is also the illustrator of a retelling of Prokofiev's "Peter and the Wolf"; presented in a comic strip format, the pictures blend the narrative with an introduction to the theater and orchestra; a cassette provides a recording of the symphony with a narration of the story. In her review in *Bulletin of the Center for Children's Books,* Betsy Hearne calls *Peter and the Wolf* "an absorbing work of art."

Awards

The Changing Countryside and *The Changing City* were given special honorable mention for nonbook illustrations by the *Boston Globe-Horn Book* Awards committee in 1977; in the same year, they were named notable trade books in the field of social studies by the Children's Book

Council and the National Council on the Social Studies. *Rabbit Island* received the Mildred L. Batchelder Award in 1979 while *Peter and the Wolf* was named a Children's Choice Book by the Children's Book Council and the International Reading Association in 1987. In 1990, Müller received Germany's Deutscher Jugend-literaturpreis for *The Animal's Rebellion*. With Jörg Steiner, he was nominated for the Hans Christian Andersen Award in 1989; in 1994, he won the award for his body of work.

GENERAL COMMENTARY

Jeffrey Garrett

SOURCE: "Jörg Müller," in *Bookbird,* Vol. 32, No. 3, Fall, 1994, pp. 9-11.

Jörg Müller was born in 1942 in Lausanne, in French-speaking Switzerland. In 1948, he moved with his family to Küsnacht near Zurich. As a child, he attended the School of Applied Arts in Zurich and Biel, graduating with a diploma in illustration. Even before turning 20, Müller moved to Paris and found work as a graphic artist with a succession of advertising firms. In 1967, he returned to Switzerland where, thanks to the financial support of his father, he was able to devote himself to realizing his plans to create picture books. The first of these was a collaboration with Bendicht Fivian, a portfolio of paintings depicting the gradual urbanization ("betonization") of an idyllic rural area. The prolix title of the original, which in German is in fact a cleverly rhymed couplet, translates quite heavily into English as "Every year the jackhammer smashes down again, or The transformation of the countryside." Entitled more simply *The Changing Countryside* in the U.S. version published by Margaret McElderry for Atheneum, this oversize work became against all expectations an enormous international success, with editions published in France, the United States, Italy, and in all Scandinavian languages. Fivian and Müller were encouraged to create a sequel on the destruction of a cityscape through untrammeled and thoughtless urbanization. The title, again oversized (but rhyming): *Hier fällt ein Haus, dort steht ein Kran und ewig droht der Baggerzahn oder Die Veränderung der Stadt* (Here a house is razed, there a crane is erected, and the bulldozer threatens us always, or The changing city). Together, these two books revolutionized a generation, giving expression and offering a "factual" (or at least convincingly visual) basis for the subliminal fears of thousands of thinking young people that "progress" in its modern sense is nothing other than a euphemism for the destruction of our world—above all as a place of fancy and freedom.

Müller's first collaboration with the writer Jörg Steiner was published that same year. It was the book version of a film project Müller had done for German television in 1974–75 and was called *Der Bär, der ein Bär bleiben wollte* (The bear who wanted to stay a bear). This book was also internationally successful and formed the basis for a collaboration which has continued—and intensified—in the two decades since. Among the numerous books Müller and Steiner have published together are *Die Kanincheninsel* (Rabbit Island), *Der Eisblumenwald* (The ice-flower forest), and, most recently and notably, *Der Aufstand der Tiere oder Die neuen Standtmusikanten* (The rebellion of the animals, or The new city musicians), a book which has attracted an extraordinary amount of journalistic and scholarly attention across Europe in the years since its publication. A film version of this work has now been completed by ZDF German television as a German-Swiss collaboration.

Müller's most recent project was the creation of a sequence of four monumental paintings—400 by 200 cm each!—for an exhibition on urban life in the Middle Ages at the Landesmuseum Zurich, *Stadtluft, Hirsebrei und Bettelmönch: Eine Stadt in 1300* (City air, millet gruel, and beggar monk: A town in 1300). Already available as a series of postcards, these paintings will soon be used to illustrate a book for young people about the Middle Ages, a period of special importance to the artist.

Josiane Cetlin describes in her documentary essay on Jörg Müller for the Swiss IBBY section the remarkable interplay between reality and imagination in his work. "Generally speaking," she writes, "one can say that his style has been inspired by photographic realism, but in fact his work is far richer and subtler than a simple painting of reality. . . . Everything in his graphic oeuvre is minutely depicted, which gives the illustrations a definite [and defining!-jg] clarity. . . . Everything is scrutinizable, can be recognized, and yet the reader knows he is in a totally imagined universe." It is not only the power of this imagination but also the conscience reflected in the message he seeks to impart as a thinking artist—a quality of all great illustrators—which the Hans Christian Andersen Jury sought to recognize by awarding Jörg Müller its highest distinction.

TITLE COMMENTARY

THE CHANGING COUNTRYSIDE (1977; original Swiss edition as *Alle Jahre wieder saust der Presslufthammer nieder,* 1973); *THE CHANGING CITY* (1977; original Swiss edition as *Hier fällt ein Haus, dort steht ein Kran und ewig droht der Baggerzahn oder Die Veränderung der Stadt,* 1977)

Publishers Weekly

SOURCE: A review of *The Changing Countryside,* in *Publishers Weekly,* Vol. 211, No. 7, February 14, 1977, p. 83.

The seven marvelous paintings in Müller's portfolio are

not accompanied by words (except for the dates of each scene) and they need none. The pictures are precisely detailed, beautiful and disturbing records of the changes wrought by "progress" on a Swiss farming community. Müller painted the same scene at intervals from the spring of 1953 to the fall of 1972. In each, we are impressed by the progressive devastation as the once inviting and pastoral country becomes unrecognizable with the encroachment of multiplying autos, trains, shopping centers and other clamorous and polluting products of industry. A companion volume, *The Changing City,* contains eight pictures of equally deplorable alterations in the section of a city. . . . Both books hold a vital message for everyone.

Amy Scholar

SOURCE: A review of *The Changing City* and *The Changing Countryside,* in *School Library Journal,* Vol. 23, No. 8, April, 1977, p. 69.

These two unusual titles by the Swiss artist are wordless portfolios of full-color paintings showing "progress" at three-year seasonal intervals. Each portfolio is a disturbingly insightful commentary on our urban/industrial culture.

The Changing City, which contains eight fold-out prints spanning 13 years, shows how a quaint neighborhood is gradually renovated into an impersonal area of highrises, parking lots, and freeways. In the process, clearly visible from print to print, the area loses all character and personality.

The Changing Countryside, which contains seven prints spanning 10 years, focuses on a tranquil country landscape which slowly industrializes and urbanizes. The once peaceful countryside is altered until its pastoral charm and appeal is all but unrecognizable underneath the asphalt and cinderblock. Müller's realistic paintings are colorful and appealing, and even though they detail devastation, they contain humorous asides (e.g., "James Dean" appears as grafitti on a bar in the 1959 . . . *City* spread.) Unique and unparalleled, both titles are sure to stimulate thought-provoking classroom discussions.

Kirkus Reviews

SOURCE: A review of *The Changing City,* in *Kirkus Reviews,* Vol. XLV, No. 9, May 1, 1977, pp. 484-5.

Jacketed like records but marketed like books, these two series of folded 33½ x 12½ paintings from Switzerland document, in a sort of primitivist photorealist style, the ugly, commercial modernization of a quiet country landscape and a human scale city neighborhood, respectively. The seven rural scenes, spanning nineteen years from 1953 to 1972, start out romantically with browsing cows, barefoot kids, a tree in bloom, and a small village squeezed up beside the railroad track. Gradually trees are chopped

and houses wrecked; storage tanks, overpasses, sterile factories, and futuristic stores intrude, until nothing is left of the original scene. In the city (eight pictures covering 1953–1976), a few blocks of charming old row houses, street level shops, and people everywhere are marred at first by neon lights and picture windows, then attacked by wreckers and builders until, despite the protest of a crowd (which is met with tear gas and clubs), it is all a shimmering nightmare of skyscrapers, signs, and expressways. Deplorable sequences to be sure, but Müller, far from moving children to any genuine response, merely programs them for stereotyped reactions. Pious and pretentious.

Karla Kuskin

SOURCE: A review of *The Changing Countryside* and *The Changing City,* in *The New York Times Book Review,* July 3, 1977, p. 11.

These two practically wordless books have so much to say that they make far wordier volumes seem inarticulate. In fact neither of Mr. Müller's works is truly a book, but rather a handsome portfolio containing separate, fold-out paintings on heavy, glossy stock. In *The Changing City,* the artist, who is Swiss, has focused on a few lovely blocks in a European city. This scene is shown at three-year intervals between 1953 and 1976. The dates preceding these urban portraits are the only text. It is sufficient. The transformation from the human scale and charm of the old into an undifferentiated segment of gray and glass metropolis literally unfolds before us. It is a startlingly dramatic short history. There are countless stories for an observant eye, and who has more observant eyes than children? Construction is wed to destruction. Buildings change their functions, decay, are torn down; new ones arise, streets are widened, the underground is built, a highway plows through. Everywhere there are abundant details of human life: the painter who loses his studio, the knife grinder who has no more knives to grind.

The Changing Countryside employs the same theme and format as its sister portfolio. This time the cement glacier of progress moves across an idyllic countryside leaving an industrial suburb in its wake. Only a tiny white cat survives the years and changes. On the last long page she can be seen dashing across the new highway as a mobile home speeds too quickly toward her. You want to cry "Watch out!" But it looks like it is too late.

Ann A. Flowers

SOURCE: A review of *The Changing City* and *The Changing Countryside,* in *The Horn Book Magazine,* Vol. LIII, No. 4, August, 1977, pp. 455-6.

A portfolio of fold-out illustrations opening out to thirty-three and a half inches depicts the physical changes in a European city over a period of twenty-three years, from 1953 to 1976. Each successive picture portrays the same scene after a period of about three years has passed. Different seasons and times of day give variety to the pan-oramas, but the great interest lies in the details of the changes in the face of the city. Fine old buildings and trees are destroyed; new highways are constructed. In almost every picture a disaster is taking place in the background—a fire, an accident, a demonstration; and some figures recur in every picture. A blind man with a seeing-eye dog represents the disaster in the final picture; he has been struck by a car. Hippies appear and disappear; increasing internationalization makes the signs more and more universal, such as Sprite, Sony, Kodak; and the dominance of the automobile has effectively removed all the appurtenances of civilized living. Certainly a graphic and powerful expression of the encroachment of technology on the city.

In a companion work the same theme is carried out in pictures of the changes taking place when a farming community turns into a suburb. The town is, in fact, Güllen, to which the highway signs point in the city pictures. Among the most notable changes shown are the steadily shrinking recreational opportunities for children; ponds, streams, hills, and fields disappear, and only one small playground is left. The factories which spring up all around and, indeed, all the industrial buildings, are remarkable for their coldly repellent modern architecture. Although European in conception and presentation, the significance of the pictures is universal.

Zena Sutherland

SOURCE: A review of *The Changing City* and *The Changing Countryside,* in *Bulletin of the Center for Children's Books,* Vol. 31, No. 1, September, 1977, p. 22.

In these two folios of loose pictures, first published in Switzerland, each painting is dated, folds out to show a scene (in one set a small square and a street with some side streets running off and in the other a rural landscape with a hamlet in the background) and documents the changes to the environment over a period of years. *The Changing City* (1953–1976) shows neon signs creeping in, subterranean construction projects, decay and demolition, new buildings going up, the gradual disappearance of a residential neighborhood and the emergence of urban monoliths and superroads. Each painting has some marvelous period details: children playing with hula hoops, new car styles, advertisements for products, etc. The pictures of the countryside show a new road coming through, then construction of a factory nearby—oil storage tanks, more and more buildings encroaching on the single farmhouse in the foreground, and finally its demolition, and a scene of superhighways and shopping center. A cold but telling commentary on social changes and destruction of the natural environment, the pictures are stunning in themselves and offer a broad range of subjects for discussion. Easily comprehensible, they can also be used by individual children for browsing. And, one hopes, thinking. This may cause problems of storage and circulation, but it should be a very useful supplemental teaching aid for art, social studies, and other areas.

Reader's Digest

SOURCE: "There Was a Little Town," in *Reader's Digest,* September, 1977, pp. 45-7.

Ten years ago, a 25-year-old German-Swiss artist named Jörg Müller decided to attempt a picture book for children, with paintings of youngsters at play. But Müller's project quickly ground to a halt: "I suddenly realized that most of the great games we used to enjoy as kids are often no longer possible today. Looking around, I discovered why—and got a new idea: to paint the gradual but irreversible changes that have led to the eradication of the flying of kites, the football game in the street, the swim in the little country stream."

The result was the publication, in 1973, of *The Changing Countryside,* a portfolio of seven paintings which make, without words, a haunting statement about progress. Each of the pictures portrays the same imaginary landscape at intervals of about three years; from the first, dated 1953, to the last, dated 1972, the devastation increases in stunning progression, until there remains only a concrete sandbox, with a length of pipe, where children may play.

In developing the series, Müller compared old photographs with pictures he snapped himself as he traveled about Switzerland. The central pink house, for example, he photographed in 1969 in a suburb of Bern. "My paintings were prophetic," he notes. "Last year I went looking for that house. It had gone—large blocks of flats had taken its place."

Few who study these prize-winning pictures will disagree with the spontaneous reaction of many Swiss children who have seen them: "I'd like to live in the first picture only."

Stefan Kanfer

SOURCE: A review of *The Changing City* and *The Changing Countryside,* in *Time,* New York, Vol. 110, No. 21, November 21, 1977, p. 66.

Jörg Müller's *The Changing Countryside,* is the pictorial equivalent of program music—an unbound suite of seven large luminous paintings that spellbind without the use of words. Though Müller is Swiss, his story, unfortunately, is universal: the gradual erosion of a natural setting by urban sprawl. Starting in the spring of 1953, with barefoot farm children in a burgeoning countryside, artist Müller takes characters and acreage through the incursions of a railroad, the depredations of bulldozer, drill and crane, and, ultimately, in the fall of 1972, to those hallmarks of Western civilization, the discount store and the parking meter. Yet Müller never stoops to cheap nostalgia or self-righteous despair. Each page is keyed to a child's comprehension; each of the meticulous landscapes shows compassion as well as irony in the face of the familiar. A companion suite, *The Changing City,* shows the same process in an urban environment, from the calm,

From Peter and the Wolf, *written by Sergei Prokofiev. Retold by Loriot. Illustrated by Jörg Müller.*

dignified arrangements of turn-of-the-century houses to the epoch of right-angle multiple housing and fast-food enterprises.

Denise Von Stockar

SOURCE: A review of *The Changing City* and *The Changing Countryside,* in *The Horn Book Magazine,* Vol. LVI, No. 3, June, 1980, p. 281.

An exceptional synthesis of old Swiss tradition with a contemporary theme has been created by Jörg Müller in his complementary masterpieces, *The Changing Countryside* and *The Changing City*. Large separate paintings without text demonstrate what can happen to a beautiful, serene landscape and a healthy, lively city in the course of time. The pictures show exactly the same segment of the scenery, but the sequence reflects the progressive destruction brought about by industrialization and urbanization, depicted in carefully executed, photorealistic paintings. The idiom of Müller's pictures is clearly Swiss; his concern, however, is international, understandable to both children and adults.

Mary M. Banbury

SOURCE: A review of *The Changing City,* in *Top of the News,* Vol. 37, No. 1, Fall, 1980, p. 46.

John S. Goodall's book, *The Story of an English Village,* and Jörg Müller's portfolio of pictures, *The Changing City,* require a sense of persistence of images. The first depicts the same view of a medieval English village at

intervals of approximately one hundred years; the second shows the same section of a contemporary European city at intervals of approximately three years. Both are beautiful and compelling statements concerning the mutability of the physical and social world. Both are vivid illustrations of spatial and temporal differences, and detailed portraits of progress and decay as well. Caught up in this panorama of life, children visually recall, compare, and contrast images, lifestyles, and social patterns. They perceive the obvious and subtle ways in which architecture, transportation, fashions, and occupations are altered, modified, and revised. These books engage children visually, cognitively, and emotionally.

📖 THE BEAR WHO WANTED TO BE A BEAR (written by Jörg Steiner, 1977; British edition as *The Bear Who Wanted To Stay a Bear;* original Swiss edition as *Der Bär, der ein Bär bleiben wollte,* 1976)

Publishers Weekly

SOURCE: A review of *The Bear Who Wanted to Be a Bear,* in *Publishers Weekly,* Vol. 211, No. 111, March 17, 1977, p. 99.

The author and illustrator have created an extremely stylish and sophisticated picture book, another one of the marvels among children's books with a strong appeal for adults as well as for the young. [Jörg] Müller's compelling pictures sustain the feeling—and the implicit moral—of [Jörg] Steiner's strange story. A bear awakes from hibernation to find that a factory has been built over his winter quarters. An officious employee accuses the bear of being a man, goofing off work by pretending to be an animal. The bewildered creature is forced to dress, shave and work at tasks he can't comprehend. Everyone who starts on page one will follow the events in the life of the misused bear to the last word. He can serve as a metaphor for any human who finds life too much at times—a familiar problem.

Kirkus Reviews

SOURCE: A review of *The Bear Who Wanted to Be a Bear,* in *Kirkus Reviews,* Vol. XLV, April 1, 1977, p. 423.

Another pseudo-sophisticated European import, this one from Switzerland. Waking after a winter's sleep to find a factory has been built over his den, Steiner's bear is mistaken for an "unshaven lazybones," bullied into a uniform, and put to work. No one will believe he's a bear until, fired for sleeping on the job as the next winter approaches, he's turned away from a motel by a desk clerk who sees through the human clothing. But Steiner's stereotyped message is as heavy as the factory's senseless machinery, and about all that can be said for the sterile surreality of Müller's airbrush paintings is that it suits the bear's predicament.

Zena Sutherland

SOURCE: A review of *The Bear Who Wanted to Be a Bear,* in *Bulletin of the Center for Children's Books,* Vol. 30, No. 9, May, 1977, p. 151.

First published in Switzerland, this engaging reversal of the familiar theme of the creature who wants to be another sort of animal is nicely told and is illustrated with amusing, sophisticated color pictures in pencil and airbrush. A bear wakes from his winter sleep to find that a factory has been built over his den; when he appears and insists he is a bear, not a man, he is scoffed at. Other bears will corroborate his claim, he says—but the zoo bears reject him (bears don't sit in the audience, they dance), so the bewildered, docile bear dons work clothes and joins a button-pushing crew. Time passes, autumn comes, the bear is sleepy; he is fired for laziness. Turned down by a motel proprietor who says that bears cannot be accommodated, the bear is satisfied to find, at last, someone who acknowledges that he's a bear. He goes off into the snowy forest, and there is a den. Last picture: a heap of clothes outside the den, and paw prints leading to it. The illustrations are handsome, especially one of the snow scenes with a harsh, acrylic blue neon sign, "Motel," and the story has a message about conformity that's a bonus for the child who sees it but that does not lessen the appeal or cohesion of the book for the child who misses it.

Ann A. Flowers

SOURCE: A review of *The Bear Who Wanted to Be a Bear,* in *The Horn Book Magazine,* Vol. LIII, No. 4, August, 1977, p. 432.

An unusual picture book, a fable for our times, it is a strange but successful mixture of fantasy and satire. A bear wakes from hibernation to find that his forest has disappeared and a factory has been built over his den. Nobody will believe he is really a bear; the guard, the personnel manager, the vice-president, the director, and the president of the company, not to mention the bears in the zoo and the circus all tell him he's "'a dirty, unshaven lazybones.'" Unhappily, he becomes a factory worker and spends every day endlessly pressing a button; but he gets so sleepy in the fall that he is fired. He tramps the roads until a clerk in a motel recognizes that he is a bear, and he thankfully finds a den to sleep in. Except for the pictures of the bear in his natural habitat, the illustrations are suitably cold, gloomy, and joyless, though amusing in their depiction of the corporate life.

M. Hobbs

SOURCE: A review of *The Bear Who Wanted to Stay a Bear,* in *The Junior Bookshelf,* Vol. 42, No. 1, February, 1978, p. 21.

This is a moving, rather terrifying story of the bear who wakes up in spring to find his forest replaced by a factory, in which he is forced to work because he cannot prove he is a bear, until his incompetence earns him the sack and blindly he seeks his natural habitat once more. It is told with deceptive and most effective simplicity, which makes all the more terrible the frustration of his attempts to establish his identity, and his rejection by his own kind in zoo and circus because he is brought to them by humans. There is a pleasing geometric Leger-like solidity of texture to the illustrations, by the Swiss artist Jörg Müller, and the muted colours of countryside and interiors are a delight.

Olga Richard and Donnarae MacCann

SOURCE: A review of *The Bear Who Wanted to Be a Bear,* in *Wilson Library Bulletin,* Vol. 60, No. 10, June, 1986, p. 65.

In Jörg Müller's illustrations for **The Bear Who Wanted to Be a Bear,** the precisely drawn monstrosities of the industrial world are relieved by scenes from nature. There is an appealing ambiguity in the tree shapes in even the most stark, snow-covered landscapes, whereas the mechanized interiors are threatening as they dwarf living creatures. In fact the human members of the cast are so desensitized by their surroundings that they deny a poor, sleepy bear his identity when he wanders into the factory built around his winter den. The plot centers around the bear's sad life on the assembly line and his eventual escape.

This Steiner/Müller narrative is a powerful parable about what technocratic societies can do to the quality of life. It produced mixed feelings in a nine-year-old informant—a blend of interest, concern, and alarm. The return to normalcy for the bear was reason for relief, but the overall encounter with the book produced the sadness that permeates the theme.

RABBIT ISLAND (written by Jörg Steiner, 1978; original Swiss edition as *Die Kanincheninsel,* 1977)

Sarah Hayes

SOURCE: "The Power of Pictures," in *The Times Literary Supplement,* No. 3979, July 7, 1978, p. 763.

The place of fear in picture books is a much debated subject. The illustrations [by Jörg Müller] in *Rabbit Island,* airbrushed surrealism against a pseudo-naturalistic background, are clever but quite horrible. The message—that Big Grey rabbit chooses to return to the "safety" of the rabbit factory because an unseen future is preferable to the known rigours of Little Brown rabbit's natural life (a sort of reverse *Watership Down*)—is a terrible one. This book is advertised as "being published simultaneously in over a dozen countries", and it oozes internationalism at its worst: a "significant" theme; style but not substance; a combination of bravura and banality.

Publishers Weekly

SOURCE: A review of *Rabbit Island*, in *Publishers Weekly*, Vol. 214, No. 3, July 17, 1978, p. 169.

An appalling experience awaits unwary readers of the Steiner-Müller collaboration. Spectacular paintings of endearing rabbits and a country landscape are boobytraps that deceive one into believing this book is fit for children. Actually, it's a reprehensible performance, capable of disturbing sophisticated adults. "Factories that make chocolate are chocolate factories; [factories] that make guns are gun factories. This is a rabbit factory. It has no chimney and makes very little noise." It's where bunnies are fattened for slaughter. Big Gray meets Little Brown, a new captive. They escape for a time but fear the unexpected in the outside world. Returning to the sterile, disquietingly methodical factory, Big Gray elects to stay because he knows what to expect in prison. The old one even loses the comfort of a friend, for the small one opts for freedom.

Merrie Lou Cohen

SOURCE: A review of *Rabbit Island*, in *School Library Journal*, Vol. 25, No. 2, October, 1978, p. 139.

Steiner writes well and Müller paints beautiful oil and airbrush pictures which are an able blend of detailed realism and dreamlike fantasy. But the talents of both are wasted in this chilly, depressing story concerning the blighted fate of two rabbits, Big Gray and Little Brown, trapped in a factory where their ultimate destination is probably a can of dog food. The smaller of the two, a new prisoner not yet adjusted to life in a sterile cage, escapes and takes his cellmate with him. But the latter is uncomfortable in nature (he has forgotten how to run, jump, and dig; prefers pellets to fresh clover; and mistakes a river for a conveyor belt), so he leaves his friend and returns to safe confinement. The moral is clear—in fact, there is little else to this dogmatic tale except for splendid illustrative technique which, in this case, does not a winner make.

Kirkus Reviews

SOURCE: A review of *Rabbit Island*, in *Kirkus Reviews*, Vol. XLVI, No. 20, October 15, 1978, p. 1135.

Another grim view of modern times like the same pair's *The Bear Who Wanted to Be a Bear,* this features two inmates of a sterile "factory" [where] small rabbits are brought in to be fed and fattened and large ones are taken away to be slaughtered. A big gray rabbit who has been there for some time and forgotten all about sunshine, clover, and such believes that the big ones are taken from the factory to a "much better place"; and when he escapes with a little brown rabbit who has just arrived, he is so frightened and inept out in nature that Little Brown has to take him back to the factory. The last page shows Little Brown alone outdoors, exchanging curious stares with a hedgehog. Again, Müller's chilling pictures undoubtedly achieve the effect they aim for, but this has less story and an even more import-laden tone than *The Bear*. . . .

Olga Richard and Donnarae MacCann

SOURCE: A review of *Rabbit Island*, in *Wilson Library Journal*, Vol. 53, No. 3, November, 1978, p. 271.

The social implications in Jörg Steiner's **Rabbit Island** are more complicated [than those in Tomie dePaola's *The Clown of God*]. The opening lines present the irony that preparing animals for the butcher is a "clean" industry.

> Factories that produce chocolate are chocolate factories. Factories that make guns are gun factories. But the factory in this story is a rabbit factory. It has no chimney and makes very little noise.

Chiefly a parable about environmental conditioning, the story also introduces thoughts about superstition and artificial life-styles. When the rabbit Little Brown arrives at the factory, his new surroundings frighten him. An older tenant, Big Gray, explains that the fattened rabbits go to a better place when they mysteriously disappear—a place where "White Watch Rabbits" protect good rabbits and punish bad ones, a place of eternal life. The two new friends escape into the countryside, but this life proves too threatening for Big Gray, and the companionship ends. Big Gray returns to a nice, safe cage.

Packed with so many different concepts, the plot requires many changes of direction. Unfortunately, these shifts are too arbitrary and abrupt; the result is a feeling of manipulation, a quality that reduces the intensity of concern we have for the characters.

Jörg Müller compensates for this deficiency with his powerfully desolate, surrealistic illustrations. The imagery is hard, dark, mechanistic, but often evocative, as in the drawing of the rabbit logo on factory buildings. Color helps articulate the minutiae in each scene, but the hues are so restrained that no warmth is generated.

Derwent May

SOURCE: "Of Mice and Mists," in *The Listener*, Vol. 100, No. 2585, November 9, 1978, pp. 626-7.

[*Rabbit Island* is] a book packed with grim social and humanitarian morals. . . . It is the story of two rabbits who run away from a battery rabbit farm, with sombre brown pictures of the massed hutches and chill violet evocations of the industrial landscape; but the rabbits are painted in a way to suppress all emotion in the reader, like stiff fur-and-wire toys that are bent into shape for each elaborate painting.

📖 *SEA PEOPLE* (with Jörg Steiner, 1982; original Swiss edition as *Die Menschen im Meer,* 1981)

Elaine Moss

SOURCE: "Moral Themes," in *The Times Literary Supplement,* No. 4156, November 26, 1982, p. 1305.

The Sea People by Jörg Müller and Jörg Steiner is a mammoth landscape-shaped picture book with a cerulean cover that suggests ancient Eastern Mediterranean civilizations. On two islands, divided by a narrow strait, live peoples of very different cultures. The Greater Island is a monarchy with a feudal society structured so that the land is developed to its utmost potential. On the Lesser Island, however, so long as there is enough fish in the sea, people laugh, dance, enjoy themselves in a simple manner. Greed tempts the Greater Islanders to steal first land, then slaves from the Lesser. But when gold is discovered beneath the sacred Red Sunstone the Greater Island is hideously threatened—for an old prophecy has foretold that if the stone should fall the islands will sink beneath the sea. The story is told directly in the manner of myth, the morality left to the reader to determine. Is work all? Do riches count for more than happiness? Is superior strength an excuse for plunder? Does "civilization" always prove a corrupting influence?

The paintings by Jörg Müller which accompany (Or perhaps gave rise to?) this apocalyptic tale are of a quality, page after page, that is truly breathtaking. In some a lemon dawn rises over seas, rock, olive trees, ramparts—each ripple, stone, leaf, rope in full focus. In others towering landscapes of Wagnerian splendour are lashed by angry seas beneath leaden skies. This is a magnificent picture book which asks more questions than it answers and has no ending because "it is about the world and as long as this world exists the story goes on and on . . .".

William Feaver

SOURCE: "From Aertex to Adidas," in *The Observer,* December 5, 1982, p. 33.

The Sea People by Jörg Müller and Jörg Steiner is a large, oblong album, permeated with good intentions. Müller and Steiner must be members of the Green Party for their story concerns the sensible use of natural resources and the folly of most industrial drive. The Greater Island goes all-out for expansion while its neighbouring Lesser Island is ruthlessly used as a source of raw materials. Eventually ecological catastrophe restores natural order. The story is illustrated with carefully detailed, 00-gauge paintings showing the progress of growth and decay. An excellent perspective on universal concerns with plenty of possibilities explored.

Stefan Kanfer

SOURCE: A review of *The Sea People,* in *Time,* New York, Vol. 120, No. 25, December 20, 1982, p. 80.

In a time beyond history, on two rockbound islands, live *The Sea People.* The Greater Island is ruled by a king, the Lesser one by an old, blind oracle. Peace reigns until the king decides to move a red sunstone. Once the rock is disturbed, the Sea People experience an absolute shower of gold. But absolute shower corrupts absolutely, and soon the islands are threatened by pride and avarice. Only the old man's wisdom can rescue them from themselves . . . This familiar tale is saved from banality by the panoramic artwork of Jörg Müller and Jörg Steiner. Gull's-eye views of the islands seem three-dimensional, and the huge pictures of ancient machinery and people have a Shakespearean sweep.

Margery Fisher

SOURCE: A review of *The Sea People,* in *Growing Point,* Vol. 21, No. 6, March, 1983, p. 4047.

A picture-book for older children with a powerful argument against power-mad ambition, following the fortunes of adjacent islands, one rich and greedy and the other poor and contented. At first the larger island seems to be succeeding in the gradual theft of stone to extend its acreage, but time and tide, and the natural need for freedom, brings destruction on the tyrannous king and his purloined domains. The large format of the book accomodates bold, striking pictures in which people of antique and anonymous appearance are massed against a huge rocky landscape; cold blue, green and brown tints suit the neo-classical architecture and symbolic details of the book, and forward its message in their own way.

📖 *PETER AND THE WOLF: A MUSICAL FAIRY TALE* (written by Sergei Prokofiev, retold by Loriot, 1986; original Moscow production as *Petya i volk,* 1936)

Publishers Weekly

SOURCE: A review of *Peter and the Wolf,* in *Publishers Weekly,* Vol. 230, No. 18, October 31, 1986, p. 61.

A theatrical tour de force, this version of [Sergei] Prokofiev's story is told as if the reader were attending a symphony performance in an ornate European opera house. We see the musicians first, then the red velvet curtains open and the play begins. As in the Tintin books, the story is told in a series of picture frames, but here the cartoon style is oddly mixed with richly detailed drawings in vibrant colors. The insects hovering over delicately drawn Queen Anne's Lace or the wolf's sharp teeth contrast unexpectedly with the Disney-like face of the fanciful bird or Peter's over-large eyes. The performance closes with eight beautifully rendered drawings of the conductor that border pictures of Peter's triumphant march. When the actors take their bows on the last page, readers will join the storybook audience in shouting "Bravo!"

Patricia Dooley

SOURCE: A review of *Peter and the Wolf,* in *School Library Journal,* Vol. 33, No. 3, November, 1986, p. 82.

The creators of this retelling of [Sergei] Prokofiev's work have tried their best to bring stage and orchestra into the book (a cassette is available separately). The title page is framed by the proscenium arch; individual musicians and their instruments are introduced; and only after the curtain has risen on Peter's stage-set hut does the scene expand naturalistically to take in meadow, pond, and forest. Large-type captions and speech-balloons accompany copious illustrations (mostly vignettes, from three to nine per page), their pace and direction set by the narrative and musical tempo. The lively comic-book layout counterpoints the well-made paintings. The tone of the text is pragmatic but not moralistic: Grandfather is not allowed to preach at the end, and the appetites of cat and wolf are not glossed over. The wolf is rather frighteningly painted, but becomes abject in captivity and is returned to the forest instead of being sentenced to the zoo. Characterization is fuller than in other versions, and an effective visual comparison of their views of the forest contrasts Peter's youthful optimism with the Grandfather's elderly caution. The book ends in the theatre again, and the duck reassuringly takes her bow with the others, before the applauding audience in the gloriously baroque hall. The book's oversized square format is its only drawback: it is awkward and requires a capacious lap when it is read. This version is richer and more developed than Erna Voigt's, and on a different scale altogether from Warren Chappell's.

Kirkus Reviews

SOURCE: A review of *Peter and the Wolf,* in *Kirkus Reviews,* Vol. LIV, No. 22, November 15, 1986, p. 1725.

The classic orchestral story in a lushly illustrated and packaged oversize (just short of 13" sq.) edition, first published in Europe. . . .

Müller's conception of the story as staged in an ornate theater is dramatically effective and allows him to depict the instrumental soloists by way of introduction. His landscapes—blossom-studded meadows, mysterious forests, distant vistas, more German than Russian—provide a lovely backdrop for vividly caricatured human figures. Unfortunately, his animals have a jarring, cartoonish quality, especially the unlikely toucan-billed bird; but the 112 various-sized paintings provide plenty of interest. . . .

Betsy Hearne

SOURCE: A review of *Peter and the Wolf,* in *Bulletin of the Center for Children's Books,* Vol. 40, No. 5, January, 1987, p. 96.

An oversize picture-book version with effects significantly different from the one illustrated by [Charles] Mikolaycak, this frames the story in its orchestral setting with an elaborate stage on the cover and title page, followed by an introduction to the characters with their representative musical instruments. The adaptation itself has humorous additions as the animals talk to themselves and each other in cartoon balloons ("A bird on the nose is better than a cat in a tree") and in the end, parade the wolf back into the forest instead of toward the zoo. The illustrations are meticulously rendered paintings in a comic-strip format that heightens the narrative and the satire simultaneously. Müller's refined line and clarity of color, combined with occasionally sudden shifts in perspective, make this an absorbing work of art, which culminates, as the curtain closes and the conductor hushes his orchestra, in a bow from the animal cast. Also available is a narrated audio cassette with music performed by the Hamburg Symphony Orchestra. Bravo!

Ilene Cooper

SOURCE: A review of *Peter and the Wolf: A Musical Fairy Tale,* in *Booklist,* Vol. 83, No. 10, January 15, 1987, p. 788.

Peter and the Wolf has long been a popular choice for introducing classical music to children. This oversize volume gets off to a good start with an impressive theater interior and boxed illustrations showing the musicians who will interpret the various characters and their instruments. The continuation of this boxed effect results in a choppy layout, however, especially when the artwork is balanced by only a small amount of text. Despite the design problems, the book has some charming pictures—especially those featuring the animals—and the sunny light and unusual perspectives that Müller uses make this fun to look at frame by frame. The book is also available with a narrated audiocassette with music performed by the Hamburg Symphony Orchestra.

Additional coverage of Müller's life and career is contained in the following sources published by Gale Research: *Contemporary Authors,* Vol. 136; and *Something about the Author,* Vol. 67.

Jan Needle

1943-

English journalist and author of books for children and young adults.

Major works include *My Mate Shofiq* (1978), *A Fine Boy for Killing* (1979), *A Sense of Shame and Other Stories* (1980), *Piggy in the Middle* (1982), and *Wagstaffe, the Wind-up Boy* (1987).

INTRODUCTION

Jan Needle is an original and varied writer of works for children and young adults. His writings cross many genres—from picture books to historical novels to television adaptations. Although different in form, Needle's works all share his distrust for authority and his hatred of class and racism. Needle's confrontations with prejudice and other social issues make his books interesting to adults as well as children—and controversial. Nevertheless, he writes for the enjoyment and excitement of children and cautions adults to judge children's literature not by their standards but by a child's.

Biographical Information

Needle was born in Holybourne, England, during World War II. He spent his happy childhood in the poverty of seaport slums and began working early: He published his first short story in a local newspaper at the age of eight. By 17, he became a junior reporter for the *Portsmouth Evening News.*

As a child, Needle read avidly, but found it difficult to identify with much of the literature available then to children. As he explained in *Books for Your Children,* "I do remember, from my own childhood, wondering why no one ever wrote about people like me. And I do think that the need not only remains today, but is getting greater by the minute. Not only do the underprivileged need a voice, but the privileged need to see and hear them suffering." Needle became that voice.

Major Works

Needle speaks in his writings through realistic subject matter and explicit dialogue. Two of his better known works—*My Mate Shofiq* and *Piggy in the Middle*—exemplify his brand of social criticism. *My Mate Shofiq,* for instance, explores the problems of an immigrant Pakistani family in a northern industrial town. The portrayal of racism and prejudice is realistic, including abusive nicknames, bleak frustration, and violent actions. In the sto-

ry, a boy—Bernard—acts as an advocate for Shofiq, a Pakistani classmate. That action pulls Bernard into Shofiq's sad world of racial discrimination and futile battles with teachers, social workers, the police, and other often misguided authorities.

Piggy in the Middle also deals with responses to racism in the community, the police, and the media. A young police officer, Sandra, resigns from the force owing to the social pressures she feels after the racially motivated killing of an elderly Pakistani changes her perceptions. The brutality with which the police interrogate the victim's son—a former classmate—disturbs Sandra, as does the harassment of the victim's family. The cynical approach of the press—of which Sandra's boyfriend David is a part—erodes her relationship with him, leaving her to make hard decisions about their future. Again, the portrait here is true to tense urban life. Sexual mores are relaxed, and Sandra's interaction with her fellow officers show the double standards held for men and women. Needle's language includes coarse "street talk" and enough references to whiskey and gin to cause one reviewer to comment that Needle might believe that "alcohol is a girl's best friend."

Critical Reception

In general, Needle's writings have been embraced by critics for their realism and serious approach to social justice. In *British Book News,* Judith Elkin counted Needle among the new writers that "make a positive contribution towards multicultural understanding." Similarly, a *Junior Booklist* reviewer called Needle an "author of . . . sensitive and committed stories about racial minority problems."

Nevertheless, an equal number find Needle's work controversial for the very same reasons. According to Ann Wright, writing in *School Librarian,* "Jan Needle's contemporary idiom and realistic subject matter have been criticised as reflections of an over-grim reality." In short, adults struggle with the harsh situations and common language of Needle's writings for children.

Needle, however, keeps his perspective about the controversy, realizing that the rhubarb is created by adults not children—his intended audience. "I would not dream of writing anything I thought might damage a child's psyche," he wrote in *Books for Your Children,* "but being confronted with tough and intractable problems of the real world seems to me to have the opposite effect. Truth helps children to grow—and unlike some adults, they are not afraid to face up to it."

Awards

My Mate Shofiq received a commendation from the Guardian Award for Children's Fiction in 1979; *A Sense of Shame and Other Stories* also received a commendation from the Carnegie Medal in 1980. *Wagstaffe, the Wind-up Boy* was named one of the best books of 1987 by the Federation of Children's Book Groups. *Piggy in the Middle* was recognized as one of the National Book League's children's books of the year in 1982.

AUTHOR'S COMMENTARY

Jan Needle

SOURCE: "On First Writing for Children," in *Books for Your Children,* Vol. 15, No. 4, Autumn-Winter, 1980, pp. 20-1.

When I started writing children's books about four or five years ago, I had no idea of the trouble I was letting myself in for. I suppose I should have guessed, because my main reason for starting was a vague feeling that so many books already on the market were soft in the extreme—middle-class, middle of the road, and middling awful. What I didn't realise was just how large and determined is the body of adult opinion intent on keeping them that way!

Let me explain my background. I was born during the war, and brought up in extreme poverty in seaport slums. Throughout my—very happy—childhood I was an avid reader, and on becoming junior reporter at seventeen began the climb into the middle classes. I now live very comfortably in a small Pennine town, about three miles from Oldham.

It's the last fact which is probably the most important one. Although I've "made it" out of the poverty trap, I'm still surrounded by poverty. What's more, it is getting rapidly, and disastrously worse. In the past six months all four textile mills in the town where I live have closed down—after more than 130 years *each* of uninterrupted trading. In the wake of the closures two clothes shops, two butchers, one chip shop, one craft shop and an electrical store have gone broke. Other closures—including that of the weekly market—are almost certainly imminent.

Now, I have nothing against nice, sweet stories about wealthy, well-educated kids having adventures with spies in the school hols á la Enid Blyton (and all her perhaps more talented, certainly more respectable and respected, followers). But I do remember, from my own childhood, wondering why no one ever wrote about people like me. And I do think that the need not only remains today, but is getting greater by the minute. Not only do the underprivileged need a voice, but the privileged need to see and hear them suffering. Poverty and unemployment can still be very easily overlooked and ignored by the better-off; but it is a perilous—and tragic—oversight.

My first book, *Albeson and the Germans,* was received with critical acclaim. The second, *My Mate Shofiq,* was a runner-up for the Guardian Award and got fantastic reviews. It was not until my third, *The Size Spies,* that an interesting phenomenon became apparent. This book, a straight-forward comic adventure, immediately sold far more copies (in hardback—that is to schools and libraries) than the other two. What is more, I got a feedback of great *relief* from many teachers and librarians that at last I'd written a book that was not *controversial.* It was nice, conventional, and above all, safe. It was, indeed, about middle-class children having an adventure involving spies! *A Fine Boy for Killing,* which was published (for older children and adults) in late 1979, really put the cat among the pigeons. Some excellent reviews, yes, but also . . . well, I am still reeling from a letter from a London school librarian and ILEA reviewer which is abusive to the point of hysteria, almost certainly libellous, and which (wilfully?) misinterprets the book to a scarcely believeable extent.

Luckily children—and I *am* writing for children, remember—are far more sensible than many of the adults who "filter" books for them. *Fine Boy* is certainly a tough, bleak tale. So are *Albeson* and *My Mate Shofiq.* So indeed is *A Sense of Shame,* a volume of stories for teenagers out this autumn. But I have yet to meet a child who has been unable to handle the difficult elements, or who has failed to be stimulated, if sometimes saddened, by them. I would not dream of writing anything I thought might damage a child's psyche; but being confronted with tough and intractable problems of the real world seems to me to have the opposite effect. Truth helps children to grow—and unlike some adults, they are not afraid to face up to it.

The danger in trying to explain myself in an article like this is that everything I've said so far probably sounds terribly smug and holier than thou, not to say downright humourless and pompous. That's a pity, and an unfortunate product of having been labelled in some quarters as a *"controversial"* writer. In fact my *main* reason for writing and everything I do is to give enjoyment and excitement to children. I try to make my stories move extremely fast, there's almost always a lot of humour, and they're meant to appeal to both sexes over a very large age spread. I also write a pretty wide range of *"types"* from social realistic, to comic fantasy to the downright nuttiness of **Rottenteeth**. Next spring's novel, **Wild Wood,** which is my favourite, has no realism, no violence, no problems, and lot of affinity with **The Wind in the Willows**. I wonder what Disgusted of Cheltenham will make of that!

Seriously, however, I am very glad that some of my books have elicited such strong responses from adults. As far as I know, the "battle" on the children's level is already won (except that children, like me until I was enlightened, never knew there was a fight on; they read the books and accept them, whether they like them or not). To the adults who think I am treading in areas best left unexplored, I can only say this: if a problem exists in life and affects children, it exists to be examined through the medium of children's fiction. I always tread extremely warily, whatever some of them claim to think; but I shall continue to tread. I hope they'll try and understand.

Jan Needle

SOURCE: "Personal View: Jan Needle," in *The Sunday Times,* London, July 31, 1988, p. G4.

There is currently a flurry of interest over the alleged decline in child readership due to the influence of television. This is, of course, nonsense. More children's books are published in Britain now than ever before, and the number is climbing steadily. Last year 5,014 titles for children were published compared to the 2,934 published in 1981. Towards the end of 1986, W. H. Smith commissioned a survey into the leisure habits of children. Out of just over 1,000 aged between eight and 15, 57% had read a book on the previous day.

Television not only drastically enhances the sales of individual children's titles, but has made both the reputations and fortunes of many authors of children's books. Even an Everyman paperback of Oliver Twist that I bought the other day bears the sticker beside the title: TV Series. But television is not perceived as being "respectable". In the world of children's writing, the respectability factor is overpowering.

Enid Blyton and Roald Dahl are the two most widely read children's authors in this country. They are also the most reviled and suppressed. I went into a famous London toy and book shop some time ago to buy Dahl's *Revolting Rhymes,* and was told with some hauteur that the book was not considered suitable for children.

The selection and possible suppression of children's books is done by adults, and adults alone, on *behalf* of the person at whom the work is directed. They use adult criteria of literary merit, intellectual worth, depth of emotion, use of language etc, which—to a child—are at best irrelevant and at worst totally destructive of enjoyment. They assume, in short, that children are merely small adults, who must be weaned off the pap they enjoy as soon as humanly possible, and set onto good, solid, meaty, useful literature. Which will, they think but do not say, Do Them Good. Most children have a taste for both beefburgers and Blyton. Most children, left to their own devices, grow out of both them naturally. In both cases, the nannyism is not only arrogant, but a waste of time.

The custodians of the respectability factor are very rarely confronted or attacked. When they are, though, they fight back valiantly and many of their arguments are quite hard to refute. Teachers and librarians will tell you, quite truthfully, that complaining parents are the problem, especially in books where "bad language" is involved. Many of them when pressed, however, will admit that they themselves "disapprove" of certain books, and therefore feel perfectly entitled not to buy or stock them.

The awarders of the annual prizes for books for children appear to have even less self-doubt: they choose books quite frankly on "literary merit", with the supposed taste of child-readers a very tiny element in their deliberations. It shows. Most prize-winning children's books are more beloved by the adults who select them than the children who are often forced to read them.

Finally, the reviewers. Most of them are literate, concerned, and middle-class. They were in the vanguard of the long war of attrition against Roald Dahl's books, and their strategy was simple, and for many years very effective: they ignored him. Nowadays they use Dahl as a weapon against anybody who writes in a "similar" vein. Only the Master can do children's horror/comedy, and the others are imitators or bandwagon-hoppers who in any case lack Dahl's brilliance, moral depth, understanding of children's psyches, and so on. (All the things, oddly, that detractors used to claim he lacked.)

Michele Landsberg, in her recent *The World of Children's Books* finds "a parallel with the Holocaust" in the violent bits of Dahl's *Charlie and the Chocolate Factory.* Her volume, a list of 400 of the "best" books by British, American and Canadian children's writers, is the "respectability factor" writ in stone. Its intention, quite simply, is to introduce children, via the adult who has read her book, to works which she deems to be "very good" and "demanding", from first-reading age to the teens. Enid Blyton and other "junk" is allowed if the child insists, but should be sandwiched "between two or three highly recommended books".

Again the total lack of doubt. Children's views of their preferred books have no actual value. If an adult thinks a children's book is "better", it must be true. If a child rejects one of the highly recommended and demanding books, the child is at fault, not the adult. The fact that Landsberg's book is now being used in colleges of education in Canada filled me with despair. British colleges will follow soon I am sure.

I have more than 20 children's books in print. Several of them have sold very well, and many are respectable enough to appear both on exam syllabuses and the shelves of W. H. Smith. But my last year's title, a fairly silly and revolting comedy called **Wagstaffe and Wind-Up Boy,** ran into the buffers of gentility. Even librarians I know as friends will not stock it. It was not reviewed and American publishers were shocked by it.

However it was recently voted one of the best books of 1987 by the Federation of Children's Book Groups, which is unique in using panels of *children* as the judges and, more to the point, the person I wrote it for, who reads books with extreme reluctance if they do not have train numbers in them, has read it 28 times.

The point is that down here in the ghetto there are some writers who think that children are capable of identifying their own taste in books. Not because they are cleverer than (or even as clever as) us adults, but because they are a different breed, marching to a different drumbeat, standing on a different rung of the ladder. Put at its simplest, they prefer fish fingers to fish. Is there some way that the silent censors can be made to realise it?

GENERAL COMMENTARY

Ann Wright

SOURCE: "Something for Everyone? A Study of Jan Needle," in *The School Librarian,* Vol. 33, No. 4, December, 1985, pp. 301-5.

Since Jan Needle's first book for children (**Albeson and the Germans,** 1977), he has proved himself to be a prolific and varied writer. His work is unified by an irreverent sense of humour which is always linked to a sceptical distrust of authority. The humour ranges from the comic vitality of his one picture book (**Rottenteeth,** 1980) to the zany situation comedy of **The Size Spies** (1979); and develops to include satiric parody (**Wild Wood,** 1981) and an ironic viewpoint which reveals the contrast between romance and reality in the stories for adolescents. Jan Needle's written style matches his subject-matter. There is a consistent tendency towards explicitly realistic dialogue and limited description: the books are not literary

in the way many of the best-known children's books are. With Jan Needle's writing the reader's perceptions accumulate as the result of progressive narrative events, and comprehension comes largely from an interpretation of outer rather than inner realities. In this way Jan Needle observes one of the conventions of writing for children, but is not totally a 'children's writer' in the more usual sense because of his persistent creative awareness of oppression, violence, exploitation and anarchy. This is usually muted for younger children and often expressed in comic vein, but it becomes more evident and more complex as the social and emotional context requires. Jan Needle's contemporary idiom and realistic subject-matter have been criticised as reflections of an over-grim reality, but they are balanced by a persuasive blend of social criticism and ironic humour.

The social realities of **Albeson and the Germans** and **My Mate Shofiq** (1978) are very persuasive, and the major characters are developed sensitively and imaginatively. Both books have lonely heroes: Albeson is isolated by his fearful fantasies about the Germans, Shofiq by his race. Albeson is seen as the victim of his circumstances, equally frightened by the thought of a spelling test and by his friend Smithie's insistence that he play truant again. His well-meaning teacher never glimpses the fear instilled in him by his grandfather's tales of war; and his father's answer to all problems is to belt him. However, the book's adventurous and lively plot is very exciting and a happy ending elegantly achieved when Albeson has to face his fears because he unwittingly takes refuge in a German cargo boat.

My Mate Shofiq is about racial prejudice and is told from the viewpoint of Bernard Kershaw, who is initially in a state of loneliness and isolation comparable to Shofiq's. Bernard has just lost his best friend, killed playing chicken on a railway line, and this horror is linked to Shofiq's ruthless and terrifying violence in the face of overwhelming odds—inter-racial gang warfare. Shofiq is proud and reticent, but Bernard's loneliness has encouraged in himself a growing recognition and understanding of Shofiq's existence and values. When Miss Todd, their teacher, misunderstands the purpose of Bobby Whitehead's attack on Shofiq, Bernard speaks up for him. This wins Miss Todd's approval and the class's dislike, but leads Bernard to understand in an interview between the head, Bobby Whitehead, Shofiq and himself that telling the truth can change your life and make it very uncomfortable. What he does not predict is the assistance and support of a mate like Shofiq. This story's narrative excitement is enhanced by the theme of friendship between Bernard and Shofiq, explored in a way that allows for the natural development of affection and respect between them. Their relationship is part of a wider concern for human values, counterpointing the potentially discouraging realism which informs Jan Needle's view of contemporary society.

In the books for younger readers this reality is tempered by a comic approach. Jan Needle's fondness for humour which arises from reversing any kind of expectation may be adult in inspiration, but **Rottenteeth** (1980), with pictures by Roy Bentley, has the power to entertain children and adults and provides a simple demonstration of Jan Needle's stylistic devices. *Rottenteeth* tells the story of a greedy pirate, most of whose teeth dropped out because he ate too much barley sugar. Defiance of simple narrative conventions is announced in the first line:

Once upon far too many cream buns and chocolate biscuits there was a remarkably fat and greedy baby with disgusting habits.

The baby grew up to be a pirate and the plot twists and turns, reversing the reader's and listener's expectations. The anarchic humour of the situation is underlined by a simple but aggressively idiomatic text; and the pictures, especially those of the ships, are a striking complement to the story's appeal which is essentially in contrast to the traditional, child-centred world of most picture books.

Jan Needle's variations on the popular family story for children fall into two categories: comic fantasies and realistic adventures. In the first category are *The Size Spies* and its sequel *Another Fine Mess* (1983) in which the same characters appear: an eccentric professor, two children (George and Cynthia), and an assortment of other characters including two spies, a mechanical dog called the Snark and not unlike Dr Who's K9, and an intimidating Elizabethan alchemist. The action is fast and furious, but the overall impression is one of too familiar, almost stereotyped characters and events. Nevertheless these are entertaining books, and children certainly enjoy the freedom from parental restriction which both portray.

The Bee Rustlers (1980) and *Losers Weepers* (1981) have the tang of the real world and are also both about the same family: a rather morose Dad, a younger Mum and two children, Carol and Tony. *The Bee Rustlers* opens with Tony sniffing miserably because his farmer father has just whacked him for driving the land-rover without permission. Eventually, however, Tony's consuming interest in anything mechanical is justified for it helps to thwart the plans of the bee rustlers and bring them to justice. The relationship between Tony and his older sister Carol is well described and shows how Tony is always on the losing end, from being afraid of bees to having to do stretching exercises to make his legs and body long enough to reach the pedals on the tractor. The villains of the story are made to look very menacing in Paul Wright's illustrations; and the description of how Tony started and drove a lorry with no ignition key, worn-out brakes and gears he could not control makes exciting reading. The book ends on a positive note with Tony no longer afraid of the bees. In *Losers Weepers* the family relationships have not changed; and an interesting feature of both books is that Carol challenges her rather ill-tempered father's authority and wins, despite her fears. The books portrays her as independent, hardworking and brave. Tony's friends admire her for her toughness and cleverness. One memorable detail in *Losers Weepers* is her annoyance at losing sight of Tony, who has run off with the treasure sword which they found near the reservoir, because she was

obliged to slow her running pace to that of her teacher, Mr Potter. *Losers Weepers* has an interesting and lively plot, but its unique quality lies in its consideration of the possession of property. The children's father wants no part of the £15,000 bounty money given for the sword and Tony's vision of trains, go-karts and motor bikes has to give way to the reality of seeing his name on a brass plaque in a museum commemorating the find. His father's attitude to money contrasts with Tony's and this moral dimension adds distinction to *Losers Weepers*.

The variety of narrative and style in Jan Needle's writing is very clearly illustrated in two other books—*A Fine Boy for Killing* (1979) and *Wild Wood* (1981). Although both books are essentially analyses of tyrannical authority, the tone of each is different. The first is a terrifying and brutally detailed description of life on a British naval vessel during the Napoleonic wars; it concludes hopelessly with the implicit statement that corrupt and established authority will always conquer rebellions, no matter how legitimate. Within this framework the complexities of human personality and moral responsiveness are strikingly described. The contrasting world of *Wild Wood* takes its metaphors from its imaginative source, Kenneth Grahame's *Wind in the Willows,* and reinterprets the narrative significance by telling the story from the Wild Wooders' viewpoint, mainly Baxter Ferret's. The Wood, much feared by the River Bankers, is the centre of a political movement stirred up by Boddington Stoat, an outsider and an agitator. The heroic uprising against oppression and exploitation, and the seizing of Mr Toad's property, are truly comic descriptions of political realities; and a precise balance is achieved between the humorous descriptions of the original text and the fearful excitement of the alternative and revolutionary version. The effect of distancing the narrative from the events gives a pleasingly historical and personal dimension to the story; it also leaves the storyteller wondering whether he fully understands the happenings which he has related.

Jan Needle's short stories for older readers are linked by their relevance to everyday life and its difficulties; they concentrate on what is contemporary and are often an expression of confusion about and even contempt for the world which adults have created and inhabit. *A Pitiful Place* (1984) includes a story about a young British soldier's reactions to serving in Northern Ireland; and *A Sense of Shame* (1980) has references to Welsh nationalism, Irish romanticism, illegitimate babies and enforced marriage. One of the most memorable stories in the second collection has a deliberately limited narrative structure and deals powerfully with legal injustice. There is a description of the court proceedings taken against a young man, Jim Barker, who became unwillingly involved as an innocent passer-by in a demonstration which got out of control. In court Jim faces a line of lying policemen, but pins his hopes for justice on an apparently sympathetic and intelligent woman magistrate. When she supports the police and places him in the category of criminals, thugs and hooligans who deserve to feel the weight of the law, he can hardly speak and realises:

They didn't believe him, or they believed in law and order more . . . five minutes later he owed the State £200 in fines . . . and not much in respect any more. Very little indeed.

Jan Needle describes the emotions of young people with unerring directness and honesty, and does not gloss over the difficulties which many have in a world where adult prejudice and animosity allow little toleration of different values or new people. *Going Out* (1983), adapted from the TV series of the same name, centres on a world that offers very little to young people leaving school with no qualifications; but *Great Days at Grange Hill* (1984) never really escapes from the confines of the original TV series about life inside and outside school. *Piggy in the Middle* (1982), by contrast, is a serious analysis of a young woman who always wanted to join the police force and 'help'. She finds herself in a world where hints of police brutality to suspects have become recognised fact and where the police are a closed society with its own rules. All these stories provide varied and provocative reading and are in striking contrast to those written for younger readers.

Jan Needle's narrative and stylistic versatility provide for a variety of reading levels and responses. As a storyteller he is interested in creating alternative and unpretentious worlds which contrast, sometimes amusingly, with the conventions of ordinary society. The different interpretations of reality to be found in his writing are strengthened by his fondness for reversing expectations and viewpoints. Comedy, with a vein of seriousness, keeps company with fantasy and adventurousness, allowing insights into any number of human situations and predicaments. Social criticism is enlivened by irony, satire and farce, adding a persuasive tone to the underlying ideas. These ideas, which are fundamentally those of social justice and humanity, are not often the subject of children's fiction. They provide a welcome addition to the range of children's reading and help to distinguish Jan Needle's unique qualities as a writer.

Fred Inglis

SOURCE: "Social Class and Educational Adventures: Jan Needle and the Biography of a Value," in *Stories and Society: Children's Literature in its Social Context,* Macmillan Academic and Professional Ltd, 1992, pp. 84-96.

It is only fair to pick [for analysis] a novelist of whom one can make serious demands, otherwise the examples simply won't stand up to the strain. I take as my example Jan Needle, strongly representative for my purposes not only because he can tell a gripping and appealing tale to such as wide range of child readers, but because he starts from a strong sense of the intrinsic value of children's needful venturesomeness, autonomy, and defiance.

He endorses, in other words, the great gains won for modern life by the claims of rights, procedural justice, equality made by all those struggling to emerge from the long human custom of immiseration and exploitation. He

speaks implicitly but eloquently for solidarity—solidarity of class (in the *Grange Hill* book-of-the-serial, in the astonishing *A Fine Boy for Killing;* in *The Wild Wood*) and of common humanity against racism (in *My Mate Shofiq* and *Albeson and the Germans*). In *Piggy in the Middle* he teaches children in school that our splendid British bobbies are, mostly, psychopathic and racist bullies, and that a mere girl can say so.

Jan Needle accepts, that is to say, as I do, the great promises held out to the future by a certain local, low-key and militantly domestic British socialism. He is powerful and interesting to so many teachers because of this (whatever his appeal to the children). He shares with the best of old British progressivism that hatred of class and racial arrogance which is the other side of a genial and generous nature. An important fraction of the schoolteaching constituency keeps faith with those antique values—with the idea of the state as at once just and compassionate, with an image of community, with the resonance of mutuality—and does so at a lowering moment in world history when jeering commentators are acclaiming the death of socialism.

Needle is a very present help to such as them and me in our travails in the class- and bookroom. He expresses in the real language of men the hazards and incoherences of modernity, but brings out as well that there is nowhere else we can live. By the time he has finished, the adventure as lived from Henty to Arthur Ransome has been changed utterly and at times terribly.

Ransome's is a pertinent name, for Needle's heroic children are as much on their own as Ransome's, especially when one of them puts to sea. Arthur Ransome, let us say, wrote at the last moment at which children could live their adventures in the old purity of diction—could go to sea like Her Majesty's Britannic Navy, to the Arctic like Scott (although with a proper respect for Amundsen) and to look for treasure with Rider Haggard. Ransome's children, who shared in that splendid vision of public duty and communal faithfulness, then went to war. Patriotism went one way and its bread and wine turned thick and sour—

> What if Church and State
> Are the mob which howls at the door?

Its fate was written out by Evelyn Waugh with Guy Crouchback in Crete.

Idealism went the other way, into international socialism, and had a hard time of it. Needle is one of its heirs.

Being an internationalist, he starts by telling children bluntly of the evils of nationalism, the delusions of heroism. His police are crude racists in *Piggy in the Middle* (the piggy is a pretty young policewoman), in sympathy to the National Front thugs who attack the quiet anti-racist demonstration; they finally drive Sandra the heroine out of the force, leaving only the one decent constable Terry to keep faith. Bernard starts out a crude nationalist and racist until his mate Shofiq changes his heart, and together they stand and fight the Bobby Whitehead gang.

Their victory is a bloody one. Their loyal friend Maureen, who fought with them, has an eye put out by a flying stone. Although Needle's imagination closes on the last fight in the final act in the way of the classic adventure, he is careful to strip fights of all glamour, even of justification. They are caused by human stupidity and unreason; you can't win.

In this he sedulously follows the best modern way. That is, he refuses any link between violence and virtue; he votes for social realism and telling children how horrible and pointless battles are; he is Richard Rorty's kind of liberal 'for whom cruelty is the worst thing there is'.

This is, as Michael Howard tells us [in *The Causes of Wars*], a fairly recent development and still not a general one: Islam, 1991 painfully showed us, retains a place in its doctrine for the ennobling values of going to war for the Prophet. But a modern left-liberal like Needle will only do battle if he absolutely must, and this leaves adventures going wrong at the end rather than right. When the Falkland Islander children meet the young and nameless Argentinian conscript in *A Game of Soldiers,* it is a matter of life and death that each terrified party puts off warfare and sees the other as a human child.

Secondly, Needle teaches the primacy of rights, of fair treatment for each individual, even going to the DSS office with Shofiq to show the readers how badly a speechless old Bangladeshi is treated. So too with that hard-to-bear stereotype of the claimants' union, the social worker stooge who comes to take Albeson to school and Shofiq into care.

But this modern lesson goes hard not only with adventure stories which have never been strong on rights and justice, but also with solidarity, which Needle and his camp-followers wish very properly to rate high. It is an aporia of modernity that in stressing the individual and his or her rights and equalities among life's chances, there is a corresponding loss entailed among the values of community and co-operation.

It is a difficulty which the French Revolution put us in and the theorists have found no way out. Classical liberalism and its fearsome progeny revolutionary socialism set out on a quest for the free development of all: one solution was the state socialism so roundly ejected from its Eastern European offices in 1989. The other was Oxford Street and Fifth Avenue consumerism. Is that the best we can do?

Needle dallies with an image or two of revolution. In his most lovable book *Wild Wood* he plays (and played early) the now-familiar game of turning round a well-known work of literature (*Rosencrantz and Guildenstern Are Dead, Wild Sargasso Sea*) in order to see it from the back.

Wild Wood tells the tale of Toad's chauffeur in old age. A dedicated car freak (it is his avocation) he can't stand the way the rich, nonchalant Toad smashes up these lovely machines out of wealth, vanity, utter irresponsibility. The chauffeur is an honest weasel, and lives in the wood itself. An Agitator comes, a working-class, industrial, voluble and discontented stoat to rouse the peasants and proletariat (Needle's Maoist or Leninist theory is a bit unclear at this point) to take over the empty Toad Hall and live in a bit of comfort for once.

Well, we know the rest. And in old age, the old boy is gentle and cheerful and forgiving. It is a heartwarming book, and does proper honour to Kenneth Grahame.

It is, however, a lapse in Needle's modernity—a lapse all of us trying to salvage socialism by teaching our children to be both nice and good must study. For at the same time as fighting for their rights and comforts, the stoats and weasels are celebrated for their working-class solidarity. But as we have learned from the social democratic history of Europe since the early purges in Russia, Germany, and elsewhere, it is damnably hard to have both. Needle's generous heart and enlightenment head go two ways at once—towards the rich communities of proletarian resistance and their reassuringly horrible enemies; *and* towards the clean well-lighted place in which autonomous individuals exercise their individual dignity and rights.

Thus the policewoman Sandra in *Piggy in the Middle* renounces the revoltingly racist and self-protective solidarity of the cops in the excellent and reliable name of her own conscience. Thus, by contrast, at the moving end of *My Mate Shofiq* Bernard, Shofiq and Wendy go together to face the music of retribution which they know will not be just but is inevitable. In *Grange Hill* the morals go either way, all the time, as those children and ours try to sort a new history of ideas, in which, in a slogan, Kant's duty, Paine's *Rights of Man,* and D. H. Lawrence's aristocracy of the spirit negotiate for a settlement.

In Needle's masterpiece, he makes his boldest effort at resolving all these contradictions. *A Fine Boy for Killing* is a small classic of the language. It also helps to kill off the adventure story. I don't know if the ancient mariner William Golding read it before launching into *his* classic sea-going trilogy ending with *Fire Down Below,* but it might help to explain his taking refuge in dazzling pastiche from the intolerable moral puzzles of the day, if so.

Needle's novel is both fable and piece of history, *histoire* and *conte*. It is set, at about the time of the 1794 Spithead mutinies, on board a Royal Navy man o'war bound on a secret mission to the Antipodes. The captain is a monster of sadism but, as Grey Derring's researches into naval punishment of the time show, not a caricature (however unfair it turns out that Charles Laughton was to Captain Bligh).

The Captain orders a fourteen-year-old midshipman, also his nephew, to pressgang a few extra men and the youngster picks up a bovine shepherd boy by making him drunk and a strong, courageous and upright yeoman caught in his wherry with some minor contraband. This is Jesse Broad, who with the young midshipman William is the focus of the story.

The story mounts through one incident after another of unrelieved brutality: rum, buggery, and the lash, as Winston Churchill reputedly said of the Navy in the French wars of the 1790s, and although Needle misses out the middle of the formula, he makes something unremittingly bleak but entirely gripping out of his catalogue of savagery punctuated by the details of bilges, vomit, latrines and storms no more terrible than stinking heat and dead calm.

In summary it sounds like cliché. Don't we have enough of this in the folk memory? But Needle knows and feels deeply his sea and sailing lore, loves it all as well, and shapes a plain, solid, terse idiom in which to tell his tale.

Behind this good craftsman's prose is a driving anger and hatred at class cruelty and arrogance which he forces any halfway decent reader to share. The urgency with which we do not want Jesse Broad and Thomas Foxford to be pressed is hardly bearable. Broad himself, a convincingly fine figure and character, he makes to carry the best of Tom Paine's beliefs. When William Bentley, a chit of a lad, jets a mouthful of spit in Broad's face, Needle brings his reader to the revolutionary moment.

Broad bears the insolence in silence, after a shuddering struggle with himself. But the captain's deliberate, unremitting cruelty and hatred of the lower deck brings the other men to the inevitable moment of mutiny. The captain has the soft, loving and stupid shepherd boy tied to a spar in appalling cold. Effectually, the experience kills him. A spontaneous, ragged and wretched insurrection takes place in which Broad and another pressed civilian with a master mariner's experience take charge in order to save lives, and put the crazed captain together with the marines and seamen, who out of sheer consternation did not mutiny, off in a long boat. William Bentley, badly wounded, remains on board.

In the desperate epilogue, Broad can barely hold the order of the ship together. But he tenderly, forgivingly, nurses William back from death's door, and in long conversations shows the boy the very best of the Enlightenment values which led on to the best of modernity. He cuts through the patriotic cant about the useless war: he speaks French and loves France. He can plainly see the stupidity of class which made the captain so mindlessly brutal and almost turned the boy into a monster. He understands how the dreadful life makes ordinary, dumb men into the scum William believes them to be. He speaks for justice and equality.

And, of course, is caught by ruling class revenge and hanged.

> Jesse Broad could not go to his death unaided, try as he might. He stood between two seamen, his legs like dolls' legs, his crippled shoulder hunched. He fought

desperately to stay upright on his own, but he could not. He had to be held. Even his head had to be lifted up so that the noose could be slipped over it. It was then his eyes met William Bentley's.

> They stared at each other for what appeared to be eternity. As if there was no one else on board, as if they were utterly alone. They stared and stared, their faces clenched and rigid. It was like an age.

> Then Jesse Broad's feet swung out and upwards with a jerk. His eyes met Bentley's just once more, and they were bulging, filled with pressured blood. Then away, high up in the air he flew, twitching on his rope. The sightless eyes, bulging out obscenely, passed across the island as he turned, then seemed to scan Spithead. Then the Gosport shore, the hill, and then he spun round back again.

William Bentley swears to the bottom of his little soul that he will testify on behalf of this noble man, save his life, and bring his hideous uncle down. His family prevent him. He is never called to the trial.

There is something in the novel of the force and simplicity—the caricature, also—of Eisenstein's *Battleship Potemkin*. But the calm tone and moral fervour, the love of the sea and the clear exposition of sailing culture and art, come together in a way which goes well beyond propaganda.

The ship restores the propinquity and comradeliness which modernity lacks. It throws abominable class exploitation into sharp relief. The work at its best is rich and resonant: it creates identity. Jesse Broad is the internationalist hero of the future. His goodness and manliness teach the boy William how to go into that future with these so hard-won historical gains. Shocking, anger-creating defeat will be turned, one day, into generous victory.

Maybe I overpraise the book a little. But it is a rare thing for a children's novelist to try to teach politics so directly and with such idealism. Then the idealism is exactly our problem. For the moral-political lessons hold much more plainly in 1794 than two hundred years later. Needle is much too intelligent, as his fable brings out, to *commend* mutiny: as I said, he goes beyond *Potemkin*. He implies reconciliation where Marxism so stoked itself up on a doctrine of vengefulness and terror. But the sailing which is the occasion for communal art and culture is now become the leisure culture of the class enemy down at the marina. Post-Fordist industrialisation prevents both identity-formation and solidarity at work. At the same time the great gains in individual rights make Captain Swift's kind of class cruelty impossible to enforce. Nobody (in Europe at least) has to bear that kind of thing any longer. The local class war is over.

Are we left, therefore, with Jan Needle as an anachronism? I realise of course that I have treated him in a crudely foreshortening way as a dominie rather than a children's novelist. But I do so, as I said, in order to honour the political purpose to teach children strong ideals and meanings at a time when these are so scarce and spectre-thin.

As he and I find, however, it is an exiguous business. Our best political past, as lived by a man like Jesse Broad, can find no present embodiment, and our best political present, glowing for a moment in the lives of the policewoman Sandra or the tough little Anglo-Pakistani Shofiq, is a poor bare thing, short of friends and without a job. Old socialism or new consumerism. It's a lousy choice, and no adventure, either way.

TITLE COMMENTARY

ALBESON AND THE GERMANS (1977)

Roy Blatchford

SOURCE: "Spirit of Adventure," in *The Times Educational Supplement*, No. 3266, January 13, 1978, p. 22.

If *Albeson and the Germans* were not built around such an absurd conceit it would be an unqualified success. Suspend disbelief that the harum-scarum Albeson starts truanting because two German children are rumoured to be joining his class, and you are left with a first-class thriller. Albeson and his tough little mate Smithie "hop the wag", start shoplifting and graduate to an orgy of vandalism in the school. Albeson runs away to sea and boards a ship which, with uncanny irony, turns out to be German; after a further chase sequence, recounted with tremendous verve and excitement, the sympathetic crew befriend the stowaway and allay his fears about the Bosche. The author's insight into the feelings and reactions of children when they trigger off events which rapidly leap out of control is remarkably forceful, and the pacing of the plot finely judged. It should not be long before Jan Needle appears on the Topliner list.

Margaret Meek

SOURCE: A review of *Albeson and the Germans,* in *The School Librarian,* Vol. 26, No. 1, March, 1978, p. 60.

Albeson's idea of Germans is gleaned from his grandfather's war stories and the comics he reads. The prospect of meeting two of them in school disturbs him so much that he truants, vandalises the school and runs away with his strange friend Smithie. It all has to end well, of course, but not before the author has shown the darker side of children's imaginings and no small amount of the adults' failure to grasp what goes on. The headmaster is a stock bully (the retribution scene is unnecessarily long), but the young anti-hero joins Ray Brown's and Bernard Ashley's men, Robert Westall's too, to make a new character group who can't escape the adults who control their lives by running away to favourite uncles. There's a new realism abroad. It will make us less comfortable, for a start, but young readers will see the point.

MY MATE SHOFIQ (1978)

Gillian Cross

SOURCE: "Brightening Up Their Lives," in *The Times Literary Supplement,* No. 3991, September 29, 1978, p. 1082.

Jan Needle in *My Mate Shofiq* shows how an exciting story can be written around the problems of racial integration. Shofiq, a Pakistani boy, arouses the wrath of the local gang by attacking them in order to defend his little sisters. Bernard, who is English, is unwillingly drawn into the quarrel on Shofiq's side and comes to understand the problems of the Pakistani boy's family, learning eventually that Shofiq is a good friend to have in a tight corner. The complicated story is excellently told and moves at a fast, exciting pace.

It is not always, however, entirely convincing. It is hard to believe that Bernard would not have known Shofiq's name, when the two of them are in the same class. Nor is it easy to accept the crude portrait of Mr Burke, the obtuse and authoritarian social worker. Nevertheless, the book is a conscientious study of a tense situation and, commendably, eschews facile solutions.

Margery Fisher

SOURCE: A review of *My Mate Shofiq,* in *Growing Point,* Vol. 17, No. 4, November, 1978, p. 3417.

Jan Needle is . . . forceful in his example of racial hostility but *My Mate Shofiq* does not read as though it had been written solely for a purpose. Here are the streets of Blackburn—the run-down houses of the Brook where the Pakistanis have clustered, Middleton Road where Bernard Kershaw lives, the derelict Jericho Mill where Bobby Whitehead and his gang lie in wait to bash their enemies, whether white or brown. This is the tale of an unlikely and dynamic friendship. Bernard is reluctant to be drawn into Shofiq's problems and the Pakistani boy in his turn does not want Bernard to know about his father's loss of a job, his mother's depression and his sister's misery at school. The two of them have many differences to sort out and they achieve friendship through quarrels, misunderstandings and artless confessions that seem entirely natural to boys of ten or so. The brutality and prejudice showed by adults and children alike are not exaggerated and the author is at pains to suggest points of view in the local government officers and teachers that vary somewhat from the sourly crude interpretations of their actions by the two boys. This gives the book a necessary balance while in no way muffling the forthright, boldly idiomatic style that carries the point of the book firmly and easily.

Margaret Meek

SOURCE: A review of *My Mate Shofiq,* in *The School Librarian,* Vol. 26, No. 4, December, 1978, p. 361.

You don't have to be a prophet to foretell that books for

children will more and more deal with the social problems that preoccupy us all. Of these, the ethnic and social mix of life in towns is bound to be pre-eminent and we are likely to see exploitations of this theme, bad and good, increasing in number. Here Jan Needle tackles, head on, the plight of Pakistani children in the working-class district of a Midland town. The hero Bernard has fixed ideas of what is 'soft'; crossing at proper crossings, for instance. The day he sees Shofiq Rahman defend little children from Bobby Whitehead's gang he finds himself involved in more than a fight. His family share all the standard prejudices about coloured workers, and Bernard's growing friendship with Shofiq puzzles them and strains natural loyalties. The author voices his views on tower blocks, social workers, services and schools, and all the confusions that arise when cultures clash. Signs of the times include Shofiq's local vernacular (it's the same as Bernard's). Altogether this is a strongly committed, outspoken book. In one sense there can be no other kind on this theme because children born here are in the midground of all racial conflicts.

G. Bott

SOURCE: A review of *My Mate Shofiq,* in *The Junior Bookshelf,* Vol. 43, No. 3. June, 1979, pp. 170-1.

An attack by bully Bobby Whitehead and his gang on a group of young Pakistani children involves Bernard Kershaw in an unscheduled friendship with Shofiq Rahman. He is none too keen but circumstances elbow him into a commitment which plunges him into the domestic turmoil of Shofiq's family. The Pakistani boy's mother is ill and is sent to hospital; his sister is bussed to the other side of town and is disturbed enough to play truant regularly; his father has lost his job; an unsympathetic welfare officer fails to appreciate the family's desire to stay together. Bernard's attempts to help end in disaster and a police chase; his feud with Bobby Whitehead culminates in a nasty brick fight.

The violence of rival schoolboy (and girl) gangs hangs darkly over the major confrontations of this lively story: the misunderstandings by adults and children of an alien culture; the barriers that are built on racial prejudice; the efforts of the do-gooders who, with the best intentions, allow administrative convenience to swamp compassion.

There is a good deal of slang, a smattering of obscenities and plenty of verbal posturing by rival groups and friends, all of which help to cement the story together effectively and realistically—and it should be stressed that this is primarily a story and not a social document disguised as fiction.

One niggle: Jan Needle has joined the ever-growing band of writers who condense the auxiliary verb 'have' into 'of' instead of ''ve'.

Leila Berg

SOURCE: "Black and White Are Beautiful," in *The Times Educational Supplement,* No. 3430, March 26, 1982, pp. 28-9.

Jan Needle will have to work hard the rest of his life, because nothing, *nothing,* will ever be better than *My Mate Shofiq. . . .*

Shofiq tells it straight, not allegorically: it is a passionately unsentimental book both accurate and truthful—about kids in a Salford Paki-bashing district, about a boy who draws a Pakistani kid into his gang, about the man from the Welfare. Which is more violent, the streets, the school, or the social security office? and can you *limit* violence? This is a very thoughtful book, utterly absorbing, exciting and moving. No one who has read it (not "no child"—"no one") will ever be the same again; which gives our society a chance of improvement.

Terry Jones

SOURCE: A review of *My Mate Shofiq,* in *Children's literature in education,* Vol. 13, No. 2, Summer, 1982, pp. 59-60.

One of the difficulties of the "social problem" novel for young readers is that the author, in seeking to convey reality—at school and at home—may paint so bleak a picture of that life that the reader is disinclined to go beyond the first few chapters. It is one which Jan Needle doesn't entirely solve and which may deter the reader from what is a provocative, sometimes disturbing, occasionally confused, but very honest novel. Certainly, the environment which he describes is uninviting—a drab school, and apparently even drabber homes, in a raw northern town in which it seems always to be raining, snowing, or blowing a gale. But one of the strengths of the novel is Jan Needle's ability to show us this environment through the eyes of his young characters. Bernard Kershaw, the reluctant "herd," lives in a block of flats covered with graffiti, in which the lifts stink of "piddle" and rarely work. His "mate," Shofiq Rahman, lives in a run-down terraced house with an outside lavatory in "blackie-land." Yet for both boys this is home—the flat and the house have qualities which adults simply don't understand. Jan Needle avoids sentimentality here just as he avoids it in the main action of the story: the slow, painful awareness on Bernard's part of the reason his mate, Shofiq, has to fight, often violently, for what he sees as his rights—and those of his family—in an apparently hostile society. If there is a sentimentality in the novel, it is in giving both boys a mother who is suffering from severe depression. But the good things in the novel outweigh that. The school life of the boys, though not described at length, is convincing enough for the most sceptical young reader, particularly in the description of the Head Teacher who, in the eyes of the more credulous of his pupils, Bernard among them, is capable of "caning a kid half to death." The racial prejudice in a town where rising redundancies lead mill workers, sadly but understandably, to blame the Pakistanis is described sensitively and honestly as Bernard struggles to understand why his father can like Shofiq but want to get rid of Shofiq's father from the mill where both work. There is violence in the book—it is possible that a girl may lose an eye as the result of a fight—but that is also dealt with in the same way. The plot is exciting, realistic, and convincing, but what comes through most clearly is compassion, warmth, and the suggestion that as Bernard and Shofiq "face the music," something good has come out of the frustration, prejudice, and violence—and that the young reader will, like Bernard and Shofiq, have learned from this.

A FINE BOY FOR KILLING (1979)

Book Window

SOURCE: A review of *A Fine Boy for Killing,* in *Book Window,* Vol. 7, No. 1, Winter, 1979, p. 32.

The writer shows great knowledge of conditions in the British Navy of Nelson's day. This material given in documentary style would be acceptable though horrifying. However as the skeleton of fact becomes clothed in the flesh of fiction an unpleasant flavour creeps into the book, and something like relish is present in the description of the fearful floggings and other brutalities inflicted on the men. The story depicts the frigate *Welfare* sailing south under sealed orders. Her captain, who wields the power of life and death over his crew, is a man without pity. A young relative of his is midshipman, and the story is concerned with how he becomes involved with a smuggler and a shepherd boy who have been illegally 'pressed' on board ship. The smuggler is a fine, robust and attractive man, the shepherd boy weak, afraid and so obviously doomed that it is frightful to pick out the threads of the story that lead to his death. The description of the foul conditions the men lived in down in the depths of the ship is masterly, and the personality given to each character is interesting and vivid, but the book is overbalanced with the emphasis on bestiality and it fails as an adventure, with the story never plunging forward to exciting events, but rather the reader is dragged on unwillingly to witness further horrors. The shocking title is warning enough perhaps.

David Churchill

SOURCE: A review of *A Fine Boy for Killing,* in *The School Librarian,* Vol. 28, No. 1, March, 1980, p. 62.

It is difficult to review this book for school libraries: the language is often crude, there is considerable brutality, suffering and sadism in the action, and good does not triumph at the end. But it is very powerfully and well written and contains strong and memorable characters. It depicts life on board a ship of the British Navy in the time of Nelson, with an evil captain exercising god-like powers over the hundreds of pressed men, criminals and others who make up his crew. His wickedness, the inev-

itable mutiny and its tragic, equally inevitable, outcome make absorbing if at times horrifying reading. Secondary-school librarians must at least consider the book, for it does demand attention.

Margery Fisher

SOURCE: A review of *A Fine Boy for Killing,* in *Growing Point,* Vol. 19, No. 1, May, 1980, pp. 3702-3.

The paths of William Bentley, fourteen-year-old midshipman, and Thomas Fox, a farmer's son a year older, cross by bitter accident outside Portsmouth: Thomas is driving twelve sheep to market, William is (illegally) seeking to press landsmen for his uncle's frigate *Welfare.* In Nelson's navy (we are told in a prefatory note) the incidence of suicide was seven times greater than on land. This savage, incisive story of a brutal captain, of flogging, disease and mutiny, is as far from the active jollity of Marryat and Kingston as it is from the sardonic humour of Patrick O'Brian. Some readers may be consoled for the unremitting horror of the story by the fact that William is shaken out of his privileged callousness by the fate of Thomas. Others may feel that, in his determination to avoid romanticising the past, the author has forced them to sup too full of horrors to respond to his book as they should.

Holly Sanhuber

SOURCE: A review of *A Fine Boy for Killing,* in *School Library Journal,* Vol. 30, No. 5, January, 1984, p. 87.

Conditions aboard the British frigate *Welfare,* commanded by madman Daniel Swift, were frightful: dirty, stinking, with rations rotting and rum the only drink. Worse still were the floggings, the daily "punishments" the men were forced to witness and the inability of the officers to understand that the seamen, no matter what their unsavory antecedents, were human beings. As the tension on the ship mounts, murder and mutiny are inevitable. So too is the justice, wholly unjust, which is meted out to the survivors. This is an engrossing story set during the time of Nelson, but it is also a book which hurts to read, with an impact which devastates readers. Violence is commonplace and described very graphically. In fact, readers may be sickened by the descriptions of floggings. In the end the title takes on added irony as one wonders whether the boy who died was not more fortunate than the one, illusions and dreams shattered, who was forced to live—and remember.

THE SIZE SPIES (1979)

Book Window

SOURCE: A review of *The Size Spies,* in *Book Window,* Vol. 8, No. 1, Winter, 1980, p. 29.

The Size Spies is an extremely funny and imaginative tale

which will appeal to both boys and girls. . . . It concerns the adventures of George and Cynthia with their eccentric friend the Prof as they try to outwit the spies and at the same time find a way of returning their parents—shrunk to doll-size by the Prof's shrinking machine—to normal size. This is a story which is at the same time fast-moving, exciting and humorous. Jan Needle provides the reader with such delightful "characters" as Snark, the electric dog and a "Thinks Computer" which is unbelievably smug and inclined to sulk, as well as the human participants. Children in the 12-13 age group will find *The Size Spies* a highly enjoyable book.

THE BEE RUSTLERS (1980)

Margery Fisher

SOURCE: A review of *The Bee Rustlers,* in *Growing Point,* Vol. 19, No. 1, May, 1980, p. 3699.

Fiction may compel belief by the shock of the extraordinary or by the reassurance of events evolving from the ordinary. Jan Needle takes the latter course in *The Bee Rustlers,* a tale that should appeal to readers of nine or ten by virtue of its short, sharp, direct narrative and the authentic behaviour and talk of Tony, who is ten or so, and his slightly older sister Carol. The children are sent up to the high Yorkshire moor to check the hives for their mother, who is laid up with a back injury. Carol has a certain immunity to stings from long practice but Tony is scared of bees and still more alarmed when they realise that the trespasser they surprise is one of an organised gang. Anger inspires the children to oppose the men themselves, since help is far to seek. Their rashness succeeds but is not commended by their father:

> Dad just let fly. How these men were professional crooks, how they were ruthless, violent and wouldn't think twice about harming a child, how if it hadn't been for the confusion caused by the bees they probably would have caught Carol and taken it out on her for getting in their way.

He is, justifiably, as hard on Tony for his reckless dash downhill in the getaway van. He does, all the same, admit that their actions were at least practical and the final celebration with Aunt Mary's elderflower champagne is one of many moments in which humour sharpens up a well-judged first-person narrative.

E. Cowell

SOURCE: A review of *The Bee Rustlers,* in *The Junior Bookshelf,* Vol. 44, No. 4, August, 1980, pp. 178-9.

Not sheep or cattle rustling but bee rustling gives this story an unusual background, although otherwise the general pattern is much the same as in other adventure stories with this theme. Two children are involved and several experienced thieves. The bees help in the defeat of the

rustlers, but the children's father is not grateful, for they have disobeyed him. Such an attitude towards two children who are covered with bee-stings in their effort to save their mother's bees, will rouse the indignation of some child readers.

The children use a great deal of slang and this can become tedious. However, there is excitement and suspense and just enough information about bees and bee-keeping to interest the reader.

A SENSE OF SHAME AND OTHER STORIES (1980)

Neil Philip

SOURCE: "Running the Race Game," in *The Times Educational Supplement,* No. 3359, November 7, 1980, p. 24.

Depth of feeling and depth of understanding are the two outstanding qualities of Jan Needle's new stories. They are often melodramatic or overstated, and there are minor pocks and abrasions on their surface which a cooler writer . . . would never allow to appear, but they are real, immediate, moving. They approach life head on. They are also often funny, and never lose their sense of the comic. They are all concerned with racial prejudice, always from a white viewpoint, and are notable for the manner in which they provoke thought and avoid preaching or sloganizing.

The title story, **"A Sense of Shame"**, can stand for all. Lorraine works for an Oldham printer in the accounts department. She is sixteen. Mohammed mends the broken machines. He is nineteen. They fall wildly, passionately, secretly, guiltily, innocently in love. Their joy is very touchingly described, all the more so for the bitter fearful edge which Needle discerns in the relationship. Tragedy is inevitable; in a short story, Needle takes the easy way out and conjures up a baby, a possible abortion, eventual adoption. So much for the dramatics: what matters in a story dealing with this touchy subject is the dynamics, and Needle gets them absolutely right.

Margery Fisher

SOURCE: A review of *A Sense of Shame,* in *Growing Point,* Vol. 19, No. 5, January, 1981, p. 3826.

Among the situations which adolescent readers are invited to reflect upon, the problem which Catholic Lorraine faces with her half-Pakistan baby is open-ended, but most of the stories depend on a sharp, surprising statement of alternatives. In 'Stung', a young husband discovers an unexpected bond with the baby he feels has destroyed the love that brought it to life; in 'The Common Good' a smug young man, mistakenly arrested in a street riot, finds justice looks different from the dock. Terse and acid, the stories address themselves, at times somewhat obviously, to a predictable average sample of the present-day 'teens.

Marcus Crouch

SOURCE: A review of *A Sense of Shame and Other Stories,* in *The School Librarian,* Vol. 29, No. 1, March, 1981, p. 54.

Jan Needle is interested in the problems of minorities. He is, on the whole, a sound observer (he seems to have been unlucky in his experience of the Welsh) and his sympathies embrace all shades of colour and most shades of society and politics. This quality, although essential to anyone writing in this area, is in itself not enough. What finally puts the seal on *A sense of shame* is writing skill. Mr Needle knows just how to twist the heart or put the boot in. His tales of Pakis and Irishmen will start profitable discussion just because of the sharpness with which he makes his controversial points.

Peter Hollindale

SOURCE: A review of *A Sense of Shame and Other Stories,* in *British Book News, Children's Supplement,* Spring, 1981, p. 27.

Jan Needle's writing goes from strength to strength. In his new collection of stories for teenagers, all of them concerned with the lives and problems of modern adolescents, he reveals the same qualities that were evident in his recent powerful historical novel, *A Fine Boy for Killing*: a passionate concern for human freedoms and decencies combined with a bitter and unsparing realism in the depiction of ugly and disturbing events. Most of the stories deal with racial and national prejudices. The blurb suggests 'prejudice' as the book's overall theme, but it would be truer to say that Needle's main characters are the unprejudiced (whether by reason of conscious enlightenment, genuine tolerance, idealism or love) and his main concern is the appalling damage done to such characters by the prejudiced society they inhabit. Needle's vision is a harsh one and he has not written mere propaganda: he is aware of hate as a two-way process, between which individual decencies are crushed and violated. Comfortless as his world largely is, it is authentic and convincing. The book deserves a wide readership, especially in schools: sensitively presented, it will provoke many adolescents to re-examine the clichés of both bigotry and tolerance.

WILD WOOD (1981)

Margery Fisher

SOURCE: A review of *Wild Wood,* in *Growing Point,* Vol. 20, No. 2, July, 1981, pp. 3906-7.

Wild Wood tells the story of 'Brotherhood Hall—Toad Hall as it is more usually known'—through 'the sharp and penetrating memory' of an 'ancient and helpful ferret'. Cedric Willoughby, driving his 1907 Armstrong Hardcastle Mouton Special Eight in the London to Brighton Veteran Car Run, crashes in a lonely spot and is rescued by elderly Baxter Ferret who, as well as repairing the car, tells him the story of Toad's extravagant escapades and the invasion of Toad Hall from the Wild Wooders' point of view. The entranced motorist in vain tried to find once more the 'cramped and secret house in the woods' where he had listened to the ferret's strange reminiscences: he died disappointed but made his friend (the author) promise to prepare his account of the affair for publication. This elaborate device to compel belief in a tall story successfully diverts attention from the fact that ferret and man meet and talk without difficulty. Like Graham himself, Jan Needle simply ignores the problem and so it ceases to exist. The reader slips into a caustic, brilliantly circumstantial version of *The Wind in the Willows* from 'the other side'.

To O.B. the weasel, Mole has changed for the worse:

> Why, last year he was just an ordinary sort of bloke with a little house and a cheery word for anyone. Now he's one of Toad's greatest pals, goes on caravan trips with him, dines at Toad Hall, and's full of airs and graces. Never had a servant in his life, nor dreamed of it neither, and now he's a River Banker through and through.

The old seafarer Wilson inveighs against 'that Rat bloke' because he is 'always out and about in a blazer and a fancy cap; expensive little light-weight rowing boat'—a professional sailor's scorn of people who mess about in boats. Baxter Ferret's mother, a redoubtable brewer of Real Ale, takes the most tolerant view of the River Bankers, the dour stoat Boddington the most extreme one: the middle view of O.B. and Baxter, the prejudiced attitude of Baxter's emotional sister Dolly, vary from day to day as Boddington stirs the Wild Wooders to rise against Toad's extravagance and his total disregard of his social inferiors. This ingenious narrative is neither parody nor satire, though it contains obvious elements of both. Certainly it is anti-romantic, and in this the words are brilliantly supported by William Rushton's incisive, brooding drawings. Perhaps it could be called a comic reversal, since Toad's motor-mania and its consequences, the main target of the book, is simply viewed from an unexpected angle; his escape from prison is re-cast as part of the plot initiated by Boddington and forwarded by the Chief Weasel, which leads to the take-over at Toad Hall. Such satire as there is seems to be directed against political cliché. If the author is putting out any message to society, it is a somewhat disillusioned one. The revolt neither wholly fails nor wholly succeeds. Toad behaves rather better towards his employees. Baxter Ferret, who had first met him when his former boss's car suffered from the conceited animals' appalling road manners, becomes his chauffeur and mechanic. The community settles into a compromise that will be only too familiar to older readers:

> Speaking purely personal, like, and I reckon I ought to be a bit ashamed of it, maybe, I never got settled to the life like I'd used to be. There was peace all right, but there was something else too. Regret's the nearest to it I can think of, but I'm probably wrong. I never did understand it all, really.

A handsome tribute to Grahame, indeed. The last chapter, 'Epilogue and Rest in Peace', indicates plainly enough that there is never any real answer to social inequality. As for the story, it is brilliantly intricate, beautifully crafted and outrageously funny, and this should be enough for anyone.

Jessica Yates

SOURCE: A review of *Wild Wood*, in *British Book News, Children's Supplement*, Autumn, 1981, pp. 25-6.

This is the 'sequel' to one of the great children's classics. It is the story of *The Wind in the Willows*, told from the viewpoint of the Wild Wooders who occupied Toad Hall while Toad was imprisoned for stealing a motor-car. Although the temptation to draw a contemporary political moral may have been strong, it has been resisted. Instead the book is an affectionate tribute, poking fun at the revolutionary aspirations of Boddington Stoat, as well as the upper-class life-style of the River Bankers. We can readily believe that Grahame was unfair to the ferrets, stoats and weasels of the Wood, the rural poor left in the backwash of the Industrial Revolution while the gentry waxed fat on their inherited incomes. The hero, with a hint of Grahame's modest Mole about him, is Baxter Ferret, a mechanical genius who gets a job patching up Toad's motor cars, and loses it when Badger tries to cure Toad of motor-mania. Then Baxter joins the Wild Wooders' militia and finds they have a plan to capture Toad Hall. From then on the story follows a course parallel to *The Wind in the Willows* to describe how Toad escaped from prison and regained Toad Hall, to the relief of the Wild Wooders who have just about exhausted their food supplies. It was a scoop for Needle to obtain the services of William Rushton as illustrator, as the style of the political cartoonist is just what is wanted. This book should become a favourite with adults as well as children.

Neil Philip

SOURCE: "New Lamps for Old," in *The Times Educational Supplement*, No. 3412, November 20, 1981, pp. 31-2.

Fairy tales, fables and fantasies are periodically attacked or "explained away" by one orthodoxy or another. One loud complaint of recent years has been that *The Wind in the Willows* is an idyll based on exploitation. The comfortable lives of Rat, Mole and Toad are an affront; why shouldn't the Wild Wooders taste the good life too? That there is real force in this argument everyone must admit. Yet Jan Needle's *Wild Wood,* an affectionate attempt to embody that argument in narrative, shows very clearly how badly it misses the mark. The social structure of *The Wind in the Willows* is unequal; the atmosphere is cosy; Toad by any realistic assessment is a homicidal maniac as well as a boastful snob. But none of that matters a jot beside the immense humanity of Grahame's prose. *The Wind in the Willows* is a book about friendship, and there

is no cruelty or hatred in it. Its unthinking acceptance of Edwardian social alignments is of minor importance, beside the richness of its comedy.

Needle's *Wild Wood* attempts to look at Grahame's comfortable, all-male riverbank world from underneath. The story is told by Baxter Ferret, a car mad Wild Wooder employed as a mechanic by Toad. The narrative hangs together well, and it is all very worthy, but Needle creates no characters to rival Grahame's. He seems constrained by his model, and his reversal of viewpoint is never as funny as it promises to be. *Wild Wood* is a good short story stretched to novel length. When we have admitted the justice of its critique, we return cheerfully to its unscarred, incomparable source.

Andrew Hislop

SOURCE: A review of *Wild Wood,* in *The Times Literary Supplement*, No. 4103, November 20, 1981, p. 1363.

Most of us read masterpieces rather than write them. Some, however, prefer to rewrite them. Such a tinkerer is Jan Needle. It is unclear though whether his rewriting of *The Wind in the Willows* is a labour of love or loathing. Perhaps, it is just an act of completion, an attempt to sellotape onto the original palimpsest the other side of the story that has been censored in Grahame's or the collective unconscious. Or it could be just a joke. Indeed, the concept is witty: to make the other side of the story the story of the weasels, stoats and ferrets who took over Toad Hall when Toad was incarcerated for grievous motoring offences; to reveal them to be not as jumped-up members of the lower orders of quadrupeds, surly squatters deservedly cudgled into submission by Badger, Mole and the liberated Toad, but fauna, with hearts and minds and social grievances, working class heroes and heroines suffering the rigours of a depression, decent folk who have been provoked into agit prop by Boddington, a stunted stoat, fixed of vision, ignorant of much but red of ken. This "only serious attempt at a full-scale workers' revolution in this country since the Peasants'" (to quote from the Epilogue written by a human of sociological bent) is thwarted in the end as much by latent social democrats and lack of class zeal as by the furry and slimy defenders of private property. The joke, though it might hold up well in a Monty Python-type sketch cannot be sustained throughout a book, especially a book which is parisitic on one of the great comic novels. *Rosencrantz and Guildenstern are Dead* is not as good a play as *Hamlet,* but it is funnier, at least it is more persistent if not more profound in its humour. *Wild Wood* though, does not begin to match *The Wind in the Willows*'s joyous, anarchic yet poignant humour, its inventiveness, its wit, the nicety of its balance between satire and the telling of a story, between the human and animal worlds. Needle's book offers itself to be compared with the most beautifully written of children's books but its language wilts besides Grahame's masterly prose. Social division among creatures great and small may be broken down in *Wild Wood* but differences in the class of creators are only confirmed. Grahame a least offers us redemption, bourgeois and individualistic though it might be; Needle merely confirms the impotence and comic absurdity of many radical groups with good intentions who fail to change the world.

Dorothy Atkinson

SOURCE: A review of *Wild Wood,* in *The School Librarian,* Vol. 31, No. 2, June, 1983, pp. 166-7.

Recently we had a sequel to *Treasure Island,* and there was an evident and rich seam in *The Wind in the Willows* for a modern writer. Jan Needle has taken up the contrast between the River Bankers, doing little that wasn't connected with pleasure and leisure, and the stoats, ferrets and weasels, the Wild Wooders, so soundly trounced by Kenneth Grahame.

An ebullient motorist runs into an old chap, Baxter Ferrett, who used to work as mechanic on Toad's motors. For six days, as he repairs the motorist's vintage car, the ferret re-creates the glorious days of 'the only serious attempt at a fullscale workers' revolution in this country since the Peasants' Revolt'. The Wild Wooders have been organised by a militant, Mr Boddington, a stoat dressed in grey, thin, serious and bitter, with eyes that glitter from his balaclava. His efforts get the River Bankers out of Toad Hall, but human nature gets them in again, for the Chief Weasel and his mates enjoy the flesh-pots as much as anyone and are having a party when the revenge attack is launched. Boddington leaves for the north to energise Manchester's workers, Baxter's friends pick up their old jobs and the Chief Weasel gets in with the Squire and buys a summer home on the River Bank. Everything returns to normal. Baxter Ferrett, a man who loves complicated jobs on cars, was a simpleton in political matters and lives out his life in regret.

In case you are a River Banker by persuasion and fear that violence may have been done to a favourite book, let me reassure you that the claim on the book jacket 'in many ways a celebration of Kenneth Grahame's masterpiece' is quite just. The writing, carefully phrased for the ungrammatical Ferrett, is nevertheless rich and interesting, notably in the car repair passages which are inspired. The book is funny and not out to score political points at the expense of narrative, though it does make such points; and the illustrations, in the manner of Scarfe or Steadman, reinforce these. It is perfectly possible to imagine that you are in *The Wind in the Willows,* but seeing things from the Wild Wood. That is an achievement.

Peter Hollindale

SOURCE: A review of *Wild Wood,* in *The Times Educational Supplement,* No. 4040, December 3, 1993, p. 29.

Jan Needle's **Wild Wood,** first published in 1981 and now reissued, is an irreverent neo-political tribute to its mentor, and the joyous expression of those "anarchic urges"

of which [Grahame biographer Peter] Green spoke. This is the alternative classic, the original story (more or less) told from the point of view of the Wild Wooders. Toad's incarceration triggers the heroic uprising of the oppressed stoats and weasels against the idle capitalists and brings the short-lived triumph of Brotherhood Hall. **Wild Wood** is a very funny, politically shrewd, iconoclastic masterpiece, a brilliant satire rooted in delight. It should never have gone out of print, and deserves to be read as long as Grahame is.

ANOTHER FINE MESS (1981)

Peter Hollindale

SOURCE: A review of *Another Fine Mess,* in *British Book News, Children's Supplement,* Spring, 1982, p. 12.

At the climax of this time-travel extravaganza we find ourselves in the middle of an Elizabethan riot, as the killjoy Puritans seek to expose the blasphemous wickedness of plays and playgoing. The ringleader of the Puritans is a formidable harridan called Mistress Maria Kassablank. For adult English readers a little unexacting translation here will reveal a piquant and delightful joke. Another such is the reported presence in Southwark of a blackamoor called Shakespeare, writing sonnets to his 'black mistress'. For those few adults (who besides reviewers?) who will read it, **Another Fine Mess** is a witty parody of old-fashioned children's science fiction, embellished with some delightful modern jokes. For children it is an action-packed romp, a tale of absent-minded professors, disastrous experiments and disobedient inventions, with the lucky presence of resourceful children to save the day. It is comic science fiction, a saga of hilarious catastrophes, such as used to be available for a few pence every week in comics. Children of seven to eleven will revel in it, as they do in its predecessor, *The Size Spies.* But why do such simple wares now need a gifted author with a taste for parody, and expensive hardbacked permanence?

M. Crouch

SOURCE: A review of *Another Fine Mess,* in *The Junior Bookshelf,* Vol. 46, No. 2, April, 1982, pp. 67-8.

Can this really be the author of those sensitive and committed stories about racial minority problems? This is altogether a different matter. Mr Needle might have made a list of all the things that adults imagine children like and then slotted them into his narrative. The result is rather like a comic in words—if that is not a contradiction in terms.

This is a sequel to **The Size Spies,** featuring again a lunatic Professor and his reluctant young friends. Through an unwise experiment with a time machine called the Cheap Day Return Transferer they, and their electronic dog The Snark are shot into what turns out to be the Elizabethan age. There they are befriended by a company of boy players and threatened by a charlatan of a magician, against whom the Prof pits his erratic scientific powers. They get back home just in time.

No one could complain that the fun is less than fast and furious. A more just criticism might be that Mr Needle tries too hard. He packs in so much that concern, involvement and even the smallest shadow of credibility go out of the window. As a picture-serial in a comic, spread out over, say, six episodes it might just be acceptable; nearly two hundred pages of print are a bit too much. Will those children who enjoy this kind of thing be sufficiently literate and energetic to follow Mr Needle on his very fluent and literary course to the end? It seems an awful waste of a very real talent.

Susan L. Locke

SOURCE: A review of *Another Fine Mess,* in *School Library Journal,* Vol. 31, No. 1, September, 1984, p. 121.

In Needle's sequel to **The Size Spies,** Cynthia and George take a second trip in one of Prof's loonier inventions, the cheap day return transferer. The main problem with Prof's time machine, as with all his inventions, is that it's not perfected; and the three are stranded in Shakespeare's London. They are held captive by an alchemist of ill repute, befriended by a group of roving players who use some trickery of their own to execute an escape and are finally rescued by two present-day friends. The book's strengths are the portrayal of the proximity of magic and science during this time period and the brief glimpse of the theater and the roving male actors who play all the parts. The weaknesses: the abundance of British expressions will hinder middle graders, yet many junior high students will not read about younger characters. A difficult but entertaining story for good readers who are interested in Shakespeare's London.

📖 *LOSERS WEEPERS* (1981)

Julia Marriage

SOURCE: A review of *Losers Weepers,* in *British Book News, Children's Supplement,* Spring, 1982, pp. 7-8.

A familiar plea from parents, teachers and librarians is for lively stories to offer the nine to eleven age group. Too often material available fails to attract because it is dull in style and presentation and has little in common with the age group. It is good therefore to have found *Losers Weepers* which is a most lively piece of writing in the Pied Piper series. Tony and Carol find an ancient sword buried in a feeder stream to a moorland reservoir. Family tensions build as the value of the sword is discovered and Jan Needle uses these tensions to underline what is essentially a fast-moving story. Child and adult characters are skilfully portrayed and developed both being shown as much prey to pressures and temptations of possible wealth

as the other. This is a good example of 'realistic' writing for a younger age group. The generous use of line drawings by Jane Bottomley adds to the overall appeal of the book.

Chris Brown

SOURCE: A review of *Losers Weepers,* in *The School Librarian,* Vol. 30, No. 1, March, 1982, p. 38.

Stories for children involving treasure usually delay discovery of it until near the end of the tale. In this book we have been taken only five or six pages into the plot when Tony and Carol recover an ancient sword. The problems resulting from the find and the developing reactions of the whole family make a provocative, lively and gripping book within the crisp format of the 'Pied Piper' series. The difficulties are resolved in a manner indicating that not all of the questions are answered, even for the most self-reliant of the characters, and this makes the book linger on in the mind after it has been read. Jan Needle has turned the treasure-hunt formula upside down with compelling effect.

📖 *PIGGY IN THE MIDDLE* (1982)

Charles Fox

SOURCE: A review of *Piggy in the Middle,* in *New Statesman,* Vol. 104, No. 2698, December 3, 1982, p. 21.

Murder rather than theft is the crime which provides an excuse, rather than the subject-matter, for Jan Needle's **Piggy in the Middle.** An Asian man is battered to death and the police question his son—but in dubious ways and for an unconscionably long time. Which disturbs Sandra, a young policewoman, not to mention her boyfriend, a local journalist. At the risk of sounding sexist, this book seems to be aimed at girls rather than boys. Which does not mean it sidesteps griminess or bowdlerises—well, not too much—the street talk (shitty, bugger and other secondary swear-words pop up from time to time). Much more disconcerting are the plethora of clichés and the fact that the prose needs to be read at a gallop, rather like a front-page story in the *Sun.*

Marion Glastonbury

SOURCE: "Teenage Psychobabble," in *The Times Educational Supplement,* No. 3473, January 21, 1983, p. 34.

As Jan Needle suggests in **Piggy in the Middle,** you may have to kiss a lot of frogs before one turns out to be a prince.

Sandra, a beautiful young policewoman, loves David, an earnest reporter on the local paper. But divided loyalties tear them apart when an elderly Pakistani is murdered and his timid son, a former class-mate of Sandra's is illegally detained and brutally interrogated at the police station. The consequences of a racist killing for which no-one is formally charged, the harassment of the victim's family, the protests of race-relations officials, the cynical indifference of the Press, are compellingly described. For a variety of reasons, the grim ironies of this complex drama need careful interpretation. It takes a mature reader to spot the disturbing double standard in operation at HQ: the predatory sexual approaches of Sandra's male colleagues, and their castigation of her "immorality" when, in one instance, she accepts.

A major doubt remains. Why is no character relaxed, no conversation comforting, without the "nectar" of whisky, or the "adored" sensation of gin? If Jan Needle had been sponsored by a federation of distillers, [he] could not press home more insistently the message that spirits are inspiriting, and that alcohol is a girl's best friend.

A. Thatcher

SOURCE: A review of *Piggy in the Middle,* in *The Junior Bookshelf,* Vol. 47, No. 1, February, 1983, p. 51.

The setting is a large seaside town, with some industry, and an ethnic population. Sandra Patterson is a trainee policewoman; her boy friend of several years, David Tanner, is a journalist on the local newspaper. When Yusuf Mansoor is battered to death, his son, Noor Allahi, who had been in school with Sandra, is arrested for his murder. The brutal and bigoted methods of interrogation which Sandra suspects were used by her police colleagues, Noor's release because the evidence is not conclusive, and his subsequent re-arrest as an illegal immigrant, sicken and confuse her. Then David, involved with members of the Racial Equality Campaign, attacks and insults her as one of the 'Pigs', who believe that any harassing behaviour is justified if it brings results. A violent quarrel ensues. Through her relationships with different fellow officers she discovers that not all her colleagues are prejudiced.

Even though Sandra can be violent, uses abusive 'gutter' language, and accepts easily the lax modern sex morality, she has a caring innocence and a conscience which will not allow her to be part of a system which she feels could be evil. So she resigns, and, at last, she and David begin to realise that they share the same principles, and have something on which to build a future respect and relationship.

A thought-provoking, deeply disturbing book, sometimes politically orientated, and a frightening indictment of life in the 1980's, the racial prejudice, and the antagonism towards the forces of law and order. The message of hope lies in the fact that she and David, and some of their generation are prepared to fight and sacrifice for what they think is right. Not to be placed in the hands of the immature reader.

Margery Fisher

SOURCE: A review of *Piggy in the Middle,* in *Growing Point,* Vol. 21, No. 6, March, 1983, p. 4029.

In *Piggy in the Middle* two young people making their way in the adult world come up against severe social pressures which affect their private response to one another. Sandra is in her first year as a police trainee and her boy friend David is starting as a reporter on the local paper, when the murder of an elderly Asian in the small town forces them to look honestly at the differences of outlook which they have carefully set aside. As investigations proceed it becomes clear that David and his colleagues want to publicise the murder as a racist act rather than reporting it as the domestic tragedy it really is; his relations with Sandra are all the more severely strained because at least one of the policemen she works with is a brutal, warped man who disregards both his professional and social obligations. Jan Needle's strong, direct prose, his gift for establishing individual voices in dialogue and his uncompromising view of urban tensions contribute to a well-planned, well-disciplined novel which, simplified as it has to be, still in its relatively short space gives a definite impression of real people in a real community. Sandra and David become recognisable to the reader because of the work they do and the compromises they have to make to do it well. By a cumulation of detail the author has created a world and a situation we can believe.

A PITIFUL PLACE (1984)

Rosemary Stones

SOURCE: "The Pity of It," in *The Times Educational Supplement,* No. 3545, June 8, 1984, p. 46.

Northern Ireland, this time seen through the eyes of a British soldier, is also the setting for one of the short stories in Jan Needle's *A Pitiful Place.* In "A Letter from Wally", Wally writes a despairing, almost affectionate letter about life as a soldier to his former class teacher, the "tubby little wanker. . . . and lefty swine" who once tried, unsuccessfully, to persuade him not to join up. Needle develops his anti-war theme in the title story, "A Pitiful Place to Die" which is set in the Falklands. This is the outstanding story of the collection with Needle's occasionally declamatory tone softened in his description of the lingering death of a 19-year-old British soldier who, ironically, bears the same name as a seal hunter of long ago who also perished 10,000 miles from home.

White working class girls are the central characters in two of Needle's stories. In "Given to Tears" 15-year-old Christine has her baby taken away from her and put up for adoption by a social worker convinced of Christine's inadequacy and of the natural superiority of a middle class environment for the child. If I did not know from direct experience that these things happen I would have found this story hard to believe. As it is I found it heart-rending, exact and told with just anger. "The Ghost of Mrs Hitler" is a tongue-in-cheek story with a bite about a group of teenage fascists looking for "targets". Their intended victim, an old Polish Jew, turns out to be more than a match for them.

"Respectable" racism is the theme of **"No Lady, Godiva"** in which "slim, lean and sexy" Dru ("her hair sun-bleached and beautiful") strips in a churchyard to demonstrate her solidarity with the "plumpish handsome" radical vicar (male waistlines again?) who has preached an anti-racist sermon to a hostile audience. This mawkish male fantasy is Needle-over-the-top and it should not have been included in what is otherwise a punchy, varied, exciting and well-told collection of stories about the political issues that affect young people today.

Patricia Craig

SOURCE: "Colloquial and Profane," in *The Times Literary Supplement,* No. 4247, August 24, 1984, p. 954.

A Pitiful Place consists of five stories, one long and four short, each dealing with a young person in a topical predicament. We start with Christine, sixteen years old and the mother of the illegitimate Sharon, at loggerheads with her father, and finally deprived of her baby by the actions of an unintelligent social worker. This—**"Given to Tears"**—is the title—is the longest piece. Next comes Wally, on active service in Belfast, and thoroughly fed up. Wally's impressions of life in the army—"It was all a game, it was all a laugh, it was all a bloody boring bind at times"—are recorded in a letter to his old teacher, with whom he didn't exactly get on during his schooldays, but for whom, in retrospect, he feels a modicum of admiration. The letter is composed in a very racy, outspoken style.

The following story concerns the opinionated daughter of conservative parents, newly returned home after a two-year stint doing voluntary work in Africa. Dru Brierley, when a suburban congregation takes exception to the pastor's plea for support in a case involving Bangladeshi immigrants, performs a striptease in the churchyard as a rather muddled gesture of solidarity with the underprivileged. Next, a voice—colloquial and profane—is manufactured for the female hanger-on in a gang of racist hooligans ("We found a couple of Pakistani corner shops, and we used to barge in shouting slogans and such . . ."). The point of this one is that Milly ("Yeah, that's my name, believe it or not") finally experiences a slight change of heart. To end with, we have a wounded soldier dying in a Falklands shack: "This shitty little war will be forgotten when there's no more votes in it, but we've been forgotten already. The unknown soldiers, disappeared on active service."

Jan Needle is on the side of the disaffected young, against bureaucracy, exploitation and all illiberal attitudes, and shapes his fiction accordingly. The result is dispiritingly didactic and banal. The social problem genre really requires some extraneous quality to make it tolerable—high spirits, wit, an ironic perspective or a distinctive tone. Unfortunately nothing of the sort is in evidence here.

Steve Bowles

SOURCE: A review of *A Pitiful Place,* in *The School Librarian,* Vol. 33, No. 1, March, 1985, pp. 59-60.

Here, as in *A Sense of Shame,* Jan Needle has taken a number of more-or-less topical issues and framed dramatic situations around them, highlighting aspects of each which are generally ignored or glossed over by the media through which children usually meet them—if they encounter them at all. The stories can seem contrived and the characters or the climactic scene inadequate. This is most noticeable in 'No Lady, Godiva'. Dru returns from somewhere in Black Africa after two years and finds herself being absorbed into the cosy complacency of her bourgeois parents' home against which she's formerly rebelled. Eventually she can take it no longer, stripping on a tomb in the churchyard to register her disgust with the congregation who've been outraged by a vaguely political sermon from a visiting clergyman. It might provide a moment's amusement, but it goes nowhere and there is no room in such a short piece to dramatise fully the smotheringly nice, liberal-Tory ethos of her home. Only those with a prior understanding of Dru's attitudes are likely to get much from the story. I don't see **'The Ghost of Mrs Hitler'** eliciting a very strong response either. Milly tells how, along with three boys playing at National Front thuggery, she breaks into a shop owned by an old Polish Jew. There is an accident after the old man discovers them, and Milly learns a little more about him while his contempt for her begins to bite through her ignorance. The narration isn't very convincing and the story hasn't sufficient drama to be particularly compelling.

The two stories dealing with the forces are better, though it's not easy to credit a young soldier in Northern Ireland writing a critique of army life to his former college lecturer—once regarded as a 'little tubby wanker with pebble specs' and 'a lefty swine to boot'—even if he knows he can never send it. The details he picks on are telling but somehow I doubt that they'd stir much more than antagonism in those already seduced by the advertising image of 'the Professionals'. They might not even provoke that much, especially as the story suffers from the tendency to tell rather than show, a besetting flaw with Jan Needle. I can't help feeling it's a pity he didn't expand this material to novel length, dealing with the army in the same way that he handled the police in *Piggy in the Middle,* in many ways his most impressive work. 'A Pitiful Place to Die' describes the lingering death of David Lowston, a member of the Special Boat Service, after a mission goes wrong during the Falklands war. As gangrene eats into his mangled leg, his pride in being an accomplished killer, 'one of the crème de la crème', is transformed into an understanding that 'It's all a put-up job, this heroism lark. Nobody really gives a shit . . . It makes the folks back home feel comfortable about sending us out to die.'

As with *A Sense of Shame,* it's the longest story which will make the biggest impression in schools. **'Given to Tears'** takes up nearly half the book and tells what happens to an unmarried, working-class mother when the social services act to 'help' her through a stormy period at home. Again, there is rather a lot of summarising at the expense of dramatising, but the story should generate sufficient sympathy for Christine to ensure an active involvement throughout.

For a skilful teacher, the stories could be very useful to promote or even initiate discussion, but most of us will find them helpful in supplementing the still tiny stock of fiction that one can offer teenage readers with some degree of confidence. They may not be brilliant but the demand for this kind of material is considerable and there are still far too few writers with the knowledge or honesty to tackle it even half-way successfully. An essential collection for secondary schools, despite the cover.

📖 *BEHIND THE BIKE SHEDS* (1985)

Pat Triggs

SOURCE: A review of *Behind the Bike Sheds,* in *Books for Keeps,* No. 30, January, 1985, p. 19.

If you had to bet on a handful of writers who might do something out of the usual run with a TV tie-in book, Jan Needle would surely be of the company. His book of the series *Behind the Bike Sheds* is certainly different. By the time you read this you may already have seen the first episodes of the not-so-everyday story of Fulley Comprehensive, its (few) pupils and its (even fewer) staff. If you have you'll realise that this is, among other things, a mad, anarchic send-up of all school TV series from *Grange Hill* to *Fame,* augmented by the usual Needle assault on the wilder lunacies of what we fondly think of as our Education System. The book is an extension of this. From time to time it deliberately reminds you that what you are reading is the book of the TV series.

> We cut now to the gymnasium, thanks to the vision mixer, Llynos. It's the school hall in fact, and also the classroom, where we've just come from. In between shots the scene shifters have removed the desks and put up the wall bars, that's all. Magic, eh? All the kids and the dancers are standing about in gym gear, waiting. Waiting for the horrible new Deputy Headmaster. Waiting for the sadist from the Acme Teacher's Agency.

The director, Peter Tabern, bawls instructions from the gallery, the actors complain to the writer that they haven't had a good line for ages. In between, what passes for the plot progresses, the narrative accompanied by a stream of comments from the author to the reader in a style of language usually referred to in reviews as 'racy'.

Not content with pushing out the boundaries of a TV tie-in, the book itself is a spoof 'Choose-Your-Own Adventure' story. You start with Chapter 23, followed by Chapter 73, and so on. There are 'choices':

If you wish to fight the orcs, turn to Chapter 88. If you wish to visit the nit nurse, put your hand up and wait.

Throughout, the book is liberally sprinkled with footnotes—all referenced to different pages so the reader has to hunt—which contain jokes, definitions, in-jokes about children's books, publishing, writing, Jan Needle etc.

Self-indulgent? Over the top? Silly? Genuinely innovative? A new cult book? Jane Nisson, Jan Needle's editor at Methuen is prepared for almost any kind of critical response and confesses to not having any idea how teenagers will react. I enjoyed it, and would probably have enjoyed it even more if I'd seen more of the TV series. This may be the first tie-in to be just what it says—a book to be read *with* the television! And I think there is something here for teachers. If you want to encourage teenagers to think about questions like: what is a book? what is a story? how is reading different from watching TV? what is the relationship between a writer and a reader?, this book could well be doing just that. At which idea Jan Needle may well be making rude noises and being sick into a paper bag. (Did he think that at last he'd written a book that teachers couldn't *use*?) Whatever his intentions, this adventure in writing inevitably becomes an adventure in reading. Like Jane Nisson I shall be watching what happens with interest.

Bill Boyle

SOURCE: A review of *Behind the Bike Sheds,* in *British Book News Children's Books,* March, 1986, p. 31.

The clever, slick parody in this, the book of the Yorkshire Television school series, should not disappoint Jan Needle's many young readers. With a list of credits ranging from **Grange Hill** and **Tucker's Luck** to **Albeson and the Germans,** Needle's popularity is assured. However, after the sensitivity and poignancy of the anti-war play/book *A Game of Soldiers,* which actually demanded a response from its young audience, it is a trifle disappointing to find him returning to the 'safeness' of this subject.

Having stated that fact, though, there is no doubt that the adventures at Fulley Comprehensive, under the benign dictatorship of headmistress Megan Bigge (Megapig, in school shorthand), contain much of the Needle tongue-in-cheek humour that makes his work as amusing for adults as it is for youngsters: 'Adams, a smallish boy with equal opportunity feet and a National Health nose . . .'; and 'AWOL comes from Bradford, and he'll never get to be a BBC Newsreader on account of he talks proper, and not like a constipated frog.'

📖 *A GAME OF SOLDIERS* (1985)

Stephanie Nettell

SOURCE: A review of *A Game of Soldiers,* in *The Times Literary Supplement,* No. 4278, March 29, 1985, p. 354.

This is Needle at his best, writing about a tough subject for young children with a simplicity of style that gives his book great impact. The novel is loosely based on his television series, the setting an unnamed stretch of cold, windswept moorland, rescued by a landing force from enemy invasion; it traces the effect on three children, moulded by very different backgrounds, of discovering a real wounded enemy in the middle of their fantasy war games. Is it true that this terrified, homesick boy is a dangerous threat to be eliminated? Their growing understanding of the nature of war is portrayed simply and painfully.

M. Crouch

SOURCE: A review of *A Game of Soldiers,* in *The Junior Bookshelf,* Vol. 49, No. 4, August, 1985, p. 189.

Jan Needle's new novel is small in scale and big in ideas. There are formidable problems, social and moral, with which the reader must grapple.

The story was originally written as a TV serial. This is the author's own 'novelisation'—the publisher's horrid word, not mine or—I suspect—his. The idea came, presumably, out of the Falklands conflict. Three children—two boys, one apparently tough, one feeble, and a strong self-contained girl—play at soldiers in country where a battle has been ranging. (What are the parents thinking of? you may ask. Well, they have their own problems, but there is not room enough in the book to explain their apparent irresponsibility. A flaw here, surely.) In one of their favourite hideouts is hidden a real soldier, one of the enemy, dreadfully wounded. The children find him. After the initial shock the story explores the individual reactions of the children to this crisis. In this the touchstone of normality is Sarah. Michael turns from hatred to understanding, Thomas, mirroring his parents' attitudes, swings between abuse and blind terror. Briefly a reconciliation is achieved; then the adult world bursts in and the story ends in tragedy. The children are, in their different ways, changed by the experience—or are they? Many questions remain unanswered.

Powerful as the book is, it gives the impression, as do so many books which originate in the medium of television, of being incompletely realized. It is as if the author has been pressed to finish his book before the effect of the TV presentation has had time to wear off. There is much that we want to know about these characters and their background. It is an acknowledgement of Mr. Needle's skill that we should, on so brief an acquaintance, care about his creations.

📖 *WAGSTAFFE THE WIND-UP BOY* (1987)

Jenny Woolf

SOURCE: "Something Nasty in the Nursery," in *Punch,* Vol. 293, No. 7660, October 21, 1987, p. 42.

Jan Needle miscalculated badly in *Wagstaffe, The Wind-up Boy,* which cackles and wheezes and nudges you in the ribs till you get scared and run away. Wagstaffe's mother and father hate him and eventually abandon him, (although really he is rather sweet). He is run over on a motorway: "Close your eyes if you get sick easily," smirks Needle—and a creepy doctor experiments on what's left of him and turns him into a mechanical boy. Then she turfs him out into various glum adventures, which culminate in his rescuing his parents from certain death. Unfortunately, that still doesn't make them love him. The whole thing somehow reminds me of Nathanael West's *Miss Lonelyhearts,* and the nasty bits are like Roald Dahl without the magic and moral standards. Jan Needle has written some magnificent, gritty and gripping stories which I deeply admire, so perhaps humour is just not his forte; yes, I think that must be it.

Chris Stephenson

SOURCE: A review of *Wagstaffe the Wind-Up Boy,* in *The School Librarian,* Vol. 36, No. 2, May, 1988, pp. 57-8.

Will Wagstaffe wind *you* up? In this gruesome little book, Jan Needle thumbs his nose at the higher aims and claims of children's literature—those 'naice' award-winning books 'put in the best place in the library by naice ladies'—and makes a play for the vulgar comedy market with a novel that is unashamedly nasty. Wagstaffe, the hero, is as loutish and repulsive as publishably possible. Moreover, reading about him is blatantly presented as subversive rather than 'improving', and adults are warned off. Some of the book's humour is supplied by this conniving against respectability. Lavatory jokes abound, but there is worse still. Take the central episode, in which Wagstaffe is run down on the M62 after catapulting an egg at the windscreen of a lorry:

> Then: Splatt!
>
> Wagstaffe, much to his surprise, is flattened right across the middle by a big double-tyred wheel. His breakfast pops out of his mouth and his stomach pops out of his trouser legs. There is blood and guts all over the place.

And as if this were not enough, zany line illustrations visualise the most awful moments with malicious glee.

After his accident, Wagstaffe is scraped up and rebuilt with clockwork guts by mechanically-minded Dr Dhondy (the NHS will not run to microchips), whom he repays by 'gobbing' in her eye. His only redeeming feature is his concern at the end of the story to save the lives of his frightful parents. Their response is so churlish, however, that we leave him dreaming of 'boiling them alive in sulphuric acid.' Clearly the whole thing is relentlessly tasteless, and Jan Needle *has* written 'naicer' books . . . But I have to confess to the odd snicker. The eleven-year-olds in my class are finding it '*wickedly* funny'—and that just about sums it up.

THE BULLY (1993)

D. A. Young

SOURCE: A review of *The Bully*, in *The Junior Bookshelf*, Vol. 57, No. 6, December, 1993, pp. 242-3.

Simon Mason may appear in the opening pages as the classic example of the bully. He is uncouth, a loner from a poor background who must rely upon violence as the only means of enhancing his self-image. The reader soon finds out that he is in fact the victim. The real bully is the tall, confident and good-looking Anna, who uses her younger brother David and her friend Rebekkah in a systematic campaign to belittle and destroy Simon. The reader will have realised this by the end of the first chapter but it takes the rest of the book for the school staff to shed their prejudices and admit that the bully could be the clever, well-behaved, perfect school-girl from such a good home and with such caring parents who run a Volvo estate. A dramatic chase ends in Simon's fall in the chalk pit resulting in a broken leg and the revelation of the identity of the true bully.

Although the chief protagonists are schoolchildren the author has fleshed out the characters of the adults, their prejudices, their attitudes and the staff-room politics so skilfully that the adult reader will find plenty to think about.

There is a concern that bullying in schools is more prevalent than we would like to think and the tendency in the past has been to deny that it exists rather than investigate it. If *The Bully* should stimulate open discussion on the topic by pupils *and* teachers it will have served a very useful purpose.

David Buckley

SOURCE: "The Bullies and the Bullied," in *The Times Educational Supplement*, No. 4052, February 25, 1994, p. 14.

At a time when schools are recognising that however many times they insist they "won't have" bullying they still do. Jan Needle's *The Bully* is a telling reminder that the victims of bullying seem to be the last minority to be taken seriously.

At St Michael's—probably a middle school though Needle is irritatingly vague about ages—staff prejudice plays a part in the school's blindness to the torment suffered by Simon Mason. When even the teachers find it hard to like unappealing isolates such as Simon, and suspect they bring it on themselves, no wonder the children are unsophisticated in their scorn.

The head, of course, loves all the children, but she loves the bright middle class ones more, and clumsy frustrated Simon is neither. He is, what's more, a "known liar"

occasionally found armed with a stone to throw at bright, elegant first generation state school Anne Royle. Only the sympathetic deputy, Louise Shaw, suspects that Simon may be telling the truth when he claims that Anne and her friend are tormenting him, and that while they cunningly evade attention, he is always caught with the weapons of tearful retaliation in his hands.

Jan Needle captures the frightening self-righteousness of a bully who believes her victim deserves punishment for not accepting victimhood willingly. The plot clicks into place with the lethal certainty of a shell being locked into the breach of a bolt action rifle. Louise, the deputy without an anti-bullying policy, is always two steps behind in her pursuit of the truth.

Her PE teacher ally depressingly favours the common sense view that Simon is probably a bully, but when the final chase leads to the crumbling cliffs of an old chalk-pit, his faithful blue tracksuit is as much of a relief as the arrival of the cavalry.

The Bully is a good case study and a cracking piece of storytelling.

Alan Horsfield

SOURCE: A review of *The Bully*, in *Magpies*, Vol. 9, No. 3, July, 1994, p. 32.

Jan Needle, author of such books as *A Game of Soldiers, My Mate Shofiq* and *Wild Wood* produces a disturbing insight into the consequences of prejudice and the labelling of a fellow human being. Simon is clumsy, bewildered, frustrated, poor and not at all streetwise—and Simon is a bully. Everyone knows it! He lives up to his reputation and two female students capitalise on his vulnerability to give themselves a sense of power. His mother is unable to help or even understand. Only one school teacher suspects that all is not quite what it seems. She gives Simon some small hope that he may regain a sense of self and worth.

Because Simon is called names and given a reputation, he begins to fear that he is incompetent. It is a self-fulfilling prophesy. It becomes easy for others to react negatively or indifferently to him even if the bullying reputation is not deserved. Needle provides a range of characters and situations for many readers to find some element of identification.

This is a good read and with bullying currently in the news the book adds another perspective to a topical issue.

Additional coverage of Needle's life and career is contained in the following sources published by Gale Research: *Contemporary Authors New Revision Series*, Vol. 28; and *Something about the Author*, Vol. 30.

Jerry Pinkney

1939-

African American illustrator of picture books.

Major works include *The Patchwork Quilt* (written by Valerie Flournoy, 1985), *The Tales of Uncle Remus* (written by Julius Lester, 1987), *Mirandy and Brother Wind* (written by Patricia McKissack, 1988), *The Talking Eggs* (written by Robert D. San Souci, 1989), *Sam and the Tigers* (written by Julius Lester, 1996).

INTRODUCTION

One of America's most highly acclaimed illustrators, Jerry Pinkney has been at the forefront of the movement to bring greater coverage of multicultural—particularly African American—subjects to picture books for children. He has illustrated for such noted authors as Virginia Hamilton, Eloise Greenfield, Verna Aardema, and Patricia Mc-

Kissack, but has received the most attention for his sometimes controversial collaborations with Julius Lester, works which have taken traditional folklore and reclaimed it for African Americans by presenting it from their perspective. Created mostly with watercolors over pencil drawings, Pinkney's dramatic illustrations are hailed for their ability to suggest movement and capture personality. Because the artist sees part of his job as creating character, he first stages his illustrations as scenes by posing models and photographing them. The resulting illustrations combine lifelike figures and realistic drawings with a strong sense of place; while his works have occasionally been faulted as overly stiff or photographic, most often they are praised for their insight and energy. As Anthony L. Manna asserts in *Children's Literature Association Quarterly,* Pinkney has "counterbalanced his technical skill with an emotional depth," using the drama of another's text to create illustrations that "spin his own compelling tale in visual terms."

Biographical Information

One of six siblings, Pinkney was born in 1939 and was raised in a supportive, all-black neighborhood in Philadelphia. He discovered a talent for drawing at a young age and was actively encouraged by his mother to develop it. Although an excellent all-around student, Pinkney chose to focus on his artistic skills by pursuing an education in commercial art. He earned a scholarship to the Philadelphia Museum College of Art and while there married his wife, Gloria, who would later join him in creating children's books. He left before graduating to join a greeting card company, but the narrow focus of the work soon spurred him to establish his own studio. Venturing into advertising and textbook illustration led the artist into the realm of children's books, and in 1964 he illustrated his first picture book, Joyce Cooper Arkhurst's retelling *The Adventures of Spider: West African Folk Tales.* Since then Pinkney has increasingly focused his energies on children's book illustration, in particular the portrayal of African American subjects in family life and folklore. He has said that his ambition is to "address the issues of being an African American and the importance of African American contributions to society" through his art, in addition to serving as a role model for aspiring artists. When not illustrating, he spends time teaching art at universities and those inspired by his example include his son Brian, himself a recipient of a Caldecott Honor citation.

Major Works

While Pinkney's early illustrations were praised for their realistic figures and composition, it was not until his work for Adjai Robinson's *Femi and Old Grandaddie* (1972) and *Kasho and the Twin Flutes* (1973) that he began to receive much notice. It was for these two original tales set in Africa that he first began using photographic models, and the resulting scenes have been cited for their fluid motion, expressive faces, and believable characters. This method similarly has proved effective for the first of the artist's Coretta Scott King Award-winners, *The Patchwork Quilt;* his illustrations for this quiet story of how a craft project draws a family together are noted for a warmth and vibrancy which adds to the drama of the tale. For Crescent Dragonwagon's *Half a Moon and One Whole Star* (1986), Pinkney uses fanciful detail, strong compositions, and expressive, deep colors to depict the nighttime visions of a little African American girl; his work for Nancy White Carlstrom's *Wild Wild Sunflower Child Anna* (1987) similarly illustrates another story of imagination with a protagonist who could be any child, but in this instance is black. The artist has not limited his subjects to African Americans, however; for Dragonwagon's *Home Place* (1990), his lush and evocative images feature both black and white families, while his cleverly designed pictures for Jean Marzollo's *Pretend You're a Cat* (1990) portray an interracial mixture of children.

Animals have also taken center stage in many of Pinkney's illustrations. For the four-volume series beginning with *The Tales of Uncle Remus,* a reworking of traditional folktales that in the past were too often filled with black stereotypes, Pinkney photographed himself as the animal characters. The ensuing paintings—which *Christian Science Monitor* critic Stephen Fraser claimed "may indeed become the definitive Uncle Remus illustrations"—have been hailed for capturing the character of the animals without making them too human. The artwork for Verna Aardema's retelling of the African folktale *Rabbit Makes a Monkey of Lion* (1989) has similarly been praised for the way Pinkney's rich watercolors create realistic animals and extend their characterizations. The artist retains a special affinity for African American stories and folktales, however, to which he brings his own memories and experiences. In *Mirandy and Brother Wind,* for instance, his warm and bright watercolors capture the spirit of the cakewalk, a traditional dance, and the warmth of a turn-of-the-century Southern black community. In *The Talking Eggs,* a dark and spooky retelling of a Creole folktale, Pinkney's paintings convey the mood of the characters and add numerous interesting details that enhance the story. Another collaboration with Julius Lester, *John Henry* (1994), takes the traditional black folk hero of the railways and reinvigorates his story by giving authenticity to the legend. In *Sam and the Tigers,* Lester and Pinkney once again reclaim a story from its previously negative connotations, taking Helen Bannerman's *The Story of Little Black Sambo* and recasting it as a fantasy set in an imaginary land reminiscent of the Old South. Pinkney's illustrations, filled with motion and interesting detail and highlighted by his extraordinarily expressive tigers, capture the mood of Lester's text. As Barbara Bader states in *Horn Book,* "the imaginary world that's home to young Sam is so instantly real, so familiar and comfortably habitable in Pinkney's opening bird's-eye view, that we don't need a word from Lester to be ready to walk along the streets of this old-time Southern town."

Awards

Pinkney received a Caldecott Honor citation in 1989 for *Mirandy and Brother Wind* and in 1990 for *The Talking Eggs.* He garnered three consecutive Coretta Scott King Awards for illustration from 1986 to 1988 for *The Patchwork Quilt, Half a Moon and One Whole Star,* and *Mirandy and Brother Wind;* earned a King Honor citation in 1980 for *Count on Your Fingers African Style* and in 1990 for *The Talking Eggs;* and then in 1997, he again received the Coretta Scott King Illustrator Award for *Minty: A Story of Young Harriet Tubman. Home Place* received the 1992 Golden Kite Award for illustration, while *John Henry* won the 1995 *Boston Globe/Horn Book* Award for picture book.

ILLUSTRATOR'S COMMENTARY

Jerry Pinkney

SOURCE: "The Artist at Work: Characters Interacting with

the Viewer," in *The Horn Book Magazine,* Vol. LXVII, No. 3, March-April, 1991, pp. 171-9.

I drew very early. I was comfortable being alone, and I spent my time drawing. I was not a great reader, but I was always looking through magazines, looking for things to draw. Early in elementary school, I became aware that by drawing my class projects, I stood out; I was noticed. I became the class artist. At home, from my mother's point of view, I was a child who was going to do something. I always had special privileges. I didn't have to be home at a certain time. My parents knew that I was off at some art or music class. When I was eleven or twelve years old, I had a newspaper stand in Philadelphia, Pennsylvania, where I grew up. I used to take drawing pads with me, and I would draw, in between selling newspapers, the mannequins in the window of Raoul's department store. I would draw anything stationary. It's amazing because I was never around anybody who drew or expressed themselves in that way.

John Liney, the cartoonist of "Little Henry," had a studio up the avenue. He took notice, befriended me, and invited me up to his studio. He even gave me drawing instruments I didn't know existed. And he gave me inklings early on that there was the potential of making a living at drawing.

For high school, I went to Dobbins Vocational School in Philadelphia, where I met my wife, Gloria. Dobbins had a commercial art program. I excelled. One of the teachers there ran a sign painting business after school; another teacher was involved with rendering. So on a high-school level I was working with an airbrush and drawing products. Then I won a scholarship to the Philadelphia Museum College of Art. I remember my drawing teacher saying he was going to have to break me in. I knew how to draw a cup of coffee and still lifes—total realism. But I was in school during the heyday of abstract expressionism. I went to art school knowing how to use an airbrush, and if you just mentioned the word, they flunked you. I was at the College of Art for two-and-a-half years. Then Gloria and I got married. The idea was for her to put me through school; it was going to be a very workable situation. But when she became pregnant with our first child, I dropped out of school, doing free-lance calligraphy for a while, and I worked in a flower store. I drove a truck for six months, and then I moved into the store and became a floral designer.

There was always a supporter or a mentor in my life. When I left school, I went to see Sam Maitin, who was a designer. I guess I went because all the students talked about him. I showed him my portfolio, and a year later he called me and said he had a friend who had just been hired by Rustcraft Greeting Card Company in Dedham, Massachusetts, outside of Boston. They wanted to get a whole new look, and they were looking for designer-illustrators. I went up to Dedham with a portfolio I'd put together quite quickly, and they hired me. So we moved to Boston—for a ten-dollar-a-week raise in salary.

At Rustcraft, I was in the studio card department, and my interest was in the use of typography with illustration. The printing component in the building was off-limits because of union rules. But I would go down there on my lunch break and find out how the presses worked. Rustcraft had an art director who was doing free-lance work in book cover design, and I was asked to do some illustrations. My vacations were spent in New York City going around to see people with my portfolio. I was starting to get work—not a lot of work, but I illustrated a piece for *Seventeen* magazine in the early sixties and soon found an agent to represent me in New York.

The Adventures of Spider [by Joyce Cooper Arkhurst] was the first manuscript I was given to illustrate. I'm fairly sure that I worked out the formatting of the book myself. Even when I look at it today, it looks like what I do now, as opposed to some of my books where I was not involved with the design. I've always thought of myself as a problem solver, and although designing a book was something I had never done before, I didn't find it to be that difficult. I began to see the marriage, or the possibility of a marriage, between drawing and design. I liked dealing with the problem of how to position the art and text on a page. Even though text and art work together, the idea is not to make one look better than the other. For me the book represents the ultimate in graphics. I tend to like working with drawing and typography first as an artist and second as a designer. Drawing gives me the opportunity to deal with the aesthetics of line, color, and expression; typography with putting parts together with respect for elements that are not as flexible as line and color. As for my drawing, it has always been important to develop a way of seeing that was my own.

At first I couldn't afford to live on what I earned creating books. For a long time, I structured my day in such a way so that from nine to five I was earning a living. By the time I was twenty-three years old I had a wife and four children and a house in Sharon, Massachusetts. And it was important to me not only that I provided, but that I provided in a certain style, one I didn't grow up with: a house and a yard—we had the whole business. And then, at night and on weekends, I would work on a book. It had nothing to do with money. It just had to do with the love of doing a book. I would do one book a year that way.

In the beginning, I was doing many folk tales from foreign lands. In 1972 my approach to illustrating books changed when I did two African tales, from Sierra Leone. There was a sharp difference in approach from *Femi and Old Grandaddie* to *Kasho and the Twin Flutes* (both [by Adjai Robinson]). *Femi* was done the way I had approached all my books, using the scrap file and almost designing the figure on the page. But with *Kasho* I started to deal with getting some kind of emotion and more action in my figures instead of the people just being part of the composition. Interaction between the characters became more and more important in my work. All of a sudden, that interaction added another dimension to my work. Now my characters became people relating to each other. When I did African folk tales, or African-American stories, I would use family.

For Mildred Taylor's *Song of the Trees*, I shot a lot of photographs in Philadelphia of my uncle and my nieces and nephews. I began to use photography more and more, getting live models to relate to one another. Trying to find the right models, and getting them to act out the text, gave my books a different look. I also began to try to make the viewer and the characters become one. Often you'll see the characters in a book looking out at you. I wanted the viewer to move around the space where the story takes place and explore. There are always things in my pictures I think readers may find interesting that support and enhance the main subject and action. In *Count on Your Fingers African Style* [by Claudia Zaslavsky], each of the participants talks directly to the reader, speaks to the reader. In *Turtle in July* [by Marilyn Singer], the reader is in contact with the creatures, and the creatures are in contact with the reader.

The production of my books has always been important to me. In the seventies, art directors and designers tried to keep me in check. I would do a book dummy, and it would come back changed. There were some battles then. But when I started working for Atha Tehon of Dial, we worked together. Atha had an attitude or philosophy about the way books were to be designed, and I think it worked well with me. She was always asking how I felt about the typography, and she made sure that I saw everything even though she was doing the design work. She was also aware that I knew how to pace a book. I was always very good at knowing just when to use an illustration in the text. And so Atha, and Cecilia Yung at Macmillan, began to give me tremendous freedom in terms of design. In the beginning, I was working only with art directors; working with editors came later—Phyllis Fogelman at Dial, Judith Whipple at Macmillan, and Bonnie Ingber at Harcourt. Now I'm even okaying color proofs; I'm involved in almost all stages of the book.

Just how detailed my dummies are now depends on the book. If you look at the initial drawings for *Mirandy and Brother Wind* [by Patricia McKissack], they're really quite sketchy, because there's a whole cast of characters. I remember working with Denise Cronin and Anne Schwartz. In our first meeting, they were so excited because of the pacing of the book. One thing I try to do while putting the dummy together is to get the feel of the story without the text. Then I cut up xeroxes of the text and place them into the dummy, laying out where I want the type to be placed. The rhythm, the initial look of the book is close to being exact. Some dummies are more finished than others, of course.

In books like [Robert D. San Souci's] *The Talking Eggs* or *Mirandy,* after the dummy is approved I search for models. For this, my wife, Gloria, is a big help. She often finds the models; they're shot with a Polaroid camera, mainly. We use family, people around us, friends and their children. There's usually a suggestion of who the characters might be through my sketches. For *Talking Eggs,* Dial needed the cover to be designed first. Sometimes, in order for them to get the flavor of the book in order to choose a typeface, they'll ask you to do a cover or a piece with color to give them a feeling for the book as a whole. For this cover character, Gloria posed, which she often does, and I created the character of the old woman. When I compared the sketch of the first drawing I did with the model we found later, it was as if I'd created the character and then found the actual character.

We bring the models into the studio. Sometimes they come together; sometimes separately. I get people to respond to me and to each other. But I don't just take a photograph and then draw from it. Sometimes I fill in a lot; certainly when there's a male figure, I'm very often that male figure, and that way I can exaggerate the action.

The next thing is getting the reference for the setting, the environment. Sometimes I find an interior through research that I think might play a role in the book. I may find the reference on an interior or landscape and then create my scene—my people responding, reacting to each other—within that particular staging. For instance, for *The Talking Eggs* I did extensive research in the library system in Louisiana. I discovered they had a whole section on fences that were unique to that part of the country. So then I had to figure out how to make use of that fence. I usually look at tons of books, and I use markers. I have codes: a star means that the object may not be in the text, but I want to use it, make it work.

When I put all these things together, I work on tracing paper. The drawings are fairly rough. I create the design background, the silhouette values, and composition. The movement, which I work very hard for, comes in the actual drawing. Those are done on a lightbox; I transfer my designs to Arches watercolor paper. The artwork develops with me working with a lightbox—turning it on and off. I have to make sure the composition is working or I'm not getting in the way of type, and then I'll continue off the lightbox. Sometimes I will find that the drawing I'm working on isn't quite working, or sometimes I find something else I want to use, maybe a table or chair. But I rarely start over; I just work with an eraser and scrub out and go back in. So if you look at some of my drawings, you'll even see the old drawings underneath. I want that to happen. I'm not creating museum paintings; I'm creating something that's going to be photographed by a camera. My intent is always to do a piece that will work well in a book. It is important that the drawing work on that level. I'm interacting with the material and the people. When I give lectures at art schools, what they like about my work is that you can almost see the process as you look at the work. So it's great for students to see what's going on. The process also gives a sense of movement to the figures. The pictures actually grow.

At one point, I mount and stretch the paper. Then I go back and forth, floating the color. Something then happens with the line. Once I put the color on, the line almost disappears; it's not defined. I go back in, and I begin to start pulling out certain things so that there's a back and forth between the color and the line. I've just started using pastels and Prismacolor pencils, and if I find I can't achieve something with watercolor, then I just move to another medium. In my drawings, there might be pastels or there might be cray-pas. I often can't say which medium I will mix for a particular drawing; I have no idea. There's a whole palette of new materials that I'm thinking about using in order to keep my work growing and changing.

Usually I'm working on at least half the book in stages. I don't finish one piece and move to another; they're all at different stages. Certainly when you're matching color, that makes sense. But it also makes sense that you don't overdevelop the first piece, because then you have to live up to that piece. I always do one piece that I feel very comfortable with; usually it is in the middle of the book. I move from the middle to the back and jump around. Then I start developing the look. With [Valerie Flournoy's] *The Patchwork Quilt,* I wanted to give the feeling that the final drawings were sketches as opposed to more finished drawings. I wanted to draw the reader into the family as if the reader was there.

I think of all the drawings for a book as one piece of art. That's a conflict, because I'm trying to get the reader to turn the page. I'm trying to get him or her to look at the page and then be curious about turning it. So I'm trying to hold you and make you move at the same time. Aesthetically, I think I have to give up something. I have to give up spelling it all out on a particular page. I have to give up having a piece stand on its own, because I need my work to be a narrative. It's a different process for a person who's done editorial art or book jackets, which stand on their own, completely say something. I often battle with myself over this process.

My animal books happen quite differently. Even the dummy itself tends to be kind of a sketchbook. I actually staple or tape the dummy together as if it were a thirty-two-page sketchbook. I always do thumbnails first. I do these on yellow legal pads. I don't know why this feels comfortable; I just feel free enough to move and make notes and things like that. In other words, the book is broken down in terms of a thumbnail, and then I move toward developing the dummy. I decide how the text is going to fall with the pages. And I draw into the dummy as one would a sketchbook. I find the reference that I need, and then I draw directly onto the dummy, as if these were finished drawings. I move the drawings around; I scrub out; and I play with them and develop them at that point. I submit the dummy to the publisher and get it approved, and then I go directly into the finishes. The animals happen not easily but generally very fast. With *Turtle in July,* it took forever to get the deer's anatomy. What I was trying to do was difficult, and I wanted it to come off as naturally as possible. But at the same time, I try to articulate the animals so one could almost feel the creatures reciting the poems. The finishes, for the most part, did not take me long to complete.

As influences, there are certain figurative artists that I tend to look at. One would be Thomas Eakins. You see his work and even his composition in my art. And Charles White is a great influence, the way he uses the African American in terms of power and dignity. I try to speak to that in the part of my work that deals with African-American life and culture; the people in my work tend to be proud and upright. Two more influences are Arthur Rackham, the way his animals work together with his people, and Alan E. Cober, because of the drawing and integrity in his figures. I am currently a professor of art at several universities, and, as a teacher, it is my hope to influence others as I have been. I spend a great deal of time on- and off-campus helping young and inspiring talent.

GENERAL COMMENTARY

Nick Meglin

SOURCE: "The Strength of Weakness: Illustrator Jerry Pinkney," in *American Artist,* Vol. 46, No. 474, January, 1982, pp. 54-9, 95-6.

It is a common educational procedure to "correct weaknesses"; if, for example, drawing or painting a figure's anatomical proportions is an artist's weak point, it is often said that one should study that discipline until one "works out the problem." While few can fault this approach, especially in the case of students who seek to improve and expand their artistic horizons, too often it is accepted as the *only* approach. At times, artists with particular "shortcomings" lose a spark of individuality as a result. Imagine an instructor directing El Greco to "work on your anatomical proportions until you get it right!" or telling Rubens to "slim down those chubby women!"

Whether resulting from a variance in visual perception or an individual way of "seeing," a "weakness" may serve as a basis for a personal approach that might just elevate an artist's work from the commonplace to the unique.

It may have been Jerry Pinkney's very lack of formal drawing and illustration training that enabled him to avoid joining the ranks of many of his contemporaries who were busy imitating the style so prevalent at the time. Having studied only two-dimensional design at the Philadelphia College of Art, Pinkney had no idea how an illustration was designed, executed, or reproduced in print. His few attempts to "put together something in the order of what I think I was looking at in a magazine" were aborted when he tried to place his figures in any reasonably convincing perspective, and so he sought refuge once again in the flat, two-dimensional design world where "shapes and forms floated in space abstractedly."

Then a college assignment that was given by both the illustration and the design departments required that the students execute an illustration. The assignment forced

Pinkney to complete a work that made him realize that his "weakness"—a flat response to perspective—might very well be his strength. His work drew attention for its strong design elements and his two-dimensional treatment of space and distance. Moreover, Pinkney approached typography as a part of the whole, not an inconvenient, albeit necessary, addition to the total graphic image.

Upon completion of two and one-half years of formal education at the Philadelphia College of Art, Pinkney married and, among other odd jobs he took to support his family, drove a truck. He finally landed a studio job in the art department of Rustcraft Greeting Cards, mostly on the strength of his design portfolio. He eventually started his own art studio with two other artist friends and, through the different requirements of particular accounts the studio serviced, found more and more opportunities to do actual illustration work. His portfolio gradually evolved to that of an illustrator rather than that of a designer, and Pinkney was able to begin free-lancing in the Boston area when the financial status of the studio made it necessary for the partners to disband.

As Pinkney's reputation as an illustrator grew, so did the scope of his assignments. He was able to earn a living for his growing family while experimenting with his craft and learning how best to use his unique approach for storytelling, using line and flat color in patterns and abstract form while maintaining representational concepts. Although this personal statement was often encouraged in certain areas of the illustration field, such as books and magazines, he was also asked to lend his "look" to certain advertising campaigns. It wasn't long before Pinkney, like many aspiring illustrators from all over the country, began dreaming of making the "big move" to the heart of the publishing world—New York City.

Regarding his move from Boston, Pinkney relates: "Boston is a big city, but like so many other big cities, it imitates New York styles and trends; in short, such big cities choose to duplicate New York instead of being an original 'somewhere else.' I found it too confining as an illustrator. I wanted to do something different and I felt the place to be was where 'something different' was what they were looking for more than 'what's *in* now.'"

Pinkney's education in new media and techniques followed the same procedure as his earlier schooling in that he learned by doing. "I did a lot of mixed media just for the experience of discovering their potential. I find that system always works best for me—do it, sweat it out, be prepared for a lot of frustration and a lot of work you don't like very much at all—and somehow, it all comes together and you stop fighting it and start using it as your own."

As acceptance of his "see flat, draw flat" style grew, Pinkney took on more assignments and received higher rates. Pinkney realized he was fortunate to have discovered an individual approach from within. He didn't rely on imitation, contrivance, or gimmicks to achieve a personal statement; instead he had only to look into his own

complex network of feelings and experiences to come up with graphic solutions. So intent was he on focusing his energies into this introspective procedure that he purposely chose watercolor as his prime color medium because he found it difficult to control. "Its difficulty let me focus on the more expressive aspects of the medium," explains Pinkney. "I was able to get a kind of looseness."

With many major fiction magazines on the decline and others limited in their budgets for quality illustration and the subsequent color plates and printing involved, the editorial illustrator's work is, for the most part, unseen by the conventional audience. The "showcase" days of *The Saturday Evening Post, Colliers, Look,* and other top-level publications that brought illustrators and their work to an appreciative public are long gone. The "institutional" publications, however, offer something different for today's illustrator. As Pinkney observes, "I don't get much editorial work to do, with the exception of book illustration. Books offer me the opportunity to work with typography as part of the total design, which, of course, is well-suited to my approach. While book illustration encourages originality, I find institutional work even gutsier and closer to what I enjoy doing. Because such publications have a limited readership—and they know that readership well—they allow the artist to experiment, to explore—in short, to *have fun* with design, media, and techniques that more conventional markets wouldn't allow. It's assignments like these that give illustrators a freedom of expression and an opportunity to grow that I don't think would have been possible in the old, traditional markets."

There are many stages an illustration goes through before it reaches completion, claims Pinkney, "and while all these stages are important—whether to progress the idea, to define the subject, or simply to improve the drawing itself in particular areas—the magical moment for me is when I lose control of it and let it go its own way." The "magical moment" for Pinkney is not unlike the experience felt by many participants in one art form or another. This ability to surrender to the impulse or feeling of a moment has often served as the turning point in a work, a response that elevates it from the mundane to the inspired. Spontaneity doesn't come easily, and it cannot be contrived. It must evolve from the work itself—from the contradictory approach of the artist who must both control and be controlled by his or her response.

While Pinkney's work was, like that of most young artists, undergoing change as experiences and influences created new awarenesses, his basic approach, concentrating on strong, two-dimensional design, remained constant. This proved advantageous to the artist, for although he, like most design and illustration students of that period, had been influenced by the style of the time, the response to his work was more favorable because of his individual emphasis. Pinkney recalls one artist friend in particular who said, "Your work looks *handmade*. A lot of the work I see today looks like it came off a conveyor belt." Pinkney was wise in taking these comments and observations seriously and fortifying his individuality, rather than bending to trends and fashions, a short-lived approach for anyone in a creative field. This very commitment to one's own responsibility for self-expression can mark the difference between success, failure, and the various stages in between. In the case of Jerry Pinkney, his success can also be measured in the strength of a weakness.

Anthony L. Manna

SOURCE: "Reading Jerry Pinkney Reading," in *Children's Literature Association Quarterly,* Vol. 16, No. 4, Winter, 1991-92, pp. 269-75.

What music is to Maurice Sendak, drama is to Jerry Pinkney. For Sendak, music is a faithful muse that rouses his imagination and steers him to "the spirit of animation, the breathing of life, the swing into action" which, as he observes in "The Shape of Music," best sustains the vigorous interplay of words and pictures in an illustrated book. Abandoning himself to the configurations of a musical score, particularly the steady course of its theme and variations, Sendak will mine a text in his restless, reflective search for visual images that will *"vivify, quicken,* and *vitalize"* the text.

For Jerry Pinkney, the muse is drama and the manner dramatic. For Pinkney, whose credits include two Caldecott honors, several Coretta Scott King awards, and a host of prizes from the graphic design establishment, the process of illustrating a text is akin to building a small-scale theater production. When Pinkney talks about working with a text en route to investing it with the lively balance of motion and stillness which, in a successful picture book, illuminates thought, feeling, and action, he is prone to think in terms of dramatic arrangement and composition and his vocabulary is apt to resemble that of actor, director, costumer, set designer, and lighting technician. He talks, for example, about staging a scene to emphasize motive and character relationships; about punctuating an incident with effective lighting to demonstrate mood, atmosphere, and emotional content; and about alternating still-life tableaux with visual impressions that shift and change to lay out a transformation in awareness and insight. "The page," Pinkney pointed out in a recent interview, "is my stage."

Envisioning the picture book page as a plane for dramatic action is, of course, a common notion among critics and artists. Barbara Bader, for one, considers the progressive movement of effective picture book art a dramatic conceptualization of what the writer offers in the way of structure and verbal patterning. In a picture book, she says [in *American Picturebooks from Noah's Ark to the Beast Within*], activity or stillness, by virtue of being "pictured and spaced out, marks time dramatically . . . or, to dramatic purpose too, [displays] gradual gathering action. . . ." Uri Shulevitz, for another, aligns the illustrator's function with the dramatist's need to show, rather than describe, character and incident. "By telling a story visually, instead, of through verbal description," Shulevitz suggests [in *Writing with Pictures*], "a picture book

becomes a dramatic experience: immediate, vivid, moving."

In Pinkney's scheme of things the dramatic principle is less a conceit that governs his aesthetic than a functional, formative strategy, first deployed in the initial stages of interpreting a text and later used when reconstructing the text in pictorial terms. By literally improvising an incident in role, for example, or enlisting live models to do the same Pinkney is able to experiment with a text's shape, texture, and movement in his effort to uncover a subtext and the visual impressions that will bring this subtext to light. What particularly jibes with his conception of how a picture book is meant to reveal character in action is the dramatist's means of manipulating time, space, and incident in order to create an illusion of immediacy. This aura of immediacy, as well as the spirit of spontaneity derived from it, is the hallmark of Pinkney's signature and the quality that, in effect, allows him to transform a two-dimensional page into a three-dimensional space in which figures seem to move about as though totally caught up in the demands of the moment.

Pinkney's Early Works

Pinkney's black-and-white pencil drawings for *Femi and Old Grandaddie,* a folktale from Sierra Leone retold by Adjai Robinson, stand out as an early affirmation of his distinctive approach to the picture book aesthetic. Sustained by the richly textured cadences of an oral telling, *Femi* tells a tender tale of the rewards a young orphan boy gains when, albeit reluctantly, he shares his treasured cassava root with Grandaddie, a weathered village elder. When Old Grandaddie uses the privilege of age to wrest the hard-earned cassava root from Olu-fe-mi ("God wants me"), he reciprocates the favor by telling the youth a riddle which, as it turns out in the deftly paced contest that constitutes the tale's emotionally charged climax, secures for Femi, the least likely suitor, a marriage to the king's beautiful daughter.

The pictures for *Femi* set Pinkney on a new course as a stylist. Compared with the generalized setting he devised for [Joyce Cooper] Arkhurst's *The Adventures of Spider,* his first book, and [John W.] Spellman's *The Beautiful Blue-Jay and Other Tales of India,* both slight volumes given to predictable story lines, primer-like language, and condescending lessons, the village in which he set Femi contains the type of unobtrusive detail that makes a setting distinct, specific, and visually interesting.

The same can be said of Pinkney's awareness of character in *Femi.* As Pinkney explains it, *"Femi and Old Grandaddie* marked the first time I dealt so consciously with the human figure in a picture book." And it shows. In *Femi,* in contrast, say, to the largely indistinguishable characters he conceived for [Lila] Green's *Folktales and Fairy Tales of Africa,* he enlarges the folktale's abbreviated suggestion of character by using simple strokes to attend to mannerisms, postures, expressions, and the like, which in turn signal attitudes, motives, and the temper of relationships. In short, the characters in *Femi* are flesh-and-blood individuals whom we care about and whose predicaments concern us. The king's jester, for example, is rendered as a delightful composite of dishevelled trickster, cunning seer, and master of meaningful disorder. He is at once an arrogant wit and a charming impresario, forged, through the illustrator's adeptness with simple, evocative line and his control of stylized movement, into an altogether compelling character.

These changes in Pinkney's technique and manner were rooted in a new-found freedom with his pencil medium and a bolder, riskier conception of page design than he had used previously. In earlier books—his black-and-white pencil drawings for [Francine] Jacob's *The King's Ditch: A Hawaiian Tale* come to mind—his illustrations are descriptive or decorative at best; they more or less serve as self-contained, text-bound visual captions that largely underscore textual details about character and action without deepening these details with the dynamic rhythm between word and picture, the pin-point visual phrasing, and the sympathetic regard for character that distinguish his later work. In *Femi* the whole page becomes Pinkney's field of action and the illusion of movement is often parlayed through an unfinished liner that extends across a double spread to thrust the story forward in a clear linear development and to capture the tensions and rhythms of an incident.

Pinkney's use of live models heralded yet another turning point in his effort to invest his art with the energy of genuinely felt experience and the immediacy of life lived in the moment. Although he first turned to models to better delineate the human figures in Adjai Robinson's *Kasho and the Twin Flutes,* Pinkney soon discovered that the process of having the models actually role play the story characters involved the kind of attention to composition and lay out which, in his words, spurred him "to think more consciously of the art of staging an incident and the way characters act, react, and interact with one another." In all but a few of his book projects since *Kasho* Pinkney has relied on the process of taking photographs of models, himself included, to help him interpret a text.

Pinkney's models served him well in *Kasho and the Twin Flutes,* which in essence is a character study that explores the conflict between self-concern and one's responsibility to others. Kasho is a likable boy in a fix. His sole purpose is to prove himself talented and loyal by learning to play the flute as competently as his father, the most celebrated flutist in the village, before his father returns from the mountain retreat where he has been recuperating from an illness. He thus has little time or concern for the chores his mother sets before him in preparation for the celebration that will welcome his father home. When he puts his mother in grave danger by using his burgeoning skill as a flutist to lure a snake into the family hut before he has learned how to control the creature, Kasho learns an important lesson in pride and patience.

Pinkney structures the tale as a compelling drama. He uses full-page and three-quarter page spreads and a continuous single line to create the nimble visual phrasing that not only propels the action forward, but also highlights the juxtaposition of tension and release that defines the movements of Kasho's escapes into music and the gentle confrontations that these escapes precipitate between the mother as pursuer and her son as the pursued. This steady, fluid visual development crests at the suspenseful, climactic skirmish with the snake and then relaxes with Kasho's new insight into the value of compromise.

Pinkney's method and manner in *Kasho* pointed the way to the gradual refinement of his black-and-white pencil medium and the increasing confidence with which he settles into a text and expresses his personal vision of the images the text calls forth. His taut, contemplative drawings for Mildred D. Taylor's *Song of the Trees* are a case in point. For this novella, Pinkney created twelve aphoristic drawings that pinpoint the spiritual significance of Taylor's bittersweet tale of a close-knit black family's encounter with the pressures of bigotry. To capture the dichotomies of dignity and pain, survival and oppression, and hope and fear which Taylor poses, Pinkney strikes a balance between the sanctity of the Logans's cherished woods and the destruction of the trees at the hands of the impudent lumbermen, between the healing power of strong family ties and the starkness of the lumbermen's cruel intrusion into the family's affairs. In this way, he implies that much more is at stake than the woods which provide the Logans with a semblance of independence as well as a safe harbor from the prejudice that rages around them. In the moral sense of things, the desecration of their land portends the demise of their spirit. The large tree that fills most of the page in the initial drawing, for example, is an emblem of the entire tale in that it signals the human dignity and courage the story celebrates and, at the same time, foreshadows the gravity of the impending conflict through moody shading and a quiet, uneasy starkness. The deeply sullen mood is emphatically struck through the artist's sympathetic understanding of a painful situation.

Song of the Trees afforded Pinkney a rare opportunity to delve into a text which, to Rudine Sims's way of thinking, represents [what she calls in *Shadow and Substance: Afro-American Experience in Children's Fiction*] "culturally conscious" fiction. Such fiction, says Sims referring solely to examples of the African-American experience in contemporary realistic fiction,

> . . . reflects[s] . . . the social and cultural traditions associated with growing up Black . . . [and] illuminate[s] both the unique and the universal humanness of the Afro-American experience from the perspective of an Afro-American child or family.

Among other things, Sims maintains, writers of culturally conscious stories " . . . recognize, sometimes even celebrate, the distinctiveness of the experience of growing up simultaneously Black and American."

While most of the books in Pinkney's repertoire address the character and temperament of various racial and ethnic groups, only *JD* (1973), Mari Evans's quarter of stories about the viscissitudes of life in an urban ghetto, broaches the issues and problems of the politics of race as directly as *Song of the Trees* does. The cultural currency in which Pinkney more characteristically deals is that of universals which signify commonalities among people. His route to expressly cultural topics and themes has, for example, coursed its way through more than a dozen books of various types of folklore such as [Barbara] Michels and [Bettye] White's *Apples on a Stick,* a collection of traditional playground verses, [Verna] Aardema's *Ji-Nongo-Nongo Means Riddles,* a gathering of riddles from various regions of Africa, and a host of folktales including Rosebud Yellow Robe's *Toneweya and the Eagles and Other Lakota Tales,* Robert San Souci's *The Talking Eggs,* a Caldecott honor book, and Julius Lester's controversial retellings of selected Uncle Remus stories. In several other books which portray children involved in experiences of everyday living, Pinkney creates a specific cultural context for texts which do not specify the racial or ethnic affiliation of the characters. In two of these "culturally neutral" books, [Crescent] Dragonwagon's *Half a Moon and One Whole Star* and [Nancy White] Carlstrom's *Wild Wild Sunflower Child Anna,* Pinkney pictures the principal character as a black child, while in *Pretend You're a Cat,* by Jean Marzollo, and Dragonwagon's *Home Place,* he presents a racial mix of characters.

Pinkney, the Colorist

Not surprisingly, Pinkney's manner of working with live models is a sturdy link in the chain that connects drama and color. As Pinkney sees it, in each of the books he has done in color, the shape of the drama his models have helped him to uncover has heightened his awareness of structure, pace, texture, and mood. Gradually, color becomes its own dramatic statement as do scale and perspective in his black-and-white illustrations.

Pinkney's illustrations for Valerie Flournoy's *The Patchwork Quilt* marked his debut into full-color. By having the models study the text for *Patchwork* and improvisationally act out key scenes from it, Pinkney happened upon a method of working with models which has become a standard procedure for finding his way into a text. According to Pinkney, the process allows him some initial distance from the material so he can gain a new or different perspective on it. What also has become essential to the method is his use of a Polaroid camera. "In front of the camera I am a model for the models," Pinkney has said, "and behind it I am their director." The copious photographs he takes of his models as they pose, gesture, and interact in a given episode often provide a stimulus for his initial sketches of character and incident. But, as Pinkney points out, the most important thing about these sessions is the collaborative enterprise they make of the challenge of bringing a text to life.

In *Patchwork* the collaboration proved its worth by opening the way to homey, unpretentious illustrations that parallel and extend the story's touching theme. The story tells of the concern that compels the members of a caring black family to rally around their ailing grandmother as she makes a quilt out of scraps from the family's old clothing. The project not only unites the family throughout a difficult year, affirming, in particular, young Tanya's love for her grandmother, but, as a result of the woman's subtle and patient prompting, also serves as a reminder of the inestimable value of memory and heritage as well as the dignity that can derive from a respect for ties that bind.

Color keeps harmonious time with the different stages of the story's unfolding, and Pinkney maintains a composed kinetic balance between color and the book's overall composition to reinforce the good feelings the story evokes. He uses varying shades of blue, yellow, red, and brown to telescope thought and feeling, and, along with changes in perspective and layout, to bring to the surface shifting moods.

The improvisational approach which Pinkney used to work his way into the heart of *Patchwork* would prove itself just as reliable when it came to solving interpretive problems in subsequent projects. With *The Tales of Uncle Remus,* the first volume in Julius Lester's three-volume set of updated—and consequently controversial retellings of Joel Chandler Harris's politically and culturally skewed versions of the tales, the problem Pinkney faced had to do with characterization. After Pinkney's editor rejected his initial sketches for the volume on the grounds that the animals were not as anthropomorphic as the tales seemed to warrant, he hit upon a satisfying solution by having photographs taken of himself as he experimented with the mannerisms and attitudes of the principal animal characters while he also attempted to retain a semblance of their basic animal features and characteristics. In this way he was led to the delicate balance he was seeking, one that has remained a distinctive feature of his animal characters ever since the Remus project: species-perfect creatures anthropomorphized just enough to give them a little personality, but not enough to turn them into cloying pseudohumans.

All three volumes of the Remus tales boast Pinkney's gallery of remarkably convincing and interesting creatures, each of them branded, as Lester's retellings would have it, with idiosyncratic qualities, quirks, or vices. Given their homespun, yet dapper clothing (" . . . what slaves wore at the time," Pinkney told Helga Tilton), their large-scale emotions, and the range of their involvement in the situations that unfold around them, particularly their involvement in the predicaments and misfortunes they either instigate, dodge, or succumb to, there is nothing precious about these creatures. As illustrated by Pinkney, the tales invite us to be privy to the machinations of a complex, amazingly diverse community that covers a full gamut of personalities and temperaments, trials and tensions, and motives and moods. Pinkney construes the animals as downhome folks who live out their days coping with the large and small challenges that come with trying to get on with one another.

In all three volumes, Pinkney's dramatic instinct is at

work from the outset. The first hint of the diversity to come is in the "stagey," brilliantly lit wraparound jacket that reveals a curious assembly of the major animal characters. Rendered in deeply layered red, grey, and violet as well as earthy green and weathered, luminous shades of tans, each jacket is a composite of stirring incongruities in appearance, posture, and relationship. There is, for example, something peculiarly ordered and peaceful about these gatherings, for creatures of this sort are hardly as staid and compatible as they appear here. These inconsistencies give the jackets the look and feel of an impromptu, slap-dash assembly; it's as though the group has been called together hastily to pose for the artist in a brief, uncertain respite from the risky business that ordinarily constitutes their affairs with each other, a fact which the tales, illuminated by several tightly executed and framed color spreads and a bevy of softly textured pencil and graphite drawings, confirm with such ample detail.

Capturing the Child's World

Of late, Pinkney the colorist has been at work on a cycle of books that takes an intimate look at children's involvement in the experience of reaching beyond their boundaries and making sense of things through dramatic play and the dictates of their imaginations. Whereas in previous books Pinkney grew to rely on dramatizations of the text and his dramatic manner of construing the picture book page to help him realize his interpretation, in several books in this cycle spontaneous dramatic play constitutes the very essence of the narrative—as it does in Carlstrom's *Wild Wild Sunflower Child Anna,* [Julia] Fields's *The Green Lion of Zion Street,* and Marzollo's *Pretend You're a Cat,* all of which show children acting out a situation without adult intervention. In the books that celebrate the child's imagination, namely, Dragonwagon's *Half a Moon and One Whole Star* and *Home Place* and [Patricia C.] McKissack's *Mirandy and Brother Wind,* Pinkney's other Caldecott honor book, the engine that drives the narrative is the drama inherent in human experience.

The texts that depict children constructing or acting out situations of their own making placed Pinkney on familiar and fertile ground. Not surprisingly, the spontaneity and immediacy which the illustrations in these books capture and the authenticity of the young characters' involvement derive largely from Pinkney's method of tracking the elements of a narrative by working with live models who play out an episode and press him toward the visuals with which he interprets it.

With *The Green Lion of Zion Street,* Pinkney experimented with a new interpretive strategy. In the manner of a playwright who refines his or her script after seeing or hearing a dramatization of it, Pinkney left the manuscript with a group of children (the book is dedicated to "the Star of Bethlehem Baptist Church Drama Committee") who, in his absence, dramatized the story line in preparation for the photography sessions which he would later direct. From these photographs Pinkney developed his initial drawings for the text.

The Green Lion of Zion Street is rooted in the type of speculation which consumes children in their dramatic play. Here, it provides a group of black city children with a conduit for playing out and confronting the fear that both entices and repels them. As they wait for their school bus on a foggy, frigid winter morning (" . . . in weather ten times colder/than a roller skate"), the children, capitalizing on the delicious eeriness of the moment, put their collaborative imagination to work to bring to life a menacing stone lion that looms large in a nearby park. The capriciousness of the incident is shaped by the carefully patterned cadences of Fields's meandering, resonating verse which resembles the movement of a jazzlike improvisation crackling with odd configurations of shape, rhyme, and rhythm.

In Pinkney's visual telling of *Zion Street* the story is less a linear narrative than a cumulative series of impressionistic beats that deconstruct the textual images so as to heighten the emotional pitch and sensory appeal of the incident. Owing to the restless energy of Fields's characters and the exuberant narrative thrust of Pinkney's pictures, *Zion Street* seems a much larger book than its relatively small size (9.5 by 8 inches) first suggests. The deep, robust watercolors, set against muted multicolored washes, contribute to the book's large-scale appearance by infusing the children's joyful apprehension of their drama with an upbeat, large-spirited urgency that, similar to Pinkney's use of perspective in *Mirandy and Brother Wind,* extends the experience well beyond the boundaries imposed by his limited page space. Coupled with Pinkney's now characteristic method of having his characters draw us into the story by occasionally focusing their attention on us through direct visual address, the technique of exaggerating action through scale and perspective makes *Zion Street* an intimate experience. As they create their fantasy out of a shared notion of the lion's electrifying power, the characters afford us the privilege of an insider's view of the special gift children have of turning an ordinary situation—a jaunt to school—into an absorbing adventure.

An insider's perspective is even better suited to the metaphorical possibilities and implications that underpin the deceptively simple situation Dragonwagon explores in *Home Place.* Reminiscent of Robert Frost's "The Pasture," *Home Place* combines a breezy colloquial formalism with spare poetic description to fix our attention on the wonder and pleasure of the imagination. On its most concrete, accessible level *Home Place* reveals the thoughts and perceptions of a group of hikers, envisioned by Pinkney as a father, mother, and daughter, when the group pauses to reflect on the discoveries it makes while trekking through the woods on a brilliant spring day. On a more subtle level the family's musings become a stately associative meditation that plumbs a number of large, ramifying truths. As the members of the family puzzle over the implications that inhere in the vestiges of an abandoned house, an ordered cluster of daffodils, and other signs of the people who once inhabited the place, they invite us to join them in forming a portrait of the people who may have once called this place a home. Embedded in the story the family builds about the everyday circumstances of an imaginary extended family (a turn-of-the-century black family, as Pinkney sees it) are provocative insights into, among other things, the relativity of time, the evocative power and permanence of simple family love, the mark every individual leaves on the course of history and the cycle of life, and the inevitable changes life promises.

Pinkney's pictures for **Home Place** are the means of transport from an outer to an inner realm, from the intimate details the family observes in nature to the optimistic affirmations about life these details signal in the mind's eye. As always, Pinkney uses his initial visual beats to forecast mood, tone, and theme. As it should be in a picture book that both extols and gives credence to the virtues of looking beneath the surface of things, every aspect of the opening matter—from the jacket and endpapers to the title, copyright, and dedication page—is designed to entice us slowly and thoughtfully into the experience, to alert us, that is, to the commitment of time and thought the experience will require. For example, the full-spread jacket illustration of the imagined family, posed portrait-like, expectant, and welcoming on the front porch of its pleasant home, presages the pensive, mystical aura and lurking philosophical themes that permeate each scene in **Home Place**. The jacket's faded, Monet-style patches of watercolor make object, flora, and human figure barely distinguishable and thus give this significant opening picture a scintillating illusory quality, while the juxtaposition of towering trees and delicate, brightly colored flowers hints at the contrast between permanence and change that reverberates throughout the narrative.

The curious images in the endpapers and title page are equally provocative in the way that they hint of things to come and rouse our attention. Only in retrospect, after having been led through the interior of the home, do we realize that the floral pattern and acorn-laden branches that fill this overture are designs from the wallpaper in the imagined family's home. With these details Pinkney plants subtle clues about the notions of time and space and transience and evanescence that the family members' revival of the past summons up. In fact, a sprouting acorn graces the dedication page and, later, a stylized acorn is used as a decorative motif (endurance? renascence?) on each of the framed pages reserved solely for the narrative.

The entire layout of **Home Place** is synchronized to support the narrative's graceful alternating movement between the present and past and to sustain the leisurely pace of the revelations kindled by the family's reverent attention to what is seen and heard and imagined. Throughout, Pinkney both distinguishes and blends reality and invention. To help the viewer differentiate past from present action the episodes which show present time appear on the right-hand pages while the imagined events appear on the left. Whereas Pinkney extends the present-time episodes to the extreme borders of the page, whenever the narrative slips into the past to tell of the daily life of the other family, the accompanying pictures are framed, giv-

ing these more formal and posed incidents the appearance of old photographs in a treasured family album. At the same time, however, present and past are linked through recurring colors, objects, and sentiments; the perceptions which emerge in the present spill into the family's musings about the past.

Pinkney's color scheme for **Home Place** also signals subtextual ideas. Through his use of shimmery watercolors and dramatic lighting he glosses the text with a daring ethereal atmosphere in sync with the reflective tone of Dragonwagon's poised poetic narrative. Whether he is immersed in the world of nature or the elusive province of the mind, Pinkney has applied his watercolors with a lighter, more delicate touch than in many of his previous illustrations. In **Home Place,** incidents, as well as the sensations that accompany them, blend and converge much as they do in the misty, illusory atmosphere that usually surrounds an unfolding dream. As a result, past and present penetrate one another and hold together as Pinkney strives, always with laudable restraint, to encompass in his vision the spiritual and emotional ties that unite the two families across a seemingly immense expanse of time and space, and, in purely pictorial terms, of race. All told, Pinkney's most quietly dramatic illustrations to date are also his most transcendent.

As Jerry Pinkney has coursed his way through more than three dozen books he has increasingly counterbalanced his technical skill with an emotional depth. This intense personal kinship with the texts he illustrates parallels, as he himself admits, his increasing comfort with the various types of language that consume him in his work. There is, says Pinkney, a curious irony about his constant preoccupation—and fascination—with words. In his youth his decision to pursue a career in art stemmed, at least in part, from the inadequacies he felt as a reader and writer. As it turns out, Pinkney has become the type of reader each of us hopes to be, the reader who, to paraphrase Eudora Welty, locates him—or herself in the pages of a book and emerges from the experience with a larger perspective, a new way of seeing and attending that enlarges both the private and public world. In Pinkney's case, the drama inherent in narrative has served him as a guiding consciousness that both accommodates his discovery of an inner text, the text that deals in universals, and spurs him to spin his own compelling tale in visual terms.

Michael Cart

SOURCE: *"Carte Blanche:* Invisible No Longer," in *Booklist,* Vol. 91, No. 12, February 15, 1995, p. 1069.

[There is hope to be found] in the growing body of literature for young readers, which also gives artful and authentic expression to the African American experience— as well as faces to the people who live it. Many of the best of these books—along with their creators, authors, and illustrators—have been honored with the Coretta Scott King Award, which recently celebrated its twenty-fifth anniversary. ALA [the American Library Association] has joined in that celebration by publishing *The Coretta Scott King Awards Book: From Vision to Reality,* edited by Henrietta Smith. Well represented in that volume is artist nonpareil Jerry Pinkney, the only three-time King Award winner for illustration. Pinkney has once again joined forces with his frequent collaborator Julius Lester (winner of two King honors himself) to give us a brilliant new version of the traditional story of that legendary steel-drivin' man, *John Henry* (1994), who, as Lester observes in a prefatory note, "continues to move us by his affirmation of something triumphant."

That "something," I think, is the human spirit, and it is celebrated in this book with style and leap-off-the-page exuberance—not only in its boisterous account of the mature John Henry's famous contest with the steam drill, but also in its narrative of his life before that. Even as an infant, it's obvious that John Henry is a force of nature; not only do all the animals come to see him, but even the sun peeps out "from behind the moon's skirts trying to get a glimpse of the new baby."

In Lester's brisk and stylishly written version, John Henry grows up quick and he grows up big; like other tall-tale American heroes, he is a work giant, and he hollers at a sleepy sun, "Get up from there! I got things to do and I need light to do 'em by."

His energy, strength, and heart are manifested early: en route to his rendezvous with the steam drill and his personal destiny, John Henry stops to help a road crew that's stymied by a boulder "as hard as anger." And when he begins the work of pulverizing that rock, swinging his pair of 20-pound sledgehammers in the process, a rainbow appears around his shoulders "like hope that never dies." It is this infusion of hope that makes Lester's telling of this story so timeless and that gives truth, as well, to the connection he makes between his hero and Dr. Martin Luther King Jr., for "both have the courage to hammer until our hearts break and leave our mourners smiling in their tears."

Jerry Pinkney's watercolor illustrations, with their rich colors borrowed from the rocks and the earth, are so beautiful that they summon their own share of smiles and tears. But more importantly, the realism of style and the artistic skill that are Pinkney's signature lend authenticity to legend, while his affection for his subject brings humanity and heart to a tall-tale hero who, in other versions of the legend, has been only . . . well, tall. Here he is every inch the folk hero.

Pinkney brings the best kinds of talent to his collaborative work as an illustrator: he consistently demonstrates not only a sympathetic intellectual grasp of an author's material, but also an empathetic understanding of its emotional content. Look, for example, at his largehearted illustrations for his wife, Gloria Jean Pinkney's two affecting picture-book memoirs: *Back Home* and the more recent *Sunday Outing.*

In the first of these two memory stories, Ernestine, an eight-year-old African American girl from the urban North, visits her family in rural North Carolina, where she was born and where her mother grew up. In the second, a prequel, we see Ernestine at home in Philadelphia dreaming of the trip south and trying to imagine ways to save her parents' money so they can afford her train fare.

These are quiet stories in which atmosphere is more important than incident, and family and the places it calls "home" are most important of all. Names of relatives are offered almost as invocations—Uncle Ariah, Aunt Odessa, Uncle June Avery, Grandmama Zulah. Their slightly old-fashioned sound suggests a setting sometime in the indeterminate past, and Jerry Pinkney's masterful use of color and light are as evocative and soft as remembered sunshine and as warm as family feelings.

TITLE COMMENTARY

📖 *THE ADVENTURES OF SPIDER: WEST AFRICAN FOLK TALES* **(written by Joyce Cooper Arkhurst, 1964)**

Priscilla L. Moulton

SOURCE: A review of *The Adventures of Spider: West African Folk Tales,* in *The Horn Book Magazine,* Vol. XL, No. 5, October, 1964, pp. 496-7.

Spider (usually called Anansi), popular and cunning trickster of West African folk tales, is the hero of six humorous how-and-why stories. The simple direct telling introduces Spider's wily ways and prepares children for more sophisticated versions of Anansi stories. A storyteller's introduction places the reader in the listening ring of a moonlit African village waiting for the "one who tells stories best" to describe "how Spider came to be the way he is." To the listener's delight, Spider frequently falls into the trap that he intended for a victim. Strikingly modern illustrations, many in bold color, amplify Spider's amusing character and the West African background. A most enjoyable and handsome addition to the limited number of folk-tale collections that second and third graders can handle themselves. For storytellers, too.

📖 *FEMI AND OLD GRANDADDIE* **(written by Adjai Robinson, 1972)**

Kirkus Reviews

SOURCE: A review of *Femi and Old Grandaddie,* in *Kirkus Reviews,* Vol. XL, No. 22, November 15, 1972, p. 1303.

An original tale by a student of African folklore, this hews to a universal theme—a poor boy wins the hand of a princess by an act of kindness. Femi's generosity is actually reluctant—decreed by his ingrained respect for the elderly and a certain fear of the creepy old Grandaddie who appears mysteriously in a canoe and demands the huge cassava Femi desperately needed as bait to trap the grorn pig that had been digging up his garden. The more dramatic moments—Femi's parents being swept away in a flood, the Grandaddie whispering the secret name of the headman's daughter, the grotesque teasing of the headman's clown—are heightened by Jerry Pinkney's fluid pencil drawings. His wonderfully expressive faces, semi-abstract landscapes and draperies, and clever use of perspective and pose keep the reader right in the middle of the action.

Dorothy De Wit

SOURCE: A review of *Femi and Old Grandaddie,* in *Library Journal,* Vol. 98, No. 4, February 15, 1973, p. 638.

An African folk tale resembling *Rumpelstiltskin.* Femi, an orphan boy, gives his food to an old man who complains of hunger in exchange for a riddle which contains the name of the king's daughter. The next day Femi pronounces her name to the king and receives her as his wife. The story is enhanced by descriptions of customs in Sierra Leone, and the writing is smooth and skillful. Occasionally the translation of the African jargon—"'My dear, darling, sweetie boy, . . .'"—makes the otherwise strong story seem saccharine. The expressive black-and-white drawings are appropriate, though occasionally too sophisticated for the simple text. But, the vivid details of the locale and the brisk story make this an interesting addition to folklore collections.

KASHO AND THE TWIN FLUTES (written by Adjai Robinson, 1973)

Kirkus Reviews

SOURCE: A review of *Kasho and the Twin Flutes,* in *Kirkus Reviews,* Vol. XLI, No. 22, November 15, 1973, p. 1260.

Pinkney's fluent soft pencil drawings—of people in motion (or dynamically at rest), splendidly poised animals, harmonious African huts and objects and rich African fabrics—add considerable texture and vitality to Robinson's tale of happy-go-lucky Kasho "who could think of nothing but playing his twin flutes" and desires only to play like his father, Shopeh, who charms the sacred snakes at the mountain spirit festival. Kasho's mother despairs of his ever leaving off the flutes long enough to get his chores done, but one day when the poisoned mamba snake he has brought home to charm escapes and prepares to attack her, Kasho plays in earnest to soothe and distract the creature. It takes a back-up from Shopeh, just home from the mountain, to completely charm and capture the mamba, but as Kasho says when his father, impressed, predicts that "one year soon" they will play together at

the festival—"A man does not climb a steep hill in a hurry."

Helen Gregory

SOURCE: A review of *Kasho and the Twin Flutes,* in *Library Journal,* Vol. 98, No. 22, December 15, 1973, p. 3702.

Kasho desperately wants to play the flutes as well as his father, whose music tames the sacred snake at the festival of the mountain spirits. One day Kasho captures a deadly green mamba to test the efficacy of his own flute-playing. Predictably, the snake escapes in Kasho's house, bringing about a suspenseful climax to this satisfying picture book. Believable family scenes of African village life are depicted and illustrated with realistic pencil sketches that capture the humor of the story and the humanity of the characters. The words to Kasho's song appear at the end of the book, but, unfortunately, just the lyrics, no music.

JI-NONGO-NONGO MEANS RIDDLES (written by Verna Aardema, 1978)

Frances Paterson

SOURCE: A review of *Ji-Nongo-Nongo Means Riddles,* in *School Library Journal,* Vol. 25, No. 5, January, 1979, p. 39.

Ji-Nongo-Nongo may mean riddles in Africa but it certainly will not mean humor to the average American child picking up this collection. Given the difficulties of translating folk wisdom from an entirely different culture, it is not surprising that most of the selections fall flat, e.g., "What thing in the forest frightens even the lion? Answer: The forest fire." or are obscure, e.g., "What does the pin say to the kente cloth? Answer: Don't hang your troubles on my neck!" The best feature of the book is its artwork—African animals and people are drawn in tones of gold and brown.

TONWEYA AND THE EAGLES, AND OTHER LAKOTA INDIAN TALES (written by Rosebud Yellow Robe, 1979)

Virginia Haviland

SOURCE: A review of *Tonweya and the Eagles and Other Lakota Indian Tales,* in *The Horn Book Magazine,* Vol. LV, No. 5, October, 1979, pp. 543-4.

The eldest daughter of Chauncey Yellow Robe, a hereditary chief of the Lakota-oyate tribe, retells stories she heard from her father as a child. . . . The stories in the collection feature her father as the young boy Chano going on his first buffalo hunt and listening to stories told by his parents, whom he loved deeply. The stories feature animal characters such as the beaver and the red-eyed ducks. Folk customs, such as rubbing blood on a young pony's nose to allay a fear of blood, are woven into the narratives. The tales are direct and simple, and the distinctive line drawings done in pencil interpret both the action and feeling of the stories in fine detail.

Robert Gish

SOURCE: " . . . and Legends from North America," in *The Christian Science Monitor,* October 15, 1979, p. B3.

In *Tonweya and the Eagles,* Rosebud Yellow Robe hits upon a most effective narrative technique when she focuses on her father, Chief Chauncey Yellow Robe (Chano), and the tales he heard (and retold again and again to his daughters and others) growing up as a member of the Lakota-oyate tribe, roaming the plains as part of the Sioux nation before domination by whites. Interpolating experiences in Chano's life with parallel legends of even earlier days, the days of Tasinagi, Chano's father, the author takes the reader beyond the moment, almost outside of time. And throughout the tellings of the 10 tales found here, the reader, like brave Tonweya lifted aloft out of gratitude by his eagle brothers, soars on the wings of myth. . . . [The] illustrator, Jerry Pinkney, adds immeasurably to making the make-believe believably real.

📖 *JAHDU* (written by Virginia Hamilton, 1980)

Ilene Cooper

SOURCE: A review of *Jahdu,* in *Booklist,* Vol. 77, No. 4, October 15, 1980, p. 332.

The magical Jahdu from Hamilton's collections, *Time-Ago Tales of Jahdu* and *Time-Ago Lost,* now appears in reader format. Jahdu is abrasive, brassy, and haughty—but he has lost his power. The child Lee Edward brushes him aside and his own shadow ridicules him, taunting him and refusing to be kicked about. Shadow says Jahdu's power belongs to CIGAM, who lies beyond the horizon, where Jahdu must not go. Jahdu does go, nevertheless, and learns that Shadow has taken his power and turned it upside down. The writing is Hamiltoniously original, poetic, and luring; and its elusiveness matches Pinkney's subtle, dreamlike realizations of the story, making the whole a challenge.

📖 *COUNT ON YOUR FINGERS AFRICAN STYLE* (written by Claudia Zaslavsky, 1980)

Nancy J. Schmidt

SOURCE: A review of *Count on Your Fingers African Style,* in *School Library Journal,* Vol. 27, No. 3, November, 1980, p. 68.

Focuses on finger counting in market places primarily in East Africa, but also in Sierra Leone, with mention of a

From The Patchwork Quilt, *written by Valerie Flournoy. Illustrated by Jerry Pinkney.*

children's finger game and two South African number words. The text is extremely general, considering the author's expertise. The black-and-white drawings are essential for comprehending the text. Most of them show market places where food is being sold. These drawings are neither ethnically nor physically distinctive of the people named in the text. Other drawings show a Maasai man selling jewelry, a Taita farmer by his house, and hands arranged in number signs of several ethnic groups. There is no map to show the places in Africa named in the text. A broader range of East African culture and more specific information about East African life are introduced in Muriel Feelings' *Moja Means One: Swahili Counting Book.*

Philip Morrison and Phylis Morrison

SOURCE: A review of *Count on Your Fingers African Style,* in *Scientific American,* Vol. 243, No. 6, December, 1980, p. 54.

Could you convey your price of eight shillings for produce to a customer who did not speak your language? Well, you might easily hold up two hands, four fingers on each, thumbs folded. That is what the Taita farmer did in front of snowy Kilimanjaro. Not far off a Masai trader waved his right hand, four fingers up, once back and forth. The Kamba fruit seller grasped with his right hand the three small fingers of his left. All had said eight.

Sometimes words retain old ideas. The Zulu still hold up the right thumb to show six; the Zulu word for six is *isithipa*, which means "take the thumb." An old echo still rings in English: the words eleven and twelve seem to contain the Old English for "left over"; they might have meant one or two left over after counting 10 fingers. In this book for young readers or those read to, who hope to learn to count well or who like far travel by way of books, we visit African markets to see the sights. Daily many people use fingers for arithmetic, a practical method when a common language is lacking. After all, ours is the time of digital mathematics; here are its origins. The detailed and evocative pencil renderings from life are the pleasure of these pages; they show striking costumes and animated crowds in the varied marketplaces of Africa, East and West, where one little Mende girl can count on her fingers nimbly up to 20 while her experienced mother carries out big sums swiftly in her head.

📖 THE PATCHWORK QUILT (written by Valerie Flournoy, 1985)

Susan Powers

SOURCE: A review of *The Patchwork Quilt*, in *School Library Journal*, Vol. 31, No. 8, April, 1985, p. 78.

Flournoy draws children into an old woman's dream of creating a "masterpiece" from the family's clothing scraps. This story of the completion of the year-long project—a quilt that has brought a family together in a new way, with a new understanding of and appreciation for each other—will leave children moved and satisfied. Creating a patchwork of family life that parallels the quiltmaking, the author details the daily events, special celebrations and the passing of the seasons with descriptive home scenes. Telling dialogue gives an added sense of the tensions, loyalties and love in this three-generational black household. Tanya, the youngest of the three children, is the pivotal character, and her special communication with her grandmother makes her the champion of what Mama impatiently views as Grandma's old and stubborn ways. Tanya's example and gentle persuasion draw her mother into helping to piece the patchwork and into becoming more and more involved in the work. When Grandma becomes ill, Tanya doggedly leads the effort, gaining sewing skills out of necessity. Eventually her two brothers take their part. Grandmother, recovered, is able to finish the quilt, now full of mementos and memories, and stitched with the message, "For Tanya from your Mama and Grandma." Plentiful full-page and double-page paintings in pencil, graphite and watercolor are vivid yet delicately detailed, bespeaking the warm physical bonds among members of this family. Giving a sense of dramatization to the text, which is longer than most picture books, the illustrations provide just the right style and mood for the story and are well placed within the text.

Tony Bradman

SOURCE: "Family Feelings," in *The Times Literary Supplement*, No. 4296, August 2, 1985, p. 862.

The Patchwork Quilt is a . . . straightforward story. Tanya is a black child, who lives with her mother and father and brothers, and her Grandma, who has decided to make a patchwork quilt. Tanya's mother offers to buy Grandma a quilt, but Grandma wants to make one the old-fashioned way and Tanya decides to help her. Later, Grandma falls ill, and Tanya takes over the quiltmaking until she recovers. The quilt, however, is more than just something to cover a bed; in Grandma's words, it's a masterpiece, something that tells a life story—or the story of the family. And all the members of the family contribute something to its making, whether it's a patch of cloth from a worn-out pair of jeans or actual sewing.

The quilt, therefore, stands as a symbol for family togetherness, and the lesson it teaches Tanya is one of belonging. Grandma connects her to a tradition which goes beyond the present members of the family and at the same time holds it together. Valerie Flournoy's story is very well written, and manages to convey these important themes in a totally painless way. What's more, for a long story it reads aloud very well. My only quibble is with Jerry Pinkney's illustrations. They are realistic, and at first glance do appear to suit this warmly human story. But there's a certain stiffness about them which stems, I think, from too "photographic" a style; some of the facial expressions seem very odd indeed. That said, *The Patchwork Quilt* is a welcome addition to the growing number of picture books which show positive images of black families.

Hanna B. Zeiger

SOURCE: A review of *The Patchwork Quilt*, in *The Horn Book Magazine*, Vol. LXI, No. 5, September-October, 1985, p. 546.

To Tanya a year seems too long to wait for the patchwork quilt Grandma has promised her. Disregarding her daughter's complaint about the mess the quilt scraps make in the clean living room, Grandma dozes off in the sunlight by the window murmuring, "'I'm gonna make a masterpiece.'" As the weeks and months pass, bits and scraps from the family are added, and Tanya says that Grandma and the quilt tell each other stories. When Grandma falls ill, Tanya and her mother pick up the task until Grandma recovers and adds the finishing touch—a dedication stitched in the corner of the quilt, including the three generations of women in their family. The illustrations extend the characterizations in the story and give us something too seldom seen in children's books: a strong, loving black family—dressed handsomely, living in a beautiful home, and sharing in the happiness of family gatherings and in their concern for Grandma during her illness. Papa fixes breakfast and comforts Mama, and the boys pick up scissors and scraps and go to work on the quilt. Jerry Pinkney's paintings of the family glow with as much warmth and vibrancy as the loveliest of quilts. In tracing the origins of the scraps of material, the story helps children see how a family's history could indeed be told from reading a patchwork quilt.

Betsy Shea

SOURCE: A review of *The Patchwork Quilt,* in *The New York Times Book Review,* October 20, 1985, p. 18.

Quilting is a domestic art form which, in its thrifty use of cloth scraps and blocks of straight stitching, produces complex results that somehow satisfy many of our longings for family closeness and traditions, for the home truths associated with everyday tasks. Such feelings of warmth, security and family love permeate [this book] about quilting for beginning readers.

In *The Patchwork Quilt* by Valerie Flournoy, Tanya, the youngest of the three children in a black, middle-class family, is fascinated by the patchwork quilt her grandmother is making. Her mother is initially impatient with the laborious process. But Grandma has time and conveys to Tanya, who is 6 or 7 years old, that things of value take time. Thought and planning are necessary in the selection of just the right colors and placement of the squares. The meaningfulness and satisfaction of doing something yourself—when you have the time—are clearly conveyed.

When Grandma is taken ill, the quilt becomes the expression of the family's love and concern for her. Jim and Ted, Tanya's brothers, cut and pile squares of fabric. With Tanya's determination and Mama's help, they all work to complete the quilt's top, and Grandma recovers to quilt it as a gift for Tanya.

There is warmth and intimacy in the richly detailed watercolor illustrations by Jerry Pinkney. One doesn't need words to sense the affection among family members or the pride they feel in their achievement, a beautiful patchwork quilt.

HALF A MOON AND ONE WHOLE STAR
(written by Crescent Dragonwagon, 1986)

Kirkus Reviews

SOURCE: A review of *Half a Moon and One Whole Star,* in *Kirkus Reviews,* Vol. LIV, No. 4, February 15, 1986, p. 301.

A dream-like lullaby poem showing how life continues through the night while a child sleeps.

When half a moon and one whole star hang in the sky, it's a sign that night is about to come. The birds and the animals prepare for night; some are going to sleep while others rouse. "Susan lies in bed, not sleeping./ Not yet sleeping, but does she doze,/ Blinking as the curtain blows?/ Yes, yes, yes, she does, sleep, Susan, Sleep." The soothing, hypnotic story continues as Susan smells summer scents of honeysuckle and green-cut lawns, and hears the whir of the crickets and the sounds of her parents talking on the porch. Forest animals stir, fish sleep in the lake, a docked ship raises its anchor and sets sail, a saxophone player plays blues through the night. The baker, powdery white in flour, bakes his bread, and Susan sleeps on. But soon—a reversal. The sky lightens, and all creatures of the night prepare for bed while the day creatures awaken.

The cadence and the sensual images of the text, coupled with the artist's direct, yet subtly disjointed pictures in vivid watery colors, combine for a harmonious nighttime symphony of sound and color. The jump in time sequence in the last three spreads, while a bit confusing, does introduce children to the concept of time's continuity; when night comes, day will follow. Pinkney's interpretation of Susan as a black child adds an interesting dimension and should broaden the range of readership.

Denise M. Wilms

SOURCE: A review of *Half a Moon and One Whole Star,* in *Booklist,* Vol. 82, No. 14, March 15, 1986, p. 1080.

A lullaby of sorts, this presents the sights and sounds of the night that surround a girl named Susan as she drowses half asleep: "Not yet sleeping, but does she doze, / Blinking as the curtain blows? / Yes, yes, yes, she does, sleep, Susan, sleep." In the darkness crickets whir, curtains stir, the Steinkamps call their good-byes, and her parents talk. Then the view shifts farther afield—to the wood where raccoons walk, to the harbor where a ship will soon raise anchor, and to a town where a sax player approaches the club where he'll play the blues. The litany of nighttime sights and scenes continues with the players carrying on their roles till dawn when they'll be ready for sleep, and Susan will wake to a hot, sunny new day. Pinkney shows a black girl snuggled in a cozy bed in a country house; his colors are jewel-like and deep, his lines made expressive by well-controlled watercolor washes. An effective mood piece that's suitable for leisurely bedtime reading and conversation.

Bulletin of the Center for Children's Books

SOURCE: A review of *Half a Moon and One Whole Star,* in *Bulletin of the Center for Children's Books,* Vol. 39, No. 9, May, 1986, p. 164.

A black child dozes, dreams, and sleeps until dawn while night creatures and night workers go their way. The paintings that illustrate this night poem are among the best work that Pinkney has done: there are fanciful details skillfully incorporated into realistic pictures that are sometimes busy but that are strong in composition and in textural quality. The poem has some lilting phrases and some sharp images; occasionally the rhyme or meter falters, but the concept of night activity and the sleeping household should appeal to the read-aloud audience.

📖 **THE TALES OF UNCLE REMUS: THE ADVENTURES OF BRER RABBIT** (written by Julius Lester, 1987)

June Jordan

SOURCE: "A Truly Bad Rabbit," in *The New York Times Book Review,* May 17, 1987, p. 32

Beautifully written, or retold, by Julius Lester, these resurrected Brer Rabbit stories raise more questions than the little tales themselves can answer: Is this folklore or children's literature? When should folk materials be extricated from the historic context of their origins? Do racist stereotypes become acceptable because the victims apparently internalize, or choose not to challenge, such notions? How shall anyone salvage "The Tales of Uncle Remus" and yet hope to escape the implications of that mythical, that happy, garrulous ol' slave whom Joel Chandler Harris used to narrate his collections of stories published between 1896 and 1918? . . .

Yes, the Brer Rabbit stories have been around a long time, but so has wife abuse. With lamentably few exceptions, the Uncle Remus stories center on a pathological hustler, a truly bad rabbit. Knavery of every sort defines this "cornerstone." Premeditated violence, compulsive cruelty, exploitation of children and regular opportunism abound. Add to these characteristics a fundamental laziness (why can't Brer Rabbit grow his own darn cabbages and carrots, for example?), plus a fulsome enthusiasm for lying all the time, and you have summarized the substance of Brer Rabbit and his not so merry misadventures.

If these folk tales were not meant for children (quiet or otherwise), then the relentless chicanery of the protagonist would not matter so much, nor would the sometimes positively homicidal humor of the material. . . .

This misbegotten resurrection is a terrible waste of very considerable talents. Julius Lester comes through at his irresistible best, as a compelling and frequently hilarious teller of tall tales. Every single illustration by Jerry Pinkney is fastidious, inspired and a marvel of delightful imagination. Perhaps Mr. Lester and Mr. Pinkney will soon collaborate on new material more worthy of their labors. Certainly, I hope so.

Margery Fisher

SOURCE: A review of *The Tales of Uncle Remus,* in *Growing Point,* Vol. 26, No. 3, September, 1987, pp. 4854-5.

The Brer Rabbit tales are for *telling:* to be fair to them reviewers do well to try them aloud. If hearing was necessary for Joel Chandler Harris's dense, dialectal sentences, it is just as necessary although the language has now been 'made accessible' in what Julius Lester calls 'a modified contemporary southern black English, which is a combination of standard English and black English.' Instead of the intermediary Uncle Remus we have an almost offhand voice, anonymous but entirely individual; instead of the continuity supplied by the exact circumstances of each of Uncle Remus's meetings with the small boy to whom he introduced Brer Rabbit and his many victims, the stories are now grouped so that we meet the trickster first in some of his most characteristic encounters with Brer Fox (among them Tar Baby, the dead horse and the luckless hunting expedition); then gradually more and more characters are introduced, with Lion, Bear and Wolf in turn trying to outwit him. Mr. Man appears in several stories, as a triumphant captor sadly discomfited, and so does Miss Meadows with the girls; in the last story the indomitable Brer Rabbit almost admits he is growing old; unexpectedly, the agelessness of a mythological creature clashes with the weakness of a small animal. Brer Rabbit is, of course, a hare, and this has been some help to the illustrator in reducing the problems of scale and posture always present in group pictures. In animal fable, humanisation can be taken for granted. It should not worry anyone (the author says firmly) if Brer Rabbit courts at one time or another a friend of Miss Meadows and the pretty daughter of Brer Wolf; the interrelation of animals and humans may be taken as perfectly natural because the storyteller refuses to think otherwise. Similarly, in the magnificent illustrations, the artist has taken for granted that the animals will wear shirts and trousers and assume human attitudes, with paws serving as hands or feet (the four stages of the Tar Baby episode are especially skilful in this respect): conversely, the landscapes in the four coloured double spreads, and the slighter suggestions of natural surroundings in the numerous drawings, remind us that these are animals in a Southern state of America as well as characters in folk-tales which served to demonstrate a particular human society. As stories speaking for the oppressed, as farcical episodes and as sharp studies of personality, these tales are now offered in a fluent, idiomatic, direct prose to new readers and to those who previously had to pursue the humour through difficult verbiage. Julius Lester in his introduction has put the stories firmly in historical context but while we need to take account of the background, such a warm, entertaining and finely produced book offers most of all a chance of enormous enjoyment. Let pedants worry about the unnatural antics and stratagems of the hare and his fellow animals (some of them, like Lion and Tiger, geographically out of place); we may appreciate these furred and feathered actors in a drama we can all ruefully recognise.

Irene Babsky

SOURCE: A review of *The Tales of Uncle Remus: The Adventures of Brer Rabbit,* in *The School Librarian,* Vol. 36, No. 2, May, 1988, p. 77.

The Uncle Remus stories that were collected by Joel Chandler Harris and published in 1896 and 1918 are problematic for the modern reader. Firstly, the dialect in which they are written is difficult to understand and, while Harris's notation of the stories was impeccable, his narrator, Uncle Remus, is by today's standards unacceptably derogatory about black people.

Julius Lester retells forty-eight of the Chandler stories in this volume. He has dispensed with Uncle Remus as a character and re-created him as a voice, so the writing is a masterly combination of black oral storytelling techniques blended with a clear, direct writing style. This combination gives the stories freshness and vitality and makes them enjoyable over a wide age range. Jerry Pinkney's illustrations are clear and detailed. They are distinguished by warmth and sensitivity, and achieve that rare attainment in the illustrators' art of adding a dimension of their own yet being entirely in harmony with the text. These retellings will become great favourites with all who read them and the writer deserves our gratitude for telling them to us so well. Yet he has done more than this. After their long wanderings, Julius Lester has brought these treasures of Afro-American culture back home to their readers and listeners at last, so sit down and welcome them—with the young of all ages.

📖 *WILD WILD SUNFLOWER CHILD ANNA* (written by Nancy White Carlstrom, 1987)

Denise M. Wilms

SOURCE: A review of *Wild Wild Sunflower Child Anna,* in *Booklist,* Vol. 84, No. 3, October 1, 1987, p. 257.

Little Anna in a sunshine-bright dress cavorts and dawdles through a country day. Her meanderings are recorded in a free-flowing poem that's expanded by Pinkney's summer-lush illustrations. "Running and jumping/ silly and loud/ is Anna/ in the morning./ Wild wild sunflower child/ Anna." She digs in the garden, picks juicy raspberries, plows through overgrowth collecting a frock full of burrs, splashes in the creek, and otherwise wiles away her hours. The watercolor illustrations feature appealing flower- and greenery-filled landscapes with Anna at the brilliant center. Though she's conceived here as a black child, she could be any child; audiences young and old will find her pleasure in the day most contagious.

Ellen Fader

SOURCE: A review of *Wild Wild Sunflower Child Anna,* in *The Horn Book Magazine,* Vol. LXIII, No. 6, November-December, 1987, p. 721-2.

Anna is an appealing and active young girl wearing a bright yellow dress and white sandals; her pigtails are tied with yellow ribbons and seem to echo her movements as she explores the world around her. "Running and jumping / silly and loud / is Anna / in the morning.

/ Wild wild sunflower child / Anna. / Flying in the field / in the greening / of the morning. / Anna drifts, / Anna glides, / Anna's arms open wide / for the sun rolling / sky falling. / It doesn't, Anna does. / Dizzy, tizzy Anna." Anna's exuberant appreciation of nature, including berries and burrs, frogs and flowers, seeds and spiders, is captured in Carlstrom's lilting verse, which is presented on the left side of each double-page spread with an illustration that calls attention to something from Anna's summer world. On the right side Pinkney's full-color pencil, gouache, and watercolor paintings perfectly complement Carlstrom's joyous free-form poetry. The one illustration that spans both pages is wonderfully startling, as Anna gazes directly at the reader. At times impressionistic, at other times full of colorful detail, Pinkney's art, reminiscent in style of his work in *Half a Moon and One Whole Star,* will draw young listeners into Anna's special world. The book is for an older preschooler than Carlstrom's *Jesse Bear, What Will You Wear?* and *The Moon Came Too*—the verse is less controlled and the subject more abstract. An exceptional treat awaits the parent and child who can lose themselves in this book.

Patricia Pearl

SOURCE: A review of *Wild Wild Sunflower Child Anna,* in *School Library Journal,* Vol. 34, No. 6, February, 1988, p. 58.

In perfect harmony of text and illustration, Carlstrom and Pinkney extol the joy of being a vigorous, curious child exploring the delights of a lovely summer day. Exuberant Anna, a pony-tailed little black girl in a bright yellow dress, frolics through luxuriant flower gardens, a raspberry patch, and weedy wildflowery meadows; rolls down a green hillside; hops across a cool, froggy stream; stands sturdily up in a tree; crouches to examine insects under a rock; and finally falls asleep in the grass. The text, in free verse form, is melodious with internal rhymes, repetitions, and varied rhythms. Exquisite full-page illustrations in watercolor, gouache, and colored pencil depict a charming girl amid brilliant floral magnificence and radiate summer warmth and beauty. The facing pages set off the verses attractively with a border of blossoms and leaves and a center portrait of an individual bloom, berry, burr, or other element from the larger illustration.

📖 *MORE TALES OF UNCLE REMUS: FURTHER ADVENTURES OF BRER RABBIT, HIS FRIENDS, ENEMIES, AND OTHERS* (written by Julius Lester, 1988)

Mary M. Burns

SOURCE: A review of *More Tales of Uncle Remus: Further Adventures of Brer Rabbit,* in *The Horn Book Magazine,* Vol. LXIV, No. 5, September-October, 1988, pp. 639-40.

"I am awed that these tales about Brer Rabbit, created by

slaves, speak so directly and with such clarity to us who are not slaves—that in these tales created by slaves is the vital voice of our humanity." These concluding phrases in Lester's introduction to the companion volume to *The Tales of Uncle Remus* precisely capture the importance of these two compilations in the contemporary world. The second volume, like the first, rings with the authentic voice of the storyteller, casting traditional tales in an idiom comprehensible to a modern audience without sacrificing their elemental strength. The imagery is remarkable, as in this description of the lovely Melody Mellifulous who captured Brer Rabbit's fancy but refused to respond to his longing: "If it had been raining and Melody had had the only umbrella in the world, Brer Rabbit would've drowned." There are thirty-seven stories in the collection, representing a variety of tale types and folkloric motifs from the *pourquoi* that explains **"Why Dogs Are Always Sniffing"** to the repetitive refrains found in **"Brer Rabbit, Brer Coon and the Frogs."** Unifying all is the motif of the Trickster "charming and likeable, surrounded . . . by an aura of innocence and vulnerability." This concept is expanded in the enlightening and entertaining introduction. Truly a collection for all ages, the book offers a tale for any audience. The illustrations are equally remarkable for their energy and synchronization with the spirit as well as with the words of the text. While the full-color illustrations are magnificent, the soft pencil sketches, as intimate and revealing as a candid snapshot, develop the characters more precisely, adding still another dimension to their personalities. Beautifully designed so that content is complemented by format, either of the two volumes of the Uncle Remus tales would be a major contribution to folklore for children in recent years; together, they outdistance all challengers.

📖 *MIRANDY AND BROTHER WIND* (written by Patricia C. McKissack, 1988)

Betsy Hearne

SOURCE: A review of *Mirandy and Brother Wind*, in *Bulletin of the Center for Children's Books*, Vol. 42, No. 4, December, 1988, pp. 103-4.

One of the surest new storytelling voices in picture books has followed up *Flossie and the Fox* with another winner, also drawn from memories of Patricia McKissack's family. Here, Mirandy is sure that she'll win the cake walk if she can catch Brother Wind for her partner, but he eludes all the tricks her friends advise. When she finally does catch him with her own quick wits, she ends up wishing instead for her boyfriend Ezel to overcome his clumsiness. Sure enough, the two children finish first in high style. "When Grandmama Beasley had seen Mirandy and Ezel turning and spinning, moving like shadows in the flickering candlelight, she'd thrown back her head, laughed, and said, 'Them chullin' is dancing with the Wind!'" This narrative gets a high score, too, for plot, pace, and characterization. Mirandy sparkles

with energy and determination, while the action dances with its own rhythm. Pinkney's watercolors are splashed with multi-hued, overlapping shapes that fill the pages with patterned ferment, occasionally threatening to overwhelm the story but never quite doing so. The translucent blue, larger-than-life figure of Brother Wind is clothed in the same historical costume as the rest of the southern black cast. Occasionally the portraits seem studied, but the rural settings are lush with laurel and wisteria, aflutter with chickens, and evocative of country communities at their best. A treat to pass on to new generations.

Denise M. Wilms

SOURCE: A review of *Mirandy and Brother Wind*, in *Booklist*, Vol. 85, No. 9, January 1, 1989, p. 792.

The junior cakewalk contest is fast approaching, and Mirandy thinks she would like Brother Wind to be her partner: "Then I'd be sure to win." She tries hard to catch him, even going to see Mis' Poinsettia, who is rumored to be a conjurer, but Brother Wind proves too slippery—until the afternoon a quick-thinking Mirandy slams the barn door behind him. "Now," she says, "you got to do whatever I ask." At the dance, Mirandy pairs herself with Ezel, the boy whose invitation she has resisted, and calls on Brother Wind for help; weeks afterward, their prize-winning performance is still the talk of the town. Several breaks in time interrupt the narrative, but Pinkney's expansive pictures sustain the reader's attention. His paintings are best viewed from a bit of distance, which makes the blurred lines and myriad shadings appear more sharply focused. Warm colors and homey scenes enhance the story's strong sense of a turn-of-the-century rural black community. Inspired by a family story, McKissack's tale is both fanciful and grounded in affectionate remembrance.

Lois F. Anderson

SOURCE: A review of *Mirandy and Brother Wind*, in *The Horn Book Magazine*, Vol. LXV, No. 2, March-April, 1989, p. 201.

The impetus for the delightful and joyful story came from a 1906 photograph of the author's grandparents after they had just won a cakewalk contest. In splendid, bright watercolors with floral tones, Jerry Pinkney captures the high prancing spirit of this Afro-American dance which became such a vital part of the American culture in the nineteenth century. Mirandy, happily anticipating the cakewalk, will only settle for Brother Wind as her partner. But the elegantly dressed Brother Wind is elusive and difficult to capture. Relentlessly, Mirandy pursues the blue spiritlike creature until, with the help of a little magic, she corners him. The reader accompanies Mirandy in a jaunty stride to the spirited finale. The author and illustrator present young listeners with an endearing glimpse into America's entertaining past.

RABBIT MAKES A MONKEY OF LION: A SWAHILI TALE (written by Verna Aardema, 1989)

Carolyn Phelan

SOURCE: A review of *Rabbit Makes a Monkey of Lion,* in *Booklist,* Vol. 85, No. 13, March 1, 1989, p. 1131.

Out of the folklore tradition in which a wily little creature outwits a big, brawny opponent comes this Swahili tale. When Rabbit and her friends Bush-rat and Turtle steal the honey that Lion claims as his, they stir up his wrath. Each time he tries to avenge his loss, one of the tricky critters manages to outsmart him, resulting in the cry, "That little rascal made a monkey of me!" Pinkney's soft-line drawings, rich with subtle, overlapping watercolors, capture the drama of the tale. The full-color illustrations depend heavily on greens and tans, which the artist uses to create a series of pleasantly varied settings. His lively characters express their emotions convincingly without becoming more or less than the animals they are. The humor, which comes mainly from the imaginative use of onomatopoeia, will facilitate the storyteller's task: "Kahta-KUM, kahta-KUM, kahta-KUM" is the sound of Lion scooping mud on top of Turtle, for example. A little long for preschool audiences, this will be a good African story to read aloud to primary-grade children.

Ellen Fader

SOURCE: A review of *Rabbit Makes a Monkey of Lion,* in *The Horn Book Magazine,* Vol. LXV, No. 3, May-June, 1989, p. 381.

Aardema has discovered another marvelous African folk tale; the original, "The Hare and the Lion," appears in the 1901 collection *Zanzibar Tales.* In her retelling Aardema eliminates much of the meandering quality of George Bateman's translation from the Swahili and enlivens an action-packed and funny story. A honey guide bird is the cause of the animals' trouble; she leads Rabbit to a bees' nest in a calabash tree, and from then on Rabbit is obsessed with eating the honey. Unfortunately, the tree belongs to Lion, who is understandably annoyed to have Rabbit and her partners in crime, Bush-rat and Turtle, raiding his property. The animals are able to evade slow-witted Lion's grasp and appetite the first time they come down the tree, but on the following day Lion captures Rabbit. Eventually, however, the tricksters outwit the king of beasts. Aardema's version of the tale reinforces the amusing trickster qualities of rascally Rabbit, making it a sure-fire choice for sharing with groups of children, who will instantly root for her success. Pinkney's lovely watercolor and pencil paintings in hues of green, brown, and gold fill the pages with lush scenes which evoke the East African setting. His creatures show an intriguing mix of animal and human qualities perfectly in tune with this folk tale.

Constance A. Mellon

SOURCE: A review of *Rabbit Makes a Monkey of Lion: A Swahili Tale,* in *School Library Journal,* Vol. 35, No. 10, June, 1989, p. 97.

The honey guide bird begins this tale by singing to Rabbit "Chee, chee! Come and see—/ A bees' nest in a calabash tree." Rabbit brings Bush-rat to help her get the honey from the first tree, Turtle to help with the second tree. Each time they must run from Lion, who is angry that the animals dare to steal his honey. Each escape is managed by outsmarting Lion, who exclaims, "That little rascal made a monkey of me!" Aardema brings these jungle tricksters to life with her lyrical version of this Swahili tale. The choice and use of repeated sounds add authenticity and rhythm to the retelling and make this version delightful to read aloud or tell. Pinkney's full-page watercolors in muted tones extend Aardema's characterizations of the animals, producing portraits by word and picture that capture the mood of trickster tales. Pinkney's animals are handsome and realistic, unlike the cartoon animals in clothing which all too frequently romp through the pages of animal folktales. Yet, through pose and expression, they show that they are rascals who live by their wits. This tale, with such favorite tricksters as Rabbit and Turtle outsmarting a lesser known opponent, Lion, is sure to delight readers and listeners alike.

THE TALKING EGGS: A FOLKTALE FROM THE AMERICAN SOUTH (written by Robert D. San Souci, 1989)

Kirkus Reviews

SOURCE: A review of *The Talking Eggs: A Folktale from the American South,* in *Kirkus Reviews,* Vol. LVII, No. 13, July 1, 1989, p. 996.

A lively retelling of a rather hard-hearted Creole version of a widely collected folktale.

Blanche does all the work while her mother and older sister Rose put on airs and treat her cruelly. To repay a kindness, a mysterious old woman leads Blanche to her magical shack deep in the backwoods, where the chickens have rainbow colors, the two-headed cow brays like a mule, and nattily dressed rabbits dance. As Blanche leaves the next morning, the woman tells her to help herself to any eggs that say "Take me." Though these prove to be the plainer-looking eggs, they yield great treasures on the journey home. Seeing her younger sister's wealth, Rose sets out to duplicate it, but behaving in her usual high-handed fashion wins her a fair reward: her eggs hatch snakes, frogs, yellow jackets, and a wolf. Blanche moves to the city, leaving Rose and her mother fruitlessly searching for the old woman.

Pinkney sets the story in an eerily tangled southern forest; his black characters glow with personality, each one distinct and believable, while the cow and chickens are rendered so matter-of-factly that it takes more than one look to discern their unusual features. Blanche's gentle ingenuousness may seem at odds with her ready abandonment of her family, but that traditional ending does keep the thematic waters unmuddied.

Betsy Hearne

SOURCE: A review of *The Talking Eggs: A Folktale from the American South,* in *Bulletin of the Center for Children's Books,* Vol. 43, No. 2, October, 1989, p. 42.

A Creole folktale about a widow and her two daughters, who "lived on a farm so poor, it looked like the tail end of bad luck," combines elements of Cinderella with distinctively southern black lore. The youngest child, abused by her mother and sister, helps an old woman who rewards her with magic eggs that produce gold and jewels. When the evil sister seeks the same old woman and disobeys her, the eggs give forth snakes, toads, and vermin. It's a strong story well told, and Pinkney's elaborate watercolor scenes play it to the hilt. The two-headed cow with corkscrew horns and a mulish bray, the multicolored, many-legged chickens that whistle like mockingbirds, and the old woman who removes her head to comb her hair are haunting images of magic, both verbally and visually. In spite of occasional stiffness in drafting of human faces and figures, there is an eerie quality to these scenes that will electrify storytelling or picture-book sharing sessions.

Lois F. Anderson

SOURCE: A review of *The Talking Eggs,* in *The Horn Book Magazine,* Vol. LXV, No. 6, November-December, 1989, p. 782.

Adapted from a Creole folk tale originally included in a collection of Louisiana stories by folklorist Alcee Fortier, this tale captures the flavor of the nineteenth-century South in its language and story line. There are four characters: a wicked mother; a girl who is sweet, kind, and "sharp as forty crickets"; a second daughter who is arrogant and spoiled; and an old woman who possesses magical charms. As expected, the good daughter does all the chores while her mother and sister dream of riches and do nothing, and she is ultimately rewarded for her goodness. Similar to Perrault's "Diamonds and Toads," the story has a compelling charm. Jerry Pinkney's watercolors are chiefly responsible for the excellence of the book; his characters convey their moods with vivid facial expressions. A wonderful book to read aloud.

Teresa Scragg

SOURCE: A review of *The Talking Eggs,* in *The School Librarian,* Vol. 38, No. 2, May, 1990, p. 70.

Adapted from a Creole folk tale from nineteenth-century

Louisiana, this story has its roots in the folk and fairy stories of Europe. It is the story of Blanche, who lives with her lazy mother and spiteful sister, and like Cinderella, has to do all the work until a mysterious old woman rewards her kindness with riches and treasures, and introduces her to a whole new world of dancing rabbits, bright coloured chickens, and talking eggs. Naturally, her sister Rose is anxious to share the prize, but her rudeness meets with a very different response.

The illustrations by Jerry Pinkney are excellent, and give authenticity to the South American setting. They enhance the bizarre nature of the story, and have lots of detail to engage fully the observant child; although younger children may be unsettled by some of the details in the text, like the fact that the old woman removes her head to comb her hair! This is a lengthy, complex folk tale, which will stimulate much interest and discussion.

📖 *TURTLE IN JULY* (written by Marilyn Singer, 1989)

Betsy Hearne

SOURCE: A review of *Turtle in July,* in *Bulletin of the Center for Children's Books,* Vol. 43, No. 1, September, 1989, pp. 20-1.

The great joy of these fifteen nature poems is the pattern of verbal rhythms that reflect the character of each subject creature. The befuddled bear emerging from hibernation in March asks "Who I?/ Where I?/ When I now?/ No matter/ Need water/ Few berries/ Fresh ants/ Not so hungry/ Or am I?" The timber rattlesnake sibilantly describes summer and winter with long coiling sounds. The beavers in November hurry here and there with the refrain, "This stick here/ That stick there/ Mud, more mud, add mud, good mud. . . ." The joy of the art is Pinkney's venture into new effects without sacrificing his characteristic style. While his human figures are sometimes studied, these animal drawings are anatomically spontaneous. The settings are lusciously simple, with spacious color and sharply focused compositions. Both writer and artist have captured the essence of the fish, fowl, and mammals featured here. Perfect to share in classrooms or story hours emphasizing themes of nature study and seasonal change.

Nancy Vasilakis

SOURCE: A review of *Turtle in July,* in *The Horn Book Magazine,* Vol. LXVI, No. 1, January-February, 1990, pp. 82-3.

A bullhead catfish lying in the sediment at the bottom of a pond sets down the underlying rhythm of the changing seasons in this symphony of verses that features an animal for each month of the year. The variety of wildlife and the corresponding changes in meter and tone, combined with Jerry Pinkney's lush, full-page illustrations in full color, create a vivid picture book that is visually as well as auditorily pleasing. By using the first person throughout, Singer captures the essence of each animal: the slow, ponderous sonority of the March bear awakening from its long hibernation; the giddy spirit of a terrier in April as it charges through the park. A subtle humor underscores the beaver's two-beat rhythmic chant as it fortifies its dam in November: "Mud, more mud, add mud, good mud / You pat / I gnaw / I pile / You store." The refrain of the timber rattlesnake, in contrast—"Warm bones / Warm blood / Strike I still can / Yes"—evokes a macabre fascination. While Pinkney's pictures are more static portrait than true illustration, the combination of text and art creates a striking effect that will draw the attention of younger readers.

📖 FURTHER TALES OF UNCLE REMUS: THE MISADVENTURES OF BRER RABBIT, BRER FOX, BRER WOLF, THE DOODANG AND OTHER CREATURES (written by Julius Lester, 1990)

Betsy Hearne

SOURCE: A review of *Further Tales of Uncle Remus: The Misadventures of Brer Rabbit, Brer Fox, Brer Wolf, the Doodang and Other Creatures,* in *Bulletin of the Center for Children's Books,* Vol. 43, No. 9, May, 1990, pp. 218-19.

The cast of characters shifts in this third volume of Julius Lester's series that began with *The Tales of Uncle Remus: The Adventures of Brer Rabbit* and continued with *More Tales of Uncle Remus.* Here, the other animals dominate, and they are a much grimmer lot than the irrepressible cotton-tailed trickster, who, when he does appear, lightens up the scenery with sly humor. Lester digresses more as narrator, sometimes with quick jabs ("The truth is that folks fool themselves a lot worse than they get fooled by others") and sometimes in longer peregrinations, as in his commentary on time, which fills a paragraph at the start of "**Brer Rabbit, Brer Fox, and the Chickens.**" He takes potshots at feminists ("next thing you know, we'll be hearing about the Foxperson and the Lionperson"), whites ("Deep down I think they want to look as good as us black folks do"), and critics: "Somebody come telling me once that it was a story about stealing and that Brer Rabbit wasn't nothing but a liar and a thief and a scoundrel. Them words hurt me in the heart so bad I had to eat a gallon of Haagen-Dazs coffee ice cream before I started feeling better." But mostly he stays in touch with his characters and their fast-paced doing with witty aplomb. Says Brer Turtle in conning Brer Buzzard: "Two heads are better than one, especially when they on different bodies." Says Brer Bullfrog in conspiring against Brer Fox: "It takes two to make a trick. The tricker and the trickee." Lester also keeps some of the rhythmic passages from Joel Chandler Harris' original collection, as in the description of Brer Rabbit's journey to Aunt Mammy-Bammy Big-Money's swamp; there are lots of quotable lines as well as a few forced jokes ("Luciano Pavarotti Sings the Blues"). Storytellers will relish recreations of Taily-po, Brer Wolf and the Pigs, Teenchy-Tiny

Duck's Magical Satchel and other variants of familiar tale types from a unique narrator. Pinkney's watercolor compositions have loosened up considerably, with more flexible lines, satisfying tonal blends, and generous textural variations.

Kay McPherson

SOURCE: A review of *Further Tales of Uncle Remus: The Misadventures of Brer Rabbit, Brer Fox, Brer Wolf, the Doodang and Other Creatures,* in *School Library Journal,* Vol. 36, No. 5, May, 1990, p. 99.

As in **The Tales of Uncle Remus: The Adventures of Brer Rabbit** (1987) and **More Tales of Uncle Remus: Further Adventures of Brer Rabbit, His Friends, Enemies, and Others** (1988), Lester has retold "Uncle Remus" tales, although fewer will be familiar than in the previous books. Mostly, the antics of other animals are featured instead of those of the perennial hero, Brer Rabbit. But they're still a lively crowd, constantly trying to outsmart, outtrick, and outfox one another with varying degrees of success. Lester's excellent retellings once again use a forceful and audacious Uncle Remus as their narrator. The prose is spirited and witty with nimble and original turns of phrases that are highly entertaining, making the text a good read-aloud choice. Pinkney's watercolors, full-page spreads rich in the use of earth tones and other colors of nature, have a strong folk verve to them.

Kirkus Reviews

SOURCE: A review of *Further Tales of Uncle Remus: The Misadventures of Brer Rabbit, Brer Fox, Brer Wolf, the Doodang, and Other Creatures,* in *Kirkus Reviews,* Vol. LVIII, No. 11, June 1, 1990, p. 800.

This third volume in Lester's widely acclaimed updating of Harris' collection of African-American folk-tales includes 33 stories, with Lester's ironic voice growing even more distinctively his own. It's still dancing with irrepressible wit (the bear cub that eats an alligator "didn't leave the tail. And he ate the shadow for dessert"), comical anachronisms (Brer Turtle looks miserable, "like he needed a dime to call his therapist"), and sage observations ("She had so much sense that it was a bother to her sometimes"). Meanwhile, Lester himself is always in evidence, his wit razorsharp as he describes Miz Rabbit threatening her husband with her consciousness-raising group or calls a remark "the funniest thing they'd heard since. . 'Pavarotti Sings the Blues.'" He also stops more often to ruminate on things—like why folks don't think alike, or the meaning of time.

Pinkney's fine drawings and paintings continue to enhance the stories; they appear to even better advantage here thanks to better quality paper. A splendid addition to Lester's unique contribution to American folklore.

◫ *PRETEND YOU'RE A CAT* (written by Jean Marzollo, 1990)

Carolyn Phelan

SOURCE: A review of *Pretend You're a Cat,* in *Booklist,* Vol. 86, No. 18, May 15, 1990, pp. 1802-3.

Challenging preschoolers to imitate pigs, cows, birds, and other animals, this upbeat picture book will appeal to their imagination and sense of fun. For each animal, there's a double-page spread with a large illustration and a smaller inset within a border. Sometimes the animals appear in the larger picture, with the children imitating the animal illustration in the smaller; sometimes this scheme is reversed, but the visual interplay between the two illustrations in composition and detail makes an interesting study in itself. For each animal, the rhymed text asks questions, such as, "Can you chew? / Can you munch? / Can you moo / During lunch? / Can you drink / from a pail? / Touch your ear / With your tail? / What else can you do like a cow?" Simple in concept and inviting in design, this book will be a popular choice for story hours.

Ellen Fader

SOURCE: A review of *Pretend You're a Cat,* in *The Horn Book Magazine,* Vol. LXVI, No. 4, July-August, 1990, pp. 446-7.

An engaging exploration of imagination, movement, and animal characteristics. Eight lines of rhyming text describe each animal—"Can you bark? / Can you beg? / Can you scratch / With your leg? / Can you fetch? / Can you roll? / Can you dig / In a hole?"—and invite the child to think of other notable attributes of the animal. The variety of animals ranges from small bee, snake, and chick to large bear, cow, and seal; the expansive, uncluttered illustrations make all thirteen recognizable to even the very youngest child. Each illustration also includes from one to five preschool-age children mimicking the animal. Pinkney's decision to separate animal and child by boxing one or the other of them on each double-page spread, therefore allowing the majority of the animals to appear as wild and natural as possible, is ingenious. The children—an active, rough-and-tumble group of both sexes and various races—appear uninhibited and eager to participate. It's hard to imagine a child who wouldn't be tempted to join in the fun. A treat for young minds as well as young bodies.

◫ *HOME PLACE* (written by Crescent Dragonwagon, 1990)

Denise Wilms

SOURCE: A review of *Home Place,* in *Booklist,* Vol. 86, No. 22, August, 1990, p. 2171.

Blooming daffodils signal the remains of a house; a fam-

ily out hiking stumbles on the site and explores its remnants. The odd bits they find—a marble, a piece of plate, a china doll's arm—conjure up images of the family who once lived there. The echoes of their lives resonate through the pages as Pinkney's drawings show us a loving black family with a daughter who braids her long, black hair; a husband and wife who sit on the bed's edge one night watching a thunderstorm; and several other scenes that could have taken place at this homesite "as it might have been, or was, before / the house burned down, or everyone moved away / and the woods moved in." This mood piece captures that quiet, reflective feeling a country hike can prompt. As always, Pinkney's watercolors are lush and memorable. Here, they shimmer with shadowy detail and deep woodland hues that make the atmosphere almost palpable.

Publishers Weekly

SOURCE: A review of *Home Place,* in *Publishers Weekly,* Vol. 237, No. 35, August 31, 1990, p. 65.

On a backpacking trip, a girl and her parents uncover a bit of the past when they chance upon some daffodils—"cups lifted to trumpet / the good news / of spring." Nearby they find a chimney buried in honeysuckle, a stone foundation, a glass marble, the arm of a china doll. The girl imagines a black family living there in the past, what they ate, how they talked, the songs they sang. With striking craft, Dragonwagon limns a forgotten family's day-to-day existence. Pinkney's characteristically stunning, limpid watercolors are lush in shades of greens and browns, with touches of vibrant yellow in the flowers. His evocative images present a joyous mealtime, a child carefully ribboning her hair and hardworking Uncle Ferd, "wiping the sweat from his forehead." A nice touch in the book's attractive design is the fact that paintings of the present are full page, while those set in the past are "distanced" by their frames. This lovely work closes as the girl reluctantly leaves her imaginings to rejoin her parents in the present.

Betsy Hearne

SOURCE: A review of *Home Place,* in *Bulletin of the Center for Children's Books,* Vol. 44, No. 4, December, 1990, pp. 82-3.

Walking through the woods, a red-haired narrator discovers the ruins of a house and imagines a black family who might have lived there. "A chimney, made of stone, . . . a round blue glass marble, a nail. A horseshoe and a piece of plate. A small yellow bottle. A china doll's arm." From these she projects the lives of a boy and girl, husband and wife, uncle and grandparents, a clan eventually disbanded when its members die or move away: "still, whether anyone sees, or not, whether anyone listens, or not, the daffodils come up, to trumpet their good news forever and forever." Dragonwagon's text is evocative, and Pinkney's graphics are intensely atmospheric here. Even the endpapers simulate peeling wallpaper. In one picture that recalls images from Toni Morrison's *Beloved,* a woman seems to step through time as she passes from sunlight to shadow through a doorway. Always at home with nature spreads, the artist has quickened his portraiture with more graceful lines and planes; the family dinner makes a powerful scene. In spite of its picture-book format, this richly illustrated prose poem is better suited to independent readers beginning to develop a sophisticated sense of time. The words and art together will have an impact on children realizing their own ancestral past as part of history.

Carey Ayres

SOURCE: A review of *Home Place,* in *School Library Journal,* Vol. 37, No. 2, February, 1991, pp. 68-9.

Pinkney's richly hued water-colors, strong with a sense of place and personality, will help draw young readers into this dreamlike reminiscence of a large, lively family whose existence echoes only faintly in the present. Deep within a lush southern woodland is the site of an old homestead, visited only by deer, squirrels, and raccoons. One spring day, a child discovers this "home place." Spurred by her curiosity about the past, she digs in the ruined foundation and discovers a marble, a horseshoe, and the arm of a china doll. These objects lead her to envision the family whose home once stood there. Children love a mystery and this is a picture book that will invite them to think about the life cycle and the riddles of the past. Primary graders may need the help of an adult in raising and exploring these questions. Dragonwagon's short, rhythmic lines, laid out like poetry, have a sometimes mystical, sometimes conversational quality. Each full-page illustration lies opposite a brief block of text printed on a soft bone-colored background. One error must be mentioned, with regret. The flowers identified as honeysuckle in the text appear as morning glories in the illustration. The book has a simple dignity that is in complete harmony with the tone set by the author and the illustrator. A wonderfully evocative work.

IN FOR WINTER, OUT FOR SPRING (written by Arnold Adoff, 1991)

Ilene Cooper

SOURCE: A review of *In for Winter, Out for Spring,* in *Booklist,* Vol. 87, No. 11, February 1, 1991, p. 1128.

Often, no doubt too often, reviewers say things like, "This book is a perfect wedding of author and artist." Well, this one is. Adoff has worked with many fine illustrators, but never has his poetry been more radiantly expressed than in Pinkney's watercolor and colored-pencil art. Using the changing seasons as a framework, Adoff captures the big and small moments that occur within a year in the life of a young black girl, Rebecca. She is the family's youngest, "So They Call Me All Day Long / My Name Is Rebecca

at Breakfast Time / Becky by Lunch / But / Becka / Beck / Beck Come Wash Your Neck / Is Daddy's Supper Song." In energetic full-page pictures, Rebecca tosses leaves in the air, sleds down a hill with her brother, and worries with her family when a spring storm is on the way. But the book's farm setting also proffers scenes of nature, as birds, insects, and plants maintain their own life cycles through Rebecca's year. Perhaps the most striking picture—and one of the most affecting poems—relates how Granny's 92-year-old legs are aching: "Her Shin Bones Have Been Hurting Clear to Winter." Burdened, sage Granny, as depicted by Pinkney, stares straight out at the audience, old in years but with a glimmer of remembered happy times in her eyes. Throughout, Adoff's poems strike the right balance between good cheer and strong emotion. Not all is carefree on the farm, as when the western wind blows, bringing the sad smells of the paper mills and burning plastic, but the overwhelming feelings here are ones of connectedness, anticipation, and love. The poetry is formatted in eye-catching designs that encourage effective reading, whether by adults or by middle-graders who will be able to handle this themselves. Pinkney's dedication reads: "In celebration of the family." What a celebration indeed.

Leda Schubert

SOURCE: A review of *In for Winter, Out for Spring,* in *School Library Journal,* Vol. 37, No. 4, April, 1991, p. 108.

These 28 poems celebrate family life and the cycle of the seasons. Rebecca, the young black narrator, lives in a rural area with her parents and older brother, Aaron; her joy in her family and in the world around her permeates the pages. Poems are about gardening, finding a stray puppy, the weather, the pleasure of walking barefoot in freshly mown grass, and other seasonal events. Activities described are consciously nonsexist: Mom mows and Dad bakes. Adoff begins and ends with the family settling in for winter. Words and letters within words spread and compress across the generously sized pages; a few of the groupings seem contrived. All words are capitalized, which makes for a staccato reading. While the meanings are readily accessible, it will take sophisticated readers to read these poems alone. Pinkney's realistic watercolors stick closely to the text, fleshing out the words with carefully observed natural scenes. A double-page spread that contrasts fireflies with the end-of-summer tomatoes is particularly striking. Page design is nicely varied.

Ruth Ann Smith

SOURCE: A review of *In for Winter, Out for Spring,* in *Bulletin of the Center for Children's Books,* Vol. 44, No. 9, May, 1991, p. 209.

"Rebecca at Breakfast Time/ Becky By Lunch" is the exuberant young black narrator of this seasonal cycle of poems. Some are her simple outbursts of joy: "I/ Send/

This/ Spring/ Song/ Out/ For/ All/ To Shout/ And Sing/ Out For Spring/ Out For Spring/ Out For Spring." Others poems are observations about the natural world, some of them suggesting an older point of view than Rebecca's: "I Hear The Usual Thump/ And Know That One More/ Robin/ Has Hit The Glass Door/ In Love With Its Own/ Reflection." Understatement is sometimes used to comic effect: "Daddy Screamed A Perfect/ Cartoon Scream And Dropped The Heavy Cream/ And Dropped His Cake Pan/ And Ran/ Out Of Our/ Warm/ Kitchen/ Faster Than The Mouse Was/ Running The Other Way." The idyllic life of this rural family is disturbed only by the threat of storms, or of polluted air when the wind blows the wrong way ("We Stay In For the Rest of the Day"). With his variegated watercolor and pencil illustrations, Pinkney captures the mood or essence of each poem. Purple crocuses burst through snow, and dead leaves come "Out For Spring," while a wary, chased-from-the-kitchen mouse looks on. A master of color, Pinkney uses a full palette of spring greens. His flora and fauna are meticulously rendered, but the human figures, though lovingly portrayed, present occasional difficulties with their awkwardly drawn heads or faces. Because the uninhibited layout of the free verse poetry may be confusing to younger readers, this book would benefit from one-on-one sharing. It certainly invites repeated readings.

THE MAN WHO KEPT HIS HEART IN A BUCKET (written by Sonia Levitin, 1991)

Stephanie Zvirin

SOURCE: A review of *The Man Who Kept His Heart in a Bucket,* in *Booklist,* Vol. 88, No. 1, September 1, 1991, pp. 62-3.

The bold watercolors that sweep across the pages of this picture book demand a strong story line. Levitin delivers a respectable one, blending familiar folk- and fairy-tale conventions into a sentimental tale of yore about a passionless tinsmith, who keeps his heart "safe" in a bucket so it cannot be broken. One day, while refreshing his heart in the water of a stream, the young man encounters a golden carp. Leaping from the water, the fish turns into a lovely maiden who steals the precious heart and runs away, challenging the tinsmith to solve a riddle in order to regain it. Subtle at the outset, the tale becomes more surefooted as the solution to the riddle is sought. The pull of Pinkney's art, however, remains constant. Each character is expressively rendered, and the paper, buff colored like an old tintype, vibrates with splashes of color and intriguing period detail.

Robert Strong

SOURCE: A review of *The Man Who Kept His Heart in a Bucket,* in *Bulletin of the Center for Children's Books,* Vol. 45, No. 5, January, 1992, p. 131.

"Jack's heart had once been broken," so now Jack keeps it safe in a bucket that he carries along while plying his trade as a metalsmith. Safe, but useless—Jack can't work up any enthusiasm for the baker's bread, the piper's music, or the holding of a baby that "squirms and cries," all three of which are offered to him in exchange for his work. But when Jack stops at the lake to get water for his heart, the story shifts from a reasonable parable to a confusing hash of the fictive and the folklike, the literal and the symbolic. A carp jumps into the pail, turns into a beautiful maiden, and steals Jack's heart, literally, and, as it turns out, figuratively, as we discover when Jack goes back into town in search of the answer to the maiden's riddle, an answer demanded for return of the heart. For some reason, Jack then melts down the bucket he had held his heart in; for some other reason the melted bucket turns into a golden heart. And, in gathering the answers to the maiden's three-part riddle, Jack discovers that he has a heart and that it is, as the townspeople point out, "in the right place after all." The riddling is irrelevant, the two hearts are confusing, the story's conclusion is filled with contradictions that have none of the mystery of paradox—they're just bewildering. Pinkney's watercolors feature his familiar rural landscapes; the facial distortions of the characters further confound the mixed messages of the story.

BACK HOME (written by Gloria Jean Pinkney, 1992)

Hazel Rochman

SOURCE: A review of *Back Home,* in *Booklist,* Vol. 88, No. 20, June 15, 1992, p. 1834.

Like Donald Crews' *Bigmama's* this celebrates an African American child's discovery of her family's rural roots. From the moment that Ernestine steps off the train in Lamberton, North Carolina, she's enfolded in the joyful embrace of her smiling aunt and uncle. Full-page sunlit paintings in watercolor and pencil set the warmly individualized portraits within a dappled summer landscape of earth tones and shimmering greens. Small pictures focus on farm implements or interior scenes, like the glowing still-life of peaches and paring knife. There's not much story here, but it is more than a simple mood piece. Even while she enjoys the flowers and the farm animals and the sweet scent of freshly baked biscuits, Ernestine yearns for her cousin Jack to like her. But he's put off by her fancy clothes and city ways. She changes into her mother's old overalls, but he still embarrasses her and treats her like a clumsy stranger. The turnaround comes one day when they drive to where Ernestine was born. She loves the abandoned farmhouse and swears that someday she'll fix it up. Then the book's one wordless double-spread painting captures the exquisite moment when Jack discovers that he likes her. Absorbed in the place, she doesn't see his startled look of admiration, and the story never spells it out. But the cousins are connected after that, friends now, both glad she's coming back next summer.

At the corner store Mr. Jessup told Mirandy that a great-aunt of his from Ipsala, Mississippi, said to put black pepper in Brother Wind's footprints. That would make him sneeze. "While he's busy sneezing, slip up behind and throw a quilt over him."

Mirandy rushed home and got the black-pepper mill and one of Ma Dear's quilts. Wasn't long 'fore Brother Wind came strolling through the meadow, his wind cape hovering gentle-like over the grasses.

Sneaking up behind him, Mirandy commenced to grinding pepper. Then she threw the quilt. But—*whoosh!* Brother Wind was gone.

From Mirandy and Brother Wind, *written by Patricia C. McKissack. Illustrated by Jerry Pinkney.*

Betsy Hearne

SOURCE: A review of *Back Home,* in *Bulletin of the Center for Children's Books,* Vol. 46, No. 1, September, 1992, p. 21.

Like Donald Crews' *Bigmama's* this depicts a city child's summer trip south to stay with country relatives. The graphic evocation of a past time and place radiates from lightfilled watercolors dappled with a blend of hues. The holding power of the story depends primarily on a friendship that develops between visiting Ernestine and the older cousin whom she yearns to please. This child's-eye view of North Carolina in the 1930s hints of neither poverty nor racism; the focus is on overalls, goats, peaches, and family dynamics. Ernestine's truck ride to the tumbledown cabin where she was born proves an episodic highlight. She's young enough to declare, with sweeping conviction, "Someday . . . I'm going to fix it up." An experience not even marred by bug bites, this is about as happy as memories get, especially visualized through the haze of Pinkney's euphoric pastorale.

Shirley Wilton

SOURCE: A review of *Back Home,* in *School Library Journal,* Vol. 38, No. 9, September, 1992, pp. 209-10.

A long train ride takes Ernestine to visit her great-uncle

and aunt in North Carolina, to sleep in the house where her mama grew up, and to visit her own birthplace. Cousin Jack teases her for her city ways, but she quickly learns about raising goats and canning peaches, and by the time she has been to church and visited her grandmama's grave, Ernestine looks forward to a future visit. This is more a reminiscence than a plotted story, warm with Southern summer and family affection, a vignette of times gone by and roots rediscovered. Jerry Pinkney's full-page watercolors complement this account of a young girl's journey several decades ago. Their sketchy, impressionistic style softens the rural poverty and strengthens the genuine family feelings that greet Ernestine. Like Donald Crews's *Bigmama's,* **Back Home** draws on personal history and celebrates the lives of an African-American family.

Ann A. Flowers

SOURCE: A review of *Back Home,* in *The Horn Book Magazine,* Vol. LXIX, No. 1, January-February, 1993, p. 83.

A nostalgic remembrance of a young girl's visit to the old family home is enhanced by Jerry Pinkney's glorious illustrations of a time not so long past. Young Ernestine goes alone by train from her home in the North to visit relatives in North Carolina. Heartily welcomed by her uncle and aunt, Ernestine also hopes her cousin Jack will like her. But he ridicules her for her city clothes and ignorance of country ways and plays mean tricks on her. Eventually, however, he is won over, and Ernestine enjoys her visit, especially a ride to see the abandoned house where she was born. The story is very simple, but the illustrations are an explosion of textures and colors—quilts and overalls, baskets and peaches, linoleum and weathered wood—and, clearly, kind and loving people. Evocative of a gentle past.

DRYLONGSO (written by Virginia Hamilton, 1992)

Hazel Rochman

SOURCE: A review of *Drylongso*, in *Booklist*, Vol. 88, No. 21, July, 1992, p. 1938.

In an understated story of drought and hard times and longing for rain, a great writer and a great artist have pared down their rich, exuberant styles to something quieter but no less intense. Drylongso is a tall boy in overalls and cap who comes to the house of a small girl named Lindy one day in 1975 during a great dust storm. Her mother and father take him in. After the storm, he gives them seeds to plant; with a dowsing rod, he helps them find water; they prepare and plant the land; and then he leaves. The characters are vital and lovingly individualized, set against a landscape washed in thick drifts of pale red dust. Pinkney's paintings in watercolor, pastel, and pencil have a flowing softness, like snow. With Lindy and her parents we feel the long, unbroken stillness and heat; then the drama of the storm, like a high brown wall moving toward them in a rusty, choking haze; then the arrival of the stranger, the planting, and the hope of renewal. Kids will get the eloquent environmental message ("Folks had overused the land. Made it rise up") and the warning of drought to come. As always with Hamilton, her scholarly note is as fascinating as the story: she explains that *drylongso* originally meant drought-so-long and eventually came to mean anything commonplace. Her words are plain, but she makes Drylongso a folk hero, both ordinary and mysterious, and reveals the mythic in the everyday.

Kirkus Reviews

SOURCE: A review of *Drylongso*, in *Kirkus Reviews*, Vol. LX, No. 19, October 1, 1992, p. 1255.

In a concluding note, Hamilton discusses the origins of the name she gives Drylongso, "a youth imbued with simple human kindness. Not only does he personify drought, but he also represents the longing for rain." Moreover, he's "a folk hero" and "the symbol of fate." The word itself, probably from the Gullah, means "drought" or, metaphorically, "ordinary" or "boring"; here, it provides a multilayered theme for an evocative story about a farm family enduring the drought of 1975 until, running in front of a dust storm, Drylongso takes refuge with them. While the storm rages outside and they battle the grit

within, Drylongso converses with little Lindy's dad and Mamalou, telling jokes and stories about other droughts and explaining how farming practices like plowing have led to the dust storms. Next morning, he presents a gift of seed corn and potatoes; before he leaves, he uses a "dowser" to locate a spring.

Told with elegant simplicity, the story's steady focus on elementals—earth, water, seed, the love of parent and child, home—gives it the mythic quality Hamilton intended. Meanwhile, Pinkney surpasses his own best work with his marvelous watercolors, their soft tones muted with the color of dust, the suble relationships among the characters enriched by every detail of stance and expression, the prairie setting and homely household evoked in spare compositions of rare harmony. A lovely tribute to all good people who still know how to negotiate peaceably with the earth on which they depend.

A STARLIT SOMERSAULT DOWNHILL (written by Nancy Willard, 1993)

Shirley Wilton

SOURCE: A review of *A Starlit Somersault Downhill*, in *School Library Journal*, Vol. 39, No. 9, September, 1993, p. 221.

A great brown bear offers to share the warmth and shelter of his hibernation cave with a small rabbit, but once he is securely tucked into the dark with his "prudent friend," a "sleeping stone," the rabbit regrets his decision. Despite frost outside and the dangers of predators, he opts to be free, to leap and somersault through snow and starlight. Willard's short, rhyming poem carries a potent message about the differences set by nature as well as a subtler message about the choice between a dull, safe existence and an exciting life filled with challenges and risk. However, some of the lines are awkward, and their meaning may be difficult for the intended audience to grasp. Pinkney's watercolor paintings in earth tones and winter whites complement the text. They fill the pages to the edges and burst forth in a last spread that unfolds to triple size. This collaboration between a Newbery medalist and an award-winning artist whose pictures enthrall results in a good book for children to see and talk about.

Ilene Cooper

SOURCE: A review of *A Starlit Somersault Downhill*, in *Booklist*, Vol. 90, No. 3, October 1, 1993, p. 355.

With a rhyme that's pleasant to the ear, if not always clearly understandable to young listeners, Willard introduces a bear who invites a bunny to share his lair during the long, snowy winter. The rabbit agrees, but as soon as the bear falls asleep, the rabbit has second thoughts: "Some go in green, some go in white. / The snow's footfall is very light. / It is not wise for us, dearbear, / when snow combs silver from her hair / and stars are shears and hills are sheep, / it will not do to fall asleep. / How inconvenient to play dead!" Like lightning, the rabbit is out the door of the cave, back into the sunlight. Pinkney's impressive two-page spreads fill the pages with stars, snow, leaves, trees, and of course, the two unlikely roommates. Graceful in both picture and word, this creates a mood that transcends the intricacies of the text.

Betsy Hearne

SOURCE: A review of *A Starlit Somersault Downhill,* in *Bulletin of the Center for Children's Books,* Vol. 47, No. 4, December, 1993, p. 136.

As she did in "Blake Leads a Walk on the Milky Way" in *A Visit to William Blake's Inn,* Willard has set up a dialogue between creatures of opposite viewpoints, here a bear preparing to hibernate and a rabbit reluctant to confine itself to the secure cave of its ursine friend: "The rabbit sighed. 'How ripe and sweet/ this patch of clover by my feet!/ The fields are broad, the hills are wide./ A pity we should stay inside.'" Even when the cold comes and the rabbit tries to settle down, the stars and hills call irresistibly. Pinkney is at ease with animal anatomy, and his warm brown watercolors, turning gray-toned as winter snows take over, are layered into double spreads of striking composition. In fact, the pictures are so realistically drafted and textured that they seem oddly literal in accompaniment to the fantastical text. For instance, one stanza—"They carried water from the spring/ and laid out all the breakfast things/ and washed their faces in the stream"—is illustrated with a scene of the bear catching a fish. This intensely dynamic view of the natural environment is slightly out of sync with the daintily anthropomorphic world reflected by the verse. Later, a wolf seems to threaten the rabbit by looming near the cave while the rabbit is deciding to emerge, but this element of conflict evaporates. As a picture book, the whole is less successful than its separate parts of verse and art, but it will nevertheless provide lilting sounds and richly rewarding sights for a preschool audience.

THE LAST TALES OF UNCLE REMUS
(written by Julius Lester, 1994)

Betsy Hearne

SOURCE: A review of *The Last Tales of Uncle Remus,* in *Bulletin of the Center for Children's Books,* Vol. 47, No. 6, February, 1994, pp. 179-80.

One way to hang onto a book you love is to slow down and read the last page over and over to keep it from ending. Such is the reluctance with which I finished *The Last Tales of Uncle Remus,* the final volume in a series of four collections celebrating the trickster who outflanked most of the animals around, be they big, little, smart, or dumb. Brer Rabbit made no allowances for political cor-

rectness. This, plus the fact that Lester updates the storytelling voice of Uncle Remus, has drawn flack from African-American literati as notable as June Jordan (*New York Times Book Review,* May 17, 1987). Alice Walker's not too crazy about Joel Chandler Harris, either (see "The Dummy in the Window: Joel Chandler Harris and the Invention of Uncle Remus" in Walker's *Living by the Word*). Uncle Remus was, after all, an Uncle Tom who accepted the outrage of slavery and passed on his priceless traditions to a little white boy. Or was he and did he? These stories are the soul of subversive irreverence, and maybe Remus/Harris had a trick up his sleeve in targeting a gullible white audience that dominated the marketplace and—all unawares of being the butt of the joke—made sure the stories went public. A more cultural point has to do with the commonality of tricksters to all societies. Any psychologically attuned folklorist (or folklorically attuned psychologist) will tell you the same thing Lester does in replying to Jordan, " . . . the trickster is in each of us. He is created in our image. Our task is to receive him and thereby uncover our humanity—if we dare." (Letters, *New York Times Book Review,* June 14, 1987). . .

Storytellers using the book as a resource will be happy to meet up with variants of other familiar tale types. **"The Adventures of Simon and Susanna"** contains motifs from Baba Yaga and several Jack tales. Both Wicked John and Big Sixteen lurk in **"The Blacksmith and the Devil." "The Little Boy and His Dogs"** is a twin of "Wiley and the Hairy Man," and **"How Tinktum Tidy Recruited an Army for the King"** recalls "Travels of a Fox." Folklore is one place where African and European influences were integrated early on. Ghost stories vie with tales of transformation. You're bound to find several suited to your own particular telling. The humor ranges from sass to slapstick violence; take your pick. Everybody gets a fair share of backhanded ridicule, including feminists, chauvinists, ageists, handicapists, and racists. Sometimes the storyteller confines himself to sideswiping one group: "that's how men can be—adding two and two and coming up with seventy-seven." Sometimes he manages to insult two with one blow, as in his under-the-breath indictment of both politicians and voters: "You don't have to be smart to be king or president. (I could name presidents who didn't have *any* brains)." Ultimately, like Brer Rabbit, he makes fun of just about anything on two, four, or seven legs.

Jerry Pinkney, as he has done for the other books, supplies realistically detailed watercolors to illustrate a rustic world of talking animals invaded by the occasional stray human. Pinkney's drafting has relaxed, smoothed out, and mellowed just as a good story does over time, and he manages to underscore Lester's sly tone by treating the cast of characters with seriously deadpan respect. Respect is a key word here. That's what Lester shows for the largest body of African-American folklore collected in this country. You can't get any more respectful of a cultural tradition than recharging the elements that helped it survive—and that affirm its kinship with other peoples of the world.

THE SUNDAY OUTING (written by Gloria Jean Pinkney, 1994)

Hazel Rochman

SOURCE: A review of *The Sunday Outing*, in *Booklist*, Vol. 90, No. 17, May 1, 1994, p. 1609.

Back Home (1992) was about Ernestine's first visit to her aunt and uncle's farm in North Carolina, where she was born. This upbeat picture book is set just before that visit, when Ernestine dreams of going on that journey "back home." Every Sunday Ernestine rides the trolley with her great-aunt Odessa to the Philadelphia railway station to watch the trains pass through; Ernestine listens to family stories and imagines herself riding south to the farm. She saves and plans and prepares with her parents and her great-aunt, and finally, all on her own, she boards the Silver Star and waves goodbye. This time the full-page illustrations in colored pencil and watercolors are of a city neighborhood, including the bustling station platform. Inside Ernestine's home the rooms are filled with light and intricately patterned clothes and furnishings. Gloria Pinkney draws on her own memories to create a sense of the period and a sense of childhood. On the station platform, Ernestine is bursting with excitement; in contrast, her father is quiet, remembering. The members of the family are strongly individualized, and they are connected. Surrounded by their love, this is one happy child.

Betsy Hearne

SOURCE: A review of *The Sunday Outing*, in *Bulletin of the Center for Children's Books*, Vol. 47, No. 11, July-August, 1994, p. 370.

In this prequel to the Pinkneys' picture book *Back Home*, young Ernestine yearns to take the train down south for a visit with her relatives. At last her aunt, with whom she makes Sunday picnic expeditions to the Philadelphia train station, suggests that she think of some way to save her folks money, "so they'll be able to buy that ticket." Ernestine gives up her new school clothes, Mama volunteers the money she's saved toward an electric sewing machine, Daddy postpones getting a new tool set at work, and Ernestine is on her way, slightly scared and wildly excited. We know from the previous book that she has an unforgettable time, but you'd better have it on hand for young listeners who want to find out what happens after Ernestine boards the Silver Star. Gloria Pinkney knows how to play out a scenario, and Jerry Pinkney's art is as lyrically decorative in an urban setting as it was in the rural outdoors. With subtle color blends, he emphasizes contrasting patterns in wallpaper backgrounds, mottled textures, and playful chiaroscuro. Fabrics are showcased in almost every illustration. In fact, Ernestine's sacrifice seems slightly diminished by her eyecatching wardrobe, but the real centerpiece of the action is a warmly supportive African-American family, and any young listener who's longed for an excursion will identify with Ernestine's anticipation.

JOHN HENRY (written by Julius Lester, 1994)

Jerry Pinkney

SOURCE: "John Henry," in *The Horn Book Magazine*, Vol. LXXII, No. 1, January-February, 1996, pp. 32-4.

[The following excerpt is Pinkney's acceptance speech for the 1995 Boston Globe/Horn Book *Award for best picture book.]*

Thank you for this prestigious award, and congratulations to my fellow award winners. It is an honor for me that *John Henry* is in the company of such notable books. Special thanks to Phyllis Fogelman for her extraordinary publishing instincts; to Atha Tehon for outstanding art direction; and to Gloria Jean for her patience, support, and enthusiasm while I was shaping the vision for this book. Finally, how fortunate I was when Julius Lester embraced the idea to create the text. For who better to take on the task than Julius, a civil rights advocate, folksinger, author, and educator?

I have always been interested in visual images and drew throughout my growing-up years—as a way of creating my own space and as a way of expressing myself. Growing up in a small house in Philadelphia, there were few books for me and my five siblings to read and few stories told. There were, however, three that I remember: *Little Black Sambo*, "Tales of Uncle Remus," and "John Henry."

Little Black Sambo was one of those few books that I owned and would read over and over again. The reds, greens, blues, and that wonderful butter yellow. A palette that is as vibrant and fresh in my mind's eye as ever.

When the Uncle Remus tales were read to me, Brer Rabbit and I became friends and have remained so—even through the labor of creating over one hundred illustrations for the four volumes of Brer Rabbit tales retold by Julius Lester. I welcomed the chance to bring life to characters who shared my growing-up years and who helped shape my interest in telling stories through pictures.

And as far back as I can recall, I have sustained the memory of the legend of John Henry, especially the part about him winning a contest with the steam drill. Whether I was told or read the tale or heard the ballad escapes me. Nevertheless, the story has stayed with me.

Little Black Sambo, Brer Rabbit, and John Henry—these three heroes from my childhood gave support and comfort in a world where almost all heroes in literature were white. Years later, these stories were held up to a different light and disappeared from bookstores, schools, and libraries.

I am not sure why it took me so long to unlock John Henry from his place in my memories. After all, he had been a part of my most cherished remembrance of African-American perseverance, along with Harriet Tubman, Frederick Douglass, and Sojourner Truth. And John Henry and High John de Conquer were the only tall-tale black heroes to come from that period in American history.

I was fascinated with the realization that black heroes did not exist in African-American folklore until after the Civil War. Before emancipation, African-American story characters, like the enslaved, had only two weapons that they were able to use: good old-fashioned common sense and—like my friend Brer Rabbit—the wiles of the trickster.

After illustrating two projects for *National Geographic*—"The Underground Railroad" and "The African Slave Trade from Ghana to South America"—I became hooked on studying and learning more about the history of the Americas. My research enabled me to place John Henry, though a mythical character, in a staging based on a real place and historic facts. Interestingly, the retellings I read of the tale did not match the images from my childhood. The vision of how best to portray John Henry came from the warm and rich feelings that I carried from my childhood into my adulthood.

At each step in my research, the doors to piecing the story together opened wider. Working with the West Virginia Division of Culture and History and the U.S. Department of the Interior at Harpers Ferry, West Virginia, I gathered information on John Henry and on his particular era of the building of America.

The story takes place in West Virginia during the time of the construction of the Big Bend Tunnel for the C&O Railroad. At that time, West Virginia was still wilderness. The John Henry that emerged from the collaboration between Julius Lester and me represents and symbolizes the men and boys who made up the crews, whose muscles built the roads and railroads in this country in the late 1800s. One can only imagine the stamina and endurance of the men, both black and white, required for such dangerous work. I tried to give reverence to the men by instilling in each person I portrayed a sense of his own history.

How blessed and privileged I am to draw upon my childhood stories and have the opportunity to share them with you through my illustrations today. For with this book we strove to create an African-American hero that would inspire all.

My dedication reads, "In memory of my father, James H., my John Henry."

Elizabeth Bush

SOURCE: A review of *John Henry*, in *Bulletin of the Center for Children's Books*, Vol. 48, No. 2, October, 1994, p. 54.

The newest version of this popular American tall tale bursts to life under the reprise collaboration of Lester and Pink-

ney. Based on published versions of the folk song and some verses from Lester's memory, this tale includes Henry's showdown with Ferret-Faced Freddy and some nifty rock smashing for a road building crew as prelude to his famous race against the steam drill. Lester's telling, while accessible to kindergartners, transcends an age ceiling with its front-porch humor and intimacy. Witty similes and shameless hyperboles abound, inclusive language advocates take a tweaking as Henry sips a "soda mom," and even the Almighty gets into the act, hollering, "It's getting too noisy down there." Had Pinkney chosen to match Lester's tone with comical sight gags, the rendering could have dissolved into farce. Instead the earthy, craggy watercolors capture the sober, thoughtful side of Henry's story—his tenuous relationship with his surroundings as both larger-than-life hero and smaller-than-nature mortal. Henry's chiseled muscles appear to be chipped out of the very mountain he conquers, and the single scene in which he clearly stands apart from the rocky terrain, framed by the tunnel's mouth and a victory rainbow, is immediately followed by that of his own conqueror—his funeral train. The successful melding of rich prose and challenging visual imagery should make this the preferred choice among extant print versions of the tale.

Jack Zipes

SOURCE: "Power Rangers of Yore," in *The New York Times Book Review*, November 13, 1994, p. 30.

It is a joy to read tall tales and legends that revise American folklore in provocative ways and are just as interesting for adults as they are for children. In the case of . . . *John Henry*, we have . . . [a poignant example] of how contemporary writers and illustrators use fabulous stories to suggest that we still have a lot to learn from folk heroes, even if they may not have existed. . . .

[There are] few well-known legends about black heroes in American history, and Julius Lester's respectful version of *John Henry*, with exquisite watercolor illustrations by Jerry Pinkney, brings out the dignity of a man who demonstrated that "dying ain't important. Everybody does that. What matters is how well you do your living."

It is unclear whether there ever was a real John Henry, but we do know that the Big Bend Tunnel on the Chesapeake & Ohio Railroad was built in the Allegheny Mountains between 1870 and 1873, and that a former slave named John Henry may have worked on the tunnel. Ballads and songs about his fabled deeds arose during the latter part of the 19th century and recounted his different exploits. At one point, it was said, he defeated a steam drill in a contest to see whether machine or man was the better worker. John Henry won but died in the end. Despite his death, his noble victory formed the basis of his legend.

Julius Lester's eloquent prose in *John Henry* incorporates

light, humorous remarks and sayings throughout the narrative. It is John Henry's integrity that becomes the central concern of the story, not his power, and Mr. Pinkney's realistic illustrations, which employ a subtle blend of colors to bring out the interconnections of the man with nature and his society, are intended to highlight John Henry's exemplary role in American folklore.

MINTY: A STORY OF YOUNG HARRIET TUBMAN (written by Alan Schroeder, 1996)

Publishers Weekly

SOURCE: A review of *Minty: A Story of Young Harriet Tubman,* in *Publishers Weekly,* Vol. 243, No. 21, May 20, 1996, p. 259.

This fictionalized account of Tubman's childhood on a Maryland plantation provides a cruel snapshot of life as a slave and the horrid circumstances that fueled the future Underground Railroad leader's passion and determination. At eight years old, Minty (so-called as a nickname for Araminta) boils with rebellion against her brutal owners and bucks their authority whenever possible. Deeming her too clumsy for housework, Mrs. Brodas banishes Minty to harder work in the fields. Toiling in the hot sun only intensifies Minty's desire to run away to freedom, and soon her father teaches her how to survive in the wild, so that she'll be prepared to make her break one day. Schroeder's choice of lively vignettes rather than a more traditional biography is a wise one. With color and feeling he humanizes a historic figure, coaxing readers to imagine or research the rest of the story. Pinkney's full-bodied watercolors evoke a strong sense of time and place. Laudably, Pinkney's scenes consistently depict young Minty's point of view, giving the harshness of her reality more resonance for readers. A formal author's note follows the text and both Schroeder and Pinkney have included personal messages about the history of the book project. A firm stepping stone toward discussions of slavery and U.S. history.

Maria B. Salvadore

SOURCE: A review of *Minty: A Story of Young Harriet Tubman,* in *The Horn Book Magazine,* Vol. LXXII, No. 5, September-October, 1996, pp. 589-90.

According to the author's note, Harriet Tubman's "cradle name" was Araminta; hence the nickname Minty. Minty—born around 1820 on the Brodas Plantation on Maryland's Eastern shore—was strong-willed, independent, outspoken; characteristics neither desired nor tolerated in a slave. So Mistress Brodas moves the eight-year-old Minty from house slave to field hand—much more arduous work—with the threat of "being sold South" always present. As Minty's desire for freedom grows, so does her unwillingness to tolerate the abuse and cruelty of plantation life. Recognizing her growing impatience, Minty's father teaches her survival skills: how to identify the North

Star (known as the "Drinking Gourd"), how to swim, how to read moss on trees. Minty knows instinctively that one day she will find the road that, "when she had the courage, would carry her to freedom." This fictionalized account of the early life of the woman who became known as the conductor of the Underground Railroad is based on facts gleaned from the 1869 biography *Harriet Tubman: The Moses of Her People.* Quick action and dialogue create a taut story, although it is illustration that shapes the characters. Pinkney's well-crafted watercolors portray a highly idealized young Harriet (as well as parents and extended family) while depicting an unswervingly angry Mrs. Brodas. Pencil lines emerge from the translucent paints to provide detail and depth.

SAM AND THE TIGERS (written by Julius Lester, 1996)

Lambeth Hochwald

SOURCE: "Little Book, Big Controversy," in *Publishers Weekly,* Vol. 243, No. 11, July 29, 1996, pp. 32-3.

If Helen Bannerman, author and illustrator of *The Story of Little Black Sambo,* were alive today, she'd have the chance to read two new interpretations of her controversial picture book, both due out this September. Most people have some recollection of *Sambo,* the mini-picture book Bannerman created for her daughters in 1899; many have a love/hate relationship with the tale. Generations of readers have loved the story because Bannerman weaves a fantasy that both children and adults can have fun with. Not only is Sambo a spunky child hero who manages to foil a pack of bullying tigers who'd like to have him for lunch, but he ends up outwitting them.

At the same time, other readers have registered complaints about the story, beginning in the late 1930s when public protest against the treatment of blacks in children's literature began. The root of the discomfort with the tale was the derogatory names Bannerman gave her characters (Sambo's parents were named Black Mumbo and Black Jumbo) and the stereotypical, turn-of-the-century illustrations: the family is depicted with minstrel-like qualities, full red lips and exaggerated white coloring of the eyes.

It's the characters' names and the illustrations that have been most criticized for decades, and form the basis for the book's removal from many libraries since 1970. . . .

Now, almost a century after *Sambo*'s publication, Dial Books for Young Readers and Michael di Capua Books at HarperCollins have reclaimed the story, casting aside the reprehensible images and character names associated with it. It's an amazing case of serendipity that Dial is bringing out **Sam and the Tigers** and HarperCollins is bringing out *The Story of Little Babaji* [by Fred Marcellino] in the very same season. . . .

Sam and the Tigers' illustrator Jerry Pinkney says he

also thought he and his partner, author Julius Lester, were the only ones working on a rendition of the story. "For me, this book is a natural step in finding stories that we can reclaim," he says. "Because I'm African American, I was touched by a lot of the original illustrations. The illustrations affected me emotionally and personally. Certainly Julius and I can bring to it some element of being wounded by the various versions."

Dial's *Sam and the Tigers* sets its main character Sam in the American South of the '20s, includes more contemporary language and has a much larger trim size than the original. This is the third time Lester and Pinkney have teamed up to place a long-maligned story into a more positive framework. In 1987, they published four new volumes retelling the Uncle Remus tales; in 1994 they retold the story of John Henry.

Lester's interest in the story was piqued by some Internet discussions he joined early on, [Dial president and publisher Phyllis] Fogelman points out. "Those discussions gave him the idea of retelling the story," she says. "Sambo has a folktale aspect to it. It's become part of black literature in a seriously negative way, whether you like it or not." . . .

It's likely that debate about Sambo will resurface with the publication of these new books. "I had always thought of *Little Black Sambo* as negative," says Pinkney. "We're trying to make it positive. If the story is frozen and we only think of it as demeaning, nothing will be served. We wanted to unthaw it, see it in the context of the time period and make something of a rich story."

Betsy Hearne

SOURCE: A review of *Sam and the Tigers: A New Telling of Little Black Sambo,* in *Bulletin of the Center for Children's Books,* Vol. 49, No. 11, July-August, 1996, p. 378.

For living such a long and argufied life, Little Black Sambo sure looks fresh here—new words coming out of his mouth, new mouth entirely, for that matter. Sam, son of Sam and Sam, all residents of Sam-sam-sa-mara, picks out his own clothes at the bazaar, thank you. "Uh-uh. That ain't me," he tells his mother, who's holding up a conservative brown jacket and white shirt. So Sam proceeds to pick out a wardrobe that only a tiger could love— a red coat, yellow shirt, silver shoes, green umbrella, and purple trousers. There's a little hitch in the logic here, because this is a land "where the animals and the people lived and worked together like they didn't know they weren't supposed to," but suddenly Sam meets five tigers out to turn him into lunch. Piece by colorful piece, Sam trades his new duds for his life; he gets them all back when the tigers turn into butter, as everybody knows, and the ensuing pancakes make a happy meal for the more civilized creatures, Brer Rabbit included (life is full of ironies). Helen Bannerman could ask for no sharper successors than Julius Lester and Jerry Pinkney (each of whom provides a note explaining his history with and interpre-

tation of the story). These two tricksters have delivered us with a politically correct but fully humorful version of a story that has survived, on the strength of an airtight plot, many justified accusations of racism. Lester honors that plot, jazzes up the style, and gives the artist a venue for roguishly tongue-in-cheek illustrations. Pinkney's tigers are perfectly proportioned, and their expressive faces and postures outstripe an already colorful cast. This is not quite as classically spare as the earliest version and those in between, but it sure is fun and you can use it in your library or classroom without a quiver of unease. Finally.

Donna L. Scanton

SOURCE: A review of *Sam and the Tigers: A New Telling of Little Black Sambo,* in *School Library Journal,* Vol. 42, No. 8, August, 1996, p. 126.

Lester and Pinkney reclaim "Little Black Sambo," the tale of a black child who outwits a pack of bullying tigers, from its negative, racist connotations. The reteller places the story squarely in the fantasy land of Sam-sam-sa-mara, a place " . . . where the animals and the people lived and worked together like they didn't know they weren't supposed to." All the humans are named Sam, which allows for a touch of Monty Pythonesque humor. Lester narrates the story in what he describes as a "southern black storyteller's voice." He deftly employs devices such as hyperbolic similes (Sam's jacket is "as red as a happy heart"), repetition, and understated humor. The rolling, lilting narrative is a model of harmony, clarity, and meticulously chosen detail, accessible to listeners as well as to independent readers. Pinkney's lively pencil-and-watercolor illustrations sprawl extravagantly across double spreads and are smoothly integrated with the narrative. The pictures are filled with motion, contrast, and appealing, often whimsical details. In their notes, both the author and the illustrator comment on the goals of their collaboration and their personal feelings about the original story. Some may feel that there is too much historical and cultural baggage attached to "Little Black Sambo" to make any retelling acceptable, but those who approach this thoughtful and entirely appealing book with open hearts and minds are in for a wonderful time.

Publishers Weekly

SOURCE: A review of *Sam and the Tigers,* in *Publishers Weekly,* Vol. 243, No. 32, August 5, 1996, p. 441.

Troubled by the racist trappings—the characters' names and the stereotypical illustrations—of *The Story of Little Black Sambo,* but drawn nonetheless to its hero and its humor, Lester and Pinkney set out to reinvent the tale. Their interpretation is more freewheeling than Fred Marcellino's (*The Story of Little Babaji*), and they depart frequently and ingeniously from Bannerman's version. The new book's protagonist is simply Sam; the setting is the land of Sam-sam-sa-mara, where *everyone* is named Sam— a touch that not only defuses any echoes of the original hero's derogatory name, but allows for many wonderfully absurd exchanges ("Sam looked at Sam. Sam shrugged. Sam shrugged back. . . ."). Using the lively Southern black voice of his Uncle Remus retellings, Lester creates a savvy, comically streetwise hero who quickly learns to anticipate the tigers' muggings ("'You know the routine,' said the Tiger. Sam nodded and took off his pants. 'Take 'em.'") while losing none of his own sass. Pinkney's lavish illustrations—a feast of figures, color, expressions and detail—pick up and run with the expansive mood of the text. A hip and hilarious retelling that marries the essence of the original with an innovative vision of its own.

Barbara Bader

SOURCE: "Sambo, Babaji, and Sun," in *The Horn Book Magazine,* Vol. LXXII, No. 5, September-October, 1996, pp. 536-47.

[*Sam and the Tigers*] has so much to offer on its own that you might wish it had nothing to do with *Little Black Sambo.* In the case of a song, either the words or the music can come first. In the case of a picture book, the words must come first, or what would the illustrator illustrate? But the imaginary world that's home to young Sam is so instantly real, so familiar and comfortably habitable in Pinkney's opening bird's-eye view, that we don't need a word from Lester to be ready to walk along the streets of this old-time Southern town, with its plain wooden fences, its snug unpainted cabins and tidy garden plots, its street stalls and pushcarts and turbaned heads bearing baskets. We are ready to greet passers-by, all lightly dark-skinned—or furred, feathered-and-beaked, leathery and gray.

Without signposts we are in the backcountry South of Uncle Remus and Brer Rabbit, of folk-Southerness today. (See the frontispiece of the first Lester-Pinkney Uncle Remus collection; see Southern cartoonist Jim MacNelly's "General Store and Center for Southern Culture.") This particular Brueghel-rama, this particular *Brigadoon,* is Lester's Sam-sam-sa-mara—"where the animals and the people lived and worked together like they didn't know they weren't supposed to." Both Pinkney and Lester add fillips of their own, extra bits of fantasy and nonsense to stash away. The bird's-eye view that introduces Sam-sam-

sa-mara is the view of a hatted and shawled stork, who is carrying a basket of *eggs* (more of a joke for adults, maybe, but one they can share with kids). And all the people in Sam-sam-sa-mara are named Sam, including of course Sam's mama and daddy, "but nobody ever got confused about which Sam was which, and that's why nobody was named Joleen or Natisha or Willie."

In pictures as anecdotally effective as a Norman Rockwell cover and pungent dialogue that would play well on stage, Sam and his parents shop for new clothes for school. At Mr. Elephant's Elegant Habiliments, Sam turns down his mother's conservative choice in favor of "a jacket as red and happy as a heart." Sam, in short, will have his bright red-green-blue toggery because boys will be peacocks, given a chance.

When the plot of *Little Black Sambo* kicks in, however, **Sam and the Tigers** gets in trouble. Sam, dressed to dazzle, leaves for school. "Not very far" from the dooryard a real-live jungle tiger appears and announces its intention to eat Sambo up. The reader is not prepared for the tiger, of all Sam-sam-sa-mara's wild animals (which include alligators, bears, and wolves), to be a predatory beast. A child might reasonably ask how come the tiger wants to eat Sam if "the animals and people lived and worked together. . . ." And making the answer more of a stumper is the fact that Miss Cat, proprietor of The Feline's Finest Finery, is not a fireside puss but a wildcat indistinguishable from a tiger, in her enveloping dress, except for the absence of stripes on her tail.

Sam himself doesn't seem much concerned; and given the script, you might suspect Lester was spoofing the whole stylized Sambo-tiger conflict. After relinquishing jacket, pants, and shoes, "Sam didn't see any point in moving, and sure enough, along came another Tiger." The tiger rejects Sam's proffered umbrella as useless, and insists he'll eat Sam up. "If you do," Sam begins, "it'll send your cholesterol way up." And the tigers are not made to look ridiculous; we never see tiger number three with Sam's shoes on its ears, or tiger number four holding the umbrella aloft. But Lester and Pinkney do stick to the climax: the tigers, squabbling, spin themselves into a pool of butter that Sam carries home to Sam-sam-sa-mara—whereupon all the animal neighbors join the striped-pancake feast. . . .

Additional coverage of Pinkney's life and career is contained in the following sources published by Gale Research: *Major Authors and Illustrators for Children and Young Adults; Something about the Author,* Vols. 41, 71; and *Something about the Author Autobiography Series,* Vol. 12.

Robert D. San Souci

1946-

American reteller and author of fiction and nonfiction.

Major works include *The Legend of Scarface: A Blackfeet Indian Tale* (1978), *Song of Sedna: Sea-Goddess of the North* (1981), *Short and Shivery: Thirty Chilling Tales* (1987), *The Talking Eggs: A Folktale from the American South* (1989), *Kate Shelley: Bound for Legend* (1995).

INTRODUCTION

A popular and prolific author whose specialty is retelling both familiar and less well-known folktales from a variety of multicultural sources, San Souci is praised for creating straightforward retellings that retain the oral quality of the tales while reflecting his extensive research into their original sources. The adapter of both collections and individual stories, some of which are taken from authors such as Washington Irving and Nathaniel Hawthorne as well as retellers such as the Brothers Grimm, Madame d'Aulnoy, Andrew Lang, and Joseph Jacobs, San Souci directs most of his works to middle graders, although he has also written several picture books. His works—which are of Native American, African American, Chinese, Japanese, Inuit, and European derivation, among others, and often feature strong, independent female heroines—are usually acknowledged as accessible introductions for children that are also good for reading aloud. In addition, critics appreciate the considerable research that San Souci's books reflect; the stories are usually accompanied by author's notes with information about original sources. Although some reviewers claim that the changes made by San Souci in his adaptations, such as replacing or deleting characters and events and sacrificing descriptions, lead to a pared down or uneven quality, other observers laud the author for successfully reshaping the folktales for their intended audience. "One always expects impeccable scholarship and a fluid storytelling style when reading a text by Robert D. San Souci," writes Mary M. Burns in *Horn Book,* and Marlene Lee adds in *School Library Journal* that the writer "has a gift for adaptations that read smoothly without cheating their folktale sources."

Biographical Information

San Souci was born in San Francisco, California, but grew up, as he wrote, "on the Berkeley-Oakland side of the Bay." He claims that he always knew that he would be a writer: "Before I knew how to read or write, I would listen carefully to stories that were read to me, then I would retell them to my younger brothers and sisters, or to my friends. But I would add new bits or leave out those I didn't find so interesting—so the storytelling

impulse was already at work in me." One of the younger brothers who heard these stories was Daniel San Souci, who has provided the illustrations for several of his brother's texts. In grade school, San Souci wrote for the school newspaper; in high school, he contributed to the yearbook and, as a sophomore, had an essay printed in a paperback called *T.V. as Art.* San Souci studied creative writing and world literature in college and did graduate work on folklore, myth, and world religions. After graduate school, he worked as a book buyer and as the manager of a bookstore as well as a promotions coordinator, editorial coordinator, and copywriter for Harper and Row publishing company; during this period, he also worked as a journalist for newspapers and magazines and as a book and theater critic. Since 1993, San Souci has worked as a story consultant for Walt Disney Feature Animation; he has also contributed to several children's magazines and has lectured in elementary and middle schools as well as at the university level. In addition to his books for young readers, San Souci has written fiction and nonfiction for adults. Of his children's books, San Souci states that he plans "to continue writing as long as I have stories to tell—and an audience that is willing to listen." He continues, "Retelling a Grimm Brothers' fairytale or a Pueblo

Indian myth allows me scope to tell a story that has a solid structure derived from the inner truths that are the kernels of all legends, myths, and fairytales. In all my writing I'm first of all concerned with the story; but (and I see this more and more as I write) I'm also using the narrative to explore ideas and suggest answers to questions about why and how the world works. I hope my books are entertaining, and I also get pleasure from thinking they may be sharing a little more substance with readers."

Major Works

San Souci's first book, *The Legend of Scarface,* is a retelling of a Plains Indians myth. The story describes a young man with a facial scar who, although despised for his poverty and disfigurement, is strong and courageous. Scarface loves Singing Rains, a young woman who has promised the Sun that she will never marry. After embarking on a dangerous quest and saving the Sun's son from attacking birds, Scarface is allowed to marry Singing Rains. With *Song of Sedna,* San Souci retells an Inuit tale that Jon C. Stott, writing in *Children's Literature Association Quarterly,* calls "[p]robably the oldest Canadian story focusing on a strong female character." The book outlines the journey of an Eskimo maiden who, after being tricked into marriage by a bird spirit and betrayed by her father, becomes a goddess of the sea. Several of San Souci's books reflect his—and his young audience's—interest in the supernatural. For example, he has retold Washington Irving's "The Legend of Sleepy Hollow" and has written two volumes of ghost stories, *Short and Shivery* and *More Short and Shivery: Thirty Terrifying Tales* (1994). San Souci's works also include several variations on "Cinderella"; one of his most popular is *The Talking Eggs,* an adaptation of a Creole folktale. In this story, a cruel widow has two daughters, spoiled Rose and mistreated but kind and good Blanche. Blanche meets an old woman and gives her a drink; later, when Blanche runs away after being abused, the woman gives her magical talking eggs that turn into gold and jewels; when Rose attempts to get a similar reward from the old woman, she receives a shower of frogs and snakes. In her review in *School Library Journal,* Leda Schubert calls *The Talking Eggs* "a unique contribution to the American folktale repertoire." San Souci has compiled two collections of American folktales, one focusing on male heroes and the other on female heroines. *Larger than Life: the Adventures of American Legendary Heroes* (1991) includes stories about such well-known characters as Paul Bunyan, John Henry, and Pecos Bill, while *Cut from the Same Cloth: American Women of Myth, Legend, and Tall Tale* (1993) includes stories about their female counterparts from a variety of North American resources; in her review in *School Library Journal,* Ruth K. MacDonald calls this collection "a cut above other such compilations." Although San Souci is best known for his retellings, he is also the author of a work of fiction for children set in the 1850s, *The Christmas Ark* (1991), and the biography *Kate Shelley: Bound for Legend,* about a nineteenth-century heroine. In *The Christmas Ark,* San Souci describes how sisters Sarah and Elizabeth, who are stuck on a fogbound clipper ship taking them to their father and a new home in San Francisco, accompany Santa Claus on an ark that takes them to places around the world that celebrate Christmas; at the end of the story, the girls decide that their best Christmas will be the one that is waiting for them. In *Kate Shelley,* San Souci tells the true story of a fifteen-year-old Iowa girl who averts a major disaster in 1881. San Souci has also written a book on pilgrims that features the art of N. C. Wyeth, a nonfiction title about the Loch Ness monster, and a prose account of Igor Stravinsky's musical composition *The Firebird.*

Awards

The Talking Eggs won the Irma Simonton Black Award from the Bank Street College of Education in 1989. *Cut from the Same Cloth* received the Aesop Award from the Children's Folklore Section of the American Folklore Society, in 1993, the same year that *Sukey and the Mermaid* won the Hungry Mind Award for picturebooks/fiction. Several of San Souci's books have been named ALA Notable Books and Notable Children Trade Books in the Field of Social Studies in their years of publication. In addition, many of San Souci's works have received child-selected awards and several have won prizes for their illustrations.

GENERAL COMMENTARY

Malcolm Jones, Jr.

SOURCE: A review of *The Talking Eggs and The Boy and the Ghost,* in *The New York Times Book Review,* January 28, 1990, p. 29.

Folk tales were the original "fun for the whole family"—the whole village, for that matter. The good tale tellers always worked the Big Room.

Robert D. San Souci, a wise adapter, knows that a good folk tale needs no more than fine tuning. He has left *The Talking Eggs* and *The Boy and the Ghost* more or less as he found them, their plots unsullied, their lingo and custom still that of the 19th-century rural South.

The Talking Eggs, by far the more elaborate, describes the fate of a young country girl named Blanche who, though "sweet and kind and sharp as forty crickets," is nonetheless afflicted with a harridan mother and spoiled older sister. One day, while drawing water at the well, she meets a strange old woman, who begs a drink of her. Before too long she is following the old woman, plainly a good witch, deep into the woods.

Before returning home, she is sent to the old woman's henhouse to gather eggs to take with her. As ordered, Blanche takes only the eggs that say, "Take me," and leaves the eggs that say, "Don't take me," even though those eggs are covered in gold and silver and jewels. Likewise she does as she is told on the road home and tosses the eggs one after another over her shoulder in the roadway, where there then appears a wealth of goods, from jewels to dresses to a carriage and a pony to draw it. When Blanche returns home with her loot, of course, her selfish mother immediately packs the older sister off to find the old woman and grab even more booty. It is easy to see what will happen next, but not how, and that's what's good about it.

Mr. San Souci has the extravagant luck of having as his partner in this venture the illustrator Jerry Pinkney, an extraordinary draftsman and colorist. One of the few benefits of living in an age when folk tales are almost never told aloud any longer but are found most often between the covers of a book is that illustrators play a new and important role. Mr. Pinkney's boldly detailed pencil and watercolor pictures complement this story so aptly that it becomes impossible to think of Blanche's adventures without seeing them through his eyes. Indeed, he has been given his second Caldecott Honor designation for *The Talking Eggs*.

Appropriately in the generation-to-generation world of the folk tale, Mr. San Souci's story *The Boy and the Ghost* is illustrated by J. Brian Pinkney, who is Jerry Pinkney's son. It is the story of a poor boy who gains a treasure by being brave enough to stay in a haunted house overnight. The ghost comes down the chimney a limb at a time. So far, the same old shoot-'em-up, the same old rodeo, but Mr. San Souci and Mr. Pinkney quietly and deftly make their young hero, Thomas, one of the all-time great deadpan actors. He couldn't care less about how the ghost comes and reassembles itself so long as he can eat his soup in peace! Or so he so bravely pretends.

In these tales the heroine and hero win out by doing the right thing—without a speck of irony. In their world one wins with fair dealing and hard work, kindness and charity, generosity and bravery. Siblings and parents can be mean and lazy; poverty is never far away. It is also a world where virtue is always more than its own reward and where you never know when you might run into a witch or a ghost or a yard full of chickens with coats like Joseph's, a plainly fabulous place where everything works out perfectly in the end.

TITLE COMMENTARY

📖 *THE LEGEND OF SCARFACE: A BLACK-FEET INDIAN TALE* (1978)

America

SOURCE: A review of *The Legend of Scarface*, in *America*, Vol. 139, No. 19, December 9, 1978, p. 440.

The hero of this Blackfeet Indian folktale is a young man who is despised because of his poverty and particularly because of the scar on his face that has given him his name. Scarface is a courageous youth, and he dares to love the chief's daughter. She doesn't notice his scar because she returns his love. But she has promised the Sun that she will never marry. Perhaps the Sun would release Singing Rains from her vow? Scarface resolves to ask him. So he journeys the long way to the Sun's lodge, guided by animals, for he is known to them as a brother and true friend. Does the Sun give Scarface his heart's desire? The entire story is told in prose that sings and in paintings by Daniel San Souci that convey the beauty of the wilds in winter and summer and show the strong and lovable traits of the characters.

Gale Eaton

SOURCE: A review of *The Legend of Scarface: A Blackfeet Indian Tale*, in *School Library Journal*, Vol. 25, No. 7, March, 1979, p. 144.

Scarface, a poor and neglected youth, finds that the chief's beautiful daughter returns his love, but she has promised the Sun that she will never wed. To release her from this vow, he undertakes a long and dangerous quest, finally reaching the Sun's lodge and befriending his young son, Morning Star. After rescuing Morning Star from savagely attacking birds, Scarface is given a sign of the Sun's blessing and sent back to marry Singing Rains. . . . The telling here, short, unadorned, and a little flat, is still strong and will be accessible to young children and to reluctant readers—who will appreciate the traditional theme of hidden goodness recognized and rewarded. The dozen paintings [by Daniel San Souci] catch both drama and a somewhat Wyeth-like sense of the mysteriousness of open space.

Virginia Haviland

SOURCE: A review of *The Legends of Scarface: A Blackfeet Indian Tale*, in *The Horn Book Magazine*, Vol. LV, No. 2, April, 1979, pp. 185-6.

A greatly abbreviated retelling of the classic hero tale so well set down by George Grinnell in his *Blackfoot Lodge Tales*. As a précis, it is skillful, keeping the mood and spirit of the original, but it necessarily sacrifices details, incidents, and minor characters. There are also small alterations; for instance Grinnell's "young woman" becomes "Singing Rains." The retelling ends as Scarface is married—"[t]he sun blessed the couple all the days of their lives, and the Moon gave them sweet dreams each night"—rather than continuing until the couple dies in old age. The twelve large full-color paintings [by Daniel San Souci] have a dramatic strength, realistically interpreting the action, the Indian characters, and the animals.

📖 *SONG OF SEDNA* (1981)

Betsy Hearne

SOURCE: A review of *Song of Sedna,* in *Booklist,* Vol. 77, No. 21, July 1, 1981, p. 1396.

Sedna is an Eskimo maiden tricked into marriage by a bird-spirit, betrayed by her fearful father, and finally deified as goddess of the sea. Markedly different in tone from Beverly Brodsky McDermott's *Sedna: An Eskimo Myth*—which fashioned a first-person narrative in a story-within-a-story frame—this is a straightforward retelling with literal, sometimes prosaic artistic effects [of Daniel San Souci's illustrations]. While the print is heavy and Sedna's features seem more Caucasian than Eskimo, the total effect of landscapes, cultural backdrop, and a woman's triumph over trials makes the book worthwhile, especially for third- and fourth-graders, who will be less daunted by the folklore's length and complex elements than would a picture-book audience.

Carole Paikin

SOURCE: A review of *Song of Sedna,* in *The New York Times Book Review,* October 4, 1981, p. 38.

Finding one's Prince Charming isn't always what it's cracked up to be, as Sedna, the young woman of this Eskimo legend, discovers. Strong-willed, beautiful and romantic, she has many suitors but holds out for a man she has seen only in her dreams. When he appears at last, all is not as she anticipated. Sedna's Prince Charming, Mattack the hunter, is really a demon bird-spirit in Eskimo clothing. He paddles her off in his umiak to his home, where she soon discovers his chameleon quality and escapes in terror with him in hot pursuit.

What follows is a journey fraught with trials: a brush with ghosts in the Kingdom of the Dead, a trip on the back of a killer whale, a crossing by foot on a narrow ledge over a bottomless canyon. At journey's end, Sedna finds immortality as Goddess of the Sea.

Beyond the literate simplicity of the text, the beauty of the book is twofold. It is an adventure story complete with interesting characters, a stark setting and a mood that is absorbing. But it is also laced with treasures. When Sedna becomes Sea Goddess, a seal-spirit advises her that anything she wishes is now within her reach but that she must use her power wisely "for a god uses power tempered by wisdom and mercy." Sedna responds by dealing compassionately with her father, who has betrayed her. This pleases the "spirit of justice who is the most powerful being of all."

The realistic illustrations complement the haunting text and contrast well with the mythical quality of the story.

If Sedna loses out on a Prince Charming, the reader only gains from this book.

Jon C. Stott

SOURCE: "In Search of Sedna: Children's Version of a Major Inuit Myth," in *Children's Literature Association Quarterly,* Vol. 15, No. 4, Winter, 1990, pp. 199-201.

Probably the oldest Canadian story focusing on a strong female character, the myth of Sedna, found across the Canadian and Greenland Arctic, is a reflection of the Inuit belief in a world filled with powerful and often terrifying and malicious spirit beings. It is extremely different from those traditional European tales that have formed the basis of much Western children's literature. Violent to the point of gruesomeness, it reflects cultural beliefs that are not only foreign but also repugnant to the vast majority of adults who are the creators and custodians of children's literature. A study of two American children's versions of the Sedna story against the cultural backgrounds of the traditional Inuit reveals both the tremendous challenges faced by modern adaptors and the mistakes that can be made when they approach it without the necessary knowledge and sympathy.

The traditional Inuit lived in a physically and spiritually dangerous and violent world. Both the weather and the animals they hunted could quickly bring death. Moreover, the spiritual beings who peopled the lands and seas could angrily turn on them for violating taboos. The most significant of these beings was Sedna, "the Old Woman of the Sea" or "the Food Basket," who lived on the ocean floor, controlling the lives of the sea mammals that provided the basic food supply of the people. Anthropologist Franz Boaz wrote [in *The Central Eskimo*]: "She has supreme sway over the destinies of mankind, and almost all of the observances of these tribes are for the purpose of retaining her good will or of propitiating her if she has been offended."

Although the myth has many variants, all contain a basic plot line. A proud woman who has refused all suitors is enticed from her home by an unknown, handsome man who professes to be a great hunter. When she discovers that he is, in fact, a supernatural petrel and that she is living among seabirds on a rocky, windswept cliff, she calls in her spirit to her father for rescue. However, the supernatural husband follows the fleeing pair, creating a fearsome storm. In terror, the father throws her over the side of his boat, cutting off her fingers as she clings to the side. As she sinks to the bottom of the sea, the amputated digits are transformed into the various sea mammals, her children, whom she fiercely protects against irreverent hunters.

Hers is a lonely and bitter life. As one Inuit song relates: "Nuliajuk [one of the names by which she is known] gave seals to mankind, it is true, but she is not friendly to people, for they had no pity on her when she lived on earth, throwing her into the sea like that to drown. So naturally she would like mankind to perish too. That is why we do our best to be as good as we can and make Nuliajuk think kindly of us" [*Eskimo Songs and Stories,* translated by Eugene Field]. In times of her greatest displeasure, Sedna can only be appeased by a visit from the angakok, the Inuit shaman. Casting himself into a trance, he travels to her abode, where he asks forgiveness on behalf of the tribe and seeks to appease her by combing her hair and removing lice, actions she cannot perform because of her mutilated hands.

The non-Inuit writer adapting this story is faced with many difficulties. Most important, the elements it contains—the necessity of marriage for continuation of the species and the wrongness of Sedna's willful, almost prideful rejection of suitors, the danger of hunting and the ever-present possibility of starvation, the terror of betrayal by a family member and the vindictiveness of Sedna, and the spiritual power of the angakok—although totally understandable within traditional Inuit culture, are very unlike Western values embodied in most children's literature. Because what would be easily understood by an audience of Inuit children might be meaningless to a Western audience, adaptors may be tempted into either rejecting the beliefs as foolish superstition or reinterpreting them to make them more consistent with their own and their readers' values. Robert and Daniel San Souci's *Song of Sedna* (1981) is so altered as to be virtually worthless as a reflection of Inuit culture. . . .

While the first half of the San Soucis's adaptation, up to the point that Sedna is thrown from the boat, is fairly close to traditional versions, the second part adds incidents and changes the character of the heroine. Throughout, the illustrations are inaccurate and the visual depictions of the setting inappropriate.

As we have seen, traditional versions explained the origins of the sea mammals and the reasons for poor hunting. In *Song of Sedna,* the seals already exist. Not surprisingly, Sedna is not portrayed as an angry and vindictive protectress of her children; they are not hers. Instead, after engaging in a quest during which she is tested, she becomes a beneficent helper to the Inuit. As she sinks beneath the waters, "a powerful blessing was on her," and two banded seals tell her, "Approach that mountain and you will find your destiny." They are, in a sense, like the guardian helpers of European folklore, helping the quester to help herself. When they urge her to avoid the temptations of the spirits of the dead who call on her "to forsake her journey and rest with them . . . [she] drew upon her inner strength and ignored the ghost-voices." The seals instruct her to use her courage to climb on the back of a ferocious looking killer whale. Finally, she crosses a knife-edged bridge of ice and, encouraged by the seals, swims to her throne.

Having achieved power, Sedna now faces a new conflict: how to use it. In the originals, she sits vengefully at the bottom of the sea. In *Song of Sedna,* however, she listens to the warning of seal spirits: "'Use your power wisely . . . for a god uses power tempted by wisdom and mercy.' Sedna realized that she was being tested. She sensed that her powers might be taken from her if she misused them. So she followed the best instincts of her heart." She forgives her father and, sitting on her throne, helps the Inuit:

"The Eskimos seek her good will whenever they need protection on the open sea or help with harvesting the sea's bounty." Clearly, the conclusion of *Song of Sedna* subverts the tone and message of the traditional myth. The warnings against refusing marriage and violating the goddess's taboos do not appear. Instead of awe, fear, and reverence, this version communicates joy and a sense of fulfillment.

The text is profusely, lavishly, and inaccurately illustrated. The pictures counteract the Inuit values the story ought to have embodied. This process begins on the half-title page, which contains a stylized killer whale. While this mammal plays a role in the story, the illustration is in the style of Native Indians of southern Alaska and northern British Columbia. The title page compounds the cultural errors. Although the story is explicitly set "beside the Arctic Ocean," an Indian totem pole is visible. Such poles were found in groups in villages of the Northwest coast; a single pole would not be located far from a village. In the foreground is a deciduous tree, at least two feet in diameter; in the distance, a large stand of evergreens. These, of course, are never found in the high Arctic. Further inaccuracies are seen in the portrayal of the characters and their artifacts. Sedna, her father, and her mate are tall, willowy figures with long, lean faces and slender, delicate hands. They bear greater resemblance to the figures depicted in the San Soucis's *The Legend of Scarface* (1978), a Plains Indian myth, than they do to Arctic Inuit. The embroidery on the parkas resembles the beadwork of the northern Cree and Ojibway, and the woven grass sails of the umiak are of a type that was found on the boats of the Bering Sea Inuit of western Alaska. The serpent the enraged husband rides while pursuing his fleeing wife bears scales like those of rattlesnakes. In form, color, and size, such a serpent would not have been imagined by traditional Arctic Inuit.

The effect of these inaccuracies is to rob the accompanying story of its cultural background. More important, it implicitly reflects an attitude that cultural accuracy in portraying a story of these people is unimportant. Approximation is sufficient. These visual inaccuracies, along with the alteration of the character of Sedna and the meaning of her story, totally invalidate *Song of Sedna* as an acceptable presentation of this story for children. The authors appear to have respected neither the culture and the story it created nor the child audience for whom they have adapted it.

In addition to containing cultural inaccuracies, the San Souci version fails to embody the major cultural fact underlying stories of Sedna and the angakok's attempt to placate her. As religious scholar [Mircea] Eliade has noted [in *Shamanism: Archaic Techniques of Ecstasy*], the shaman/angakok "in a manner re-establishes the situation that existed *in illo tempore,* in mythical times, when the divorce between man and the animal world had not yet occurred." In the story of Sedna, the girl's double betrayal is a kind of fall that results in the Mother of the Seals maintaining a very tenuous relationship with human beings, a relationship that, when broken, can only be re-established by the angakok. In essence, the story embodies dualities: land and sea, spirit and human, human and animal, faith and betrayal, love and anger, breach and reconciliation—that is, physical, spiritual, and psychic life and death. Only when opposing tensions are reconciled is a unified, whole life possible. The story of Sedna is a classic example of the dualities which Claude Lévi-Strauss has maintained provide the essential structure of mythology.

THE LEGEND OF SLEEPY HOLLOW: RETOLD FROM WASHINGTON IRVING (1986)

Eleanor K. MacDonald

SOURCE: A review of *The Legend of Sleepy Hollow*, in *School Library Journal*, Vol. 33, No. 4, December, 1986, p. 108.

San Souci's retelling of the American classic retains the basic plot of the tale but sacrifices the rich descriptions of place and character that give the original its status. While more accessible to young readers, this version of Ichabod Crane's encounter with the headless horseman is little more than a simple, rather conventional ghost story. [Daniel San Souci's] illustrations are richly colored in the manner popularized by Michael Hague, and the final chase, with its dark skies, spectral moon, and ghostly trees is dramatic. However the early illustrations in the book, particularly those showing Ichabod's courtship of Katrina, are flat, and the figures are uniformly static and curiously unattractive. Only Ichabod, with his almost comic face and figure, comes across as a real person. While this version may be useful to introduce the "tale," particularly at Halloween, young readers who are exposed only to this version will miss both the richer language of the original and the fine draftmanship of earlier editions, notably those illustrated by Arthur Rackham and Leonard Everett Fisher.

Barbara Elleman

SOURCE: A review of *The Legend of Sleepy Hollow*, in *Booklist*, Vol. 83, No. 10, January 15, 1987, p. 788.

Retold from Washington Irving's famous classic, this spooky story of a superstitious schoolmaster's skirmish with a headless horseman will continue to send shivers down children's backs. Though the narrative does not have Irving's original rich cadences and lyrical presence, it does maintain the atmosphere and sense of character. The full-color illustrations, done mainly in earthy colors and night-time blues, add a rustic and ghostly tone—especially in the backgrounds. Daniel San Souci's caricatured faces lack depth, but his glossy full-color dust jacket with the clouds forming a wraithlike headless horseman riding over a quaint village will surely attract readers. This tale will also make a good read-aloud; the text is short and the illustrations are all single-page spreads, easily seen in a small-group setting.

THE ENCHANTED TAPESTRY: A CHINESE FOLKTALE (1987)

Kirkus Reviews

SOURCE: A review of *The Enchanted Tapestry*, in *Kirkus Reviews*, Vol. LV, No. 6, March 15, 1987, p. 475.

Here, a hybridization of several versions of a Chinese folk tale that relies more on quiet effects than the usual folk-tale picture book, and is the stronger for it.

San Souci's text retains the pared-down quality of the versions of folk tales most familiar to American readers: the sentences are generally declarative and reveal without irony or understatement the story of an old woman who weaves the finest tapestry of her career when she chooses to weave for beauty instead of commerce. Family strife and discord occur, when two of her three dependent sons beg her to sell the masterpiece, but a mighty wind tears the cloth from its loom and sends it flying out of sight. All three sons attempt to find it; the first two fall prey to a sorceress' offer of gold, but the third overcomes the obstacles. In retrieving his mother's masterpiece, he comes upon a beautiful fairy, who ingeniously insinuates herself into his life in a happy-ever-after ending with a particularly charming twist.

[Laszlo] Gal's use of ochres, salmons, olive greens and smoked whites re-creates the emotional quality of Chinese drawing; his three-dimensional modelling lends drama to his characterizations. And the delicate overlays of color, stroke and stipple, wash and line, evoke the technique and form in tapestry work. Author and artist are well paired here; children should be enchanted.

Barbara Elleman

SOURCE: A review of *The Enchanted Tapestry: A Chinese Folktale*, in *Booklist*, Vol. 83, No. 18, May 15, 1987, p. 1450.

Using the same Chinese folktale that Marilee Heyer retold in *The Weaving of a Dream*, San Souci creates a simpler, more direct rendition. A beautiful tapestry woven by a Chinese widow is stolen by the fairies of Sun Mountain. After its loss, the woman becomes gravely ill and asks first her eldest son and then her second son to retrieve the weaving she has worked on for so long; however, both are seduced by a few gold coins and fail to do her bidding. Finally, her beloved youngest son sets off, and despite many obstacles, arrives at Sun Mountain, where he retrieves the tapestry and falls in love with the red-robed fairy. Upon returning home, he finds the fairy has woven herself into the cloth and is there too. The happily-ever-after ending is extended when the mercenary brothers return only to be whirled far away by magic. [László] Gál's elegant illustrations are done in muted, earthy colors, and the background flowers, buildings, and arched bridges reflect an Oriental atmosphere. The robed characters and deliberately expressionless faces blend with the settings, providing an overall mood rather than an individualized interpretation of specific people and events. For a folktale this effect works well; the story is not overpowered by the art as often happens in todays's renderings. The illustrations, diffused with a gauzy white, appear almost as opera backdrops with the story's events happening on center stage.

SHORT AND SHIVERY: THIRTY CHILLING TALES (1987)

Mary Lathrope

SOURCE: A review of Short & Shivery: Thirty Chilling Tales, in Booklist, Vol. 84, No. 7, December 1, 1987, pp. 637-8.

Demons, vampires, skeletons, goblins, werewolves, witches, wizards, and ghosts aplenty inhabit these tales from various parts of the world. Most have been adapted, more or less loosely, from traditional sources, and San Souci explains just how much tinkering has been done in a carefully annotated, appended notes and sources section. In "The Golem," for example, he has created an entirely new story inspired by versions of the old Jewish tale. Children, however, will probably not be concerned with such documentation and will just enjoy encountering strange new creatures such as the Nuckelavee from the Orkney Islands, the Cegua from Costa Rica, and a monstrous white spider from Japan, as well as renewing an acquaintance with Grimms' "Robber Bridegroom" and the Appalachian "Tailypo." While [Katherine Coville's] soft gray drawings faithfully depict the action they are much too realistic to contribute any feeling of eeriness. Librarians will welcome a new collection of spooky but not terrifying yarns, especially for Halloween, and will also find some of them suitable for year-round storytelling.

Annette Curtis Klause

SOURCE: A review of Short and Shivery: Thirty Chilling Tales, in School Library Journal, Vol. 34, No. 5, January, 1988, pp. 82-3.

A collection of spooky stories, competently adapted and retold (sometimes quite freely) from world folklore, including Japan, Africa, and Latin America, as well as Europe and the U.S. Fairy tales are represented, from Grimm's "The Robber Bridegroom" to the modern urban folktale "Lavender," a reworking of the phantom hitchhiker story. Some tales are familiar, appearing in one form or another in various collections, e.g., "Tailypo," but many are not. Stories have also been adapted from the work of Nathaniel Hawthorne, John Bunyan, and Washington Irving. The stories drawn from collections of regional American folklore are not only the freshest, but often the scariest. Sources are fully documented at the back of the book. The cover has just the right touch of gruesomeness to attract

readers, with bats, rats, weird faces, and a skeleton arm escaping from the grave. Almost every story is illustrated [by Katherine Coville] with a full-page picture in pen-and-ink and wash. These are well crafted but, with some notable exceptions, don't always capture the true terror of the tales, and don't enhance the text in a spine-tingling manner. Many of the stories will be effective as read-alouds. There are some delicious shivers here, with plenty of fodder for an active imagination, as well as excitement.

THE SIX SWANS (1988)

Louise L. Sherman

SOURCE: A review of The Six Swans, in School Library Journal, Vol. 35, No. 12, August, 1989, p. 138.

The Grimms' tale is retold by San Souci with a somewhat tighter plot. In the original there is no connection between the witch whose daughter marries the king and turns his sons into swans and the mother-in-law who steals the faithful sister's babies and smears blood on her mouth. Here, instead of the mother-in-law, it is a wicked aunt who is also the witch of the wood. It is in her house, not a robbers' den, that the brothers show their human form to their sister. Here the witch's daughter is disposed of in the end, while the Grimms don't mention her again. This makes a somewhat more satisfying although less "authentic" tale. The retelling is smooth. Less sentimental (and less poetic) than Andersen's retelling of The Wild Swans, this faithfulness-rewarded story has great appeal. It is also one of which there are not many picture-book versions. [Daniel] San Souci's somewhat formal watercolor illustrations provide a well-focused medieval setting and add drama to the story. . . . This story will make a good read-aloud for middle elementary grades.

THE BOY AND THE GHOST (1989)

Kirkus Reviews

SOURCE: A review of The Boy and the Ghost, in Kirkus Reviews, Vol. LVII, No. 15, August 15, 1989, p. 1250.

Derived from two "negro ghost stories" published in 1898, a variant on the story of a traveler who stays overnight in a deserted house and is visited by a ghost who arrives in pieces. Here, the story is extended by describing Thomas as the middle child in a large, poor family, off to look for work; since he survives his fearful experience, the ghost gives him his treasure—on the condition that he share it with others who are also poor. Though not especially spooky, the story reads well. In his first picture book, [J. Brian] Pinkney—whose style resembles that of the well-known illustrator of that name—makes a promising debut, especially in his pictures of sturdy, self-reliant Thomas.

Barbara Rollock

SOURCE: A review of *The Boy and the Ghost*, in *The Five Owls*, Vol. IV, No. 1, September-October, 1989, p. 7.

Storytellers will recognize this variant of the folktale, *The Tinker and the Ghost*. Instead of the hills of Toledo, Spain, however, the setting is rural America and the hero is a poor farm boy whose politeness and kindness are justly rewarded.

San Souci traces this version based on two "Negro ghost stories" back to an 1898 printing in *The Southern Workman*, and *Hampton School Record* later reprinted it in 1906 in the *Journal of American Folk-Lore*. Accordingly, [J. Brian Pinkney's] illustrations show an African-American family and both the protagonist and ghost have similar racial features, although the ghost is robust and striking with his red beard and hair.

This ghost, portrayed in pastel wash and pen strokes, appears less forbidding than the disembodied specter the tinker faced, and Thomas, the boy, is more polite though dauntless as he offers some of his soup to the ghost, who reassembles parts of his body before him. Even the ghost appreciates and acknowledges kindness, and his directions to Thomas about digging for treasures are less menacing and result in a more benign ghost story than the retelling by Boggs in *Three Golden Oranges*. Nevertheless, it is still a good story for reading aloud and Halloween story times.

Denise Wilms

SOURCE: A review of *The Boy and the Ghost*, in *Booklist*, Vol. 86, No. 3, October 1, 1989, p. 355.

This tale's story line will be familiar to readers of *Esteban and the Ghost*, though the locale is different. Here, the adventure is set in the South and features a self-possessed black boy who braves a night in a haunted house and effectively deals with a ghost that tumbles down the chimney in pieces. Details are also changed. Thomas, the middle child in a poor family of seven, wants to earn some money to help his parents. On his way to look for a job in town, he meets a stranger who tells him about a haunted house with a hidden treasure. Thomas decides to try his luck at staying all night in the place, and later that evening discovers the ghost's mission—to show the treasure to someone who will give half of it to the poor, allowing the ghost to rest in peace. Thomas, of course, is happy to carry out the specter's wishes, and returns home to improve his family's fortunes. Pinkney's line-and-watercolor drawings show deft composition and a flair for the dramatic. Scenes of shanty, family, and hot fields are quiet and restrained, but those involving the ghost are considerably more dynamic. A handy pick for story hours, especially around Halloween. Author's note on the tale's origin appended.

THE TALKING EGGS: A FOLKTALE FROM THE AMERICAN SOUTH (1989)

Leda Schubert

SOURCE: A review of *The Talking Eggs: A Folktale from the American South*, in *School Library Journal*, Vol. 35, No. 13, September, 1989, p. 244.

This adaptation of a Creole folktale contains familiar European fairy tale elements, but certainly stands on its own and is a unique contribution to the American folktale repertoire. In imagistic language spiced with Southern folk flavor, San Souci tells of a cruel mother and her two daughters, Blanche and Rose. Rose is just like her mother, while Blanche is good and kind, and consequently abused. One day Blanche meets an old woman and treats her with a "spirit of do-right." Soon they meet again, when Blanche runs away from mistreatment and the old woman takes her back to her house. And what marvels Blanche finds there—a two-headed cow, multicolored chickens, abundant food from nothing, a hostess who takes off her head to comb her hair (the illustrations spare readers most of this last detail), and a glorious scene of rabbits engaged in country dancing. For being obedient, Blanche is rewarded with magic talking eggs that turn into everything she's ever wanted. As expected, her greedy family wants to get in on the action, but Rose, of course, fails to follow the old woman's instructions, and gets nothing but a plague of snakes, toads, frogs, and the like. This lesson about virtue rewarded and greed punished is illustrated with [Jerry] Pinkney's lush, detailed watercolor and pencil art, which literally interprets the story and provides abundant detail. The characters are black, the setting rural, and the themes universal.

Betsy Hearne

SOURCE: A review of *The Talking Eggs: A Folktale from the American South*, in *Bulletin of the Center for Children's Books*, Vol. 43, No. 2, October, 1989, p. 42.

A Creole folktale about a widow and her two daughters, who "lived on a farm so poor, it looked like the tail end of bad luck," combines elements of Cinderella with distinctively southern black lore. The youngest child, abused by her mother and sister, helps an old woman who rewards her with magic eggs that produce gold and jewels. When the evil sister seeks the same old woman and disobeys her, the eggs give forth snakes, toads, and vermin. It's a strong story well told, and [Jerry] Pinkney's elaborate watercolor scenes play it to the hilt. The two-headed cow with corkscrew horns and a mulish bray, the multicolored, many-legged chickens that whistle like mockingbirds, and the old woman who removes her head to comb her hair are haunting images of magic, both verbally and visually. In spite of occasional stiffness in drafting of human faces and figures, there is an eerie quality to these scenes that will electrify storytelling or picture-book sharing sessions.

Lois F. Anderson

SOURCE: A review of *The Talking Eggs,* in *The Horn Book Magazine,* Vol. LXV, No. 6, November-December, 1989, p. 782.

Adapted from a Creole folk tale originally included in a collection of Louisiana stories by folklorist Alcee Fortier, this tale captures the flavor of the nineteenth-century South in its language and story line. There are four characters: a wicked mother; a girl who is sweet, kind, and "sharp as forty crickets"; a second daughter who is arrogant and spoiled; and an old woman who possesses magical charms. As expected, the good daughter does all the chores while her mother and sister dream of riches and do nothing, and she is ultimately rewarded for her goodness. Similar to Perrault's "Diamonds and Toads," the story has a compelling charm. Jerry Pinkney's watercolors are chiefly responsible for the excellence of the book; his characters convey their moods with vivid facial expressions. A wonderful book to read aloud.

Margery Fisher

SOURCE: A review of *The Talking Eggs,* in *Growing Point,* Vol. 28, No. 5, January, 1990, p. 5274.

[An adaptation] of a Creole folk-tale collected in the last century in Louisiana, *The Talking Eggs* shows its European origins in the familiar situation of good sister Blanche and crabby sister Rose and their differing fortunes. Banished from home after she has given an old woman a drink, Blanche goes to a house where the same old woman lifts off her head to dress her hair, which Blanche views with surprise but not with fear. Her kindness is rewarded and her virtue exemplified when she is told to take eggs from the hen-house—not the richly jewelled eggs but those that say 'Take me'. The honest girl returns home with rich clothes and gold, driving a pony and trap, and her jealous mother sends greedy Rose to try her luck, with predictable results. Jerry Pinkney's illustrations in wash and pencil line match the story in action and give movement to the characters and especially to the various animals who play their parts (traditional dances performed by a rabbit troupe are especially entertaining). A rich forestal setting and a smattering of Creole idiom in the dialogue help to make this a fresh and individual retelling.

📖 *THE WHITE CAT: AN OLD FRENCH FAIRY TALE* (1990)

Kirkus Reviews

SOURCE: A review of *The White Cat: An Old French Fairy Tale,* in *Kirkus Reviews,* Vol. LVIII, No. 14, July 15, 1990, p. 1012.

One of the courtly tales of Mme. d'Aulnoy: to choose a successor, a king sends his sons on three quests; the young-est is helped by a cat who turns out to be an enchanted, marriageable queen. Long a favorite for its entrancing details and adventures, this gracefully retold story is elegantly illustrated [by Gennady Spirin] with sumptuous paintings set in the *ancien régime.* A handsome edition.

Linda Boyles

SOURCE: A review of *The White Cat: An Old French Fairy Tale,* in *School Library Journal,* Vol. 36, No. 10, October, 1990, p. 112.

A king's youngest son, sent on a quest by his father, stumbles on a mysterious castle, where he is welcomed by the White Cat. The prince is quite taken with the charming and elegant cat whose generosity and unique powers help him fulfill not one request of his father's, but two. When the prince learns that the White Cat's happiness is threatened by impending marriage to a wicked wizard, he valiantly defends her, thereby winning her hand. She is, of course, a lovely enchanted princess. San Souci has done an excellent job of retelling Madame d'Aulnoy's long, ornate tale. While many elements of the older story have been left out, the romance remains and the mystery is heightened, making a tighter, more direct story that will appeal to young readers. The formal tone of the story is carried out in [Gennady] Spirin's elaborate, detailed illustrations. Their soft, golden glow evokes an appropriate sense of the past, as if the scenes were being viewed across the ages. A ferocious sea battle and a dramatic confrontation between the wizard, disguised as a dragon, and the prince are depicted in two marvelous double-spreads that afford special pleasure for the eye and imagination. The only jarring note is the face of the White Cat, which often looks cruel rather than lovely. Still, this is a fine addition to folk and fairy-tale collections that will serve as an accessible introduction to this relatively unknown story.

Margaret A. Bush

SOURCE: A review of *The White Cat,* in *The Horn Book Magazine,* Vol. LXVI, No. 6, November-December, 1990, p. 740.

Opulent costumes and spirited battles mark this elegant version of the old French tale by Madame d'Aulnoy. The youngest son, "who was the handsomest and smartest of the three," makes the requisite three journeys in search of the items by which his father will decide who is to rule the kingdom. The convolutions and elaborations found in many versions of the story have been pared down, but San Souci's simple narration retains plenty of the colorful detail. On his first visit to the strange palace, the prince passes the time amicably with the white cat; the second year is more lively, with the cats waging a fierce naval battle with an army of rats. During the third year, the source of the enchantment is revealed when the wizard-dwarf Migonnet arrives to claim his bride. His chariot is drawn by a dragonlike salamander, faced by the prince in a voluptuous double-page scene. Gennady Spirin's paintings include beautiful court costumes for the cats and many small details embedded in the scenes that are both lively and dreamlike, cast in tones of pale ocher. . . . Both the American author and the Russian illustrator exercise skillful constraint in interpreting and elaborating the story elements. The exotic events set in a familiar scheme are played out to a rich, satisfying dénouement.

THE CHRISTMAS ARK (1991)

Joanne Schott

SOURCE: A review of *The Christmas Ark,* in *Quill and Quire,* Vol. 57, No. 10, October, 1991, p. 39.

In *The Christmas Ark* Robert San Souci attempts something more complex [than many holiday stories]. Sarah and Elizabeth are fogbound on Christmas eve, on the clipper that is taking them to their father. Santa finds them, arriving in an ark like the toy they have been playing with. They accompany him around the world and may choose one place the ark visits for their special place to celebrate Christmas. The tour includes their former home in Maine, a great temptation, but when they visit the San Francisco hotel where their father has prepared wonderful things for them, they decide to go back to the ship "because that's going to become this Christmas, too—when we land." The dream adventure will come true, but the visits to the old home and new make the resolution predictable. The devices of the ark and the choice are awkward and have nothing inherently to do with Christmas. Because the girls must have a way to make their sensible, family-affirming decision, the conclusion too obviously guides the plot. Daniel San Souci's illustrative style is becoming more impressionistic and its richness works especially well in cityscapes and scenes on the ship. In some of the ark's visits, chances are lost to use it to best advantage, though the book is a very attractive one. Its appeal lies in its visual strength, the realistic characters, and warm conclusion, though the story itself fails to be entirely convincing.

School Library Journal

SOURCE: A review of *The Christmas Ark,* in *School Library Journal,* Vol. 37, No. 10, October, 1991, pp. 32-3.

An elaborately written and lavishly illustrated story of two young girls traveling by ship with their mother from Maine to San Francisco in the 1850s to join their father. It is Christmas Eve, they are fogbound, and Sarah is worried that St. Nicholas will not be able to find them. But he does, of course, arriving by ark to take the girls on a Christmas Eve journey around the world so they may choose, out of all the Christmases they see, the one they would most like to have as their own. The long voyage leads them to realize that their ideal Christmas is one shared with their family, no matter where they are, and St. Nicholas returns them to the ship. San Souci's comfort

and familiarity with so many themes from a variety of literary traditions gives an added depth and richness to his story. However, after taking such pains to provide a geographically detailed itinerary, he leaves readers with an ending that is abrupt and not completely satisfying.

SUKEY AND THE MERMAID (1992)

Hazel Rochman

SOURCE: A review of *Sukey and the Mermaid,* in *Booklist,* Vol. 88, No. 11, February 1, 1992, p. 1034.

In a romantic folktale drawn from various African American traditions, a beautiful, brown-skinned, black-eyed mermaid saves a poor, unhappy girl. Sukey's step-pa's a bossy do-nothing man who drinks and works her too hard. When she cries for help, a mermaid hears her and takes her below the sea to a gentle place without time or pain. But Sukey longs to return to the world, even though hurt and hunger are never far away. In the neat ending, she gets all she wants: a loving husband, the mermaid's treasure, and her step-pa dead. San Souci's source note describes how he traced the rare tale of a black mermaid. His telling is vivid and immediate, casual and colloquial ("How do, my lady. . . . Come into the water and cool off"). [Brian] Pinkney's brief artist's note describes his technique of working in scratchboard and oil pastels, which allows him to sculpt as well as draw the images. . . . The mermaid looks like a West African princess decked in gold. She's a powerful woman, and she helps make Sukey strong.

Kirkus Reviews

SOURCE: A review of *Sukey and the Mermaid,* in *Kirkus Reviews,* Vol. LX, No. 4, February 15, 1992, p. 260.

Weary of the unreasonable demands of Mister Jones, her new stepfather, Sukey escapes to the water's edge, where she meets "a beautiful, brown-skinned, black-eyed mermaid"—Mama Jo—who befriends and comforts her and each day gives her a gold coin. Mister Jones drinks up most of the money; eventually, he tries to capture the mermaid, who escapes and takes Sukey to her undersea kingdom. Homesick, Sukey bargains for a chance to go home and is also given a dowry and the promise of a fine husband, to be named Dembo. Wicked Mister Jones steals the dowry and kills Dembo; but Mama Jo appears one last time to bring him back to life.

A careful note explains that this eventful, richly complex story was based on a folktale from the Sea Islands of South Carolina, as well as on Caribbean and West African sources. [Brian] Pinkney's delicately tinted scratchboard illustrations are his best yet; the many fine lines swirl through the dramatic black ground, catching the sea's luminous glow and softening the sturdy figures with diaphanous garments. An unusually handsome presentation of an appealing tale.

Betsy Hearne

SOURCE: A review of *Sukey and the Mermaid*, in *Bulletin of the Center for Children's Books*, Vol. 45, No. 7, March, 1992, p. 192.

An organic blend of fantasy and South Carolina island folklore, this exemplifies the best ongoing tradition of storytelling in picture book format. The heroine is young Sukey, who, to escape from her oppressive stepfather, goes daily to the seashore for a visit with a brown-skinned mermaid: "Thee, thee, down below, / Come to me, Mama Jo." After trying to capture the mermaid with Sukey's summons, the angry stepfather works the girl nearly to death. She escapes underwater and returns with a dowry of gold, only to have her true love struck down; twice more the mermaid intervenes, once to revive Sukey's betrothed and once to drown the villain. It's a long story, but one supported with strong writing and some of Brian Pinkney's most expansive illustration. . . . From her black eyes to her deep-green tail, the mermaid is a natural extension of the wild seascapes. However tenuous the narrative connection with West African sources—and San Souci cites some research in a brief author's note—the language and art together take on rich African-American hues in this newly imagined version.

Martha Rosen

SOURCE: A review of *Sukey and the Mermaid*, in *School Library Journal*, Vol. 38, No. 5, May, 1992, p. 108.

From West Africa via the Caribbean to the Sea Islands off South Carolina's coast come the story fragments melded in this unusual, haunting tale. San Souci's eloquent prose, matched by [Brian] Pinkney's handsome illustrations executed in scratchboard and oil pastel, tells the tale of a black girl's special relationship with a benevolent mermaid. As the arresting cover illustration suggests, Mama Jo is no ordinary water spirit. This fabulous creature, with opulent jewelry and golden combs in her sea-green hair, offers Sukey more than a gold coin at day's end. The time spent in the sea with the mermaid provides respite from the hardships of life with her mother and shiftless stepfather. Although the Cinderella theme is most apparent, there are references to many others. What provides this book with depth and richness, however, is the smooth transition from the mermaid's magical kingdom to the harsh reality of the girl's life on land. Sukey is a likable heroine, determined, clever, and compassionate. This is a realistic coming-of-age story, combined with fantasy.

Mary M. Burns

SOURCE: A review of *Sukey and the Mermaid*, in *The Horn Book Magazine*, Vol. LXVIII, No. 5, September-October, 1992, pp. 593-4.

Many familiar motifs can be identified in this tale of a child, abused by her stepfather, who finds succor through the magical intervention of a beautiful African-American mermaid. Yet, the diction of the narrator sets it in a specific locale and gives it a unique flavor. The central character is Sukey, who, one hot afternoon, sings a snatch of half-remembered song: "Thee, thee, down below, / Come to me, Mama Jo." The mermaid thus summoned listens to her woes, gives her a coin to appease her parents, and becomes her friend. As Sukey's lot fails to improve, the mermaid offers her the endless comfort of the kingdom beneath the sea—which refuge Sukey accepts until longing for the world becomes too strong and she wins the right to return by posing a riddle to her protector. Although grieved by the outcome, the mermaid lives up to her side of the bargain and generously provides for Sukey's future. But, in the last analysis, it is not the mermaid's gifts but Sukey's own integrity which wins Sukey freedom and love. [Brian] Pinkney has captured Sukey's innate dignity and strength through the demanding scratchboard medium. The figures are given sculptural dimension; the undulating waves from which the elegant mermaid emerges suggest a magical world without becoming fey; the color is commanding—mysterious, deep, almost hypnotic. The combination of text and illustrations is indeed as powerful as it is appealing. According to the appended author's note, this captivating retelling of a South Carolina story is "one of the relatively few authenticated African-American folktales involving mermaids." In fleshing out the brief narrative that was his original inspiration, San Souci did considerable research and concluded that the earliest version was, in all probability, African. It is this documented attention to detail that gives the story additional credibility and value for folklore collections—a fine blending of scholarship and the storyteller's art, complemented by an outstanding visual interpretation.

THE TSAR'S PROMISE: A RUSSIAN TALE (1992)

Kathryn Jennings

SOURCE: A review of *The Tsar's Promise*, in *Bulletin of the Center for Children's Books*, Vol. 46, No. 2, October, 1992, p. 53.

Romantic watercolors with golden borders [by Lauren Mills] illustrate a story retold from Andrew Lang's *Green Fairy Book*. Trapped by his father's foolish promise, a Tsar's son finds himself the prisoner of a water-demon. Fortunately for Ivan, he is loved by Princess Maria, a talented magician who helps Ivan outwit the demon. The adaptation of this complex tale is simply and smoothly written, moving convincingly from the demon's tricking of the Tsar to Maria's and Ivan's difficult escape. In the illustrations, Mills has successfully combined a Russian flavor with the universal fantasy of folklore, with gnarly demons contrasting well with the noble beauty of Maria and Ivan. For the young lover of fairy tales, this attractive, action-packed book will become a favorite.

Kirkus Reviews

SOURCE: A review of *The Tsar's Promise,* in *Kirkus Reviews,* Vol. LX, No. 22, November 15, 1992, p. 1448.

A simplified version of the Russian tale entitled "King Kojata" in Lang's *Green Fairy Book.* The Tsar is tricked into promising his baby son to an evil demon; once grown, Ivan sets out to honor his father's word. With the help of an enchanted maiden, Maria, he finds the demon's underworld kingdom and is given three impossible tasks to win his freedom. Maria helps accomplish the first two; since the third is beyond her power, they flee, with the demon's minions in pursuit. Maria's magic changes them into a church where the demon has no power, and they escape his clutches. Interestingly, the prince of the Lang version is more feckless and the heroine stronger; San Souci omits the ending in which Ivan forgets his rescuer and is on the point of marrying another when he is reminded of his first love by the wedding cake she's baked. Also, the men in Lang's story cause trouble that women must set aright; San Souci emphasizes the clash of good and evil. [Lauren Mills's] illustrations, set against soft gold, contrast the protagonists' beauty (and their jewels and brocade) with the grotesque demon, his ragtag troll servants, and their chimerical steeds, with enough claw-like fingers, pointy ears, and warty noses to populate a nightmare—fairy-tale telling-and-showing at its most romantic.

Chris Sherman

SOURCE: A review of *The Tsar's Promise,* in *Booklist,* Vol. 89, No. 8, December 15, 1992, p. 741.

San Souci's retelling of this old Russian tale includes all the elements that have long ensured the popularity of folktales: evil demons with horrific powers, a handsome couple, fearsome tests, dramatic flight and pursuit, enchantment, and true love conquering all. When he's unwittingly promised to a demon by his father, the young Tsarevitch, Ivan, honors the promise and surrenders himself. The demon offers Ivan freedom if he can perform three impossible tasks. Ivan is helped by Maria, a beautiful princess stolen by the demon, who has learned some of the demon's magic. Eventually, Ivan and Maria foil the demon, but a marvelous tension builds until the couple is finally safe and married happily ever after. A frightening depiction of demons and trolls enhances the eeriness of the tale, but the mood is softened by [Lauren] Mills' dreamy, golden watercolors and by the beauty of Ivan and Maria.

Denise Anton Wright

SOURCE: A review of *The Tsar's Promise,* in *School Library Journal,* Vol. 39, No. 2, February, 1993, pp. 86, 91.

Returning from a long journey, Tsar Kojata is captured by a hideous demon who demands to have what awaits the ruler at home. Thinking that nothing is worth risking his life over, Kojata agrees. But once home, he discovers that his son was born during his absence. Because Kojata forgets his promise to the demon, it is Prince Ivan who must honor it. Aided by Maria, a beautiful young woman who is also a prisoner of the demon, the young man completes each seemingly impossible task he's asked to perform and eventually returns to his homeland safely with Maria as his wife. San Souci draws largely upon the Russian folktale "King Kojata" found in Andrew Lang's *The Green Fairy Book* (1969). Although his retelling is competent, several key incidents providing much-needed character motivation have been left out. Unfortunately, the book's illustrations do little to clarify the story line. . . . Despite good intentions, this picture book never quite hits its mark.

THE SAMURAI'S DAUGHTER: A JAPANESE LEGEND (1992)

Kirkus Reviews

SOURCE: A review of *The Samurai's Daughter,* in *Kirkus Reviews,* Vol. LX, No. 20, October 15, 1992, p. 1316.

From medieval Japan (as detailed in a careful note), a wonderful legend about the dauntless Tokoyo, whose beloved father Kuma has taught her the samurai virtues, plus such manly arts as riding; and who insists, despite her noble birth, on learning to dive for pearls, a traditional skill of women of the Oki Islands. When Kuma loses favor and is unjustly exiled, Tokoyo follows, braving ghosts, battling a sea monster, and bringing up a submerged statue of the ruler. Thus she ends the statue's curse and dispels the ruler's madness: he summons Kuma home, honoring him and his courageous daughter. The action-filled story is admirably retold, while newcomer [Stephen T.] Johnson offers dramatic, elegantly balanced paintings in rich, subtly harmonious colors; his tender compositions depicting Kuma and Tokoyo at their parting, and again at their reunion, are especially fine. Like Merrill's *The Girl Who Loved Caterpillars,* an unusual glimpse of an independent-minded girl in long-ago Japan; a handsome book that will have many uses.

John Philbrook

SOURCE: A review of *The Samurai's Daughter,* in *School Library Journal,* Vol. 38, No. 11, November, 1992, p. 86.

Tokoyo, daughter of a loyal samurai in 13th-century Japan, sets off on a perilous journey to be reunited with her unjustly exiled father. En route, she slays a sea serpent and, by sheer serendipity, lifts the curse that has caused the paranoia of the supreme ruler. Her father is restored to favor, suitably rewarded, and both return home to enjoy "peace and prosperity for the rest of their lives." San Souci's retelling of this Kamakura Period folktale is smooth, lively, and makes a resonant read-aloud. [Stephen T.] Johnson's pastel and ink illustrations capture authentic small details yet remain dreamily impressionistic. Pictures match the text well, although Tokoyo is often depicted in overly melodramatic poses that may detract from one-on-one reading, but become quite effective at a distance for group sharing. The strong, independent female protagonist will inspire many admirers.

Hazel Rochman

SOURCE: A review of *The Samurai's Daughter*, in *Booklist*, Vol. 89, No. 15, November 1, 1992, p. 517.

In an old story set in medieval Japan, the hero, Tokoyo, is a brave young woman; her quest is to free her father; and on her difficult journey, she must dive deep to fight the demonic serpent who lives at the bottom of the sea. Trained as a samurai warrior, Tokoyo has learned from the women on her island to dive and harvest the wealth of the ocean. San Souci tells the tale quietly, in a direct storytelling style that allows the mythic elements to work their mystery. [Stephen T.] Johnson's full-page pastel illustrations in rich colors show Tokoyo as a strong, long-haired beauty. When her father is forced into exile, their parting embrace is as heartfelt as their reunion at the end, when her loyalty and courage have restored him to home and honor. In contrast are the wide-open scenes of her diving through the ocean, hair swirling as she attacks the coiling monster. In an introductory note, San Souci explains the source of the legend and relates it to the diving women of the Oki Islands, who continue their "time-honored occupation" even today.

Mary M. Burns

SOURCE: A review of *The Samurai's Daughter*, in *The Horn Book Magazine*, Vol. LXVIII, No. 6, November-December, 1992, pp. 733-4.

One always expects impeccable scholarship and a fluid storytelling style when reading a text by Robert D. San Souci; this latest venture continues to enchant readers. The beautiful daughter of a samurai, raised in the traditions of that class, follows her father into exile, slays a malevolent sea monster, and restores the sanity of the ruler who had banished her parent. The tale, as a brief but informative author's note informs us, is based on a legend from medieval Japan. In addition to the primary sources cited, San Souci also indicates his use of collateral materials—especially those related to the diving women of Shima province—giving depth and authenticity to the narrative, [Stephen T.] Johnson's illustrations, rich and glowing, match the dignity of the plot yet develop the warm relationship between father and daughter. Thus, the central character emerges as a real personality—triumphantly feminine without seeming anachronistic in the par-

ticular historical setting. An exemplary and stunning collaboration.

FEATHERTOP: BASED ON THE TALE BY NATHANIEL HAWTHORNE (1992)

Publishers Weekly

SOURCE: A review of *Feathertop*, in *Publishers Weekly*, Vol. 239, No. 48, November 2, 1992, pp. 70-1.

Portions of Nathaniel Hawthorne's short story "Feathertop: A Moralized Legend" have been, of necessity, greatly altered for this picture book adaptation. Robert San Souci's retelling, however, preserves a surprising amount of drama—even in this truncated form, the plight of the scarecrow who loves a mortal girl retains its affecting overtones. Mother Rigby, "one of the most powerful witches in early New England," transforms her ragtag scarecrow into a flesh-and-blood man and sets out to humiliate her antagonist, Judge Gookin, by having the manikin woo the judge's daughter. As might be expected—and hoped for—in a work for this age group, true love wins out, and even Mother Rigby seems a trifle calmer at book's end. Brisk pacing, a believable conflict and even a certain amount of depth are skillful substitutions for the original story's disturbing psychological issues. Daniel San Souci's handsome watercolors, in pinks, plums and browns, effectively capture the garb and architectural details of mid-18th-century New England; more than that, they imbue the story's small cast with the child appeal of a solid folktale. Though literary purists may object to this abridgement, youngsters will relish cheering for hero and heroine and booing a nasty witch indeed.

Shirley Wilton

SOURCE: A review of *Feathertop: Based on the Tale by Nathaniel Hawthorne*, in *School Library Journal*, Vol. 38, No. 12, December, 1992, p. 90.

Bright orange, purple, and gold color the autumn landscape of a colonial New England town in which a soft-hearted witch and a pumpkin-headed scarecrow play out a drama of magic and romance in this well-told tale. In order to trick Judge Gookin, old Mother Rigby turns her shabbily dressed scarecrow into a handsome gentleman and sends him to woo the judge's daughter as Master Feathertop. Falling truly in love with Polly, he regrets the deception and retreats to his original state as a straw man. But Polly's love is also true, and with the help of Mother Rigby's magic, she changes the ragged scarecrow back to her handsome Feathertop. Adapted from a little known moral tale by Nathaniel Hawthorne, the story has been modernized to bear the contemporary theme of love and its power. The smoothly flowing oral quality of Robert San Souci's text is matched by the interpretation in brilliant colors and lively action of Daniel San Souci's pictures, making **Feathertop** a highly effective picture book for any season of the year.

📖 *CUT FROM THE SAME CLOTH: AMERICAN WOMEN OF MYTH, LEGEND, AND TALL TALE* (1993)

Janice Del Negro

SOURCE: A review of *Cut from the Same Cloth: American Women of Myth, Legend, and Tall Tale*, in *Booklist*, Vol. 89, No. 16, April 15, 1993, pp. 1508, 1510.

This well-intentioned collection contains 15 stories retold by San Souci, who's put together his versions from a variety of secondary sources. Divided loosely by geography (**"Women of the Northeast," "Women of the South,"** etc.), the tales feature Native American, African American, Hawaiian, Eskimo, and Anglo American heroines. Each tale begins strongly with [Brian] Pinkney's black-and-white scratchboard portrait of the heroine, but San Souci's retellings are uneven, lacking both definitive voice and focus. The inclusion of **"Drop Star"** (a "place legend," popularized by white settlers, about the kidnapping of a three-year-old white child by Indians) as an implied example of Seneca Indian heroism (it's listed in the table of contents as "Seneca Indian") is misleading at best—the character Drop Star barely appears. What's more, the use of pseudodialect in several of the African American tales is highly questionable. While there is a recognizable need in children's literature for folktales with strong women heroines, this will not fill it satisfactorily. The bibliography will be useful for storytellers who are trying to create their own folktale heroines, but the book is recommended only for large comparative folktale and professional collections.

Betsy Hearne

SOURCE: A review of *Cut from the Same Cloth: American Women of Myth, Legend, and Tall Tale*, in *Bulletin of the Center for Children's Books*, Vol. 46, No. 10, June, 1993, pp. 328-9.

Grouped by region—Northeast, South, Midwest, Southwest, and West—these fifteen stories offer a satisfying balance to the male-dominated tall tale figures so familiar from books such as Paul Robert Walker's *Big Men, Big Country*. There's also a good ethnic mix here: six of the heroines are Native American, four African American, two Anglo American, one Mexican American, and one Hawaiian. If any particular characteristic seems to distinguish these superhumans from their male counterparts, it's the fact that the women's deeds tend to be less staggering than haunting. The Miwok legend of Hekeke, for instance, in which Hekeke is kidnapped by a cannibalistic giant and must watch him consume his victims until she destroys him, has a tone more reminiscent of Odysseus' experience in the cave of the Cyclops than of any Paul Bunyan-type feats. Otoonah's determined survival after being abandoned on an island by her brothers during a period of starvation is as adventurous a quest as you'll find anywhere. Others, such as **"Molly Cottontail,"** are lighter-hearted or, like **"Sweet Betsey from Pike,"** sharp-

edged. San Souci has varied his retellings to suit the style of each story, and his introductions, source notes, and bibliography are commendably thorough. Brian Pinkney's signature scratchboard illustrations, one of which introduces each tale, are particularly well tuned to the heroic mode. This is a first-class resource for school media centers where students work with tall tales, or for public libraries where parents and professionals read folklore aloud and do storytelling.

Ruth K. MacDonald

SOURCE: "Off the Map: The Journals of Lewis and Clark," in *School Library Journal*, Vol. 39, No. 6, June, 1993, p. 122.

In many ways, this volume continues the work of Ethel Johnston Phelps's *Tatterhood and Other Tales* (1978) as it offers authentic folk and fairy tales about heroines. Here, however, San Souci confines himself to North America and organizes his selections by region, moving from east to west. The women come from the Native American, African American, Mexican American, and Canadian traditions. Although they differ in many ways from their male counterparts, there are still tricksters, sweet talkers, and brave and strong protagonists like those found in hero stories. There has been some retelling, some modifications of dialects, some reshaping of open endings, but the plots have not been tampered with. Each story is illustrated with an engraving of some sort [by Brian Pinkney], with black background and white lines that give the pictures an antique quality like a woodcut or copper engraving. Notes on the stories and an extensive list of further reading are appended. An impressive and gratifying collection that's a cut above other such compilations.

📖 *THE SNOW WIFE* (1993)

Hazel Rochman

SOURCE: A review of *The Snow Wife*, in *Booklist*, Vol. 89, Nos. 19 & 20, June 1 & 15, 1993, pp. 1848, 1850.

Reminiscent of San Souci and [Stephen T.] Johnson's last handsome picture book *The Samurai's Daughter*, this also focuses on a beautiful, bold young woman with thick, spreading black hair. Based on a traditional Japanese legend, it has connections with stories everywhere about the hero's perilous journey to expiate his betrayal of a secret. The landscape is a desolate, wintry mountain, and Johnson's watercolors and pastels show swirling snow and wind-swept precipices. In the opening scene, "the winds howled like demons," and the young woodcutter Minokichi is saved by a mysterious, beautiful woman in white, who makes him swear he will never speak a word about her. Later, he marries a woman of grace, but when he tells her about the creature in the storm, his wife cries, "The woman you saw was I!"; because of his broken promise, she swirls away in a white mist. Then he must journey to the shrine of the Wind God on the peak of

Bitter Mountain and overcome fierce monsters before he can persuade the god to make his wife mortal again. The monster figures in the storm are compelling—almost like grotesque versions of the mysterious snow wife—and story and pictures blend the human and natural worlds with beauty and fear.

Kirkus Reviews

SOURCE: A review of *The Snow Wife*, in *Kirkus Reviews*, Vol. LXI, No. 16, August 15, 1993, p. 1079.

A ghost story based on an ancient Japanese legend. The young woodcutter Minokichi, happily married to lovely Yuki, doesn't know she's an icy spirit in thrall to the Wind God. When a broken promise exiles Yuki back to the spirit world and she loses all memory of their happy life together, Minokichi undertakes a perilous quest to the capricious god's shrine to plead for her return. His desperate journey through mountain wastes, where he eludes fearsome creatures, has the drama and power of the Orpheus myth—with a happy ending. [Stephen T.] Johnson's pastel-and-watercolor art features marvelously subtle colors, mysterious light, mists, and vapors, and extravagantly imaginative portraits of the grotesque beings on Bitter Mountain. An excellent edition of a fine story.

Betsy Hearne

SOURCE: A review of *The Snow Wife*, in *Bulletin of the Center for Children's Books*, Vol. 47, No. 5, January, 1994, pp. 166-7.

Kids intrigued by yetis will find this retelling of a Japanese legend eerily appealing: it starts when a supernatural woman freezes an old woodcutter but spares his young companion, Minokichi, who later meets her in human form and marries her. Then Minokichi breaks a promise not to mention his wintry brush with death, whereupon he must trek past a threatening Mountain Man and cannibalistic ogress to win back his wife from the Wind God. [Stephen T. Johnson's] paintings are as coldly spooky as the story, with awesome demon-figures and impressionistic layers of color overcast by snowy white. Even the adaptation (no source cited) has a trace of cool wit: "Circumstances—a white hairy ogress to be exact—forced my disrespectful act," says Minokichi to the Wind God. Try this for variety at Halloween or any old time you need a ghost story.

Linda Boyles

SOURCE: A review of *Snow Wife*, in *School Library Journal*, Vol. 40, No. 3, March, 1994, p. 218.

The team that created *The Samurai's Daughter* (1992) turns again to Japanese legend, bringing their considerable talents to bear on a tale with a familiar folklore motif. Caught in a terrible blizzard, two woodcutters take shelter in a mountain hut. During the night, Minokichi, the young-

er, finds a coldly beautiful woman bending over his companion. Seeing Minokichi's terror, she says that she feels "pity and something deeper" for him, and spares his life, extracting his vow not to tell anyone what he has seen. As she drifts away, he sees that his friend is dead. Returning home, he tells no one of his vision until years later, when he tells his wife of his strange dreamlike experience. His broken promise brings disaster, for before his eyes, Yuki changes into the Woman of the Snow and fades into the mist. Seeking the help of the Wind God, Minokichi undertakes a dangerous journey through mountains inhabited by fierce supernatural beings to win back his beloved snow wife. San Souci spins a compelling, atmospheric tale, enhanced by Stephen T. Johnson's equally evocative paintings. His cool, misty watercolors and textured pastels create a strong sense of the snow-filled landscape, underscoring the drama of the retelling. A fine addition to any collection.

📖 THE HOBYAHS (1994)

Janice Del Negro

SOURCE: A review of *The Hobyahs*, in *Booklist*, Vol. 90, No. 11, February 1, 1994, p. 1006.

In one fell swoop, San Souci has redefined the "classic version" of a popular, traditional tale about goblins called Hobyahs. Rather than eliminating plot elements, his retelling contributes to what is already in place. San Souci's little dog Turpie has four dog friends, and instead of losing limbs to the draconian old man, the dogs run off into the woods. When the Hobyahs come upon the unprotected house, they still tear down the walls, eat the old man and woman, and carry the little girl off in a bag. After being rescued by her faithful dogs (who gobble up the Hobyahs), the little girl returns with her dogs to build a new house—"and if they haven't gone away, they must be living there still." The addition of rhyming quatrains at key moments in the plot turns the book into a storytelling treat, and [Alexi] Natchev's just-a-little-scary illustrations are great for showing to groups during reading aloud. With notes on sources, this definitely has a place in children's collections.

Kirkus Reviews

SOURCE: A review of *The Hobyahs*, in *Kirkus Reviews*, Vol. LXII, No. 6, March 15, 1994, p. 403.

In Joseph Jacob's version of this classic tale (in *More English Folk and Fairy Tales*), faithful Turpie tries to warn his owner of the wicked Hobyahs who come by night, intent on evil; but the old dog's ungrateful owner only punishes him for barking. He cuts off Turpie's tail, his legs, finally his head, till Turpie can bark no more. Then the Hobyahs return, destroying all but a kind little girl who's saved by a hunter and his dog. Much of the story's power comes from the horror that builds, night by night, with the Hobyahs' menace and the old man's cruelty. Here, in reducing the violence, San Souci loses much of the drama. He includes five dogs that are merely chased away one by one; in the end they all come back to rescue the girl. In his energetic illustrations, [Alexi] Natchev blends the natural and fantastical to create a dark, mildly eerie landscape. The dogs are as much comical as fierce; the Hobyahs—round-eyed, cat-like creatures in striped nightgowns—are not very scary. For those who relish the older tale, a disappointing substitute. San Souci explains his alterations in a scrupulous source note.

Dot Minzer

SOURCE: A review of *The Hobyahs,* in *School Library Journal,* Vol. 40, No. 4, April, 1994, p. 122.

An adaptation of an English tale about a little girl who lives with an old man and an old woman in a house made of hemp stalks. Night after night, the dreaded Hobyahs come out of the woods to "tear down the hemp stalks, eat up the old man and woman, and carry off the little girl." But each time they are chased away by the barking of the old man's five dogs, a change from the original version's sole little dog Turpie. Bothered by the barking, the ungrateful couple beat the dogs and send them away, one by one. Finally, there is no one to frighten the Hobyahs away. They eat the old man and old woman and carry off the little girl, but she is rescued by the banished dogs, providing the tale with a happy ending. San Souci's smoothly written text with repetitive lines creates a rhythm that captures a listening audience. It is offset by short poems that provide an eerie tone while they signal each change of action in the story. [Alexi] Natchev's first-class, full-color illustrations add to the drama and suspense. . . . While the original tale was extremely violent, be warned that this tamer version will still cause some kids to wince as, one by one, the dogs are beaten and cast out. That aside, it remains a fun scary book that will be a hit as a read-aloud.

📖 *MORE SHORT AND SHIVERY: THIRTY TERRIFYING TALES* (1994)

Stephanie Zvirin

SOURCE: A review of *More Short & Shivery: Thirty Terrifying Tales,* in *Booklist,* Vol. 90, Nos. 1 & 2, June 1 & 15, 1994, p. 1796.

Like San Souci's earlier collection *Short & Shivery* (1987), this contains a sampling of folktales in which supernatural elements take center stage. Vampires, disembodied heads, ghosts, and evil entities of varying descriptions terrify unsuspecting mortals, the nice as well as the nasty kind. Several of the 30 stories—for example, the often anthologized **"King of the Cats"** from the British Isles and **"Knock . . . Knock . . . Knock,"** a popular North American urban legend—may be known to scary-story fans. But most of the tales, which have been gathered from countries as far flung as Russia, Haiti, Iceland, and Nigeria, will be unfamiliar. . . .

Though creepy enough, San Souci's straightforward retellings (he sometimes uses dialogue) keep the grisly details well under control, and his thorough source notes can lead readers on to other collections of folklore, fairy tales, and myths.

Kirkus Reviews

SOURCE: A review of *More Short & Shivery: Thirty Terrifying Tales,* in *Kirkus Reviews,* Vol. LXII, No. 16, August 15, 1994, p. 1138.

This collection reads more like a cultural anthropology text than a book of ghost stories. San Souci (*Cut from the Same Cloth,* 1993, etc.) retells 30 "scary tales" from around the world. But, stripped of much of their gruesomeness, these stories fall completely flat. The ethnic details, which are placed rather awkwardly in the narrative, disrupt the flow further so that whatever suspense might have been created is utterly lost. The only time the author writes a story that is even a little frightening is when he sticks to urban myths and avoids "other cultures" completely, but even then his narration is too rushed and casual to involve the reader.

The prolific San Souci has not managed to create a campfire classic in this book—even the most squeamish will remain unfazed.

Patricia A. Dollisch

SOURCE: A review of *More Short & Shivery: Thirty Terrifying Tales,* in *School Library Journal,* Vol. 40, No. 9, September, 1994, p. 235.

This volume of 30 scary stories from around the world is an absolute delight. The breadth of the collection is impressive. Some of the tales are old friends (**"The King of the Cats"** from England and **"The Devil and Tom Walker"** from the U. S.), while others seem familiar (**"Escape up the Tree"** from Nigeria is a lot like "Wiley and the Hairy Man," and **"Knock . . . Knock . . . Knock"** from the U. S./Canada is a story that youngsters have been telling each other at camp for years). There are still others (**"Sister Death and the Healer"** from Mexico/American Southwest and **"The Greedy Daughter"** from Italy) that are unfamiliar but will soon be well loved. San Souci's fine ear for dialogue is reflected in his retellings, and he deserves a medal for the detailed source notes he provides. Each selection is illustrated [by Katherine Coville and Jacqueline Rogers] with a dramatic, full-page black-and-white painting. A book that's equally appropriate for the classroom or under the covers.

Deborah Stevenson

SOURCE: A review of *More Short and Shivery: Thirty Terrifying Tales,* in *Bulletin of the Center for Children's Books,* Vol. 48, No. 2, October, 1994, p. 65.

Transmogrified snakes, vengeful ghosts, seductive but lethal spirits—all these and more appear in this followup to *Short and Shivery Tales*. As with the previous volume, the tales here are drawn from a wide variety of locations, including Japan, Russia, Britain, and the U.S. San Souci's retellings are more literary than elemental, which tends to make the tales into short stories rather than sinister yarns (the retelling of the classic urban legend "The Boyfriend's Death" as **"Knock . . . Knock . . . Knock,"** for instance, is still compelling but far less ominous); the use of dialect sometimes makes a story denser rather than more atmospheric. The pan-ethnicity of the collection, however, makes for entertaining breadth, and the stories will make good readalouds for older kids on a dark and thundery afternoon. San Souci's exemplary and complete notes on the stories appear in the back of the book. The occasional black-and-white illustrations [by Katherine Coville and Jacqueline Rogers] provide some eerie visual entertainment.

SOOTFACE: AN OJIBWA CINDERELLA STORY (1994)

Carolyn Phelan

SOURCE: A review of *Sootface: An Ojibwa Cinderella Story,* in *Booklist,* Vol. 91, No. 4, October 15, 1994, p. 433.

In this Ojibwa tale, Sootface is a young woman who does all the cooking, mending, and fire tending for her father and her two mean and lazy older sisters. When the mysterious invisible warrior announces through his sister that he will take for his bride a woman with a kind and honest heart, only Sootface proves worthy. The tale has been told before, even in picture-book format, but the San Souci version reads aloud well, and the watercolor artwork [by Daniel San Souci] illustrates the story with quiet grace. A satisfying picture book for reading aloud or alone, and a good choice for classes studying Native Americans or comparative folklore.

Venessa Elder

SOURCE: A review of *Sootface: An Ojibwa Cinderella Story,* in *School Library Journal,* Vol. 40, No. 11, November, 1994, p. 101.

Sootface's mother is dead, her sisters beat her, and her father doesn't intervene. Her face is always smeared with soot, and her hair is horribly singed from the cookfire. In spite of all this, she remains resilient—she knows that one day she will escape her circumstances. A mighty warrior who has the power to make himself invisible decides to marry the woman who is kind enough of heart to see him. Several attractive maidens, including Sootface's sisters, try and fail. Now, Sootface is resourceful—no fairy personage shows up to magically bestow finery upon her or to fix up her hair. She prepares herself the best she can and goes off to meet him. She exclaims on

the beauty of his bow—it's made of a rainbow and strung with stardust. He materializes, renames her Dawn-Light, and they are betrothed. The retelling is lively, flows well, and brings out the harshness of the heroine's situation, and yet it is not without humorous touches. [Daniel San Souci's] full-page watercolors dramatically convey the natural woodland setting, the jeers of Sootface's sisters and fellow villagers, and the serenity and kindness of the warrior and his sister. Sootface's dazed expression remains rather similar throughout—until the end, when she is transformed by love into a beautiful girl. Altogether a refreshing and rewarding "Cinderella" variant.

THE FAITHFUL FRIEND (1995)

Ilene Cooper

SOURCE: A review of *The Faithful Friend,* in *Booklist,* Vol. 91, No. 16, April 15, 1995, p. 1499.

From the collaborators who gave us **Sukey and the Mermaid** (1992), a rich tale that adds Caribbean spice to the folklore stew. Based on a story from the island of Martinique (via Europe), this begins with two friends, Clement and Hippolyte, who have been raised as brothers. Clement has fallen in love with the beautiful Pauline, so the duo head off to woo her. Pauline readily accepts Clement's proposal, despite the fury of her uncle, Monsieur Zabocat, who is rumored to be a wizard. The three young people return to Clement's plantation, but in the dark of night, Hippolyte spies three zombies, who have been ordered by Monsieur Zabocat to make sure the wedding never takes place. Anyone who reveals the zombies' murderous plans will be turned to stone. After a slow start, the story ignites with dark and glorious elements. Love, hate and death take shape in [Brian] Pinkney's impressive scratchboard-and-oil artwork, which is given full range in the dramatic two-page spreads. In his informative afterword, San Souci notes that one appeal of the book lies in its emphasis on the friendship of black and white characters (Clement is West Indian, Hippolyte, French), and while this is true, it is really the brooding elements of the netherworld and the promise of redemption that give the story its potency.

Marlene Lee

SOURCE: A review of *The Faithful Friend,* in *School Library Journal,* Vol. 41, No. 6, June, 1995, pp. 104-5.

On the beautiful island of Martinique in the 19th century, good friends Hippolyte, the son of a French-born widow, and Clement, a rich landowner's son, set out to meet a young woman Clement has fallen hopelessly in love [with] through her picture. At their destination, they encounter the prospective bride's frightening uncle, Monsieur Zabocat, purportedly a *quimboiseur,* or wizard, of the worst degree. After overcoming Zabocat's several curses, which lead both young men into many true tests of friendship, the couple is married and all ends happily. [Brian] Pinkney's scratchboard and oil artwork switches from bright daytime hues for most of the book to purples and grays for scenes with the zombies and snakes, which are very effective. An afterword gives valuable information about the origins of the tale, and a glossary with pronunciation makes reading aloud and/or telling the tale a real pleasure. This excellent title contains all the elements of a well-researched folktale, and convincingly conveys the richness of the West Indian culture.

Betsy Hearne

SOURCE: A review of *The Faithful Friend,* in *Bulletin of the Center for Children's Books,* Vol. 49, No. 1, September, 1995, pp. 28-9.

Like Ehrlich's Italian variant *Pome and Peel,* this celebrates a friendship threatened by forces of evil: when the Caribbean plantation owner's son, Clement, falls in love with beautiful Pauline, his white friend Hippolyte protects them from her guardian's zombies, first by turning the couple away from poisoned water and mangoes, then by hiding in their bridal chamber to kill a deadly serpent. Alas, the snake disappears. Hippolyte is accused of planning to kill his friend out of jealousy, and, just as the zombies have threatened, he turns to stone when he explains the black magic. Fortunately, he's brought back to life by an old beggar resurrected, just for this purpose, from the grave where Clement and Hippolyte had paused in their travels to give him a decent burial. If it sounds complicated, it is, but San Souci has a gift for adaptations that read smoothly without cheating their folkloric sources. His informed note discusses the tale type, placing this West Indian variant from Martinique in a broader cross-cultural context and describing changes he's made along with the reasons for them. Older picture-book audiences will relish the story's suspense, which is enhanced by [Brian] Pinkney's brooding illustrations. The tension of his sophisticated ghostly white linework against backgrounds of dark forest or dim interiors exposes a twilight side to characteristically brilliant Caribbean colors.

📖 *KATE SHELLEY: BOUND FOR LEGEND* (1995)

Mary Harris Veeder

SOURCE: A review of *Kate Shelley: Bound for Legend,* in *Booklist,* Vol. 91, No. 21, July, 1995, p. 1877.

In this picture book for older readers, San Souci reconstructs a slice of history. After the railroad bridge near her home collapsed during a summer storm in 1881, 15-year-old Kate Shelley walked to the nearest railroad station to make sure the passenger train from Chicago would be stopped before it reached the broken bridge. To get to the station, she had to crawl across a 700-foot-long railroad bridge, with a raging river below. The train had been stopped by railroad officials before she arrived, but her courageous efforts still saved two lives and won her a

national reputation. Along with dramatic descriptions, San Souci presents a convincing portrait of Kate's personality, depicting her as a strong, supportive part of her family long before that summer's night. [Max] Ginsburg's realistic oil paintings of the storm and the bridge crossing are particularly effective.

Martha Rosen

SOURCE: A review of *Kate Shelley: Bound for Legend,* in *School Library Journal,* Vol. 41, No. 9, September, 1995, p. 197.

A lyrical account of 15-year-old Kate Shelley's feat of averting a major train disaster during a tremendous storm on the night of July 6, 1881. Based on scholarly research, as well as on Kate and her younger sister's own commentary, the story helps readers to feel the tension building to a crescendo, mirroring the fury of the storm, as Kate realizes what she must do to stop the midnight express from flying off the destroyed Honey Creek Bridge. The young woman battles not only the ferocious elements and the clock as she makes her way across the railroad ties of the Des Moines River Bridge to Moingona Station, but also her personal fears. Kate's story has been told adequately in Margaret Wetterer's *Kate Shelley and the Midnight Express* (1990), but San Souci's version better captures the drama, as it also gives life to the characters, particularly Kate and her widowed mother. The excitement is enhanced by the luminous oil paintings, as each page evokes an emotional response to Kate's predicament and difficult choices. [Max] Ginsburg's illustrations of the night scenes are superb. The image of Kate, halfway across the bridge and threatened by an uprooted tree swept along in the angry water, is illuminated simply by a bolt of lightning splitting the dark sky. This powerful painting emphasizes the magnitude of the heroine's struggle and the enormity of her accomplishment.

Roger Sutton

SOURCE: A review of *Kate Shelley: Bound for Legend,* in *Bulletin of the Center for Children's Books,* Vol. 49, No. 4, December, 1995, pp. 138-9.

Kate Shelley braves the stormy bridge once again, in this picture-book biography that sticks more closely to the facts than did Margaret Wetterer's *Kate Shelley and the Midnight Express.* Something of a folk hero in her native Iowa, Kate Shelley made her way through a fierce summer storm in 1881 to tell the stationmaster that an engine had gone down in Honey Creek; even more desperately, she needed to stop the eastbound express to Chicago before it reached the now-severed bridge. San Souci points out, as Wetterer does not, that the express train had already stopped because of the storm; while Kate Shelley was certainly brave, she was also unwittingly beside the point. (San Souci and Wetterer also differ in their accounts of the wrecked engine, with only San Souci mentioning fatalities.) The newer book is the fuller account, probably too full for story hour and better appreciated as a choice for individual reading. [Max] Ginsburg's illustrations are painterly and studied, not particularly well-matched to the dramatic story.

Additional coverage of San Souci's life and career is contained in the following sources published by Gale Research: *Contemporary Authors New Revision Series,* Vol. 46; *Contemporary Authors,* Vol. 108; and *Something about the Author,* Vols. 40, 81.

David Wiesner

1956-

American author and illustrator of picture books.

Major works include *The Loathsome Dragon* (with Kim Kahng, 1987), *Free Fall* (1988), *Hurricane* (1990), *Tuesday* (1991), *June 29, 1999* (1992).

INTRODUCTION

Noted for his distinctive, intricate watercolors and fantastic themes, Wiesner has quickly become a critical and popular success with picture books that explore the world of the imagination. Taking as their premises such surrealistic events as flying frogs, floating vegetables, and adventure-filled dreams, Wiesner's books employ realistic illustrations with witty details, rather than text, to accentuate the humor or drama inherent in the story. Critics have praised the artist's attention to form and design, his inventive use of perspective, and his skill with light and color, frequently comparing his work to that of fellow Caldecott-winner Chris Van Allsburg. An advocate of the wordless picture book format, Wiesner leaves the interpretation of his stories open to readers by concentrating each tale's development within his artwork; as a result, a *Publishers Weekly* critic says, Wiesner's work "makes the picture book format seem limitless."

Biographical Information

Born and raised in Bridgewater, New Jersey, Wiesner enjoyed an upbringing that indulged his imagination. His neighborhood, with a nearby river, woods, cemetery, and dump, was the ideal environment for fantasy games; as one of several creatively inclined siblings, he found encouragement for his interests in art and drawing. Preparing for a career in fine arts, Wiesner attended the Rhode Island School of Design. Although one of his assignments there later became the genesis for his Caldecott honor book *Free Fall*, it was not until visiting lecturer Trina Schart Hyman saw his work and offered him the cover of *Cricket* magazine that he considered creating children's books as a career. He started by illustrating the work of others—including authors such as Jane Yolen and Avi—shortly after graduation; by 1987 he had collaborated with his wife Kim Kahng on his first book, *The Loathsome Dragon*. With his next work, *Free Fall*, Wiesner ventured into the wordless picture book format which has since earned him much acclaim. His purpose in eliminating most or all of a book's text is to allow the reader to collaborate in the story: "There is no author's voice telling the story," the artist said in his acceptance speech for his Caldecott Medal-winning picture book *Tuesday*. "Each viewer reads the book in his or her own way. The reader is an integral part of the storytelling process."

Major Works

A retelling of an English fairy tale about a bewitched princess, her loyal brother, and their vengeful stepmother, *The Loathsome Dragon* provides Wiesner with a medieval setting which highlights his skill in developing perspective and creating detail. This traditional telling also features touches of Wiesner's trademark visual humor, as when Princess Margaret's ladies-in-waiting first behold her draconic transformation. *Free Fall* takes a young boy through a fantastic, continuous dream sequence in which objects inside each double-page spread gradually metamorphose to create a new scene. Wiesner's illustrations earned widespread acclaim for their technical brilliance; some critics, however, found the lack of text and plot confusing, although others believed the format would provide readers with an enjoyable game. Based on an actual incident from the author's youth and full of autobiographical visual details, *Hurricane* is another celebration of imagination as two brothers use a giant elm tree felled by a storm to transport themselves to the jungle, the ocean, and even outer space. While the book contains a brief text, it is the artist's illustrations, with their inventive use of light and perspective, that create excitement and interest. Perspective also plays a great part in *Tuesday,* as a flock of frogs levitates through the air on their lily pads. Several amusing encounters in a nearby town are portrayed in dark, rich watercolors that range from panoramic skyscapes to close-up portraits. Unusual sights also fill the skies in *June 29, 1999,* as a young girl's science experiment seems to result in an epidemic of giant vegetables appearing above cities all over the country. As the brief, alliterative text eventually reveals the humorous solution to the mystery, Wiesner's illustrations include the kinds of unusual perspectives, realistic drawings, and imaginative details that have earned him recognition as an innovative and entertaining creator of picture books.

Awards

Free Fall was named a Caldecott Honor Book in 1989, while *Tuesday* won the 1992 Caldecott Medal.

AUTHOR'S COMMENTARY

Susan F. Caroff and Elizabeth B. Moje

SOURCE: "A Conversation with David Wiesner: 1992 Caldecott Medal Winner, *The Reading Teacher,* Vol. 46, No. 4, December, 1992-January, 1993, pp. 284-9.

Interviewer: *It is an honor to have the opportunity to talk with you about your book* Tuesday *for which you received the Caldecott Medal. Please share your thoughts about winning the Caldecott for the book* Tuesday.

WIESNER: Well, it's pretty amazing to win the Caldecott. Having looked at the books that have won over the years, and gradually getting to know some people who have won, it seems pretty unbelievable that I won the Caldecott. I certainly felt confident about my work, but to actually know that my name will be added to the list— well, that is a stunning moment. It's a very satisfying feeling to be recognized.

INTERVIEWER: *We are interested in knowing something about how you wrote the book* Tuesday. *Would you tell us a little bit about your process of visual storytelling?*

WIESNER: Wordless books have been my passion for a long time. It's something that goes way back. I've always liked telling stories with pictures, more than just painting a single painting. If I came up with an image that I really liked—with characters that I liked—I would always be interested in seeing what had happened before or after the particular image I had painted. Growing up drawing and painting, or telling a story with pictures, was always more comfortable for me than using words.

When I was in college at the Rhode Island School of Design, a number of things began to have a big impact on me and the way I thought about telling stories. Probably foremost was a book called *Mad Man's Drum* by Lynd Ward, who I later found out worked mostly on children's books and was a Caldecott Medal winner. Ward wrote novels for adults completely in woodcuts with no words. They were very complex stories dealing with a lot of complicated themes and imagery, such as life, death, spirituality, and good and evil. These themes involved a remarkable range of emotions, and Ward composed these 250-page novels *with no words.* I saw *Mad Man's Drum* in my sophomore year. Ward just amazed me—the process from page to page and the way he conveyed information and paced images. His ideas fit in with things I had begun to think about. So, as a student, I began to play around with wordless storytelling. This culminated in my senior degree project, where I constructed a wordless picture book. I took an adult story, threw away the text, and attempted to tell it in pictures. When I got to the point where I was ready to finally write my own books, I decided on the wordless book. My first attempt was **Free Fall.** Then I wrote **Hurricane,** my first attempt at writing text (which is a whole other story). After **Hurricane,** I wanted to come back to the wordless book because there were still a lot of things I hadn't yet explored.

INTERVIEWER: *How did you come up with your idea for writing* Tuesday?

WIESNER: *Tuesday* came about from a cover for *Cricket,* the March 1989 issue. In this issue, they had stories about St. Patrick's Day and frogs. Green, I guess, was the main link there. St. Patrick's Day didn't particularly interest me, but frogs seemed like they would be fun because frogs are visually very interesting. I got out some *National Geographic*s and started looking at frogs. They are sort of round and bumpy and really funny looking. It was when I drew one on a lily pad that the shape they made together—the round blob on the flat saucerlike bottom—reminded me of a flying saucer. I saw the unit of a frog on a lily pad in the air flying, and I came up with an image for the cover of the *Cricket* issue. It is very similar to the first double-page spread in **Tuesday.** When I finished the cover I liked the painting, but I also really liked the frogs. They just seemed like real interesting characters that had these personalities to them.

With all my books, I usually start in a sketch book, where on a single page I'll do small thumbnail drawings of all the pages of a book. This way I can see the entire layout of the book in very small, quick drawings. In each of the pages I try to block out how I see the flow of the story. For example, when I started to think about **Tuesday** and frogs and decided that they could fly, I placed them in a swamp. Then I thought to myself "What if I were a frog and could fly? What would I do?" and "Where would I go?" My wordless picture book emerged within about an hour. The whole book was written and remained pretty much unchanged from this stage to the finished story. It really came together very naturally, including the layout and the use of the panels and the graphic look of it, which

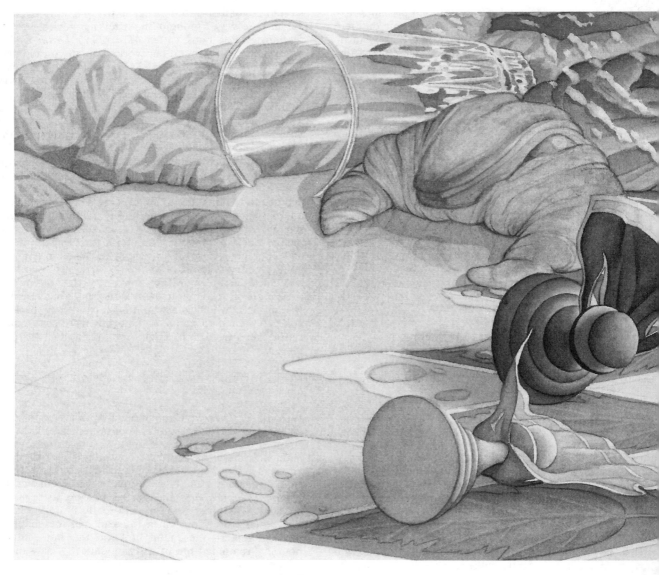

From Free Fall, *illustrated by David Wiesner.*

goes back to my love of comic books as I was growing up. The book immediately seemed wordless—except for the punctuation, that is, the times of day. This led to a mysterious element—that all of these events happened on Tuesday evening. To highlight the mystery I used clocks, such as the clock tower on the cover, clocks scattered throughout the pictures, and the times of the day in the text.

INTERVIEWER: *When you were writing* **Tuesday** *you used several ideas including your interest in frogs. Who do you consider as your audience when you write?*

WIESNER: When I am doing a book I am only thinking about me as the reader and how I would respond. I don't think there is any way to guess or gauge what anyone else will think of a book. I'm thinking about myself as an adult and myself as a child. I have a very good recall or link to not only what I did as a kid, but to the things I felt as a kid. I finished the full-sized dummy of **Tuesday** from the sketch book thumbnail drawings. It is a 32-page cut-paper fold-up version where I ruled out all of the panels and all of the page layouts. Essentially, it was a version of the actual book in pencil that I could show someone else. When I took **Tuesday** to my editor, and this was literally about a month after I finished **Hurricane,** I had no idea what anyone else would think of it, and I didn't even know if she would publish it. The story really appealed to me, and it just felt like a truer representation of some of the things I had been wanting to do. But I didn't know if anyone else would find it funny or if they would think it was too weird. When I walked in I was thrilled because Dorothy Briley, who is my editor at Clarion Books, just cracked up as soon as she saw **Tuesday.** Then

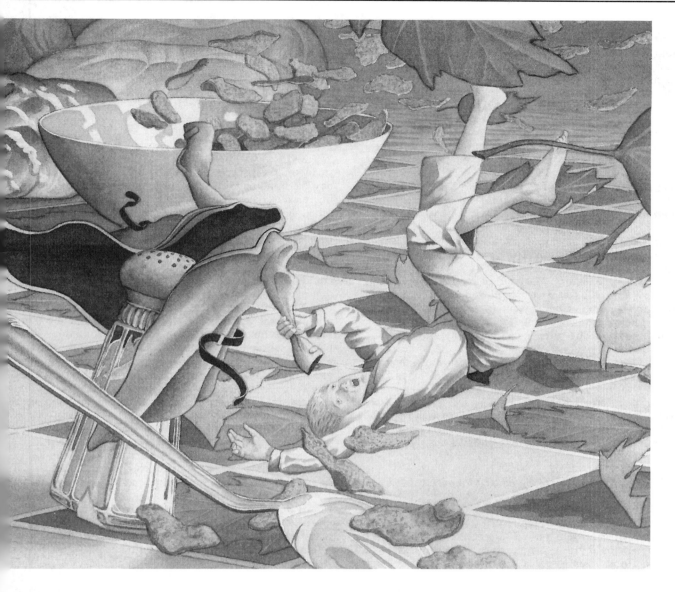

one of the other editors came in and we all sat around making frog and pig noises. So I just started right in on the finished book. It was great! That first reaction was something that happened right down the line whenever anyone saw **Tuesday.** Clearly I had hit on something, but as I was working on **Tuesday** I certainly was not thinking about what anyone else would think. So, no, there is usually no audience consideration as I'm working on books.

INTERVIEWER: *How would you like to see* **Tuesday** *used by teachers and children in the classroom?*

WIESNER: I have heard many people's reactions to *Free Fall* and *Tuesday.* And, you know, it has been amazing, just wonderful. All sorts of creative writing classes have responded to my books. I have received many versions or continuations of my stories. Classes put sets of stories together and send them to me. Students use my books as a stimulus for creative thought. I have heard from teachers who have used **Tuesday** in a children's drama class, during creative writing, in English as a Second Language class; and as a story that students could tell in their own words. I think it's great because I didn't have any grand uses in mind. I'm always intrigued to hear what other people come up with.

INTERVIEWER: *So, any creative use of your books is okay with you?*

WIESNER: Oh, absolutely. The whole point of the book is that it is a flight of imagination and a way to stimulate unbridled thoughts and fun. I think it's great that the book has inspired creativity. One of the nice things about wordless books that makes them different from books with text is that they need the reader to complete the book. The author's voice isn't there in the form of a text telling the story. It's up to the children or adults who read the wordless picture book to essentially tell the story and interpret it themselves. And the pictures really have to be read. There is a lot going on within the various details that adds to the story. Everyone who reads a wordless picture book is going to interpret it in a different way, which is great. I have my own version of *Tuesday* but it's no more valid that anyone else's who reads it.

INTERVIEWER: *Do children also send you letters about your books? What kinds of things do they say about* **Tuesday?**

WIESNER: Yes, I have received a lot of letters. It is nice to know that students and teachers are reading and responding to my books and that they are having fun with *Tuesday* and generating that kind of imaginative enthusiasm. Usually children write about their favorite parts in *Tuesday.* And they really want to know what happens next—particularly what happens with the pigs at the end. Children's letters are often accompanied by drawings, and some of their versions of what happens next are pretty funny. One class had a theme running through their responses wherein they had various items and things from their school beginning to fly—not only frogs, but things like scissors attacking math books. The students were telling little revenge fantasies! These letters showed the students' enthusiasm and how much they liked the book and the frogs. Or, these stories showed their desire to fly!

INTERVIEWER: *Is there a sequel to* **Tuesday?**

WIESNER: That's what I'm deciding right now. I have an inherent dislike of sequels, just as a sort of general principle. It seems like a good film is often ruined for the sake of attempting to do it one more time to make more money. Books clearly are a different matter. In a book there really isn't a whole lot of space to always do everything you want to do. So I know what the story is for a sequel to *Tuesday,* and I just have to decide whether or not I am going to do it. I probably will, because I don't want to leave that world created in *Tuesday* quite yet.

INTERVIEWER: *Tell us about some of your current projects.*

WIESNER: I'm finishing a book right now that should be done within a few weeks. It took about 11 years for me to figure out what the story would be. The idea grew out of a picture that I did in 1980 or 1981 as a sample piece for my portfolio. It was one of those illustrations that I did attempting to show a certain imagery I wanted to draw. I had hoped I could find stories to fit the illustrations. When no one knew how to react to the pictures, I realized that *I* had to write the stories myself. The book [*June 29, 1999*] is about a young girl in third grade and her science experiment with giant vegetables. It's unusual in some sense because I finally did a story about a female

protagonist. People seem to comment on the fact that I do these "boy books," although I don't think of them that way.

INTERVIEWER: *Several times you talked about how you generated new ideas for books, such as going back into your portfolio or revisiting the piece you created for the* Cricket *magazine cover. Can you tell us about your processes as an author-illustrator?*

WIESNER: First, my schedule is very, very flexible. Instead of asking myself, "What am I going to do in a day?" I think about, "What do I want to accomplish during a week?" Within that larger time frame the actual schedule really shifts around, especially in the conceptual stage. It's hard to schedule my ideas. I can't say, "I'll start at this point and by five o'clock I'll have the idea ready." Ideas come on their own time and pace. That can be infuriating sometimes; it would be nice if the process could be more controlled. I keep a sketch book that is full of visual ideas and brief notes of things that intrigue me or are visually interesting. I think most of my books grow out of visual images, and the trick is finding the story behind the image. To accomplish this I sometimes look back over sketches or notes that I made years ago or just recently completed. For example, when I sat down to think about *Tuesday* I looked back at my sketches from the *Cricket* cover to see if I could find a chronology or story in them. In examining the sketches and notes I saw little flashes of images—almost indecipherable to anyone else— like a frog in front of the TV set. What happens at the point where I'm looking at this visual information and I make a connection to a story line is impossible to say— I don't try to analyze it too much. I'm just glad that it happens. I often start out with a particular imagery that I want to try to work with. But it may be that by the time I'm into the book the original inspiration no longer fits into the story line and it has to be discarded. I may, however, try to come back to the original inspiration again later and see if I can do something else with it.

INTERVIEWER: *Earlier you referred to* **Hurricane** *as the first book in which you actually wrote a story in words. Could you tell us more about this process?*

WIESNER: Writing is a whole different process. The visual part of writing, drawing and painting, is something that I have always done, shown people, and talked about, particularly at art school. The art class situation was set up so that each week students brought in their work and put it up on a wall. Everyone talked about and critiqued each other's work. It was a constant give and take. Consequently, I am very comfortable showing my work to others and talking about it. Writing, however, was the kind of thing that I never really did in a public forum. It was a much more personal experience, and I was less comfortable showing my writing to anyone else. This seemed rather intimidating to me. Also, writing a children's book is a special discipline. The text has to be very concise, and usually the shorter the better. My tendency at first was to write a lot of description; I wrote far too much

Writing for me is a back and forth process of working on the text and then working on the pictures. Working on the pictures shows me all the things I do not need to say in the text because there is no need to describe everything that is happening in the pictures. It was a great learning experience to constantly hack away at the text. Engaging in this process made my current book, *June 29, 1999,* which has a text, far easier. *Hurricane* was a great learning experience.

INTERVIEWER: *The notion of going back and forth between the text and illustrations is interesting, particularly when you are both the author and the illustrator of a book. When authors collaborate with an illustrator, I wonder if the process of fitting the text and illustrations together is the same as you described.*

WIESNER: No. Being both author and illustrator really makes it interesting. I define a lot of what is happening as I write by creating the pictures and actually realizing the characters on the page. Doing this helps me define the characters' personalities even more. It helps me look at the text again and shape it by seeing the story visually. It may seem backwards to most authors but it works well for me.

INTERVIEWER: *I am going to reread* **Hurricane** *with that in mind. I think understanding your process as an author-illustrator will be fascinating to teachers and students who are learning about being authors.*

WIESNER: Additionally, the story behind *Hurricane* is true, too. It is about an incident that happened to me when I was young. I started by including my entire family, a memoir of my youth. I had put in all sorts of details that would be fun to include but ultimately had no real business as a part of the story that I was trying to tell. In the book it wouldn't work to have a friend stay over during a hurricane, so my friend became my brother. My brother is 7 years older than me, but in the story the brothers are close in age, though I still used his name. I used my brother's name, my name, the house, the yard, the bedroom, and even the wallpaper—description based on my house where I grew up, right down to the furnishings that were in the house. I wanted to put everything about my memories in the pictures, even though the description is not in the text.

INTERVIEWER: *And the cat in* **Hurricane** *was a part of the family?*

WIESNER: Yes. That's the same cat that we had when I was growing up. So little things from one's life can be included that add that extra note. On page 32 in *Hurricane* the cat is looking out the window just like the real cat did. All through the book the cat is accompanying the kids as they fantasize on their various adventures on the fallen tree. It was fun to be able to end the book with the cat looking out the window at the rain envisioning his personal fantasy—having rainbow trout floating by outside. Using the cat fantasy illustration was a last-minute decision. I had finished all other parts of the book and

suddenly saw the image of this cat in the window imagining the fish, and I did the picture in one afternoon. I took it in to my editor and asked, "What do you think?" It seemed to sum up the story nicely. As you can see, writing is an ongoing process.

INTERVIEWER: *Thank you for sharing your thoughts about the writing process. We look forward to seeing your future books and we'll appreciate them even more because of the insights you've provided us.*

GENERAL COMMENTARY

David Macaulay

SOURCE: "David Wiesner," in *The Horn Book Magazine,* Vol. LXVIII, No. 4, July-August, 1992, pp. 423-8.

There are three things about David Wiesner which stand out in my mind. The first is his imagination. The second is his skill. The third is his reserve. Actually, there is a fourth—the speed with which number three disappears when the conversation turns to the process that employs numbers one and two. David's passion for making pictures—particularly pictures that tell stories—is clearly evident not only in his books but also in the enthusiasm and sincerity with which he animatedly describes their creation. Honored by his request to write the Caldecott Medal winner's profile for the *Horn Book,* I found myself playing amateur reporter. David and I chatted one Sunday afternoon in March as I scribbled away. While I had no idea how or even if it would all come together, I was nevertheless delighted at having the opportunity to get to know a little better one of my very best former students turned colleague. Whether or not the following is what he actually told me, it is definitely what I heard.

On Sunday, February 5, 1956, the population of Bridgewater, New Jersey, increased by one. Born to Julia and George Wiesner on that day was their fifth child and second son in ten years. In addition to populating their house, the elder Wiesners also imbued it with a nurturing atmosphere in which creative endeavor, while never forced, was always encouraged. This, at least, is how David remembers it. In fact, the cunning with which the minds of the unsuspecting Wiesner kids were shaped is perhaps best illustrated by the achievement-oriented wallpaper found on page thirteen of David's unpaginated and highly autobiographical book, *Hurricane.* The stimulating pattern of rockets, magnifying glasses, elephant heads, ships in bottles, books, and, believe it or not, medals comes directly from the walls of the very room in which he played, slept, and dreamt for the first eleven years of his young life—the formative years. I never did find out what the rest of the wallpaper in the house looked like, but whatever it was, it seems to have worked. His eldest sister and his brother were both artistically inclined and generously passed down their used or unneeded art supplies, along with a fair amount of natural reinforcement. His second oldest sister trained in opera. Her artistic impact on David has yet to reveal itself.

While it might seem presumptuous, or at least premature, to suggest that David was destined to become an artist, his early years could not have been more appropriately spent. Even trips to the local paint and wallpaper store were filled with special pleasures. There, in a small section devoted to art supplies, David found himself scouring the shelves and opening the drawers, to see, touch, and ultimately sniff the various materials housed in this exotic treasury.

The first nonfamily member whose artistic impact David readily acknowledges was the goatee-toting, plaid-clad, coolest-of-artists—Jon Gnagy. The granddaddy of television art teachers, Gnagy took to the airwaves every Saturday morning, after the agricultural shows, and took over the imaginations of thousands of impressionable viewers, and young David and his similarly inclined siblings were among them. Introducing the ideas of a light source and simple perspective, Gnagy made one drawing a week in which he transformed circles into form and straight lines into depth. In the brief fifteen-minute process he transported a ten-year-old New Jersey boy to new heights of ecstasy and ambition. Over the months and years that followed, David faithfully completed almost every sequential exercise in the accompanying workbooks, learning not only how to create illusion but also about the joys of drawing from direct observation. As his ideas and skill grew, so did his interest in storytelling through pictures—an interest fed both by comic books and repeated television showings of such classics as *King Kong.*

David's early artistic education was not just an indoor activity. In fact, whatever familial life did for young David's imagination, it was at least equaled, if not surpassed, by life outside. His Bridgewater neighborhood was one of those perfect places to grow up because it encouraged playing outside. First, there were people to play with. Like his house, but on a larger scale, the neighborhood was populated with kids of different ages. The older ones invented games for the younger ones, who in turn looked up to, idolized, and in time became the older ones. Second, there were many wonderful places to play. A network of lawns, trees, and shrubs linked the houses, while at the edge of the neighborhood there were woods and a brook. Armies could freely chase and stalk each other through the vegetation, but once they hit the sidewalks, the rules changed. Because these were the rivers, both feet had to be kept on the ground at all times. Fleeing the enemy was now much more problematic since only very small steps were allowed and you had to carry your stick—which was loaded—over your head to keep it dry.

As the neighborhood kids grew, their games became more sophisticated. In UFO, a favorite, a wire coat hanger was bent into a circle and attached to the open end of a plastic bag. Across the diameter of the circle another piece of wire supported a wad of burning fabric. As the bag filled with hot gas, the whole flimsy contraption lifted into the

air and drifted dangerously away. The journeys of these do-it-yourself hot-air balloons sometimes covered two miles and were tracked by the walkie-talkie-bearing pyromaniacs, either on foot or by car.

Meanwhile, at home, the older Wiesner siblings were slowly moving on and, more importantly, out. David eventually occupied his own second-floor room, and into it came one of his prize possessions—a sturdy oak drafting table lugged home by Dad. Its very presence underscored the importance of the act of drawing and transformed a mere bedroom into a studio. Now, with a suitable environment, the young artist increased production. There is a price, however, for the extraordinary pleasures associated with the primarily solitary process of making art. Whether or not David's increasing artistic conviction grew in response to a pre-existing shyness, or whether it helped create it, is neither here nor there. The fact is that he was an extremely reticent youngster. It wasn't until high school that his self-esteem got a boost from his growing identity as class artist. Although this did nothing to seriously elevate his status, Wiesner, like all teenagers, was grateful for any identity.

By this time, David had become familiar with the images of such artists as Da Vinci, Dali, De Chirico, Brueghel, and Dürer—all available in the Time-Life Books of Great Artists and all contained within the Wiesner home. Fed by these artists' often fantastical landscapes, David's imagination touched everything before it was rendered. He realized that just by changing his point of view, the Derailleur gears on his bike or even the vacuum cleaner could become an amazing technological landscape—jumping-off places for invention and creativity. Nowhere is the power of point of view more clearly displayed, or more masterfully handled, than in *Tuesday.* In addition to the creation of his own comics, which described the exploits of anti-hero "Slop the Wonder Pig," David and his high-school friends produced a live-action vampire film entitled *The Saga of Butchula.* This silent classic was accompanied by a taped musical soundtrack which was best played on a variable-speed tape recorder so that the music and the action could be kept more or less in sync. One of David's most "satisfying moments" came at the senior talent show where, during the film's screening, people laughed at the right times—to his relief and amazement.

It is hardly surprising that Bob Bernabe, the art teacher at Bridgewater Raritan High School, would be the first in a series of in-person teachers, as opposed to television or book folk, to influence and encourage young Wiesner. He was undoubtedly delighted just to get someone in his class looking for more than credits or a rest. In this case he got someone looking for much more. Motivation was never an issue, and Bernabe soon had his eager pupil working well beyond the assigned problems, exploring the possibilities of print making, photo silk screens, and watercolor. An important, out-of-school experience was a trip to the Museum of Modern Art in New York City. When young Wiesner first saw *Guernica,* he was bowled over by the power and size of the work—and Picasso's work finally began to make sense. On that same trip he also saw Dali's *Persistence of Memory*—only in this case he couldn't believe the smallness of a work he found so powerful.

For better or worse, high school, as those of us who have experienced it know, doesn't last forever, and there is always that nagging question of what comes next. For David, this question was answered while he was still a sophomore. Sometime in 1971 Mr. Bernabe's art class was visited by a college student who showed films he had made and with great humor talked about something called art school. For David the experience was both revealing and reassuring. "You mean there are places where I can go? You don't have to have a real job? Wow!" And in one fell swoop, the school's guidance counselor was off the hook. It would no longer be his or her responsibility to figure out what to do with this very shy, intensely curious, and passionately creative young man.

In September of 1974, David left New Jersey to study illustration at Rhode Island School of Design. He left behind a mountain of drawings but brought with him an imagination and level of commitment which those of us who had the pleasure of working with him quickly realized was exceptional. As a sophomore, he produced a ten-foot-long by forty-inch-high mural in response to a problem called "metamorphosis." In it orange slices turned into sailboats, which turned into fish. He recalls putting it up and hearing a deep, reassuring chuckle from his teacher, who was standing at the back of the room. The teacher went on to point out all the things which came naturally to David—such as choosing unique points of view, or pushing things up to the front of the picture to enliven the composition and reinforce the depth. The metamorphosis that evolved on paper encouraged another, albeit slower, transformation from shy, retiring person to confident, retiring person. It also served as the genesis of a wordless book that would emerge some thirteen years later and win David his first Caldecott Honor Medal.

Also during his sophomore year, David began oil painting. Although he valiantly struggled with it, he never enjoyed it and eventually returned to watercolor. Under the tutelage of Professor Tom Sgouros, David found that his technical and conceptual skills continued to soar. The extent of Sgouros's influence and the importance of his contribution are best illustrated by the fact that it is to him that *Tuesday* is dedicated.

During his senior year, having been inspired by a Lynd Ward wordless picture book, David designed and began producing one of his own. Although he finished only two watercolors, he thoroughly explored the process, creating mounds of sketches. A department-wide problem called "series" resulted in another sequence of wordless images. In eight steps the image of King Kong on top of the Empire State Building gradually became Leonardo's famous study of human proportion. The simpler and more open-ended the problem was, the more inventive would be David's solution. He remembers students continually asking one professor questions about a problem he had

assigned and thinking that each answer, while illuminating, was also a kind of restriction. The more ambiguous the problem, the more he liked it, and the better it served his inventive mind.

By June of 1978 we had done all we could for David Wiesner, so we graduated him. From Rhode Island he traveled to New York and began his career as a free-lance illustrator. In March of 1979, he was commissioned to do a cover for *Cricket Magazine*. Three years later, he found himself working on his first jacket and interior art for a book called *The Man from the Sky* by someone named Avi. He has just been asked to create a new jacket for the book's reissue. This he agreed to do as long as the publisher promised not to use the original illustrations. David's standards have been growing along with his self-confidence.

In 1983 an apartment fire destroyed all his possessions, including work done up to that time. Also lost in the fire was the precious oak drafting table his father had retrieved. But it would take more than a fire to stop this smitten bookmaker; *The Loathsome Dragon,* a story retold by David and his surgeon wife Kim Kahng, was published in 1987. Take a look at the watercolor landscapes it contains and tell me you don't see a little Da Vinci in there. In 1988 came the Caldecott Honor Book *Free Fall,* a direct descendent of that ten-foot-long mural and either the second appearance of the loathsome dragon or a very close relative. In 1990, *Hurricane* blew into town. It is no coincidence that the names of the two young boys who play on the tree toppled by the storm are David and George—alias the brothers Wiesner—since the story is based on a real incident. And finally in 1991 came the glorious culmination of his efforts to date—which brings us back to *Tuesday.*

"So, why frogs?" I asked. In 1989 David was asked to create his second *Cricket* cover. When he asked what kind of an image they were looking for, they wisely suggested that he should do whatever he wanted. The only clue they offered was the theme of that particular issue: Frogs. And that, as usual, was all it took.

TITLE COMMENTARY

📖 *THE LOATHSOME DRAGON* (written with Kim Kahng; 1987)

Publishers Weekly

SOURCE: A review of *The Loathsome Dragon,* in *Publishers Weekly,* Vol. 232, No. 18, October 30, 1987, p. 70.

This tale of enchantment and familial devotion is the retelling of a lesser known English fairy tale. Bamborough Castle is the home of a widowed king and his lovely daughter Margaret and son Childe Wynd. The King falls in love with a beautiful but wicked enchantress who, in a jealous rage, turns the princess into a dragon. The story of Childe Wynd's quest to free his sister casts a spell on readers. The traditional telling is enhanced by Wiesner's classic watercolors. Few artists depict the medieval world or labyrinthine castles, venomous enchantresses and fair damsels as well; he is attentive to detail, with richly brocaded costumery of the period and architecturally correct renderings of castles and their interiors. The subtle palette of greens, grays and blues achieves a peaceful tonality.

Phillis Wilson

SOURCE: A review of *The Loathsome Dragon,* in *Booklist,* Vol. 84, No. 5, November 1, 1987, p. 486.

The storybook castle called Bamborough is the setting for Wiesner's distinctive staging of this little-known English fairy tale. A widowed king meets a beautiful enchantress

and brings her to the castle as his wife, where she, true to stereotype, becomes flushed with jealousy at the sight of the king's beautiful daughter, Princess Margaret. The queen chants her spells deep within the ominous dungeon, summoning her magical wraiths. Wiesner's sense of dramatic effect and deft humor is at its best in the next scene; Margaret, who went to sleep as a fair princess, awakes as the Loathsome Dragon. Upon discovering this scaly green inhabitant, who engulfs a cavernous four-poster bed, the ladies-in-waiting drop cutlery and crockery to the floor before fainting away. The Dragon then slithers out and wends its way to Spindlestone Heugh rock, devouring all in its path. After consulting his scrolls of knowledge, a mighty warlock tells the people to send for Margaret's brother, Childe Wynd, who rescues his sister. Once more in human form, Margaret returns to the castle and the queen, staring in shock, slowly shrivels into a Loathsome Toad. Wiesner evokes a sense of a theatrical performance: each double-page spread is handsomely bordered, creating a proscenium effect, and his skilled use of perspective heightens the dominant emotion of each scene.

From Hurricane, *written and illustrated by David Wiesner.*

Constance A. Mellon

SOURCE: A review of *The Loathsome Dragon*, in *School Library Journal*, Vol. 34, No. 7, March, 1988, p. 178.

Jealous of her lovely stepdaughter, the new Queen of Bamborough Castle changes Margaret into a loathsome dragon until Childe Wynd, her brother who is traveling the world, returns and kisses her three times. Thus begins this "little known English fairy tale." While the retelling is not distinguished, it follows traditional patterns and rhythms and is written in a form simple enough for young children to follow and enjoy. The illustrations are delicate, misty, and enchanting, extending and harmonizing with the traditional motifs of this fairy tale. The dragon is pictured with softly rounded contours so that the imagination can believe that Princess Margaret lies beneath its green scales and sad blue eyes. The portrait of the queen, shriveled into a Loathsome Toad, with robes and full head of red hair still flowing about her, will bring delight to justice-minded children. This fairy tale picture book will be welcomed by storytellers and by those who enjoy reading aloud and sharing handsome illustrations with young listeners. Both the quality of the illustrations and the fact that this tale will be new to most readers make *The Loathsome Dragon* a good addition to any collection of "retold" folktales.

FREE FALL (1988)

Publishers Weekly

SOURCE: A review of *Free Fall*, in *Publishers Weekly*, Vol. 233, No. 11, March 18, 1988, p. 87.

Wiesner creates a wonderful dream sequence in a wordless exploration that makes the picture book format seem limitless. Gray-and-green gingham squares of a sleeping boy's coverlet flow into the patchwork fields of a landscape, with mountains in the blue-green distance. Onto this checked ground, figures like chess pieces appear, pages turn to castles and turrets with knights and moats—

still using the shapes and colors of the first bedroom scene. The dreaming boy, clad in his pajamas, visits castles and slays a mottled green dragon. Next he sprawls like Gulliver among the Lilliputians, and then journeys into an urban dreamland: tenements instead of castles, rooftops with aerials instead of parapets. A last ride up on a swan's back, over a green-checked seascape of waves and shadows brings him ashore, and back to his bed. This unbroken dreamscape is artfully carried through a blending of ancient and modern motifs; the book is an exceptional choice for children and visually enticing for older readers as well.

Betsy Hearne

SOURCE: A review of *Free Fall*, in *Bulletin of the Center of Children's Books*, Vol. 41, No. 9, May, 1988, p. 193.

This really could have been entitled "*Free Association*," and it's an excellent replication of a dream . . . for what that's worth to the picture book audience. Unlike many books of this kind, the artist has made a clear transition from reality, showing the boy asleep with a subsequent double-page spread fading from blanket to landscape. There follows a sequence of a chessboard becoming a medieval setting, complete with castle, knights, and a dragon that the child overcomes. Then the pages of the book reshuffle themselves as he escorts a caravan, glimpses a familiar cityscape, and falls through the air into images of breakfast. Spilled juice suggests water, including swans and fish, and the boy wakes up to see his goldfish and other objects from the dream highlighted by sunshine. These are skillfully rendered transitions; the question is one of reception. Although there is progression, there is no plot, and the concept may be more appealing to adults, who can analyze it, than to children, unless they can perceive it as a game.

Kirkus Reviews

SOURCE: A review of *Free Fall*, in *Kirkus Reviews*, Vol. LVI, No. 9, May 1, 1988, p. 699.

In an imaginative wordless picture book, Wiesner (illustrator of [Dennis Haseley's] *Kite Flyer*, 1986) tours a dream world suggested by the books and objects in a boy's room. A series of transitions—linked by a map in the book that the boy was reading as he fell asleep—wafts him, pajama-clad, from an aerial view of hedge-bordered fields to a chessboard with chess pieces, some changing into their realistic counterparts (plus a couple of eerie round-headed figures based on pawns that reappear throughout); next appear a castle; a mysterious wood in which lurks a huge, whimsical dragon; the interior of a neoclassical palace; and a series of fantastic landscapes that eventually transport the boy back to his own bed.

Most interesting here are the visual links Wiesner uses in

his journey's evolution; it's fun to trace the many details from page to page. There's a bow to Van Allsburg, and another to Sendak's *Night Kitchen*, but Wiesner's broad double-spreads of a dream world—whose muted colors suggest a silent space outside of time—have their own charm. Intriguing.

Ellen Mandel

SOURCE: A review of *Free Fall*, in *Booklist*, Vol. 8, No. 19, June 1, 1988, p. 1680.

Clutching a large, leatherbound volume, a boy sleeps. As he slumbers, the book—an atlas—tumbles from his grasp, opening his dreams to the exotically historical locales represented between its covers. With meticulous refinement and unbridled imagination, Wiesner charts the youth's course, as objects magically transform into different images with the turn of each page: the boy's plaid blanket breezily billows into a patchwork of farm fields that, in turn, regiment themselves into a chessboard whose figures greet the pajama-clad visitor. Crossing the board into a medieval castle whose winding stone walls startlingly evolve into a menacing dragon and whose turrets become tall trees, the youngster escapes the fearful beast in a forest of books where the dragon is squashed between pages until only his tail remains dangling like a limp bookmark from a closed volume. Riding a pig's back along a canyon ledge, falling through air amid tumbling map pages and slices of mountains and city buildings, the boy floats back to bed aboard a swan, while around him are strewn the diverse elements incorporated into his bizarre dream. Reminiscent of Salvador Dali's surrealistic paintings and at times of *Gulliver's Travels* and *Alice's Adventures in Wonderland*, this wordless journey into the mind's fantasies—at one point the map pages even chart regions of the brain rather than areas of the world—needs textual grounding to guide children through its remarkable spreads; the brief verse on the dust jacket isn't a satisfactory compass through the maze of this brilliant illustrator's imagination. But older and gifted children may well relish the challenge of interpretation, while the sheer artistry will intrigue all ages.

Julie Corsaro

SOURCE: A review of *Free Fall*, in *School Library Journal*, Vol. 35, No. 9, June-July, 1988, p. 95.

In an odd wordless picture book about a dream, a fair-haired boy falls asleep while reading an ominous looking atlas. As he floats through sky and slumber, the boy's green checked bedspread is transformed into an aerial view of the earth. He then descends upon an enormos chess board complete with mortal playing pieces. This medieval welcoming party leads the youngster to their mazed castle where he continues his search (although this is not always clear) for an elusive map. The nameless protagonist's ensuing adventures are confusing, complicated, and illogical. Transformations abound in this surrealistic universe. Floating leaves change into swans, fortress walls become dragons, building fronts turn into mountains. The influence of such literary classics as *Gulliver's Travels, The Wizard of Oz,* and *The Water-Babies,* along with the artistry of Raphael, Escher, and Sendak, is apparent. Soft shades of green, blue, and yellow dominate the action. Technical virtuosity is the trademark of the double-page watercolor spreads. Especially notable is the solidity of forms and architectural details. While many of the illustrations are stunning, if somewhat slick, they work better as individual pieces than as a whole. This book lacks the sequence and logic required by young children, and it will have limited appeal among older children.

HURRICANE (1990)

Publishers Weekly

SOURCE: A review of *Hurricane,* in *Publishers Weekly,* Vol. 237, No. 35, August 31, 1990, p. 66.

The Caldecott Honor recipient for the dreamlike picture book *Free Fall* offers another work to delight children and spark their imaginations. Wiesner's detailed, exquisitely rendered paintings draw the reader into his story of a hurricane's progress with all the sweep and immediacy of a film sequence. As the sky grays and the leaves swirl by in a "green blizzard," David, George and their parents share a cozy supper by the fireplace. The next morning, the boys discover that a big elm which had stood on their lawn now lies stretched across their neighbor's yard. The old tree becomes the vessel that whisks the pair to adventure, as they joyously explore exotic jungles, confront pirates on the seven seas and travel to the stars. Sometimes they just relax, enjoying "their private place, big enough for secret dreams, small enough for shared adventure." One day, though, reality intrudes as workers arrive to remove the tree from their neighbor's yard. Glum all afternoon, the boys brighten when their dad announces that another storm is on the way: maybe a second tree will fall, this time into *their* yard! This is an exuberant, absorbing slice of life.

Patricia Dooley

SOURCE: A review of *Hurricane,* in *School Library Journal,* Vol. 36, No. 10, October, 1990, p. 104.

However worrisome for adults and insurers, hurricanes can be the stuff of lifelong memories for children. Wiesner draws on just such memories for this book. It begins in the kitchen, where groceries are being stockpiled, and misses few highlights: the taped glass storm door, supper on the floor in front of the fireplace, a hurricane lamp at bedtime, and excited speculation about what the storm is doing outside the snug house. The brothers here, about seven and ten years old, get a bonus when a big elm blows down. For days it serves as a fantasy prop, becoming a spaceship, a jungle, a caravel—a place "big enough for secret dreams, small enough for shared adventure."

This dream ends in a cord of firewood, but another threatened storm brings hope springing eternal. The child-focused, low perspective gives even ordinary scenes an extra measure of drama, and the fantasy spreads are detailed delights. It's fun to find the cat, Hannibal, who registers subtle degrees of disgust, disgruntlement, and hauteur at the disruption of his domain. We wouldn't wish a real hurricane on children, but this book will give them a taste of the magic of the moment when the lights go out.

Roger Sutton

SOURCE: A review of *Hurricane,* in *Bulletin of the Center for Children's Books,* Vol. 44, No. 3, November, 1990, p. 74.

Like the author's *Free Fall,* this picture book explores imaginative extensions of reality, but is all the more involving for its basis in ordinary child life, rather than in the murky depths of a dream. A hurricane is coming, and brothers David and George enjoy the drama of the "green blizzard" of leaves, the creaking of the house, the lights going out, and a cozy supper by the fireplace. The hurricane leaves in its wake a legacy of a large fallen-down tree, "a sleeping giant" that provides the boys (and their cat) with a vehicle for fantastic journeying as they imagine themselves on safari, riding the seven seas, in space, and sometimes just sitting enjoying the view. "It just feels good being here." With the hurricane providing its own meteorological excitement, the imaginary games allow Wiesner plenty of scope for phantasmagoric landscaping; *Jumanji*-like, all the games are foreshadowed in the wallpaper pattern in the boys' bedroom. The tree makes a likely-looking space capsule landed on a distant planet, or pirate ship awash in stormy seas; its allure in plain dappled sunlight is also apparent, and readers will share the boys' dismay when the chainsaw turns it into firewood. But as the book closes, the wind is kicking up, and another tree just might fall. Robust and real, this one is guaranteed to get them outdoors.

Polly Shulman

SOURCE: A review of *Hurricane,* in *Voice Literary Supplement,* No. 91, December, 1990, p. 36.

David Wiesner writes about—or rather, draws about—transformation, so it's not surprising that his new book is really two stories shading into each other. The first concerns a hurricane, which David and George weather in their suburban home with their parents and cat. In his naturalistic watercolors, Wiesner catches the fear and the coziness of the situation, the wild winds, the candles and flashlights, choosing appropriate angles to maximize the drama. The second story is about a tree the wind knocks over, and how the boys turn it into a boat, a jungle, a spaceship. Their make-believe games give Wiesner an opportunity to perform the realistic, impossible alterations he does so well.

From Tuesday, *written and illustrated by David Wiesner.*

Kathryn LaBarbera

SOURCE: A review of *Hurricane,* in *Booklist,* Vol. 87, No. 8, December 15, 1990, p. 863.

Wiesner's paintings highlight the text in a tale of two brothers who find a hideout in a tree felled during hurricane season. Momentum builds as the hurricane closes in on the family. Then, in the tradition of *Free Fall,* successive double-page spreads set the boys and their tree in the heart of a jungle, in a ship sailing the seven seas, and on some faraway planet. But the best illustration captures Wiesner's feel for the security of a secret and a friend—two boys sipping milk through straws as sunlight flickers across their faces, hidden from the world by the many branches and leaves of their downed tree. When men come to saw the tree and take it away, the boys know an era has ended. But another storm is whipping up—another tree may fall! Wiesner's perspectives, lighting, and rich colors express tension and anticipation as well as comfort and protection.

Nancy Vasilakis

SOURCE: A review of *Hurricane,* in *The Horn Book Magazine,* Vol. LXVII, No. 1, January-February, 1991, pp. 61-2.

The natural disasters that one survives are usually among the best-remembered signposts of childhood. In this handsome book, David Wiesner captures perfectly the aura of a giant storm from a child's perspective. Careful preparations are made for the impending hurricane—the win

dows taped, the family cat rounded up—while outside the world grows dark, with whirling leaves creating a "'green blizzard.'" Weather reports add to the realistic tone created by the author-artist's paintings, which resemble formal family portraits. When the lights go out and the family is sitting by the fireplace in a darkened room, "it felt safe with everybody together, even though there were creaks and groans and sometimes great roaring sounds coming from outside." Realism gives way to fantasy once the two boys in the family enter the post-hurricane yard the next day. A great fallen elm provides opportunity for much imaginative play. It becomes the background for romps through jungles, encounters with pirate ships, and interplanetary travel. A perfect playground, the tree is "big enough for secret dreams, small enough for shared adventure." When workers arrive with chainsaws to cut it up and haul it away, the children are despondent, until

they remember that a neighboring tree still stands—potential victim to another storm. Not an adult's fancy, this wish, but one that children will appreciate. Pairing the book with Seymour Simon's *Storms* affords opportunities for sharing information, fears, and dreams of adventure.

📖 *TUESDAY* (1991)

David Wiesner

SOURCE: "Caldecott Acceptance Speech," in *The Horn Book Magazine,* Vol. LXVIII, No. 4, July-August, 1992, pp. 416-22.

[*The following essay is Wiesner's acceptance speech for the Caldecott Medal he received in 1992.*]

Bufo marinus, the Australian cane toad, secretes a toxic substance when it is attacked. This substance is lethal to nearly all predators, including dogs and other large animals, and it can have an incapacitating effect on humans.

In the early 1970s, some adventurous young Australians discovered an interesting use for the cane toad. After the toad is boiled down into a broth, or a resin, it can be ingested as a liquid or smoked as a powder. The toxin, bufotenin, produces a hallucinogenic reaction in the user. To this day, it is a criminal offense to smoke a cane toad in Australia.

I'm often asked where I got the idea for **Tuesday.** The question is usually accompanied by a suggestion or two. Did I have a pet frog while growing up? Do I live near a swamp? Do I have a "thing" for frogs? I have discovered only recently that quite a lot of people have a special affinity for frogs. My favorite comment, though, was a rhetorical question from Laurence Yep, who gave me a funny look and asked if I had been importing cane toads.

The truth is that the imagination needs no outside stimulus. To watch children at play is to see the mind in all its uninhibited glory. Growing up in New Jersey, my friends and I re-created our world daily. The neighborhood would become anything from the far reaches of the universe to a prehistoric jungle. To believe that giant Pterodactyls were swooping down on us required only a small leap of faith.

Dinosaurs were an important part of my world as a child. Just as the caves of Lascaux, France, are full of images of the animals hunted by prehistoric man, so my room was full of drawings of the dinosaurs I hunted in my backyard. In an attempt to make them more real and alive, I drew them over and over again.

I had many books about dinosaurs. My favorites were the ones that had the best pictures, and the pictures I liked were in a *World Book Encyclopedia* supplement about the evolution of the Earth. It wasn't until many years later that I realized the pictures were by the artist Charles Knight, the man who first visualized what dinosaurs looked like, and on whose work all subsequent dinosaur renderings were based.

The dinosaurs were executed in exacting detail, with solid musculature, giving the animals a real presence. Thinking about it now, I'm aware it probably wasn't the greatest printing job, but back then the washed-out quality of the black-and-white reproductions created a real sense of atmosphere for me. I thought they were photographs. Even after I should have known better, I thought they just might be photographs.

The realization that the pictures were painted by an actual person was a revelation. The reality I perceived in those scenes was totally captivating. At the time, I couldn't imagine being able to paint so convincingly. But now, as I work, I'm continually trying to recapture for myself that total belief in the world I'm creating on paper.

As I moved on from dinosaurs, I discovered other imagery that exerted a powerful hold on me. In the stacks of Bound Brook (New Jersey) Public Library, I would sit and pore over the Time-Life books on the history of art. I was drawn immediately to the Renaissance artists—Dürer, for one, Michelangelo, and Da Vinci—before they were Ninja Turtles. The *Mona Lisa* is a compelling portrait, but it's the landscape she sits in front of that I found fascinating. It's a wonderfully alien-looking place, more like Mars than Italy. Hieronymus Bosch made a deep impression on me, too, and the landscapes of Pieter Brueghel the Elder fascinated me even more. Your eye can wander in and out of his paintings, from the extreme foreground to the distant horizon, with incredible clarity and detail. I was also intrigued by the surrealists—Magritte, de Chirico, Dali—who depicted the dream world with an unsettling precision.

Every painting seemed to be a scene in a story, like a frame in a film. I longed to be able to switch on a projector that would show me what happened before and after the image that was captured on the canvas.

And, of course, I went on trying to put my own reality down on paper, not always with welcome results. When I was in the fourth grade, we'd find a short assignment on the blackboard every morning that we were supposed to work on until the bell rang to start class. This was called "a.m. work," and we did it on paper that was about six by nine inches and sort of an ochre color. It was cheap paper, but it had a nice bit of tooth to it and was great for drawing. One morning I looked up from a scene I was creating to find our teacher, Miss Klingibel, standing next to me. She was not amused. She took my picture and wrote an angry note home to my mother: "David would rather be drawing than doing his a.m. work." In my opinion, that was the most astute comment she made all year.

I went on to study at the Rhode Island School of Design. I was finally in a place where *everyone* would rather be drawing than doing "a.m. work."

During my freshman year, my roommate, Michael Hays, casually described to me a book that would become a catalyst for many of my own visual ideas. He had seen this book in the rare books collection in the Hunt Library at Carnegie-Mellon University. It was an allegorical novel for adults about good and evil, life and death, and spirituality. And it had no words. The story was told in a series of about 130 woodcuts.

I couldn't get the idea of this book out of my head. A year and a half later, I visited Mike in Pittsburgh. I arrived in the evening, and we were at the library the first thing the next morning.

The book is called *Mad Man's Drum* and is by Lynd Ward, whose book *The Biggest Bear* won the 1953 Caldecott Medal. Sitting in the artificial air of the library's climate-controlled rare-book room, I read the book in amazement. Each turn of the page opened a door in my mind a little wider.

Back at school, I began to explore the possibilities of wordless storytelling in some of my assignments. It was in my senior degree project that I had the chance to investigate the form more fully. I created a forty-page wordless book based on Fritz Leiber's short story "Gonna Roll the Bones." I began to understand the process by which a story is distilled, and the essential information presented in visual terms.

When I graduated and began working as an illustrator, my goal was eventually to publish a wordless picture book of my own. I was very fortunate to make a connection with Dorothy Briley, who believed in the vision I had and let me bring it to fruition in an uncompromised form. *Free Fall* was the culmination of many ideas about an impressionistic kind of storytelling that I had been forming since art school.

There were many other possibilities I wanted to explore. I longed to do a book that was wildly humorous, almost slapstick. When I talked about this, people who knew my work found it a little hard to believe. I was offered a number of manuscripts to illustrate, but none of them seemed to fit the particular mood and tone I had in mind. I knew that I would have to make up my own story someday. That "someday" turned out to be *Tuesday.*

So what was the inspiration for the book?

My first professional job, which I got while I was a senior at RISD, was the March 1979 cover for *Cricket Magazine.* So when I was asked to do the March 1989 cover for *Cricket,* I was very pleased—two *Cricket* covers exactly ten years apart would make nice "bookends" for my first decade in children's books.

Another reason why I was happy to accept this job from *Cricket* is that their instructions for a cover are the perfect assignment: "Do anything you want to do." They let me know, as food for thought, that because this was the March issue, there would be stories about St. Patrick's Day and about frogs—the link there being green, I think.

St. Patrick's Day didn't strike a chord—but frogs, they had potential. I got out my sketchbook and some old *National Geographic*s for reference. Frogs were great fun to draw—soft, round, lumpy, and really goofy-looking. But what could I do with them?

I drew one on a lily pad. That shape . . . the round blob with the saucerlike bottom. Suddenly, old movies were running through my head: *Forbidden Planet* and *The Day the Earth Stood Still.* Together the frog and lily pad looked like a fifties B-movie flying saucer! As I drew, I saw that the frogs and toads weren't actually flying. It was the lily pads that had the power of flight, like a carpet from *The Arabian Nights.*

For the *Cricket* cover I showed a group of frogs rising up out of a swamp, heading off to who knows what mischief. I liked the picture a lot, and I began to like the frogs and toads themselves. They had distinct personalities. They looked pretty silly, yet up in the air they clearly felt dignified, noble, and a bit smug. I wanted to know more about them. As I did when I looked at a painting as a child, I wondered what happened before and after this scene. Now I could find out.

Appropriately, I was in midair when I finally got around to thinking seriously about "the frog book." I was sitting in an airplane, looking through my sketchbook, and I thought, Okay, if I were a frog, and I had discovered I could fly, where would I go? What would I do?

Images quickly began to appear to me, and for fear of losing them I hastily scribbled barely legible shapes onto the page: a startled man at a kitchen table; a terrified dog under attack; a roomful of frogs bathed in the glow of a television. A chronology began to take shape, and within an hour I had worked out a complete layout, which remained essentially unchanged through to the finished book. Everything was there: the story, the use of the panels, the times of day, and the title.

At least as often as people ask me where I came up with the idea for the book, they want to know, "Why Tuesday?" When I decided to punctuate the story with the times of the day, it became clear that the mysterious element had to do with the particular day of the week when these strange things happened. So I tried to decide what the funniest day of the week was. I immediately discounted the weekend; Saturday and Sunday had too many connotations, as did Friday. Monday was next to go, being the first day of the work week, which left Tuesday, Wednesday, and Thursday. Wednesday's spelling had always bothered me, so it was out. Thursday was all right, but the more I said "T-u-e-s-day," the more I liked the "ooze" quality it had. It seemed to go with frogs.

A wordless book offers a different kind of an experience from one with text, for both the author and the reader. There is no author's voice telling the story. Each viewer reads the book in his or her own way. The reader is an integral part of the storytelling process. As a result, there are as many versions of what happened that Tuesday night as there are readers. For some, the dog in the story is rightfully defending his territory against amphibian invaders, and their sympathy lies with the dog when the frogs get the best of him. For others, the dog is a humorless bully who gets his comeuppance. As the author of a wordless book, I don't have to concern myself about whether the reader's interpretation of each and every detail is the same as mine. My own view has no more, and no less, validity than that of any other viewer. Since my intent was for the book, as a whole, to make people laugh, all that matters is that the pictures are funny.

A series of individually funny pictures, however, does not necessarily add up to a successful story. The book was very carefully plotted, and details were developed in ways that move the story forward as logically as possible, from the full moon that rises slowly in the sky that first Tuesday night to the gibbous moon that appears a week later at the end. By placing my characters in the context of familiar reality, I hoped to entice readers to take that great leap of faith and believe that frogs, and perhaps pigs, too, could fly—if the conditions were just right.

One result of winning the Caldecott Medal is the opportunity to travel and meet a wide variety of people who are interested in my book. Readers can be quite passionate about their perceptions. I've heard heated arguments over what *Tuesday* sounds like. Some people are sure it's a silent squadron of frogs gliding through a still summer night. Others are equally positive it's full of zooming cartoon sound effects accompanied by Wagner's "Ride of the Valkyries."

It has been great hearing children tell me how much they love "those frogs" and how funny they think the book is. One first-grade class wrote their own book, *Wednesday*. In it, their school is subjected to some interesting revenge fantasies involving scissors and math papers.

I keep waiting for letters telling me how frightening *Tuesday* is. I'm waiting only because many people—and by *people* I mean adults—keep bringing up this possibility, whether I'm at a signing, a speaking engagement, or on the "Today" show. Fortunately, kids know funny when they see it. If, after reading *Tuesday* one evening before bed, they look out the window and see frogs flying by—well, we should all be so lucky.

I'm always delighted when teachers and librarians tell me about the ways they use wordless books. These books have become springboards for all kinds of writing, bookmaking, and even drama classes. Teachers of English as a second language tell me that wordless books are particularly useful in helping students express their thoughts in English. The students aren't inhibited by the burden of having to translate literally. That kind of interaction between books and children is very exciting. To know that my own pictures may be inspiring imaginations with the same wonder I felt as a child is a very satisfying feeling.

In 1989, when *Free Fall* was given an Honor Medal, I felt supported in my interest in the wordless format. By awarding *Tuesday* the 1992 Caldecott Medal, this year's committee has challenged the perception of the wordless book as a novelty. I thank all the committee members for the great honor of being included among the distinguished roster of medal winners. I hope Lynd Ward would be pleased.

I would like to thank a few others who have played a part in my being here tonight.

My thanks to my family for a lifetime of encouragement and support.

To Tom Sgouros and David Macaulay, two unfailingly generous teachers.

To everyone at Clarion for making it such a fun place to publish books, and to Carol Goldenberg and Dinah Stevenson for good advice and great humor.

To Dorothy Briley, who was the first person to give me a chance to be an author. When I presented her with the pencil dummy of *Tuesday*, which was not the book she was expecting, I thank her for laughing.

To Dilys Evans, who has been with me every step of the way, always ready with biscuits and a pot of tea.

Finally, to my wife, Kim, who is a part of every book I do. Thank you for asking me to the Sadie Hawkins Dance.

Kirkus Reviews

SOURCE: A review of *Tuesday,* in *Kirkus Reviews,* Vol. LIX, No. 5, March 1, 1991, p. 325.

On Tuesday, just as the full moon is rising, the lily pads take off flying—each topped by a serene, personable frog. This extraordinary flock startles some dozing birds and blunders into a line full of sheets before joining a woman drowsing by her TV; with dawn approaching, the frogs set out for home but don't quite make it before their magic carpets fall to earth, leaving the frogs to hop back to the pond while passing humans marvel at the unusual debris in the road. This is a nearly wordless book (its few words only add confusion: if the frogs' adventure is linked to the full moon, next Tuesday won't duplicate the magic as suggested). In the illustrations, the fey events are depicted with beguiling realism, the plump frogs washed in luminous moonlight, drifting silently on their eerie escapade. Wiesner varies his double spreads with occasional insets and frames, and provides plenty of intriguing visual details to ponder. Nifty.

Publishers Weekly

SOURCE: A review of *Tuesday,* in *Publishers Weekly,* Vol. 238, No. 11, March 1, 1991, p. 73.

In this nearly wordless picture book, Wiesner again takes readers on an imaginative voyage, using everyday reality merely as a touchstone. Here, a squadron of frogs soars through the night air one Tuesday, squatting upon lily-pads that they use as flying carpets. Apparently intending no harm, these mysterious visitors to a suburban development leave a minimum of disruption as evidence of their eerie flight: a few startled eyewitnesses, some scattered lily pads and a spooked dog. Wiesner's visuals are stunning: slightly surrealistic, imbued with mood and mystery, and executed with a seemingly flawless command of palette and perspective. But, perhaps because this fantasy never coalesces around a human figure, it is less accessible and less resonant than his tales that center on a child protagonist.

Roger Sutton

SOURCE: A review of *Tuesday,* in *Bulletin of the Center for Children's Books,* Vol. 44, No. 9, May, 1991, p. 231.

Only briefly surprised that their lilypads can suddenly float and fly, the frogs by the thousands are soon carooming through the night sky. That's it, for premise *and* wordless story, as the frogs surprise a man (Wiesner himself) at his late night snack, sail into a clothesline of sheets, watch T.V. while an old lady sleeps unaware, and pester a dog who should have known better. Come the dawn, the frogs, Cinderella-like, are on their own, leaving behind lots of now-stilled lily pads while they march back to the marsh. Watercolor paintings are lavishly and deeply colored, but what saves this book from simply being a gorgeous gallery of paintings is its warmth and humor: these frogs are having a lot of fun. One gives a dapper wave to the midnight-snacker; another operates the TV remote control with its long pink tongue. In the same spread, one different drummer gazes longingly at a landscape painting on the wall while all its fellows are mesmerized by the video glow. And words aren't needed to convey the feeling of *whoops* when the midair frogs are grounded by the sunrise. Compositions are naturalistic but strongly patterned, with the occasionally Escher-ish design made all the more effective by realistic details. Realistic? Of course. And pigs might fly—they do here, on a *gotcha* final picture.

Patricia Dooley

SOURCE: A review of *Tuesday,* in *School Library Journal,* Vol. 37, No. 5, May, 1991, p. 86.

As the full moon rises over a peaceful marsh, so do frogs on their lily pads—levitating straight up into the air and sailing off, with surprised but gratified expressions. Fish stick their heads out of the water to watch; a turtle gapes goggle-eyed. The phalanx of froggies glides over houses in a sleeping village, interrupting the one witness's midnight snack, tangling with some laundry, hovering briefly before a TV left on. A dog chases one lone low-coasting frog, but is summarily routed by a concerted amphibious armada. Suddenly the rays of the rising sun dispel the magic; the frogs fall to the ground and hop back to their marsh, leaving police puzzling over the lily pads on Main Street. In the final pages, the sun sets on the following Tuesday—and the air fills with ascending pigs! Dominated by rich blues and greens, and fully exploiting its varied perspectives, this book treats its readers to the pleasures of airborne adventure. It may not be immortal, but kids will love its lighthearted, meticulously imagined, fun-without-a-moral fantasy. *Tuesday* is bound to take off.

Carolyn Phelan

SOURCE: A review of *Tuesday,* in *Booklist,* Vol. 87, No. 17, May 1, 1991, p. 1723.

While technically not a wordless picture book, this has no text other than occasional markers of time, "Tuesday evening around eight" or "11:21 p.m.," to guide viewers through one remarkable night and suggest what happens one week later. On the first night, frogs rise from their ponds on lily pads that magically float like flying carpets. Leaving their country home, the frogs fly into town, where they peek through windows, enter a house to watch television, and terrorize a dog. At dawn the magic ends, and the frogs hop back home, leaving wet lily pads in the streets to puzzle the townsfolk and the police. The following Tuesday at dusk, pigs rise into the air, like helium balloons. Then the book ends, leaving viewers to imagine the magic and mayhem to follow. As in *Free Fall,* Wiesner offers a fantasy watercolor journey accomplished with soft-edged realism. Studded with bits of humor, the narrative artwork tells a simple, pleasant story with a consistency and authenticity that make the fantasy convincing. While this trip may not take children far, its open-ended conclusion invites them to carry on the fantasy, allowing for unexpected magic in everyday, modern settings.

JUNE 29, 1999 (1992)

Kirkus Reviews

SOURCE: A review of *June 29, 1999,* in *Kirkus Reviews,* Vol. LX, No. 19, October 1, 1992, p. 1262.

A follow-up to *Tuesday*: this time it's flocks of gigantic vegetables wafting through the air, landing all over the US—turnips larger than trees in the Rockies, plane-sized artichokes in Anchorage, limas in Levittown. At first it seems to be the result of young Holly Evans's experiment—she launched seedings (by balloon) "to study the effects of extraterrestrial conditions on vegetable growth" —but species are landing that she never sent up. The answer to the mystery makes an amusing conclusion; meanwhile, Wiesner has a lot of fun with details— imagine climbing a giant stalk of broccoli or roping down buoyant bell peppers, to say nothing of marketing these elephantine comestibles—and even more fun with the surreal visual effects. One of the best is some hilariously puzzled, slightly jaded sheep and a couple of Native American farmers investigating the canoe-sized pea-pods that have landed in what might be Monument Valley. The brief tongue-in-cheek text is a plus for story time, but these witty, wonderfully imaginative pictures reward closer study, too. Hurray for Wiesner, and his grand sense of humor!

Stephanie Zvirin

SOURCE: A review of *June 29, 1999,* in *Booklist,* Vol. 89, No. 4, October 15, 1992, p. 443.

Reality and fantasy humorously collide in Wiesner's newest picture book, which, like *Tuesday,* has us looking skyward for unusual flying objects. But this time, Wiesner supplies a narrative that leaves a little less to the imagination. Intending to "study the effect of extraterrestrial conditions on vegetable growth," budding botanist Holly Evans attaches small container gardens to orange balloons and launches the weird contraptions into the heavens on May 11, 1999. The results exceed her wildest dreams: on June 29, giant vegetables float to earth—"cucumbers circle Kalamazoo; parsnips pass by Providence." Obviously, there's something amiss. But what? Wiesner relies on understatement in the illustrations to convey most of the humor. Generous enough in size to make the book good for use with small groups, his watercolors spread luxuriously across pages, using marvelous aerial perspectives and close-ups to evoke a 1999 classroom and community remarkably like today's. The laugh-out-loud surprise comes at the close, when tentacled aliens bemoan the vegetarian feast they've accidentally jettisoned to earth. The final joke is a little obscure, and Wiesner's dry wit and calculated pictorial references (to the tabloid *Star* and to Ronco, a name probably known only to kitchen gadget lovers) will be lost on lots of kids. But what child can resist so bizarre a notion as waking up to find broccoli in the backyard and space aliens in the sky, especially when the images are delivered with such glee and in such glorious "photographic" detail.

Publishers Weekly

SOURCE: A review of *June 29, 1999,* in *Publishers Weekly,* Vol. 239, No. 47, October 26, 1992, p. 69.

Caldecott Medalist Wiesner once again presents an offbeat premise and unconventional artwork to tempt youngsters into his deliciously skewed landscapes. In this thoroughly winning flight of fancy, it seems the strange events that occurred on *Tuesday* still continue. Wiesner here leaves the boggy, froggy swamp for suburbia and beyond, setting this work in "Ho-Ho-kus, New Jersey." There Holly Evans sends boxes of planted vegetable seeds into the ionosphere as part of her ambitious third-grade science project—"her classmates are speechless." What happens next may or may not be the result of Holly's experiment, but the country is never the same. Giant specimens of produce begin to bombard various regions, as "cucumbers circle Kalamazoo," "artichokes advance on Anchorage" and "cauliflower carpets California." (On the same date, it turns out, a space-ship's cook has inadvertently jettisoned mega-vegetables from his galley. Perhaps a bizarre coincidence, perhaps not.)

Wiesner's dry humor, irony and artistic wizardry have been masterfully marshalled into a visual and literary feast. Kids will relish rolling amusingly alliterative phrases off their tongues almost as much they delight in these wryly rendered paintings. From the huge broccoli reminiscent of the fallen tree in *Hurricane* to the Mount Rushmore-like faces carved from potatoes, readers will adore this imaginative romp. Though several picture books of late have attempted to combine drollery and sophistication, only to end up with results far over youngsters' heads, this work succeeds notably on several levels. Spectacular

to look at, great fun to read—it is, in sum, executed with consummate skill.

Roger Sutton

SOURCE: A review of *June 29, 1999,* in *Bulletin of the Center for Children's Books,* Vol. 46, No. 3, November, 1992, pp. 93-4.

It's certainly no coincidence that June 29, 1999 is a *Tuesday.* A few Tuesdays before that date, budding scientist Holly Evans had sent aloft helium-held vegetable seeds; now, giant vegetables are descending: "Cucumbers circle Kalamazoo. Lima beans loom over Levittown. Artichokes advance on Anchorage." Although the joke goes on a little too long, this benevolent invasion provides Wiesner with some delectable opportunities for illustrative aplomb: the big vegetables peacefully settling into the backyards of America (giant broccoli in Holly's) look like just another part of the scenery, their luscious greens beautifully at home, their size a source of wonder, manna from heaven. The American ethos soon takes over, and giant veg-

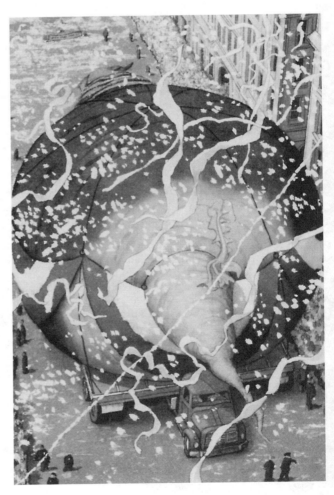

From June 29, 1999, *written and illustrated by David Wiesner.*

etables are traded around the country, becoming a source of several new ventures, some unsuccessful, such as a perishable Mt. Rushmore: "Potatoland is wisely abandoned." In a picture visually and thematically reminiscent of Wiesner's **Hurricane,** Holly turns her broccoli into a tree house where she ponders the unexpected results of her experiment; concluding that these aren't the same vegetables, she wonders what happened to hers. You'll see.

Luann Toth

SOURCE: A review of *June 29, 1999,* in *School Library Journal,* Vol. 38, No. 11, November, 1992, p. 81.

As in the mysterious goings-on of that particular *Tuesday* not long ago, Wiesner again takes off on a flight of fantasy, this time set in the not-too-distant future. This sci-fi adventure begins with Holly Evans, a visionary third grader who launches some seedlings into the ionosphere as part of a science experiment. And so the fun begins. Cabbages fill the sky in one part of the country, turnips in another. "Lima beans loom over Levittown." "Parsnips pass by Providence." Yankee ingenuity reigns supreme as the mammoth veggies are put to some rather creative uses. Of course, there's an extraterrestrial twist to this healthful tale and the true fate of Holly's project is at last revealed. The exquisite watercolors are truly out of this world. The three-quarter page paintings utilize unusual perspective and are filled with clever detail. The photorealistic quality of the figures and background vistas only underscores the absurdity of the gigantic airborne produce and accentuates the deadpan humor. By all accounts, *June 29, 1999* is a date to remember.

Linda Perkins

SOURCE: "Hocus-Pocus in Ho-Ho-Kus," in *The New York Times Book Review,* November 8, 1992, p. 31.

Look! Up in the sky! It's a bird! It's a plane! It's a giant turnip!

Not only gigantic turnips but towering forests of broccoli and other massive vegetables soar through the air in David Wiesner's new storybook, *June 29, 1999.* It seems Holly Evans's science project may be the cause of this astonishing phenomenon. Studying "the effects of extraterrestrial conditions on vegetable growth and development," the budding young scientist launches vegetable seedlings from her home in Ho-Ho-Kus, N.J. on May 18.

On June 29, a hiker in the Rocky Mountains of Montana is shocked to witness enormous turnips gracefully floating through the mountain passes. This is but one sighting. Throughout the country, startled Americans behold astounding visions. "Cucumbers circle Kalamazoo. Lima beans loom over Levittown. Artichokes advance on Anchorage. Parsnips pass by Providence."

Holly follows the television news accounts, methodically recording each vegetable and final landing site. With the report of arugula in Ashtabula, Holly realizes something is terribly wrong. Arugula was not part of her experiment. Nor were eggplant, avocado and rutabaga. Sitting in her broccoli tree house, Holly wonders, "What happened to *my* vegetables? And whose broccoli is in my backyard?"

The answers, as it turns out, are truly blowing in the wind. The final scene and ensuing explanation may prove a disappointing *deus ex machina* for adults, but the final fantastic twist will amuse and satisfy children.

On June 28 of this year, Mr. Wiesner was awarded the 1992 Randolph Caldecott Medal for *Tuesday.* Presented annually by the American Library Association, the medal honors an artist for distinguished contribution to American children's book illustration.

In *Tuesday,* a fleet of frogs, drifting on lily pads, flies through the air and into homes as a community slumbers. They do no more damage than play with a television remote control, disappearing by dawn and leaving only a few traces. In the last few pages, shadows and appendages of pigs suggest a future invasion of flying porkers.

The similarities of the two books are readily apparent. Mr. Wiesner's distinctive watercolors portray contemporary American life in extensive detail from a variety of perspectives, angles and views, reminiscent of Chris Van Allsburg. Perfectly conventional communities experience bizarre atmospheric conditions in both stories. Plot twists in the last few pages stimulate thoughts of further adventures that might occur after the final page. Both tales, full of visual whimsy, are very funny, and in 1999, June 29 will fall on a Tuesday.

If the story pattern is similar, if the reality versus-magic theme reappears and if Mr. Wiesner's surrealistic images again spark humor, some may grouse that he has become formulaic. These are the same people who complain about plot structure in Marx Brothers films. They miss the whole point. Mr. Wiesner has not resorted to cliche or routine. His images continue to be original, imaginative and delightful, and he's added some new dimensions.

The juxtaposition of science and science fiction is a new source of humor. Holly is so serious and so exacting a scientist that a freak intergalactic occurrence seems doubly funny.

In Mr. Wiesner's earlier books, the text has been flat, or merely a means of tying illustrations together. Sometimes he has avoided narrative altogether, producing virtually wordless stories such as *Tuesday.* The succinct story of *June 29, 1999* provides just enough background with perfect deadpan wit and even a few alliterative flourishes, and packs a final punch of its own.

David Wiesner's real strength is vivid, innovative illustration. The image of tethered red bell peppers hovering off the coastline is as silly as the sedate flying frogs in *Tuesday.* Sheep, looking appropriately perplexed, graze among mammoth string beans in the Southwest with desert buttes in the distance. Peas from Peoria dwarf boats on the Mississippi, as a train hauls an immense purple eggplant from Mobile.

The landscapes show a variety of urban and rural settings and are uniformly handsome. Human figures, often an illustrator's shortcoming, look very real, natural and expressive. The best part of Mr. Wiesner's watercolors, however, is the sly details that may escape the first or even second reading. Don't miss, for example, the expressions on the animals or such magazine headlines as "4,000 Lb. Radish Has Face of Elvis!"

The larger-than-life vegetables floating above recognizable national landscapes make this a visual tall tale in the best American tradition. In an era of Big Macs, Whoppers and colossal hot dogs, vegetarians won't be the only ones to welcome these jumbo veggies—fit for Paul Bunyan himself.

Ellen Fader

SOURCE: A review of *June 29, 1999,* in *The Horn Book Magazine,* Vol. LXIX, No. 1, January-February, 1993, p. 81.

On May 11, 1999, Holly Evans sends vegetable seedlings into the sky as part of her science experiment "to study the effects of extraterrestrial conditions on vegetable growth and development." By the end of June, gigantic vegetables are spotted in the sky. Playful, alliterative language catalogues the sightings: "Cucumbers circle Kalamazoo. . . . Artichokes advance on Anchorage." But Holly knows something has gone awry in the "airborne vegetal event" when vegetables she did not include in her research begin appearing; she decides that the huge specimens that have captured the attention of the country are not the result of her experimentation. As she sits in her vegetable treehouse, pondering the imponderable—"'and whose broccoli is in my backyard?'"—the scene shifts to the ionosphere, where the source of the giant vegetables, as well as the fate of Holly's seedlings, is disclosed. It is the alien Arcturians' great good fortune that Holly's vegetables happen to float by their spaceship, because, on June 29, 1999, a cook on their starcruiser accidentally sent their entire supply of food drifting toward Earth. Thanks to Holly and their Mega-Veg Growth Accelerator, the Arcturians now have a feast in the making. Caldecott-medalist Wiesner clearly remains entranced with the incongruity of earthbound objects flying, as explored in *Tuesday;* here an understated, fairly straightforward text is a perfect foil for the outrageous scenes of vegetables run amok. Realistic watercolors reveal red peppers that need to be roped down, beans with bemused Arizona sheep clambering over them, and gargantuan peas floating down the Mississippi like logs to the sawmill. Fans' of Wiesner's offbeat sense of humor will be delighted.

Sian Griffiths

SOURCE. A review of *June 29, 1999,* in *The Times Educational Supplement, Part 2,* No. 4129, August 18, 1995, p. 18.

New Jersey, 1999, Surrounded by books (Marie Curie biog, *The Greenhouse Effect*) Holly Evans, aspiring girl-scientist, launches trays of seedlings into the sky. The aim: "to study the effects of extra-terrestrial conditions on vegetable growth." So when, weeks later, giant vegetables drift across America the conclusion seems obvious . . . But when exotic veggies like arugula and rutabaga appear, Holly realises that the data no longer fits her hypothesis. So whose giant broccoli is in her backyard?

Not until the last page is the "truth" revealed and the ethos of scientific realism exposed. An Arcturian space ship accidentally jettisons its food supply. The joke comes full circle as the hungry aliens consult a scientific manual on how to turn Holly's seedlings into mega veggies. . . .

"Is this real?" asked my six-year-old reader half way through. "Nah, not real", she announced at the end. Wiesner brilliantly captures that line where science and sci-fi cross, highlighting the limitations of the scientific approach and its aim of discovering. "facts" about the natural world—in the face of a galaxy which largely escapes scientific measurements and about which, perhaps, the visual imagination can be equally perceptive.

Clues to the surprise ending are scattered throughout— from the first picture of Holly's seedling-trays, attached to balloons, looking just like miniature space-craft, to the discarded tabloid (*National Inquirer?*) blaring "Man kidnapped by well-dressed space aliens".

A sophisticatedly sceptical picture book raising pertinent questions about the scientific method.

📖 *NIGHT OF THE GARGOYLES* (written by Eve Bunting; 1994)

Julie Cummins

SOURCE: A review of *Night of the Gargoyles,* in *School Library Journal,* Vol. 40, No. 10, October, 1994, p. 86.

What child hasn't looked at a sculpture or creatures carved in stone and wondered what would happen if they came to life? Bunting's canny phrasing and Wiesner's ominous black-and-white illustrations answer the question perfectly. When night comes, the gargoyles on a museum building come alive. They "gargoyle-hunch" with friends around a fountain, "rumble-laugh" at the night watchman, and resume their stone facades with empty eyes unblinking when morning arrives. If anyone could bring gargoyles to life pictorially, it's Wiesner. High-rise angles and perspectives are peopled with pigeons and squirrels;

light is played against dark, forming menacing shadows; spreads and panels zoom in on narrow and wide-angle views; all creating a deliciously eerie, spooky scenario. . . .

This is not for very young children, but it's sure to have enormous appeal for older audiences. From stony-eyed stares to their merry scorn of humans, it's gargoyle gleefulness.

Hazel Rochman

SOURCE: A review of *Night of the Gargoyles,* in *Booklist,* Vol. 91, No. No. 3, October 1, 1994, p. 331.

In a macabre and funny picture book, those stone gargoyles that squat all day on public buildings get free at night and come down from their shadowy corners. Bunting's words are creepy and poetic, scary because they are so physically precise. The stone creatures are "pockmarked," their tongues "green-pickled at the edges." They have unblinking, bulging eyes and their mouths gape like empty suits of armor in museum halls. Wiesner's duotone charcoal illustrations capture the huge heaviness of the stone figures and their gloomy malevolence as they bump and fly and tumble free in the dark. They are so ugly. They're like fiends that come from the graves at night. They're also very human. Wiesner's funniest scene is a double-page spread of a group of gargoyle creatures hunching and grunting together at a spitting water fountain. They could be the gossips and grousers at your local neighborhood hangout. This book is more a situation than a story, but it makes you face what you've always feared but hadn't quite seen. Even the word *gargoyle* makes you choke.

Elizabeth Bush

SOURCE: A review of *Night of the Gargoyles,* in *Bulletin of the Center for Children's Books,* Vol. 48, No. 3, November, 1994, p. 82.

Bunting sets the scene for an exposé on the midnight rites of the grotesque title beasts. Free verse that tolls as steadily and solemnly as a church bell is rich with moody imagery: ". . . rain/ that pours in torrents through/ their gaping lips/ and chokes their throats/ with autumn's leaves") and the promise of some child-pleasing menace. But when it comes to the big question—What do gargoyles *do* in the dead of night?—the answer is disappointing. They lurk and they creep and they peer and they swoop, and then they gather and complain about the weather, make rude faces at the museum guard, and go home. Wiesner, with his sharp insight into the nocturnal antics of frogs (see *Tuesday*), seems the ideal artist to illuminate Bunting's theme. Indeed, his grainy, deeply shadowed charcoal images, which are bound to be compared with Van Allsburg's Conté pencil work, expertly blend frolic and fright; vertical panels cleverly incorporated into the book's design offer an appropriately Gothic look. But absence of plot provides Wiesner little to work with, and so his stone figures mostly pose and mug. A provocative title and enticingly creepy cover art are certain to attract and even please browsers, but youngsters looking for a good scare will only find a mild shudder.

Additional coverage of Wiesner's life and career is contained in the following source published by Gale Research: *Something about the Author,* Vol. 72.

CUMULATIVE INDEXES

How to Use This Index

The main reference

Baum, L(yman) Frank
1856-1919 .... **15**

lists all author entries in this and previous volumes of *Children's Literature Review.*

The cross-references

See also CA 103; 108; DLB 22; JRDA;
MAICYA; MTCW; SATA 18; TCLC 7

list all author entries in the following Gale biographical and literary sources:

AAYA = *Authors & Artists for Young Adults*
AITN = *Authors in the News*
BLC = *Black Literature Criticism*
BW = *Black Writers*
CA = *Contemporary Authors*
CAAS = *Contemporary Authors Autobiography Series*
CABS = *Contemporary Authors Bibliographical Series*
CANR = *Contemporary Authors New Revision Series*
CAP = *Contemporary Authors Permanent Series*
CDALB = *Concise Dictionary of American Literary Biography*
CLC = *Contemporary Literary Criticism*
CLR = *Children's Literature Review*
CMLC = *Classical and Medieval Literature Criticism*
DAB = *DISCovering Authors: British*
DAC = *DISCovering Authors: Canadian*
DAM = *DISCovering Authors Modules*
　　DRAM: dramatists module
　　MST: most-studied authors module
　　MULT: multicultural authors module
　　NOV: novelists module
　　POET: poets module
　　POP: popular/genre writers module

DC = *Drama Criticism*
DLB = *Dictionary of Literary Biography*
DLBD = *Dictionary of Literary Biography Documentary Series*
DLBY = *Dictionary of Literary Biography Yearbook*
HW = *Hispanic Writers*
JRDA = *Junior DISCovering Authors*
LC = *Literature Criticism from 1400 to 1800*
MAICYA = *Major Authors and Illustrators for Children and Young Adults*
MTCW = *Major 20th-Century Writers*
NCLC = *Nineteenth-Century Literature Criticism*
PC = *Poetry Criticism*
SAAS = *Something about the Author Autobiography Series*
SATA = *Something about the Author*
SSC = *Short Story Criticism*
TCLC = *Twentieth-Century Literary Criticism*
WLC = *World Literature Criticism, 1500 to the Present*
YABC = *Yesterday's Authors of Books for Children*

CUMULATIVE INDEX TO AUTHORS

221

CUMULATIVE INDEX TO NATIONALITIES

CUMULATIVE INDEX TO TITLES

Title Index

Title Index

Title Index

Title Index

Title Index